CW00673112

# Investment Risk and Uncertainty

Founded in 1807, John Wiley & Sons is the oldest independent publishing company in the United States. With offices in North America, Europe, Australia, and Asia, Wiley is globally committed to developing and marketing print and electronic products and services for our customers' professional and personal knowledge and understanding.

The Wiley Finance series contains books written specifically for finance and investment professionals as well as sophisticated individual investors and their financial advisors. Book topics range from portfolio management to e-commerce, risk management, financial engineering, valuation, and financial instrument analysis, as well as much more.

For a list of available titles, visit our website at www.WileyFinance.com.

# Investment Risk and Uncertainty

*Advanced Risk Awareness Techniques for the Intelligent Investor*

STEVEN P. GREINER

John Wiley & Sons, Inc.

Cover design: John Wiley & Sons



Published by John Wiley & Sons, Inc., Hoboken, New Jersey.
Published simultaneously in Canada.



***Library of Congress Cataloging-in-Publication Data:***

Greiner, Steven P.
Investment risk and uncertainty : advanced risk awareness techniques for the intelligent investor / Steven P. Greiner.
pages cm. — (Wiley finance series)
Includes index.
ISBN 978-1-118-30018-3 (cloth); ISBN 978-1-118-41966-3 (ebk);
ISBN 978-1-118-42141-3 (ebk); ISBN 978-1-118-65373-9 (epdf)
1. Investments. 2. Risk. 3. Investment analysis. I. Title.
HG4521.G7234 2013
332.601–dc23

2012040847

Printed in the United States of America

10 9 8 7 6 5 4 3 2 1

# Contents

**Foreword** xiii

**Preface** xv

**Acknowledgments** xvii

**INTRODUCTION**
**Why Risk Management Is Mostly Misunderstood** 1
*Steven P. Greiner, PhD*
Quantitative Risk Management Beginnings 3
Quantitative Risk Management Successes 8
Quantitative Risk Management Failures 11
Warren Buffett's Risk Management Strategy 14
Defining Risk Management 16
Fat Tails, Stationarity, Correlation, and Optimization 18
Managing the Risks of a Risk Management Strategy 23
The Risk Management Opportunity Set 25
Notes 29

**PART ONE**

**CHAPTER 1**
**Exposed versus Experienced Risk Revisited** 33
*Steven P. Greiner, PhD, and Andrew Geer, CFA, FRM*
Exposure Hedge versus Dollar Hedge 37
How the Credit Crisis Moved Risk Management to the Forefront 47
Risks beyond Volatility 49
What Risk Management Should Provide 51
Clarifying Expectations of Risk Management 54
An Example 55
Notes 58

**CHAPTER 2**
**Definitions of Tractable Risk** **59**
*Steven P. Greiner, PhD, and Andrew Geer, CFA, FRM*
The Effect of Uncertainty on Objectives 59
Identifying and Measuring Risks 63
Forecasting and Hedging Risks 71
Portfolio View versus Security-Level View 75
Total Risk View of Multi-Asset-Class (MAC) Portfolios 82
Stability and Accuracy 84
Note 86

**CHAPTER 3**
**Introduction to Asset Class Specifics** **87**
*Steven P. Greiner, PhD; Andrew Geer, CFA, FRM; and William F. McCoy, CFA, PRM*
Equities 87
Fixed Income 96
Conclusion 117
Notes 118

**CHAPTER 4**
**Commodities and Currencies** **121**
*Steven P. Greiner, PhD, and William F. McCoy, CFA, PRM*
Commodities 121
Introduction to Currency Risk 138
Conclusion 143
Notes 144

**CHAPTER 5**
**Options and Interest Rate Derivatives** **145**
*Steven P. Greiner, PhD; William F. McCoy, CFA, PRM; and Mido Shammaa, CFA, FRM*
Short History of Option Pricing 145
Volatility Smile 149
Implied Volatility Model 151
Baroni-Adesi Whaley (BAW) Option Pricing Methodology 161
Other Option Pricing Methods 162
Swaps, Swaptions, Forwards, and Futures 165
Conclusion 181
Notes 182

**CHAPTER 6**
**Measuring Asset Association and Dependence** 183
*Steven P. Greiner, PhD; Andrew Geer, CFA, FRM; Christopher Carpentier, CFA, FRM; and Dan diBartolomeo*
The Sample Covariance Matrix 183
Estimation Error Maximization 184
Minimizing the Extremes 185
The Copula, the Most Comprehensive Dependent Structure Measure 193
The Model Covariance Matrix 196
Notes 197

**CHAPTER 7**
**Risk Model Construction** 199
*Steven P. Greiner, PhD; Andrew Geer, CFA, FRM; Jason MacQueen; Laurence Wormald, PhD*
Multifactor Prespecified Risk Models 199
Principal Component (Statistical) Risk Models 205
Customized Hybrid Risk Models 212
Notes 229

**PART TWO**

**CHAPTER 8**
**Fixed Income Issues** 233
*David Mieczkowski, PhD, and William F. McCoy, CFA, PRM*
Variety. Illiquidity. Size. 235
Empirical Evidence 240
Test Portfolios and Methodology 241
Test Metrics 242
Computational Efficiency 248
Conclusion 249
Notes 250

**CHAPTER 9**
**Interest Rate Risk** 251
*David Mieczkowski, PhD, and Mido Shammaa, CFA, FRM*
The Term Structure 252
Term Structure Dynamics 258

Factor Models 258
Stochastic Differential Equations 267
Interest Rate Risk Exposures 273
Risk Forecasting 278
Conditional Duration and Expected Tail Duration 281
Conclusion 282
Notes 283

**CHAPTER 10**
**Spread Risk** **285**
*David Mieczkowski, PhD, and Sameer R. Patel*
Spread Basics 286
Reduced Form Approach 290
Structural Approach 292
Spread Exposure 295
Spread Volatility 296
Derived Spread Approach 297
Euro-Sovereign Spreads 308
Factor Model Approach 312
Conclusion 322
Notes 324

**CHAPTER 11**
**Fixed Income Interest Rate Volatility, Idiosyncratic Risk, and Currency Risk** **325**
*David Mieczkowski, PhD, and Steven P. Greiner, PhD*
Fixed Income Interest Rate Risk 325
Fixed Income Idiosyncratic Bond Risk 346
Fixed Income Currency Risk 352
Conclusion 367
Notes 368

**CHAPTER 12**
**Portfolio Risk Measures** **369**
*William F. McCoy, CFA, PRM, and Steven P. Greiner, PhD*
Coherent Risk Measures 370
Commonly Used Risk Measures 370
Marginal Contribution 375
Stress-Testing 377
Notes 399

CHAPTER 13
Risk for the Fundamental Investor 401
*Richard Barrett, CFA, FRM; Roberto Isch, CFA, FRM; and Steven P. Greiner, PhD*
Fundamental Investing versus Other Approaches 401
Typical Risk Controls for Fundamental Investors 403
Implementing Risk Management Strategies into a Fundamental Process 405
Optimization 421
Conclusion 428

CHAPTER 14
Portfolio Optimization 429
*Sebastian Ceria, PhD, and Kartik Sivaramakrishnan, PhD*
The Enhanced MVO Model 432
Constraints and Objectives in EMVO 434
Further Improvements to the Enhanced MVO Model 441
Factor Alignment Problems 443
Constraint Attribution 445
Specially Structured MVO Models 448
Extreme Tail Loss Optimization 450
Incorporating Nonlinear Instruments in the EMVO Model 452
Algorithms for Solving MVO Models 453
How to Choose an Optimizer 456
Notes 459

PART THREE

CHAPTER 15
The SunGard APT Risk Management System 465
*Laurence Wormald, PhD*
Introduction to Statistical Factor Models 465
APT Factor Model Estimation—Equities Models 468
Selection of the Core Universe for Factor Modeling 469
Choosing the Number of APT Factors 470
Estimating the Risk Profiles in an APT Factor Model 471
APT Multi-Asset-Class Factor Model Estimation 474
Modeling Derivatives and Other Nonunderlying Securities 477
User-Defined Assets within APT Models 479

Conclusion 480
Notes 481

CHAPTER 16
**Axioma Risk Models** **483**
*Bill Wynne; Melissa Brown, CFA; and Sebastian Ceria, PhD*
Background 483
Risk Model–Based Reporting 484
Role of Risk Models in Investment Decisions 485
Axioma Value at a High Level 486
Daily Risk Models, Delivered Daily 487
Multiple Risk Models 488
Empirical Results 489
Details of Axioma Innovations 492
Conclusion 506
Notes 506

CHAPTER 17
**Distinguishing Risk Models** **507**
*Steven P. Greiner, PhD, and Richard Barrett, CFA, FRM*
History 507
Risk Model Details 508
Risk Model–Based Reporting 510
Conclusion 520
Notes 521

CHAPTER 18
**Northfield's Integration of Risk Assessments across Multiple Asset Classes** **523**
*Dan diBartolomeo, PRM, and Joseph J. Importico, CFA, FRM*
A Unified Framework 524
Interest Rate Risk 526
Credit Risk 527
Equity Factor Representation of Corporate Credit Risk 528
Default Correlation 529
Complex Instruments and Derivatives 531
Private Equity 532
Direct Real Estate and Geographically Localized Assets 536
Concluding Example 540
Conclusion 543
References 544

**CHAPTER 19**
**R-Squared** 547
*Jason MacQueen*
Why Build Stock Risk Models? 547
Generic Risk Modeling 548
Practical Risk Modeling 551
Statistical Factor Models 552
Defined Factor Models 554
Estimate Factors or Estimate Betas? 555
Practical Consequences at the Stock Level 557
Practical Consequences at the Portfolio Level 557
A Short Digression 558
Hybrid Risk Models 559
The R-Squared Short-Term Hybrid Risk Model for Global Equities 560
Summary 565
Note 565

**CHAPTER 20**
**The Future of Risk Management and Analytics** 567
*Steven P. Greiner, PhD; David Mieczkowski, PhD; William F. McCoy, CFA, PRM; Andrew Geer, CFA, FRM; Daniel S. Mathon, PhD, CFA; Viviana Vieli; Christopher Carpentier, CFA, FRM; Mido Shammaa, CFA, FRM; and Sameer R. Patel*
The Increasing Regulatory Environment 569
The Impact of Regulations with Technology 571
The Future View 572
New Types of Risk Models 573
Stress-Testing Your Way to Event Risk Preparedness 577

**Index** 579

# Foreword

For many years, I have written and edited finance books as well as read the works of many others covering a wide range of topics. What is immediately recognizable about this book, however, is that it touches on many difficult and deep topics all under the same roof. *Investing Risk and Uncertainty* is able to do so by gathering the expertise of several highly qualified contributors and seamlessly organizing it all in one place for the reader.

Although the book does have some financial mathematics throughout, that is not the focus—the core message is about multi-asset class risk measurement, on-going monitoring, and mitigation. It is a formal practitioner's guide to the topic of risk, from first principle's definitions through to the latest mathematical construct of sophisticated risk measures calculations. To deliver that topic, the book starts with simple definitions of risk and in particular, introduces risk, its management, and its interpretation in historical context. This is an essential element often left out of books on the subject, leading a less informed reader up the learning curve much quicker than they might arrive naturally.

Since the Great Financial Crisis of 2008, there has been much discussion in the media about risk management failures. Likewise this on-going crisis has seen the promotion of risk managers to positions offering more authority over portfolio assets than they've ever had before. This has led to greater attention paid to the risks of portfolios and assets along with the development of new techniques for risk estimation. But the context of why that's necessary is completely missed if one doesn't understand the current useful measures of risk, understand their assumptions, their credible theories and how the current suite of risk estimation procedures came to be. The book's main author Steven Greiner captures that sentiment when he says:

> *When financial failure happens, everybody's life is touched because of the massive amount of money that is involved. As a result, every carbon-based life unit on the planet feels they have something valuable to say about it. Opinion and baseless facts construct the everyday perception of the situation since they are the dominate voices, and the realities are morphed far away from the truth.*

Thus, this volume seeks first to offer a wider perspective on which to understand why risk management is necessary, beginning in its early days, and ending with explaining why we need more of it in the future.

The book's main achievement is its ability to form a co-operative of competing risk vendors assessment of methodologies available for measuring risk. Nowhere else can one flow from SUNGARD-APT's to R-Squared's risk model(s) while covering Northfield's, Axioma's, and Barra's along the way, in a single work and have their founders and experts in the risk community work together to form a complete volume on risk. Surely this feat alone must mean the crisis of the last decade and its systemic risks to the field and business must have been obscenely egregious compared to past financial crisis.

Finally, every investor needs global exposure these days and in many different asset classes. The largest companies in the world are no longer "attached" to their local economies. Globalization is not only being encouraged, it cannot be stopped. Technology has made the world too small and pensions, hedge funds and every other investor is thinking globally, if not traveling globally unlike ever before in history. Before recently, most firms measured or estimated risk in specific asset classes separately, then aggregated the risk to attempt full risk estimation across all asset types and portfolios. This was done first in countries and regions, and then combined to form their global risk assessment. In doing so, the risks were obviously over-estimated simply because diversification across assets was not ascertained. Recently though due to the aforementioned crisis, attention has been on forming better estimates of risks globally and across asset types. This involves a careful estimation of the covariance matrix, or more importantly, asset association of which covariance is just one type of measure. Additionally, the software and hardware technology is just beginning to allow these very large calculations to be performed in "almost" real-time and there is pressing need for it. This book addresses all of the major concerns with this kind of overall risk measuring process and on some level covers every topic related to it. I cannot think of a more comprehensive and concise book on the subject.

Within this volume, the authors set about writing the requirements for a multi-asset class global risk model and do so with a good mixture of theory and real world examples. Practitioners on every level should prepare themselves to be pleasantly surprised by the information found here and the unique, collaborative approach of its authors.

FRANK J. FABOZZI<br>January 2013

# Preface

## HOW THE BOOK IS ORGANIZED

This book is divided into three parts. The first part will discuss risk at a very high level, 30,000 feet if you reside in the United States and 10.000 meters if you live somewhere else. The beginning chapters will lay the groundwork giving the perspective on risk, outlining the hat you should wear when beginning to think about applying a risk management strategy. In this part we'll describe risk exposures versus experienced risks, provide the working definitions of the risk measures (what exactly we are calculating at the portfolio level), and then delve qualitatively into various asset classes to bring out the fat, those verbal descriptions of what is risky about these assets, what is a calculably reliable measure of risk, and what isn't. Thus the specifics of risk measuring for equities, the myriad fixed income types of securities, commodities, currencies, futures, and options will all be given a risk overview, definitions made, and the various ways of incorporating their pricing algorithms for risk forecasting explained. Interest rate derivatives will be reviewed as well.

The covariance matrix will be introduced, discussed, and dissected; and its comparison to using a copula will be explained and their respective tradeoffs reviewed. Descriptions of multifactor risk models, which are the most common type of risk model, will be explained. Risk models created using principal component analysis will be introduced, and how one combines the two to produce hybrid risk models will be reviewed. Part One will have little or no mathematics in it, but the results of mathematical computations may be shown from time to time.

The second part will develop a more rigorous approach to defining risks. This part starts out with raising the issues associated with developing risk models for fixed income assets. A large part of this discussion will address each of the individual risks that a bond offers. We'll address the risks that are covered in FactSet and what's needed to be able to calculate them. We'll discuss risk model construction, historical risk, and the ARCH and GARCH techniques, showing some examples of how these work as of today's computational capabilities, their usage, and where and how they'll probably be used in the future.

The mostly widely used and commonly reported risk measures will be discussed and formulas for their calculation will be shown. Then, and throughout, some computational modeling pitfalls will continuously be reviewed. A whole chapter is dedicated to how fundamental managers can use risk models, and will identify insights that risk models bring to the investment process specifically from the perspective of fundamental managers. In this chapter we'll discuss what they can use the covariance matrix for and how it can be used to ascertain and shine a light on risks they're not used to examining directly. This is where the "Warren Buffett is a covariance matrix" analogy will be (sort of) emphasized.

When it comes to risk forecasting, a very commonly used methodology involves mean-variance portfolio optimization, especially for equities. We'll have a chapter on optimization, which will be reviewed in significant detail. Part Two will have lots of mathematics and statistics, but presumption on the audience will be avoided as much as possible, which we'll strongly emphasize.

Part Three will review the risk products available in FactSet with working examples. This part will provide detailed overviews of the most prominent risk modeling capabilities within the industry. Vendors of renown such as Axioma, SunGard APT, and R-Squared will be featured prominently. For its historical significance, Barra will be discussed, as it was the first risk vendor, launched by Barr Rosenberg in the mid-1970s. Professor Rosenberg pioneered the use of quantitative methods for formulating risk metrics and investment strategies, and no discussion about equity risk would be complete without this review.

The book concludes with some modest forecasts of our own. Although most readers are aware that prognosticators and fortune-tellers have a large standard error between forecasts and realization, we will utilize some obvious trends combined with future computing speed (which never ceases to increase) to postulate where risk management might find itself in a few years.

A variety of authors and editors contributed to this encyclopedic detailing of risk models and management. It's on shoulders I stand and it's with their expertise that I offer this exposition for the benefit of an industry I love so much.

## WATCH THE VIDEOS

*Investment Risk and Uncertainty* is accompanied by eight videos you can watch on your computer or mobile device. Three of the videos are FactSet or other risk vendor heads of research answering questions put to them on a conference risk panel. The remaining videos are how-to videos for using FactSet products.

When you see a box like this in your text, you will be directed to a video that relates to what you are reading. Go to www.wiley.com/go/greiner to see the full listing.

# Acknowledgments

This book would not have been possible without the support from FactSet Research Systems and particularly from Chris Ellis, the senior head of product development, who in many ways is the original thought leader for risk on FactSet. Likewise, the chapter authors from FactSet's risk vendors include Jason MacQueen, Laurence Wormald, Sebastian Ceria, and Daniel diBartolomeo, to whom we owe a hearty thanks for offering their expertise freely and also for their advice from time to time on technical matters and with clients. Sebastian graciously wrote the chapter on optimization, which was a special help, along with his colleague Kartik Sivaramakrishnan. Additionally, Melissa Brown and Bill Wynne from Axioma collaborated with Sebastian on writing a very user-friendly, easy-to-read chapter with good examples on using their products within FactSet.

I have great pleasure working at FactSet, which has some of the nicest people on the planet. These include the authors and editors Bill McCoy, David Mieczkowski, Richard Barrett, Christopher Carpentier, Mido Shammaa, Sameer Patel, Roberto Isch, Joe Importico, Viviana Vieli, Daniel Mathon, and Andrew Geer. Andrew in particular spent an inordinate amount of his time editing many chapters and offering help in formatting throughout the text. Katherine McCabe, Michelle Bova, and Mathew Ward also contributed, and it is Mathew's magic that makes the product videos sprinkled throughout the book come to life. Without these people, this book would not have been written, let alone a hope or possibillity. Their contributions have been substantial.

I speak for all the authors collectively that we hope our clients use this book in such a way as to aid them in improving their investment process. Moreover, many of the issues we are involved with day to day are of such detail that the often cited 30-minute phone call with a client just doesn't do them justice. For this reason I was inspired to write this book for their longer-term benefit, heavily assisted by the aforementioned contributors, who gladly joined my vision. It is hoped this volume will sit on clients' desks as a quick and detailed reference for many years to come.

On a personal level, I dedicate this book to my daughter Vanessa. As of this writing she has started her first year in college, where I wish her more than luck and my sincerest well-wishing, even above what my heart cannot evoke in words.

Last, my wife Veronica continues to offer a steady hand, which I know I lean on more than I'd like to admit. Her love is constant, inveterate, and resolute. A thank you to her doesn't convey properly all that she deserves.

# Introduction

# Why Risk Management Is Mostly Misunderstood

*Steven P. Greiner, PhD*

When we hear the term *risk management* (RM), our thoughts are instinctively directed to muse about the subject from what we know about insurance, drafted from the multitude of car insurance commercials on television. That is, we search our memories for accidents that occurred in our own lives, such as car collisions, falling down stairs, our grandmother tripping over the runner down the central corridor of her old home in South Wherever. If we're slightly educated in a field where that term is vaguely familiar, we may entertain deeper thoughts about the subject simply because we recognize the distinction between the words *risk* and *management*, which to some is an oxymoron in the first place. However, if we're deeply involved or employed in finance, the insurance industry, or asset management, this term has major consequences when its application fails. It's the failure of risk management that is inherent in the fear that registers cognitively upon hearing the term. The emphasis of the word *risk* often overwhelms the second word, *management*. If instead we sort this phrase so that it's termed *management of risk*, the fear subsides a bit and one can concentrate on the purpose of the phrase. It is from this perspective—the management of risk—that this book is written.

There have been calls for better and more comprehensive risk reporting for some time now, accentuated by the credit crisis of 2008 and the even more recent sovereign debt crisis in the Eurozone. The cry for better reporting is ubiquitous. A 2010 report by a British institute of accountants found investors wanting major changes in how banks present risk, for instance.[1] This awareness, however, is an attempt to narrow the gap between what risk reporting is versus what it can achieve. Unfortunately, the expectations of risk reporting are usually too high. That is, it can never be expected to forecast future extreme events or foresee so-called unknown unknowns. When thinking about the credit crisis today, for instance, pundits still are having difficulty ranking the hierarchy of causes even after it happened, let alone forecasting it before it occurs!

Forecasts are somewhat subjective even if using historical data in risk model development, just as varying purveyors of the art use different methods. Additionally, the assessment of estimates, forward-looking statements, and subjectivity in preparing financial statements is eventually validated or not, simply due to a firm's profits and losses coming to fruition. Risk reporting, in contrast, involves an estimation of something that *could* occur, not that it *will*. The fact that it didn't happen doesn't mean it couldn't have, meaning a risk forecast that doesn't occur cannot be used as a data point in decision making about whether a risk-measuring strategy is accurate. It cannot be that some asset manager is wrong to identify it as a potential risk or to take hedging action though a forecasted possibility doesn't come to pass. The risk assessment isn't at fault simply because a forecasted risk didn't occur. Similarly, if a risk that is predicted with a 1 percent chance of occurring does occur, this does not mean the risk assessment was wrong. Suppose the probability of the event occurring is only 0.01 percent and it occurs? Is the risk forecast at fault? It's not the risk forecast that should be retooled necessarily, but the hedging strategy or risk mitigation strategy put in place given the risk description. This highlights that reviewing the overall risk management strategy should be a continuous activity for the enterprising investor.

It's difficult to make customized risk reporting available for a given firm, simply because the correlations between firms mean, by definition, that most major risks are common. By reviewing the risks that occur over time, such as what went wrong, what we have learned from that event, whether outcomes have matched forecasts regularly or irregularly, one obtains an overview of the risk management and reporting methodology that continually improves the process in a disciplined fashion. Investors have most to lose from poor risk reporting and most to gain from installing a better reporting process. The drawback is that if firms don't review and overhaul their risk management process themselves and instead leave the task to regulatory authorities, it may be too blunt, too one-size-fits-all, to yield enough specific information useful for risk management, and may even accentuate systemic risks.

For instance, consider liquidity risk as outlined in Undertakings for Collective Investment in Transferable Securities (UCITS) documentation and banking regulations.[2] They necessitate that a firm should consider its exposure to liquidity risk and assess its response should that risk materialize.

These guidelines include establishing a monitored liquidity risk tolerance while maintaining a cushion of liquid assets. These guidelines are uniform in their conditions on the asset cushion:

- Able to meet redemption requests at least bimonthly.
- Monetized quickly with little loss of value under stressed market environments, given trade volume and time frame.
- Low credit and market risk.
- High confidence of base valuation.
- Low correlation with other assets.
- Listed on an exchange, not over-the-counter (OTC).
- Actively traded within a sizable market.
- Flight to quality candidates.
- Assets must be unencumbered and not collateralized.
- Proven record of liquidity in past stressed markets (e.g., credit crisis of November 2008).

Now, these guidelines suggest that regulatory authorities are mandating a common risk-reduction strategy across firms, where they include the descriptions of the safe assets that managers can invest in. They may indeed begin to compress the universe of investable assets such that it makes all firms look similar in terms of risk since they cross-own so many of the same assets, raising the correlations between firms and resulting in an increase in systemic risk, the exact opposite of what the overregulation is supposed to achieve. The goal of regulation in this regard should be about increasing diversification across firms, not concentrating it. We won't say much about that type of governmental risk other than to draw attention to that possibility, but this strongly suggests it's in the interest of investors to review their risk accordingly in regular intervals and create their own set of decision rules for RM implementation.

## QUANTITATIVE RISK MANAGEMENT BEGINNINGS

Though risk management as a profession is quite evolved and mature, its infancy sprang from a demand for business to insure a loss against some catastrophe. In this regard, it was Black Swan events (obsidian uncertainty, popularized by Nassim Taleb today) that occurred with sufficient frequency that made insurance (the spreading of risk among many participants) the easy-to-understand and affordable tool of choice in the field. In this vein, Lloyd's of London was involved in risk management as far back as the 1700s; unfortunately, this endeavor was to the detriment of Africans since

Lloyd's was the number-one insurer for slave-trading vessels in that period, a very large British enterprise at the time. The fact that, of the 10,000+ ships carrying over three million people in a century, there were more than a thousand lost vessels says that one in 10 ships, or more properly one in 10 voyages, was to be written off. This meant that a premium was required to be a small percentage of the nine successful voyages' profit to insure 10 percent failure rates.

Since Lloyd's began as a news service for shipping interests, having at its fingertips most of the data for estimating losses (which it could maintain secrecy over), this allowed the process of insurance price discovery to be calculable and premiums set just above estimated losses. In this way Lloyd's could arbitrage the difference between estimated and realized losses with more than a little padding. As time wore on, the estimates got better, along with the skill in aggregating risks across many different vessels, owners, and operators, all to the benefit of Lloyd's of London. Thus the first principle of RM is observed by this activity in the historical record. That is, before you can manage risk, you must have a sufficient amount of valid data to describe, measure, and monitor it. Additionally, defining the risk is a necessary but insufficient condition, and isn't useful if you cannot measure the risk. One should focus on avoiding losses with the same attention one gives to taking profits. Said another way, RM is managing the probabilities about future losses, and it should require as much of our thinking as managing future profits does.

As the years progressed and insurance became a commodity, other fields emerged that needed risk management. Nowadays risk management has even transformed itself to include firmwide RM that insurance companies and consulting firms proudly emphasize they can provide. This very broad definition of the concept concerns any type of risk affecting the business, from warehouse accidents between forklift drivers to the sinking of a transpacific ocean freighter to errors and omissions failures of registered and regulated fiduciaries. This definition is wider than mere insurance against some catastrophe, because it codifies aggregating risks from multiple sources of business concerns. Imagine that a company has risk of loss from the sinking of a ship as in previous examples, but also risk due to off-balance-sheet activities, failure to meet regulatory compliance, sales from foreign entities with various currency exposures, or loan defaults, as well as legal risks, risks due to employee fraud, or liquidity risk simply due to short-term demands on working capital exhausting the supply of cash on hand. As the sophistication and complexity of business needs grew, so did the opportunity for losses to arise from many sources. In this regard, firmwide risk management is involved in first comprehending and identifying a loss, whether directly or indirectly, from failed business methods or processes due to exposure to externally ill-defined events. Then, secondarily, this leads to defining the methods and processes for mitigating the loss or rendering it not so concerning. The major activities of risk management then are in three parts, which are defined as identifying the risk, measuring it, and offsetting it. Unfortunately, risk assessment is a complex undertaking based on often uncertain information; hence the practice of it works to improve its accuracy and predictive ability.

As an important aside, the preponderance of quality management introduced by W. Edwards Deming and used in General Electric, Xerox, AlliedSignal, and many other companies brought risk management techniques to the cutting edge of manufacturing in the latter half of the twentieth century. Deming was the father of what we call Total Quality Management (TQM). He made his mark with the Ford Motor Company in the 1950s, where his impact on teaching in Japan came to the forefront. In the period following World War II, Deming spent two years teaching statistical quality control to Japanese engineers and executives. Later, while investigating why Americans preferred U.S.-made automobiles with Japanese-made transmissions, it came to Ford's attention that though both the United States and Japan were building transmissions within the same specifications, the Japanese tolerance ranges were narrower. The result, of course, was fewer defects in the Japanese-made versions.

Deming's first degrees were in mathematics and physics. Statistics is a natural application of the tools math and physics provide and often comes easily to those trained in such hard sciences. When Deming moved out of the research laboratory at Bell Labs, having been a student of Walter Shewhart, he first started rewriting Shewhart's Rube Goldberg applications of statistical quality control. Deming became famous for engineering error-reduction methods that lowered recalls, reducing customer complaints and increasing their overall satisfaction. Subsequently, a company's profits would rise while its risks would fall. Ultimately, Deming's methods and philosophy evolved to initiate the Six Sigma revolution used in worldwide manufacturing, aiming for the reduction of defects to one in a million or six standard deviations from the mean under the normal approximation. Though the application of risk management is perhaps more readily visible in Deming's methods, applying these methods to portfolio and asset management is part and parcel of what we're trying to communicate in this work.

In the current embodiment, we focus primarily on the uncertainties that asset managers generally need to consider when managing a fund. Measuring and mitigating these uncertainties, just as Deming did in manufacturing, is a proper application of risk management. In this way, we define risk simply as the effect of uncertainty on objectives. To understand this, we begin by describing the typical scenario for establishing an investment objective, which revolves around setting priorities for objective achievement. At this point, the finance committee overseeing the fund is thinking at the strategic level in light of the overriding liabilities the invested assets seek to cover. Uncommonly described in performing this activity, however, is that the finance committee is already actively performing RM by even establishing a fund to cover liabilities. These priorities are usually followed by guidelines set to achieve these objectives, which are established by the board of directors, committee, or members of the managing counsel who have the fiduciary responsibility. Then, objectives stated and priorities attached, the next step involves restrictions or constraints that are designed to mitigate obvious losses of capital or abhorrent risks that the fiduciaries believe themselves unqualified to handle. Often at this time moral conditions, such as socially conscious issues, can be imposed in the form of constraints on the management of the assets. For instance, the fund may be restricted from investing in tobacco or gambling companies.

Thus far we've described the process for establishing the criteria for investing (from a very high level), a procedure that is regularly performed by pension fund, mutual fund, and endowment fiduciaries, and even cash management facilities at banks. Next, capital is deployed into the mandate. This step is critical, as the portfolio manager (PM) must now balance the activities of choosing the best assets to meet the objective while simultaneously ensuring there are no constraint violations. Nowadays, this involves legal and governmental regulatory oversight that may be, but often is not part of the official investment objective document. In this regard, legal or regulatory compliance may overwhelm the risks associated with loss of assets. Consider the situation where the fine for being out of compliance is larger than reasonable investment losses might be in regular market conditions. Consider a $150 million portfolio, where a loss with a 5 percent chance of occurring in a month could typically be around 3 to 4 percent of assets, amounting to $4.5 million to $6 million, while a regulatory body could levy a fine of $8 million for not utilizing some required risk measure calculation or statistic. Ludicrous perhaps, but not an unreasonable expectation in light of UCITS regulations in Europe and Dodd-Frank fallout in the United States that have been imposed since the credit crisis.

So with the establishment of investing safeguards consisting of the constraints set in the investment objective document as well as any legal or regulatory oversight, the poor soul whose job it is and who has the decision rights to deploy the mandate does so in trepidation. This far along in the time line of establishing the fund, a whole litany of risk management has already been performed but mostly in the form of handrails or safeguards to keep the manager from inadvertently stumbling over a perceived edge. It's also at this point, just after proceeds are invested, that risk management as we will come to describe in 99 percent of this book is mustered and brought to good effect.

At a high level, the form of RM applied on an existing portfolio of assets involves two broad categories of risk. There are those risks that involve specifying the variance of returns of a portfolio (or variance of a collection of assets) and those that do not. Those that do not are extreme events and are the extinction-level externalities one can neither prepare for very easily nor forecast very well. We delay describing these obsidian uncertainties for now and focus on a qualitative description of risk whose management brought successes to the modern world.

Before doing so, however, we mention that risk management has been commonly, routinely, and soundly misspecified in the media these days (in the shadow of the global financial crisis), where it is often misstated that methodologies in portfolio risk management (particularly those methods related to variance measurement and forecast) have been of no help in preventing losses or preventing the financial crisis. We would argue that it's just easy pickings for self-aggrandizing, opportunity-seizing, and attention-gathering people of the Snidely Whiplash variety to level these accusations.[3] It's perhaps a failure of the RM profession and its organizations (Global Association of Risk Professionals [GARP], Quantitative Work Alliance for Applied Finance, Education and Wisdom [QWAFAFEW], Professional Risk Managers' International Association [PRMIA]) along with CFA Institute to properly explain the market situations, roles, and methodologies of risk management to the media, proletariat, and middle classes that allows this blame. However, it's easy pickings to blame risk management methods for their failure to halt risk, simply because that's RM's perceived job.

Consider being a risk manager, as described in the earlier part of this Introduction. The less educated—or, more accurately stated, uninstructed—media representatives will say that "you failed to manage that risk" since their perception of the title is that one's job is to prevent an accident or, as with insurance, to contribute funds in event of that accident. Along with the accusation of the person comes the accusation of the methods employed in the operation of RM. It's this latter perception that the beginnings of this book will help address as we seek to clarify how risk management works, how its methods apply, and exactly what information is obtained in the measurement and forecast of risks. Most of this explanation involves the details of variance risk estimates, but under the topics of stress testing, the enablement of just what to do when an obsidian uncertainty arises will be discussed.

Now, I take great consolation from Andrew Lo and Mark Mueller, who wrote a working paper in March 2010 titled "Warning: Physics Envy May Be Hazardous to Your Wealth!" and we reproduce a snippet here:

> *Among the multitude of advantages that physicists have over financial economists is one that is rarely noted: the practice of physics is largely left to physicists. When physics experiences a crisis, physicists are generally allowed to sort through the issues by themselves, without the distraction of outside interference. When a financial crisis occurs, it seems that everyone becomes a financial expert overnight, with surprisingly strong opinions on what caused the crisis and how to fix it. While financial economists may prefer to conduct more thorough analyses in the wake of market dislocation, the rush to judgment and action is virtually impossible to forestall as politicians, regulators, corporate executives, investors, and the media all react in predictably human fashion. Imagine how much more challenging it would have been to fix the Large Hadron Collider after its September 19, 2008 short circuit if, after its breakdown, Congress held hearings in which various constituents—including religious leaders, residents of neighboring towns, and unions involved in the accelerator's construction—were asked to testify about what went wrong and how best to deal with its failure. Imagine further that after several months of such hearings, politicians, few of whom are physicists, start to draft legislation to change the way particle accelerators are to be built, managed, and staffed, and compensation limits are imposed on the most senior research scientists associated with the facilities.*

The hyperbole works beautifully and is not far from the truth. When financial failure happens, everybody's life is touched because of the massive amount of money that is involved. As a result, all the carbon-based life units on the planet feel they have something valuable to say about it. Opinion and baseless facts construct the everyday perception of the situation since they are the dominant voices, and the realities are morphed far away from the truth. This leads us to testify about the myriad ways RM has influenced successful outcomes that improve our everyday lives.

## QUANTITATIVE RISK MANAGEMENT SUCCESSES

Our first examples involve everyday experiences.

- You live in a city of less than a million people and drive 11 miles to work each day through the center of town. You purchase a brand-new

Volkswagen Passat for $26,319, putting $5,000 down and financing the rest over three years. Your insurance costs are $493 semiannually for a $500 deductible policy.
- Your parents live on a slight embankment along the Arkansas River in northeast Oklahoma that has been prone to flooding for over 50 years.
- You're in Las Vegas or Monaco with $400 that you plan on risking for a few hours of entertainment at a $15 minimum bid blackjack table.

How is risk management applied successfully in these three situations? First, the financing of the automobile for over $21,000 is possible because many depositors at your credit union have collectively allowed their savings and checking cash flows to be accumulated, aggregating the net between borrowing and lending activities of the credit union financing the loan. Continual monitoring of the cash position as well as calculating estimations of cash demand from deposits, all risk managing activities, allow for lending at not unfavorable interest rates. Second, a home insurer sells flood insurance across a wide geographic area, covering many different potential flood areas. It simultaneously collects historical weather and rainfall data across these regions, analyzing the frequency and occurrence of flooding as well as historical flood damage costs while considering inflation rates for repair costs. Given this knowledge and assuming *stationarity* of weather patterns, the insurer forecasts future flooding and future costs of damage. Then it can calculate a viable premium for flood insurance. Last, as a gambler you would not put all $400 on any single hand. You would spread your risks by investing small portions for each hand and would further itemize your bets in a single hand based on the first cards dealt. You may even purposefully stop betting (e.g., you obtain a king and an eight of hearts as the first two cards) to mitigate a future potential worst loss.

Though these are obvious instances of RM, think of the outcomes without its application. It's the continual defining, measuring, forecasting, and hedging of risks that improves the outcome for us as individuals as well as for society. The difficulty in observing when RM is applied successfully becomes obvious when one considers the nonevent of its application. Overengineering the Golden Gate Bridge so that it can hold three times the weight of bumper-to-bumper traffic in rush hour isn't reported. However, should it fail, you could watch the event on the Internet within three minutes of it happening! This is often the way it is with the proper application of risk management techniques: quiet and subversive.

In many ways, it's easy to point out famous losses that occurred and then state, "They should have done so-and-so." The nonapplication of RM techniques is also easily identified and need not be confined to only those methodologies given by mathematical models and statistics. The greatest application of risk management methods comes from government, and an excellent example is documented in *This Time Is Different* by Reinhart and Rogoff called "Default Through Debasement," which is Chapter 11 in their book.[4] This chapter describes the centuries-old practice of currency devaluation (debasement). Now, in their review of this risk management strategy, they refer to the negative viewpoint the citizens of these countries would take. We counter that from the government's perspective, currency debasement was active risk management.

The illustration of this alternative perspective is useful, because it documents why a single risk management technique for an entity may be beneficial to that entity, but may be quite painful for those on the other side of the trade. In essence, a single strategy in risk management may have negative consequences for the parties that the risk is transferred to, though favorable to the RM's employer. To explain, consider a long-standing practice of coinage *seignorage* whereby governments, kings, and various sovereigns would earmark a coin's value by the amount of silver in the coin, and then, over time, reduce the amount of silver in the coin while keeping its rated value constant. Henry VIII began debasing his currency in 1542, continued the practice through his reign, and passed the RM strategy down to his successor, Edward VI. The British pound lost 83 percent of its value during this time, though a pound was still a pound. Reinhart and Rogoff give tables of currency debasement in differing countries from the years 1258 through 1900. From the point of view of the sovereign, this was prudent. Why not reduce your debt by application of this risk management strategy? The risk of default goes down as the debt falls. Why this is important has to do with an equivalent perspective of an equity option put buyer on, say, Exxon Mobil Corporation (XOM).

The buyer of that XOM put transfers the risk of default of the company's stock to the seller of that put. Better yet, the put buyer transfers the risk of just a loss, not as severe as default. If the put seller has only that one asset, and if XOM's stock price moves below the strike of that put before expiration, the put seller in turn would acquire a loss. If the put is exercised, the put seller will be required to buy XOM from the put buyer at the strike price, which is higher than the market price of XOM. One could use credit default swaps (CDSs), too, for this example. This is akin to the holders of Henry VIII coins. The analogy (maybe even hyperbole) works because though it may be wise for the holder of XOM to buy a put for RM applications, if the seller of that put hasn't also applied risk management to his or her holdings from a strategic portfolio-wide point of view, the seller is like the British subjects of Henry VIII. Though in reality there may not have been much his subjects could do in the way of RM, from Henry's perspective it was a wise strategy to limit his risks. Today, however, there's much the sellers of puts can do to protect themselves. That is, put sellers can apply RM strategies as well.

Unfortunately, nations continue this strategy of debasing currency through either deliberate printing of fiat currency or in combination with inflation. From 1977 to 1981, the U.S. dollar was devalued by 50 percent due to inflation, for example. Fiat currency is currency that has no intrinsic value and is demanded by the public because the government has decreed that no other currency may be used in transactions. Thus inflation and debasement are nothing new; only the tools and currencies have changed through the years. Nevertheless, it's one way for governments, central banks, kings, sultans, monarchs, dictators, queens, sovereigns, princes, and princesses to apply RM to manage their risk of default, though extreme and not advantageous for their subjects, unless their subjects can apply RM for themselves and hedge. We'll talk more about this in further chapters, but the key takeaway is that the application of risk management strategies may benefit only the entity employing them, not necessarily all parties involved, which is a subtle and hidden topic of conversation but should be a consideration, particularly if you have exposure to the counterparty risk.

## QUANTITATIVE RISK MANAGEMENT FAILURES

Currency debasement can also fall on the failure side of the coin. There are unfortunately failures of risk management galore. They may involve the failure to apply any RM or they may involve applying the wrong strategy to one's situation or assets. The time line depicted in Figure I.1 represents the VIX from the Chicago Board Options Exchange (CBOE) plotted through time with its one-month counterpart over the recent past. The VIX is highly correlated with the actual realized 30-day standard deviation of the S&P 500 index. Its value is a compendium of a chain of S&P index option implied volatilities, so it is a trader's view of what the future expected volatility will be for the S&P 500 over the next 30 days. Moreover, it is strongly negatively correlated with the returns of the S&P 500. Annotations (labels) were written by Joe Mezrich from Nomura, taken from an August 2011 conference call of his.

Each annotation represents an opportunity for a portfolio manager, albeit of almost any asset type, to have used RM to mitigate the risks of such an event. These events almost entirely represent the obsidian uncertainties that occur from time to time, much more often than events predicted by a normal distribution (Gaussian curve) would forecast.

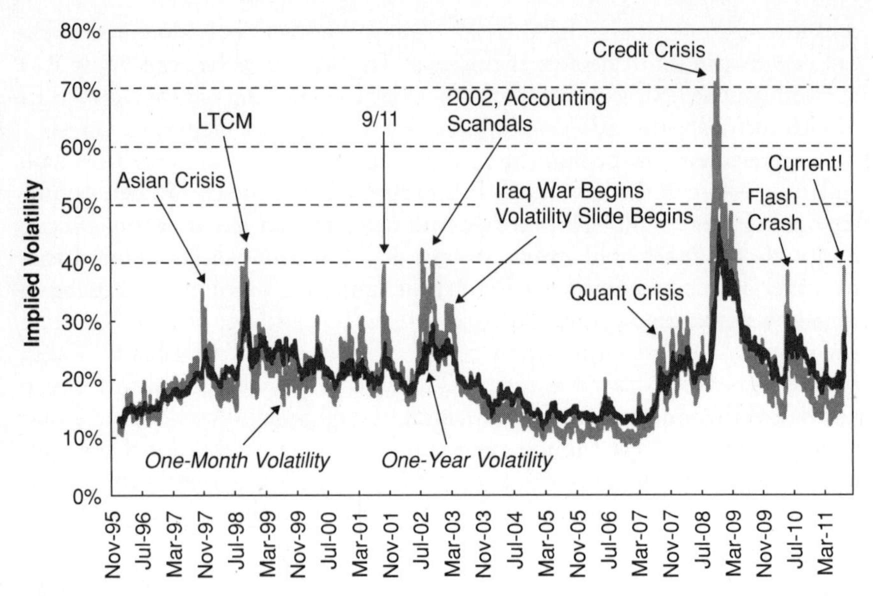


**FIGURE I.1** Time line of the VIX (lighter) and one-month VIX (darker) over more recent events where risk management appeared to the public to be wrongfully applied or if applied failed to hedge the exposed risk.

If one had foreknowledge that these events were going to occur, then there would be no risk. This time line serves to remind us that losses were incurred during each event and that a lack of properly applied risk management allowed these losses. Risk management did not lead to losses as is usually the notation applied in the general media; its misapplication merely allowed losses to occur. In most of these situations, the "this time it's different" syndrome was applied, too, albeit it wasn't different. There are three commonalities associated with most crises: increasing correlations across assets, downward-trending market prices, and higher volatility. Additionally, one can argue that these situations are driven by fear and panic, which results in a decoupling of fundamentals with securities as investors are more concerned about macro risks than firm-specific risks. The three are preponderant, however, and are almost universal constants, allowing us to say, "This time it's the same," which readers should make their default supposition going forward whenever a crisis occurs. Moreover, the VIX can be used at a glance to reference when time stationarity breaks down. Generally and usually, when the VIX spikes, the covariance and correlations across assets make a break from the historical relationship. Therefore, if the VIX jumps to local highs, it is likely that existing risk modeling processes that use historical asset prices and returns to estimate the covariances across assets will subsequently produce covariances and estimates that are too low.

Interestingly, notice that the Internet bubble is not annotated here. The fact that its crash did not result in a severely spiking VIX indicates "that time it *was* different." Particularly, though quite an event in the United States, the Internet bubble was not—nor did it precede—an economic crisis, banking failure, or currency crisis. It was unique in that construct relative to the events labeled on the short time line of Figure I.1. In fact, Reinhart and Rogoff hardly mention the Internet bubble in their book *This Time Is Different* except to say it was not related to economic debacles. It was a nonevent when it comes to crisis definition, though it led to huge losses for many. Similarly, Black Monday of October 1987 was also not associated with any other crisis. As Nobel laureate Paul Samuelson famously quipped, "the stock market has predicted nine out of the last five recessions"; market run-ups are notorious for generating false signals when it comes to predicting financial crises, and we call attention to their difference for the average reader.[5]

Now, these event risks are often described by the media as risk management failures. Whenever an exposed risk is experienced, we hear or read about the losses associated with it and this is what catches a reporter's attention. The current crisis of 2008 (continuing even as we write) involving housing bubbles, credit crunches, currency issues (Eurozone), and the overwhelming developed world debt, hangs over us, making news every day. Why? The losses experienced in 2008 and the potential for additional future losses create a perception that if risk management techniques are being applied, they have been and may continue to be ineffective.

The annotations on this chart are illustrative of global crises of economic origins where the application of RM, as observed by the economy as a whole, appeared to have failed us. However, at the individual portfolio level, applications of RM had lowered risk substantially. For instance, in 2007 and 2008 a risk attribution report demonstrated that a large-cap portfolio of a manager we know had significant exposure to volatility. Seeing the VIX hike up to very high levels during 2007, this enterprising PM began rotating his portfolio toward lower-volatility assets. Since broad market returns are generally negatively correlated with the VIX, during 2008 he outperformed the S&P 500 by over 800 basis points. The old portfolio would have roughly performed the S&P's negative –37 percent return had this application of RM not been employed.

## WARREN BUFFETT'S RISK MANAGEMENT STRATEGY

Many people do not know that Warren Buffett was a student of the famous value investor (often thought of as the father of value investing) Benjamin Graham. Now, Ben Graham never liked the term *beta*. In a *Barron's* article, he said that what bothered him was that authorities equate beta with the concept of risk.[6] Price variability yes, risk no. "Real risk," he wrote, "is measured not by price fluctuations but by a loss of quality and earnings power through economic or management changes." Similarly, in Warren Buffett's 2003 Letter to Shareholders of Berkshire Hathaway we read:

> *When we can't find anything exciting in which to invest, our "default" position is U.S. Treasuries. . . . Charlie and I detest taking even small risks unless we feel we are being adequately compensated for doing so. About as far as we will go down that path is to occasionally eat cottage cheese a day after the expiration date.*

Buffett does not take risks that are inappropriate in relation to their resources. Additionally, in the Berkshire 2010 Letter to Shareholders in regard to hiring a new investment manager, he said:

> *It's easy to identify many investment managers with great recent records. But past results, though important, do not suffice when prospective performance is being judged. How the record has been achieved is crucial, as is the manager's understanding of—and sensitivity to—risk (which in no way should be measured by beta, the choice of too many academics). In respect to the risk criterion, we were looking for someone with a hard-to-evaluate skill: the ability to anticipate the effects of economic scenarios not previously observed.*

Ben Graham and Warren Buffett believed there are times in the market when prices are just too high for investors to be buying stocks at that time. In this sense, they believe companies have intrinsic values. The trader's mentality, however, says that if prices are too high in the market, maybe it's time to short them. The market maker's mentality uses the art of price discovery to seek that right price, and if Warren or Ben feels the market is too high for a long position, then they should short it. But we digress; not buying a security because you believe it is overvalued is a form of risk management for a long-only portfolio that has been successfully executed. Risk for Buffett and Graham was/is really the potential for losses, not variance or volatility of returns. Beta is an attempt to capture both volatility and correlation between a portfolio (or security) and its benchmark in a single measure. Neither Ben nor Warren believed beta is a valid definition of risk. However, by carefully and thoughtfully extending their estimate of a company's future cash flows, they are in fact estimating volatility or variance of returns (albeit perhaps unknowingly), since stock returns are correlated to cash flow and asset volatility. Yet, since Warren is not a relative investor, the concept of beta isn't useful to him, simply because it is more akin to a *relative* volatility measure, separate and distinct from his view on general volatility.

Buffett's and Graham's ideas about risk management are often the template for many fundamental investors. That is, when researching a company, they simultaneously ascertain its potential for return and its potential for losses. In doing so, these two are complicit in understanding that they have a responsibility to determine who are the firm's customers and clients, its competitors, as well as its vendors and suppliers. By making themselves aware of this interacting chain of connectedness between companies, while simultaneously judging the business environment impact down and up this chain, they are essentially capturing the covariance between these companies in a qualitative sense—though they probably never thought about these concepts mathematically that way.

Warren Buffett and Charlie Munger study their target acquisition so deeply they construct an alpha estimate as well as a covariance matrix for risk forecasting, but all in their heads. They consider event risk by forming a judgment about how the company will do in different economic environments, and weigh the impact of the company's sales ability to its customers, its ability to obtain suppliers, and the associated costs, and form an opinion about how the company's competitors will fare in such environments. This is exactly what the process involves for covariance matrix estimation, albeit completely mathematically. We cannot know for sure whether this is a conscious activity on their behalf (i.e., if you ask Buffett if he considers the covariance across companies he owns, he'd probably say no), but doing this well helps to explain the strong investment performance Berkshire Hathaway has achieved through the years.

One might be tempted to believe that Warren Buffett thinks of companies as independent entities (statistically speaking, independent and identically distributed [i.i.d.]) and that the covariance across assets doesn't enter his mind at all in evaluating risk. The fact that he doesn't consider beta a useful risk metric implies he doesn't consider return or price volatility as useful measures of risk, either. That mind-set would lead to ignoring the covariance across assets, which is a proxy for understanding the interdependence between a company and its customers and suppliers. Additionally, it would lead to ignoring stock price volatility, a proxy for cash-flow volatility, but we know he does both of these activities. Thus, it's difficult to come to terms with his magnificent investing record if he indeed doesn't account for these, even if he does so subconsciously and just as a result of his deep research.

After reading letters to shareholders from Berkshire Hathaway over the years, one pictures Warren Buffett as an investor who applies rigorous risk management techniques. We would argue that his method of applying RM isn't condensed to mathematical equations, but his focus and attentiveness to the loss of principal, the stability of cash flows, and the contagion of risks from unforeseen events and different economic environments is in essence the personification of a covariance matrix. Warren Buffett is a covariance matrix. You heard it here first.

## DEFINING RISK MANAGEMENT

If you read your typical mutual fund prospectus, you'll get prose outlining the major investment risks the investor will assume by investing in the fund. These could include market risk, foreign currency exposure, industry concentration, interest rate risk, credit risk, issuer risk, liquidity risk, derivatives risk, prepayment risk, leverage risk, emerging market risk, management risk, legislative risk, short sales risk, and so forth. Risks of these natures are explicitly defined because lawyers and compliance personnel require it. However, many of these definitions are incredibly and often deliberately vague. Consider this definition of issuer nondiversification risk lifted from a mutual fund prospectus:

> **Issuer Nondiversification Risk:** *The risk of focusing investments in a small number of issuers, including being more susceptible to risks associated with a single economic, political, or regulatory occurrence than a more diversified portfolio might be. Funds that are "nondiversified" may invest a greater percentage of their assets in the securities of a single issuer (such as bonds issued by a particular state) than funds that are "diversified."*

Now seriously, would the average investor have a better understanding of how this risk would impact an investment in the fund? How about the majority of investors? What does this really mean? How is this illustrative? The litigious society we live in has led to this description of risk and is a wonderful example of why risk management is mostly misunderstood. This leads us to make distinctions between quantifiable and nonquantifiable risks.

For instance, take human risk (fraud, incompetence, and theft), process or technology risk, litigation risk, and operational risk. Though we all agree these are important risks to consider, we probably have large disagreements on how to measure them. Can we attach a probability of fraud to each employee, determine employee correlations, and aggregate the fraud risk across the firm? Probably not; fraud risk is nonquantifiable, and thus for these kinds of risks we usually form policy guidelines and have people sign off that they have read them on an annual basis rather than use hard, calculated metrics.

Likewise, how would you estimate litigation risk for a software company? Can a metric for patent infringement be ascertained? What can a firm do to first characterize this risk and then minimize it? These kinds of risks have high interest, of course, but are not the focus of our discussion. Instead, we devote this book to dealing with quantifiable risks and teaching the art of using these metrics to control and manage risks. There are numerous ways to define risk management, but for the purposes of discussion in this work, we are speaking mainly about mathematical, statistical, and probabilistic assessment of risks. In this vein, we first need to clarify the risk problem we hope to solve, the assets whose risks we'll measure, and the methods to measure or characterize these risks; then, once we have measured the risks, we discuss how to mitigate them.

First, however, consider a remark from an old friend of ours, now president of Manning & Napier Advisors, Jeffrey Coons. When asked years ago, "Do you engage in any hedging?" he responded, "Our best hedge is not to own the asset." Unfortunately, even for bright and experienced investment managers this is often the flippant response, but this is actually only a minor risk-reduction process, not a risk-removing process. This is because, though one may not own an asset, most likely one owns several assets correlated with it, in which case if the unowned asset tanks, it will affect those closely correlated to it and take them down with it. This is what contagion is all about and is similar in essence to the earlier discussion about Warren Buffett's methods. Applying successful risk management strategies properly means accounting for the cross-correlations between assets and in fact is the crux of risk management's chore. Thus, behaving as if a single market asset is completely decoupled from all others is not well thought out.

Now Jeff is certainly aware of this; he just had the equivalent of a senior moment earlier in his career. I'm sure he would answer that question differently today and we know he employs the Buffett methodologies discussed earlier, but the story lends itself to making the strongest point one can about risk management methodologies, which is that measuring, characterizing, and forecasting correlation risks are some of the most important aspects of risk management. All other decisions about portfolio asset allocation build off of them (if one has an alpha estimate, too, even better). Whether or not this is possible is what's argued in the press and why Nassim Taleb adorns revolutionary garb and gets all up in arms about it. We'll address these topics continually throughout this book.

To complete this introduction, we must address the most important and earliest approximation in risk management, and that is the normal (Gaussian) approximation. In general, this was the de facto distribution used for estimating and forecasting risk for a very long time. It has two basic correlated fallacies: one, that returns are normally distributed, and two, that event risk (obsidian uncertainties, market bubbles, credit crisis, Asian contagion, and so forth) occurs far less frequently than it actually does.

There are plenty of books that cover this topic in detail, so we won't spend much time on it. A decent example of why the normal approximation has held hegemony for so long is reported by David Esch.[7] Though he attempts to make the case that departing from the normal distribution to characterize asset returns is ill-advised, he doesn't add that perhaps the chief reason has to do with the computational proclivity of the normal distribution. The finance community (in general) is finally coming to recognize the limitations of the normal distribution, and in light of the credit crisis of 2008 and an emphasis from regulatory authorities (UCITS), there is an increasing focus on extreme risks these days. However, and with regret, the normal distribution isn't a sufficient characterization to accurately describe tail risks. Throughout this book, references to the normal distribution will be made and the reader should be aware of why this is. It's primarily due to the historical use of it in finance literature, the familiarity with it most people and technicians have, and the significant ease of use and simplification of the mathematics and concepts in explaining results. That being said, in today's highly computationally capable environment, it is being used less and less and will go the way of the Edsel (manufactured by Ford in the late 1950s). The normal distribution is earmarked by being too symmetrical and not fat-tailed enough; it is too conservative. These are ideal properties, mind you, but will incorrectly model the empirical return distribution of most tradable assets.

## FAT TAILS, STATIONARITY, CORRELATION, AND OPTIMIZATION

One major concern today is with tail risk. There are publications on this topic from Svetlozar Rachev too numerous to mention, stretching back before this century began. One prominent book in particular by Rachev, Menn, and Fabozzi[8] acts as the treatise on the subject for general readership. In addition, one would like to answer why returns are nonnormal. Are deviations from normality significant and stable through time? Can we forecast them, or will the nonnormality vanish with time? It's not just whether asset returns are normally distributed and whether that is too simplistic an approximation to describe them, but that asset returns are also not independent. If asset returns are correlated, nonnormal, and fat-tailed, then even mean-variance optimization isn't optimal. The efficient frontier under these conditions must be suspect.

These days, this issue has enough attention from the finance community and asset managers that a software company has existed for a decade that has a production-ready product for performing mean-fat-tail (mean expected tail loss, or mean-conditional value at risk [mean-CVaR]) portfolio optimization, so easily found that all you have to do is type "fat-tailed optimization" in Google to locate it. There are even several patents issued on this (e.g., U.S. Patent 7,778,897) and related technologies. Several books document the impact of fat tails, kurtosis, and skewness on returns, their distribution descriptions, and expected tail loss optimization effects.[9]

It's important to recognize that in all portfolio construction or asset allocation optimization methodologies a chief underlying assumption is the stationarity of the underlying time series, return distributions, and covariance. Even in direct risk forecasts, let alone optimization, this assumption is paramount. Though this has been partially answered in Campbell et al.,[10] all modern-day risk vendors that estimate a covariance matrix wouldn't have a business if this didn't hold. Without that—without withholding in one's worldview a sudden structural change in the covariance matrix like when a Black Swan or obsidian uncertainty occurs (as in the 2008 credit crisis)—the resultant optimized solution cannot be expected to be useful to any investor, nor can it be expected that realized risk will follow forecasted risk very well. That volatility and covariance regimes exist long enough so that the estimates are useful most of the time in regular markets is what gives these methods their credence to investors. This is an obligatory condition for the usefulness of mean-variance or mean-fat-tail optimization; without it, risk management methodologies are not useful. Even a simple tracking error forecast is useless if one doesn't have some element of time-stable covariance across assets.

When you start talking about tail correlations, stationarity becomes an even more important assumption. Multivariate modeling of the dependence of extreme outcomes comes to mind in this regard. Tail correlations can fluctuate more than the overall covariance matrix through time, much like a dog's tail is more volatile than the dog (except when the dog is sleeping, and covariance never sleeps). One might consider that the typical investors' opportunity set is comprised of the cross section of return capabilities, as opposed to the time series of returns, which is what typically defines fat tails. That is, at any given moment an investor has to choose among assets, and does this cross section of returns have a fat-tailed distribution with an economic origin? Might there be some warrant for asymmetrical distribution of returns across the opportunity set on any given day?

There is a huge volume of literature discussing sample covariance calculations versus parametrically modeling for covariance estimation. That is, one can compute an asset-by-asset covariance or correlation matrix from a database of their historical returns quite easily nowadays. However, is its use thereafter a better forecaster of risks than one created using a variety of techniques to construct a more parsimonious covariance matrix? These methodologies, termed *parametric*, are defined by using a common set of properties whose values determine the characteristics of asset returns (or prices). Since the common factors are, say, between 50 to 100 versus the number of assets, which could be 30,000 or more, one creates a smaller, more parsimonious covariance matrix to describe the common or market returns with concomitant noise reduction in the estimate. That is, when you directly compute covariance estimates from sample returns, spurious correlations are likely among the true covariances. A parametric covariance estimate will tend to "signal average" away spuriously noisy results. There are so many ways the parametric approach allows for better forecasting of risks than a sample covariance matrix.

Many FactSet vendors offer mean-variance portfolio optimization. However, one has to be careful when invoking any asset allocation or optimization technology simply as a force-fed method to offer diversification. The default portfolio construction assumption is that once you've arrived at more than 60 assets (the number used to be 30 before the credit crisis) you have a diversified portfolio. What optimization offers as a solution to portfolio construction is a better way to inhibit assuming you've achieved diversification simply by gathering a collection of securities together. It does so by deriving a solution based on solid economic principles, offering reproducibility, robustness, and higher-quality control over the investment process. Considering that the investment process is the embodiment of the investment philosophy, optimization works in situ to help define the investment structure and is more than mere implementation methodology. The two major ingredients needed to use optimization in asset allocation applications are alpha forecasts at the stock-specific level and a risk model (which includes the covariance matrix).

Mean-variance optimization offers a methodology that utilizes both the investors' estimates of alpha and their estimate of risk.

During the early stages of professional asset management, attention was mostly given to the alpha side of the trade-off between risk and reward. The landscape started to change in 1975 when Barra, Inc. produced its first risk model, meeting a need that traditional financiers, MBAs, and investment managers had neither the wherewithal nor the training to do alone—model risk. At this time the financial engineering profession didn't exist, so so-called quants weren't around with the math skills to offer much in regard to modeling covarying risk. For this reason, chief investment officers (CIOs) kept their people busy working on the alpha side, and they mostly outsourced the risk measuring, monitoring, and calculating to Barra. Similarly, having risk forecasts and alpha forecasts in numerical form allowed the application of mean-variance optimization as invented by Harry Markowitz to become practical.[11] Thus, with Barra came actionable mean-variance optimization, much before anybody was thinking about fat tails and asymmetric risk forecasting. This methodology grew and many people began using optimization, and its spread gave rise to many other risk vendors, many of which have been integrated into the FactSet workstation, wonderfully so. For many, especially in regard to relative risk or benchmark relative investing, mean-variance optimization is a wonderful tool for determining the most appropriate security weights. Mean-variance optimization at the very least is better than aligning security position weights (whether active or absolute) proportional to one's alpha assessment alone. This is because so often the alpha estimate from an investor is independent and identically distributed (i.i.d.) while the risk estimate used in mean-variance optimization accounts for asset covariance. This leads us to distinguish between active weight and active exposure, often thought to be one and the same.

The fact that active exposure is not the same thing as active weight is extremely important in asset allocation. Consider an investor's portfolio with a benchmark relative active weight of 5 percent in the information technology (IT) sector. Now, what other assets in the portfolio have correlations to this sector? For that matter, which securities have been assigned to the IT sector that have significant correlation to another sector? Consider a software company whose clients are all in the asset management business. Would you think this IT company has exposure (i.e., correlation) to the financial sector? To pull a Sarah Palin moment, "you betcha." Thus the concept of exposure gets expressed in the results of a mean-variance portfolio optimization because asset correlation is contributing to the exposure of an asset to other factors and other companies. This isn't ascertained or utilized when setting security weights proportional to the individual assessment of alpha alone. Exposure is not just a function of industry, country, or currency classification (e.g., Standard & Poor's Global Industry Classification Standards [GICS]) but also accounts for an asset's stationary correlation with the groups that it has not been assigned to.

Now, there is a reason to offer statistical resampling of optimized portfolios due to optimization having the side effect of emphasizing the extreme components of the covariance matrix. That is, for any given covariance matrix, whether created from a parametric model or from a sample covariance matrix, the effect of optimization pivots on accentuating those matrix elements that are the extrema of the matrix. Thus if many elements are small (in absolute value), but there are a few extremes (large in absolute value), the optimized portfolio can be dominated by these extreme values. Additionally, there's no reason to believe these extreme values in and of themselves don't have major contributions from spurious correlations between assets making the individual elements larger than they should be. Applying statistical resampling of the optimized portfolio to account for this can help. This method demonstrates an ability to help lower estimation error, which is written about in great detail,[12] but it's still an open question whether resampling of optimized sample weight percentages or computing a parsimonious covariance through a parametric risk model contributes more to estimation error reduction. Shrinkage methods can also be applied on the covariance matrix to essentially lower or draw in the extreme covariance matrix elements, but this method is more art than science.[13]

When speaking about fat tails, even in their time-series form, one should include a discussion of their underlying properties, as we did earlier for exposure. As asset correlations reach extreme values during a market shock, they're accompanied by negative downtrends in asset pricing, which are the main drivers of the negative tail. There are several examples where mean-CVaR optimized portfolios outperform mean-variance optimized portfolios in back-tests. For instance, a simple example is noted in Xiong and Idzorek where they give evidence of multiple portfolios' demonstration of this attribute when properly accounting for fat tails.[14] They yield better results and higher risk-adjusted portfolio returns, too, relative to mean-variance optimized portfolios, but only when the asset classes have fat tails. They compare the risk defined by variance versus the risk defined by expected tail loss, and offer insight into the risk measure, though they do not give a comprehensive review of the subject and offer very limited references.

Now, if the investment manager is a relative manager, performing portfolio optimization against a benchmark with many hard constraints, the advantage of mean-CVaR optimization is less consistent and mean-variance optimization is suitable and easier. This is because, though a return series of a portfolio may be fat-tailed, if the benchmark has a similar return distribution, their difference is usually normal, and active weight solutions through mean variance then vary as the difference between two fat-tailed distributions (it is easy to think of it that way). In particular, the distribution of tracking error through time is normal then, for instance.

Another important question to answer is whether the tail correlation itself or the mathematical specification of the fat tail is the greater contributor to mean-fat-tail outperformance over mean-variance optimization. If the fat tail is incorrectly specified, will the optimization overcome it anyway? David

Esch believes one reason to avoid moving away from a normal description of assets has to do with just this—that mathematically specifying the tail is so difficult that one introduces errors simply by trying. This is relatively trivial to answer, however, and is worth noting that it describes a typical scenario the physics community deals with continually, and lends itself to describing why risk management is such a multidisciplinary approach nowadays. Fat tails can have significant importance for portfolio formation, which is well and widely known. But we would like to offer a rational economic discussion for why fat tails exist and comment on the important outstanding issues on the subject; we will cover that in future chapters.

## MANAGING THE RISKS OF A RISK MANAGEMENT STRATEGY

In general, when the modeling of risks, however performed, doesn't characterize them correctly and the time stationarity behavior of assets doesn't hold, the covariance matrix computed isn't the one of the latest extreme event (e.g., credit crises) resulting in diversification being an illusion, risks concentrating, and losses occurring. Thus the proper application of RM will entail accounting for these risks of RM itself. The users or implementers of the risk measurement system must be acutely aware of the shortcomings of the methodology, and must know how the risks are calculated and what approximations are used. They must also be widely cognizant of both short-term risks as well as the longer-term forecasts. What risk models do well is predict the persistent trends, the levels less so. Moreover, keeping one's mind's eye on the stationary of the covariance between assets is important, and continually examining the correlations between assets is a necessary chore to be monitored daily at various horizons for the enterprising portfolio manager. For example, by monitoring the CBOE's VIX, one can keep an eye on how well the expected risk forecasts should be working. For when the VIX spikes, it's very likely that risk forecasts underestimate the true risk for equities simply because VIX spikes are associated with spikes in the covariance between assets, so that the covariance estimated from historical values isn't representative of the current situation. It is an uncommon philosophy that one must be a risk manager of one's own risk management strategy, but it should not be understated. This should be the practitioner's modus operandi.

Likewise, monitoring the balance between common risks and security-specific risks from one's risk model is helpful in determining when the risk model should be trusted more or trusted less. If common factor or market risks are increasing as a percentage of the total risk, most likely the market is increasing its correlation between assets and one should be prepared for a dislocation to occur between fundamentals and securities. This also leads to when stock pickers should have a higher probability of market outperformance. When the risks are increasing into stock-specific residual risks as a percentage of total risks, market risks are falling and fundamentals increasingly matter. We'll give examples of this in future chapters. In effect, this is an example of how one can remedy model risk; given all the risk-forecasting strategies one might be using, each is subject to model risk, and hedging model risk is all about proactively validating the model's assumptions on a continuous basis. This is particularly true when complexity is involved in the risk estimation models or the risk management overall strategy. This means that a culture of risk assessment should be grown and fostered within an organization. Does preventing a $1 million loss have the same emphasis and support as a $1 million gain? When it does, then we believe the appropriate level of risk awareness has been reached making risk management an integral part of the operating process of the firm. A firm is less likely to overexpose itself to a single investment asset or theme (as MF Global did in 2010 with a huge bet on euro sovereign debt and went bankrupt) when the risk managers have the same veto rights in the portfolios as the portfolio managers. This equivalence of veto rights is found more commonly in European and Asian asset managers than in the United States.

We have written that risk models predict persistent trends with more accuracy than the actual levels of risk. Often the users of risk models, however, have expectations for the risk modeling process that demand accuracy at computing portfolio-level values and even expect this accuracy to be maintained at the individual security level. However, if risk managers turn the question around and ask these analysts and PMs responsible for selecting the assets for this same kind of accuracy in their alpha estimate, their response would be that it's impossible. In fact, they'd be told, "That's why we hold a portfolio: we cannot be certain of the alpha we're expecting from any single name, so we diversify." Thus, I find it troubling when these same people have expectations for risk forecasts at the security level to supersede their alpha forecasts for these same securities. That is something akin to forecasting their alpha within +/–5 percent over some time frame whereas they want risk forecasts within +/–1 percent over the identical time period.

Often quantitatively minded PMs will estimate alphas for their portfolios over, say, 1,000 securities. In essence they rank them by their computed alpha from some model (or investment team's consensus opinion). Then, they're quite conscious that their investing process cannot discriminate between a stock ranked 78th versus one ranked 81st. However, they then use a risk modeling software or vendor program and get worried that the reported risk for some security is 2.563 for one security and 2.565 for another, and they behave like the security with a risk assignment of 2.565 is actually a more at-risk security than the one with the 2.563 standard deviation rating over some fixed horizon.

Even fundamental investors will behave this way. We've seen fundamental managers obfuscate a bit when asked to rank their best bets versus their worst, simply because they do not have high confidence in discriminating one security from another. In addition, the weights they select for the securities are often ad hoc and proportional to their estimation of a security's alpha contribution even though they're not sure. It's funny then when they scrutinize a risk model (and RM process) and demand accuracy from it that they themselves cannot purport to offer on the alpha side of the investment process. This comes about from misunderstanding what risk management and modeling are about and is one impetus for this book.

It's important to understand that the accuracy of the risk forecast cannot be much greater than the accuracy of the return forecast for a security, and while forecasting volatility is generally a bit more accurate than forecasting return, it is not nearly to the degree that many professional investors believe it to be. In the risk forecast, the common factor risks of the portfolio are the nondiversifying component of risk and are usually much larger than the idiosyncratic pieces. For different risk models, the actual level of this common factor or market risk component will be different simply because the factors will be different. However, what two different risk models will do well is track the risk trend through time quite similarly. Though their levels may be different, the difference between their particular level and the true risk is quite stationary and slowly evolving. In essence their difference sparks a true cointegrating time series.[15] Thus, tracking the real risk is accurate though the level is off a bit. Think of the model risk level as being parallel to the true realized risk, and in this fashion the risk model becomes highly useful over time at the portfolio level. However, given this amount of error at the portfolio level, the individual security components of risk estimation have larger errors and are less reliable for basing investment decisions on. Thus, one important characteristic of risk model usage is to maintain the same risk model for a while. Managing to a given risk model's forecasts through time means one is managing the risk at a constant relative relationship to true risk. If one keeps changing risk models, then the level of true risk you manage the assets to moves around as well. We'll discuss how to choose a risk model in tune with one's investment process later.

## THE RISK MANAGEMENT OPPORTUNITY SET

Anyone responsible for measuring and managing risk, globally or within a particular market, should benefit from having a perspective about the sizes of different investment markets. Of course these size measures are good only for the period in which they're calculated because as prices move around, so does a market's total capitalization. The numbers reported in Table I.1 are average values and are meant only to give the reader a rule of thumb understanding of their relative size. Unfortunately, if you examine multiple sources for economic data on the same country, you often get varying numbers. The enterprising reader should be mindful of the errors about their levels, similar to reported risk numbers.

We deliberately avoid attaching a date to the references as we want the reader to use these very roughly. Nevertheless, the entire U.S. public equity market is approximately $15 trillion, depending on the day (if you include stocks trading at low liquidity), comprising roughly 6,000 stocks whose total market capitalization nears the size of the U.S. gross domestic product (GDP); this is out of a total global stock market of almost $70 trillion.

To create Table I.1, we downloaded all common stocks within the FactSet database in January 2012 with trading liquidity larger than 10,000 shares per day, and merely sorted by region. While we're not giving historical values here, it's noteworthy that the market capitalization of Europe is now larger than that of North America, while the number of opportunities to invest (number of different companies) from Asia dwarfs both Europe and the United States. This wasn't the case just a few years ago.

**TABLE I.1** Approximate relative size of global regional stock markets as of January 2012.

| Region | Number of Stocks | Market Cap (USD in millions) | % of Total Stocks | % of Total Market Cap |
|---|---|---|---|---|
| Europe | 3,670 | 26,113,983 | 14.66 | 37.78 |
| North America | 6,051 | 20,566,375 | 24.17 | 29.75 |
| Asia | 13,632 | 19,251,563 | 54.46 | 27.85 |
| Nordic countries | 515 | 1,532,384 | 2.06 | 2.22 |
| Middle East | 804 | 602,330 | 3.21 | 0.87 |
| Africa | 229 | 574,574 | 0.91 | 0.83 |
| South America | 127 | 478,837 | 0.51 | 0.69 |
| Grand total | 25,031 | 69,120,408 | | |

*Source:* FactSet.

Mutual funds contain roughly $11.1 trillion in assets, including equity funds $4.8 trillion, balanced funds $0.78 trillion, and bond funds $2.8 trillion. It's interesting that although the bond market is much larger than the equity market, the largest share of assets under management in mutual funds is comprised of equities.

Derivatives are more difficult to assess, but they are believed to have a notional amount closing in on $800 trillion. The notional amount is the market capitalization of the derivatives' underlying securities. Of this, the wide majority are basic fixed-for-floating interest rate swaps. The notional amount of credit default swaps (CDSs) is roughly $26 trillion. This notional amount refers to the par amount of credit protection bought or sold that is used to derive the CDS premium. The net amount is only $2.3 trillion.[16] (Yes, we said "only.")

Currencies are harder to measure, but suffice it to say that the Bank for International Settlements has some statistics for this most liquid market in the world. The daily trading volume of foreign exchange (FX) is just shy of $4 trillion as of this writing. If you combine total foreign exchange to include spot, forward rate agreements, foreign exchange swaps, currency swaps, and options, one arrives at about $79 trillion a month trading and, extrapolating, to just shy of $1.0 quadrillion a year in FX trading! That's $\$10^{15}$ equivalent traded, or a million billion dollars (equivalent) per year! Given this, why is it that when one travels abroad one has to pay such a huge commission to convert a measly $100 at Heathrow to British pound sterling for taxi money? Well, that's another story.

The U.S. debt market is roughly $9.85 trillion when you combine Treasury bills, notes, and bonds.[17] If you add in intragovernmental holdings of $4.7 trillion, you arrive at $15.1 trillion in outstanding U.S. government debt. Compare this with China's domestic debt market of about $3 trillion. Following (in trillions of USD) in the United States we have: municipal bonds $3.7, mortgage-related securities $8.5, corporate debt $7.7, federal agency debt $2.3, money markets $2.6, and asset-backed securities $1.8, with the final tally at $36.3 trillion for U.S. debt in totality. The global bond (debt) market stands at about $82 trillion.

Who owns the U.S. debt? The top 10 foreign exchange reserves holdings of U.S. debt in billions of USD listed from the December 27, 2011, *Wall Street Journal* are: China has $3,200 billion, Japan $1,300 billion, Russia $526 billion, Saudi Arabia $525 billion, Taiwan $388 billion, Brazil $352 billion, Switzerland $347 billion, India $316 billion, South Korea $311 billion, and Hong Kong $282 billion, accounting for $7.54 trillion or about 60 percent of all U.S. debt outstanding. Throw that debt on top of about $30 trillion of unfunded Medicare liability, and the United States owes a lot of money. U.S. governments might easily decide that such promises like

Medicare and Social Security have a better claim on tax revenues than the rights of foreign debt holders one day.

Compare these to the Eurozone's government debt-to-GDP levels as seen in Table I.2.

From this chart, the GIIPS countries (Greece, Italy, Ireland, Portugal, and Spain) have debt-to-GDP levels that are obviously higher than the average, though Spain is the least of their worries. The U.S. GDP is approximately $15 trillion, while the U.S. debt is of the same magnitude before you add in all municipal and government agency debt, and then it's much higher; Medicare liabilities approach $30 trillion. Given the debt levels of the United States, it won't be long before the Grecian formula must be applied to the United States, too. The United States' saving grace is that it can print its own currency, though Greece might be able to soon as well, if it is vanquished from the Eurozone. The United Kingdom looks relatively fiscally responsible compared to other European nations in terms of debt-to-GDP level. The 27-member Eurozone has a collective GDP of roughly $16.2 trillion, with total sovereign debt about 85 percent of that level. China's GDP is on the order of $5+ trillion and growing while its debt to GDP is reportedly somewhere between 18 percent to 34 percent,

**TABLE I.2** Approximate gross sovereign debt to GDP as of December 2010.

| | | | |
|---|---|---|---|
| France | 86% | Lithuania | 38% |
| Germany | 81% | Luxembourg | 19% |
| Italy | 121% | Malta | 72% |
| Austria | 72% | Netherlands | 64% |
| Bulgaria | 15% | Poland | 56% |
| Cyprus | 68% | Portugal | 106% |
| Czech Republic | 40% | Romania | 34% |
| Denmark | 47% | Slovak Republic | 43% |
| Estonia | 6% | Slovenia | 44% |
| Finland | 45% | Spain | 66% |
| Greece | 154% | Sweden | 37% |
| Hungary | 77% | Belgium | 98% |
| Ireland | 102% | United States | 100% |
| Latvia | 45% | United Kingdom | 77% |

*Sources:* The data is from the bank of England and European Central Bank websites and the U.S. Treasury Summary Report of November 2011.

depending on who is reporting it, but one must consider China's huge trade surplus of over $3 trillion when considering its debt-to-GDP ratio. Japan's debt-to-GDP ratio is over 200 percent.[18]

One should be aware that the growth of global sovereign debt has been awesome since 2001. Local-currency government debt stood at an outstanding $11 trillion in 2001, whereas by the end of 2011 it was at $32 trillion. We see a doubling in investment grade foreign currency debt, securitized debt, and investment grade corporate debt from 2001 to 2011.[19]

Though the size of the various markets seems unrelated to risk management as a topic, we believe it's helpful to be able to put these numbers in perspective when considering the task of applying RM methods appropriately in various markets and asset types.

## NOTES

1. Nigel Sleigh-Johnson, "The Great Expectations of Risk Reporting," *Financial Times*, November 28, 2011.
2. Basel Committee on Banking Supervision, "Principles for Sound Liquidity Risk Management and Supervision," September 2008.
3. Nassim Taleb, *The Black Swan*, 2nd ed. (New York: Random House, 2007); and Scott Patterson, *The Quants* (New York: Crown Business, 2010).
4. Carmen M. Reinhart and Kenneth Rogoff, *This Time Is Different* (Princeton, NJ: Princeton University Press, 2009).
5. Paul Samuelson, "Science and Stocks," *Newsweek*, September 19, 1966.
6. Excerpt from *Barron's*, September 23, 1974.
7. David N. Esch, "Non-Normality Facts and Fallacies," *Journal of Investment Management* 8, no. 1 (2010).
8. Svetlozar Rachev, Christian Menn, and Frank J. Fabozzi, *Fat-Tailed and Skewed Asset Return Distributions: Implications for Risk Management, Portfolio Selection, and Option Pricing* (Hoboken, NJ: John Wiley & Sons, 2005).
9. For example, see Svetlozar Rachev and Stefan Mittnik, *Stable Paretian Models in Finance* (New York: John Wiley & Sons, 2000).
10. Rachel A. J. Campbell, Catherine S. Forbes, Kees G. Koedijk, and Paul Kofman, "Increasing Correlations or Just Fat Tails?" *Journal of Empirical Finance* 15 (2008): 287–309.
11. Harry M. Markowitz, "Portfolio Selection," *Journal of Finance* 7, no. 1 (1952): 77–91.
12. Bernd Scherer and R. Douglas Martin, *Introduction to Modern Portfolio Optimization* (New York: Springer, 2005).
13. Olivier Ledoit and Michael Wolf, "Honey, I Shrunk the Sample Covariance Matrix," UPF Economics and Business Working Paper 691, June/November 2003; David J. Disatnik and Simon Benninga, "Shrinking the Covariance Matrix," *Journal of Portfolio Management*, Summer 2007.

14. James X. Xiong and Thomas M. Idzorek, "The Impact of Skewness and Fat-Tails on the Asset Allocation Decision," *Financial Analysts Journal* 67, no. 2 (March/April 2011).
15. Clive Granger, "Some Properties of Time-Series Data and Their Use in Econometric Model Specification," *Journal of Econometrics* 16 (1981): 121–130.
16. International Swaps and Derivatives Association, December 2011 report.
17. Securities Industry and Financial Markets Association (SIFMA), October 2011 report; U.S. Treasury Monthly Statement of Public Debt, November 30, 2011.
18. *The World Factbook*, United States Central Intelligence Agency website, accessed January 2012; European Commission Eurostat, accessed January 2012; Trading Economics and International Monetary Fund, accessed January 2012.
19. *Economist*, February 11, 2012, 71.

# PART One

CHAPTER 1

# Exposed versus Experienced Risk Revisited

***Steven P. Greiner, PhD, and Andrew Geer, CFA, FRM***

If you ask five different investment professionals what the term *exposure* means to them, you'll probably get five similar, yet distinctively unique, answers. For instance, when equity portfolio managers (PMs) are discussing currency risks, they will interchangeably confuse the word *exposure* with position size in some denominated currency. Likewise, active investment management professionals often refer to a portfolio's active weight in an industry, like information technology (IT), to be its exposure to that industry. Neither of these is a correct interpretation of the term. In a nebulous sense, exposure simply represents a contribution to future portfolio risk from some source, and that's how it's mostly interpreted. In a strict sense, it represents a measurable characteristic to the portfolio such as style, industry, currency, or country association. It more exactly represents a value that, when multiplied by the portfolio's beta to the factor, yields the factor's contribution to return. This is, of course, for risk models predicated on the (somewhat) standardized methodology of using cross-sectional regressions of return for a given time period. Exposures are the actualization of stock-specific or stock-dependent values in this sense. For instance, if a risk model contains the price-to-book (P/B) ratio as a factor, exposure is a stock's P/B. If the risk model contains stock price momentum as a factor, then exposure is the stock's price momentum value, calculated by one of the many mathematical definitions of momentum. A regression of security returns versus the exposure yields the factor beta for a given time period. If you run these cross-sectional regressions for many periods, you obtain a time series of these betas, and by monitoring these time series one can ascertain information about the stability and stationarity of the underlying process.

Let's review an insightful example of exposure analysis based on a client's inquiry about risk model exposures for Axcelis Technologies Inc. (ticker ACLS). The risk model showed a suspicious exposure to Italy, although Axcelis has no operations there. Furthermore, according to its 10-K, ACLS should have a large exposure to Asia-Pacific countries and currencies, but it had zero exposure according to the risk model.

Now, we caution that just because a company claims that it has risk somewhere does not mean it is so. For instance, on page 15 of Axcelis's 2011 10-K we read:

> *Axcelis is subject to the risks of operating internationally and we derive a substantial portion of our revenue from outside the United States, especially from Asia.*

It's merely their opinion, not one determined from statistical analysis, and in particular, one needs to consider that it is a company's fiduciary responsibility to make that statement in a material report. Think of a mutual fund's risk disclosures; the smallest potential risk has to be enumerated even if it's infinitesimally small. Lawyers and regulators have moved the industry in this direction. So if an analyst is looking to understand why the foreign exchange (FX) exposure for Asia-Pacific countries is not detected in the risk model, she must read the fine print from Axcelis's 2011 annual report (reproduced next from several sections) where Axcelis announces that it bills in USD! When you bill in USD, you substantially reduce any FX risk that will come through in the risk model if USD is your base currency. More generally, if a company bills in the same currency a PM measures performance in, one would tend toward lowering the reported currency exposure.

> *Our international operations involve currency risk.*
>
> *Substantially all of our sales are billed in U.S. dollars, thereby reducing the impact of fluctuations in foreign exchange rates on our results. Operating margins of certain foreign operations can fluctuate with changes in foreign exchange rates to the extent revenue is billed in U.S. dollars and operating expenses are incurred in the local functional currency. During the year ended December 31, 2011, approximately 21% of our revenue was derived from foreign operations with this inherent risk. In addition, at December 31, 2011, our operations outside of the United States accounted for approximately 37% of our total assets, the majority of which was denominated in currencies other than the U.S. dollar.*

**Foreign Currency Exchange Risk**

*Substantially all of our sales are billed in U.S. dollars, thereby reducing the impact of fluctuations in foreign exchange rates on our results. Operating margins of certain foreign operations can fluctuate with changes in foreign exchange rates to the extent revenues are billed in U.S. dollars and operating expenses are incurred in the local functional currency. During the years ended December 31, 2011 and 2010, approximately 21% and 24% of our revenue were derived from foreign operations with this inherent risk. In addition, at both December 31, 2011 and 2010, our operations outside of the United States accounted for approximately 37% and 34% of our total assets, respectively, the majority of which was denominated in currencies other than the U.S. dollar.*

**Other Income (Expense)**

*Other income (expense) for the year ended December 31, 2011 primarily consisted of foreign exchange gains compared to foreign exchange losses in 2010, as a result of U.S. dollar currency fluctuations against the local currencies of certain of the countries in which we operate. For the year ended December 31, 2011 the Company incurred $1.2 million of foreign exchange gains. For the year ended December 31, 2010 the Company incurred $1.9 million of foreign exchange losses. Included in foreign exchange losses in 2010 are $0.3 million of foreign exchange losses relating to currency hedging activities.*

Additionally, Axcelis Technologies' own estimates of FX gain and losses are less than $2 million on revenues of $287 million. Its FX risk is inconsequential even from an accounting standpoint, and the risk model confirms that. In our experience, risk models are able to accurately identify factor exposures—often more accurately than a company's accountants and CFO can. Furthermore, while risk models are also often good at identifying the sources of risk that an individual security is exposed to, they lack an ability to forecast the level of risk with much precision. In aggregate, risk models are best suited for portfolio risk where the cumulative estimation errors on a single asset's risk number decreases substantially as the number of assets in the portfolio grows.

One should remember that if the FX exposure's contribution to an asset's return is statistically undetectable, then it won't be pointed out in the risk exposure analysis. This is what risk models do: measure the sensitivity to FX, to the return, and ultimately to the risk. The more FX exposure a firm actually has, the more FX will contribute to its return, which will be detected by the risk model during its construction process.

Last, the order of the regressions in the construction of a risk model matters. If one regresses returns against currency FX before country and industry, it's quite likely the currency effects will gobble up any explanation of variance before one gets to the country and industry factors. This is because currency, country, and industry factors are all correlated with each other in their natural state. So if we allow the currency factor to have the first bite of explaining a stock's variance, it is not going to just capture the stock's pure currency risk; it's also going to grab its covariance with the country and industry factors, including, in this particular case, ACLS's presumed sensitivity to Italy.

In time-series regressions to factors, the exposure is the regression parameter and the beta is the factor being regressed, the exact opposite definition of cross-sectional regressions. Usually these time-series factors involve currencies, industries, and country or regional indexes (or composite indexes). In these situations, the regression of a stock's time series of return yields the exposure, and the beta is defined and would be given by, say, the foreign exchange time-series, for instance.

If you consider setting the exposure to some currencies or industries in some risk model to 1 (as if we're using dummy variables for sensitivities to industries and currencies), then there is no reason to run regressions. One is implying by doing so that a given security has an exposure equal to its assigned denominated currency and assigned industry, designated by a governing or standardizing body or listed exchange like the Standard & Poor's (S&P) Global Industry Classification Standards (GICS). The security has no exposure to any other currency or industry. The stock would have exposure to only one currency, one industry, and one country or region using this technique. Historically, this was the method utilized in risk model construction started by Barra in 1975.

If one utilizes this technique, the portfolio exposure will correspond directly one to one with the respective weights of holdings in the portfolio. For example, if 21 percent of the portfolio's holdings are information technology (IT) companies, the portfolio exposure to information technology will appear to be 0.21 because the portfolio exposure is a linear sum of security exposure times its weight in the portfolio.

Consider, however, the operations of large-capitalization global companies. They often have vendors and suppliers across multiple industries and countries invoicing in multiple currencies. Further, they have costs and payroll in multiple currencies and customers in numerous countries and industries paying for their services and products in multiple currencies. Therefore, it's unlikely a company of global proportion would actually have an exposure to only a single country, currency, and industry. This can be revealed statistically by using a risk model that determines the exposures through the regression of industry, country, and currencies in a time-series manner. In practice, this methodology does in fact often calculate exposures for global securities that vary substantially from 1. The exposure's value could be more or less than 1 and even negative. In this case, the net exposure to the factor would be quite different from the weight of the securities in the portfolio.

To illustrate this idea further, consider a company with an exposure of 0.8 to information technology and 0.45 to consumer staples that also has a simultaneous exposure to the euro of 0.7 and the Aussie dollar of –0.15. If a portfolio contained many like securities, with multiple exposures to multiple currencies and industries, then the portfolio exposure to the Aussie dollar is the sum over all security weights times each security's exposure to the Aussie dollar. The AUD exposure would be quite different from just the total weight of all securities listed on the Australian exchange.

## EXPOSURE HEDGE VERSUS DOLLAR HEDGE

To begin, we start with a description of the situation today in the Eurozone. Given the state of the Eurozone's 17 member countries that use the euro after the credit crisis of 2008, currency risk has recently become of increased interest. The standard methodology for producing a currency hedge of a global portfolio or index involves determining the total position size of all securities denominated in a currency. Once that's done, the hedge is simply selling currency forward contracts equivalent to the position size and buying the base currency of the investor. For example, if the total market value of all securities denominated in Japanese yen, reported in a base currency of a U.S. investor equivalent to and in USD, is $32,546,208 and the portfolio also owns $237,814 yen in cash, the hedge involves selling their sum of $32,784,022 in yen forward one-month contracts and buying the equivalent magnitude in USD. In so doing, the absolute exposure to yen is hedged in the portfolio, so it is thought. If the portfolio owns multiple currencies, this process is repeated for those currencies. If the report currency is something other than USD, the euro, say, then the process would still sell forward yen contracts but purchase euros in cash, the report currency, rather than USD. This has made good sense and historically has been how one hedges currency risk in a typical long-only portfolio. The only drawback is that it is wrong to suppose that the weight in a denominated currency is the portfolio's exposure to it. The fact that a security is listed on the London exchange doesn't necessarily mean that when you own it 100 percent of the currency risk exposure is pound sterling.

This process for hedging doesn't take into account the covariance between FX rates so that exposure is assumed to be only the currency the asset is denominated in. To account for total exposures due to covariation between currencies and assets, one needs to determine the association between the securities with a suite of currencies, and this is usually provided in a risk model. Then, the method for hedging a portfolio's currency exposure is a little more complicated but provides a better hedge. The reason has much to do with the fact that an asset that is denominated in one currency may have a strong correlation with FX for some other currency, implying it also has partial exposure to this other currency. Mark Kritzman said, "To minimize risk, the amount of the forward contract to sell as a fraction of the total portfolio equals the portfolio's beta with respect to the foreign currency."[1] Hence the determination of currency betas is paramount for forecasting the risk and for hedging.

An excellent way to reveal the differences between exposure-based risk analysis and active (or absolute) weights being interpreted as the exposure is through currency hedging. We will demonstrate this by comparing results of the standard methodology for forming a foreign currency hedge to those of the exposure hedge approach. First, we are mindful of the devaluation of the U.S. dollar over the past decade, as is seen in Figure 1.1. This is a plot of the USD versus 17 major global currencies since December 31, 2001, until the end of 2011. Values have all been normalized to 1 at the start date and represent each currency's cumulative return relative to the USD.

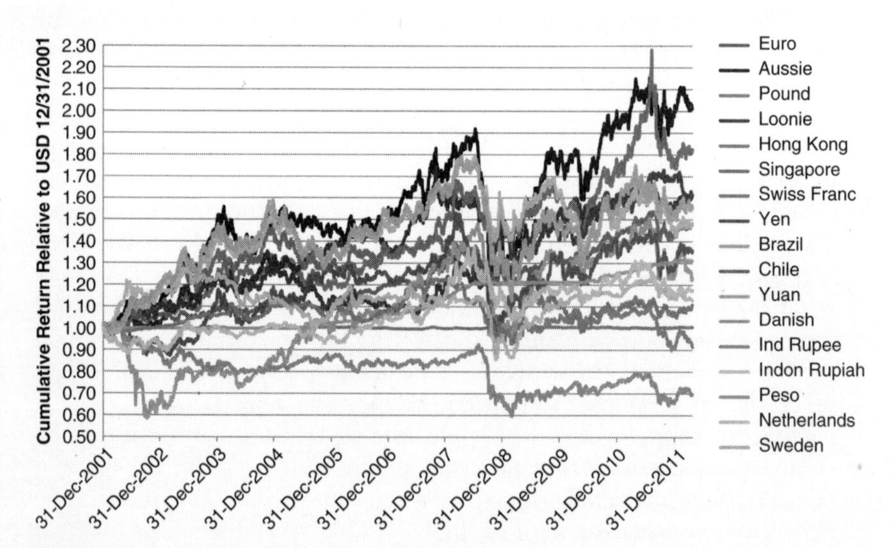


**FIGURE 1.1** Normalized and indexed currency exchange rates versus the U.S. dollar from 12/31/2001 until 12/31/2011.

Clearly the U.S. dollar has fallen against all major currencies over this time frame (except for the Mexican peso) with the exception of when there was a so-called risk-on macro trade and when investors ran for quality (least worst, actually) in the credit crisis of 2008. The U.S. dollar being the world's reserve currency (though the U.S. balance sheet mirrors Greece's these days) was the "butt of the run." Since that time, foreign currency has begun its long march increasing against the USD. What this means is foreign investors in the U.S. market have been getting shortchanged because of their USD exposure, while U.S. investors in foreign markets have been making gains in which many investment managers, ignorant of FX rates over this time frame, have benefited from the falling dollar while thinking those gains were from their skill. Chief investment officers (CIOs) take notice: Was it skill or was it dollar devaluation? Was the foreign currency exposure of the portfolio greater than the mandate's benchmark? Did the PM purposefully take this risk or was it mere happenstance? These considerations should be given weight in the managers' compensation schema—but we digress.

The decision to hedge FX should be made neither haphazardly nor reactively. It should be made because of the increased risk that currency exposure adds to a portfolio. Moreover, if the portfolio manager has explicit currency views, these should be part of the asset allocation decision, not a policy, investment guideline, or risk management (RM) decision. Last, currency returns do not wash out over the long run. That is just an urban legend. So the beta of securities to FX is paramount to establishing the currency hedge. Hence a risk model that determines the beta of the portfolio to FX rates is necessary to be able to compute the exposure hedge or simply to compute the true FX exposure.

How does Morgan Stanley Capital International (MSCI) form its currency exposure hedged indexes? From the MSCI website accessed in the autumn of 2011, we read the following from its methodology dated Geneva, July 5, 2002:

> *The MSCI Hedged Indices integrate the hedging of each currency in the index for one month against the base currency by selling the base currency at the one-month Forward rate. The amount of forwards sold represents the value (or the market capitalization) of the index as of the close of the last trading day of the month, i.e. reflecting changes in the composition implemented as of the close of that day. This approach is designed to replicate the hedging process of portfolio managers who typically sell Forwards for an amount corresponding to the value of their portfolio as of the close of the last trading day of the month.*

This is tantamount to admitting that managers do not form the exposure hedge. They merely sell forward with monthly rebalancing the position size, or the absolute weight of the amount of a security's position in its base currency. They do not determine the beta of each position to a suite of FX currencies as Kritzman suggested. For clarification, Table 1.1 demonstrates this standard method for hedging currency exposures.

We show the denominated assets of a small portfolio on the left along with their position size from the perspective of a U.S. investor. The conventional way MSCI is referring to for hedging involves simply selling forwards equivalent to each position size in the denominated currency, effectively taking a short position in the listed securities' base currency. One tallies the data and buys the equivalent amount of USD to cover the shorts.

Contrast this method with Table 1.2. The top portion of this chart shows the betas of the securities to various FX. Notice that all securities have a beta to the euro as well as betas to their home currencies.

Obviously there's a beta to each stock's base currency (Table 1.2), but in addition each has a beta to the euro. The bottom portion of this chart multiplies each beta times the position size for each currency. The amount to sell forward is the product of beta times the position size.

If one multiplies those betas times the position size in each denominated currency, one gets the figure shown on the bottom of Table 1.2. Notice that the shorted forwards of other currencies exist as well as for the euro, but buying the equivalent USD to cover the total of all shorts is still required. Comparing Table 1.1 with the bottom of Table 1.2 shows a striking contrast. The conventional hedge is long $1.5 million USD to cover while the exposure hedge is long $5.0 million to cover and is also short euro along with the other currencies.

We also state that in the conventional hedging methodology MSCI proposes, Table 1.1 represents exactly a 100 percent hedge ratio, referred to here as the dollar hedging strategy. The exposure-based hedging methodology of Table 1.2 is another way of defining the hedge, and its hedge ratio is also 100 percent. But because the hedge construction methods are very different, their 100 percent hedge ratios mean entirely different things. Consider that the result of forming the dollar hedge is what happens when you consider weight in a portfolio as the exposure. However, when you consider the exposure as the result of accounting for covariance and correlations between assets and factors in a portfolio, you obtain a very different result. In this case, the conventional dollar hedging methodology is an *underhedge* from the viewpoint of the exposure hedging methodology. We say underhedged because not enough foreign currency was sold short to effectively cancel the currency impact. Experiments we've run on hedging the MSCI All-Country Asia Ex-Japan index, for instance, result in the dollar hedging

**TABLE 1.1** A standard typical currency hedge: The amount of currency forwards shorted is the position size equivalent of the asset held in the denominated currency.

| Report Currency: U.S. Dollar | | Purchase | Sell Forward in USD Equivalents | | | | |
|---|---|---|---|---|---|---|---|
| | Position Size | USD | U.S. Dollar | Euro | Swiss Franc | UK Pound | Japanese Yen |
| **British Pound** | | | | | | | |
| Rio Tinto PLC | 485,656 | 485,656 | | | | −485,656 | |
| Standard Chartered PLC | 218,973 | 218,973 | | | | −218,973 | |
| Xstrata PLC | 151,991 | 151,991 | | | | −151,991 | |
| BP PLC | 71,566 | 71,566 | | | | −71,566 | |
| **Japanese Yen** | | | | | | | |
| Toshiba Corp. | 409,410 | 409,410 | | | | | −409,410 |
| **Swiss Franc** | | | | | | | |
| ABB Ltd. | 189,071 | 189,071 | | | −189,071 | | |
| Nestle S.A. | 57,748 | 57,748 | | | −57,748 | | |
| **U.S. Dollar** | | | | | | | |
| General Electric Co. | 358,200 | | | | | | |
| Totals | | 1,584,415 | | | −246,819 | −928,186 | −409,410 |

**TABLE 1.2** The risk model determined betas of the portfolio positions with various currencies.

| Report Currency: U.S. Dollar | | Risk Model Determined Betas | | | | |
|---|---|---|---|---|---|---|
| | Position Size | U.S. Dollar | Euro | Swiss Franc | UK Pound | Japanese Yen |
| **British Pound** | | | | | | |
| Rio Tinto PLC | 485,656 | | 0.81 | | 3.00 | |
| Standard Chartered PLC | 218,973 | | 0.74 | | 2.47 | |
| Xstrata PLC | 151,991 | | 1.15 | | 3.00 | |
| BP PLC | 71,566 | | 0.44 | | 2.16 | |
| Japanese Yen | | | | | | |
| Toshiba Corp. | 409,410 | | 0.66 | | | 0.80 |
| Swiss Franc | | | | | | |
| ABB Ltd. | 189,071 | | 1.32 | 1.41 | | |
| Nestle S.A. | 57,748 | | 0.41 | 0.88 | | |
| U.S. Dollar | | | | | | |
| General Electric Co. | 358,200 | | 1.38 | | | |

| | | Purchase | Sell Forward in USD Equivalent | | | | |
|---|---|---|---|---|---|---|---|
| | Position Size | USD | U.S. Dollar | Euro | Swiss Franc | UK Pound | Japanese Yen |
| British Pound | | | | | | | |
| Rio Tinto PLC | 485,656 | 1,847,984 | | −391,016 | | −1,456,969 | |
| Standard Chartered PLC | 218,973 | 703,556 | | −162,730 | | −540,826 | |
| Xstrata PLC | 151,991 | 631,263 | | −175,290 | | −455,973 | |
| BP PLC | 71,566 | 186,391 | | −31,528 | | −154,863 | |
| Japanese Yen | | | | | | | |
| Toshiba Corp. | 409,410 | 596,605 | | −268,662 | | | −327,943 |
| Swiss Franc | | | | | | | |
| ABB Ltd. | 189,071 | 515,346 | | −248,980 | −266,366 | | |
| Nestle S.A. | 57,748 | 74,892 | | −23,875 | −51,018 | | |
| U.S. Dollar | | | | | | | |
| General Electric Co. | 358,200 | 492,530 | | −492,530 | | | |
| Totals | | 5,048,568 | | −1,794,611 | −317,383 | −2,608,631 | −327,943 |

strategy to be an *overhedge* from the viewpoint of exposure hedging. In this case, too much currency would be required to be sold short to cancel out the impact of currency in the MSCI index. The only way to perfect the hedge, buying and selling the correct amount of each currency, is through exposure hedging. Figure 1.2 further illustrates this notion by showing the impact of the two different currency hedging methodologies over a series of monthly rebalancing for a portfolio over 2011. We show the unhedged raw portfolio of these eight stocks as the black dotted line. We show the dollar hedged cumulative returns in dark gray, the exposure hedged cumulative returns in black, and the pound sterling versus USD FX rate in light gray.

The dotted line in Figure 1.2 is the raw unhedged portfolio, the dark gray line represents currency hedging using the standard dollar hedging methodology, and the black line hedges the currency using the exposure-based methodology, determined from a risk model.

We normalized all of them at the start of 2011 so they fit on the same graph. From the beginning of 2011 the pound rose versus the U.S. dollar for the first half of the year. Given that, any portfolio with pound exposure (from a U.S. investor's perspective) should rise relative to a portfolio that owns the same assets but has no GBP exposure. So let us look at the first half of the graph. Since the portfolio obviously has pound exposure, it rises in tandem with the pound rising versus the USD.

The dollar hedged strategy owns the same securities and is short forwards (including the pound) and is long USD required to cover the short positions. We see that it cannot keep up with the unhedged portfolio simply

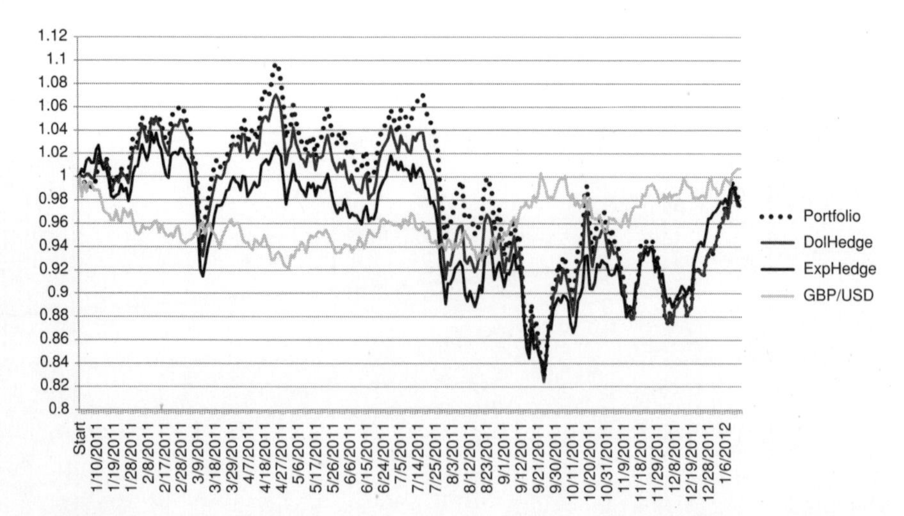


**FIGURE 1.2** Three portfolios' cumulative returns throughout 2011.

because it has partially hedged the rising pound, so it will not participate in these gains. Now look at the exposure hedged portfolio. It trails the dollar hedged portfolio, which indicates that the dollar hedged portfolio still has pound exposure; otherwise the exposure hedged portfolio wouldn't trail it. The exposure hedged portfolio has eliminated exposure to the pound while the dollar hedged portfolio has only lowered the exposure. Also, this example involves a 100 percent hedge ratio for the dollar hedged and exposure hedged portfolios, so even though we had a 100 percent hedge ratio in the dollar hedged portfolio (one-to-one correspondence between position size, and shorted their forward equivalence) it wasn't enough to hedge the pound. Obviously the impact of yen and Swiss franc are part of this result, too, but one can see that since the largest exposure is due to pound sterling, the effect is most easily observed with the pound as the focus of the contrast.

We comment again that if the portfolio manager had a view on, say, pound sterling, it should have been part of the asset allocation in the first place (i.e., the manager would have taken pound exposure on purpose). In this example we're detailing results as if the manager had no view on currency and the goal was to hedge all currency exposure, pound included.

We now shift our attention to examining the daily standard deviation of return for the three portfolios shown in Figure 1.3. One can see that even though the dollar hedged portfolio (middle bar) is underhedged, albeit with a 100 percent hedge ratio, it still results in lower volatility than the unhedged portfolio. The exposure hedged portfolio has lower volatility still, which can be generalized as the expected outcome. One can be sure that exposure hedging creates the minimum-variance portfolio (only in regard to currencies) and that once one moves beyond a 100 percent exposure hedge

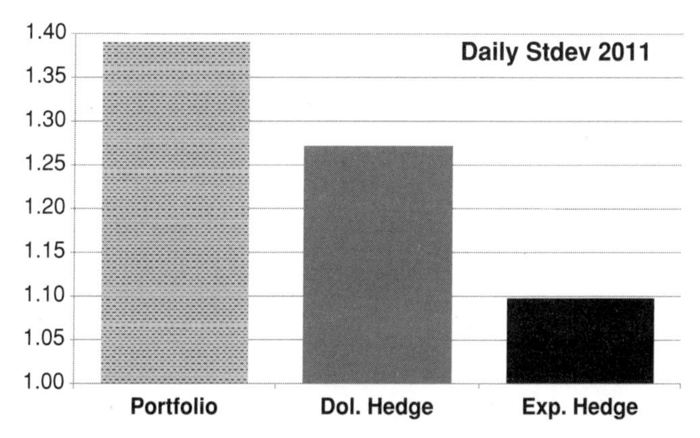


**FIGURE 1.3** Comparison of the daily standard deviation of return for the three portfolios.

ratio, the variance of return will increase. However, the 100 percent hedge ratio under dollar hedging is not a minimum-variance portfolio. These portfolios have their hedging rebalanced monthly.

Whether one is of the opinion that assets have exposure to one currency, country, and industry or many, what we can agree on is that exposure represents a future sensitivity to an event or factor movement. It is strongly connected to and labels a source of future asset price dislocation that may never occur and that never may be realized but offers potential for risk. Additionally, it's only if that factor's movement multiplied by that exposure results in losses that the risk of that exposure is really defined; thus experienced risk is exposure coming to fruition through losses. It's the realized risk.

If the loss comes through an unidentified source, this would imply that some unforeseen risk, not labeled or identified, happened. The purpose of risk analysis is to identify the most probable and common sources of risk exposures. If this analysis is relevant and thorough, there shouldn't be any experienced risks that come to realization that the manager wasn't aware of beforehand. Thus, exposure analysis is a tool that one can use to judge risk managers (RMs) and portfolio managers (PMs) by. If a risk manager identifies an exposure that the portfolio manager takes no action on and it later comes to fruition through losses, reward the risk manager and hold the portfolio manager accountable for the losses. Conversely, if the portfolio realizes a loss that the risk manager had not identified, blame the risk manager, but do not reward the portfolio manager in this instance, either.

Historically in the asset management business, rewards have accrued to portfolio managers for outperformance despite their having experienced risks that had been identified for them in advance and that they still weren't able to avoid. Yet it is entirely possible to outperform one's benchmark and still experience a risk one knew of and took no action to avoid. Consider a U.S. investment manager who outperforms an index, but fails to outperform an index's sector. For example, suppose an asset manager had been told her decision to overweight the technology sector has realized no alpha historically and that she has actually underperformed the technology sector within the benchmark on a consistent basis. Moreover, it's a small-cap growth fund and this portfolio has had consistently high systematic risk in the technology sector, over and above all other sectors in full knowledge that the stock picking bottom-up methodology favors higher stock-specific risks as a percentage of total risk, but this manager has overweighted the information technology (IT) sector even when this wasn't the case[2]—in essence ignoring the risk exposure analysis and historical empirical results that the risk manager had reported. In fact, the PM overall had achieved her objective, but left money on the table. Managers' compensation should consider money left on the table if potential losses identified beforehand weren't acted upon. Typically, the risk managers just obtain their salary and some small percentage of the PM's bonus in this situation when in fact they performed admirably. Chief investment officers need to empower and reward their risk managers more in line with their portfolio managers, in my view.

## HOW THE CREDIT CRISIS MOVED RISK MANAGEMENT TO THE FOREFRONT

We use the previous illustrations to draw contrast between exposure versus experienced risk. Profits that could have been earned but were not should be treated as losses in a PM's track record, assuming they've been identified. This elucidates the greater role risk managers can play in the asset management business and also illustrates why losses can occur even when risks have been identified beforehand; the PM typically has veto rights over the portfolio (especially in the United States) and may not take any action on exposures that the RM has brought to the PM's attention. It has been demonstrated consistently that asset managers have overconfidence in their abilities and this leads to overruling equally capable risk managers when they have the authority to do so.[3] Moreover, the financial rewards have been asymmetric as well, favoring the portfolio manager over the risk manager. This would suggest that the portfolio manager has more talent and adds more value than the risk manager. We argue that this is not because portfolio managers have an inherently better skill set, but rather because the organizational structure restricts the amount of value that the risk manager can add.

Consider the trade-off between risk identification before realization versus what's experienced as a balancing act. On one hand, nobody has complete foreknowledge of the future and exogenous events; things coming out of left field do happen. On the other hand, investing in something in which the risks have been well identified without consideration of their potential impact on loss isn't wise. It may even be a breach of regulatory fiduciary obligation in some circumstances. Fiduciaries may find themselves in a lawsuit if they identified potential avenues of loss, took no action, and later this loss was realized for an investor, particularly with the growing usage of models in asset and risk management.

Consider what happened with AXA Rosenberg. In 2009, during a model update, a significant bug was discovered in the code. The bug dated back to 2007. Internal analysts raised the issue with management, and were told to keep it quiet. Finally, in March 2010, at the urging of the analysts, management discussed the bug with their lawyers, and contacted the Securities and Exchange Commission (SEC) and clients. During the time period of the bug, and especially after the bug's discovery, AXA Rosenberg responded to client concerns over the model's performance by indicating the model was working as expected. As a result of the SEC investigation, AXA Rosenberg was forced to pay over $200 million to clients for the lost performance, and was fined an additional $25 million. Barr Rosenberg himself was barred from the securities industry for life. This was all over just a bug in a model. Consider clients' outrage should it be known that a fundamental investment manager was forewarned by the risk manager that the overweighting in a sector hasn't historically added alpha, and returns were left on the table. Clients want what's on the table, and one can argue that since this risk was identified and the manager took no action to hedge it, they're entitled to it. Obviously, if the risk isn't identified beforehand, one cannot be held responsible—but that's a different avenue to run down.

Risk management does play a larger role among asset managers outside the United States, but the 2008 credit crisis was what really pushed risk management to the forefront and expanded its influence in the portfolio management decision-making process. As is often the situation after a crisis, government regulators and elected officials sat up and started paying more attention. Across Europe and in the United States, legislation has been introduced in an attempt to remedy bank failure, or at a minimum an automatic intrusion into corporate life. The Dodd-Frank Wall Street Reform and Consumer Protection Act was voted into our lives on July 21, 2010. At thousands of pages, it is 23 times longer than the Glass-Steagall Act, enacted after the crash of 1929. The summary alone amounts to 16 pages and is a reaction from elected officials to preempt the Great Financial Crisis (in the Asia-Pacific region, it's commonly referred to as the "GFC") from ever happening again. In brief, it does nine things:

1. Establishes the Financial Stability Oversight Council.
2. Makes it tough for banks to get too big.
3. Regulates nonbank financial companies.
4. Is meant to break up large, complex companies by allowing the Federal Reserve with a two-thirds vote of the chair to force a company to divest holdings.
5. Creates a new Office of Financial Research.
6. Attempts to make risks transparent.
7. Allows no evasion of supervision by the Federal Reserve.
8. Raises capital standards.
9. Discourages "too big to fail" bailouts.

Items 5 and 6, along with member agencies, will give the Council (item 1) data that has been collected and analyzed to help identify and monitor emerging risks to the economy, making this information public in periodic reports and testimony to Congress every year. In essence, it is a far-reaching policy institutionalizing risk management. It gives risk managers veto rights over the "entire portfolio" and elevates the role risk managers will play in portfolio management. This legislation will start with banks and ultimately expand to encompass mutual funds, exchange-traded funds (ETFs), and any other SEC-regulated entity, as well as force less regulated hedge funds into compliance and oversight. In particular, most of the details are left for regulators to draft at their discretion, for of the 400 rules it mandates, only 93 were finalized as of February 2012.[4] Some law firms in New York were charging $100,000 just to read and write a review on the bill. The so-called Volcker Rule alone includes 383 questions, which, if answered affirmatively, itemize into 1,400+ further questions. Is it really going to mitigate risky proprietary trading by banks? Or will it lead to a concentration of risk by legislating away diversification opportunities between banks? One can only hope that all this excess regulation doesn't squeeze the life out of the home of the laissez-faire, free enterprise economy.

In the end, a common benefit of the credit crisis aftermath is that we now call into question the old way of doing business for banks, their proprietary trading desks, hedge funds, and asset managers. If it makes us rescind the decision rights we've given to portfolio managers a bit and forces their involvement with risk managers, that's a good thing ultimately. We do fear, however, that the goal to lower systemic risks will force the hand of compliance such that the earmarked safer assets result in an overly crowded trade and actually raise systemic risk. It will be a few years before we know for sure whether the new regulatory environment is preventive.

## RISKS BEYOND VOLATILITY

There are types of risk that go beyond measuring the volatility of return. These are in many ways the types of risk the Dodd-Frankenstein bill is meant to mitigate: the Black Swan and obsidian uncertainties of exogenous sources. We revisit our reference in the introduction to Warren Buffett's teacher, Ben Graham. He never liked the term *beta*. In a 1974 *Barron's* article he said what bothers him is that "authorities" equate beta with risk. "Real risk," he wrote, "is measured not by price fluctuations but by a loss of quality and earnings power through economic or management changes." He argued further that a certain amount of price volatility is normal and to be expected and does not signify real risk. If he were here today, how would we argue to him that his recorded superior investment performance would have benefited had he incorporated risk models in his investment process?

Risk models are meant to identify contributions to variance or volatility risk. Might they have outlined where he was leaving money on the table as in the example in the beginning of this chapter?

In reality, what Ben Graham would have ascertained using a risk model is precisely what exposure analysis reveals, unintended bets. It shines a light on factor tilts, and identifies what systematic sources the portfolio is exposed to, whether the manager intended it or not. If it wasn't intentional, it's now up to the manager to decide what to do next. But that conversation is a digression from the type of risks Ben Graham was more conscious of: fear of loss or fear of a company losing its cash flows and subsequently failing.

Risks beyond volatility include the extinction-level events (ELEs) that Nassim Taleb's book *The Black Swan* was focused on. In effect, a bubble like the Internet craze of 1999 was really only a minor ELE, a mere obsidian obsession, for there wasn't an economic shock, a banking crisis, or a loss of currency confidence involved with it. It was a hyper-market born by human greed, but it popped before great lasting damage to the economy could be realized. Though we know a few investors, even CFOs, who overallocated to technology during those go-go years and bore large losses, few institutional asset managers fell for companies with no earnings or book values selling for awesomely, egregiously high values born of the ridiculousness. The investment bankers bringing these companies to their initial public offerings made enormous sums, but most investors who bought these companies and harvested losses were retail investors. There are some thematic ways of dealing with these kinds of exogenous risks ill-defined by portfolio variance. These include macroeconomic decision trees (i.e., demand for commodities by China and other Asian countries) and the decade-long devaluation of the U.S. dollar (2000 to 2012) exclusive of the credit crisis when a run to quality (i.e., least worse) led to pile-on for USD currency. Likewise, one can break from single-asset-class investing and introduce other asset classes into the portfolio with low correlations to hedge these risks—for instance, buying commodity ETFs in an equity portfolio. Stress-testing can also be used to shine a light on accentuated risks in a portfolio. That is, given one has undue exposure to some factor, how does the portfolio behave should that factor be stressed? If 10-year Treasury yields go up 150 basis points (bps), are the estimated losses to your portfolio 40 bps or 400 bps? This is a simple example, and there are many ways to stress-test a portfolio that we will cover in later chapters, but one should think of stress-testing as investing in preparedness. Last, putting the portfolio in a situation where favorable consequences are more probable than unfavorable ones is also a top-down mind-set for investing. For instance, if institutional flows are moving heavily into the materials sectors, be careful betting on the contrary.

There are still other risks not defined by variance or categorized as the exogenous obsidian uncertainties. These risks involve regular market returns given by a return distribution that may have fat tails. We spoke about fat tails in the Introduction, and even if one doesn't want to go way out in the tail to describe risks, there are methods for estimating higher-order moments such as coskewness and cokurtosis (third and fourth moments of the return distribution, respectively) that minimally widen the risk forecast possibilities.[5] Though they are not mathematically trivial, their equations can be solved quickly with modern-day technology.

## WHAT RISK MANAGEMENT SHOULD PROVIDE

A primary role of risk management is to institute a system that measures a portfolio's exposure to known and common sources of risk. Secondarily, it's to construct a process for the continual monitoring of potential risks from these known sources. This involves monitoring the active risk exposure between the mandate, its benchmark, and the investment guidelines. Importantly, a methodology should be set up that allows for the orderly lowering of exposures should they be found higher than prescribed.

Additionally, today's software and technology make it relatively easy to exercise a portfolio and determine risks unforeseen and uncommon across assets through stress-testing. Though these methods cannot be expected to be clairvoyant, they can shed light on expectations of major events shaping our world. For instance, how will a 30 percent rise in oil prices affect a given portfolio? If the USD/euro FX rate falls by 10 percent, will German exporters suffer consequences, and how will that affect the portfolio? Will the impact be a magnitude of 100 bps or 450 bps? The possible scenarios of stress-testing are limited only by our imagination, and it's our recommendation that stress-testing become a bigger component of the portfolio management process. Using the software applications available today to measure and forecast risk, it's far easier than ever before to identify and then set up solutions for the unwanted risk exposures in a portfolio. Then, risk mitigation through hedging can be designed and readied should it be needed. In many cases, the investment policy statement and guidelines can be edited to account for the tactics prepared in advance that may be applied in the event a forecasted risk becomes realized. We cannot say enough about stress-testing. It's a necessary tool for the intelligent investor.

It is important for those who are a step removed from the risk management process, and especially important for those who oversee it, to understand the following: the risk management process is not intended to predict event risk, ELEs, or Black Swan situations. These risks are beyond volatility, and, while unlikely, they are extremely hazardous because they blindside everyone when they do occur. The best offense against these events is a rigorous stress-testing system. Such a system should outline a process for the forecasting of losses given exogenous event shocks, which may allow for loss prevention during a catastrophic financial crisis simply because the size of losses can be quantified beforehand and prepared for accordingly. But one should not misconstrue these tests as a guarantee of event detection itself, let alone risk mitigation. If we turn the question around and ask, "What could hurt me the most?" the answers are probably going to be the best foundation for a risk management policy going forward.

In simple terms, the RM process should have eight steps:

1. Define how risks will be measured and set acceptable levels in the form of thresholds that correspond to the investment process of the manager.
2. Identify the unintended bets and confirm the intended bets of the portfolio.
3. Itemize these risks with as much granularity as possible (trade-off between accuracy and estimation error).
4. Forecast these risks and monitor a time line of realized versus forecasted risks.
5. Estimate the size of the losses associated with each risk.
6. Convey model risk appropriately. Be completely transparent on the accuracy of the expected forecasts and loss estimation. Confidence limits can work well here.
7. Suggest ways to hedge the unintended identified risks in concert with the investment guidelines and compliance constraints.
8. Document the process.

We inform the reader that risk management is always better at trend analysis than at forecasting the actual level of risk, so one has to keep a record of these risks through time as suggested in step 4. For instance, monitoring forecasted tracking error and comparing it to realized tracking error through time is a useful practice to gain confidence in your RM process and also allows one to gauge estimation error and model risk. Plotting a time line of systematic risks through time provides an insightful illustration of increasing or decreasing market risks for the portfolio.

Too often step 6 is neglected in risk management systems. Risk estimates almost always involve their forecasted level errors. For instance, suppose the 99 percent one-month VaR forecast is 4.5 percent of assets. How much more informative is it to read: 99 percent one-month VaR of 4.5 percent of assets +/–1.6 percent at a 95 percent confidence interval (CI)? A confidence level on top of an estimate is much more informative. This relates to step 3 since confidence levels can help itemize risks to a granularity that is commensurate with the accuracy of the process. If we report the marginal contribution to tracking error for stock X as 2.3 percent +/–0.9 percent and for stock Y as 2.7 percent +/–1.2 percent, it becomes clear that one cannot differentiate their contributions. The bar chart in Figure 1.4 illustrates this. One cannot be certain that stock Y is riskier than stock X when you plot the error bars in addition to the level of the forecasts. Think of the error bars as corresponding to the individual estimation error at the security level.

It appears in Figure 1.4 that stock Y has larger tracking error as computed using Monte Carlo methodologies; however, when one overlays the error bars on top of the raw values, one can see stock X's and stock Y's tracking errors are indistinguishable.

In our hypothetical example, a wise risk manager would understand that this RM process is not suitable for this level of granularity and would back up the risk forecasts to a lower level. For instance, determining whether it is possible to differentiate between the riskiness of industries is a logical next step for this analysis.

The process of steps 1 through 7 is sequential but should include feedback and involvement from the portfolio managers and analysts throughout the implementation process. Further, it is important to note that the risk management process is never done. The steps outlined should be updated and practiced continuously; they will evolve with the market and the rest of the investment process. We argue that using a risk model in the process is a gigantic aid. Which risk model to choose is dependent upon one's investment process, and we'll cover that in later chapters.

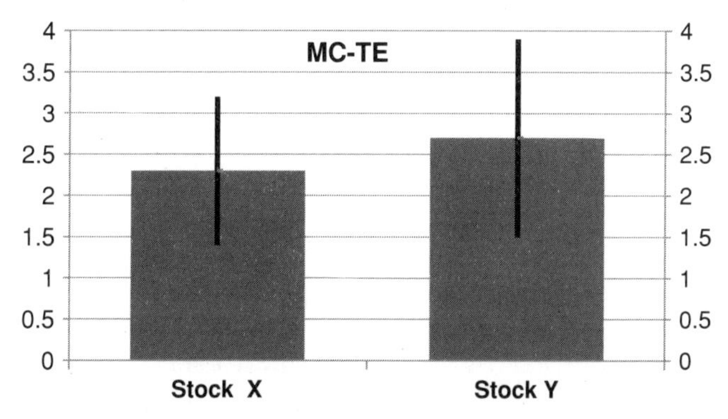


**FIGURE 1.4** Indistinguishable tracking errors in stocks X and Y.

## CLARIFYING EXPECTATIONS OF RISK MANAGEMENT

Once a risk management process is agreed upon by the investment team, risk managers, and compliance personnel, the next step (usually forgone) is to set the expectations or deliverables of the process. This is crucial as portfolio managers usually have veto rights over the asset selection process, which generally means that risk managers, quants, and researchers report to the PMs, regardless of whether there is a direct arrow in the organizational chart. At a minimum, agreeing on the deliverables will minimize finger-pointing should performance suffer from an unknown source of risk. Ideally, foreknowledge of this risk will enable the portfolio manager to act upon it before it is too late.

So what are the expectations and deliverables of a good RM process then? Start by defining what RM cannot do (identification by elimination). As stated earlier, it cannot predict exogenous events. However, stress-testing can prescribe loss estimates should a scenario you hypothesize occur. A deliverable of the stress-testing process can therefore suggest preemptive steps to take to hedge should that risk materialize.

RM cannot guarantee general safety. The level estimates and confidence intervals are just that, estimates with confidence, much like weather forecasting. To the extent that your risk horizon forecast is short, the more reliable the forecast should be. If asked to give a weather forecast for the next two hours only by looking out your office window, that two-hour forecast will certainly be more accurate than if asked to give a 24-hour forecast via the same method. It is similar with risk forecasting because markets are as complex as the weather, but less so than climate, so the analogy is a good one. A daily forecast is more reliable than a monthly one, which is more reliable than an annual one. By "more reliable" we mean that the forecast's deviation from realized risk measured by value at risk or tracking error, for instance, will most likely be smaller.

To set the expectations for the portfolio managers, CIOs, and clients of an investment management firm that is beginning the RM process that meets the seven criteria mentioned previously, we then propose six steps:

1. Agree on an acceptable reporting frequency and a forecast horizon.
2. Define the categories (level of granularity) you're going to report on, and the type of risk measures you'll be monitoring (tracking error, common risks, idiosyncratic risks, marginal contributions to risk, value-at-risk confidence levels, information coefficient, and so forth).
3. Define the factor exposures you are most concerned with and will monitor closely, including style and fundamental factors as well as exogenous (macro) factors such as currency, industry, or country if

appropriate. These should be taken into account for the selection of the risk model, too.
4. Define the size of acceptable-level estimates along with their confidence intervals that you're going to report for a given factor exposure. These are the levels whose breaching requires action on the part of the investment team.
5. Agree on steps to mitigate potential risks should their levels or exposures be breached.
6. Document the process.

It's fair to say that the factor risks from step 3 do not have to be described in a risk model, but they should be related to the investment process regardless of how they are determined. Obviously, step 5 is of paramount importance, as is ensuring that if a risk level is breached and about to be acted upon, it is one of consequence. The earlier steps are the vanguard for alleviating that tension.

## AN EXAMPLE

In designing a risk management program, there are some tests that can be done to elucidate exactly what the major concerns for the mandate might be. This involves stress-testing again, which shines a light on exactly what factor exposures could lead to the largest losses.

To yield some color, then, as to how to proceed to find answers for steps 1 through 4, we're going to walk through a hypothetical situation for a portfolio manager whose investment process is already in place but lacks a system for risk management. Let's further assume that it's a global equity long-only strategy and that the portfolio is constructed simply by assigning asset weights linearly proportional to the universe ranking. The universe is comprised of investable securities on listed exchanges only (no illiquid stuff), and the portfolio is limited to only 100 names. The weight of the most highly ranked asset could be 2 percent while the 100th security would take a weight of roughly 50 bps. The assets are ranked simply by the investment process or alpha model, 1 to $N$ where $N$ is the number of assets in the investable universe.

So how does one proceed to outline RM objectives and expectations given an investment process of this nature? First, the answer will be biased so the reader should understand it's just one possible solution. We're going to suggest a risk model predicated on factors that are similar to the PM's investment process and that offer risk forecasts at horizons commensurate with the rebalancing frequency. Assuming the PM rebalances quarterly (whether through portfolio optimization or heuristics), then he needs to be able to forecast risks out to a three-month horizon. Generally, short-term risk models can signal long-term risk trends, but long-term risk models cannot signal short-term risk trends, so the former is more appropriate. We'd suggest a prespecified multifactor model over a statistical one since the PM is not a high-frequency trader and because his alpha model suggests investment preferences that are based on financial statement variables that are consistent with a bottom-up process. Additionally, we live in a parametric world, not a statistical one, so it's just much easier for people to understand a multifactor model.

Next, we'd suggest using the risk model to reveal the portfolio's factor exposures, focusing on styles, currencies, and countries. Care should be taken to ensure that there are positive factor exposures for those used in the PM's alpha model or the investment process if the manager is more fundamental than quant. Moreover, since it's a global portfolio we assume the PM has developed a view on currencies and countries and should use the model to verify that the exposures to each are directionally consistent with those opinions. For instance, the portfolio might have high exposure to currencies appreciating against USD and negative exposures to currencies like the Mexican peso that have fallen relative to USD over the past decade, both of which can be easily verified through the lens of a risk model. Similarly, if the manager is agnostic on country bets, that exposure can be allowed to flow through the bottom-up stock ranking methodology. The size of those tilts can be verified by examining country exposures as described by the risk model.

Moreover and very importantly, assume the PM purposefully underweighted the positions of a GIIPS country (Greece, Italy, Ireland, Portugal, or Spain) relative to her benchmark and thus assumes that would have reduced her exposure below that of the benchmark—only to find through exposure analysis that she owns other stocks that are highly correlated with this particular country even though they are not incorporated there, which results in adding to her exposure of the very country she wants to underweight. She probably wouldn't know this without performing risk exposure analysis, because active weight analysis does not take into account covariance across assets and cannot account for contributions from other securities not in the predefined country. The correlation/covariance across assets is why you have more or less exposure than the active weight indicates, and this leaking of correlation from two assets in different countries, for instance, means they increase or decrease the exposure of each other simply because their movements are associated. That's what correlation does and why exposure is truly ascertained only by considering the covariance across all assets in the portfolio. Using a risk model to identify these tilts in the portfolio can help ensure you're accurately assuming the risks you intend. To simplify, if we reduce the scenario to a two-stock portfolio consisting of one energy name and one utility name that we know are correlated, why would anyone assume the portfolio's exposure to utilities is captured solely by the weight of the one utility name? If the utility stock falls and brings the energy stock with it, who wouldn't conclude the energy stock has some utility exposure?

So at this point we've reviewed how the PM decomposed her portfolio to reveal its exposures and has a list of the exposures she wants from her investment process versus the list of unintended (and previously unknown) exposures. Now given these exposure levels, she will decide thresholds above which exposures are too much and below which they are too little and adjust the portfolio accordingly so that each is within the desired range. The portfolio manager could do this in a systematic fashion with a portfolio optimizer, reconfiguring the portfolio after explicitly setting the ranges on factor exposures. Based on the importance of exposure analysis relative to active weights analysis as described earlier, we would even encourage her to use soft constraints on the active weighting so that the exposure settings take priority in the optimization results.

An alternative approach to rebalancing the entire existing portfolio is to create the hedge portfolio to mitigate unintended exposures. For instance, the manager could choose a hedge ratio and set aside the necessary amount of the portfolio's capital that will be used to construct the hedge. A hedge ratio of 20 implies building the portfolio with 80 percent of the assets before performing the risk exposure analysis, and then after exposure analysis using 20 percent of assets set aside to construct the hedge.

As an aside, usually the investment mandate has some compliance and investment policy guidelines that may command active weighting levels in sectors or industries relative to the mandate's benchmark. However, usually there's some leeway, allowing a range of active weights. One has to be mindful of these as well.

The next step in the process would be to repeat these activities based on a previously determined frequency. The reporting frequency should be higher than the rebalancing frequency and timed so that the analysis is delivered well in advance of the portfolio rebalancing, perhaps the previous week. That way, the portfolio manager will have time to consume the information and take the appropriate action.

Last, we haven't yet suggested any stress-testing that could be introduced into the risk management process. To perform stress-testing one starts with the portfolio constructed at the end of the aforementioned sequence or one could have a separate practice of stress-testing the benchmark. The results of these, however, are to elucidate potential loss sources in terms of their trend and magnitude. Stress-testing should be done on all major risks and is a great way to examine exogenous factors' influences on return and risk that are independent of the factors in the investment process and/or risk model. One should be careful to look for risks that drive returns steeply negative, especially during time periods when assets are stressed (under a correlation environment similar to the credit crisis, for instance). They should also be carried out minimally on a monthly frequency. Clear procedures should be articulated for design and ongoing testing as well. What one does with these reports from stress-testing, however, is almost personal. We would think they should be used to help outline required steps to be taken should the events tested begin to be realized.

## NOTES

1. Mark Kritzman, "Currency Hedging around the World," *Economics and Portfolio Strategy*, Peter L. Bernstein research report, January 15, 2005.
2. That is, when stock-specific risks are higher than average and systematic risks are lower than average, stock picking tends to perform better. When systematic (or common factor) risks are larger than average, it generally means market risks are quite high and stocks are moving collectively together in the same trend, usually downward. Additionally, when return dispersion separates widely, stock selecting (stock pickers) tends to do well, too. Stock volatility, correlation, and cross-sectional return dispersion are all related.
3. Alexander Puetz and Stefan Ruenzi, "Overconfidence among Professional Investors: Evidence from Mutual Fund Managers," *Journal of Business Finance and Accounting* 38, issue 5–6 (June/July 2011): 684–712.
4. "Over-Regulated America," *Economist*, February 18, 2012, 9.
5. Lionel Martellini and Volker Ziemann, "Improved Estimates of Higher-Order Comoments and Implications for Portfolio Selection," *Review of Financial Studies* 23, issue 4 (2009): 1467–1502.

CHAPTER 2

# Definitions of Tractable Risk

*Steven P. Greiner, PhD, and Andrew Geer, CFA, FRM*

The first step in discussing risk with a portfolio manager or investor is defining how it is going to be measured and calculated. The definitions need to be clear and understandable and specify what types of data are required to perform the calculations. This chapter outlines many of the ways risk can be measured and calculated and lays the foundation for several of the chapters to come.

Go to www.wiley.com/go/greiner to see video titled "Steven Greiner."

## THE EFFECT OF UNCERTAINTY ON OBJECTIVES

We would argue that risk is about uncertainty, but is not uncertainty. Consider a risk calculation as a *methodology* for calculating the risk of some event, but not whether the result of that calculation is *meaningfully precise*. That is, uncertainty isn't about whether the calculation methodology is correct per se. Uncertainty is about our inability to calculate the risk accurately. Precision comes to mind in this regard. We may be quite accurate about how we are going to calculate a risk measure, but to what precision can we do this? This lack of precision is the uncertainty about an objective. Think of risk as the level you're calculating and precision as how many decimal points out you can calculate this level to. Uncertainty defines the level of precision with which one can ascertain the risk. The greater the uncertainty, the lower the level of precision with which you can calculate the risk.

Gambling naturally comes to mind. Consider a game like roulette. The payoffs in this game are set in stone. That is, the risk of placing a bet is quite accurately known, given the bet you place, to uncanny precision—out to thousands of decimal points—given the identical probability of having the roulette ball land in any of the wheel's slots. A casino knows with complete certainty the odds of you winning or losing if you place a euro on a red nine or bet for the color black. Hence, a gambler faces only risk here. There is no uncertainty. Likewise, shooting a bullet out of a gun is completely determined. If the angle of the gun and the velocity of the bullet are known when it leaves the barrel, one can calculate with incredible accuracy where the bullet will land given the velocity of the wind and the effect of gravity. These examples demonstrate that uncertainty is zero in the first case and quite low in the second, which means accuracy and precision are high for both.

Now consider playing Texas hold 'em with three other people. In this game, two cards are dealt face-down to each player, and then five cards are placed face-up by the dealer. Because the cards are dealt randomly and outside the control of the players, each player attempts to control the amount of money in the pot based on handling one's holdings using the five community cards the dealer has dealt face-up. At the end of the hand the pot is awarded to the player with the highest hand. Thus, there is a combination of skill and luck involved in winning, and one's odds are a dynamic variable depending on many things, incalculable simply because one does not know what cards other players may have, let alone who's bluffing. A gambler in this poker game faces risk and large uncertainty.

Likewise, consider your odds of correctly forecasting the weather two hours from now within two degrees of the current temperature by looking out your window. Consider the odds if you must forecast only within a range of values given by a confidence interval of +/–10 degrees. Consider your odds if you can go to the roof of your building and see 360 degrees and give the forecast with the same confidence interval of +/–10 degrees instead of only being able to look out of your window. Now consider your odds if the forecast horizon changes from two hours to six hours and then to 24 hours. Intuitively, one can tell that uncertainty is an increasing function of the forecast horizon and narrowness of the confidence interval. Similarly, one may be accurate in the risk calculation but may not be able to offer it with high precision. Said another way, all of the underlying causes of risk may be properly identified, but that does not mean collectively they can offer a precise forecast. This is why risk reporting with confidence intervals offers more information than forecasting only the level of risk. Additionally, reporting numbers out to multiple decimal places is usually unwarranted because the level of the estimate isn't known with a high degree of precision. This also leads us to recommend forecasting not using point estimates, but offering a perspective of risk that changes over time. So observing a time series of risk estimates puts in perspective the variability in the estimate more than just calculating a single point in time number. Graphs of risk as a function of time offer a visual aid that is more easily gauged by our human experience because often confidence intervals aren't as easily understood or may not even be estimable under certain circumstances.

For risk forecasting in equity and fixed income securities markets, risk can be broken into model risk, which has specification error and estimation error. *Specification error* has to do with whether all the underlying causes of risks are identified and whether they are identified correctly within the model used to compute the forecast. Further, it is possible that a cause of risk has been identified but cannot be translated into mathematical terms well enough to include it in the model. This might happen if one has empirical evidence that some phenomenon contributes to risk and explains its causes but cannot account for it in the model because the data is poor or too hard to obtain. In this case, there is model risk because the model is misspecified (even if only slightly).

One analogy in physics to help explain model misspecification can be found using perturbation theory. In perturbation theory, one calculates the major contributions to risk, then uses those major contributions in a way to affect calculations of minor contributions (not strictly speaking, more allegorically). Consider a model where one only considers the top eight influences that contribute to the risk even though there are actually many more. In this case one accepts that there are contributors to risk that are real but might be too small to consider, too complicated to model, too intractable to describe mathematically, or too difficult to collect data for, or might require excessive computational time. In this case you're omitting them and voluntarily giving up precision to make the problem feasible because accepting lower precision for practicality is often admissible. In these situations, we're accepting that there is model risk because it may be that either the factors are not a complete set or they're misspecified from the beginning. They may be correctly identified but mathematically poorly prescribed or they're incorrectly identified but modeled well or both. One may even use a proxy for some contributing factor where there's no data, because the proxy's data is easier to come by. So model misspecification exists almost all the time in greater or lesser amounts, and its causes can be identified and understood.

*Estimation error* is more akin to uncertainty. Estimation error arises even when you define a *complete* set of underlying causes for market risk, because some of them are not identified well enough for an estimate to be computed with a high enough degree of precision. So it's both the neglect of some small but contributing factor and the sum of factors accepted that are known inaccurately that can contribute to overall uncertainty in a risk measure. For example, consider artillery firing while in a gale. If the angle of projectile launch and velocity are known but strong varying winds are blowing crosswise, the deterministic calculation using Newton's equations of motion to calculate where the artillery shell will land is now only an estimate because the wind adds uncertainty to the final results. If there's no wind, the trajectory is completely known with accuracy and high precision. If there's a strong storm with varying incalculable wind all along the trajectory, then the landing point will have been calculated with very poor precision and is basically a best guess. In one case you may be able to calculate the landing spot to within half an inch whereas in the windy case you can calculate it only within 20 yards over a trajectory of two miles. This is uncertainty and yields estimation error.

In a risk model, therefore, consider valuation ratios like price-to-book (P/B) or price-to-earnings (P/E) that risk managers often use as explanatory factors to forecast risk. To what precision are these values known—four decimal places, two decimal places? Earnings estimates made by sell-side analysts are often out to just one decimal place, which makes sense given that forecasted earnings have uncertainty by their very definition. Therefore, when creating a risk model that uses these factors, the precision of the supplied data should be relied upon to help determine the precision of the model's forecasts. In fact, the factor with the lowest precision is the determinant of the model's precision. If there are two factors, one known to three decimal points and the other known to one decimal point, a model created from these factors should not have higher precision than one decimal point. In Japan, it's common for risk managers to report risk statistics out to six decimal points. Frankly, this is completely ludicrous, for not one factor in most commercial risk models is known with this degree of accuracy. The Japanese have a saying for this, "精度基準が過剰である," which means "the accuracy standard is excessive" because clearly those asking for this precision are too sensitive about it.

Another result of the estimation error uncertainty manifests itself in portfolio optimization. In the typical multifactor prespecified risk model, where one has both model (specification error) risk and estimation error, the model is calibrated based on historical exposures and subsequent returns. Then, it's likely that the largest covariance element between factors in the matrix is too high and the smallest covariance matrix element is too low. This uncertainty collects in the extreme values. If this covariance matrix is used in portfolio optimization, the process will pivot on these extrema and the resulting portfolio, though mean-variance minimized, may be exaggerated because its result superfluously hinges on the estimation error magnified in the largest and smallest values of the covariance matrix. Often shrinkage methods are employed to deemphasize these extrema.

Given these issues, it is important to note here that being aware of model misspecification and estimation error is a prelude to measuring, monitoring, and managing risk well.

## IDENTIFYING AND MEASURING RISKS

Risk must be defined, both conceptually and statistically, before an acceptable level of uncertainty can be determined. Chapter 12 will delve into great detail about the numerous approaches available to measure risk. For instance, tracking error (TE), the most ubiquitous equity risk measure, came about because consultants, the gatekeepers of institutional asset management, decided they needed a way to measure how far from or how close to a benchmark an asset manager was. In this sense, TE is a yardstick invented to beat the heads of asset managers with. It calculates the standard deviation of the distribution of portfolio returns versus the benchmark returns. It's the standard deviation of portfolio return minus benchmark return in a mathematical sense. It says nothing, however, about what the mean of returns is, so it's possible for two portfolios to have two different mean returns and have the same tracking error. In fact, one portfolio could outperform its benchmark and another could underperform its benchmark and yet both portfolios could have the same tracking error.

Figures 2.1a, 2.1b, and 2.1c illustrate this shortcoming. In the first graph, Figure 2.1a, the dark line represents weekly excess returns for a fictitious portfolio whose mean excess return over 52 weeks is 0.45 percent, while the light gray line represents weekly excess returns for a fictitious portfolio with a mean excess return of –0.45 percent. Despite the discrepancy in performance, the portfolios have an identical tracking error. Portfolio 1's returns have a correlation with the benchmark of –9.55 percent while portfolio 2 has a correlation with the benchmark of 1.12 percent. This analysis was done by using Monte Carlo simulation for random number generation normalizing each 52-week draw such that the returns are minimum and maximum constrained between –10 and +10 percent.

To show that this is not the result of an error in the simulation, we present similar results for 52 weekly returns generated from draws from a normal distribution (Figure 2.1b) and from random draws from a Student's t-distribution with 12 degrees of freedom (Figure 2.1c). It takes many simulations to find a match of tracking error and excess return, but eventually you'll produce a match out to whatever precision you want to simulate. In both cases, the tracking errors are identical but the mean returns are of opposite signs (consistent with the analysis in Figure 2.1a). The mean excess return could have any value for a given tracking error, however. We chose

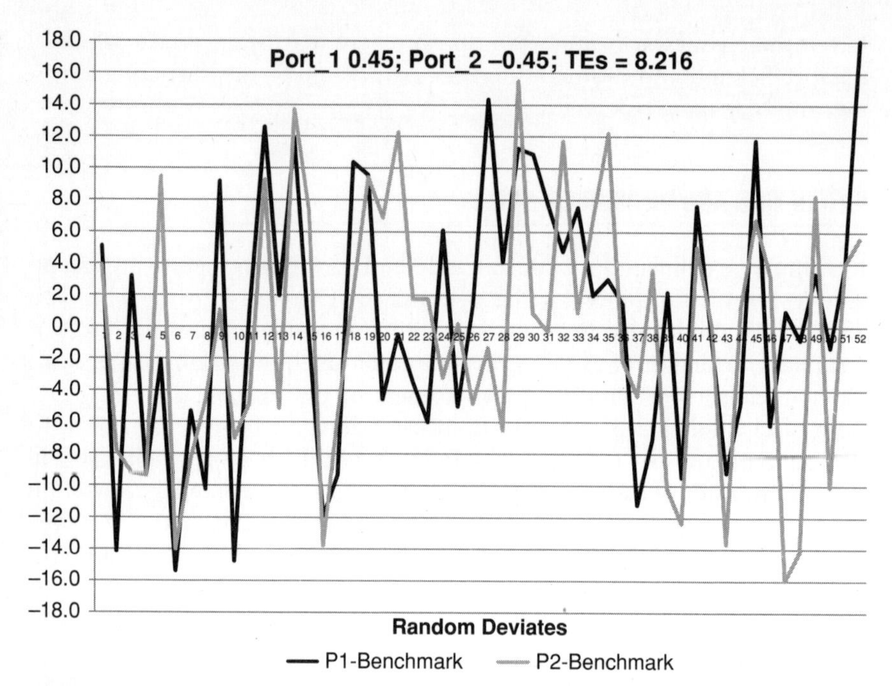


**FIGURE 2.1a** Tracking errors are identical with the benchmark of 8.216 for each portfolio.

to display only those that were mirror images across the zero point, but there were many to choose from. We selected only those whose mean excess returns were of opposite signs while having identical tracking errors.

The simulated results demonstrate that TE and correlation may not be meaningful when examined without additional insights from complementary risk measures. How informative can it really be if two portfolios with very different performance records can have the exact same TE value? Clearly, tracking error alone is not enough for a robust risk management system.

Thus we really have to think carefully about the risk measures we choose to regularly calculate and remind ourselves that how we calculate the measure, what we calculate, and how it's interpreted must be done in concert with other risk measures collectively. It is very important to think carefully about the statistics one includes in the risk management process, and it must be understood that no single measure is enough. The risk management process should include a number of measurements to calculate and dissect risk and be used collectively to validate and challenge one another. The goal is to understand the portfolio, and often a risk measure analyzed

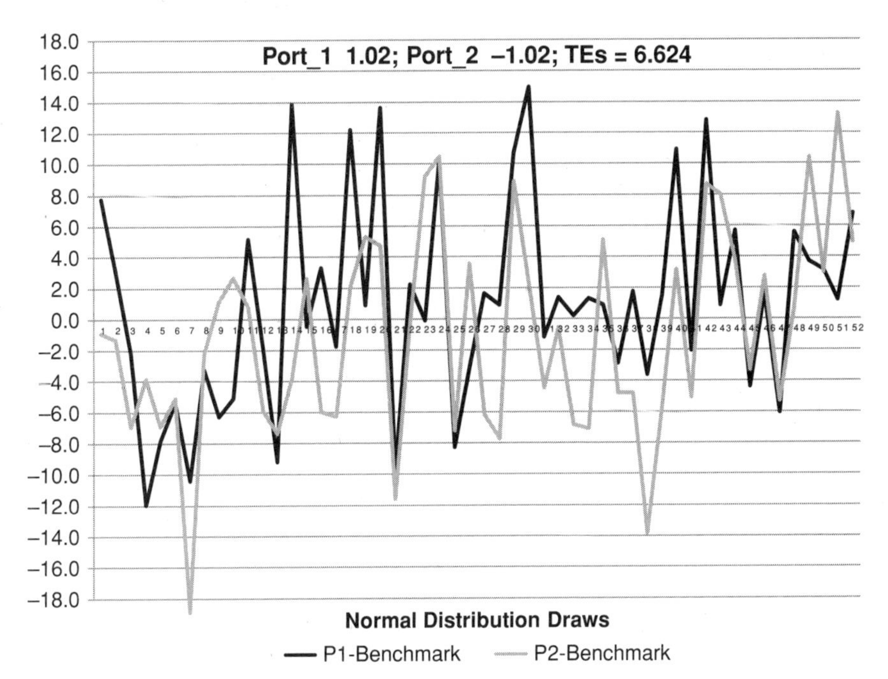


**FIGURE 2.1b** Results for 52 weekly returns generated from draws from a normal distribution similar to the previous figure. Tracking errors are identical.

on its own misses the perspective of what the total risk picture provides, as it's just too easy to get caught up in a number.

We further illustrate this "no single number" concept with an inquiry from an actual client. This client was running stress-testing experiments to shock crude oil down 30 percent, using one of the commercial risk models available on FactSet, in order to estimate how the client's portfolio would perform under this circumstance. In an ordinary situation, a return estimate using a typical multifactor model is performed by multiplying the exposures for each factor times each factor's factor return (or beta) and summing over all factors. In a stress test, we first have to calculate the beta between the time series of returns of crude oil with each and every factor in the risk model. Then, a new factor return is calculated for each risk model factor by multiplying this new beta (ascertained over time between the shock and risk factor returns) times the size of the shock. This generates a new factor return. Multiplying this new factor return times each exposure gives one a return estimate given the stress.

A client was noticing that the factor returns change every month. For a given industry factor like "Airlines" in the risk model, one month the factor

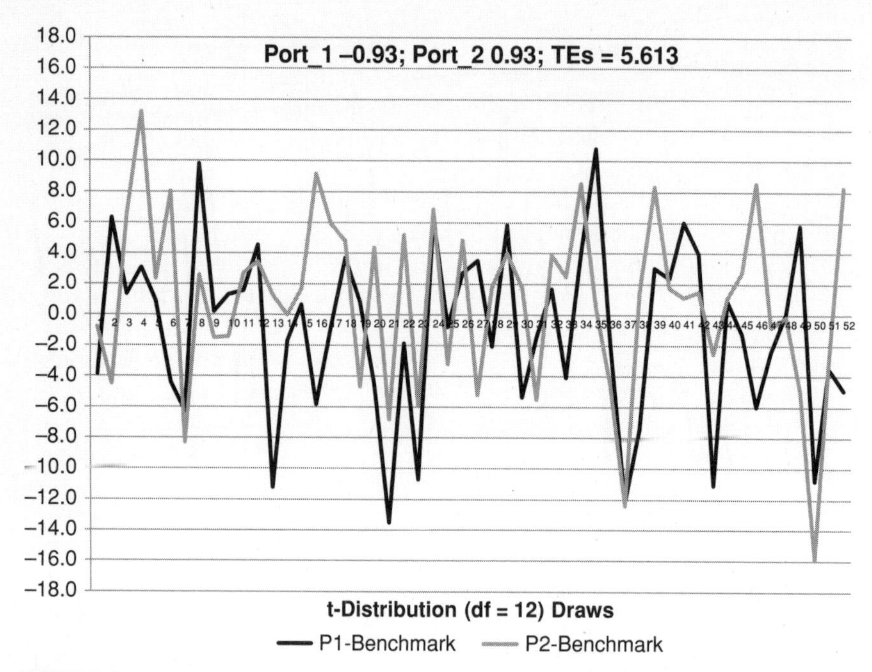


**FIGURE 2.1c** Simulated results for 52 weekly returns generated from draws from a Student's t-distribution similar to the previous figures. Their tracking errors are identical.

return could be –1.59, the next month –1.98, the next month 4.01, and so forth. Likewise, other factor returns also might have quite a bit of volatility. Thus, when you compute the beta between the shock time series and the factor's time series, then multiply the new beta times the shock, and do this for all factors, and then multiply them by current portfolio exposures of the factors and estimate the return for several months, what one may observe is that the time series may not be very stable. The client was interpreting the change in the monthly numbers with a heavy reliance on their values and was missing the much larger picture. The client's concern was that if the original factor return was changing sign every month, then the monthly stress-testing forecast was changing sign, too; therefore, how useful was the forecast? It's a good question to offer a teaching moment, but represents an example of too much scrutiny on details and not enough on the bigger picture. It's much like questioning the temperature gauge's reading on a hot Chicago summer of 90 versus 91 while ignoring the fact that the temperature forecast is for 90s all week with no rain. Seldom does 90 or 92 degrees matter; it's whether the temperatures will hover in the 80s with rain or the 90s with sunshine that matters.

To answer the question and offer a better perspective, we ran a simulation through time of a stress test to show the client a larger picture. In this stress test, we were examining the impact of Spain leaving the Eurozone, reissuing its currency the peseta again, and having it devalue. Without giving the details of how we created the time series of a new peseta currency, we just plot the stress-testing results for 15 different portfolios/indexes from around the world, performed for all months of 2011 (see Figure 2.2). Focusing on the Nikkei simulation toward the right-hand side of this graph, we see that it has a very large positive estimate of return should the peseta devalue by –5 percent relative to the euro in March 2011, whereas previously in February the estimates were near zero and afterward in April quite small in relative terms. What the client needed help understanding was that one single estimate is far less reliable than a sequence of observations. Context is everything in a risk forecast.

For the client's specific oil shock, the trend in the estimate is more important than the change in monthly values. This is because all betas have some oscillation in their monthly time series. The values may swing from 0.4 to 0.25 or from 0.1 to –0.15, but the volatility is the same even though the sign changes in one simulation and stays positive for the other. Statistics and empirical evidence would demonstrate that betas of between 0.2 and –0.2 are essentially zero in practice. So the client feigns understanding of the details of the calculation enough, to attempt to make a decision based on normal monthly estimate variability while ignoring the fact that the estimation error is so large in this stress-testing calculation that only the trend is meaningful.

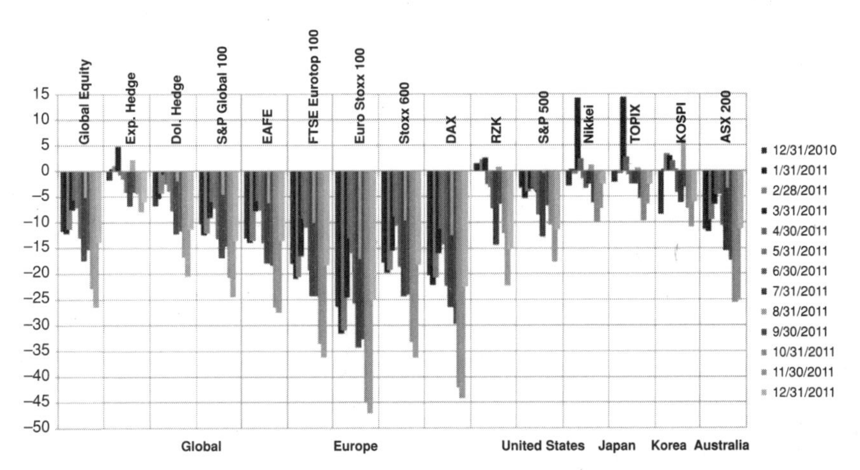


**FIGURE 2.2** The effectiveness of examining risk in a broader perspective than single point calculations.

Stress-testing is a way of estimating the direction and magnitude of a portfolio's response to an event, but the method utilized in this simulation is facile, and while it has a sound economic rationale, it isn't very precise. Monthly differences have variance. However, often the total picture matches strongly with one's intuition, which in the Eurozone example is that portfolios with concentrations of European stocks will have much larger consequences than will global, U.S., Asian, and Australian portfolios should a GIIPS country leave the Eurozone, issue currency, and devalue it. The level of precision in this calculation is poor, however, and the data makes sense only on a relative basis. In this situation, the client was interpreting the absolute value of a single point estimate and didn't understand how to interpret the accuracy or precision of the forecast. The client was missing the context.

In Figure 2.2, we show a stress testing estimate of losses that could occur each month for various index portfolios from around the world, given Spain leaving the Eurozone, issuing a new currency, and having it devalue by 5 percent, on each month ending. Five percent devaluation was the market's implied devaluation as measured from sovereign bond spreads of Spain versus Germany (on average) through this time period.

Particular to stress-testing, generally, a large number of simulated risk values are needed to determine the meaning of any single number. This is where calculating a time series of risk becomes important. Hence, it is a best practice to have a risk review committee be presented with multiple levels of risk measures, analysis, and interpretations of a wide range of outcomes before making a change to the portfolio in order to mitigate risk.

There are many statistics used today to identify, measure, monitor, and mitigate risk. We offer an abbreviated list:

- Tracking error.
- Portfolio variance.
- Portfolio standard deviation.
- Dollar value at risk (at various confidence intervals and horizons).
- Percent value at risk (at various confidence intervals and horizons).
- Information ratio.
- Sharpe ratio.
- Systematic risk.
- Idiosyncratic risk.

Later chapters will cover these in greater detail.

For the interested reader, Figure 2.3 is a screen shot of some risk measures offered on FactSet.

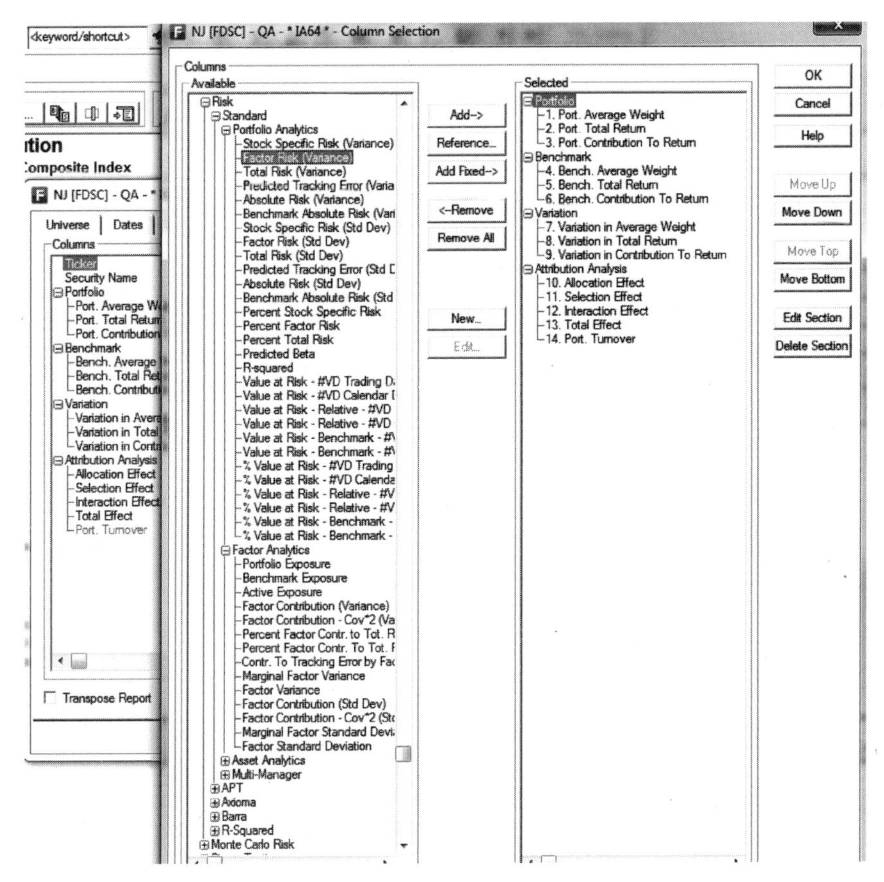


**FIGURE 2.3** Some of the risk measures offered on FactSet.

Many of FactSet's risk measures are self-explanatory, but other statistics, such as risk model R-squared values and various marginal to risk values, are unique to the FactSet offering.

These are total portfolio-level risk calculations. Often, one wants to see group- or security-level risk values, which are often percentage contributions and marginal contributions to the portfolio's overall risk. Percentage contributions are the amount that each asset (group or factor) contributes to the portfolio's overall risk. Marginal contributions are usually calculated by increasing the weight of a single security in the portfolio while readjusting all other securities' weights pro rata and then recalculating the total, systematic, and idiosyncratic components. This calculation is performed for each asset in the portfolio. Once you have that, the change in the risk from the original value to the one with the weight increase for the asset is the *marginal contribution to risk*. It answers how much the portfolio's risk will change given a 1 percent increase in an asset's weight. Luckily, this calculation doesn't require much more than rebalancing the weight vector, as the exposures and covariance don't change; it's mostly a quick matrix algebra operation and can be performed easily even for a 1,000-stock portfolio.

There are other ways to calculate the marginal contribution to (some) risk measure that involve taking the numerical derivative of risk as a function of asset weight. There exists certain security-dependent risk numbers like spread and duration for bonds and the Greeks for options. In these cases, each asset type has its own unique risks that are a function of how each behaves.

Up to this point of the discussion all we've been focused on is *ex post* measures of how a portfolio has behaved in times past (except for stress-testing). The interpretation of the risk measures are, however, called *ex ante* because they're usually used in practice as forecasts whereas the risk measures *after* the forecast are called the *ex post* measures. Generally, consider any forecast as *ex ante* and any realized values as *ex post*. The risk management process so far is backward-looking because the idea is to examine what just happened over some period back in time. In the ongoing continuous monitoring of risks, *ex post* realized risks would then be compared with the *ex ante* forecasts that occurred before, like the example for stress-testing on Eurozone currency debasement.

Another analytical framework often included in risk management processes is the Brinson attribution method. This framework measures total effect of excess return over a historical horizon and breaks it down into contributions from allocation, selection, and interaction. They are the result, however, of assuming that exposures and active weights are of identical constructs, though we've already demonstrated they are not. Nonetheless, these kinds of attribution measures are quite useful on their own, as they describe the equivalent of baseball scores for the portfolio and do so in a concise, reproducible process. The analysis is quite helpful from a quality assurance point of view, too.

Typically, the analysis is performed by grouping the portfolio by sector or industry; grouping by denominated currency and grouping by country are also common approaches for global portfolios. The results of the attribution illustrate how leanings and tilts in the portfolio have paid off or not and to what extent. For instance, from attribution analysis an RM can determine whether a persistent tilt in consumer discretionary or Canadian dollars translated into positive or negative alpha for a PM. Thus, Brinson-style attribution sheds light on how an investment style or process works (or doesn't work) over some historical time horizon. However, there are limitations to its usefulness if the tilts or leanings are small relative to the benchmark, for then it is likely the active weights are not reflective of true exposures. For example, if a portfolio is overweight financials by 10 percent versus the S&P 500, it is probable that the portfolio's true financial exposure is also overweight. The same assumption is less likely to be true if the overweight in financials is only by 1 percent or less. This is because there are likely to be other nonfinancial securities in the portfolio that have correlations with the financial sector and the active exposure would be more along the lines of active weight +/–2 percent, depending on those correlations. Furthermore, correlations change through time, underscoring the fact that the +/–2 percent will change, as will the portfolio's true exposure to financials. Today, the exposure might be active weight –2 percent, and a month from now it might be active weight +1 percent, and so on. Thus, besides normal market volatility of prices moving exposures around, one has to account for the compounded effect of correlation volatility moving exposures, which active-weight-based measures do not consider. This is an important point.

On average, fundamental investors consider only active weight as their exposure, and changes in active weight due to pricing changes of their portfolio positions are the only way they think that exposure changes. In reality, the correlations between portfolio assets change along with the pricing, inducing exposure fluctuation that can be much higher than believed. Brinson attribution can hide much of this contribution to exposure.

Nevertheless, Brinson-style attribution, though based on active weighting rather than true exposures, is a useful measure as long as one is mindful of its level of precision and doesn't read the allocation effect down to three decimal places, for instance. This is because there is uncertainty and estimation error introduced into attribution due to its methodology, not considering covariance between assets where true exposures lie. If you think of a portfolio as a collection of independent entities and trust assigned classifications by standards organizations (like S&P, Reuters, etc.), Brinson attribution more clearly mimics your investment process, though it will miss true exposure. However, if you're a quant shop, you'd be much better off with risk attribution. Moreover, a "quantamental" process would probably require both types of attribution.

## FORECASTING AND HEDGING RISKS

Once you've settled on what risk you're going to measure in an ongoing investment process, you would turn your attention to forecasting risk normally. Consider that at this point you would have defined what risk measures you're likely to want to measure consistently. You'll have chosen them because you believe they shed light on your investment process and unfold what risk your portfolio managers might have tucked into the portfolio. Next would come the discussion of forecasting these chosen measures to obtain the fundamental manager's equivalent of a forward-looking perspective on risk. In addition, the results help set expectations going forward, at least as far out as the risk horizon one is calculating for.

The risk horizon should typically be not much further than the period of your rebalancing frequency. Consider if you're a deep value shop with 30 percent turnover a year. If so, then your investment horizon can be quite long, maybe two years or more. However, your *risk* horizon has to be much shorter. This is because risk calculations cannot be assumed to be that useful for extended periods—not necessarily because their mathematics are bad or the model is misspecified, but because too many things will change over the lifetime of a long risk forecast. So in this example, you should forecast maybe a quarter or so out and do this forecast on a weekly or monthly frequency. In this way, you'll be painting a new risk view yielding insight as to how to readjust the portfolio while you simultaneously determine the time to eject a security from the portfolio.

If, on the other hand, the portfolio turnover is 100 percent a year, then the risk horizon of the forecast should be approximately one month and the frequency of forecasting would move to every day or at least once a week. Regardless of the horizon and update frequency of the risk forecast, it should aid in decision making around the rebalancing process.

The horizon of the risk forecast is also dependent on the risk model itself, and choosing a model that is compatible with the investment process is important. Typically, a model using daily data and a one-year look-back period will have about a three-month forecast horizon. This would be the edge of usefulness, however, and shorter horizons are better for a model of this nature. For a medium horizon model using daily data with a two-year look-back period, one might expect higher precision in risk estimates and perhaps greater time stationarity, but the accuracy of the level estimate for the portfolio wouldn't increase by much. The look-back period should be considered in conjunction with the exponential time decay utilized, as this determines how much weight is given to each observation. For example, if the half-life is one year for two different models, one that uses a one-year look-back period and another that uses a two-year look-back period, then even with two years of data, the second model isn't really using twice as much history in the estimate. This is because the earlier data aren't accounting for much since the data at the end of the first year are one-half the weight of the current period and the weight two years back is one-fourth of the current period, which is a function of the exponential time decay. Given this, the risk forecasts, especially if the models use identical factors, are going to be very similar. This means the data beyond one year in the longer risk model make little contribution to the resulting risk estimate.

Longer time-horizon models use monthly data with look-back periods of five-plus years. The estimate horizon on longer-term models should be a minimum of two months. They do still, however, suffer from the fact that obsidian uncertainties happen, and are susceptible to regular changes in correlations that are not reflected as quickly in the model data. Moreover, the portfolio will likely have been rebalanced before the risk horizon is met, and position weights will change daily with market prices, as will the covariance between assets (even if only slightly). Yet, none of these changes will be reflected if the risk estimates are not updated. Thus, a six-month risk forecast, even for a risk model with a seven-year look-back period, would be precisely accurate only if the portfolio weights and covariance structures don't change over the course of the forecast. That's true for any model for any forecast horizon, but it's exacerbated by longer-horizon forecasts simply because the odds of things moving around increase with time. So even for long-horizon risk model forecasts using a long look-back model, forecasts should be repeatedly made on at least a monthly frequency even for six-month risk forecasts for refreshing purposes. The reason is the compromise of the loss of model reactivity due to using only monthly updating compared to the increased chances of prices and exposures moving around as time proceeds. The frequency of running risk reports using a long horizon (long look-back) risk model is also governed by a little-known (little-known to the finance community) signal-processing barrier called Nyquist sampling.

Importantly, in signal processing there's a substantial barrier that risk modeling suffers from and cannot overcome, and it involves what's known as the Nyquist sampling theorem. This theorem is responsible for the hallucinating effect of watching the propellers of a turboprop airplane, where you see the blades rotating in one direction and as they accelerate you seem to observe them reverse direction. You can also notice this by watching the wheels of an accelerating automobile. The Nyquist sampling theorem states that you cannot forecast any phenomenon at a frequency higher than twice the data frequency. The sampling frequency should be at least twice the highest frequency contained in the sample. To understand this, consider a sine wave of 1 Hz. If we sample at 1 Hz, we will sample the signal at the same point in time for each wave and hence what we will observe will be a straight line. We won't know that the underlying is actually a wave. Now, if we sample this sine wave at 2 Hz, we can capture each peak and trough, and if we sample it at 3 Hz (or greater), we now have more than enough data to reconstruct the original wave.

When you're watching a propeller begin turning or an automobile accelerate from a standing start, in those first few seconds your mind's-eye connection is processing the images you see at a rate fast enough to interpret what they see. But as the car or propeller's speed increases beyond your brain's capacity to interpret it, you see the result of "aliasing" and your mind will interpret the speed as half your processing rate. If a piece of music is sampled at 32 KHz, for instance, any frequency components above 16 KHz will cause aliasing, and since humans' upper frequency range is about 20 KHz, a listener will hear distortion for those sounds at frequencies between 16 and 20 KHz. This is why audio digital signal processing uses a Nyquist filter to remove any frequencies above the Nyquist limit, allowing better fidelity in stereo sound.

The implications in risk forecasting on Nyquist limits are usually overlooked, even by risk vendors. But, this means that if you're using a risk model with monthly updates in data, the shortest forecast horizon you can make is two months out. Thus the adage that one can use short-term risk models for long horizon forecasts but you cannot use long-term risk models for short horizon forecasts is based on solid theory. If it were not true, your brain would not subject itself to "aliasing" in the aforementioned examples. Even intuitionally speaking, how can monthly data forecast a risk that varies on a weekly time scale? It's totally impossible. Even if it varies monthly, if it's cyclical it could be at nearly the same point of the cycle at the same day of the month and you'd never notice it, as described in the sine wave example. Imagine realized risk cycling like a sine wave with a 30-calendar-day period. A monthly updating risk model would sample the exposures at the same point of the cycle each month, allowing risk calculations that would trend horizontally. It would entirely miss the midmonth trough. This observation excludes the normal variation with risk that would tend to hide the cyclicality if it existed in the first place.

This leads to criticizing the argument that because your exposures change every day due to price movement, it's wise to run a risk report every day using a model that updates monthly to pick up this new information. The failure of the true sampling frequency to offer reliable estimates due to Nyquist violations far exceeds the value gained from changes in the exposures. This is in addition to the factor returns and exposures (through covariance) in the risk model increasingly becoming stale the further you are from the last update. If you need daily forecasts, a model that updates twice a day is required. Even a daily updated risk model can only report a risk horizon of two days. Otherwise, you'll be reacting to noise and aliasing using a monthly updating risk model for submonthly forecasts. If you can, one should employ both a long-term and a short-term risk model for risk management.

Similarly, there's a natural limit in the ability to use daily frequency risk models for long-term forecasts. This, however, has more to do with the exponential time decay utilized in most daily models than anything else. Primarily, daily risk models are larger, require a higher computational effort, and are still a relatively new innovation by commercial risk model providers. Due to this, they haven't been set up yet to use five-year look-back periods effectively, and most models look back only two years or less. Combining the limited look-back period with a half-life of a year limits their long-range risk forecasting ability. So besides choosing risk models predicated on matching the factors with one's investment process as closely as possible, the portfolio turnover (rebalancing frequency) should also be considered in selecting a risk model, commensurate with its expected precision at the chosen forecast horizon.

We comment that market memory probably doesn't follow an exponential decay, anyway. That is a construct used by academics to mimic the long memory processes of markets. What market participants most probably remember are events. That is, they look back at the VIX index over the past 20 years and see where spikes have occurred. These spikes correspond to crises and are what participants mostly remember, and earmark the major covariance structural changes in the market. A risk model that uses weightings predicated on events is still waiting to be created, so for now we'll have to live with exponential decay weighting.

The results of forecasting risk can also suggest what type of hedge should be applied to lower the estimated risk forecast. Hedging, as we've stated, should be with respect to exposures preferably, not with respect to active weighting, and the example of currency hedging in Chapter 1 illustrated this difference clearly. We don't address the instruments to use for a hedge, as that topic requires its own chapter. Additionally, the assets used to create the hedge usually will be governed by the investment policy statement and compliance and are outside the scope of topics here. The main point is that hedges should be against true exposures, not attributions masquerading as exposures realized from Brinson-type analysis.

## PORTFOLIO VIEW VERSUS SECURITY-LEVEL VIEW

Considering the review we've given about risk level estimates for a portfolio, it should be of no consequence to understand that error aggregation works to lower uncertainty and increase precision in risk forecasts for the portfolio as a whole. However, a single asset is not able to diversify away the error in estimates by itself. If this is so obviously true, why do analysts, portfolio managers (PMs), and risk managers (RMs) usually expect the same level of precision at the security and portfolio level? It's the aggregation of both positive and negative biases from security-level risks that yields the precision of the forecast of risks at the portfolio level, and if the estimation errors are normally distributed at the security level, their aggregation across a portfolio will tend toward averaging these errors away as well. Given that biases at the security level are unknown and estimation errors are larger as a percentage of the risk, expectations of accuracy for security-level estimates should be far lower than for portfolio-level estimates.

When risk specialists are asked in a survey about using vendor risk models at the security level, most would acknowledge that their usage at this degree of granularity should be limited. It depends on the risk model and type of risk measure, but given a hierarchy of the portfolio, countries, sectors, industry groups, industries, subindustries, and finally securities, we'd recommend generally using risk values no more granular than industry or sector groups.

So where or of what use are marginal contributions to risk for securities, as defined earlier? Or, for that matter, why are individual security risks utilized in mean-variance optimization? Well, in the first case it's a matter of relative sizing and changes in risk through time. To use security-level risk forecasts cautiously is to understand that their level forecasts are weak, but their trends and changing trends through time are less so. If you sort 100 securities' marginal contributions to risk and weigh them relative to one another, you have *some* information. However, the risks of any small adjacent grouping are less reliable, so that two securities sorted by marginal contribution to risk, if separated by 30 securities, are meaningfully different, whereas if separated by four securities they are much less so, if at all. Risk models are not precise enough to separate out the risks of similar securities. For example, marginal risks are usually produced without confidence limits, as in the example presented in Table 2.1.

This risk report shows the results of a large-cap growth portfolio and its benchmark, the Russell 1000 Growth index, analyzed by three different U.S. risk models in USD base report currency. The Axioma U.S. 2 MH Fundamental model and R-Squared Risk Management Limited's Daily Global Equity model, USD Version 2, are daily updated models, while the Northfield (NIS) U.S. Fundamental model shown in the middle is a monthly updated model. We display the marginal contribution to tracking error and the marginal systemic tracking error for Global Industry Classification Standards (GICS) sectors and each individual security, all easily accomplished within FactSet. Where you read negative contributions to tracking error (TE) as in the financials sector, it's by owning those assets that one has a lowering of relative risk to the benchmark.

The energy sector is expanded in this chart, and the stocks are sorted by their contribution to tracking error (low to high) using the Axioma model. So in practice, we would interpret this forecast to mean that HollyFrontier

**TABLE 2.1** The results of a large-cap growth portfolio and its benchmark, the Russell 1000 Growth index, analyzed by three different U.S. risk models in USD base report currency. This type of report is produced directly from FactSet's Portfolio Attribution module.

| Percent of Total Holdings<br>LCG_US_PORTFOLIO vs. Russell 1000 Growth<br>3/27/2012<br>U.S. Dollar | | | | Axioma U.S. 2 MH Fundamental | | NIS U.S. Fundamental Model | | R-Squared Daily Global Equity Model USD V2 | |
|---|---|---|---|---|---|---|---|---|---|
| Ticker | Long/Short | Portfolio Weight | Benchmark Weight | Contr. to Tracking Error | Marginal Systematic Tracking Std. Dev. | Contr. to Tracking Error | Marginal Systematic Tracking Std. Dev. | Contr. to Tracking Error | Marginal Systematic Tracking Std. Dev. |
| | **Total** | 100.00 | 100.00 | 3.917 | — | 6.049 | — | 3.355 | — |
| | **Long** | 100.00 | 100.00 | 3.917 | 5.641 | 6.049 | 8 244 | 3.355 | 6.606 |
| | Consumer Discretionary | 26.24 | 14.43 | 1.093 | 6.163 | 1.874 | 9.712 | 1.413 | 6.548 |
| | Information Technology | 21.68 | 30.53 | 1.075 | 5.220 | 1.437 | 7.693 | 0.748 | 6.562 |
| | Health Care | 15.21 | 10.40 | 0.500 | 5.487 | 0.781 | 8.349 | 0.493 | 6.051 |
| | Energy | 11.87 | 9.97 | 0.683 | 6.238 | 0.761 | 6.099 | 0.772 | 8.112 |
| FTI | FMC Technologies Inc. | 0.64 | 0.16 | 0.024 | 5.993 | 0.018 | 6.250 | 0.044 | 7.510 |
| EQT | EQT Corp. | 0.63 | 0.04 | 0.030 | 5.651 | 0.016 | 4.840 | 0.054 | 7.183 |

*(continued)*

**TABLE 2.1** *(continued)*

Percent of Total Holdings
LCG_US_PORTFOLIO vs. Russell 1000 Growth
3/27/2012
U.S. Dollar

| | | | | Axioma U.S. 2 MH Fundamental | | NIS U.S. Fundamental Model | | R-Squared Daily Global Equity Model USD V2 | |
|---|---|---|---|---|---|---|---|---|---|
| Ticker | Long/Short | Portfolio Weight | Benchmark Weight | Contr. to Tracking Error | Marginal Systematic Tracking Std. Dev. | Contr. to Tracking Error | Marginal Systematic Tracking Std. Dev. | Contr. to Tracking Error | Marginal Systematic Tracking Std. Dev. |
| RRC | Range Resources Corp. | 0.68 | 0.13 | 0.031 | 5.944 | 0.027 | 7.030 | 0.064 | 8.052 |
| CXO | Concho Resources Inc. | 1.04 | 0.14 | 0.041 | 5.350 | 0.037 | 5.086 | 0.093 | 7.739 |
| HP | Helmerich & Payne Inc. | 0.84 | 0.07 | 0.045 | 6.121 | 0.034 | 4.778 | 0.101 | 8.695 |
| OIS | Oil States International Inc. | 0.81 | 0.05 | 0.048 | 6.793 | 0.046 | 7.042 | 0.109 | 9.436 |
| RES | RPC Inc. | 0.63 | 0.01 | 0.049 | 6.555 | 0.009 | N/A | 0.098 | 8.834 |
| CLR | Continental Resources Inc. Oklahoma | 0.76 | 0.05 | 0.049 | 6.433 | 0.059 | 8.291 | 0.080 | 8.078 |
| CRR | CARBO Ceramics Inc. | 0.53 | 0.03 | 0.050 | 7.023 | 0.025 | 5.938 | 0.070 | 8.126 |
| OII | Oceaneering International Inc. | 0.92 | 0.08 | 0.052 | 6.601 | 0.053 | 7.463 | 0.093 | 8.266 |
| CLB | Core Laboratories N.V. | 0.94 | 0.08 | 0.060 | 6.744 | 0.040 | 6.601 | 0.082 | 7.289 |

| | | | | | | | | | |
|---|---|---|---|---|---|---|---|---|---|
| PXD | Pioneer Natural Resources Co. | 1.23 | 0.14 | 0.067 | 5.805 | 0.062 | 5.723 | 0.129 | 8.057 |
| PXP | Plains Exploration & Production Co. | 1.18 | — | 0.083 | 6.292 | 0.106 | 6.917 | 0.144 | 8.020 |
| HFC | Holly Frontier Corp. | 1.04 | 0.09 | 0.083 | 6.239 | 0.040 | 4.898 | 0.147 | 8.106 |
| | Industrials | 11.67 | 12.49 | 0.263 | 5.368 | 0.633 | 8.085 | 0.007 | 6.434 |
| | Consumer Staples | 6.87 | 11.79 | 0.285 | 5.138 | 0.475 | 8.869 | 0.168 | 5.843 |
| | Materials | 2.57 | 5.25 | −0.012 | 5.338 | 0.067 | 7.586 | −0.169 | 6.571 |
| | Financials | 1.37 | 4.27 | −0.039 | 4.110 | −0.035 | 4.632 | −0.161 | 6.960 |
| | Utilities | 1.26 | 0.08 | 0.027 | 4.140 | 0.013 | 3.051 | 0.042 | 4.701 |
| | Telecommunication Services | 1.26 | 0.80 | 0.042 | 5.620 | 0.044 | 5.927 | 0.041 | 5.915 |

Holdings Data As Of
LCG_US_PORTFOLIO 12/31/2011
Russell 1000 Growth 3/27/2012 Risk Model As Of
Axioma U.S. 2 MH Fundamental 3/27/2012
NIS U.S. Fundamental Model 2/29/2012
R-Squared Daily Global Equity Model USD V2 3/27/2012
Hidden: Benchmark-Only Securities and Groups

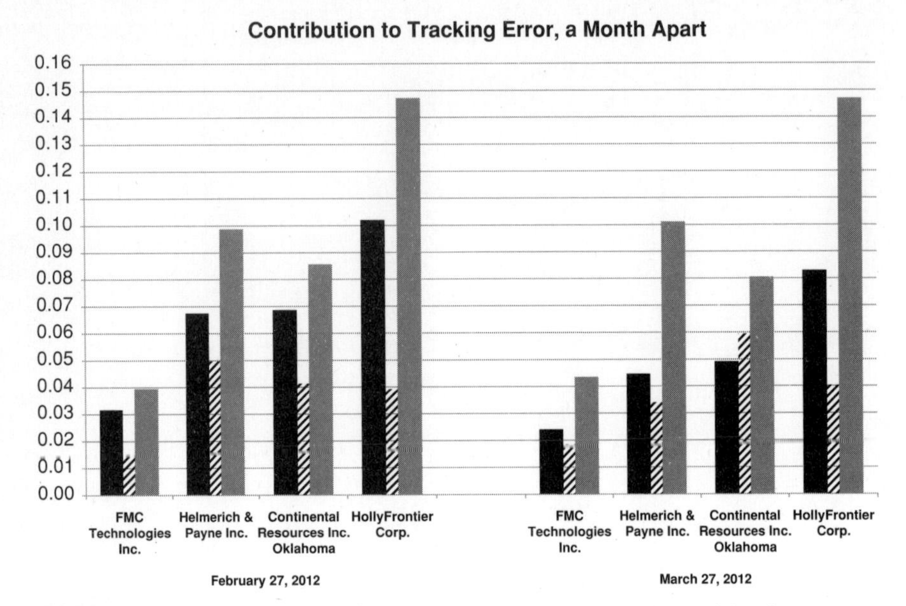


**FIGURE 2.4** The contribution to tracking error from three risk models (the Axioma U.S. 2 MH Fundamental model, the R-Squared Daily Global Equity model USD Version 2, and the Northfield (NIS) U.S. Fundamental model) on February 27, 2012, on the left, and on March 27, 2012, on the right.

Corporation (HFC) with a value of 0.083 out of a TE of 3.917 is riskier than FMC Technologies (FTI) with a contribution of 0.024. Their relative contributions to TE are 2.1 and 0.6 percent, respectively. On the other hand, Helmerich & Payne (HP) and Continental Resources (CLR) with values of 0.045 and 0.049, respectively, could indeed have the same risks. Exactly where the values are that allow discrimination versus where they do not is hard to say, given this report. Since there are no statistically estimated confidence intervals, one cannot know for sure. That assumes the methods of using risk models to forecast have already triumphed over the critics of backward estimation in the first place.

Figures 2.4 and 2.5 will now be used to illustrate how one can obtain sensitivity to relative risks among these securities. Figure 2.4 illustrates the contribution to tracking error from the three risk models on February 27, 2012, on the left, and on March 27, 2012, on the right.

In this bar chart, one can see the estimates from the three risk models for a single security as described by the height of the bars. The Axioma model is the left-most of each group (shown in black), Northfield in the middle is crosshatched, and R-Squared is gray on the right. A working

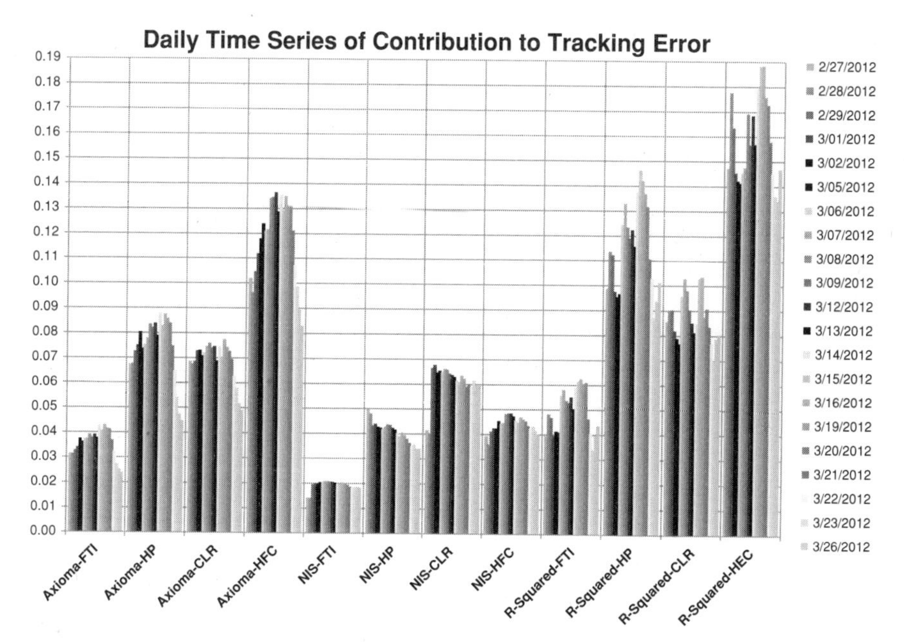


**FIGURE 2.5** The daily time series of contribution to tracking error for the four stocks between February 27, 2012, and March 27, 2012, offering an alternative view of estimation error. The left four collections of bars are the results using Axioma's risk model, the middle four are with using Northfield's model, and the rightmost four are using R-Squared's model.

rule of thumb for error estimates on a given security might entail the relative sizes of the values from different risk models. So, for instance, the difference between the risks of the Northfield model (usually the smallest, the center bar of each group) and the R-Squared model (the largest, the rightmost bar of each group) may substitute or act as a proxy for the confidence interval, say, on the Axioma model's risk estimate on the left. If one makes that assumption, then it's easy to see why FMC and HollyFrontier have completely different risks whereas Helmerich and Continential are probably not distinct, and this carries over from one month to the next.

Figure 2.5, which shows the daily time series of contribution to tracking error for the four stocks between February 27, 2012, and March 27, 2012, offers an alternative view of estimation error.

Strictly speaking, the NIS model is a monthly updated model, so a daily time series of risk forecasts is picking up only changes in exposures, not covariance changes, and thus it suffers from the Nyquist impact mentioned earlier. Nevertheless, we ran it concurrently with the daily risk models and plot its evolution through time in Figure 2.5. The left collection of four bars represents the results using Axioma's model, the middle four are with Northfield's model, and the rightmost four are using R-Squared's model. Consider the disparity in risk forecasts over a month for a given risk model as a proxy for estimation error on the security. If we do that and focus on the leftmost group of four bars, we again see how we can discriminate between FTI and HFC but not HP and CLR with the Axioma model.

The Northfield models, on the other hand, do not allow discrimination between HP and HFC now but show it for HP and CLR, which appear distinguished. But, since it's a monthly updating model, the exposures haven't changed over the time period of the display; only price and weighting have, so to use it for daily risk discrimination means one has greater estimation error in its results than the other two risk models. Finally, the R-Squared model allows discrimination of all four securities, as it appears to offer a clear grouping of risk for each asset over the entire month. These time series of risk presentations offer the context in which to discriminate between individual security risks that single point estimates and single level estimates cannot provide.

In summary, the interpretation of risk forecasts at the security level involves an analysis that utilizes multiple risk forecasts with multiple models over multiple time periods. Clearly, trying to draw such conclusions using a single risk model with a single point in time estimate is questionable. Regarding the use of security-level risk estimates in portfolio optimization, we draw an analogy to return estimates from analysts and portfolio managers, with one caveat: risk estimation has historically been easier to do than return estimation. Estimating the variance of return is widely known to be a better estimate than is a return forecast for the same portfolio. However, both of these are inputs to basic portfolio optimization, and they each come with concomitant estimation error. The mitigation of this error compounding in the optimization process is what some patents[1] are about and what shrinkage covariance estimation techniques (discussed later) aim to avoid. Nevertheless, there's evidence that security-level estimates are useful when examined properly, as we've demonstrated, and studies have shown that various portfolio construction techniques result in outperformance on both an absolute basis and a risk-adjusted basis.

## TOTAL RISK VIEW OF MULTI-ASSET-CLASS (MAC) PORTFOLIOS

In the recent great financial crisis of 2008, the losses that ensued ensnared all asset classes. The run to safe assets was confined to U.S. Treasuries,

UK gilt, German Bund, yen, the almighty U.S. dollar, and gold. The world deviated thereafter to "risk-on" and "risk-off" sentiment, yielding a bifurcation in groups of investable assets consisting of the risk-off assets just described (the "safety of principal" assets) and everything else. This led to a deleveraging of the developed world when assets increased their correlation, and equities, commodities, currencies, and fixed income (except risk-off safe assets) all trended identically. From that time onward, the macro trade was all that worked for several years and global macro funds had quite outsized returns when they called it correctly. Huge losses in equities, commodities, and currencies in 2008 led to many outspoken critics of risk modeling and risk managers (touched on earlier), and even the institution of regulation toward managing global risk better. In Europe, UCITS III freed investment managers from style restriction somewhat, which also created more demand for multi-asset-class risk forecasting and measuring solutions.

The risk management profession thereupon also began to emphasize that risk needs a more holistic view. Historically, individual asset class risks were often estimated individually and then aggregated together, which usually led to overestimating risks but also sometimes led to underestimating risk—especially when risk-on sentiment was leading the charge. This led to conversations about how one can combine the risk estimation techniques to uncover and estimate the total covariance matrix across many asset types, simply because conventional RM has been argued to fail when multiple standard deviation events (obsidian uncertainties) occur. Additionally, these asset classes were believed to have low correlations with one another and had not previously been involved in risk contagion. It has also led to a prominent sentiment that if you cannot estimate the risk of an asset you shouldn't invest in it, and that flies in the face of asset managers, who generally want as large an investable universe as possible. Portfolio managers do not seek to constrain their options, given a choice.

Since the risk modeling methodologies of Barclays' POINT, Yield Book, Polypaths, RiskMetrics, Moody's KMV, SunGard APT, New Frontier Advisors, Axioma, Barra, Northfield, R-Squared, FinAnalytica, and others are each different for separate asset classes, risk managers and modelers were faced with many questions. For instance, how do you combine interest rate risk for yield curve simulations for bond sensitivities with multifactor equity risk models? How do you determine the risks of commodities in the framework of a conventional multifactor risk model? Further complications ensued based on the rationale for why one invested in a particular asset class. Managed futures traders are strongly interested in roll yield, while in 2007 large institutional equity managers were buying gold simply as a dollar hedge and all they wanted was exposure. The commodity trading advisers (CTAs), then, have a different perspective on risk than do long-only equity managers, yet they were purchasing the same asset. How do you simplify and create the crux of all risk modeling, the total covariance matrix? These are the questions that kept risk managers up at night and perhaps still do, and while solutions do exist for the buy-and-hold investor from the front and middle office, none have surfaced that truly address the needs of a trader. The trading floor needs a covariance matrix on the time scale of minutes.

The three major challenges to address this need are:

1. How to overcome the discrimination between exchange-traded, relatively liquid securities and illiquid securities such as structured products, private equity, real estate, infrastructure, and timber.
2. How to ascertain an all-encompassing covariance matrix where the matrix elements are the result of forecasts from data of similar frequency (Nyquist sampling error mitigation, for instance).
3. How to differentiate the MAC risk model from firmwide risk management applications.

Though the risk management field may not converge to one set of answers for these challenges, progress is being made. At FactSet, the multi-asset-class risk model we have developed seeks to address the first and second challenges while taking into consideration client needs for implementation and execution. Chapter 3 will spend considerable effort outlining and explaining how the components of a MAC model interact.

## STABILITY AND ACCURACY

The outstanding questions about stability and accuracy in a risk model come down to construction of the model. They involve data availability, look-ahead and survivorship bias, and overcoming these difficulties. Additionally, the type of model, whether multifactor, principal component, or some other variation consisting of cross-sectional followed by time-series regression followed by PCA, has a bearing on the stability and accuracy of the risk model. Likewise, so does the data frequency, as already discussed. Equity risk models of most vendors typically use point-in-time databases without restatement. This means the data utilized in model construction has only what the marketplace knew on the date, not any data restated some time later and put back into the data at the date the data was found to be in error. So if earnings released in mid-April of some year were restated in August of that same year, the risk modeler's database wouldn't have that earnings correction put in its data back in March. Likewise, even a simple earnings announcement for the first calendar quarter released on April 17 for some company would not be back-filled to March 31. These all overcome look-ahead bias. Moreover, an older method of model construction used lagged data to overcome look-ahead bias; but this is relegated to much older models—no current vendor I know of uses lagging anymore.

Survivorship bias is different and involves building models only from surviving and prospering companies or securities. Those that fall out of the database are the losers; hence they don't contribute to the model, leaving the model overly optimistic in its estimates. To correct this bias, modelers should ensure they include all companies that actually traded on each historical date and not just those that are still around today. Survivorship bias has greater ramifications in return forecasting especially when evaluating mutual fund performance than it does for risk modelers of individual assets; however, historical risk estimates may be incomplete if dead companies are omitted from the estimate because they were not included in the risk model estimate universe.

For equity risk model construction for use with a portfolio manager and/or process that is relative to a benchmark, one avoids the survivorship bias issue somewhat. This is because the data utilized to build the model loses the same securities as the benchmark when a firm bankrupts and falls out of the database. Thus, when measuring relative risk or performance, the difference in risk or return is measured against a benchmark with the identical survivorship bias, thus canceling the effect considerably.

For narrow estimation universes for country- or industry-specific models, for instance, data availability and scarcity certainly impact accuracy and model stability. As one can imagine, in creating a Canadian risk model where the TSX is composed of about 250 securities and the whole Toronto Stock Exchange has far fewer securities than the New York Stock Exchange (NYSE), the systematic risks are quite large as a percentage of the total. So one is missing diversity across assets, which is one strong component that assists in lowering estimation error in the covariance estimate.

Last, time stationarity of a risk model is central and paramount to its usefulness. One would hope that the set of betas (factor returns) determined from a model has stable behavior through time. They are totally dependent on the exposures chosen to represent the risks. Ideally, the factors in a model are those that have shown stable correlations and are founded on sound economic reasoning. To that extent, they do indeed explain the variance of returns. The statistical estimation methods employed in risk modeling are successful in seeking to select a comprehensive set of factors with minimal correlation with each other as well as maximum correlation with returns. Still, even if a model does have the best set of factors for explaining the variance of returns, this does not mean that everyone should always use it. Aligning the risk model factors with the investment philosophy is still an important criterion, in addition to choosing a model with a forecast horizon that is consistent with the average portfolio turnover and rebalancing frequency.

To summarize, we showed a qualitative example to illustrate precision in risk forecasting for the security-level estimate. At the portfolio level, higher precision is more regularly achieved. The advent of risk regulations like UCITS where 99 percent VaR cannot be violated more than four times a year is adequately achieved with modern risk models (fulfilling 99 percent VaR corresponds to breaching the VaR 2.5 times in about 250 trading days).

The barriers to higher accuracy in a risk forecast pertain to the central issue of time stationarity, where the actual covariance structure across assets in the future changes little from today's estimate. The persistence of volatility regimes makes risk model forecasts as reliable as they are.

Now we move on to an in-depth review of the risks associated with different types of asset classes.

## NOTE

1. Richard O. Michaud and Robert Michaud, "Portfolio Optimization by Means of Resampled Efficient Frontiers," U.S. Patent 6,003,018.

CHAPTER 3

# Introduction to Asset Class Specifics

*Steven P. Greiner, PhD; Andrew Geer, CFA, FRM; and William F. McCoy, CFA, PRM*

Chapter 3 begins with equity risk and in particular earmarks the concerns that equity investors have when it comes to determining risk. The focus is on defining what risks equity investors are most concerned about (or should be concerned about if not) and, in later chapters, illustrating the main methods for calculating these risks. Additionally, we visit fixed income (FI) risks in the latter half of the chapter and elucidate how they historically differ from both conventional risk analysis and equity risk management.

Go to www.wiley.com/go/greiner to see video titled "Risk Measures."

## EQUITIES

To begin, equity risk can be categorized quite easily in terms of just two descriptions, given you accept that variance risk is your proxy for real risk. These are classified as systemic risks and idiosyncratic risks. *Systemic risks* are those defined by common factors or contributions to risk that affect all securities in kind. There is, unfortunately, a confusing plethora of terms for this kind of risk, and the variety of names include common, factor, systematic, and market risks. We've heard them all used for defining systemic risks by various vendors and risk management professionals when speaking about those connecting risks across equity securities.

*Idiosyncratic risks* are those risks that are specific to individual companies. This becomes clearer when you consider that these stock-specific risks are essentially anything that is not a systemic risk. It's a definition that really comes from first excluding all risks that are common and systemic. What's left over is placed into the category of idiosyncratic risk. Mathematically, it's usually defined as those risks that come from the residuals of regressions where the factors in the regression are the common systemic risks. So by defining what systemic risks are, one simultaneously defines idiosyncratic risks simply by exclusion, without detailing what the stock-specific risks are. They are whatever systemic risks are not.

If one starts deriving systemic risks, the first experiment run involves measuring correlations over some look-back period between economic or fundamental factors and stock returns. The estimation universe selected whose stock returns go into this equation will be determined by the allowable securities the investing mandate will yield for purchase or shorting. The investment mandate would also stipulate the holding period. Then correlations between the economic time series and stock return holding periods would commence. This would occur for three blocks of factors: true economic or macro factors, financial statement variables, and, finally, trading factors.

### Macroeconomic Risks

If your investing time horizon is of the order of two years or more, you'd find that the largest correlations with return occur with the macro factors. If the holding period is comparable to standard mutual fund holding periods of the order of about four months to two years, then financial statement variables derived from balance sheet, income statement, and the cash flow statements offer the largest correlation block. If your holding periods are three months or less, down to daily values, then short-term price momentum and reversals, trading volume, bid-ask spreads, and so forth will tend to have the highest correlation with return. Thus the final set of systemic risk factors depends to some extent on the holding period of investments for equities. The idiosyncratic risks therefore are not these, but what's left unexplained from regressions of these variables with return.

The macroeconomic factors selected depend on the analysts, quants, and portfolio managers building out the risk criteria. We can use investors like George Soros or Ray Dalio as our prototype global macro investor for indicating the thought process for determining macro factors. First, *global macro* is where the macro factor triggers by finding mispricings or speculating about where mispricings should occur in an asset class, and the global divide comes from looking for these mispricings anywhere in the world.

For example, consider Dalio's moderate bullishness on the U.S. economy after the credit crisis. Though the Federal Reserve had been slow in responding to the housing market crash of 2008, Fed Chairman Ben Bernanke was thought to have handled well the necessary bank liquidity that was needed along with instituting interest rate policies that mitigated the pain of the recession. Moreover, since the other competing developed societies were embroiled in the Eurozone sovereign debt crisis, and with Japan continually in a stall (Japan is a bug looking for a windshield), there was no other place for capital caught in a risk-off trade to go to other than the United States. Even with the slowdown, the United States was still the leading horse of the three developed economic zones in 2009 through 2012. Hence, risk for Ray Dalio was defined by not allocating capital to the United States. In the risk model of his mind's eye, it was the expectations and forecasting of how central banks were going to act that defined his actions at the strategic level. Additionally, as of this writing he believes we're currently in a deflationary environment, but with a longer-term view of inflation rising significantly, however, over the next years. Asia and the Tigers are still growing, albeit with a slight setback lasting anywhere from one to three years, out to 2015. The U.S. dollar will maintain some strength as long as the Eurozone is unsettled and, with U.S. interest rates low, the carry trade in foreign exchange (FX) markets is supported by borrowing USD and going long other higher-yielding currencies. Finally, quantitative easing 3.0 will begin soon as some contagion of the Eurozone problems leaks back to the United States. This is the Dalio risk worldview as of spring 2012.

It's interesting that on September 13, 2012, Dalio proved right with Federal Reserve Chairman Bernanke announcing the Fed would spend $40 billion a month purchasing mortgage debt through the end of the year, leaving open this continued policy until conditions improve thereafter.

At the tactical level, then, employing these common risks of gross economic nature to use is more difficult, simply because they're not so easily quantified. However, they key in examples of where to collect macroeconomic factors. Certainly changes in gross domestic product (GDP) and debt levels, foreign exchange rates, bond yields at the sovereign debt level, credit default spreads, and, to borrow from Roll and Ross,[1] surprises in inflation, investor confidence, and yield curve shifts, levels and changes are all worthy factors for contention as risk contributors at the macro level. Last, commodity levels and returns are worth adding. A set of factors like these leads to a slow impact on stock returns, which is why they're most useful to investors with long time horizons.

Another way of using these measures is to form the top-down perspective for aiding or assisting asset allocation decisions. This can be performed either fundamentally or quantitatively through the use of a model layover strategy. In this design, a model for asset allocation can be devised using macro factors. A great example of this exists with Leila Heckman's Heckman Global Advisors, who are specialists in country allocation modeling.[2]

### Financial Statement Variables

The suite of factors from financial statement data for defining common risks consists of most of the usual collection of factors fundamental analysts have been keying on for decades. They are divided into four categories: valuation, fundamental, momentum, and exogenous factors. The first category involves factors like price to book (P/B); price to earnings (P/E); earnings before interest, taxes, depreciation, and amortization (EBITDA) to price; or any number of other valuation metrics. Essentially, any data that has stock price in either the numerator or the denominator can be thought of as a valuation measure of some sort.

The standard vernacular among equity quants is to call any financial statement variable that doesn't have price in its definition a fundamental factor, the second category. These include factors that are constructed from earnings and growth estimates, sales changes from year to year or from quarter to quarter, estimate dispersions, operating cash flow to invested capital (EBITDA to capex)/net sales, accruals, research and development (R&D)/sales, net margin change, working capital changes, and so forth. Also, numerical derivatives of these factors or changes in these factors are also termed fundamentals. Almost all sell-side quants have lists and lists of factors in these two categories of valuation and fundamental variables, along with a third classification, the technical or momentum factors.

Historically speaking, *market technician* or *chartist* was a term given to analysts on Wall Street who believed in forecasting the direction of prices through the study of past market price action, including volume. This practice has a decent theoretical basis, however, involving behavioral finance for its explanation of return. The action of market participants is believed to result in price trajectories of stocks that exhibit predictable patterns in the data that have forward prediction characteristics. It's a very old practice that began well before modern computers and numerical digital/signal processing existed. In today's parlance, chartists are replaced with numerical methods associated with pattern recognition and momentum trading. Any recent graduate of physics or mathematics or their subdisciplines immediately sees the archaic methodologies employed in this old discipline, and that it cannot keep up with modern numerical methods invented to interpret radar and sonar reflection, radio and communications data, and numerous applications of analog-to-digital conversion in the huge variety of products in our modern society. This is not to say the old chartist methods didn't work, as there is both empirical and anecdotal evidence that they did; it's just to remind the reader that the natural evolution of the market technician's toolbox is toward algorithmic implementation. These days, in the simplest cases they're implemented in most risk modelers' lists of momentum factors, of which there is a very wide variety of formulations. In essence, pattern recognition is the modern interpretation of technical trading. Pattern recognition's chief embodiment is in high-frequency trading these days in the modern sense of the field.

The last set of data to include in the financial statement variables list, then, involves some exogenous factors that still operate on the time scales of the valuation, fundamental, and momentum factors, which include things like market capitalization (size) and outstanding share count. The enterprising risk modeler would choose these four categories of valuation, fundamentals, momentum, and exogenous factors in collecting a suite of factors for ascertaining their correlations with stock returns in time horizons from quarterly up to two, maybe three years at best. One would find the correlations with return to be highest with this suite of factors, given these holding periods versus macro and trading factor suites.

In summary, the so-called style factors many risk model vendors speak of fall into this category of financial statement–oriented variables for common risk specification and are usually associated with valuation and fundamental factors.

Additionally, currencies, countries (or regions), and industries can be used to model common risks. The particular category they fit in is a little harder to settle on, however. They're harder to classify because they appear to be of a hierarchy that identifies well with macro factors, yet they operate on time scales closer to financial statement risks, because the factors are constructed from the time series of returns due to currencies, industries, sectors, or regions. In any event, they must be and usually are included in most vendor risk models in varying ways these days.

The sticky part in modeling comes when any factor is also an asset you're holding. This generally isn't a case with the first two classes of factors of macro and financial statement common risks (how can you buy a "B/P"?), but when you begin to include commodities or currencies, it's entirely possible those risk factors can become assets, too, and that can be problematic with risk estimation.

Up to this point in this chapter we've been speaking in terms of factor classification, but this should not be misconstrued as meaning something different from exposure. To build out a risk model, the data that actually goes into filling out a factor is typically called the exposure value. Thus changes to investor sentiment and price to book are actual values filled in to create the data that will ultimately be used in regression with stock returns. So when we reference exposure in calculating risk, we mean the values, the data that are used in the regression for the most part. This subtle but important distinction is separate from a discussion on risk attribution, where exposure means the aggregated sensitivity to a factor.

For instance, if I'm a U.S. investor and my exposure to pound sterling is 10 percent, I'm saying the aggregated sensitivity to changes in FX between USD and GPB is 10 percent of the portfolio's value. I would have an exposure in the risk model of FX, too, an actual time series of the USD and GPB exchange rate in which covariance between assets and FX is measured. Risk model exposure is a concrete set of data, a column in a matrix, whereas portfolio exposure is the result of ascertaining the beta between assets and the risk model exposure and multiplying the beta times each asset's position size. Typically, statistical testing is performed iteratively to decide whether the beta between an asset and an exposure is statistically significant. If it's found to be insignificant, the beta is set to zero and the asset isn't assigned that exposure.

### Higher-Frequency Risks

The highest turnover portfolios (as in high-frequency trading) are outside the discussion of this book for the most part. The data for short holding periods certainly involves a lot of price momentum, signal processing, trading volume, and bid-ask spread data of intradaily and daily time series, and their correlations with short-horizon returns can be useful for creating a risk model for these time scales, but we won't say more about them.

### Subcategorization of Risks

Once the common risks are identified through the correlation analysis applied to the assets, a check of factor cross-correlations also must be applied to weed out those factors that share a large amount of correlation. If kept in the model, they would result in collinearity issues in model construction.

Given that one has chosen a set of factors for estimating common systemic risks, the idiosyncratic risks just fall out of the risk model construction process. They're not chosen per se, but it is the Boolean "not common" that defines them.

The next step in identifying risks for equities involves the partials or marginal contributions to risk. This can only be performed after computing the portfolio risk from the risk model, which is a matrix algebra operation between portfolio weights, exposures, and the covariance matrix. The result is a single number giving the estimate of the portfolio's risk in variance units for a given time horizon. Likewise, the idiosyncratic risks are a product of weights times a unit matrix with idiosyncratic variance on the diagonals or, more accurately, the variance of the regression residuals. The sum of the two is the total (variance) risk of the portfolio.

The way marginals are conventionally computed involves increasing the weight of a single security by 1 percent of the portfolio, prorating the weight of all other securities with the typical long-only constraint that weights sum to 1, and recomputing the total risk. Prorating is required since the sum of all weights must equal 1 in a long-only strategy. For a long/short strategy, the sum could be to some other net positive or negative result, however. The risk calculation involves only weights, exposures, and the covariance matrix. Since the latter two are unchanged with weight, a simple programming loop over all asset weights quickly computes the marginal contribution to risk for each security in a very facile manner.

The factor contributions to risk are also a desired entity. Unfortunately, there are no closed-form solutions to determine an individual factor's contribution to common risks and then total risk. The form of the risk calculation is matrix multiplication in most cases, meaning the columns of exposures and covariance that constitute the factors are mixed and not disentangled algebraically. Hence a method for computing the factor risks is invented within FactSet that involves resorting to the factor exposures and the resultant covariance matrix allowing for marginals absolutely and relative to a benchmark. We can therefore calculate the marginal systematic tracking variance (you've heard of tracking error; this is the square of that number), for instance by multiplying the covariance matrix times the difference between asset-level active exposures of the portfolio and its benchmark.

Likewise, if one multiplies the absolute exposures times the covariance matrix, one obtains a security-level marginal contribution to variance risk. Since the exposure matrix is $n \times m$, where $n$ is the number of assets, and the covariance matrix is $m \times m$, where $m$ is the number of factors, their product yields a matrix that is $n \times m$, and the asset level marginals for a given factor are picked up in the columns. Any individual stock's factor contribution to total risk is simply one-half the matrix element's value, irrespective of its weight, for that particular factor. The one-half divisor comes about from double counting in the covariance matrix since elements $j, k$ equal elements $k, j$, and they both are used in the matrix multiplication sequence. In this fashion, then, we can itemize risks apportioned to individual risk model factors for each asset in the portfolio.

In practical everyday usage, these tables of numbers are confusing to most users. Many don't understand the significance of the numbers and because of their confusion cannot use the information provided very well. While the numbers literally are component risks for securities with units of exposure variance, that means nothing to most of us. The simplest application is to use them in a relative sense, one to another for a given factor, to outline the size of the contribution to common risk variance. For instance,

Figure 3.1 illustrates just such factor contributions relative to the portfolio's benchmark.

The securities are listed at the left, and for a given risk model consisting of regional factors predicated on certain styles like growth, value, liquidity, and so forth we see the factor contribution to relative variance, and the raw values along with their percentage contributions. From this screen shot of FactSet's software for this portfolio, we can immediately ascertain that for the North American growth factor, Dell contributes a diversifying effect to this risk factor of –0.018 percent, while the entire information technology sector contributes only 0.121 percent to North American growth, so this portfolio in general has quite a tilt away from growth. These numbers are for a specific portfolio and, if relative, then are benchmark specific as well. They serve to educate the portfolio manager of the relative importance and direction of portfolio risk contributors if used properly. If graphed through time, they even can yield the trend in risk contributions of the portfolio's evolution through time. This can sometimes be extrapolated for forecasting as well, provided rebalancing in the portfolio isn't large.

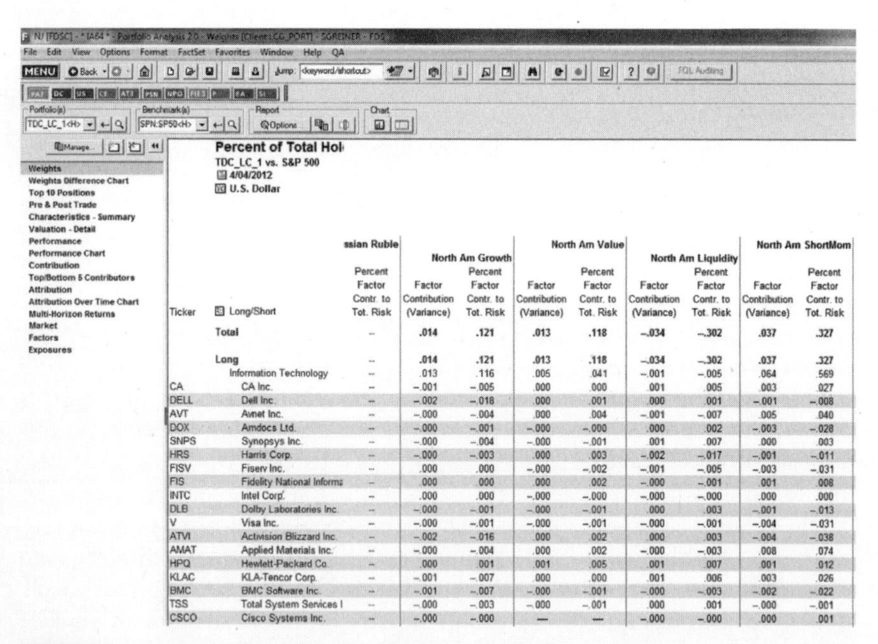


Percent of Total Hol
TDC_LC_1 vs. S&P 500
4/04/2012
U.S. Dollar

| Ticker | Long/Short | ssian Ruble Percent Factor Contr. to Tot. Risk | North Am Growth Factor Contribution (Variance) | North Am Growth Percent Factor Contr. to Tot. Risk | North Am Value Factor Contribution (Variance) | North Am Value Percent Factor Contr. to Tot. Risk | North Am Liquidity Factor Contribution (Variance) | North Am Liquidity Percent Factor Contr. to Tot. Risk | North Am ShortMom Factor Contribution (Variance) | North Am ShortMom Percent Factor Contr. to Tot. Risk |
|---|---|---|---|---|---|---|---|---|---|---|
| | **Total** | -- | **.014** | **.121** | **.013** | **.118** | **–.034** | **–.302** | **.037** | **.327** |
| | **Long** | -- | **.014** | **.121** | **.013** | **.118** | **–.034** | **–.302** | **.037** | **.327** |
| | Information Technology | -- | .013 | .116 | .005 | .041 | –.001 | –.005 | .064 | .569 |
| CA | CA Inc. | -- | –.001 | –.005 | .000 | .000 | .001 | .005 | .003 | .027 |
| DELL | Dell Inc. | -- | –.002 | –.018 | .000 | .001 | .000 | .001 | –.001 | –.008 |
| AVT | Avnet Inc. | -- | –.000 | –.004 | .000 | .004 | –.001 | –.007 | .005 | .040 |
| DOX | Amdocs Ltd. | -- | –.000 | –.001 | –.000 | –.000 | .000 | .002 | –.003 | –.028 |
| SNPS | Synopsys Inc. | -- | –.000 | –.004 | –.000 | –.001 | .001 | .007 | .000 | .003 |
| HRS | Harris Corp. | -- | –.000 | –.003 | .000 | .003 | –.002 | –.017 | –.001 | –.011 |
| FISV | Fiserv Inc. | -- | .000 | .000 | –.000 | –.002 | –.001 | –.005 | –.003 | –.031 |
| FIS | Fidelity National Informa | -- | .000 | .000 | .000 | .002 | –.000 | –.001 | .001 | .008 |
| INTC | Intel Corp. | -- | .000 | .000 | –.000 | –.000 | –.000 | –.000 | .000 | .000 |
| DLB | Dolby Laboratories Inc. | -- | –.000 | –.001 | –.000 | –.001 | .000 | .003 | –.001 | –.013 |
| V | Visa Inc. | -- | –.000 | –.001 | –.000 | –.001 | –.000 | –.001 | –.004 | –.031 |
| ATVI | Activision Blizzard Inc. | -- | –.002 | –.016 | .000 | .002 | .000 | .003 | –.004 | –.038 |
| AMAT | Applied Materials Inc. | -- | –.000 | –.004 | .000 | .002 | –.000 | –.003 | .008 | .074 |
| HPQ | Hewlett-Packard Co. | -- | .000 | .001 | .001 | .005 | .001 | .007 | .001 | .012 |
| KLAC | KLA-Tencor Corp. | -- | –.001 | –.007 | .000 | .000 | .001 | .006 | .003 | .026 |
| BMC | BMC Software Inc. | -- | –.001 | –.007 | –.000 | –.001 | –.000 | –.003 | –.002 | –.022 |
| TSS | Total System Services I | -- | –.000 | –.003 | –.000 | –.001 | .000 | .001 | –.000 | –.001 |
| CSCO | Cisco Systems Inc. | -- | –.000 | –.000 | — | — | –.000 | –.000 | .000 | .001 |

**FIGURE 3.1** FactSet's Portfolio Attribution module demonstrates some marginal contribution to risk for a couple of factors from a risk model in a large-cap core U.S. portfolio.

The risks for holding equity securities coming from first principles involve an understanding of what the company does, what its competitive landscape looks like, the current state of the industry cycle, the quality of management, new product cycles, and use of free cash flow, for instance. Basic fundamental investing undertakes the analysis of companies either from the top down or from the bottom up in an effort to determine the aggregate value of a claim on the series of a company's cash flows. It may focus on business, balance sheet, and counterparty credit risk for large corporations. Growth, margin, asset turns, and discount rates all have an impact on valuing these cash flows. It's this evaluation of the free cash flow generating capacity of a firm that determines its valuation now and into the future. This led Ben Graham to believe that prudent investors should leverage an old principle involving waiting for periods of depressed business and market levels to buy firms since they are unlikely to be able to acquire stock at other times except at prices they may regret later. He believed some measure of volatility is normal and not alarming, nor to be confused with real risk.

Risk models put the fundamentalist's view in quantitative terms for the enterprising investor and allow for identification of when risk is too high. Likewise, the factor exposures bring the fundamentalist's perspective to bear on defining where returns come from and where the fluctuations of return (i.e., risks) come from. This is why choosing a risk model that fits one's investing process is so important.

At this point, one can see why model misspecification error arises, too (so-called specification error). The choices of economic variables selected to model common risks are vast and there is no one right set, only reasons for choosing a set. Given that intelligent, rational people select a suite of factors for modeling risks they deem appropriate, this only serves to support the view that reasonable people can reasonably disagree on a topic. It is why there are more than 200 risk models on the FactSet platform as of this writing. No one model is perfect, but each is created for individual portfolio specificity and mandate. The art for the FactSet client is to choose the one most appropriate for the client's mandate, investing style, and process.

### Principal Component Risk Identification

It must be said that parametric risk modeling has a deeper and longer history of usage within asset management than statistical methods such as those employed by SunGard APT, for instance. This is not because they are better in most measures, but has more to do with the legacy of asset management being dominated by those individuals trained in economics and business schools who assess both return potential and risk through the eyes of variables defined in economic and accounting terms. They live in a parametric world and prefer explanatory variables they understand and have experience with. However, with the availability of high-performance desktop computing, along with the abundance of personnel trained in the art of scientific computing and statistics, principal component analysis (PCA) methodologies can now be applied to risk forecasting and assessment as well, especially when forecasting is the main concern as opposed to building models for explanatory purposes.

The PCA process usually begins by constructing a covariance matrix from the sample returns from some estimation universe. Then the eigenvectors and eigenvalues are deduced from the matrix, and principal components (PCs) are calculated. The PCs are orthogonal and have no correlation with one another. They're not easily interpretable, however, either. People will often regress the PCs against fundamental and economic variables to try to add interpretation to them, but that prompts the question of then why not use a parametric model in the first place. The PCA process, however, still allows for systematic or common portfolio risks to be calculated along with idiosyncratic risks with accuracy commensurate to parametric risk models.

Another similar application involves what's known as factor analysis and latent structure analysis. It's often confused with PCA methods, but they are different. In conventional PCA, the model attempts to account for the entire variance of return, while factor analysis accounts for just the common variance, the common sources of risk. Additionally, in oblique factor analysis the factors may not even be orthogonal. In some situations however, the factors derived using factor analysis offer an easier interpretation than the principal components would. It's expected that factor analysis may begin to be used more and more in risk modeling.

## FIXED INCOME

The rest of this chapter is about the evolution of fixed income (FI) risk assessment. Fixed income has taken a different approach to risk assessment than equities, but the two are beginning to converge. Bond portfolio managers convey the risk of their portfolios through duration and rating distributions. These statistics in turn measure the interest rate and credit risk of their portfolios. However, as equity-style risk models for fixed income become more popular, more portfolio managers are using statistics such as value at risk (VaR) or tracking error. Moreover, since the instruments of fixed income risk calculations can be more diverse than equity, any risk assessment tool needs the capacity to capture that diversity. Therefore, this section introduces the reader to the following topics:

- Main sectors of the fixed income markets.
- Calculation of interest rate and spread risk.
- Evolution of these measures.

The diversity and rapid evolution of the fixed income market forces this thin section to be only a brief introduction to the topic.[3] Moreover, many FI risk vendors tend toward creating factor models for assessing FI risk. At FactSet we provide a valuation model for risk modeling.

Finally, we offer two clarifications on the type of risk this section will be reviewing. First, risk is traditionally siloed into market, credit, and operational risk. *Market risk* is the measurement of risk due to price moves. This approach will be the main focus here, and it will be viewed from the perspective of a portfolio manager. *Credit risk* is the measurement of risk due to the loss of principal. It extends beyond the performance of a portfolio, and captures counterparty default as well. While important, we will be making the assumption that the markets will capture the perceived probability of default through the price, and not focus on the binary risk of default. Finally, *operational risk* is outside the scope of this book for the most part, except in regard to portfolio risk management, which is one contribution to operational risk.

The second clarification is: "Are we managing the risk versus . . . what?" This section covers both absolute risk assessment, and by extension, risk assessment versus a market benchmark. However, fixed income portfolios can be managed versus types of situations, too. For instance, there is matching the cash flows of a known set of payouts, as in pension plan liabilities. Another example is in transforming insurance company liabilities, such as deferred annuities, into replicating bond portfolios. Unfortunately, these examples are also outside the scope of this chapter in its entirety.

### Duration Risk

The mainstream measurement of fixed income risk is through *duration*. However, duration isn't really risk in the conventional definition of risk. Duration captures interest rate movement, while ratings and sector classification capture movements in interest spreads. Fixed income risk assessment has traditionally taken a different direction than equity risk, which reflects the differing approaches to valuation. There is an old saying: "Equity management is all about accounting, whereas fixed income is all about math." With equities, there is a presumed association between the company's accounting or financial statement data and the future price returns. However, this association isn't so easily ascertained and can be thought of as operating through some hidden market process usually. This hidden process can be revealed through the application of statistical (principal component) and parametric risk models, discussed earlier and again in later chapters. Meanwhile, in fixed income, the orderly cash flows of a bond lead to no-arbitrage rules on the valuation of the bond. In turn, these no-arbitrage rules have led to the ready identification of the sources of value, which in turn has led to the development of different risk measuring techniques. However, the future of fixed income risk assessment is to tie fixed income valuation measures with equity-based and statistical risk models for a more comprehensive multi-asset-class (MAC) view of risk.

To begin fixed income risk assessment, the first thing to consider is what makes fixed income *fixed*. With a traditional, plain-vanilla bond, there are regular coupon payments. Over a specified horizon, these coupon payments lead to two known aspects of the return of a bond. First, there is the accrual and receipt of the coupon payments. However, there are other interim cash flows that should be estimated due to the passage of time. For instance, there are sinking funds, calls, and prepayments that must be predicted. The second aspect assumes that everything remains unchanged, except time is advanced. The bond can be revalued with everything unchanged except the valuation date. Consider the changes that occur over one year on a three-year, 3 percent coupon bond, using the yield curve as shown in Figure 3.2. The bond starts with a price of par, or $100. However, over the course of one year, and assuming the yield curve doesn't change, what was once a three-year coupon would be valued at the now two-year rate, the two-year coupon would be valued at the now one-year rate, and so forth. In this example, the old three-year bond is now valued at a 2 percent yield with two years left of maturity. The price of the two-year, 3 percent coupon bond at a 2 percent yield is 101.95, which leads to a price gain of 1.95 percent. Since the yield curve is typically upward sloping, valuing these coupons at lower rates introduces a price appreciation, called "riding down the yield curve."

Historically, in risk management, the impact of accruals and riding down the yield curve assume fixed, unchanging environments and are ignored. These sources of return are usually excluded when measuring tracking error. However, for value at risk (VaR) calculations, where the entire valuation of the security is considered, these fixed values must be included.

Let's now move to the largest source of variation in a bond's price, which involves interest rates. During the 1980s, interest rates on government bonds were in the teens. However, while everyone knew what the price of a bond was given its yield, there was no risk measure to describe the

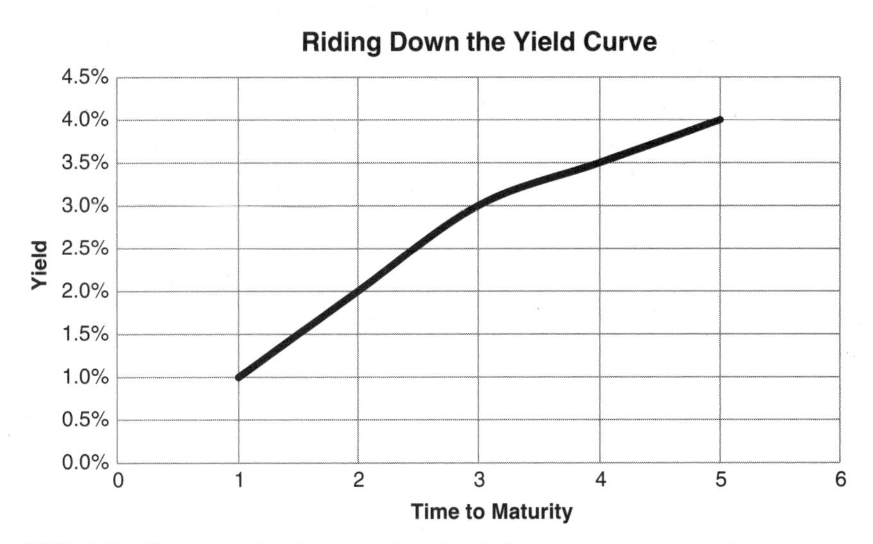


**FIGURE 3.2** The price of a three-year bond with 3 percent coupon, repriced one year later where it achieves a 2 percent yield (at two years to maturity). The price return of $100 at par to $101.95 one year later is 1.95 percent.

sensitivity of bond price with respect to yield changes. What changed fixed income was the rediscovery of the work of Frederick Macaulay. Macaulay took the first derivative of the price/yield equation with respect to yield, and named this derivative *duration*.

Without going through the math, duration equates the percentage change in the price of a bond, given a change in yield. The formula can be viewed as the weighted average time to receipt of the cash flows of a bond, where the weights are the present values of each cash flow relative to the total present value of the bond. Graphically, duration can be thought of as the fulcrum where half the present value of the bond is on each side of the duration. An example is shown in Figure 3.3, for a five-year, 4 percent coupon bond at a 4 percent yield. The bars represent the weighted average time to receipt of each cash flow. The fulcrum is at 4.4, which is also the duration.

Duration is typically quoted in years, as time is the unit remaining in the derivative.

A short digression on the variables in the duration equation is useful. While Macaulay duration is sparingly used today, these influences are still true for more complex duration measures. The influences that are important are maturity, coupon, and yield.

Increasing the maturity of the bond increases the duration. This part should be obvious, as the payments are increased and would move the

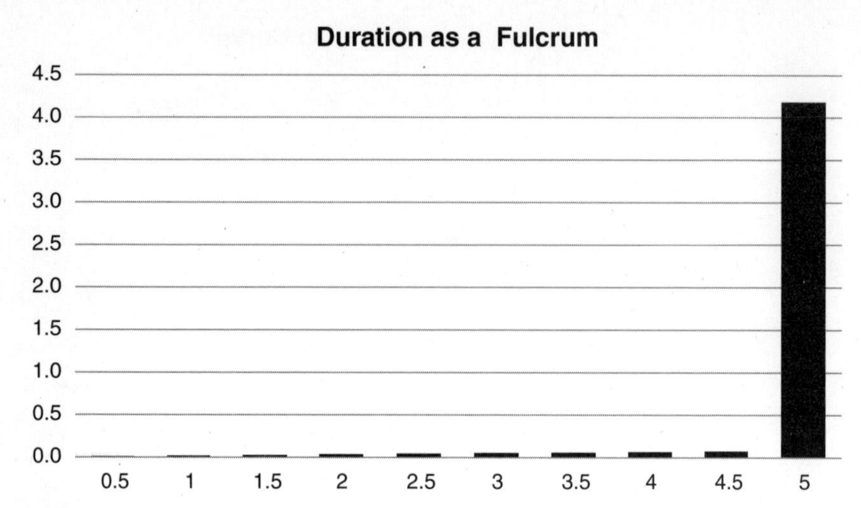


**FIGURE 3.3** A five-year, 4 percent coupon bond at a 4 percent yield.

fulcrum to the right. Figure 3.4 shows how increasing the maturity one year moves the fulcrum from 4.4 to 5.2.

Increasing the coupon of the bond decreases the duration. While the coupon increase is even across all payments, the present value is different for each payment. The earlier coupons are discounted less, and therefore shift

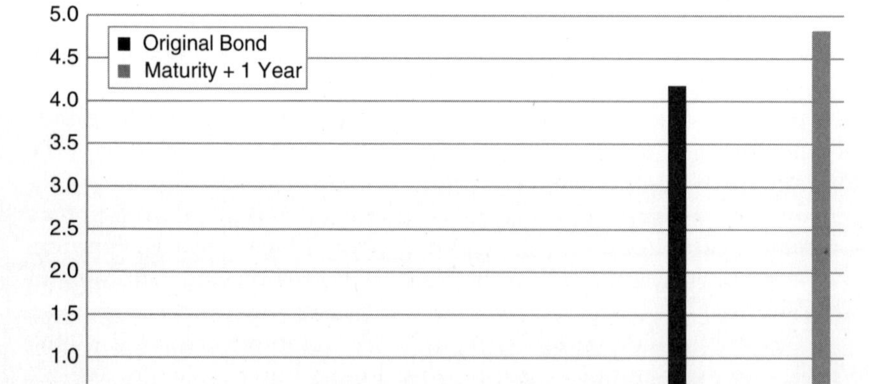


**FIGURE 3.4** Increasing the maturity one year moves the fulcrum from 4.4 to 5.2.

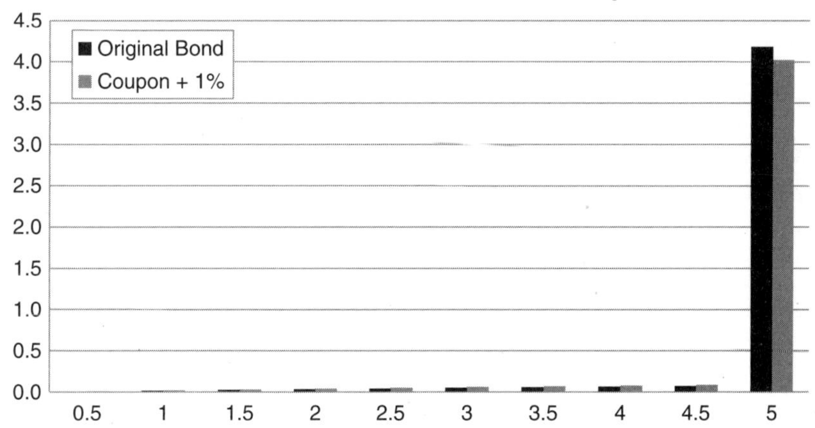


**FIGURE 3.5** If the coupon is increased 1 percent, there is a slight increase in present value in each coupon payment, and the final principal payment is less important as a percentage of the bond's value.

the fulcrum to the left. This effect is shown in Figure 3.5. If the coupon is increased 1 percent, there is a slight increase in present value in each coupon payment, and the final principal payment is less important as a percentage of the bond's value. The fulcrum decreases from 4.4 to 4.3.

Finally, increasing the starting yield of the bond decreases the duration. The later payments of the bond are discounted at an exponential rate, and so are worth less faster. This in turn shifts the fulcrum to the left. This effect is demonstrated in Figure 3.6, where the yield is increased by 1 percent. Here the effect is smaller, and the fulcrum shifts only from 4.40 to 4.39.

It is also useful to calculate the second derivative of price with respect to yield. This term is called *convexity*. Convexity starts to reflect the nonlinearity of the price/yield relationship. From mathematics, the Taylor rule shows how any complex function can be approximated in terms of the sequence of its derivatives. Duration and convexity show how the complex price/yield formula can be described by a linear component (duration) and a curvature component (convexity). For fixed income, positive convexity reflects the fact that as yields increase, the price doesn't drop as much as implied by the duration move, and as yields decrease, the price rises more than implied by duration, which leads to the Tarzan definition, "convexity good, convexity friend." We will discuss convexity more when we introduce optionality in bonds.

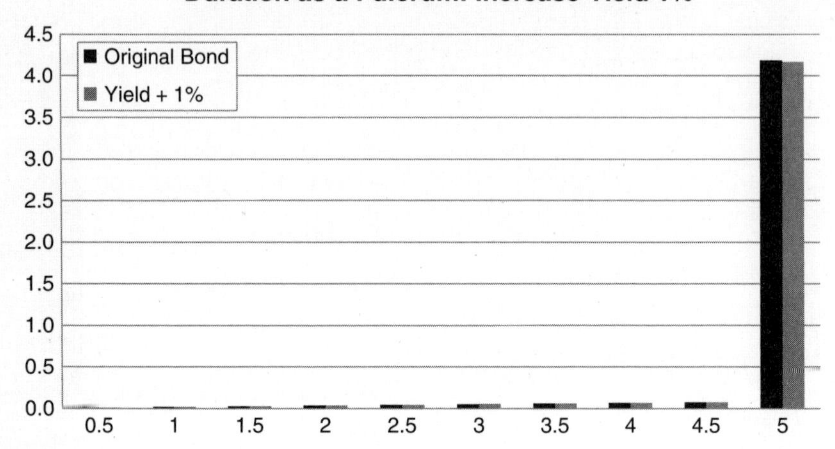


**FIGURE 3.6** Increasing the starting yield of the bond decreases the duration.

During the 1980s, the combination of high yields, changes in pension accounting, and the revival of duration and convexity led to a fixed income strategy called immunization. As laid out by Granito,[4] if you are trying to fund a fixed liability with a bond portfolio, you could immunize the liability to changes in interest rates if:

- Market value of bond portfolio equals market value of liabilities.
- Duration of bond portfolio equals duration of liabilities.
- Convexity of bond portfolio is greater than or equal to convexity of liabilities.

This strategy allowed pension fund sponsors to lock in their current levels of funding at the attractive rate levels of the 1980s and, through the use of duration and convexity, to maintain that funding level as interest rates changed.

The ability to measure sensitivity to interest rates continues to this day in more advanced forms such as using effective duration or key rate duration. However, the complexity of fixed income securities uncovered some drawbacks of Macaulay duration, which caused the statistic to be little used today. The first drawback to surface for duration was the reliance on yield. If a bond has a price, it has a yield. Yield is specific to a bond, and changes as the price of the bond changes. However, there is a conceptual inconsistency in yield when comparing two dissimilar bonds. When going from yield to price, each cash flow of a bond is discounted at the same yield.

With a typical, upward-sloping yield curve, longer-maturity bonds have higher yields than shorter-maturity bonds. However, two bonds with different maturities, but with the same cash flow occurring on the same date, will use different yields for discounting. For example, consider a three-year bond yielding 6 percent and a two-year bond yielding 4 percent. The two-year coupon on the two-year bond is discounted at 4 percent, while the two-year coupon of the three-year bond is discounted at 6 percent. An investor should be indifferent to whether the money came from the two-year bond or the three-year bond, and should apply the same discount rate to the money regardless of its source.

Wall Street made lots of money taking advantage of this inconsistency through the issuance of zero coupon Treasury bonds. This investment vehicle was the foundation for securitization. However, for some unknown reason, the vehicles all had feline names, such as CATS (Certificates of Accrual on Treasury Securities), TIGRs (Treasury Investment Growth Receipts), or LIONs (Lehman Investment Opportunity Notes).[5] The associated valuation advance came in the derivation of a spot yield curve.

A *spot yield curve* is the yield of a single cash flow at any future point in time. It is different from a yield curve, which is the plot of yields of specific bonds versus their actual maturities. A spot curve allows each cash flow of a bond to be valued at its own discount rate. In that sense, a spot curve is common to all bonds, whereas a yield belongs to a specific bond at a specific price. However, Macaulay duration is based on yield moves. As we have discussed earlier, yields are specific to individual bonds. The second problem with Macaulay duration comes from the corporate bond market, to which we turn next.

### Corporate Securities: Interest Rate and Credit Sensitivity

Corporate bond issuers reacted to the high interest rates of the 1980s by issuing debt with embedded call features. When interest rates finally dropped, the call option gave the issuer the chance to redeem the bonds, not pay the higher coupon rates, and issue debt at the lower rate. This was so evident that CFOs who didn't call their bonds were not allowed to play in any more CFO games.

The problem for Macaulay duration was that the calculation depends on fixed cash flows. However, with an embedded call option, what are the fixed cash flows? They may not be fixed if the bond is recalled. Some practitioners considered valuing the bond and the call separately using the Black-Scholes formula on embedded call options. However, Black-Scholes has a serious shortcoming for callable bonds. Interest rates are assumed constant in Black-Scholes, but interest rates are in fact the random variable in determining the value of the call. Because of this, Black-Scholes is little used in fixed income. The formula is mainly used as a quoting convention for caps and swaptions, with implied volatility taking the place of a price quote. Additionally, the Black-Scholes formula prices options that are exercisable only at maturity, called European options. Most callable corporate bonds can be exercised at any time prior to maturity and are American option exercisable, where a Black-Scholes must be replaced with a binomial, trinomial, Monte Carlo, or finite differencing methodology for pricing the optionality.

In 1979, Cox, Ross, and Rubinstein developed a particular option pricing model, called a binomial tree, for pricing American options. At each discrete point in time, there are two possible outcomes for stock prices, an up move with a designated probability and a down move with a potentially different probability. At each time step, the option price is calculated with and without exercising. If it's found to be more highly valued if exercised than not exercised, that becomes the option's price. If not, then the Black-Scholes price is used. If you shorten the time interval between successive steps, the binomial tree moves from a discrete to a continuous process, giving both American-style and European-style option pricing.

Mathematically, the Cox-Ross-Rubinstein model is the discrete-time equivalent of the continuous-time Black Scholes model. The discrete-time nature of the Cox-Ross-Rubinstein model allows for evaluation of the American options, which is needed for callable corporates. However, the problem remained of how to properly account for changing interest rates.

The Ho-Lee and the Black-Derman-Toy models of interest rates modeled interest rates changing over time using binomial trees.[6] These models assume that interest rates evolve, starting from today's spot curve, and according to a set of conditions that produce a price for existing noncallable bonds consistent with the prices observed in the market. Like Black-Scholes, these models would construct riskless portfolios at each point in time. However, their contribution was to change interest rates in such a way so as not to permit arbitrage. From each point in the tree, called a node, there are typically two or three future outcomes. The models would then value the bond at maturity, where the maturity value is known, and work backward in time to today. At each node, the model evaluates the price of the bond versus its call price. This backward induction through the tree of potential interest rates can derive the value of the embedded call option quite accurately.

The Ho-Lee and Black-Derman-Toy models were more dynamic in the evolution of spot rates than Macaulay's view of yield. In addition, the models include an estimate for interest rate volatility. Interest rate volatility is typically estimated from the term structure of swaptions, which we'll talk more about later and which is a wonderfully rich topic on its own.

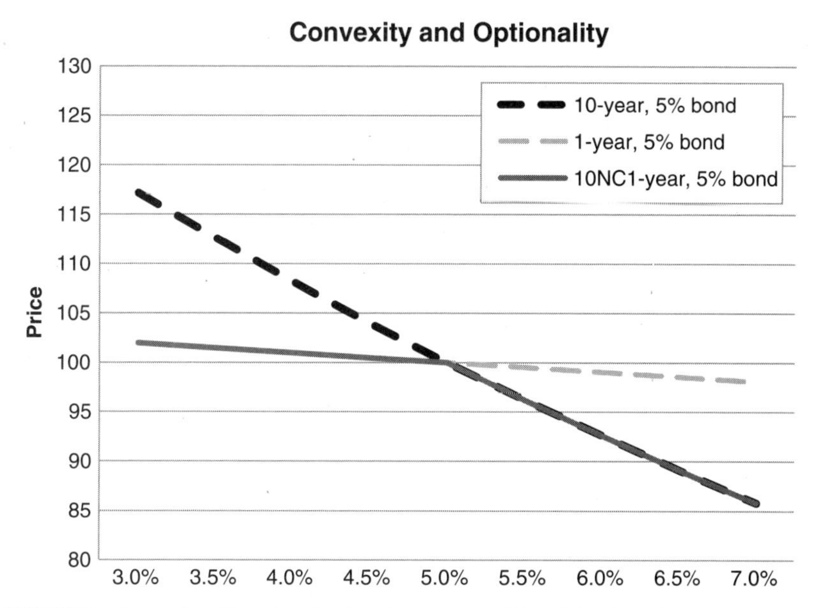


**FIGURE 3.7** A graph of bond price for the given yields of two bonds.

However, for the purposes of this chapter, it should now be clear that interest rate volatility influences the price of callable bonds, and thus needs to be included in any estimate of price risk. Let us return the conversation to convexity and through a simple example describe the influence of volatility on interest rate risk measures.

Imagine the graph of price given the yield of two bonds as shown in Figure 3.7.

Assume both bonds have the same 5 percent coupon and price, while one bond has a 10-year maturity and the other a one-year maturity. The yield curve is level at 5 percent. As expected, if yields rise, the one-year bond outperforms the 10-year bond, and if yields fall, the 10-year bond outperforms the one-year bond. Now, imagine you own a 10-year bond, which is noncallable for one year, at the same coupon and price. This bond is labeled as 10NC1 in Figure 3.7. If yields rise above 5 percent, the call is not likely to be exercised and you get the performance profile of the 10-year bond. However, the bond you want is the one-year bond. Similarly, if yields fall below 5 percent, the call is likely to be exercised, and you would obtain the performance profile of the one-year bond, while the bond you want is the 10-year. Thus, a 10-year noncallable one-year bond performs like a combination of the 10-year and one-year bonds.

There are two things to be learned from this example. First, the full impact of convexity is seen in the kinked price performance. That is, convexity really becomes important when there are embedded options. Second, in both cases, the embedded option forces you into holding the less desired bond. So why would anyone own a callable bond? The answer is because you're paid to. The callable bond has a yield premium associated with it. The higher yield reflects the value of the embedded call, and it is up to the analyst to decide if that value reflects fair compensation for the undesirable performance during interest rate volatility.

In the end, duration and convexity are measures of interest rate sensitivity, not measures of interest rate risk, and that is an important distinction. They denote the percentage price change should yields or interest rates move, not the percentage price change fluctuation. Today at this point, duration and convexity are revealed to be useful tools in understanding fixed income price sensitivity versus yields and interest rates. However, we find it quite useful to demonstrate the limits of this thinking.

Duration and convexity make no statement regarding the magnitude or the comovement of the varying interest rates. In addition, unlike equity risk, interest rate risk is nondiversifiable. A collection of bonds will not mitigate this underlying risk, since the bonds' prices will all move in the same direction given any interest rate moves. You can only take more or less of the risk. From that perspective, portfolio duration is a useful statistic, in that it captures how much exposure to interest rates you have taken, however interest rates may move.

Where duration and convexity fall apart, though, are the cases where volatility and correlation matter, which unfortunately is almost always. For instance, consider a multicurrency portfolio of bonds. The portfolio duration has the implicit assumption that the different yields in the portfolio will all move at the same time by the same amount. That's true in one currency. But, in this case, the relative volatility of the different currencies, and their relative movement to each other (i.e., FX rates), drives the true interest rate risk of the portfolio.

Just as global government yields don't move in lockstep, corporate bond yields don't move in lockstep. Corporate bonds are typically quoted as a spread to their sovereign or swap curve. The interest rate risk is captured in the curve movements, and the corporate-specific risk is captured in the spread movements. The spread is thought to predominantly contain the default risk of the corporate issuer.[7] Spread risk is commonly quoted by exposures to different ratings and sectors. The exposure assumes no model underlying the mechanics of the spread, but assumes that the rating captures the probability of default, while the sector captures the common influences on the bonds. This is unlike the equity risk approach, where a model is almost always used to capture the underlying mechanics of volatility.

Thus, ratings can be used as a shorthand for default risk. Standard & Poor's (S&P) and Fitch, two of the big three ratings firms, claim their ratings measure probability of default, while Moody's claims its ratings measure probability of loss. All three agencies base their ratings on the long-term outlook through an economic cycle. They all produce multiyear reports supporting the validity of their ratings. In these reports, they produce statistics showing how the ratings can rank order the likelihood of default or loss over time, and across asset types in fixed income. Ratings show up in investment guidelines and enjoy a special, legislated place in investments by virtue of their Nationally Recognized Statistical Rating Organization (NRSRO) status. All that said, ratings should be the starting point for credit analysis, not the end for the inquiring investor.

This brings up one differentiator of the FactSet MAC model versus other vendor risk models for FI risk: it's quite easy to regress the constituents of bond index returns against these gross classifications and produce an FI risk model in a multifactor approach like equity risk modeling. FactSet's FI risk model, on the other hand, offers a valuation approach, pricing the bond based on duration/convexity sensitivity to yield curve, interest rates, and spreads more directly.

## Credit Analysis

For corporate debt, credit analysis is similar to but not identical to equity analysis. In equity analysis, the goal is to identify companies that will enjoy superior earnings compared to those expected by the market. While that is generally a virtue in credit analysis, the goal in credit analysis is to find companies that will avoid default and make good on repayment. A company with attractive growth prospects could achieve that by taking on loads of debt, thus benefiting the shareholders at the expense of the bondholders. At the opposite end of the spectrum, for companies near default, the equity is wiped out, and high-yield analysts are valuing the assets of the company versus the bond's place in the capital structure. In both cases, the analyst is thinking in terms of individual investments, and not in terms of total portfolio volatility. Such is the case often with fundamental investing. In constructing a corporate bond portfolio, the portfolio manager should seek to diversify and thus minimize the spread risk due to covariance, which is a real and natural cause of risk.

There exist analytical tools for the evaluation of corporate credit in the marketplace. The Merton model, which recognizes that equity can be viewed as a call option on the assets of the firm, is one of the oldest.[8]

The equity holders enjoy the assets of the corporation in excess of the bond value, and put the bondholders with assets if the assets are less than the bond value plus other liabilities. This model is the foundation for firms like KMV, now Moody's Analytics.[9] The other flavor of models in use is statistical in nature. Again, among the oldest is Altman's widely used Z-scores, which rank the likelihood of default by different company-level statistics.[10]

Another approach to corporate credit analysis comes from the single-name credit default swap (CDS) market. Credit default swaps have been used to derive probabilities of default. In a CDS, the two parties agree that:

- The protection buyer makes regular payments until the expiration of the contract or the default of the reference entity.
- The protection seller pays the protection buyer the net difference between the face value of the contract and the expected recovery of the reference entity.

An example of the payments from the perspective of the protection buyer is shown in Figure 3.8. Consider a one-year CDS based on $1 million notional amount of bonds, with a 5 percent rate and 2 percent up-front fee. The up-front fee can be viewed as the price to enter the contract.[11] Thus, the

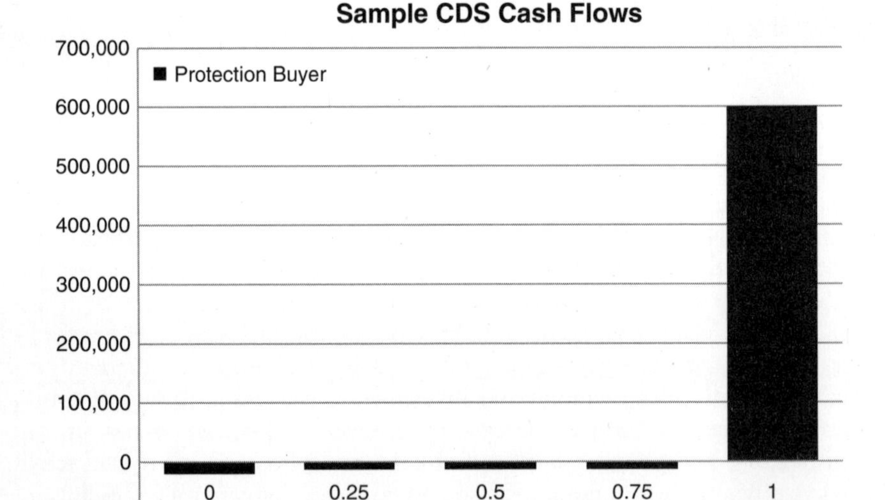


**FIGURE 3.8** The cash flows of a CDS from the perspective of the protection buyer for a one-year CDS, based on $1 million notional amount of bond coverage with a 5 percent rate and 2 percent up-front fee.

buyer pays 2 percent of $1 million to enter into the contract, and quarterly payments of the annual 5 percent rate. Now assume that the reference entity defaults at the end of one year. The recovery of the obligor's bonds is set at ~40 percent. Under bond settlement, the protection buyer delivers to the seller $1 million face amount of bonds, and the protection seller then sells the bond at 40 percent of their face value. Under cash settlement, the protection seller simply pays the protection buyer 60 percent of the face value.[12]

Assuming both parties agree that the payment amount is fair, and the recovery is known ahead of time, the probability of default can be derived for each time step in a binomial option pricing methodology. Once the first time step is known, then iteration can be used to derive the next time step, and so on.[13] These probabilities of default are also known as *hazard rates*.

As an aside, CDSs have nearly undefined interest rate durations. That is, the cash flows on both sides of the trade are opposite and nearly equal. With no cash flows, there is no impact on the security's price if interest rates change. However, the sensitivity can be derived based on a shift of the hazard curve. In practice, the hazard rates are assumed to increase and decrease, and the existing CDS contract is revalued under the new hazard rates. This imputed price change is used in the duration formula, but this time to represent a change in credit sensitivity.

Credit analysis extends beyond evaluation of corporate bonds. For municipal bonds, the goal is to evaluate the ability of the municipality to repay its obligations through taxes and project revenues. For asset-backed securities (ABSs), the goal is to evaluate the ability of the ultimate borrower to repay, and then track these repayments and any losses through the deal structure. Finally, outside credit guarantees, such as bond insurance, add an extra dimension to the credit analysis. With guarantees, the statistic of interest is the joint default of the obligor and the guarantor. The other three possible outcomes produce no loss to the bondholder. In short, credit analysis is similar to equity analysis in the broadest sense, but ultimately very specific to the type of bond, whether it's an ABS, a corporate bond, or a municipal bond.

So, let us return to the appropriate duration for spread risk. Spread duration measures the percentage price change given a change in spread. If the analyst is using Macaulay duration, then these statistics are the same. However, using more advanced models, discussed later, then spread duration measures the change in spread while holding the cash flows constant. There are two things to note. First, spread duration measures any spread of the bond over its sovereign or swap curve. Off-the-run sovereign debt (on-the-run is a most frequently traded, newly issued bond), mortgage-backed securities, and anything that by design doesn't trade flat to the sovereign curve has a spread; therefore, spread duration captures the change in price for the change in spread. However, if everything has a spread, exactly what does the portfolio spread duration measure? Second, unlike interest rate risk, spread risk can be diversified. Therefore, portfolio-level spread duration would tend to overstate your sensitivity to a change in spreads.

### Securitized Bonds: Interest Rate and Prepayment Sensitivity

Taking a step back to fixed income securities, the other big innovation of the 1980s was the acceptance of mortgage-backed securities (MBSs). Banks and insurance companies for years had been lending money for homeowners to purchase houses. In general, homeowner default rates to high-quality borrowers were low and the recoveries high. However, the capital markets were reluctant to invest in this sector, given the heterogeneity of the loans, the small loan size, and the time-consuming process of evaluating each loan. In response, government-sponsored enterprises (GSEs)—the Government National Mortgage Association (GNMA or Ginnie Mae), Federal National Mortgage Agency (FNMA or Fannie Mae), and Federal Home Loan Mortgage Corporation (FHLMC or Freddie Mac)—would buy the mortgages from the banks, collect similar mortgages together into pools, and then, for a small fee, put a guarantee on losses of principal. This guarantee opened the MBS sector to the capital markets. The underwriting decision rested with the originating banks and the mortgage agencies, while the interest rate risk rested with the capital markets.

However, MBSs presented their own challenges to evaluation. MBSs are typically broken into prime and subprime categories. Prime MBS are those of the highest quality, and can be securitized by the mortgage agencies. Prime MBSs in the United States allow homeowners to prepay their loans at any time. Subprime mortgages are lower-quality loans, where default or delinquency of payment becomes a concern. Prepayments and defaults, in the presence of guarantees, act the same as a call in a corporate bond. The key difference is that callable vanilla bonds are path independent, in that if the bond is assumed alive at any point in the model's pricing tree, then the decision to call is independent of how interest rates got there. MBSs, however, are path dependent. The behavior of homeowners to prepay their mortgages is different when rates go below their current mortgage coupon the second (or third) time than when interest rates pass below the first time. Also, the decision to prepay the mortgage is scattered across the multiple homeowners in the pool, and thus subject to a variety of differing incentives, rather than concentrated in the hands of a CFO as in a callable corporate bond.

For this reason, there needed to be two analytical innovations for the evaluation of MBS. First, prepayment models were developed to forecast the likelihood of prepayments by homeowners of different characteristics over time and across interest rate changes. While initially very simple, these models have evolved into complex analyses of heterogeneous homeowner behavior. Second, the interest model changed to a carefully tuned, randomly generated path of future interest rates. These paths have the same no-arbitrage properties as the interest rate trees, discussed earlier, only the evaluation of the security is done forward in time (versus backward in time as discussed for trees). Simply, the interest rate path is first generated. Starting at the beginning of time, the prepayment model derives the prepayments given the current and past interest rates. In this way, a stream of expected cash flows is derived for the chosen interest rate path. A price for the path is derived by starting with the final cash flows, and discounting the price one period back in time by the appropriate short rate. Today's price along this path is found by discounting the future value, plus cash flows, at the short rate back to the present. The price across all paths is the simple average of the per-path prices.

Clearly, the key uncertainty in MBS evaluation is the future prepayments, which in turn are related to future interest rates. However, this risk is more in the realm of a misspecified prepayment model than in a market risk. The next prepayment to be received from month to month can be predicted fairly accurately, and is known several weeks in advance of its receipt. However, the prepayment to be received many years from now is largely unknowable. The sensitivity of an MBS to changes in prepayments is captured in prepayment duration. The MBS is run using the current model, and then at a faster and slower multiple of the model. The percentage price change is computed given these changes in the model. In a later chapter, we will cover how prepayment duration can be used for MBS risk evaluation.

Prepayments hampered the introduction of MBSs. While participants developed a sense of the overall prepay speed of mortgages, the cash flows at the end of the life of an MBS could be cumbersome given their small size and long-lived nature. In response, Wall Street started placing a structure on top of MBS cash flows and creating bonds out of these structures. The initial structures were called collateralized mortgage obligations (CMOs). The MBSs for the CMOs were placed in a trust, and the trustee enforced a set of rules as to how the principal and interest cash flows were to be paid out to the CMO bonds. The bonds had a sequential structure, in that the first bond in the CMO got all the principal payments until it was paid down, and then the second received all principal payments, and so on. While the eventual maturity was still not known, at least there were short, intermediate, and long bonds. The engineering of these bonds grew more complex. Bonds with stable payments were created, floaters and inverse floaters were devised, and a whole alphabet soup of custom securities came into being.[14]

These new securities could be analyzed using only a Monte Carlo option pricing model. The CMO structure introduced an extra step in the evaluation. To determine a price, as before, interest rates are generated from today to the final payment of the MBS. The prepayment model then projects the principal and interest payments of the underlying mortgages. The new step is that these payments are then run through the CMO rules, called a waterfall. The ultimate cash flows of the CMO bonds are then valued.

CMOs proved to be popular with investors, and extremely profitable for their creators. The next step was to work with MBSs that were not backed by the GSE. The new wrinkle was that the non-GSE MBSs, called whole loans, did not have the guarantee against loss of principal. The loss feature required a new set of waterfall rules for the allocation of mortgage defaults. Once securities that could suffer a loss were securitized, then almost any asset with regular cash flows could be securitized. Commercial mortgage-backed securities (CMBSs), auto loans (CARS), and credit card receivables (CARDS) are some of the more widely securitized asset types, with obvious acronyms.

In terms of fixed income risk, structuring does not add a separate risk element to this new security. The structure redirects principal and interest cash flows and losses. The price of the resulting security, which we're focusing on for risk, is subject to the usual components of interest rate, spread, and volatility variability.

The alert reader will note that we've been introducing more complex security types where the fixed cash flow assumptions of Macaulay duration break down. The development of fixed income option pricing models has captured the dynamism of the underlying bonds, but has left Macaulay duration behind. In its stead, effective duration has become the preferred method to quote interest rate sensitivity. As we noted earlier, Macaulay duration is the first derivative of price with respect to yield. However, there are also numerical techniques to calculate a derivative, when a closed formula is not available. Specifically, the numerical method here is to instantaneously shock interest rates up and down, use the option pricing model to recompute the price in the up and down shifts, and then take the average change in price relative to the average change in interest rates.

While simple to describe, this method has several important implications. First, the risk factor changes from yield, which is particular to a bond, to interest rates, which are generic to all bonds. Second, it is possible to derive other risk measures. We've alluded to spread and prepay duration already in this chapter; however, it is also possible to define volatility duration. Finally, as described here, effective duration can be viewed as a stylized simulation. Effective duration is the result of two simulations of possible interest rate environments. However, it is possible to define other simulations to measure

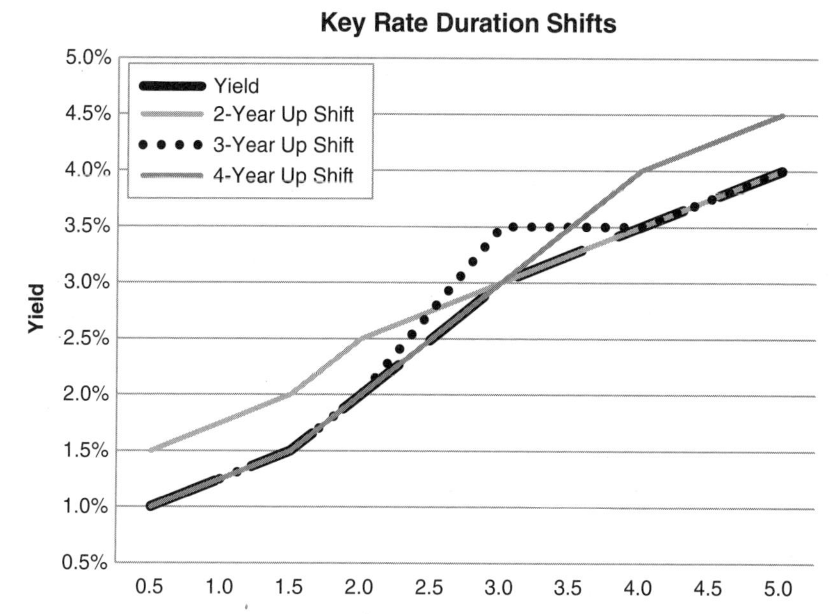


**FIGURE 3.9** We use the word *tented* to characterize the depiction of a cover over three interest rate points as observed here, where the shifts of the yield curve at the two-, three-, and five-year points are dramatized.

risk. For instance, effective duration measures the sensitivity of a parallel shift in interest rates. But interest rates rarely move in a parallel fashion. Instead, we can define a stylized simulation of rates doing a tented shift around a certain point. We use the word *tented* to characterize the depiction of a cover over three interest rate points as observed in Figure 3.9, where the shifts of the yield curve at the two-, three- and five-year points are shown.

We can then calculate duration based on up and down tented shifts. Such a calculation is called *key rate duration*. If these tented shifts are done simultaneously, it is equivalent to a parallel shock, and can be viewed as a decomposition of effective duration. Key rate durations are extremely powerful in defining the sensitivity of a security to nonparallel interest rate movements.

Duration has one disturbing philosophical problem, though. It is not possible to observe whether the computed duration is the true duration. It is possible to use an option pricing model to see if the shifted price matches the price implied by the duration. However, given that the option pricing model was used to calculate the duration in the first place, it's a little like using a word in its own definition. It is possible to observe actual interest rate moves and the resulting market prices. Unfortunately, if the two prices don't match, the difference is then attributed to spread change. The analysts must develop their models as best they can, and cross their fingers.[15]

One thought is to skip the duration calculations, and directly calculate more sophisticated fixed income risk measures. However, the one constraint to this approach is computation time. If we were to use a Monte Carlo framework to generate a VaR on a portfolio of MBSs, then each risk-based Monte Carlo path would require a valuation-based Monte Carlo option pricing run to generate the resulting price. This "Monte Carlo on Monte Carlo" means that we need to be clever in how we reprice securities when generating a VaR, to overcome these nested, time-consuming algorithms.

Up to now, we've spent the majority of time discussing duration and its variations as a fixed income risk measure. We've also pointed out the shortcomings of duration when there is correlation involved. Let's turn next to the case involving yield curve movements. Key rate durations can highlight when a barbell yield curve strategy is in place. However, they cannot describe the correlations involved in yield curve movements, or the total variance of such a strategy. To do so, we need to be able to describe yield curve movements statistically.

### Statistical Analysis for Fixed Income

The first step is to understand the types of yield curves and their main uses. There are three main equivalent ways to describe yield curves. The par or swap curve provides a direct link to observable markets and is an important source of information on market views of interest rates and implied volatility. The coupon-bearing bond is the most traded type of plain-vanilla fixed income security, while the swaption, an option written on a par rate, is the most traded type of plain-vanilla interest rate option. As discussed earlier, however, par yields suffer from the drawback in that the same cash flow gets a different discount rate depending upon which maturity bond it is associated with.

The most natural curve to use for isolating the exposure of a security or portfolio to a specific cash flow is the spot yield curve. Spot yields are the yields of zero coupon bonds, and therefore provide a natural curve for measuring exposure to individual cash flows. In particular, the spot curve allows for calculation of durations of individual cash flows, and the duration of any bond is then just the price-weighted average of its individual cash flows. This makes the spot curve the most natural one for discounting, calculation of durations, and reference curve for the determination of spreads. The relationship between spot yields and par yields has the effect of averaging spot yields.

The forward curve provides a crucial link to market expectations of the future. A par rate can be expressed as a portfolio of forwards, while today's forwards will become tomorrow's short rates, and therefore provide a view of what the short rate will look like in the future. Because of this, the forward curve is very important for derivatives pricing, especially for path-dependent bonds that are sensitive to both par and discount rates, such as MBSs, and is the natural curve off which to base interest rate dynamics. As with the par curve, however, the forward curve does not provide a natural curve for isolating exposure to specific cash flows, and so does not provide the best choice for the determination of durations. The relationship between the spot curve and the forward curve is that of holding period returns, where the holder of a security is indifferent between either holding to maturity at the spot rate or rolling at expected forward rates.

To be honest, all three yield curve conventions are used in and for risk modeling. However, whichever method is picked, it is important for the analyst to be consistent between the choice of yield curves and the associated duration calculation. The preference of this author is for spot yields for the reasons noted earlier.[16]

The traditional technique for interest rate risk is to describe yield curve movement through principal component analysis (PCA). PCA is a way of taking correlated data over time and extracting vectors of importance in ranked order. Thus, the principal component with the largest explanation of overall variance tends to be a near-parallel move in interest rates. The second principal component tends to be a twistlike move of interest rates, where short rates change relative to no movement in the long end. Traditionally, three or four principal components are used, with catchy names like *shift*, *twist*, or *hump*. However, there are many more principal components available, though without descriptive names and with low explanatory value.[17] In addition, the PCA process offers the added feature of capturing the correlations between short, medium, and long-term rates. That is, the 10-year rate rarely moves without influencing the rates that are longer and shorter than it is.

Please note that one problem in the statistical analysis of yield curves lies with the short maturities. Typically, the short end is controlled by the region's central bank, and does not move in a continuous fashion. However, ignoring the short end means an incomplete description of the yield curve. Unfortunately, the analyst must find the proper balance between statistical anomaly and completeness.

After describing yield curve moves through the PCA process, the next set of statistics focuses on spread. At this point, the traditional method is to assign bonds to some sector, derive the option-adjusted spread, and then do a statistical covariance analysis across the sectors, as well as analysis across the bonds within the sector. The primary concern here is the number of sectors, which translates into the number of factors. Looking at corporate bonds, the sector could be corporate, industrial, finance, utility, or government related, or the sectors could be finer still, down to the GICS sector level. In addition, the factor definition is usually expanded to include rating as a dimension as well. Statistically, as the number of factors increases, there need to be more data points to support a valid inference. In short, the analyst needs to be judicious in the selection of sectors, and must balance data availability, statistical validity, and explanatory power.

Most fixed income risk models also include a term for implied volatility. As discussed earlier, this volatility is used as the input to the appropriate option pricing model. However, as discussed in the section on derivatives, implied volatility has all the dimensions of yield curve analysis, plus some additional ones. First, due to the cap and swaptions market, each interest rate has its own curve of implied volatility over time. Linking together several interest rates, these curves form a surface of implied volatility. Second, the implied volatility surface is for at-the-money volatility. There is a third dimension coming out from the surface to account for moneyness.[18] The statistical models to capture market-realistic movements in this cube are very complex.

If investors buy bonds denominated in other than their home currency, currency risk needs to be managed. Just as currency exposure is separable for equity investing, so currency exposure is separable for fixed income investing. Fixed income investors use many of the same tools to control currency risk as equity investors use. It is possible to enter into customized derivatives that will completely swap out the currency risk of a bond, but in practice, the price of the derivative itself is too expensive. Typically, global bond investors will hedge the currency exposure with forwards or swaps. However, the hedge size is not always one for one. Covered interest arbitrage and market realities can imply hedges other than the notional size of the currency exposure. Statistical analysis is required to determine the proper hedge ratios. The critical issue is the relative size of currency risk versus fixed income risk. Currency risk is an order of magnitude larger than fixed income risk. This mismatch in risk can lead to unhedged exposures dominating the risk profile of an otherwise low-risk portfolio.

This brings us to the data problems of dealing with fixed income. First, unlike the equity market, where the number of investable stocks is on the order of 5,000 in the United States and approximately 35,000 globally, the fixed income market is multiple times larger. The number of large, fixed-rate, investment grade bonds is over 8,000. There are over a million U.S. municipal issues outstanding, as well as over a million U.S. MBS pools. For once in statistics, more data is a curse. There simply is too much data, and too many flavors of bonds, to handle accurately in a model. Second, not all bonds trade every day. Most are locked away and held to maturity. Thus, accurate pricing is confined to a handful of benchmark bonds. And since there is no centralized fixed income exchange, price discovery itself is difficult. Most of the quoted bond prices are the result of pricing services, where the quality of the price is discovered only at the time the bond is actually traded. For fixed income, illiquidity is ubiquitous and price discovery is limited, the opposite of publicly traded equities.

The quality of pricing of fixed income has implications for risk modeling. It is traditional in most equity risk models to have a term for idiosyncratic risk, the analysis of variation in price after systematic or market factors have been removed and accounted for. This risk is literally obtained from the residuals of the regressions of returns versus the common factors. However, when there is not agreement on the final price, there are no returns, and it is difficult to define idiosyncratic risk.

For discussion purposes, let's split fixed income into corporates, MBSs, and sovereign debt. The lack of a centralized exchange for corporates means there is wide disparity in the ending price. A quick analysis of the three principal corporate indexes in the United States as of December 31, 2011, indicates that the average pricing dispersion for the 20 largest holdings is 0.77 percent. This is during a month when corporates returned 1.9 percent. Differences of this magnitude confound any statistical analysis to separate common factors from idiosyncratic risk. For MBSs, the U.S. benchmarks report returns based on composite pools, and not actual, investable securities. Again, it would be difficult to identify idiosyncratic terms for these securities when accurate pricing on individual pools is not available. About the only fixed income sector where idiosyncratic risk can be readily identified is sovereign debt. Here, there is much greater unanimity on the final price, and a proper statistical analysis can be performed. The reality, though, is that the magnitude of the variation for sovereigns is much smaller than what is expected in the other sectors.

The last issue to consider is the risk horizon. As discussed earlier, some bonds can take a considerable amount of time to reprice, thus making full repricing impractical. Instead, the analyst is required to use duration for repricing. A complicating factor in the repricing is the impact of the time horizon. A 10-year bond one year later has different sensitivities than the same 10-year bond at issue. There has to be the appropriate decay of the associated durations to capture this aging.

## CONCLUSION

In this chapter, we began outlining the factors most usually involved in accounting for equity risks. We discussed how they're combined and how to interpret a model with these factors and the various ways they can be put together. We then covered the broad sectors of the fixed income market today, and the models used for their valuation. Duration and credit were introduced as the primary risks of a fixed income portfolio. Duration was traced from its beginnings as a measure of interest rate risk to a generalized sensitivity to all risk sources. Credit was similarly traced from a dependence on ratings to more sophisticated approaches, including credit default swaps. While the future of fixed income will evolve into statistical models joined with duration sensitivities, the nature of fixed income markets leads to some special considerations. It's truly an exciting time for fixed income risk.

## NOTES

1. Richard Roll and Stephen Ross, "An Empirical Investigation of the Arbitrage Pricing Theory," *Journal of Finance* 35, no. 5 (1980): 1073–1103; Stephen Ross, "The Arbitrage Theory of Capital Asset Pricing," *Journal of Economic Theory* 13, no. 3 (1976): 341–360.
2. http://heckmanglobal.com/wp/; Heckman Global Advisors, 317 Madison Avenue, Suite 1004, New York, NY 10017; (646) 588-4831.
3. For more information on the different sectors of the bond market, the reader is encouraged to study *The Handbook of Fixed Income Securities*, 8th edition, by Frank J. Fabozzi (New York: McGraw-Hill, 2011). For more information on valuation methods for fixed income, the reader is directed to *Fixed Income Securities*, 3rd edition, by Bruce Tuckman and Angel Serrat (Hoboken, NJ: John Wiley & Sons, 2011).
4. Michael R. Granito, *Bond Portfolio Immunization* (Lanham, MD: Lexington Books, 1984).
5. The arbitrage was simple. Strip the coupon cash flows off a bond, and sell them at different yields than the yield of the original bond. This practice continued until traders recognized the relationship between the yield of a bond and the yields of its component cash flows. The practice is now institutionalized in the Treasury's STRIPS (separate trading of registered interest and principal securities) program.
6. T. S. Y. Ho and S. B. Lee, "Term Structure Movements and Pricing Interest Rate Contingent Claims," *Journal of Finance* 41 (1986); F. Black, E. Derman, and W. Toy, "A One-Factor Model of Interest Rates and Its Application to Treasury Bond Options," *Financial Analysts Journal* 46, no. 1 (January–February 1990): 33–39.
7. However, research indicates that illiquidity and taxation are also significant components of that spread. See Jack Bao, Jun Pan, and Jiang Wang, "The Illiquidity of Corporate Bonds," *Journal of Finance* 66, issue 3 (June 2011): 911–946, or P. Colin-Dufresne, R. Goldstein, and S. Martin, "The Determinants of Credit Spread Changes," *Journal of Finance* 56:2177–2208.

8. Robert Merton, "On the Pricing of Corporate Debt: The Risk Structure of Interest Rates," American Finance Association meeting, December 1973.
9. Stephen Kealhofer, "Quantifying Credit Risk," *Financial Analysts Journal.* Part I: "Default Prediction" appeared January/February 2003, while Part II: "Debt Valuation" appeared May/June 2003.
10. Edward Altman, "Financial Ratios, Discriminant Analysis and the Prediction of Corporate Bankruptcy," *Journal of Finance*, September 1968.
11. Like most things in fixed income, most terms have multiple meanings. The upfront fee is really the price of the contract, and can be positive or negative. However, the convention for the quoted price is 100 up front.
12. This brief paragraph is intended to fit CDSs in the framework of fixed income risk. However, the details of what constitutes default and how CDS payments are resolved are wonderfully nuanced. And don't get me started on CDSs on ABSs.
13. Dominic O'Kane and Stuart Turnbull, "Valuation of Credit Default Swaps," Lehman Brothers *Quantitative Credit Research Quarterly* 2003-Q1/Q2:28–44.
14. A wonderfully detailed introduction to the topic is in *Elements of Structured Finance*, by Ann Rutledge and Sylvain Raynes (New York: Oxford University Press, 2010).
15. Massoud Heidari and Liuren Wu, "What Constitutes a Good Model?" unpublished paper, August 2004.
16. Gerald Buetow Jr., Frank Fabozzi, and Bernd Hanke, "A Note on Common Interest Rate Measures," *Journal of Fixed Income*, September 2003.
17. One of the earliest references is "Common Factors Affecting Bond Returns" by Robert Litterman and Jose Scheinkman, Goldman Sachs Financial Strategies Group, September 1988. However, the author is aware of earlier publications and implementation at JPMorgan Investment Management in an unpublished research piece, "Multi-Factor Duration and Immunization," by Michael Granito, Gregory Harris, Janet Kappenberg, and Laurence Smith.
18. The most complete source I've seen on this topic is *Volatility and Correlation: The Perfect Hedger and the Fox*, by Ricardo Rebonato, Wiley Series in Finance (Hoboken, NJ: John Wiley & Sons, 2004).

CHAPTER 4

# Commodities and Currencies

*Steven P. Greiner, PhD, and William F. McCoy, CFA, PRM*

## COMMODITIES

In modeling the risks of commodities, it's important to consider the futures that investors buy and the available host of exchange-traded funds (ETFs) and mutual funds that exist for such purposes. First, a managed futures account, unlike the usual long-only institutional fund, can typically take both long and short positions in futures contracts and options on futures. Of course, managed futures accounts are usually trading in commodities, interest rates, and currency markets.

Typically, these futures are traded using any number of strategies, the most common of which are momentum (or trend following) strategies. Momentum strategies involve buying futures that have been recent winners over some time scale and shorting securities that are recent losers (relative to the winners). Variations in trend following managers include duration of trend captured (short-term, medium-term, or long-term trend), as well as definition of trend (i.e., what is considered a winner or a loser). Many of these strategies go long in uptrending futures and short positions in futures that trend down.

There are other strategies (managed futures) that managers use, including discretionary strategies, fundamental strategies, option strategies, pattern recognition, arbitrage strategies, and so forth; however, trend following and variations of trend following are predominant by a long shot.

Of extreme importance in many of these momentum strategies is what's called *roll yield*. Negative roll yield occurs when distant delivery futures prices exceed near delivery prices, which implies that investors lose out even as prices rise for a commodity. This scenario occurs when the futures are in *contango*, so that further maturing futures are priced higher than near-term maturing futures. When the further maturing futures are lower in price than the near-term maturing futures, we have what's called *normal backwardation*. Both of these scenarios are depicted in Figure 4.1.

On the left, we see that if we are rolling out of a one-month futures contract into the two-month maturity futures contract, we're rolling from a higher price to a lower price and have a positive roll yield. Conversely, on the right, we see a commodity in contango. In rolling from a near-term one-month maturity contract to a two-month contract, we have to pay up to maintain the commodity exposure via the futures, creating the negative roll yield. Of course the short end of the curve could be in contango and the longer end in backwardation, which was the oil curve in January 2006, for instance.

So in indexes, ETFs, or long-only managed futures accounts, the roll yield can subtract a significant loss over time if the commodity is stuck in contango. Two major indexes for managed futures, Standard & Poor's (S&P) GSCI and Dow Jones (DJ)-UBS, are managed using this simple roll methodology, both of which are offered on FactSet. What's nice about these indexes is that they have long history, they roll to the nearest front month contract for you with all the accounting implicit in the indexes' construction, and they have subindexes of each of the underlying commodities that make up the composite. In addition, many of the composite indexes have very different asset allocation among the different commodities that make up the index.

Now imagine you are able to short the futures contract, in particular one whose futures chain may be in contango. Then, you'd be able to attain a positive roll yield for contracts with increasing price with maturity. There are several managed future ETFs that go long or short in their management

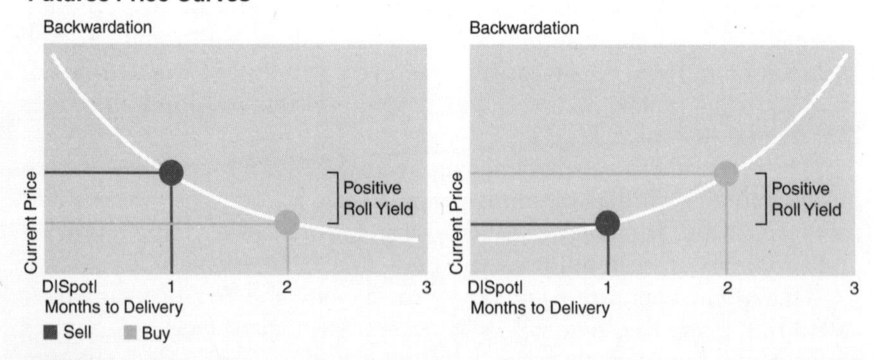


**FIGURE 4.1** The typical commodity futures term structure in backwardation (left) and contango (right).

style, including products from Morningstar, S&P, and Lucas Management. As you might guess, their long-term returns to the investor outperform the long-only indexes. Thus, many investors are seeking strategies that better manage roll yield, and a better benchmark for these strategies involves these long/short indexes.

From our clients we learned that their holdings are raw futures, ETFs of single commodities, and composite ETFs, with only occasional holdings of the physical asset. In addition, our clients' risk definitions fall within those of our purview in our Balanced Risk and multi-asset-class (MAC) products and in concert with most of our risk model vendors (MSCI-Barra, Northfield, SunGard APT, R-Squared, and Axioma) and FactSet's own multi-asset-class short-term model. In particular, FactSet users prefer exposures to common factors, variance contributions, tracking error, value at risk (VaR) numbers, and equity-like risk decomposition as opposed to risk issues more relevant to a professionally managed futures account like cost of carry, cost of storage, forward versus spot differentials, contango versus backwardation curve shapes, supply/demand fundamentals, and options coverage for hedging the yield role.

Taking these issues into consideration, as well as the major issue of index roll yield management, leads us to a commodity risk model that's devoid of supply-and-demand fundamental factors, historically the drivers of raw commodity physical prices, albeit not the main drivers of the more speculative fervor driving futures prices these days (though some say it's speculative that speculators are the major drivers of commodities). Since the vast majority of FactSet clients obtain exposure to commodities through ETFs, front-month continuous roll yield futures, and mutual funds, the factors involved in modeling commodity risk therefore have to be chosen from equity-like factor constructs. Thus we're not building a risk model using economic variables of supply and demand as would be used in a top-down macro investment strategy. We want to identify risks similar to risk definitions used in regular equity portfolio analysis, which describe the risks of variance and the covariance of assets in a portfolio. This strategy leads us to choose the factors for the model, which we'll discuss in detail next.

### Model Methodology

The commodity model on FactSet is predicated on risk factors of two categories; one set of exposures for cross-sectional regression consists of the following five factors:

1. T-statistic (of a correlation of a security's price with a 45-degree straight line) measured for the past 10 days (10-day momentum).

2. Another t-statistic factor for 30 days (30-day momentum).
3. Idiosyncratic commodity volatility (standard deviation of asset return measured over 22 trading days).
4. Ordinary least squares (OLS) determined slope coefficient of past five days' price divided by most current price (five-day beta).
5. OLS slope coefficient of past 20 days' price divided by most current price (20-day beta).

These five factors constitute the momentum of the commodity estimation universe assets, albeit very differently constructed. Thus each security (commodity) in the estimation universe would have these five factors calculated from its price time series, and each would constitute its exposure to said factor with differing look-back periods defining each factor. The cross-sectional regression ensues by regressing the forward daily return to these exposures where the ending date of the time series used to compute each exposure is one day before the dependent variable's. All exposures are Z-scored before they are applied in the regression with raw daily returns.

The following equation represents how we connect returns to factors. For a given asset $i$ with its one-period-forward daily return $R$ for a given time period $t$, we model $R$ by:

$$R_{i,t} = \sum_{k=1}^{n} X_{k,i,t}\beta_{k,t} + \varepsilon_{i,t} \tag{4.1}$$

where $X$ is the predefined asset factor exposures 1 through 5 listed earlier earmarked by $k$, $\beta$ is a coefficient determined by regression called a factor exposure for each factor $k$ at time $t$, $\varepsilon$ is an asset-specific residual of the regression, and $n$ equals 5.

Hence, the exposures lag the dependent variable by one day. Using this model, we can make the math simpler by creating vectors $R$ consisting of $m$ asset returns, each for a given time period, and exposure matrix $X$ of "size $m$ by 5" for each time period; we then solve for the regression coefficients $\beta$ and compute residuals. The betas determined in this cross-sectional regression are fixed for all assets for a given time period. The look-back period for the risk model is one year consisting of 250 $R$ vectors where we have to calculate 250 regressions for the ~250 trading days within one calendar year.

The second set of factors to be used for time-series regressions consists of the following 10 factors:

1. S&P GSCI index.
2. DJ-UBS Composite index.
3. Reuters-CRB Total Return Commodity index.

4. VIX (CBOE S&P 500 Volatility index).
5. Exchange rates of USD/EUR.
6. Exchange rates of USD/JPY.
7. Exchange rates of USD/GBP.
8. Exchange rates of USD/CAD.
9. Exchange rates of USD/AUD.
10. London Interbank Offered Rate (LIBOR).

Factors 1 through 3 each have very different returns and volatilities, so measuring a commodity portfolio's exposure to these separate composite indexes offers differing perspectives. This is a result of factors 1 and 2 being long-only commodity indexes, while 3 is a long/short index, in addition to the fact that their asset allocations across the commodities that make up the indexes are very different. The currency exchange rates are useful additions to help explain variance of return to commodities, as are the VIX and LIBOR. In addition, the highest volume of futures trading involves the currencies of USD, EUR, JPY, GBP, CAD, and AUD, which capture the majority of commodity trades.

The time series used is the daily return of each factor. The regression coefficients (betas) determined through the time-series regressions are fixed for a given look-back period but are asset dependent. All factors are Z-scored before being applied to regression with residuals from the output of cross-sectional regressions. LIBOR is chosen to offer a risk-free asset return to the model. Likewise we chose the VIX to represent equity volatility simply for its ease of use, but any suitable major stock market index volatility measure could work.

We must acknowledge that in building a risk model, the factors chosen must be comprehensive so that their contribution to individual asset returns is common across all assets. The whole idea of building a risk model is the parsimonious reduction of the covariance matrix built from asset returns. In so doing, to proxy asset real returns by model returns, the factors must be such that all assets have correlations with the chosen factors; the term *common* came about to describe factors that have this quality. This distinction prohibits the introduction of asset-specific factors like gold, silver, or corn futures pricing to be factors in this model as well as more obscure currencies. To have asset-specific factors in a risk model would be like having an individual stock's return time series in an equity risk model rather than an industry-specific factor like information technology. One wouldn't have IBM or Siemens returns as factors in an equity risk model; likewise one wouldn't use platinum as a factor in a commodity risk model. We emphasize this point because investors don't have much experience with a commodity risk model and by default, and out of context, casually think of a commodity risk model as having commodity factors.

The regressions involve two separate stages, with the residuals of one being the input to the other. Through experiment, we've found that first performing cross-sectional regression followed by inputting their residuals into the time-series regression factors is the better process. In the cross-sectional step, we regress the asset daily forward returns against the five exposures, where each exposure was created from a look-back period specific to that factor. Thus for a given date, we regress a vector of asset-specific returns against a multifactor model of vectors from each factor of the same length. We do this 250 times (one year of trading days) and collect 250 betas for each of the five exposures. These betas constitute a time series whose length is given by the look-back period of the risk model: 250 days.

The output of this regression sequence results in a matrix of residuals that is 250 times the number of assets in dimension, which feeds as the input to the time-series regressions in the following manner: for a given asset, regress all 250 of its residuals against a multifactor model made up from the 10 time-series vectors, each of which is 250 elements long. We do this for all assets, which results in a single regression coefficient for each asset for each of the 10 factors.

Due to the higher-frequency nature of this model (daily updating), the model should not be used for investing activities of commodity assets generally. Typically, daily models of this nature do not include the ramifications of trading costs. We use this daily model only in return forecasting to measure its efficacy versus realized returns as a step in designing a good risk model and do not mean to suggest it should be used for investing purposes (e.g., selecting which commodities to invest in). In the results of the model we show later, we present in-sample performance measurements of the model's asset rankings. We do not mean to imply that this is a good use for the model overall, but rather a check for consistency and robustness of the risk model while developing it.

## Risk Calculation

To calculate the common risks, we must build up the factor return matrix and take its covariance. The factor return matrix consists of the five regression coefficients (betas) time series from the cross-sectional regressions and the 10 factor time series. This is compiled by loading the columns of a matrix, first by the betas obtained in the cross-sectional regressions so that the first five columns consist of these betas, one row for each date (~250). The next 10 columns contain the actual time series of the daily returns of the factors used in the time-series regressions. Thus, the original time-series factors act as betas in this instance when building up the factor return matrix.

Once the factor return matrix is built, we exponentially weight the factor returns so that the furthest back in time (250 days ago) contributes 60 percent of its value and the closest in time (current) contributes a full 100 percent. This amounts to a half-life of around a year. Next, we take the covariance of the matrix, column against column. Ultimately, this results in a 15 × 15 covariance matrix. If we add the intercept from the cross-sectional regressions, too, it becomes a 16 × 16 covariance matrix. In this way, the vectors of the factor return matrix proxy the dependence structure that we would achieve if computing a covariance matrix of size (number of assets × number of assets) from the original asset return data. This calculation results in the parsimonious structure desired from the risk model and substantially lowers estimation error in the covariance matrix by integrating rigorous structure into its calculation, lessening the advantage of applying shrinkage methodologies that you would apply if you created a covariance matrix from raw returns.

Our next step to compute risk is to reconstruct the exposure matrix. This is not the same one used for cross-sectionally regressing commodity returns against, which was only 5 × 5. This exposure matrix is of size (number of assets × 15), evaluated at the most current time period. We first start to fill rows of the exposure matrix using the five factors from the cross-sectional regression process evaluated at the most current date. For example, the first column consists of the exposure to t-statistics for all the assets in the estimation universe. The next column contains the next exposure for all assets, and so forth. After all five factors used in the cross-sectional regression process are added, we start filling columns of the exposure matrix with the betas obtained from the 10 time-series regressions, one for each asset. Thus the regression coefficients obtained from the time-series regression act as exposures in this step.

To summarize, betas from cross-sectional regressions and time-series factors constitute what goes into the factor return matrix to compute the covariance matrix. The factors from the cross-sectional regressions, along with betas from time-series regressions, go into formulating the exposure matrix.

The last step is to use the asset weighting, the exposure matrix, and the covariance matrix to compute the total common risk through the equation:

$$\begin{aligned}\text{Common risk} &= \text{Weight} \times \text{Exposure} \times \text{Covariance} \\ &\quad \times t(\text{Exposure}) \times t(\text{Weight}) \end{aligned} \tag{4.2}$$

where all multiplications in this equation are matrix multiplications and $t$ corresponds to matrix (vector) transpose.

We now need to compute the idiosyncratic risk. After both regression sets have been performed, the final residuals from the time-series regressions become the idiosyncratic risk piece. This is created by determining the variance of the residuals, ignoring their covariances, and populating a diagonal matrix (ResidsDiag) with those values, yielding a matrix of the dimensionality of the number of assets. The idiosyncratic risk is then simply:

$$\text{Idiosyncratic risk} = \text{Weight} \times \text{var(ResidsDiag)} \times t(\text{Weight}) \quad (4.3)$$

The convention in the risk management community is to assume the residuals are independent and identically distributed, and we do, too; hence, we ignore the covariance of the residuals and concentrate only on the diagonal elements consisting of the residual variance. In truth, these covariance values are quite small if the model specification (i.e., the chosen cross-sectional factors and time-series factors) is good, because the regressions would have explained almost all of the variance/covariance of return anyway. In FactSet's multi-asset-class risk model, these final residuals are subjected to principal component analysis (PCA), but this is because the estimation universe of 35,000+ global securities has a lot more signal left in the residuals after application of the multifactor model. Even so, the prudent application of PCA on residuals in this fashion involves comparisons of PCA derived from white noise. In commodities, the estimation universe is quite small and the commodity risk model has much higher explanatory power when the residuals are left closer to being independent and identically distributed in actuality.

The total risk in units of variance is the sum of the common and idiosyncratic risk pieces. The square root of the total risk is the standard deviation risk measure.

The marginal contribution to risk is also easily determined in the model. Starting with an equal weighting of all assets in the estimation universe, it's easy to iterate over equations (4.2) and (4.3) to calculate the total risk given an increase in each asset's weight by 1 percent (current weight + 1%) one at a time. We don't need to make any changes to the exposure or covariance matrix, nor do we need any further regressions since only the weight vector is changing in this calculation. In so doing, all the other asset weights are identically readjusted downward so that the sum over all weights is 1 (for long only). The differential between total risk calculated at the current weight and that with the 1 percent increase is performed for all assets and easily reported. In this fashion, we can ascertain whether the increase in asset weight pushes the total risk higher or lower so that the asset is diversifying, identifying the greatest and least risky assets and all those in between. Of course, the total risk surface isn't sampled entirely in this manner, but the estimate is a good one and one of convention performed by most risk model vendors on FactSet.

### Estimation Universe

The estimation universe consists of 38 commodity indexes, the top 14 traded continuous front-month futures contracts, and 184 commodity ETFs and mutual funds, many of which have history of more than a decade. We add assets to the estimation universe continually as ETFs and other commodities come into the FactSet databases.

Obviously, all clients' assets will have to be mapped to this set if they own something not in our universe. Even if they own a specific futures contract, it will have to be mapped back to one of our assets in the universe. In this estimation universe are the subindexes of the factors of the time-series regressions S&P GSCI Energy and Oil, for instance, allowing for any of the major categories of commodities to have a similar ETF (gold futures with GLD, oil with S&P GSCI Oil index, etc.).

It is the intent of FactSet to grow the estimation universe over time as the new commodity ETFs and futures become available.

### Model Results

We can demonstrate the efficaciousness of the return forecasting portion of the model as well as show risk statistics. To begin, the ultimate test of a risk forecasting model lies in testing its forecasts versus realized risk. However, before that can be done, we need to test the building blocks of the risk model, which are the returns-forecasting abilities of the model.

The explanatory power of the model can be ascertained by examining the adjusted R-squared from the cross-sectional regressions, followed by examining the adjusted R-squared from the time-series regressions of the residuals of the cross-sectional regressions.

Remember, the look-back period of estimation in the risk model is 250 trading days (one year). The graph in Figure 4.2 plots the adjusted R-squared for all 250 cross-sectional regressions performed over the time period used to estimate the December 2, 2010, covariance matrix (from December 2, 2009, to December 2, 2010). The ordinate is the R-squared value, and the number of days away from the current day is plotted on the abscissa. We can observe that the R-squared values fluctuate some, as expected for a daily model, but appear bounded and average 17 percent to 18 percent. This is a reasonable expectation considering the simplicity of the five factors in the cross-sectional regression model and well within the reported R-squared numbers from many of our vendors' risk models.

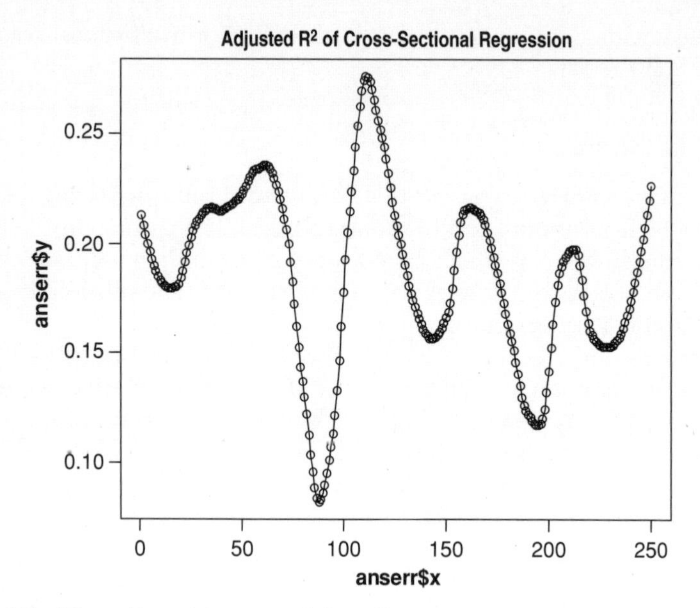


**FIGURE 4.2** The adjusted R-squared for all 250 cross-sectional regressions performed over the time period used to estimate the December 2, 2010, covariance matrix (from December 2, 2009, to December 2, 2010).

We wouldn't expect higher R-squared values from a model using only momentum-like components. With commodities, there really are no fundamental variables to add unless we want to consider supply/demand fundamentals for the underlying commodity. However, that effort would be much more involved and would obviate our general approach to making a simple, parsimonious model to work well with the MAC model. Moreover, these kinds of macroscopic variables of economic origin are hard to identify, and there's much dissension in academic literature on what they indeed are.

Figure 4.3 shows the adjusted R-squared from the time-series regression of the residuals from the cross-sectional regression. The time-series regressions, remember, are of 250 daily individual asset returns against the 10 factors' time series of returns of equal length. Thus there are 236 regressions from each of the assets in the estimation universe, whose R-squared values are plotted. The ordinate is the R-squared value, and the abscissas are individual assets in the estimation universe. To interpret this plot, consider that assets that still have a lot of signal (i.e., unexplained return variance left in their residuals after application of the cross-sectional and time-series regression) would have the low R-squared here, which implies the time-series model of their values is weak. The minimums around asset

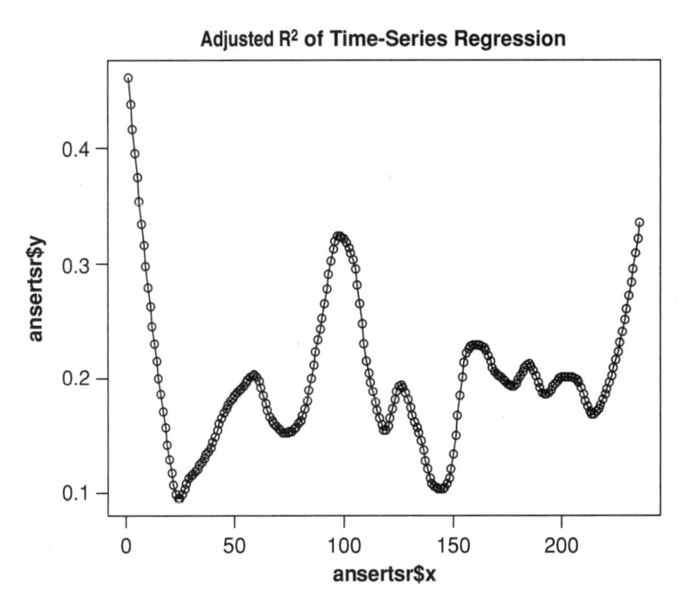


**FIGURE 4.3** The adjusted R-squared from the time-series regression of the residuals from the cross-sectional regression. The time-series regressions are of 250 daily individual asset returns against the 10 factors' time series of returns of equal length. Thus there are 236 regressions from each of the assets in the estimation universe, whose R-squared values are plotted here.

#25 (platinum and palladium) and #145 (aluminum and tin) show the model is weakest in explaining return and risk of these asset groups; however, they're thinly traded and we shouldn't expect a model to capture these outlier risks well, given this type of risk model construction. Even so, the adjusted R-squared values are within acceptable limits and average about 20 percent, demonstrating that the residuals have little predictable variance in them and offer credibility to the model.

The first 38 assets to the left of the graph are made up of commodity indexes, and, since they have high values there (other than platinum and palladium), this means the cross-sectional regression hadn't explained as much of their return variance as other assets further to the right of the graph, so that the time-series factors still have significant contribution to explaining return. Overall, the values achieved by the R-squared here are again in line with expected occurrences given this type of model.

The next two graphs in Figures 4.4 and 4.5 illustrate the time series of returns of the top and bottom quartile of the model. We divide the estimation universe returns into four equal-number fractiles based on their

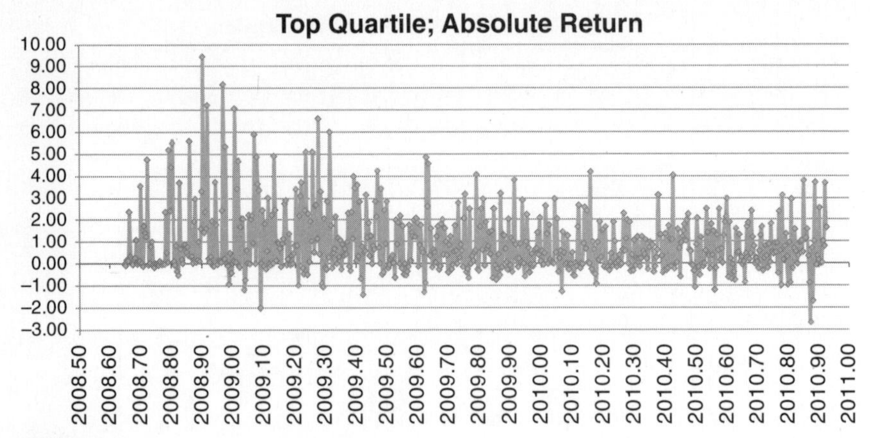


**FIGURE 4.4** We divide the estimation universe returns into four equal-number fractiles based on their rankings from the model. Then we collect realized return from those commodities in each fractile, average their realized returns across the fractile, and plot the result for every day of the in-sample estimation period of the model. This is a graph of the monthly returns of the top quartile.

rankings from the model. Then we collect realized return from those commodities in each fractile, average their realized returns across the fractile, and plot the result for every day of the in-sample estimation period of the model.

What we illustrate are the realized returns to the top quartile of forecasted returns over the look-back period of the model. It's a necessary condition that the top fractile outperforms the bottom fractile over time, and

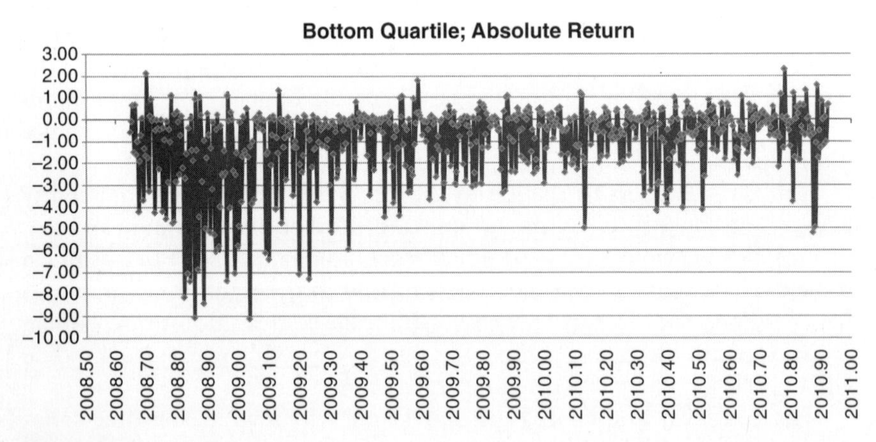


**FIGURE 4.5** Returns of the bottom quartile from the risk model estimation universe, all in-sample.

that is demonstrated here and observed in the time-series plots. This is a necessary and sufficient condition for any return and risk forecasting model in asset management; that is, the top quartile must outperform the bottom quartile of the estimation universe in-sample. Due to the overall weak statistical properties of the regression statistics of economic models in general, a "proof" of model efficacy is in the back-tested returns forecasting capabilities, though we might add that past performance is no predictor of future performance. Time stationarity and a stable covariance matrix are necessary conditions for this to be true. The best we can hope for is their slow variation relative to the reactance time of the model.

The summary distribution data produced from this time series is shown in Table 4.1. We tabulate the average returns, median, standard deviation of return, and the minimum and maximum values for each quartile along with the skewness and kurtosis. Last, we show the average return over the standard deviation of return for the quartiles, akin to a Sharpe ratio less the subtraction of risk-free returns for the four commodity time series.

We've shown the time series of the bottom quartile of returns with identical ordinate values for easy comparison. This is, of course, the in-sample realized return from model forecasts. If this model were built to be used as a return forecasting or ranking model for some portfolio manager, the sequence of construction would be much different. But since this model ultimately is to be used as a risk model, in-sample validation of return forecasting is suitable and sufficient.

We also include Table 4.2, a table of values with hit rates as calculated from the data.

**TABLE 4.1** Summary distribution statistics from the returns of the quartiles of the risk model—performance numbers.

| | Bottom | Two | Three | Top | Top – Bottom |
|---|---|---|---|---|---|
| Average | –0.984 | –0.261 | 0.240 | 0.922 | 1.906 |
| Median | –0.451 | –0.030 | 0.095 | 0.511 | 1.486 |
| Standard deviation | 1.687 | 1.284 | 1.207 | 1.435 | 1.679 |
| Minimum | –9.140 | –6.165 | –3.969 | –2.679 | –0.835 |
| Maximum | 2.300 | 3.148 | 5.445 | 9.436 | 10.131 |
| Skewness | –1.848 | –0.988 | 0.556 | 1.721 | 1.605 |
| Kurtosis | 4.295 | 2.556 | 2.318 | 4.700 | 3.231 |
| Return/standard deviation | –0.585 | –0.203 | 0.199 | 0.643 | 1.135 |

**TABLE 4.2** Hit rates of the model's quartile return results. The first column shows the percentage of time the quartile offers a positive absolute return over the whole of the testing period of July 2008 through December 2010 (look-back periods of July 2007 to December 2009). The second column reports the within-quartile hit rate, meaning the percentage of assets in each quartile that offered a positive return (on average through time).

| XS B4TS | Return | Standard Deviation | ~Sharpe Ret/Std |
|---|---|---|---|
| Bottom | –0.984 | 1.681 | –0.585 |
| 2 | –0.261 | 1.284 | –0.203 |
| 3 | 0.240 | 1.207 | 0.199 |
| Top | 0.922 | 1.435 | 0.643 |
| | **Hit Rate** | **Within-Quartile Hit Rate** | |
| Bottom | 28.247 | 24.440 | |
| 2 | 44.643 | 35.456 | |
| 3 | 56.006 | 45.561 | |
| Top | 71.104 | 54.673 | |

Hit rates come in two varieties. The first column shows the percentage of time the quartile offers a positive absolute return over the whole of the testing period of July 2008 through December 2010 (look-back periods of July 2007 to December 2009). The second column reports the within-quartile hit rate, meaning the percentage of assets in each quartile that offered a positive return (on average through time). The efficacy of the model is quite good, as the numbers tell us the top quartile obtained a positive return 71 percent of the time with more than 54 percent of the assets in this fractile doing so (on average), while the bottom quartile offered positive return only 28 percent of the time with only 24 percent of assets in this fractile doing so.

Figure 4.6 displays information coefficients, which are the correlation of assets' forecasted returns through all time with their realized returns. That is, each asset is ranked 1:*N* for each time period, and its realized return is recorded for that time period. The realized returns are ordered, and the correlation of the forecasted rank with the realized return rank is calculated. This is the information coefficient.

In Figure 4.6, we show correlation on the ordinate and individual assets (from the estimation universe) on the abscissa. A reading of the chart for a given asset would show the correlation over time of the asset's predicted return with its realized return. We would hope to find positive

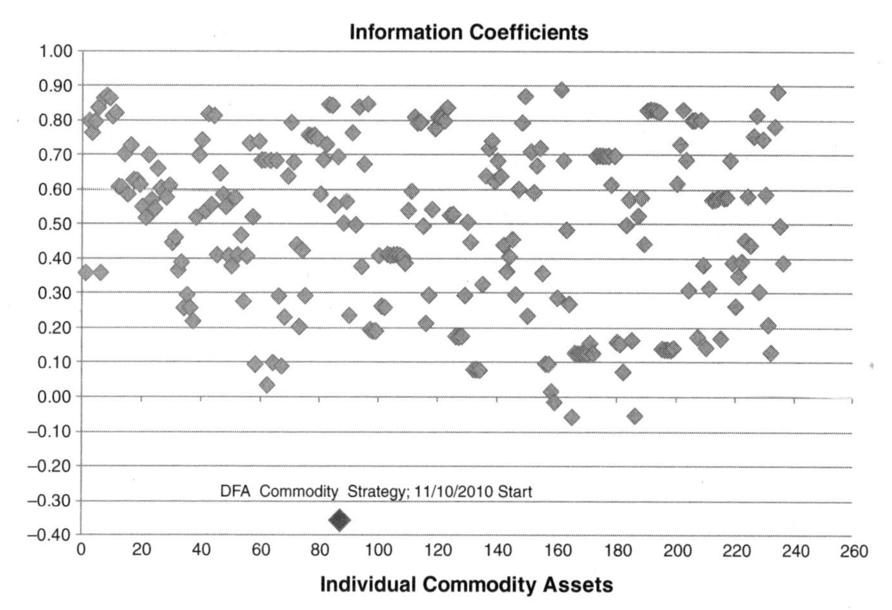


**FIGURE 4.6** This figure displays information coefficients, which are the correlation of assets' forecasted returns through all time with their realized returns. Essentially, all assets are ranked 1:*N* for each time period from the model, and each asset's realized return is recorded for that time period. The realized returns are ordered, and the correlation of the forecasted rank with the realized return rank is calculated. The point at the bottom of the plot labeled "DFA Commodity Strategy" represents a commodity fund that began on November 10, 2010, and therefore had insufficient data.

values, the higher the better. In general, the distribution of information coefficients demonstrates a good model. The point at the bottom labeled "DFA Commodity Strategy" is for a commodity fund that began on November 10, 2010, and therefore did not have enough data to determine this point. The information coefficient there is quite poor, but is the result of a data issue, not a poor reflection of the risk model's predictability.

Figure 4.7 is a chart of the realized risk (standard deviation of return) of a portfolio over a rolling 22-day (one-month) period and consisting of the equal-weighted estimation universe. This is shown as the line with the circles overlaid. This is empirical data from the time series of returns of the commodity assets. The solid thin line on the graph is that of the forecasted risk from the risk model. This is essentially the square root of the sum of equations (4.2) and (4.3) through time. At this point, risk model vendors

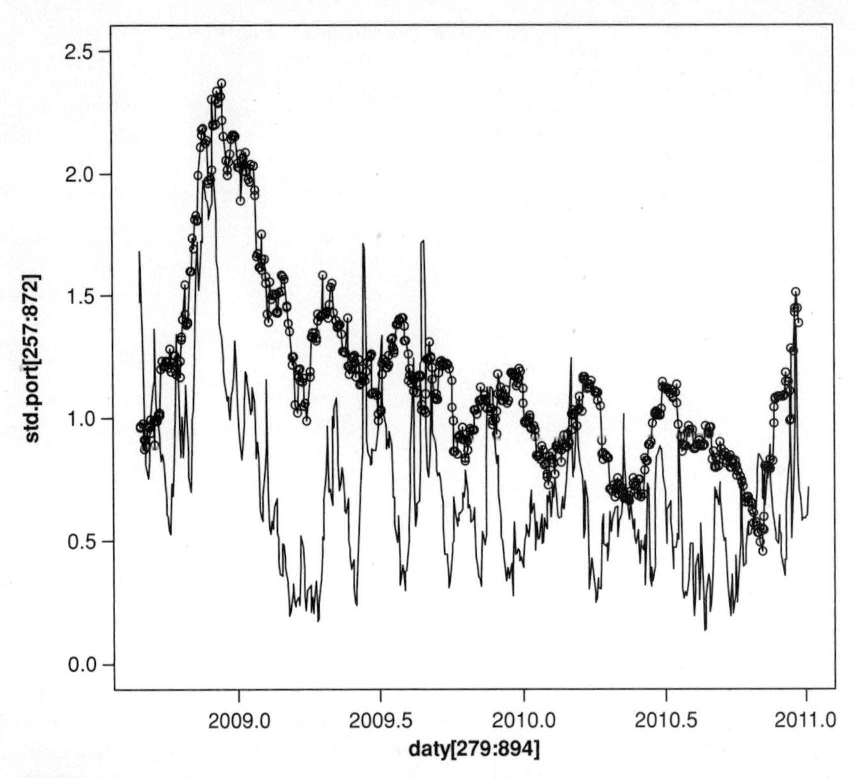


**FIGURE 4.7** Realized risk (standard deviation of return) of a portfolio over a rolling one-month period (22 trading days) and consisting of the equal-weighted estimation universe.

often apply an empirical adjustment to the model to bring the average level of risk nearer to the historical measured risk. We did not do so, and yet the empirical risks are of quite similar magnitude to the forecasted risks, ~0.5 to 1.5 standard deviations. The fact that the average value of the risk model's forecast is this close to the empirical value is quite sufficient since the main users of the model should be aware that the trend of the model's forecast is more important than the level.

In most long-horizon risk models, the model will do a reasonable job of averaging the microstructure of short-term risks and offering insight into the longer-term macro-volatility structure. However, because our model is a daily risk model, we tend to forecast the microstructural movements of volatility rather than the smoother volatility of a longer-horizon model. Thus, if this model were used directly to generate trading signals, it would

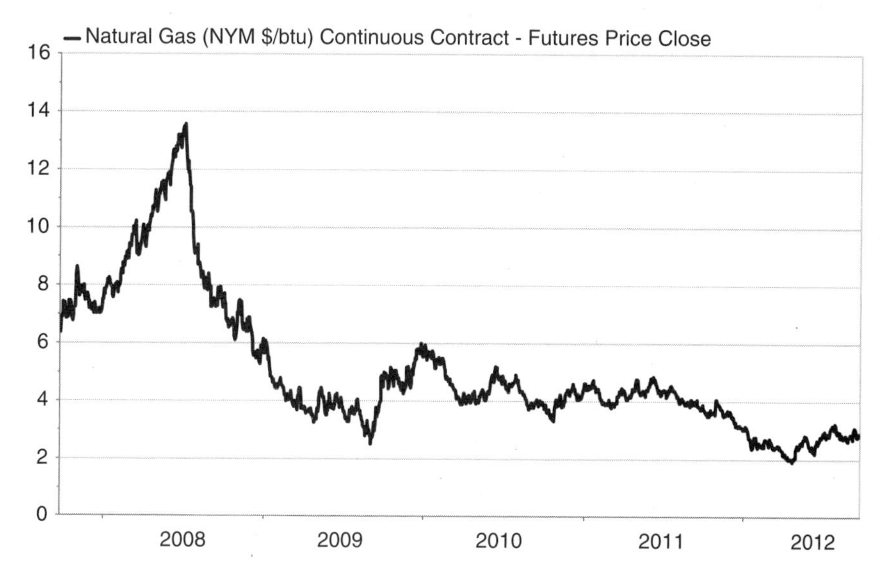


**FIGURE 4.8** Natural gas price history shown as the line from early 2007 until 2012.

be costly to implement its results due to the microstructure volatility (the volatility of volatility) and would result in significant portfolio turnover.

The next data set is of natural gas price alone, shown as the line from early 2007 until 2012 in Figure 4.8. The look-back period of the model is one year, giving us forecasts starting in early 2008 for the risk going forward each day thereafter.

The risk forecast then made from this model for natural gas is shown in the next graph. In Figure 4.9, the graph is the single asset risk (standard deviation) of realized 22-day rolling risk (circles) versus the forecast from the risk model, shown as the solid line. The volatility of the risk estimate is high again because the forecast is of a daily horizon rather than of a longer horizon where the microstructure is averaged away. However, the short-term trend is captured in the data and easily observed in the figure.

If you compare the ordinate values of this natural gas risk plot versus those in the equal-weighted asset portfolio risk plot in Figure 4.7, you'll notice the absolute values of risk for the natural gas are around 3, while the equal-weighted portfolio averaged between 0.5 to 1.5 standard deviations. Thus the diversifying episode of more securities is strongly captured by the model, with no introduction of any risk scaling parameters in either graph. Yet we see the level of forecasted risks similar to the empirical risks in each case.

In conclusion, FactSet created a commodity risk model from an estimation universe of 236 highly liquid commodity indexes, continuous front-month

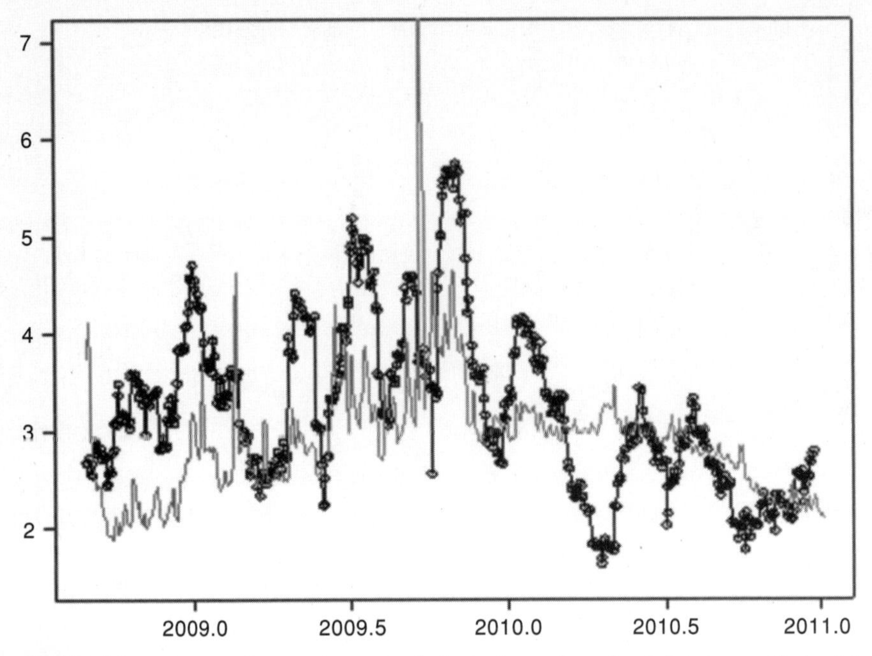


**FIGURE 4.9** The single asset standard deviation of realized 22-day rolling risk (circles) versus the forecast from the risk model, shown as the solid light gray line.

futures contracts, ETFs, and mutual funds. The model consists of five cross-sectional factors predicated on short-term momentum measures along with nine time-series factors chosen to be most common across assets. Because the model is constructed to be intuitive, simple, and with a fully transparent methodology that complements the multi-asset-class model used in FactSet's Balanced Risk product, it works for balanced portfolios of equities, fixed income, currencies, and commodities. The model has sufficiently high explanatory power along with fairly accurate risk forecasts. It is our intent to reconstitute the estimation universe from time to time as commodity assets become available either as futures or as ETFs.

## INTRODUCTION TO CURRENCY RISK

This next section of Chapter 4 is about currency risk. Currencies are unusual assets compared to standard equities, fixed income, or commodities in that they are not dividend paying, have no earnings or cash flows, and have no real intrinsic value. This is because they're mostly fiat, meaning they derive their value solely from government authority and are not backed by hard assets such as gold for the most part in today's global economies. FactSet clients usually hold currencies in portfolios while waiting for expedient opportunities to invest or trade into other assets. However, the risk of currencies mostly involves debasement and inflation risk. The two are not independent and their interrelationship is a central bank controlled or influenced phenomenon.

To the regular investor, however, the major risks involve foreign exchange (FX). This is the risk of uncertain changes in the exchange rate between the investor's base currency and the currency being invested in either directly or through the purchase of other assets denominated in the other currency. If you're a company or global investor exporting or importing goods or services in some other currency, if the FX rate moves against you, you may suffer losses inconsequent to the assets themselves. However, we add that debasement or FX movements in themselves are not risk for the investor. If the magnitude and timing were known, there would be no risk. It's the uncertainty as to the direction, magnitude, and timing of FX moves that creates risk, just like for any other asset.

Generally, there are three types of FX risk. One involves transactions, another economic direct exposure, and last is translation exposure. The first category involving transactions comes about when there are contractual cash flows being imported or exported, as for example in a currency swap. Currency swaps in their simplest sense may involve a structure to exchange only an agreed-upon principal or cash flow at a specified point in the future at an agreed-upon rate now. They're usually over-the-counter (OTC) transactions. This functions as a cost-effective way to fix forward or future rates. But FX swaps may involve loans and be combined with an interest rate swap, too, for instance. The most common FX swap involves swapping only interest rate payment cash flows on loans of the same size and terms, like fixed USD interest payments for floating rate in EUR, a cross-currency interest rate swap. The risk is that the FX exchange rate might not move in your favor.

Economic exposure to FX comes about when a firm has its market value or enterprise value subject to exchange rates. That of course can affect the firm's standing in many ways: relative to its competitors, whether it can continue to exist in a benchmark, or within some investing mandate's universe of acceptable securities. It also will affect the net present value of future earnings and cash flows of a company. Consider a multinational firm that has businesses in many countries, with vendors, suppliers, customers, receivables, and payroll in many different currencies. This direct economic exposure in many cases is hedged but often not in smaller firms. If the company's overseas payroll is in an appreciating currency relative to its home/base currency where the majority of its sales lies, then the FX risk is depleting earnings and is a real risk.

A firm that has reporting requirements in multiple currencies and countries can be subject to what's known as translation risk simply because of the markup or markdown of balance sheet or treasury assets in various currencies affecting its tangible book numbers based on regulatory accounting requirements. A firm could also be awaiting something as simple as a project bid that if accepted becomes an immediate receivable in some foreign currency if paid at project acceptance. In this case, it's like waiting for an FX futures contract to be realized, but with a floating maturity date. The uncertainty of when the deal could close results in a translation risk because it's difficult to hedge an uncertain transaction date.

The good news for currency risk occurs because currencies are the most liquid assets (markets) in the world, making the relative costs to hedge FX cheaper than most other types of hedging. The important characteristics of hedging involve calculating the exposure properly. Chapter 1 has already alluded to some of these developments. Though for firms with transaction, economic, or translation exposure, there are a number of creative ways to hedge this risk through accounting practices in currency invoicing using lagged or leading time stamping, mixing with multiple FX contracts, and so forth, for the regular investor FX risk is usually either hedged through the sale of FX forwards or ignored. Many global and international portfolio managers have told us their clients want the FX exposure, but this may be misleading due to a misunderstanding of where the risk comes from in a portfolio with foreign-currency-denominated assets.

To dramatize the impact of FX on a portfolio, consider six investors purchasing the Euro Stoxx 600 index in their home currencies of USD, EUR, GPB, CAD, JPY, and AUD in December 2007 and holding this index until March 2012. Figure 4.10 shows the index levels for each investor denominated in the home currency.

It's clear that the returns and subsequent volatility that each investor experienced over the holding period are completely different, even though they all owned the same identical portfolio/index! The bottom price trace is the Japanese investor, while the top price trace is the British. The only thing that made the Japanese investor lose the most was the value of the JPY relative to the other currencies, whereas the UK investor had the most favorable currency move over the period. The whole return/risk differential here is completely due to currency risk; there is no other cause. Professional global investors should either be encapsulating their views of currency moves into their investment process or be hedging this risk. One might argue there's a neglect of fiduciary responsibilities if they take an action without specifically addressing currency risk in their investment mandate or guidelines.

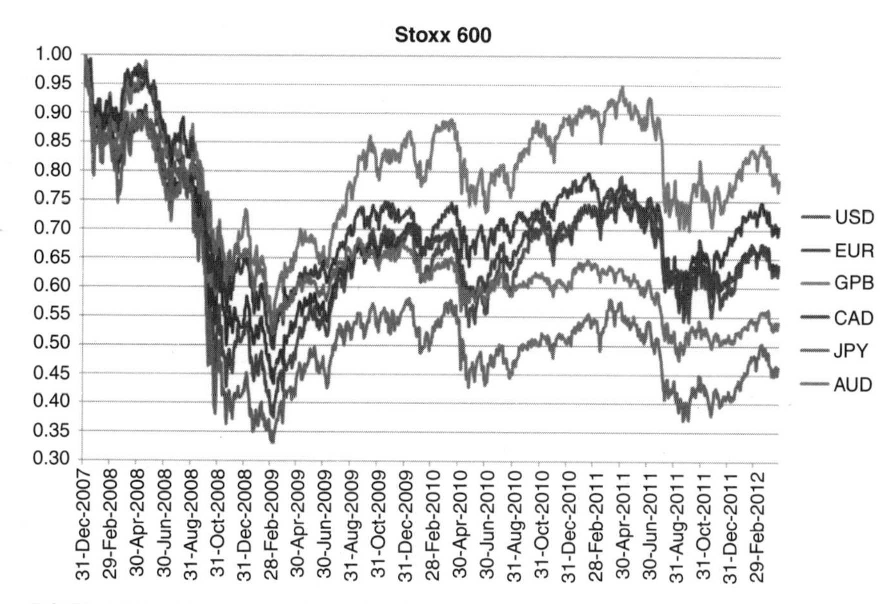


**FIGURE 4.10** Six investors investing in the Euro Stoxx 600 in December 2007 and holding the identical assets until March 2012. Their returns and risks are completely different even though they own the identical index. Their experienced return and risk profiles are solely due to currency effects and serve to demonstrate the FX impact.

For the average FactSet client, there are a couple of tools that help to reveal the FX exposure to a portfolio. The easiest is to use the "Add Currency Hedged Benchmark" or "Modify Currency Hedged Benchmark" tool kit found in FactSet's Portfolio Viewer. This method just assumes the active weight in denominated currency is the exposure and sells FX forwards equal to the position size of the long asset, or purchases FX forwards equal to the short asset. It then buys (or sells) the base currency to cover. It readily identifies and creates the basic standardized currency hedge that investors have come to know and love. Literally, however, it can yield a portfolio that is over- or underhedged because it doesn't identify the exposure properly, as Mark Kritzman discusses.[1] A portfolio could be underhedged if the resultant betas with some FX curve are greater than 1, for instance, for some assets and it only sells forwards equivalent to the position size alone. Then the amount of currency forwards sold short, for instance would be too small if based on only position size if the beta to the currency is, say, 1.2. Likewise, if the betas between the assets and FX are less than 1, the amount sold short would be too much and an overhedged situation could occur.

Global and international investors (i.e., portfolio managers) often recite the benefits of foreign investing as diversifying due to their FX exposure. However, this view is overly accentuated because it focuses on the covariances between local asset returns and their associated currency returns, which usually are quite small. Said another way, if you invest in a U.S. listed stock from the perspective of a U.S. investor, you don't worry about fluctuations in the dollar versus other currencies too much. Moreover, it's likely many portfolio managers are unaware of the size of FX risks. But consider if you reside in Australia, obtain wages in AUD, shop in AUD, and are expecting to retire and live in an economy that uses AUD. Now when you invest in the United States, you have more concern about how the FX rate between AUD/USD changes. Thus, one should not overlook the covariance between the base currency one is investing in versus the currency the assets are denominated in, which can be quite high because a large percentage of foreign asset risks are due to the FX fluctuation. Thus, the beta between the assets and the FX is what governs the diversification, and hedging must be with respect to this beta.

Alternatively, therefore, in FactSet's Risk in Portfolio Analysis, there exist the R-squared equity risk models and the multi-asset-class (MAC) risk model that properly identifies the currency exposure by determining the beta between the assets and up to 30 foreign currency exchange rates. In this fashion, one can determine true exposure and so create a proper FX hedge, if that is desired, by selling forward the product of the position size in the base currency with the beta to the FX. At a minimum, it reveals where a portfolio will be subject to FX swings, allowing portfolio managers to decide whether they want a particular currency portfolio tilt.

In addition to pure FX exposure, the assets related to FX involve foreign exchange spot (raw currency), forwards, swaps, options, and combined interest rate and foreign currency options and swaps. These all exist to help mitigate FX risk or take positions in risky FX assets if so desired.

While FactSet hasn't many clients at this time who are strictly currency managers, the fact that all of our clients hold cash and assets denominated in other currencies means it's nice to be able to reveal for them that FactSet can identify their currency exposures and even suggest a hedge if that is what's wanted.

For the raw currency investor, however, knowing that the largest currency risk factor is the return on the highest minus the return on the lowest interest rate currency helps to explain the cross-sectional variation in the average currency excess returns.[2] This information hasn't been widely disseminated among global and international equity managers, however, but will serve to offer alpha opportunities when digested appropriately, meaning the FX exposure can turn into an intended tilt rather than a spurious outcome of the investment process, and FactSet's currency exposure modules can help identify and recognize this attribute for both risk and alpha purposes.

In fixed income, currency risks need to be carefully managed. Fixed income is supposed to be a low-volatility investment. The significantly higher volatility of currencies can dwarf a fixed income strategy, similar to a balanced portfolio consisting of equities and bonds where the variance of return is dominated by the equity portion. Most of the instruments for currency hedging are also used in fixed income, and in the same way.

Still, there are three special cases that should be noted for FI currency risk. First, simple currency exposure (and hedging) can easily be picked up by investing in cash or cash equivalents. FactSet has a comprehensive database of terms and conditions on the publicly available markets, and security modeling tools for the nonpublic securities. Second, longer-term instruments, like cross-currency swaps, can be viewed as long a bond in one currency and short a bond in another. This mental decomposition readily shows that these instruments contain both currency and interest rate sensitivities. Finally, bond futures are a shortcut way to take hedged bond exposure. While not truly hedged, given the limited cash outlay to establish the position, the true currency exposure is limited to the margin. Again, FactSet has an extensive database of global bond futures.

## CONCLUSION

FactSet's commodity risk model is predicated on sustaining the methodology of the MAC model and in fact is designed to work in conjunction with this risk model inside FactSet's Balanced Risk product, though it need not be used in that way. The model is comprised of both cross-sectional regressions (implicit factor model) and time-series regressions (explicit factor model) similar to R-Squared's method for the customized hybrid multi-asset-class model but without principal component analysis on the residuals.

This commodity model was written with the idea to readily move from daily forecasts to longer-horizon risk attribution when that need arises. Right now, scaling from daily values to longer-horizon values (out to two months) is easily accomplished and is supported by theory. At FactSet, we tend to appreciate the short-horizon models for use in Balanced Risk for the reason many equity analysts examine both the 50-day and 200-day moving averages of stock prices they're interested in. That is, analysts want to see the shorter-term trending of a stock simultaneously with the longer view. Because FactSet offers many longer-horizon risk models from multiple vendors, we settled on a short-horizon model for completeness.

Our commodity model is not predicated on top-down macro variables (supply and demand fundamentals) that describe the movement of commodity prices over longer horizons. Given the shorter-term nature of the risk model and its goal of describing risks congruent with standard portfolio risk model variables within FactSet, we chose factors that fit this mode of thinking and that work well in the practice of a portfolio holding commodity assets.

Last, commodity traders implicitly trade the futures generally and avoid ETFs and their ilk for capturing the exposure to commodities. If one wishes to trade those instruments actively in a managed futures strategy, then this risk model is less appropriate for managing roll yield and trading calendar spread strategies, for instance. Though continuous front-month futures contracts are part of the estimation universe, futures with expiries are not. Thus, quantifying the risk in holding commodities is the aim of this type of risk model, and it does this very well by constructing a parsimonious set of common factors for commodity risk that works in conjunction with our multi-asset-class risk model to build a robust covariance matrix.

Exposure analysis is straightforward also, and one can observe the highest exposures and use them quite readily in a stress test, for example, with this model. We'll have a lot more to say about stress-testing in Chapter 12, where we discuss how the largest exposures in any portfolio are the pivot points that stress-testing should be focused on.

Currency risks are larger than most portfolio managers realize, we believe. Moreover, they're certainly larger than most clients realize. It's only a responsible reaction to manage these risks, and to do so requires that their magnitude be measured or estimated. FactSet offers several ways to annotate these risks, estimate their size, and gauge their consequence to a global portfolio. Moreover, FX risks can creep into almost every asset class. One can determine the FX exposure through our models even to commodities. It's the prudent application of risk modeling that reveals where these risks congregate and offers solutions as to what the best hedge might look like. Then FactSet offers a full database of applicable hedging instruments should the investor seek to mitigate these risks in an active fashion.

## NOTES

1. Mark Kritzman, "Currency Hedging and the Risk of Loss," *Journal of Alternative Investments*, Winter 2000, 27–32.
2. H. Lustig, N. Roussanov, and A. Verdelhan, "Common Risk Factors in Currency Markets," Paris December Finance International Meeting, May 3, 2011.

CHAPTER 5

# Options and Interest Rate Derivatives

*Steven P. Greiner, PhD; William F. McCoy, CFA, PRM; and Mido Shammaa, CFA, FRM*

## SHORT HISTORY OF OPTION PRICING

Stock options in general have been well studied since before the October 19, 1987, Black Monday debacle, when the Dow Jones Industrial Average fell 22.61 percent, markets in Hong Kong fell 45.5 percent, and Australia fell 41.8 percent; by October's end the contagion had swept the developed world extensively. Later this crisis was diagnosed as being due to program traders, or "algos" as they are now called, using synthetic portfolio insurance, but this is still disputed somewhat. The father of portfolio insurance, Mark Rubinstein (also an inventor of the Cox-Ross-Rubinstein binomial option pricing model), had issued several papers recounting the role of portfolio insurance in the crash both right after and a decade later. He said that any investors who reduced their holdings of stock, shorted stock, covered long futures positions, or increased open sold futures positions on October 19 contributed to the crash.

The concept of portfolio insurance of course involves inverting the Black-Scholes arbitrage argument that states an equity call option can be perfectly hedged by a short stock sale and in so doing yields the riskless rate, which is simply:

$$\text{Long call option} - \text{Stock} = \text{Riskless rate}$$

You can easily rearrange this to be:

$$\text{Long call option} = \text{Stock} + \text{Riskless rate}$$

So, alternatively, by dynamically hedging a stock with a risk-free asset one can create an option. To quickly see how this synthesis is accomplished in greater detail, consider a long stock portfolio that is also long an option put. Considering the prices of the stock and put, $S$ and $P$, while using the Black-Scholes option pricing equation for $P$, then:

$$S + P = S - S * \exp(-dT) * [1 - N(d_1)] + K * \exp(-rT) * [1 - N(d_2)]$$

rearranged to yield:

$$S + P = S * [1 - \exp(-dT)] * [1 - N(d_1)] + K * \exp(-rT) * [1 - N(d_2)]$$

which rearranges further to give:

$$P = S * A + K * \exp(-rT) * B \quad (5.1)$$

where:

$$A = [1 - \exp(-dT)] * [1 - N(d_1)] - 1$$

$$B = [1 - N(d_2)]$$

In this equation $r$ is the annual interest rate, $d$ is dividend yield, $K$ is the option strike, and $T$ is the time to expiration, whereas $N(d_1)$ represents the probability of a normally distributed random variable having a value less than $d_1$. The two parameters $d_1$ and $d_2$ will be defined later, but they're functions of stock volatility (or implied volatility).

Now, the right-hand side of equation (5.1) is a number, $A$ times the current share price, since $[1 - \exp(-dT)(1 - N(d_1)]$ evaluates to a constant, plus the discounted value of $K$, an option strike through the $\exp(-rT)$ function. Then $[1 - N(d_2)]$ just evaluates to a scalar value $B$, so it's really just another number multiplier. The $K * \exp(-rT)$ term can be interpreted as the current value of a U.S. Treasury bill, with a life of $T$ years and a par value of $K$. This means one synthesizes the value of the put position by distributing funds across the appropriate Treasuries or other risk-free assets while owning the stock of weight $A$. (Interpreting Treasuries as risk-free these days, however, might be hazardous to your financial health—but that's another story.)

This latter process could then be used for an entire portfolio rather than just for a single asset, and presto, portfolio insurance was unveiled on September 11, 1976,[1] by Leland and Rubinstein. Given that many outstanding futures contracts were shorted as part of portfolio insurance strategies during the developing October crash, the buildup of time-varying volatility certainly contributed to the ultimate crash on the 19th, which required portfolio (i.e., insurance) rebalancing. What may still be in dispute is only how much portfolio insurance contributed to the crash, though estimates suggest that about 12 percent of the trades in stocks and futures were due to portfolio insurance strategies, apparently the major recognizable reason for trades.[2]

Interestingly, one would presume that these so-called insurers would have been buying exchange-traded out-of-the-money index puts simply to reduce their hedging costs as well, which would have put pressure on the option implied volatility skew, or so one would think. Thus an option volatility smile may have been present earlier than originally thought. We'll revisit this later.

Further exciting history of options takes us back to the 1970s. The remarkable 1973 paper by Fischer Black and Myron Scholes titled "The Pricing of Options and Corporate Liabilities" outlines a recipe for valuing an option (the famous Black-Scholes model). In their paper, they claim that inspiration for the work came from Jack Treynor, and they thank Eugene Fama, Robert Merton, and Merton Miller for comments on earlier drafts and of course the Ford Foundation for funding. They also outlined the idea that corporate liabilities in addition to warrants may be viewed as an option. Though Merton gets the credit for developing this thought more thoroughly, the idea came from Black and Scholes. They also give evidence for some observations that may be for the volatility smile:

> *We have done empirical tests of the valuation formula on a large body of call-option data. These tests indicate that the actual prices at which options are bought and sold deviate in certain systematic ways from the values predicted by the formula. Option buyers pay prices that are consistently higher than those predicted by the formula. Option writers, however, receive prices that are at about the level predicted by the formula. . . . Also, the difference between the price paid by option buyers and the value given by the formula is greater for options on low-risk stocks than for options on high-risk stocks. The market appears to underestimate the effect of differences in variance rate on the value of an option.*[3]

Dr. Black stated emphatically in 1976: ". . . if the volatility of a stock changes over time, the option formulas that assume a constant volatility are wrong."[4] In 1975 Black also stated that options that are way out-of-the-money are overpriced, and options that are way in-the-money tend to be underpriced. Thus he presumably means they trade at higher volatilities when out-of-the-money and lower volatilities when in-the-money, that is, with an asymmetric smile.[5] Since he uses the words *overpriced* and *underpriced*, he must mean these prices are not justified and that the volatilities should be equal as in the Black-Scholes model. He goes on to say that one explanation for the pattern is that he left something out of the B-S formula but dismisses it as not accounting entirely for the observed pattern. Jonathan Reiss of Analytical Synthesis LLC rightly believes that though the empirical evidence of the volatility smile became overwhelming after the 1987 crash, there is evidence that it showed its "smiley face" earlier, along with the recognition that stock pricing processes had characteristics that would cause that to make sense. Black concludes in 1975 with: "At the moment, I think we have to say that we don't know why some kinds of options are consistently overpriced according to the formula and others are consistently underpriced."

In so doing, he acknowledges his belief that his formula is right and market prices are wrong, a not uncharacteristic philosophy of many academics and inventors.

The Black-Scholes formula, even with all of its misgivings, is still extraordinary.[6] The six simple approximations for its derivation involve:

1. The short-term interest rate is known and constant through all time.
2. The stock price follows a random walk, is continuous in time with a variance proportional to the square of its stock price, and has no memory.
3. The stock pays no dividends.
4. The option is exercisable only at expiration (European style).
5. Stocks can be bought at margin for short-term interest rates.
6. Short selling is possible with no penalties.

Under these conditions, the option's value is dependent on the price of the stock, time to maturity, interest rate, constant volatility, and option strike price only. The option value then is given by the following equation:

$$C = S \exp(-dT)N(d_1) - \exp(-rT)KN(d_2) \tag{5.2}$$

where:

$$d_1 = [\ln(S/K) + (b + \sigma^2/2)T]/(\sigma\, T^{1/2})$$

$$d_2 = d_1 - \sigma\, T^{1/2}$$

where $r$ is the riskless interest rate, $\sigma$ is implied volatility, and $b = r - d$ with $d$ equal to the average annualized dividend yield throughout the option's life. $N(.)$ is the cumulative univariate normal distribution so that $N(d_1)$ implies the area under the standard normal density to the left of $d_1$ regularly. Drawbacks of the Black-Scholes model include: it does not allow stock dividends (modified here), it's not continuously exercisable, and it doesn't account for volatility expressed as function of strike (skew of volatility smile) or time to expiration, nor varying interest rates with time to maturity.

## VOLATILITY SMILE

There is an issue with modeling options that concerns accounting for what's called the volatility smile or skew. This volatility skew (or smile, depending on the underlying), as it's called, generally means the Black-Scholes option pricing equation would have a different implied volatility (IV) for each option at a given strike to be accurate. This is not to mean actually that there are indeed different realized volatilities for every option; it's just a drawback of the B-S methodology in pricing options that results in this phenomenon. The option volatility has been well studied, and this phenomenon has been modeled by a variety of techniques (Gatheral 2006).[7]

Figure 5.1 is a plot exhibiting the volatility smile. Here we show the empirical implied volatility backed out of the price of Apple puts on 4/1/2011, each with 15 days left to expiration. The closing price for Apple on this day was $344.56 and you'll notice for strikes in-the-money (left side of chart) and out-of-the-money (right side of chart) that the implied volatilities are higher than for the at-the-money values in the center.

The slopes for the volatility skew on the left and right decrease with increasing expiration, and this is easily observed from the volatility surface of Apple created from its option chain on 4/1/2011. We show in Figure 5.2 the empirical volatility surface for Apple puts with sufficient open interest, determined from option prices. From this graph, notice that as one moves further out in expiry, the surface flattens out and becomes more and more independent of the option strike. However, the influence remains, as there's

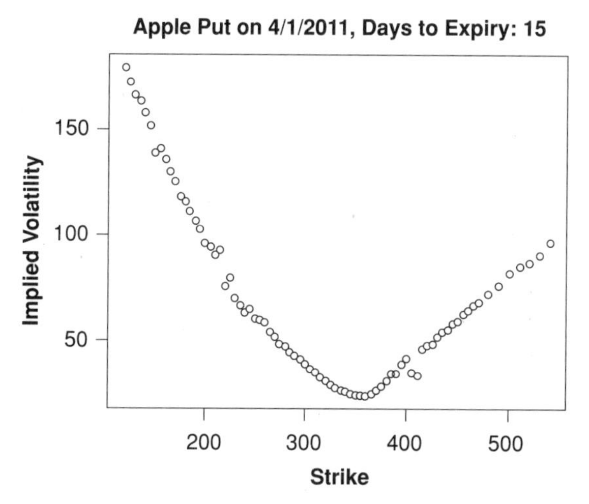


**FIGURE 5.1** The volatility skew, or smile, for Apple.

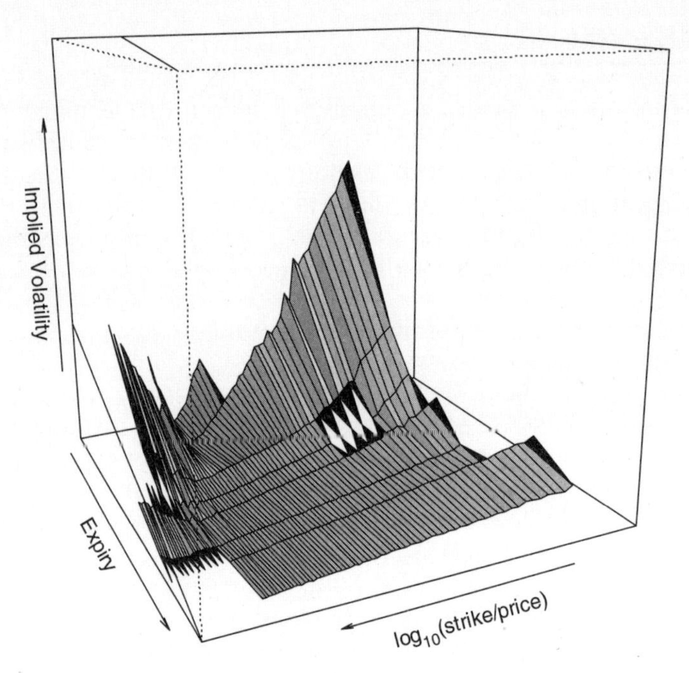


**FIGURE 5.2** Perspective plot of the empirical implied volatility (IV) surface for the option chain of Apple on 4/1/2001. We have IV versus *k*-values [$\log_{10}$(strike/price)] and days to expiration.

still a slope with the strike. Also, a fair amount of the surface has no IV values. These are the holes, the combinations of strike and days to expiration (dte) that have no active options trading on a given day.

When we want to price options, we need to be able to obtain the correct implied volatility given the strike and days to expiration (dte) of the option. Then we can reprice the option given the correct IV, underlying stock price, interest rate, strike, and dte. So, for example, consider a portfolio owning an at-the-money (ATM) option while running some risk calculation for a long horizon. If the horizon is long, that means that the resulting pricing of the underlying security could be quite far from its current value simply due to the impact of volatility, which has a multiplying effect the farther the horizon one forecasts. A stock price would normally move farther from its current price in a week than a day, and farther in a month than a week generally. So if a portfolio owns a current ATM option priced at today's current stock price, when repriced in some risk calculation, the underlying could be far from its current value, moving the option way out-of-the-money or way in-the-money. To reprice the option effectively, we'd need to know what the

IV is for an option that far in- or out-of-the-money as a function of time to expiration and to use that IV in an option pricing formula.

Thus a key to modeling the IV surface is to parameterize the implied volatility as a function of just two variables, those being strike and time to expiration from the empirical data.

However, a difficulty exists with illiquid options or for stocks with just a few options trading. How do you compute a semi-accurate IV surface from scarce data? To overcome this difficulty, the FactSet process works by downloading the option chain for each stock every day, followed by combining weighted rolling five days of data with a fit of the empirical IV to a polynomial function of log(strike/stock price) and log(dte). By using the past five days of data consisting of IV, strike, and dte, we mitigate the scarcity issue while creating a more accurate model for forecasting the IV in a weighted regression technique.

Our objective is to predict portfolio risk; it's not to compute such accurate option prices that a high-frequency trading schema can trade on these individual option prices. Thus, we use an analytical approximation method known as Baroni-Adesi and Whaley (BAW) methodology for our option pricing mechanism while also avoiding the heavy calculation of the IV from first principle solutions of partial differential equations. We choose to use past empirical data to model the IV, and create a model IV surface from that data with a five-day weighted rolling look-back period. Then, the application of the BAW pricing methodology gives an acceptable solution for pricing the option in a very fast algorithm necessary for real-time feedback.

## IMPLIED VOLATILITY MODEL

The methodology we follow is really quite simple and is calibrated for each stock in our database each and every night. The equation for each stock's option chain (*separating puts and calls*) is:

$$\text{Implied volatility} = a_1 k/m^3 + a_2 k^2/m^2 + a_3 k^2/m + a_4 k + a_5 m + a_6 \quad (5.3)$$

where:

$$m = \ln(\text{dte} + 1.01)$$

$$k = \log_{10}(\text{strike/stock price})$$

We call attention to the natural logarithm in $m$ and the log base 10 in $k$. There are five coefficients determined from an ordinary least squares (OLS) fit plus an intercept ($a_6$) obtained representing the IV level on a stock-specific basis. For a typical U.S. large-cap stock, one obtains about 50 to 100 options of varying strikes and days to expiration each day, and we use five days of data, so the regression is generally sufficient for decent goodness-of-fit measures.

For example, take a stock like Apple. On April 1, 2011, there were 530 reported put option IVs consisting of 89 strikes or *k* values and eight different dte's. Thus the full IV surface is of size 89 * 8 = 712 elements, but the empirical data offers only 530 combinations. Thus, there's only enough empirical data to populate 74 percent of the surface. On the same date, Wal-Mart has put options covering 19 strikes and six dte's, defining an IV surface of 19 * 6 = 114 values, of which there are only 81 reported IVs covering 71 percent of the surface. Now, then, this leaves two reasons for modeling the IV surface: first, so that one can fill in the holes—that is, the combinations of strikes and dte's that have no reported option IVs, allowing a user to perform option analysis and pricing in FactSet; and second, so that if under Monte Carlo (MC) value at risk an underlying stock price is generated at some value outside the reported range of IVs, or at some level of price that the *k*-value [log(strike/price)] has no corresponding IV, we are still able to ascertain what the IV would be in that situation and hence calculate an estimated price for the option.

There are some securities with so few reported options that only 50 percent or so of the IV surface is populated and one needs a model to generate the remaining surface for any option analysis. This is the purpose of performing a good fit of the implied volatility surface. In addition, due to the scarcity issue, we've found that by combining the option data from five consecutive days in sequence, we can build up a larger data set per security, obtain higher-confidence regressions, and obtain higher granularity in the model results.

For instance, referring back to Wal-Mart, since over five days we get five different stock prices each day, it generates 19 new *k*-values each day. In addition, since dte decreases by 1 each day, we also obtain six new dte's every day, all corresponding to whatever IVs are reported. This increases the data for the regression for each stock by combining five days of data together. However, it also increases the size of the IV surface, too, while not diminishing the accuracy of each IV surface hole that needs to be filled. In fact, it allows the creation of a more precise surface due to the increased granularity of the surface and the better fitted model of IV obtained from equation (5.3) because we can use more data.

We perform weighted OLS regression such that the current day's data has weight 1, yesterday's has weight 0.9, the day before has a weight of 0.8, and so forth, with the fifth day's weight being 0.6. This emphasizes the more recent data for the surface creation. From each high-resolution IV surface, we need to trim them for the current day's suite of $k$-values (strikes) and dte's. To summarize the methodology, the following seven-step recipe is utilized overall:

1. For each stock, form stacked columns of five consecutive days of option implied volatilities, $\log_{10}$(strike/price) and ln(dte + 1.010), sorted most recent to most distant. Gather puts and calls data separately.
2. Create the weights vector, 1, 0.9, 0.8, 0.7, and 0.6 for the current to last day's data. This vector needs to be the identical length of the columns from step 1. Notice that the weights vector is not linear, but stepped.
3. Run an ordinary least squares regression using equation (5.3) prescribed earlier. Save the required statistics and parameters from each stock's fit each night.
4. Separately, form Excel-like pivot tables of $k$-values in rows and dte's in columns where the values are the empirical implied volatilities from over the five days. Essentially, this pivot table is created from the empirical data collected in step 1.
5. The next step involves using the parameters from equation (5.3) found in step 3 to calculate and populate the pivot table's missing values, using the $k$-values from the rows and dte's from the columns as factors in the model. In essence, we create the pivot table from empirical data to obtain the row and column values and use model parameters in hole filling.
6. Create a new surface by using the current day's $k$-values and dte's, computed from the current day's stock price and option chain information, and extracting the subset of all IV values in the rows and columns matching the current day's $k$-values and dte's. This describes a smaller surface appropriate just for the current day's IVs.
7. Next day, repeat the process, and do this for all securities.

A given horizon for which a Monte Carlo (MC) VaR is being run would impact the dte one needs to use to price the option in the Balanced Risk product for VaR.

Another example involves a stock price generated from the MC-VaR process resulting in a $k$-value outside the range stored. Then one would have to use the regression parameters to compute the option price using the BAW methodology (described later in this chapter). The formulation of equation (5.3) allows for extrapolation quite easily from the in-sample data to out-of-sample data and is another reason for fitting the surface well in the first place. For example, the two plots in Figure 5.3 are for Apple, where we shifted the $k$-values up and down respectively from the empirical surface by a small amount, in effect modeling the IV surface out-of-sample.

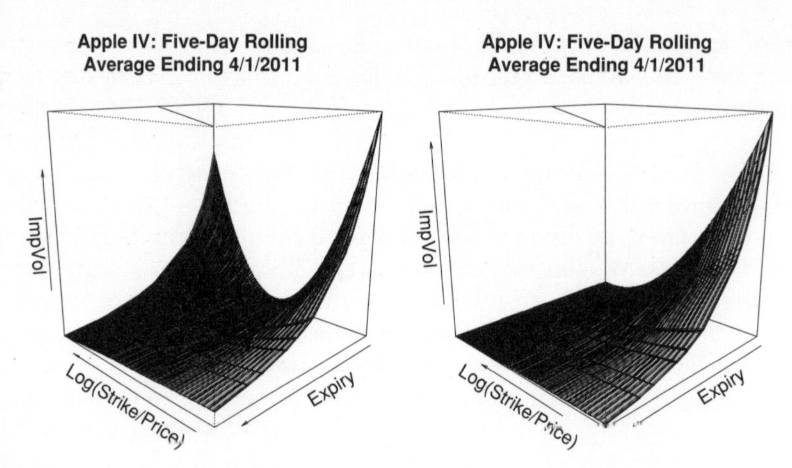


**FIGURE 5.3** Five-day rolling average implied volatility surface using equation (5.3).

Thus, equation (5.3) allows for the extrapolation of $k$-values and dte's without much error for small deviations from the empirical IV surface, built up from five days of option chain data. This probably wouldn't happen very often, as most of the usage of the MC-VaR is for shorter-horizon risk calculations, so the $k$-values determined from MC-VaR–generated stock prices would usually be found within the space of existing $k$-values (in-sample) for the IV surface.

## Some Results

What we want to be able to demonstrate is how well the polynomial of equation (5.3) reproduces the IV surface for some random stock options. The next data we'll review includes perspective plots of the IV surfaces of the empirical data and those created using equation (5.3).

The plots of Figure 5.4 exhibit the empirical IV surface on the left for Exxon's option chain and the surface created from the model designed by equation (5.3) on the right for data downloaded from FactSet on 4/1/2011. We've filled the holes of the empirical IV surface with values from the model, ascertained from modeling the five days of option chain data. Notice that the larger discrepancies between the two surfaces occur at small dte's (low expiry), which is where the smile is most prominent across $k$-values and where very large IVs occur relative to the rest of the surface. Given the scarcity of the Exxon data, for instance, of which there were 145 puts available across seven dte's, it's quite difficult to forecast well the large IVs found on the far side of the perspective plot at low dte count, and the error between the empirical and modeled surface plotted here at those dte's are about 17.7 percent. This would be quite expected given the modulation of the low-dte Exxon IV empirical surface. Even if one models over 90 percent of the surface well (as the model does in this example), the extreme levels of IV found in the empirical data are not easily reproduced by a polynomial expansion of strike with expiry, though from the picture we do a good job.

Luckily, most institutional portfolio managers, if they own options this close to expiration, handle them individually; they are well aware of the market prices of those securities and aren't so worried about their contribution to portfolio risk since they'll either be exercised or are already written off if they're expiring out-of-the-money, particularly when the time to expiration is shorter than the time horizon for the risk measure. Thus it's more important to accurately model the IV surface past the first dte or beyond one week or so before expiration.

The next set of perspective plots examine the empirical IV surface on the left and the modeled IV surface on the right for Apple, Berkshire, Pepsi, Google, and Procter & Gamble (P&G), all created from a single day's data with holes filled with model data from the five-day surface. As the reader gives these plots a cursory inspection, be mindful that these are created from scarce data per plot. This is why we want to aggregate data each day for the previous four days plus the current date for all stocks' option chains.

For instance, examine the two plots of Apple in Figure 5.5. The one on the left (from Figure 5.2) is the empirical surface with the holes, and the one on the right is with the holes filled. Apple has a fairly large option chain with fewer holes than most stocks, yet one can observe a large area of surface missing in the left plot.

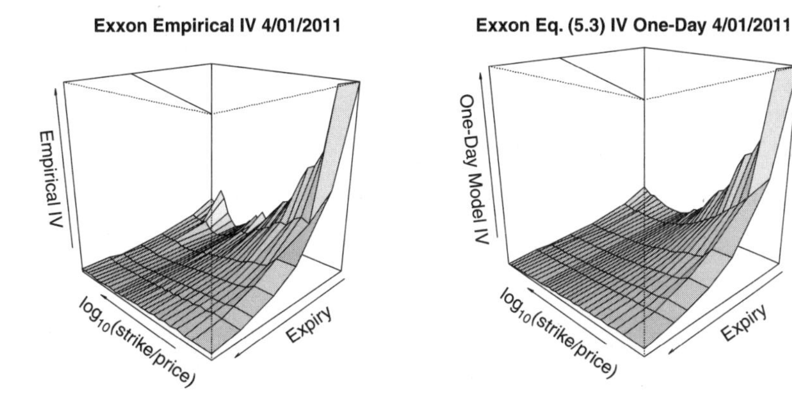


**FIGURE 5.4** The empirical IV surface on the left for Exxon's option chain and the surface created from the model designed by equation (5.3) on the right for data downloaded from FactSet on 4/1/2011.

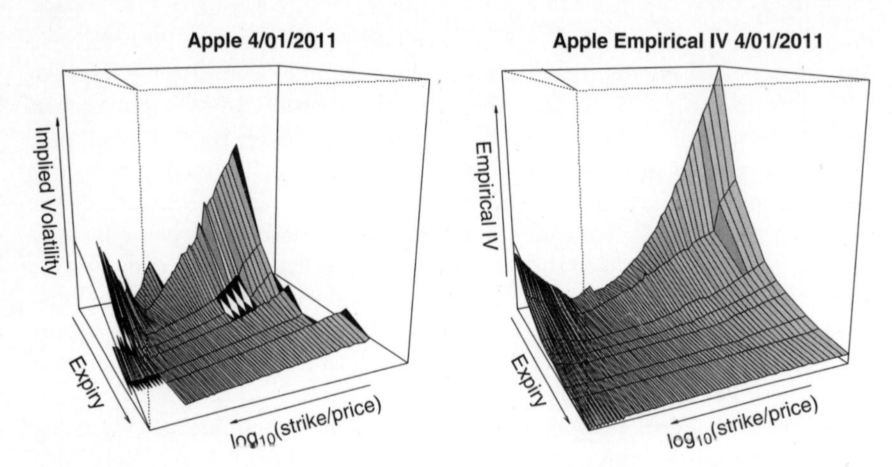


**FIGURE 5.5** The plot on the left is the empirical surface with the holes, and the one on the right is with the holes filled. Apple has a fairly large option chain with fewer holes than most stocks, yet one can observe a large area of surface missing.

Thus in the ensuing charts, we show the empirical surface on the left with the holes filled versus the modeled surface on the right for a single day's IV surface, all plotted from the same perspective to allow easy comparison.

The data for Berkshire Hathaway (Figure 5.6) and PepsiCo (Figure 5.7) are good examples to highlight how imperfect the empirical surfaces are. Yet they're modeled better than Exxon at the near expiration and high $k$-values

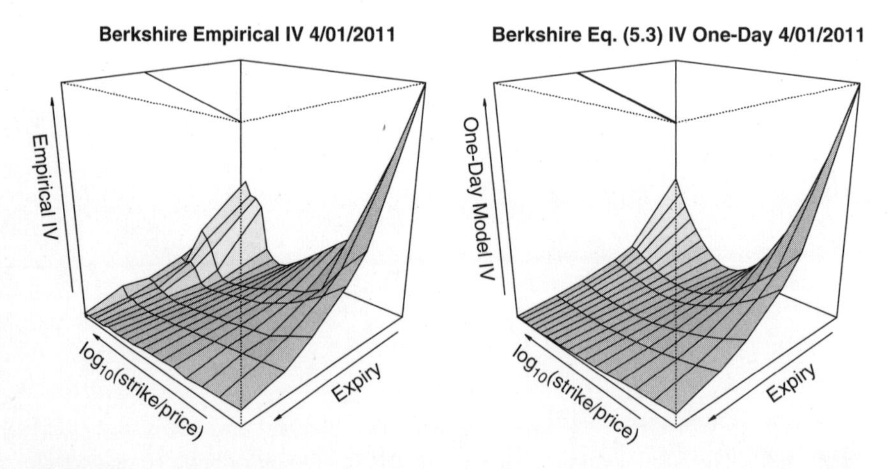


**FIGURE 5.6** Berkshire Hathaway implied volatility surface on the left and the modeled surface on the right.

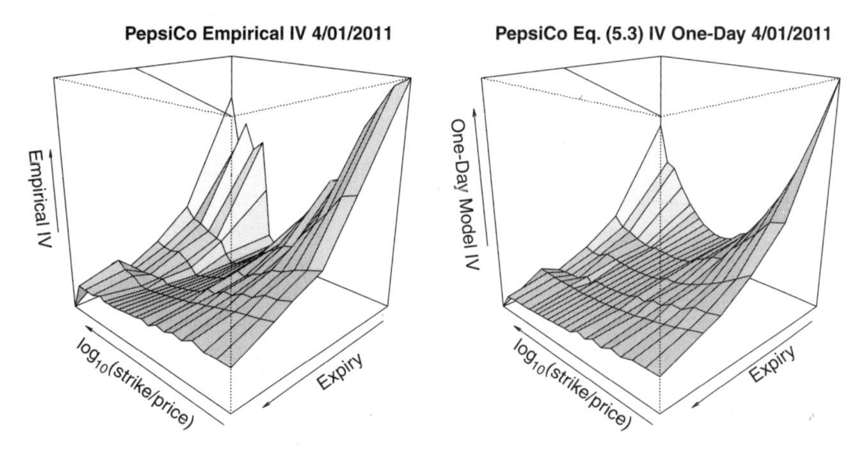


**FIGURE 5.7** Why using a five-day look-back with weighted regression to construct the surface yields richer information.

(far sides of perspective plots), even though one can imagine that the sparse data on these surfaces leaves a large amount of hole filling that has to be done to actually make them usable in risk analysis. In addition, for Pepsi there are still undulations on the modeled surface as its empirical surface is still quite rough. These examples demonstrate precisely why a single day's data is often not enough with which to build a model of the IV surface.

The set of data for Google (Figure 5.8) has higher density due to the much larger number of options available in a single day for that stock, which

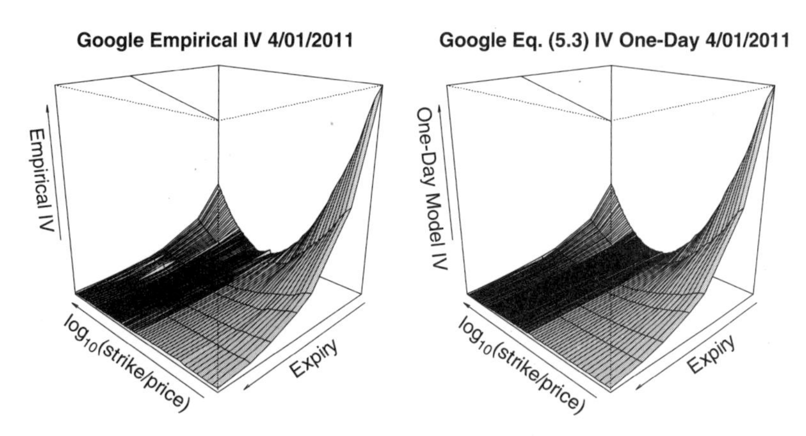


**FIGURE 5.8** The set of data for Google has higher density due to the much larger number of options available in a single day for that stock, which results in a denser surface, though there's still a number of holes to be filled.

results in a denser surface, though there's still a fair amount of holes to be filled. One can see that P&G (Figure 5.9), in contrast, has scarcer data and is more difficult to model generally. These one-day surfaces are illustrative in that they point out the differences between stocks' IV surfaces quite nicely, simply because one can visualize the dependence on the implied volatility of strike and time to expiration so easily. The visualization of the surfaces, however, looks like a decent goodness of fit, an observation corroborated by the relatively small errors displayed in Table 5.1.

The empirical surface of a single day's option chain is quite noisy itself and unreliable simply because of its highly modulated character, especially for short-expiration options or options without much open interest. As it is, filtering of the option data by removing options with little to no open interest trims the usable number of options considerably. This is why the data aggregation technique over five trading days is utilized in our methodology.

One cannot infer from these perspective plots alone that the relative accuracy the modeled surface created from OLS regressions of equation (5.3) fits to the empirical surface, however, and is why we calculated the errors displayed in Table 5.1.

Once the parameters are obtained via data aggregation over the five days and weighted regression for each stock, it's relatively simple to plot the surfaces or cross sections of the surfaces (IV as a function of expiry or strike) using the empirical data with holes filled from the model, or the model surface itself. Likewise, conversion to moneyness or option delta for

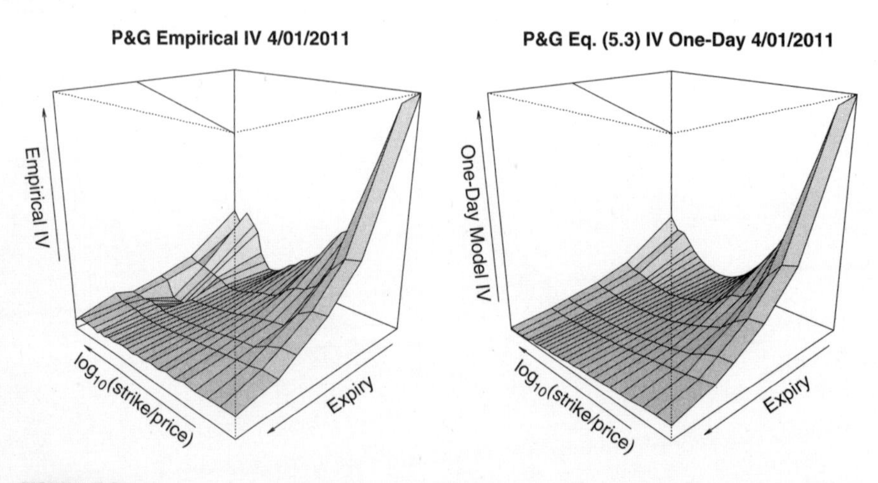


**FIGURE 5.9** One can see that P&G has scarcer data than Google and is more difficult to model generally. It's necessary to include previous days' option chain information to construct P&G's IV surface to a sufficient accuracy.

**TABLE 5.1** For the IV surface of each of the six stocks, we compute the percentage difference between the empirical surface at different days to expiration averaged across all *k*-values versus the modeled surface in the top data set, rows 1 through 8. The bottom data set lists the R-squared from the weighted regression of equation (5.3) with the five days' values of empirical IV data for a variety of dates.

| Average Percentage Error of Equation (5.3) from Empirical IV Surface | | | | | | | | |
|---|---|---|---|---|---|---|---|---|
| | Mean | 5.4% | 1.5% | 1.0% | 2.7% | 2.0% | 1.5% | 0.9% |
| | Std. | 5.9% | 2.1% | 1.0% | 2.9% | 2.6% | 1.0% | 1.1% |
| | | **Exxon** | **P&G** | **Google** | **Pepsi** | **Brk.A** | **Apple** | **NLV** |
| Shortest dte | 1 | 17.7% | 2.0% | 0.0% | 0.5% | 7.9% | 0.8% | 0.3% |
| Next shortest | 2 | 5.5% | 0.9% | 2.4% | 7.7% | 0.8% | 1.0% | 0.1% |
| " " | 3 | 8.8% | 6.3% | 0.2% | 4.4% | 2.9% | 0.9% | 2.9% |
| " " | 4 | 4.5% | 0.4% | 2.0% | 2.1% | 2.2% | 2.4% | 0.3% |
| " " | 5 | 0.6% | 0.7% | 1.7% | 1.5% | 0.4% | 3.0% | 0.8% |
| " " | 6 | 0.1% | 1.7% | 0.5% | 5.7% | 1.9% | 1.4% | |
| Longer dte | 7 | 6.1% | | 1.4% | | | 0.1% | |
| Longest dte | 8 | | | | | | 2.5% | |
| **Daily $R^2$'s from Regression** | | | | | | | | |
| | Mean* 100 | 94.6 | 86.2 | 86.0 | 88.6 | 85.2 | 89.6 | 89.6 |
| | Std* 100 | 2.43 | 4.32 | 5.54 | 2.85 | 6.17 | 3.23 | 3.23 |
| | Min*100 | 87.8 | 77.0 | 75.9 | 83.7 | 71.2 | 83.8 | 83.8 |
| Date | | **Exxon** | **P&G** | **Google** | **Pepsi** | **Brk.A** | **Apple** | **NLV** |
| 4/01/2011 | 1 | 0.878 | 0.863 | 0.889 | 0.874 | 0.809 | 0.927 | 0.677 |
| 3/31/2011 | 2 | 0.888 | 0.895 | 0.887 | 0.869 | 0.826 | 0.870 | 0.664 |

*(continued)*

**TABLE 5.1** *(continued)*

| Date | | Exxon | P&G | Google | Pepsi | Brk.A | Apple | NLV |
|---|---|---|---|---|---|---|---|---|
| 3/30/2011 | 3 | 0.968 | 0.885 | 0.854 | 0.862 | 0.899 | 0.887 | 0.542 |
| 3/29/2011 | 4 | 0.964 | 0.892 | 0.916 | 0.888 | 0.898 | 0.921 | 0.493 |
| 3/28/2011 | 5 | 0.957 | 0.901 | 0.773 | 0.875 | 0.884 | 0.882 | 0.666 |
| 3/25/2011 | 6 | 0.965 | 0.874 | 0.821 | 0.841 | 0.731 | 0.873 | 0.704 |
| 3/24/2011 | 7 | 0.947 | 0.912 | 0.916 | 0.866 | 0.912 | 0.925 | 0.749 |
| 3/23/2011 | 8 | 0.949 | 0.951 | 0.921 | 0.860 | 0.868 | 0.855 | 0.452 |
| 3/22/2011 | 9 | 0.925 | 0.872 | 0.896 | 0.873 | 0.833 | 0.870 | 0.650 |
| 3/21/2011 | 10 | 0.955 | 0.809 | 0.895 | 0.837 | 0.880 | 0.878 | 0.687 |
| 3/18/2011 | 11 | 0.950 | 0.893 | 0.885 | 0.883 | 0.847 | 0.937 | 0.609 |
| 3/17/2011 | 12 | 0.926 | 0.788 | 0.764 | 0.881 | 0.885 | 0.868 | 0.579 |
| 3/16/2011 | 13 | 0.925 | 0.821 | 0.793 | 0.877 | 0.869 | 0.838 | 0.682 |
| 3/15/2011 | 14 | 0.946 | 0.770 | 0.827 | 0.865 | 0.855 | 0.902 | 0.751 |
| 3/14/2011 | 15 | 0.960 | 0.880 | 0.802 | 0.924 | 0.912 | 0.889 | 0.741 |
| 3/11/2011 | 16 | 0.955 | 0.850 | 0.861 | 0.924 | 0.895 | 0.934 | 0.850 |
| 3/10/2011 | 17 | 0.947 | 0.843 | 0.759 | 0.911 | 0.731 | 0.874 | 0.758 |
| 3/09/2011 | 18 | 0.968 | 0.870 | 0.941 | 0.949 | 0.884 | 0.912 | 0.743 |
| 3/08/2011 | 19 | 0.961 | 0.806 | 0.855 | 0.906 | 0.899 | 0.882 | 0.758 |
| 3/07/2011 | 20 | 0.955 | 0.840 | 0.845 | 0.910 | 0.794 | 0.877 | 0.943 |
| 3/04/2011 | 21 | 0.956 | 0.858 | 0.886 | 0.919 | 0.712 | 0.954 | 0.835 |
| 3/03/2011 | 22 | 0.967 | 0.885 | 0.928 | 0.903 | 0.919 | 0.955 | 0.941 |

NLV—net liquidating/liquidation value.

the axis is also not difficult. All index option chains can also be utilized for index implied volatility surfaces.

Last, it's fairly easy to create composite IV surfaces as well for collections of stocks within GICS classifications or any other categories one wishes to cluster assets by.

## BARONI-ADESI WHALEY (BAW) OPTION PRICING METHODOLOGY

As we stated in earlier sections, we fit the option implied volatility surface each night and store the results on FactSet's servers for each stock and the classes of indexes. Then, once we generate the IV surface model and we need to price the option, we use the following methodology from Giovanni Barone-Adesi and Robert E. Whaley.[8] Though it's not the most accurate technique available for pricing an option these days, it's sufficient for VaR calculations and is much faster than most more accurate methods.

To price the option, first we have to solve for a critical price $S^*$ below which the option's call value is given by the Black-Scholes equation and above which is given by its exercisable proceeds $(S - K)$ where $K$ is option strike value. The equation to solve for $S^*$ is:

$$S^* - K = c(S^*,T) + [1 - \exp\{(b - r)T\}N(d_1(S^*))]S^*/q_2 \qquad (5.4)$$

where $r$ is the riskless interest rate and $b$ is the cost of carry, making the method applicable for commodities, for instance. If it's a dividend-paying stock, then $b = r - d$ with $d$ equal to dividend yield and the exponential collapses to $\exp(-dT)$. If we're talking about non-dividend-paying stocks, then equation (5.2) will give the price of the option with $d$ equaling zero for European-style expiration. $N(.)$ is the cumulative univariate normal distribution. The function $c(S^*,T)$ is just the Black-Scholes formulation, equation (5.2). The implied volatility "$\sigma$" in the equation below comes from the fit shown previously in equation (5.3). Other parameters are:

$$d_1 = [\ln(S/K) + (b + 0.5/\sigma^2)T]/(\sigma\, T^{1/2})$$

$$d_2 = d_1 - \sigma\, T^{1/2}$$

$$q_2 = [-(n - 1) + \text{sqrt}\{(n - 1)^2 + 4m/k\}]/2$$

$$m = 2r/\sigma^2$$

$$n = 2b/\sigma^2$$

$$k = 1 - \exp(-rT)$$

After solving for $S^*$, the critical price solution, we place it into an analytical equation involving the addition of an early exercise premium with the Black-Scholes formula. This is:

$$C(S, t) = c(S, t) + A_2\,(S/S^*)^{q_2} \tag{5.5}$$

where $A_2 = S^*/q_2\,[1 - \exp\{(b - r)T\}\,N(d_1(S^*))]$.

There are similar equations for put options. The final call option's value is $C(S,T)$ and is evaluated for every MC-generated price of the underlying for VaR calculations. For equity options, it's quite easy to calculate VaR using Monte Carlo with this methodology and it's quite fast. This method is used to price the IV surface and create the pricing surface, stored each night on FactSet servers, as well as use it on the fly when $k$-values generated by the MC process are outside the IV surface extrema and extrapolation using equation (5.3) is needed to compute a representative IV value for pricing using the BAW method.

Since that paper, numerous pricing formulas have arisen and the academic finance literature is replete with options valuation formulas. These days, dividends, multiple interest rates, multiple foreign exchange rates, multiple barriers (strikes), stochastic volatility, and continuously exercisable option valuations have all been implemented in pricing algorithms. Options on equities, equity-linked securities, interest rate options, currency options, fixed income options, commodities, futures, and indexes are all available, both over-the-counter and exchange-traded. The option analogy is even being utilized in pricing private equity and corporate projects these days.

## OTHER OPTION PRICING METHODS

Since the Black-Scholes model for pricing was developed for European options and non-dividend-paying stocks, there was considerable interest that led to splicing the model to account for early exercise and dividends. Additionally, the B-S model and its derivations found application in currency, futures, and interest rate derivatives as well. There was an early emphasis also on computational speed for option pricing. Apparently, during the earlier days of exchange trading or open-outcry auction for options, the traders couldn't obtain new pricing fast enough in the pits to react for trading purposes. This led to the hiring of numerically trained physicists, who really were the best people to develop algorithms for fast execution and real-time option pricing due to their heavy training in numerical methods and freestyle modeling.

In 1979, John Cox, Stephen Ross, and Mark Rubinstein published a paper outlining how to price an option using a binomial tree model.[9] The no-arbitrage condition and risk-neutral valuation were applied along with assuming random walking for stock prices to create an easily implementable option pricing algorithm. The method begins by setting up a long stock position and its respective short option position in a way that there is no uncertainty about the portfolio and the option's valuation at expiration. Then, since the portfolio has no risk, it must offer the risk-free rate to an investor. It follows naturally that if we're short one call option, there must be some long stock position in $X$ number of shares that satisfies an equality between the long and the short such that the overall position is riskless.

This is generalized in the following way. Assume the stock can move up from \$50 per share to a new level, \$50$u$. At this level the option's valuation is $C_u$. Also, the stock can move downward to a lower level \$50$d$; the option's value there is $C_d$. The portfolio's value at $u$ is $\$50uX - C_u$ and at the lower level it is $\$50dX - C_d$. Since it's a riskless portfolio, these two portfolio values are equal, and more generally for stock price $S$ and number of shares of the stock $X$:

$$SuX - C_u = SdX - C_d$$

and after rearrangement to solve for $X$ we have:

$$X = (C_u - C_d)/S(u - d)$$

Additionally, since the portfolio is riskless, the portfolio must be discounted by $\exp(-rT)$ such that the portfolio's value has a present value (PV) of $(SuX - C_u)\exp(-rT)$ or $(SdX - C_d)\exp(-rT)$. This leads to defining a final option pricing equation for the two legs of the tree of state $u$ and $d$ to arrive at:

$$C = \exp(-rT)[pC_u + (1 - p)C_d]$$

where $p = [\exp(rT) - d]/(u - d)$.

What lies to the right of the exponential, then, is the option's value at expiration. With this interpretation, the payoff of the option is its expected future payoff discounted at the risk-free rate. This enables us to easily determine the price of the option in various two-stage legs (binomial) and work backward to determine the present value of the option. In this way options are valued at the end of the tree at expiration and worked backward. For a call, the value at expiration is $\max(S_T - K,0)$, that is, the maximum of the difference between the stock's price at expiration minus the strike or zero, whichever is greater. Due to the tree living in a risk-neutral world, the value of the option at a tree node at time $T$ at expiration is the same as the value at $\delta = T - t$ just discounted by $\exp[-r(T - t)]$. In this way, knowing the terminal value of the option for various prices of the stock easily allows back-calculating to get prior nodes and ultimately to determine the present value of the option today.

Of course even the binomial pricing algorithm is old today and there have been long developed handy recursive relations for evaluating the option at every node given the terminating value of the option even for American (right to early exercise) put options described by:

$$C_{i,j} = \max\{K - S_o\, u^j\, d^{i-j};\ \exp(-r\delta t)\ [p\ C_{i+1,j+1} + (1 - p)C_{i+1,j}]\}$$

To use this equation, consider that the time from now to expiration of an option is divided into $N$ equally spaced time intervals of length $\delta t$, and refer to the $j$th node at time $i\delta t$ as the $i,j$ node, where $0 <= i <= (N - 1)$ and $0 <= j <= i$.

The final nodes at time $N$ valuations for a put option are given by:

$$C_{N,j} = \max\,(K - S_o\, u^j\, d^{i-j};\ 0)$$

where $j = 0, 1, 2, \ldots, N$.

To value a call, just replace $K - S$ with $S - K$ nomenclature and continue. The binomial is highly flexible and can be used to evaluate options on stock indexes, currencies, and futures contracts. The only difference involves yield, which for stocks is dividends, for currency it's the foreign risk-free interest rate, and for futures it's the domestic risk-free interest rate. Let us call yield "$q$" for further definition.

There's one last important consideration in the use of this pricing model, then, which is to relate volatility to the model through the parameters $u$ and $d$. When you do so, $u = \exp(\sigma\sqrt{\delta t})$ and $d = \exp(-\sigma\sqrt{\delta t})$, in which case $\sigma$ represents stock volatility. Do not confuse $d$ here with dividend yield, however; it simply means downward. Considering these definitions, then:

$$p = [\exp\{(r - q)\delta t\} - d]/(u - d)$$

One has all that's required to program one's own binomial tree for pricing using these equations. We can add that the option Greeks or partial derivatives used in hedging are rather easily calculated through the binomial model, too. When hedging, the reaction of the option price to small changes in $S$, $\sigma$, $T$, and $r$ is to be protected. Hence a delta neutral, gamma neutral, theta neutral, and rho neutral portfolio are the holy grail to an option trader. We remind the reader that a delta hedge is simply $\delta C/\delta S$, which is the rate of change of option price with stock price. If one can get an estimate of small changes like we did in freshman calculus class, one can estimate the delta, which in the binomial model for a node is simply:

$$\Delta = (C_{1,1} - C_{1,0})/S(u - d)$$

Now gamma, theta, vega, and rho are a little more difficult to estimate but still formulaic and can be found in Hull.[10]

There are various other methods for pricing options, too, finite difference and trinomial trees along with Monte Carlo methods with applications to many other assets like currencies or other option types, including barrier, Asian, and exotic options. We refer the reader to other books detailing these methods.[11]

## SWAPS, SWAPTIONS, FORWARDS, AND FUTURES

Compared to the complexity of fixed income securities, fixed income derivatives can be relatively tame. Most of the well-publicized derivative catastrophes involving complex fixed income structures have occurred in physical securities. In contrast, the mortgage to-be-announced (TBA) market, which is a short- to intermediate-term mortgage forward, is very liquid and largely devoid of system-rattling failures.

The mainstream use of derivatives began in 1976 with the launch of a futures contract on U.S. government bonds by the Chicago Board of Trade. In 1981, the Chicago Mercantile Exchange launched the Eurodollar futures contract. Given the high and volatile interest rates of the time and the desire to manage interest rate exposure, these futures contracts came to dominate trading volume at their exchanges.

Government bond futures are available for most countries with liquid bond markets, and often include multiple maturities. For instance, in the United States, six different maturities are available. However, what constitutes good delivery changes from market to market. In Australia, bond futures are based on a theoretical bond and are cash settled. In South Africa, bond futures are based on a specific bond. In the U.S. bond futures, the trading is based on a theoretical bond, currently a 6 percent, 20-year bond, which can be settled by delivery of one of more than 20 U.S. government bonds.

A bond forward contract can be viewed, and valued, as long the bond and short the bill to the forward date. A bond futures contract is simply a standardized bond forward. The standardization creates some optionality and opportunities for savvy traders. However, the breadth of good delivery creates some valuation challenges.

As just mentioned, trading in the U.S. bond contract is based on a 6 percent, 20-year bond. The contract can be satisfied by delivery of any U.S. government bond with 15 to 25 years of remaining maturity. There exists a conversion factor that translates the theoretical bond price into a delivery price of a specific bond. For each of the deliverable bonds, it is possible to compute the financing cost of:

- Buying the bond.
- Financing it until the futures settlement date.
- Then delivering the bond versus a short bond futures contract at today's price.

Among the deliverable bonds, the one with the highest repurchase agreement (repo) rate is called the cheapest to deliver. The original method of determining the futures contract's duration was to derive the duration of a bond forward based on the cheapest to deliver.

The volatility of interest rates causes the cheapest to deliver to change, and this change causes the duration and convexity of the bond futures contract to be different from that implied by a simple bond forward. At FactSet, we use a Monte Carlo interest rate process to simulate the changes in the cheapest to deliver, and the impact on the futures contract price.

In contrast to bond futures, which are futures on price, Eurodollar futures are futures on interest rates. Specifically, the Eurodollar futures contract is cash settled, and based on the interest rate of a three-month Eurodollar deposit starting as of the settlement date. For a one-year Eurodollar future, this is equivalent to a three-month forward rate, one year hence. The ability to control and speculate on portions of the yield contract led to the Eurodollar futures trading contracts every three months, out to 10 years. In the early days of the interest rate swap market, there was active arbitraging between the swaps market and the Eurodollar futures stack.

However, it was the collapse of Long Term Capital Management (LTCM) in 1998 that caused interest rate swaps to be the preferred product for hedging spread product. LTCM and others hedged the interest rate risk of their spread bets with Treasuries and bond futures. During the crisis following the collapse, spread product widened out, causing a loss on that leg of the trade. However, in the flight to quality, prices of Treasuries rose, causing a loss for those who were short Treasuries as a hedge. In contrast, interest rate swaps fell, accruing a gain to those who used them as a hedge.

Hedging with futures or swaps is primarily a duration analysis. The simplest method is to match the effective dollar duration of the portfolio with an offsetting amount of dollar duration in the hedge vehicle. Unfortunately, most participants would not find it palatable to hedge a typical bond

**TABLE 5.2** A simple example of how to understand the impact of interest rates on swaptions.

| Makes Money If ... | Receiver Swaption | Payer Swaption |
|---|---|---|
| Call | Rates go down | Rates go up |
| Put | Rates go up | Rates go down |

fund with the near-term Eurodollar contract. Thus, most participants also consider the key rate duration profile of both the portfolio and the hedge instrument in constructing the hedge.

The valuation of options on futures or interest rate swaps is fairly straightforward. Most market participants use variations of the Black-Scholes model. Again, details can be found in Hull. However, there are a few points to note. Earlier, we had pointed out the shortfalls of Black-Scholes for fixed income embedded options. For options on bond futures, the horizon is usually short enough not to be a problem. For options on interest rate swaps, called swaptions, the rate strike is translated into the fixed annuity of the strike rate.

The real complicating factor with swaptions is getting the nomenclature straight versus the interest rate risk. With an interest rate swap, the duration exposure comes from the fixed leg. The swaption nomenclature tracks the fixed leg. Thus, a receiver swaption is an option to receive fixed, and a payer swaption is an option to pay fixed. Table 5.2 might be useful in keeping track of the interest rate exposure.

Of course, don't forget to switch the signs on the exposure, depending on whether you are long or short the option.

Hedging swaptions is a little more difficult than hedging swaps. The difficulty comes from the second-order effects, called convexity or gamma, depending on whether you're a bond trader or an options trader. Street practice is to hedge out the second-order effects first, usually with other options, and then hedge the remaining duration or delta with simpler securities or derivatives.

### Government Bond Futures

Government bond futures are contracts for future delivery of sovereign bonds, and hence their prices move with the underlying bonds that can be delivered by the seller of the futures contract to the buyer. They are exchange traded and may be linked to either a basket of bonds such as in the case of U.S. Treasury futures or the yield of a synthetic bond as in the case of Australian government bond futures. The exchanges where these instruments trade set the contract specifications, delivery requirements, and standards, as well as regulate the market participants and clear their trades. In addition to Australia and the United States, FactSet covers Canadian, German, Italian, Swiss, French, Swedish, UK, Japanese, and Spanish government bond futures. Each country may have more than one contract traded or just one active contract.

Government bond futures are widely used to quickly alter the duration exposures of fixed income portfolios. Effective or partial durations for government bond futures can be computed numerically in the same way as other fixed income securities. As we've mentioned before, not all durations are created equal, and in what follows we will provide an example of how interest rate risk does not end with parallel shifts of the spot curve.

One advantage of using key rate durations over effective duration to estimate the price performance of government bond futures can be seen by the following comparison in Table 5.3 of a hedge of a 30-year Treasury with a 10-year note future and again with a 30-year bond future in Table 5.4. In the first report a U.S. Treasury bond position is hedged with a 10-year Treasury futures short position where the amount of the hedge is calculated using the ratio of the instruments' effective duration. From a value at risk perspective it is clear that a traditional measure such as effective duration is insufficient when used to construct a hedge, and may actually increase the VaR.

In Table 5.3, we show the portfolio on the far left and the securities in it: the U.S. Treasury bond and 10-year T-note. This represents a screen shot of the FactSet software. The portfolio's market value, effective duration, and convexity are listed. Note that the market value of the futures contract does not factor into the portfolio's market value but does affect its sensitivity to interest rates. This is because futures contracts are marked to market and do not require any cash to enter into except for posting a margin, which is satisfied by owning the U.S. Treasury bond.

The three columns on the far right compute the VaR for a 30-day horizon at a 95 percent confidence interval (CI) in market value, the stand-alone VaR and (the rightmost column) portfolio VaR as a percentage of the portfolio. Stand-alone VaR is the VaR just of the instruments singly, not in a portfolio where their covariance would normally interact to lower the portfolio risk.

This report lists the 30-trading-day, 95 percent VaR as 5.32 percent, meaning there's a 5 percent probability that within 30 days, a minimum loss amounting to 5.32 percent of the portfolio could occur. The risk increased by adding the 10-year T-note into the portfolio, moving the VaR from 5.21 percent to 5.32 percent, though it is thought that the futures contract would have lowered the risk since its application is as a hedge.

**TABLE 5.3** A portfolio composed of a long U.S. Treasury bond position hedged with a short position in a 10-year Treasury note futures.

**Valuation Analysis**
**5/18/2011**
**FactSet/R-Squared Daily Global Multi-Asset-Class Model (USD)**
**U.S. Dollar**

| Ticker | | Portfolio Ending Market Value | Ending Price | Portfolio Ending Effective Duration | Portfolio Ending Effective Convexity | Portfolio Ending Dollar Duration (Effective) | MC Value at Risk 30-Day, 95% | MC Stand-Alone Value at Risk 30-Day, 95% | MC % Value at Risk 30-Day, 95% |
|---|---|---|---|---|---|---|---|---|---|
| | **Portfolio** | **1,521,157.00** | | **5.55** | **221** | | **80,859.44** | **80,859.44** | **5.32** |
| 912810EZ | Government of the United States of America 6.625% 15-Feb-2027 | 1,521,157.00 | 150.43 | 10.59 | 1.46 | 161,042.47 | 79,220.08 | 95,604.49 | 5.21 |
| TYZ1 | 10Y T-Note (CBT) Dec. 11 | −1,200,000.00 | 120.00 | 6.39 | −0.96 | −76,693.09 | 1,686.23 | 50,836.62 | 0.11 |

Holdings Data As Of BNDFUT 5/18/2011
Risk Model As Of FactSet/R-Squared Daily Global Multi-Asset-Class Model (USD) 5/18/2011

**TABLE 5.4** A portfolio composed of a long U.S. Treasury bond position hedged with a short position in a 30-year Treasury bond futures.

Valuation Analysis
5/18/2011
FactSet/R-Squared Daily Global Multi-Asset-Class Model (USD)
U.S. Dollar

| Ticker | | Portfolio Ending Market Value | Ending Price | Portfolio Ending Effective Duration | Portfolio Ending Effective Convexity | Portfolio Ending Dollar Duration (Effective) | MC Value at Risk 30-Day, 95% | MC Stand-Alone Value at Risk 30-Day, 95% | MC % Value at Risk 30-Day, 95% |
|---|---|---|---|---|---|---|---|---|---|
| | **Portfolio** | **1,521,157.00** | | **2.17** | **2.06** | | **–861.86** | **–861.86** | **–0.06** |
| 912810EZ | Government of the United States of America 6.625% 15-Feb-2027 | 1,521,157.00 | 150.43 | 10.59 | 1.46 | 161,042.47 | 67,740.07 | 95,771.50 | 4.45 |
| USZ1 | 30Y T-Note (CBT) Dec. 11 | –1,219,680.00 | 121.97 | 10.50 | –0.75 | –128,038.19 | –68,588.92 | 86,913.01 | –4.51 |

Holdings Data As Of BNDFUT 5/18/2011
Risk Model As Of FactSet/R-Squared Daily Global Multi-Asset-Class Model (USD) 5/18/2011

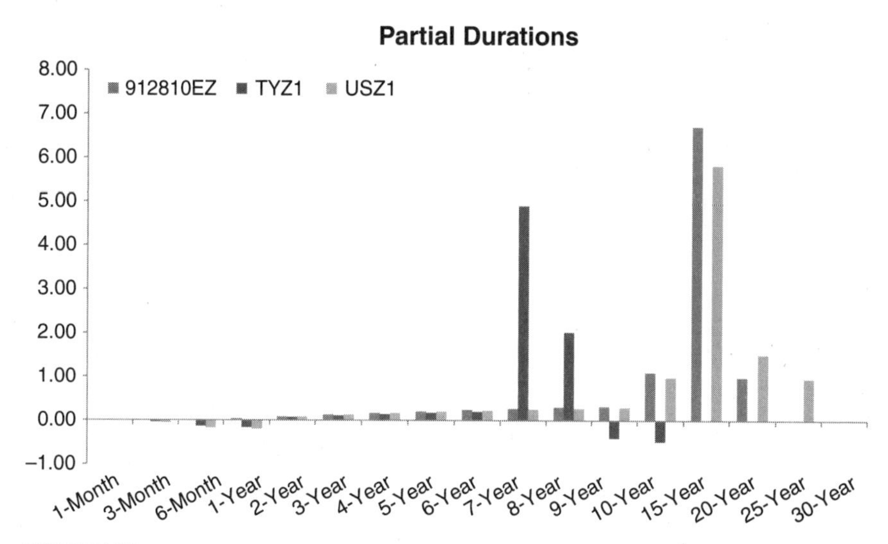


**FIGURE 5.10** The partial duration profile of the U.S. Treasury bond, the 10-year note futures, and the 30-year bond futures.

In contrast, in Table 5.4, the same security hedged with a 30-year bond futures short position has its risk reduced, as can be seen in the valuation analysis chart. Here the VaR is drastically smaller and obtained a negative value such that the 30-year Treasury bond is actually more diversifying (i.e., the overall risk of the portfolio is lowered by having the asset in the portfolio).

This is because the partial durations (i.e., sensitivities of the security to parts of the yield curve) of the 30-year bond futures match the partial durations of the U.S. Treasury bond better than the 10-year note futures, as can be observed in the next chart. The bar chart in Figure 5.10 has the interest rate tenor on the $x$-axis and partial duration level on the $y$-axis. We show the 912810EZ (bond) in black, TYZ1 in light gray, and USZ1 in dark gray. Notice how at seven-year key rates and higher, the TYZ1 has significantly larger partial duration sensitivities compared to USZ1 and the bond. At lower key rates we hardly see an impact for any of the instruments, but at longer key rates the rate sensitivity of the 30-year Treasury futures USZ1 would offer a more complete hedge for the bond's interest rate risk.

### Options on Government Bond Futures

Options on bond futures come in handy when portfolio managers try to alter their convexity exposure. Positive convexity is a good thing when you are long fixed income instruments, because it reduces the decline in a bond's value as rates rise and accelerates its gain as rates head lower; but in search of yield, managers may acquire securities with prepayment or call options attached to them. Mortgages are a prime example; they have negative convexity, which minimizes their gain from falling rates due to price compression. To hedge those effectively, one must pay attention to their convexities. In the next illustration (Table 5.5), the risk exposure of a mortgage pass-through is shown on its own, then a short position in 30-year bond futures is added as a hedge, and finally a put option on that same contract is added to the portfolio. The VaR of the portfolio declines more after adding a put option on a bond futures. The first portfolio, which consists of the mortgage-backed security (MBS) by itself, the VaR is about 64,000, but hedging it with a short position of half a million in 30-year Treasury futures reduces the VaR to 28,000. Notice, however, that the convexity of both the futures and the MBS is negative. In the third portfolio the two instruments are combined with a put on the 30-year Treasury futures, which has a positive convexity, to reduce the VaR to 25,000. Of course the MBS has additional risk exposure to MBS factors that instruments derived from U.S. Treasuries do not have exposure to.

Options on bond futures are repriced in the same rigorous fashion as bond futures themselves, where their sensitivities to the discount curve are calculated and then multiplied by the simulated rate changes coming from the Monte Carlo simulation rather than using the option Greeks.

### Interest Rate Swaps

A swap contract is essentially an agreement to trade cash flows between different interest rate sources (e.g., fixed to floating for a plain-vanilla swap) between two parties with different comparative funding advantages, economic outlooks, or liability exposures. The buyer of the swap is the fixed rate payer, while the receiver is the seller. In FactSet the swap is thus modeled as two separate legs with identical notional amount and maturities, and the buyer would be short the fixed leg and long the floating leg so that the buyer pays the fixed interest amount and receives the floating.

In the example in Table 5.6, a portfolio with a long position in a five-year swap is shown, composed of a short position in the SWAPFIX_Payor (fixed rate paying leg portion of the swap) to indicate payments of the fixed interest rate and a long position in SWAPFLT_Payor (the floating rate leg) to indicate that the holder will receive the floating rate payments. We show the portfolio market values, effective duration, contribution to effective duration, and three separate value-at-risk calculations at 95 percent CI for 30 trading days. The first VaR is in portfolio market value, while the last is the percentage of the portfolio; stand-alone VaR is in the middle.

**TABLE 5.5** Risk profile changes for a holding of a mortgage pass-through, when held on its own, then hedged with a short position in U.S. bond futures, and finally hedged with the futures and an option on the bond futures.

**Valuation Analysis**
**5/18/2011**
**FactSet/R-Squared Daily Global Multi-Asset-Class Model (USD)**
**U.S. Dollar**

| | Portfolio Ending Market Value | Ending Price | Portfolio Ending Effective Duration | Portfolio Ending Effective Convexity | Portfolio Ending Dollar Duration (Effective) | MC Value at Risk 30-Day, 95% | MC Stand-Alone Value at Risk 30-Day, 95% | MC % Value at Risk 30-Day, 95% |
|---|---|---|---|---|---|---|---|---|
| FGLMC 3.5 2011 3.500% ll-Aug-2015 | 2,023,305.60 | 101.00 | 6.10 | −0.86 | 123,372.48 | 63,890.10 | 64,057.35 | 3.16 |
| Hedged with a Bond Futures Position | | | | | | | | |
| 30Y T-Note (CBT) Dec. 11 | −609,840.00 | 121.97 | 10.50 | −0.75 | −64,019.09 | −16,469.69 | 44,394.62 | −0.81 |
| FGLMC 3.5 2011 3.500% 11-Aug-2015 | 2,023,305.60 | 101.00 | 6.10 | −0.86 | 123,372.48 | 44,301.71 | 59,527.22 | 2.19 |
| | | | | | Total | 27,832.02 | | |

(continued)

**TABLE 5.5** *(continued)*

| | Portfolio Ending Market Value | Ending Price | Portfolio Ending Effective Duration | Portfolio Ending Effective Convexity | Portfolio Ending Dollar Duration (Effective) | MC Value at Risk 30-Day, 95% | MC Stand-Alone Value at Risk 30-Day, 95% | MC % Value at Risk 30-Day, 95% |
|---|---|---|---|---|---|---|---|---|
| | | | | Hedged with a Bond Futures Position and Options | | | | |
| 30Y T-Note (CBT) Dec. 11 | −609,840.00 | 121.97 | 10.50 | −0.75 | −64,019.09 | −17,438.04 | 44,394.62 | −0.86 |
| USZ1P123 | 4,200.00 | 4.20 | −174.38 | 129.58 | −7,324.04 | −2,651.64 | 3,690.76 | −0.13 |
| FGLMC 3.5 2011 3.500% 11-Aug-2015 | 2,023,305.60 | 101.00 | 6.10 | −0.86 | 123,372.48 | 45,119.68 | 59,527.22 | 2.23 |
| | | | | | Total | 25,030.00 | | |

**TABLE 5.6** A swap modeled in FactSet as two instruments and their corresponding analytics and VaRs.

Valuation Analysis
SWAPPORT—1/04/2012
FactSet/R-Squared Daily Global Multi-Asset-Class Model (USD)
U.S. Dollar

| Ticker | | Portfolio Ending Market Value | Portfolio Ending Quantity Held | Portfolio Ending Effective Duration | Portfolio Contribution to Ending Effective Duration | MC Value at Risk 30-Day, 95% | MC Stand-Alone Value at Risk 30-Day, 95% | MC% Value at Risk 30-Day, 95% |
|---|---|---|---|---|---|---|---|---|
| | Portfolio | –67,135.94 | | 84.46 | 84.46 | 26,001.99 | 26,001.99 | 43.31 |
| 912810EZ | SWAPFIX_Payor | –1,059,073.40 | –1,000,000 | 5.51 | 86.85 | 28,000.89 | 28,081.89 | 46.64 |
| USZ1 | SWAPFLT_Payor | 991,937.46 | 1,000,000 | 0.16 | –2.40 | –2,017.72 | 4,410.87 | –3.36 |

Holdings Data As Of SWAPPORT 1/04/2012
Risk Model As Of FactSet/R-Squared Daily Global Multi-Asset-Class Model (USD) 1/04/2012

The VaR of each leg counteracts the other, but the fixed leg's larger sensitivity to interest rates risk gives it a VaR that dwarfs that of the floating rate leg. This is a result of the construction of the swap where by virtue of its longer duration the fixed portion of the swap has greater interest rate risk compared to the floating rate leg, which floats and resets quarterly to LIBOR three months. It is also worthwhile to note that the large MC % VaR value is usual for instruments like swaps because of their low present values despite their large notional amounts. It is therefore important to include the absolute MC VaR amount in the reports.

### Credit Default Swaps

Credit default swaps (CDSs) are insurance contracts on an issuer's credit. In Balanced Risk they are linked to the issuer of the debt through their exposure to the credit spread factor. Generally, a short position in the CDS indicates a purchase of credit insurance. This is mainly due to the fact that in exchange for that insurance, the holder of the CDS will have to make quarterly cash payments to the counterparty who is acquiring that risk. This premium is generally expressed in percentage of notional terms, and market convention is to quote the CDS in terms of the premium, or fair credit spread, which gives the CDS a zero present value.

Like an interest rate swap, a credit default swap has two legs: a premium payment leg and a default payment leg. A protection buyer is long the default leg and is short the premium leg. While both legs of the swap have some interest rate exposure, unlike an interest rate swap, the predominant risk of a CDS is due to changes in the fair credit spread. This also distinguishes a CDS from a corporate bond written on the same reference entity. A corporate bond exposes the holder to both interest rate and credit risk, while the risk of a CDS is concentrated mainly in the latter.

Another important distinction between a corporate bond and a credit default swap is in how the exposure to credit risk is expressed. Because a CDS generally has a very small (or zero) present value relative to the notional amount, exposure to credit risk is not naturally expressed in terms of spread durations. This is because duration measures percentage change in value for a given change in spread, which for a CDS can be undefined due to the zero PV. For this reason we measure credit exposure of a CDS as pure price sensitivity.

Last, when hedging the credit risk of a bond, one usually would match the average duration of the bond(s) with the maturity of the CDS purchased. In this way, the duration is hedged. Likewise the convexity is also hedged in actuality; however, in FactSet MAC, although we calculate partial derivatives in the Taylor series expansion of the bond price out to fourth-order derivatives, for the CDS we take it out only to the first order; thus convexity isn't accounted for in the formulas we use.

Specifically, we would calculate the first-order market value impact of holding a CDS due to a credit spread change as follows:

$$\Delta\text{Spread} \times \frac{dP}{dCDS} = \text{CDS price change from spread change}$$

This is in contrast to the calculation for a corporate bond, which would be calculated as:

$$\Delta OAS \times \text{Spread duration} \times \text{Price} = \text{Bond price change from spread change}$$

To illustrate this, take a look at the portfolio attribution charted in Table 5.7. The chart shows a portfolio consisting of a DuPont bond combined with a credit default swap that references DuPont and has a similar maturity profile. You can see how VaR for the DuPont bond is reduced by adding CDS on DuPont.

As one can see, the bond's spread duration and the dP/dCDS of the CDS almost equal each other (2.33 versus –1.17, respectively), and when it comes to their effect on the portfolio, they offset each other nicely after accounting for the difference in their relative weight.

## Eurodollar Futures

In the swap example, the portfolio was left with a considerable VaR due to the fixed leg's relatively large interest rate sensitivity. The portfolio's factor exposure to the key rates are illustrated in the next graph (Figure 5.11), which shows the risk factor contribution by partial rate point for the interest rate swap discussed in the previous section. We can see that the exposure to the six-year point of the LIBOR curve is the major source of interest rate sensitivity.

To hedge this we can use Eurodollar futures, which are contracts to fund or borrow a three-month deposit pegged to the forward three-month LIBOR rate. They are useful because they are sensitive to isolated areas of the yield curve and a portfolio manager can cherry-pick the exposure. Eurodollar futures are also widely used to replicate forward rate agreements, as they are their standardized equivalent.

**TABLE 5.7** A portfolio of a DuPont bond and a credit default swap on DuPont with similar maturity with FactSet-generated analytics and risk exposures.

**Valuation Analysis**
**5/18/2011**
**FactSet/R-Squared Daily Global Multi-Asset-Class Model (USD)**
**U.S. Dollar**

| | Portfolio Ending Market Value | Ending Price | Portfolio Ending Effective Duration | Portfolio Ending Dollar Duration (Effective) | MC Value at Risk 30-Day, 95% | MC Stand-Alone Value at Risk 30-Day, 95% | MC % Value at Risk 30-Day, 95% | Portfolio Ending Spread Duration | Portfolio Ending dPdCDS |
|---|---|---|---|---|---|---|---|---|---|
| Portfolio | 1,022,758.90 | | 2.33 | 2.33 | 4,094.52 | 4,094.52 | 0.40 | 2.33 | −1.17 |
| DUPONT3YR Credit Default Swap | −496,560.00 | 0.99 | N/A | N/A | −8,685.58 | 6,841.52 | −0.85 | N/A | 2.41 |
| E.i. Du Pont de Nemours & Co. 1.75% 25-mar-2014 | 1,022,908.90 | 102.08 | 2.33 | 2.33 | 12,806.91 | 19,189.88 | 1.25 | 2.33 | — |

Holdings Data As Of
CDS 11/09/2011
Risk Model As Of
FactSet/R-Squared Daily Global Multi-Asset-Class Model (USD) 11/09/2011

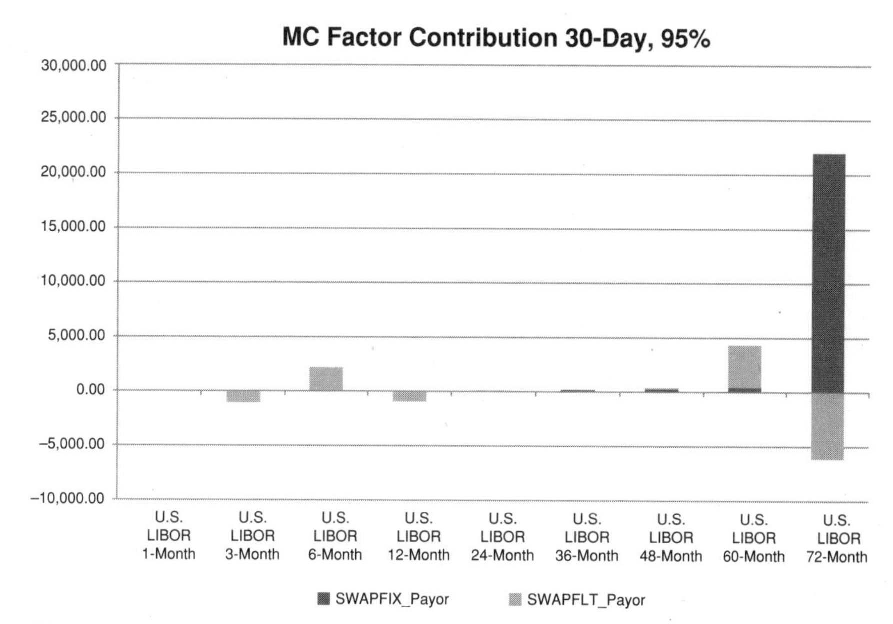


**FIGURE 5.11** Monte Carlo factor risk contribution profile by partial rate for an interest rate swap.

The Monte Carlo factor contributions shown in Figure 5.11 are the market value effects of the instruments on the total portfolio value due to changes in the specified factors. The values are sampled at the Monte Carlo scenarios that are used to calculate the 95 percent VaR for the portfolio.

In the portfolio shown in Table 5.8 the portfolio manager added $4 million in the Eurodollar futures contract expiring in December 2016 to try to balance out the 72-month U.S. LIBOR factor exposure. Again note that the futures position does not impact the total market value of the portfolio, because it is a cashless instrument to enter into and only requires a margin.

Figure 5.12 shows the MC factor contribution by partial rate point of the combined portfolio and illustrates how the VaR is reduced substantially because the Eurodollar futures contract has partial duration exposure to only the 60-month and 72-month points; therefore, the portfolio's factor exposure ends up looking more balanced at the 72-month point, as seen in Figure 5.12.

**TABLE 5.8** Analytics for a portfolio that combines an interest rate swap and a Eurodollar futures contract.

Valuation Analysis
SWAPPORT—1/04/2012
FactSet/R-Squared Daily Global Multi-Asset-Class Model (USD)
U.S. Dollar

| Ticker | | Portfolio Ending Market Value | Portfolio Ending Quantity Held | Portfolio Ending Effective Duration | Portfolio Contribution to Ending Effective Duration | MC Value at Risk 30-Day, 95% | MC Stand-Alone Value at Risk 30-Day, 95% | MC % Value at Risk 30-Day, 95% |
|---|---|---|---|---|---|---|---|---|
| | **Portfolio** | **–67,135.94** | | | | **20,198.34** | **20,198.34** | **33.64** |
| | Eurodollar (CME) Dec. 16 | 3,899,000.00 | 4,000,000 | 0.25 | –14.23 | –5,866.91 | 6,686.81 | –9.77 |
| 912810EZ | SWAPFIX_Payor | –1,059,073.40 | –1,000,000 | 5.51 | 86.85 | 27,496.32 | 27,893.33 | 45.80 |
| USZ1 | SWAPFLT_Payor | 991,937.46 | 1,000,000 | 0.16 | –2.40 | –1,477.57 | 4,436.49 | –2.46 |

Holdings Data As Of
SWAPPORT 1/04/2012
Risk Model As Of
FactSet/R-Squared Daily Global Multi-Asset-Class Model (USD) 1/04/2012

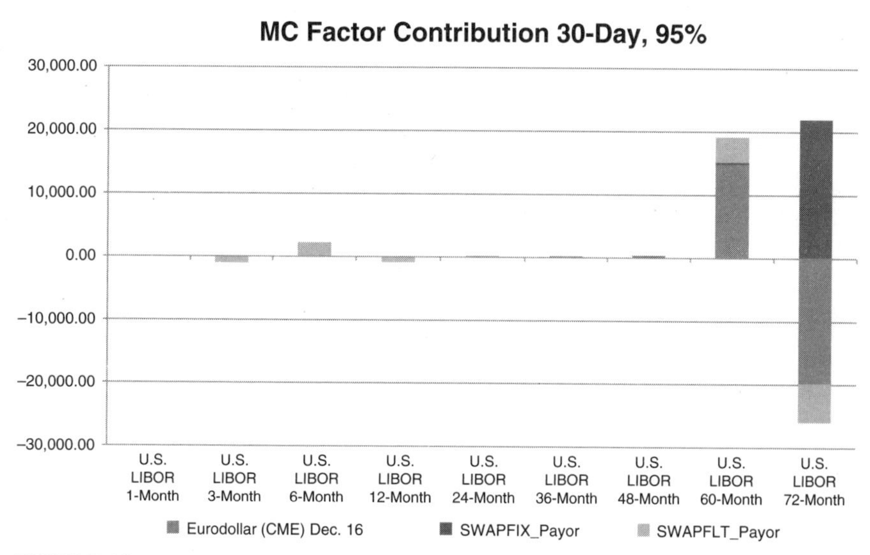


**FIGURE 5.12** Monte Carlo factor risk contribution profile by partial rate for an interest rate swap combined with a Eurodollar futures contract position.

## CONCLUSION

In this chapter we visited some interesting history of options; discussed deviations from Black-Scholes, volatility skew, and implied volatility surface modeling; and of course went over several types of derivative instruments that are used to reduce portfolio risk. We showed how we can achieve superior risk reduction by properly attributing the interest rate exposure of interest rate futures rather than using a one-dimensional measure such as effective durations. We then looked at how second-order effects can also be addressed by adding interest rate options to a mortgage portfolio. We also showed how Eurodollar futures can be efficiently used to target specific portions of the interest rate risk profile of a swap position. Eurodollar futures can be used in baskets of maturities that can target several such points. In addition to interest rate risk, we showed how credit default swaps modeled within FactSet can be used to reduce the credit risk due to holding corporate bonds. A portfolio manager can effectively create an almost riskless position by combining a corporate bond, a CDS, and a selection of interest rate derivatives in a portfolio. FactSet's balanced risk product will correctly treat all those risk exposures because it addresses the partial durations, convexities, and cross-partial (diagonal) interest rate effects, as well as any spread effects in modeling and simulating risk factors.

## NOTES

1. H. E. Leland and M. Rubinstein, "The Evolution of Portfolio Insurance," in *Portfolio Insurance: A Guide to Dynamic Hedging*, ed. Donald Luskin (New York: John Wiley & Sons, 1988).
2. Mark Rubinstein, "Comments on the 1987 Stock Market Crash: Eleven Years Later," Society of Actuaries and personal correspondence.
3. Fischer Black and Myron Scholes, "The Pricing of Options and Corporate Liabilities," *Journal of Political Economy* 81, no. 3 (May–June 1973): 637–654.
4. F. Black, "Studies of Stock Price Volatility Changes," Proceedings of the 1976 Meetings of the American Statistical Association, Business and Economic Statistic Section, 177–181.
5. F. Black, "Fact and Fantasy in the Use of Options," *Financial Analysts Journal* 31 (July/August 1975).
6. Black and Scholes, "Pricing of Options and Corporate Liabilities."
7. Jim Gatheral, *The Volatility Surface*, Wiley Finance (Hoboken, NJ: John Wiley & Sons, 2006).
8. G. Barone-Adesi and R. Whaley, "Efficient Analytic Approximation of American Option Values," *Journal of Finance* 42, no. 2 (June 1987).
9. J. Cox, S. Ross, and M. Rubinstein, "Option Pricing: A Simplified Approach," *Journal of Financial Economics* 7 (1979): 229–263.
10. John C. Hull, *Options, Futures and Other Derivatives*, 7th ed. (Upper Saddle River, NJ: Pearson Prentice-Hall, 2009): 413–414.
11. Stefano M. Iacus, *Option Pricing and Estimation of Financial Models with R* (Hoboken, NJ: John Wiley & Sons, 2011).

CHAPTER 6

# Measuring Asset Association and Dependence

***Steven P. Greiner, PhD; Andrew Geer, CFA, FRM; Christopher Carpentier, CFA, FRM; and Dan diBartolomeo***

## THE SAMPLE COVARIANCE MATRIX

Ascertaining the association between assets is one of the fundamental considerations of risk analysis. Security association is dependent on many factors, but estimating their covariance has historically been the objective for asset managers, pension owners, banks, insurers, and firms that hold assets against liabilities of some sort. Regardless of the asset class, if one can ascertain a reliable estimate of the association between assets (assuming stationarity), one is at least halfway to determining the risk of a portfolio holding such assets.

Before we discuss measures of asset association, however, first we draw attention to the importance of stationarity. Stationarity is what makes risk estimates useful. Without it, the estimate itself is unreliable. It also implies that the correlation and nonlinear dependence structure between securities exists for a long enough period of time that an estimate of risk based on the historical period most recently experienced will persist as far into the future as the horizon is forecasted. This persistence through time for both idiosyncratic volatility and asset association is a necessary condition for risk modeling to be dependable.

It's the structural dislocation of asset association that is the domain of so-called Black Swans. In simple terms, when major economic events happen like the financial crisis of 2008 instigated from the subprime mortgage debacle in the United States, the association between assets changes abruptly, seemingly similar to how earthquakes are the result of tectonic fault slippage away from some underlying equilibrium. During economic crisis, investors tend to flee from and to similar assets in their run for coverage. This lemming effect of investor behavior aggregates risk, resulting in correlations rising between all types of assets. In so doing, the dependence structure dislocates from its long-term trend, away from the most recent dependence regime. This regime is often termed a *volatility regime*, but that's the reflexive interpretation of the underlying asset dependence structural equilibrium that is in effect. Characterizing the phenomenon as a *covariance structural regime* is the more appropriate term.

The first-line measure of this dependence structure involves the covariance matrix of assets. Covariance is a linear measure of association offering "no comment" on nonlinear association. For that, one needs a copula. The term *copula* was coined in 1959 by Abe Sklar in the theorem that now bears his name describing the functions that join together one-dimensional distribution functions to form multivariate distribution functions. In general terms, given two time series produced from some underlying returns-based generating process, each has its own probability distribution, while combined they have a joint probability distribution. The utility of the copula comes from its ability to unite these two seemingly separate distributions to form a multivariate distribution, where the marginal distribution of one is simply its probability distribution while averaging over the other. A copula basically confines the joint distribution function to be a function only of the marginals. In this way, the marginals can be completely nonlinear, whereas in covariance we have only a scalar representing how one marginal changes with another (a betalike representation), not a function.

Due to the lack of computational resources available to Harry Markowitz in 1952, he restricted his analysis to covariance rather than semivariance, which he had espoused in its favor in the first place. Copulas were used before 1959, when Sklar coined the term, but since they were too mathematically complex when applied to more than a few assets, they were unavailable in practice.[1] This directed efforts in risk management and portfolio construction toward adopting covariance as the most suitable and practical approach for risk estimation, the hammer for every nail, so to speak.

## ESTIMATION ERROR MAXIMIZATION

It has been known for some time that utilizing a covariance matrix in portfolio optimization tends toward overweighting assets that have large alpha estimates, negative correlations, and small variances. Likewise, a covariance matrix is known for underweighting securities with converse properties. In effect, it leverages estimation error.[2] However, the alpha estimates generally contain larger errors than the risk model's covariance matrix, which can be observed from an analysis of *ex ante* versus *ex post* alpha and risk estimates. Typically, the risk of a portfolio is more accurately forecasted than the return, and risk trends show high correlation between their forecasts and realizations, unless a Black Swan strikes. The radical and dynamic upheaval of the covariance structure introduced by a Black Swan event isn't tracked closely by most risk models because they usually aren't calibrated to react quickly enough. There has been active research to deal with the estimation error problem, including Black-Litterman[3] and Bayesian methods, but this approach has focused on the estimation error issue from the alpha side of the optimization. These methods hinge on lowering alpha estimation error by utilizing reverse optimization to determine the market's implied returns. Afterward, the users can add, edit, or modify the market's estimates of alpha with their own. In this fashion, the mixing of the market's implied alphas with the investors' can be expected to anticipate true return more closely than outright individual investor forecasts alone. Michaud's solution to the problem involved resampling the alpha and covariance estimates from the empirical data and feeding the resamples into the optimizer again and again. The optimal portfolio solution was the average of all the outcomes from this process. He patented this approach.[4]

MSCI-Barra has documented for sample covariance estimates the ratio of estimated to true variance scales as $\sim(1 - n/T)$, where $n$ is the number of assets and $T$ is the number of time periods.[5] Ratios below 1 indicate that underforecasting bias is present. The researchers go on to demonstrate that when using a parsimonious risk model to construct the covariance matrix rather than a sample matrix, the bias scales as $\sim k/T$ as opposed to $n/T$, where $k$ is the number of factors in the risk model. Then estimation error affects a $k \times k$ matrix versus an $n \times n$ matrix, which, having fewer dimensions, has lower susceptibility for bias introduction.

Axioma, in contrast, deals with estimation error during optimization by including the uncertainty in the input parameters simultaneously in the optimization.[6] This robust optimization methodology is quite sophisticated but produces portfolios that have a higher correlation between *ex ante* forecasts and *ex post* risk realizations.

If one approaches dealing with this issue from the covariance matrix construction viewpoint, shrinkage methods come to mind. In this process, the covariance is attacked directly and the extreme elements are drawn toward less exuberant values by utilizing simple averaging techniques.

## MINIMIZING THE EXTREMES

To discuss the topic of shrinkage and why we recommend it, we copy from two references as opposed to restating the obvious. These quotations lay the groundwork for the motivation of developing and implementing this schema in the FactSet Balanced Risk product.

The central message to "Honey, I Shrunk the Sample Covariance Matrix" by Olivier Ledoit and Michael Wolf is:

> *[N]obody should be using the sample covariance matrix for the purpose of portfolio optimization. It contains estimation error of the kind most likely to perturb a mean-variance optimizer. In its place, we suggest using the matrix obtained from the sample covariance matrix through a transformation called shrinkage. This tends to pull the most extreme coefficients towards more central values, thereby systematically reducing estimation error where it matters most. Statistically, the challenge is to know the optimal shrinkage intensity.*[7]

From "Shrinking the Covariance Matrix" by David Disatnik and Simon Benninga we read (abridged):

> *Estimation of the covariance matrix, like any other estimation process, is subject to error, whether sampling error or specification error. The traditional and probably the most intuitive estimator of the covariance matrix is the sample covariance. This estimator often suffers from the curse of dimensions; in many cases the stock return time series period used for estimation is not long enough compared to the number of stocks considered. As a result, the estimated covariance matrix is ill conditioned. Several authors were recently shown to have concentrated on estimators using monthly data, assuming both return stationarity and that sample variances are good estimators of the stock variances. A fundamental principle of statistical theory is that there is a trade-off between sampling error and specification error. Hence, in order to develop a better estimator, one must reduce the huge sampling error of the sample matrix without creating too much specification error.*
>
> *The findings of others suggest that the best estimators of this type are shrinkage estimators and portfolios of estimators. Roughly speaking, in our context, a shrinkage estimator is usually a weighted average of the sample matrix with an invertible covariance matrix estimator on which quite a lot of structure is imposed and whose diagonal elements are the sample variances. As a result, the off-diagonal elements of the shrinkage estimator are shrunk compared to the typically large off-diagonal elements of the sample matrix while the variance elements in the diagonal are kept untouched.*[8]

Experiments run by these authors strongly suggest that optimization with shrinkage has improved Sharpe ratios and meant smaller differences between *ex ante* versus *ex post* returns and risks for various simple shrinkage recipes. In FactSet's Balanced Risk product, there is impetus to utilize shrinkage in the multi-asset-class (MAC) risk model to lower estimation error. In the construction of the MAC covariance matrix, there is a look-back period of one year, with factors numbering well into the hundreds, which include equity factors of style, industry, currency, and region along with commodity factors and fixed income factors for interest rate movements and spread risks for many asset types. We bump up against having $k$ greater than $T$ readily. While at this writing the product is not associated with any optimizer, it's clear that estimation error is inherently within the matrix elements. So even though we use a parametric risk model construction reducing the $N$ by orders of magnitude (there are ~40,000 global equity securities alone), one still has estimation error sensitivities to deal with in a parsimonious risk model of the MAC variety.

To account for this issue, we ran simulations to help set some guidelines on the type of target shrinkage matrix to use and gauge an estimate of acceptable shrinkage coefficient ranges, assuming a linear adaptation of a shrinkage model such that:

$$\begin{aligned}\text{Covariance matrix} = {} & \text{Original covar* } (1 - \text{Coefficient}) \\ & + \text{Target covar* Coefficient}\end{aligned} \tag{6.1}$$

The target matrices examined, while not a complete set, have the conditional constraint that they are evolved from the identical data from which the original sample covariance matrix is contrived. There are four target matrices and two controls. The data set consists of 2,564 global stocks, commodities, and currency time series of daily returns from December 31, 2007, until May 8, 2012. In total, 1,098 daily return values were obtained. The target matrices were:

- *Historical matrix:* A target matrix obtained by taking the covariance of the original data set using all the data's history since inception. It does not have any time decay. The diagonals were replaced with those of the original sample covariance matrix (to be specified) so only the covariance or off-diagonal elements were kept.
- *Eigen matrix:* This method takes the sample covariance matrix, computes the eigenvalues and eigen functions, and then determines how many eigenvalues should be kept to account for 70 percent to 80 percent of the variance. The appropriate number of eigen functions was then used to replicate a return distribution that is the basis for a new set

of covariance calculations. This last covariance matrix is then used as a target matrix. The diagonals were replaced by the sample covariance diagonal matrix's values.

- *Local averaging:* This matrix is produced by making a copy of the original sample covariance, replacing the diagonals with zero values, retaining the upper tri-diagonal elements, and then forming a box of size (4 × 4) and/or (5 × 5) around each off-diagonal element and averaging all values within the box. A final target matrix is created by replacing the original sample matrix off-diagonal elements with these box-averaged off-diagonal elements. The original diagonal elements were retained.
- *Off-diagonal average:* This matrix averages *all* off-diagonal elements and replaces the original off-diagonals with this tri-diagonal average. All covariance values were identical for this target matrix.
- Two controls were created consisting of the *original sample covariance matrix*, time-weighted (half-life of approximately one year) with a one-year look-back, and another that is a matrix consisting only of the *diagonals* of the sample covariance matrix, where all off-diagonals were set to zero. Shrinkage techniques were not applied to these matrices and they were used in the experiment as they were.

Once these matrices were created, a series of simulation experiments were performed. The ultimate goal was to create a minimum variance portfolio of assets that resembled an actual strategy of this nature, and to compare its realized performance and risk to corresponding forecasted values. To do this, cheap alpha estimates were created to feed into the mean-variance optimization. The sequence of operations consisted of the following seven steps:

1. Given a time series of daily returns for 2,564 global stocks, commodities, and currencies, the first 252 trading days were used to specify a working time period for sample covariance matrix and target matrix construction. Subsequently, a rolling time period consisting of 252 trading days, incremented by 21 days (approximately one month), was utilized in the simulation. The first time period was day 1 through day 252 of the data set, the second time period was day 23 through 274, and so on.
2. For each 252-day time period, random portfolios were created with 70 to 100 assets.
3. Alpha estimates were obtained by using two technical factors, each constructed by using a three-month (66-day) look-back period. One factor was idiosyncratic daily volatility (1/vol, specifically since volatility and return have negative correlation), while the other utilized an ordinary least squares regression determined slope coefficient of the

last (66th) day's price divided by the most current day's price. This was adapted from the R-Squared equity model, which resides on FactSet and is also used in cross-sectional regressions within FactSet's commodity risk model. Every security randomly selected for the portfolio had an alpha estimate created for each of these two measures for every time period; they were then Z-scored and added together to form a total alpha estimate for each security.

4. Using equation (6.1), shrunk matrices were created from each of the *four* targets for *five* shrink coefficients of 0.1, 0.3, 0.5, 0.7, and 0.9.
5. For each of the *five* shrunk matrices created from the *four* targets, including the two control matrices, ordinary mean-variance optimization was performed for long-only constrained portfolios to maximize utility of the following form:

$$\text{Utility} = \text{Alpha}^{*}\ \text{Weight} - [t(\text{Weight})^{*}\ \text{Covar}^{*}\ \text{Weight}] \quad (6.2)$$

6. For each portfolio, the optimal solution's return was measured from the initial date of optimization and the next month's optimization, when the portfolio was subsequently rebalanced. The optimization date was selected as the ending date of each 252 daily period used for sample covariance matrix estimation. In this fashion, the results were out-of-sample.
7. The daily standard deviation of returns for the optimal solution portfolio was collected and measured against its forecasted risk for the initial date of optimization. In this way a time series of *ex ante* minus *ex post* risk, or forecasted minus realized risk, was measured and averaged.

In summary, every 22 days a sample covariance matrix was ascertained, shrunk matrices created, optimizations run, and performance measured sequentially from start to finish over the 1,098 daily return values for random portfolios constructed from 2,564 assets. One hundred randomly generated portfolios, using a variety of settings, were run through this sequence.

The results are displayed in Figures 6.1 through 6.3. We find the best discriminator to be that of realized total risk (variance) versus forecasted total risk (variance), averaged through time across all portfolios. The first chart is for 100 optimized portfolios of 75 assets, each with a one-year look-back, a box size of 4, and eigenvalues kept to account for 80 percent of the original return variance. We show five results for each target as a function of the shrink coefficients.

In Figure 6.1, we display the control, sample covariance matrix (org-covar) on the left. Obviously, since it's not shrunk, the results are identical for all coefficients. Oddly, the eigen matrix, though shrunk, barely budges

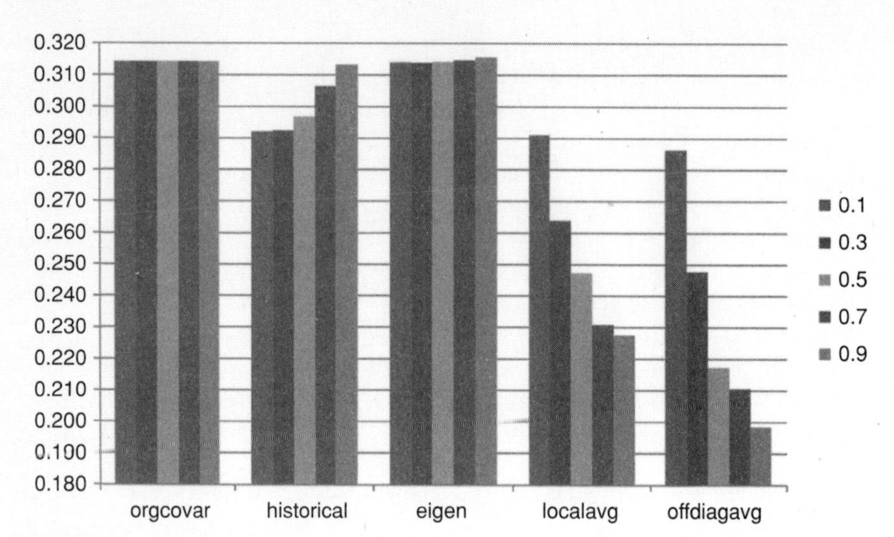


**FIGURE 6.1** We display the control, sample covariance matrix (orgcovar) on the left, which is not shrunk. The shrunk target matrices, including the historical covariance matrix from the whole time period, the eigenvector matrix, and the two from local averaging over a box size and from averaging all off-diagonal components, are listed consecutively, left to right. The legend lists the shrinkage coefficients for each run from equation (6.1).

for different shrinkage coefficients. It must mimic the original covariance matrix too much and, by observing random off-diagonal components of its resultant covariance matrix, they aren't too different from the original. Enough eigen functions were kept to account for 80 percent of the variance (not shown), and the covariance matrix wasn't different enough from the originals. The local averaging and off-diagonal averaging methods show the most significant reduction between realized and forecasted risk.

The next chart, Figure 6.2, dramatizes similar results for 100 optimized portfolios consisting of 100 assets each, using one-year look-back for formation of the covariance, with a box size of 4 and keeping enough eigen functions to account for only 70 percent of the variance of the original returns. In this chart, we include the diagonal control matrix as well (far right). Obviously, for this latter matrix there are no covariance values, so a minimum variance portfolio would have larger risks than the original sample covariance matrix depicted on the far left. The data illustrate that truth. The shrunk target matrices are the four outcomes in the middle as a function of shrinkage coefficients.

Here we can see that the eigen matrix is beginning to differentiate now as a function of shrunk coefficient; however, the discrepancy between the

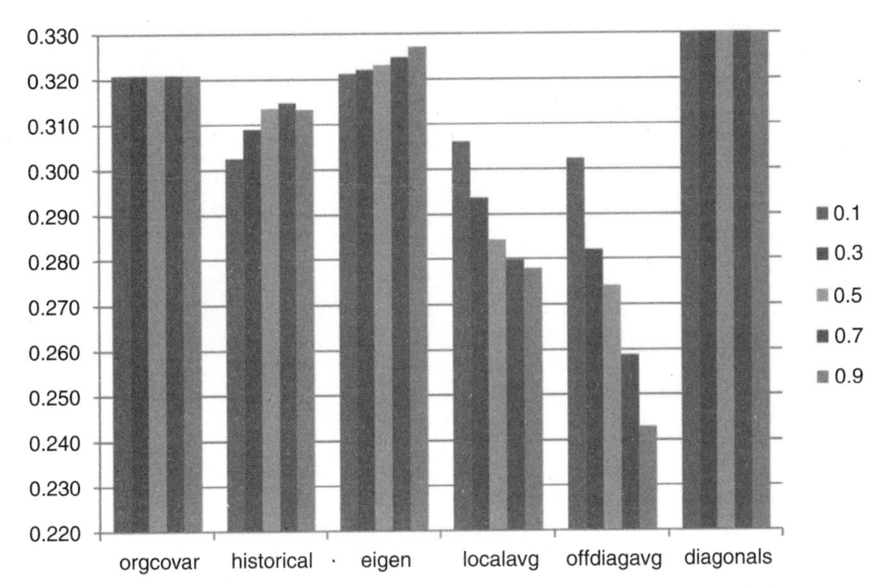


**FIGURE 6.2** Similar results for 100 optimized portfolios consisting of 100 assets each, one-year look-back for formation of the covariance, with a box size of 4 for the local averaging method, and keeping enough eigen functions to account for only 70 percent of the variance of the original returns. The legend lists the shrinkage coefficient options.

realized and forecasted risks is increasing, not decreasing. The local averaging technique, along with the off-diagonal method, shows similar results as before, which is closing the difference between forecasts and realized risk.

Our last experiment (see Figure 6.3) is designed to push the usage of shrinkage toward what it really should be used for, underdetermined risk forecasts with high estimation error. For this example, we limit the look-back period for each portfolio to only 70 days while forming random portfolios of 100 assets. We show the chart for 100 random minimum variance portfolios of 100 assets each for a box size of 5 and keeping enough eigen functions to account for 70 percent of the original return variance.

In this last chart (Figure 6.3), we can see that the covariance estimate has tighter results between realized and forecasted risk (far left) for the original sample matrix relative to using just the diagonals (far right), which uses only individual security variances for portfolio optimization and subsequent risk forecasts. When a portfolio is optimized using a covariance matrix consisting of only variance estimates and no covariance off-diagonal estimates, the amount by which realized risk exceeds the forecast is greater than when covariance estimates are included. This probably has to do with

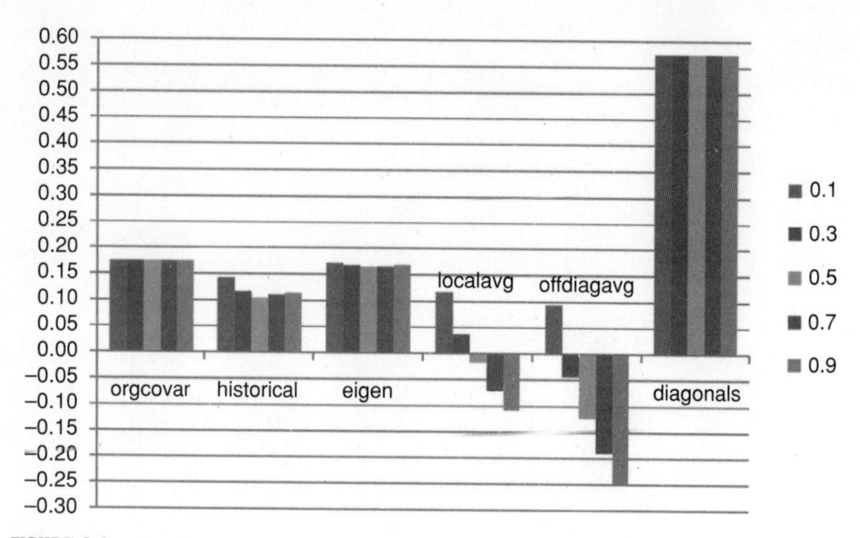


**FIGURE 6.3** Our last experiment is designed to push the usage of shrinkage toward what it really should be used for underdetermined risk forecasts with high estimation error. For this example, we limit the look-back period for each portfolio to 70 days while forming random portfolios of 100 assets. We show the bar chart for 100 random minimum variance portfolios of 100 assets each for a box size of 5 and keeping enough eigen functions to account for 70 percent of the original return variance. Therefore, we have an underdetermined covariance matrix here with significant estimation error.

not realizing a real minimum-variance portfolio during the optimization so that the outcome is a portfolio that could be anywhere within the efficient frontier, not actually on it. This anecdote does not have any bearing on the shrinkage methodology, but is deemed a worthwhile observation to note.

For the shrinkage portfolios, we can see that the difference between the realized versus forecasted risk variance is driven toward zero (on average through time and for all portfolios) for middling shrinkage coefficients approaching 0.5 for the local averaging method and below zero for the off-diagonal method. This tells us that by applying shrinkage heavily (large coefficients) we can actually achieve portfolios with less risk than the forecast. That is rare in risk analysis and it demonstrates that estimation error really is important when the time series of stock returns used for estimation ($T = 70$) is not long enough relative to the number of securities ($N = 100$).

The results of shrinkage applications are dependent upon the portfolio, number of assets, time period of the covariance estimate forecast, and the shrinkage coefficient. Thus it's difficult to identify the optimal criteria in a deterministic way for any portfolio or estimation universe. Using simulations across different assets, different portfolio sizes, varying look-back periods, and different setup parameters, we conclude that a good choice for shrinkage application involves the local averaging or off-diagonal methods. Likewise, shrinkage coefficients of approximately 0.2+/– may be most appropriate, erring on the smaller side for the off-diagonal method.

## THE COPULA, THE MOST COMPREHENSIVE DEPENDENT STRUCTURE MEASURE

We have to discuss why the copula is not more widely utilized among today's risk modeling construction techniques. Similarly, why has the covariance matrix and its subsequent legacy remained so strong given the modern computational prowess of the desktop PC and server farms when the copula is a much better measure of the asset dependence structure? One might assume the answer is obvious. For large portfolios, computers still aren't fast enough for dependence structure ascertainment, risk decomposition, and back-testing under a copula framework, and you'd be right, but that isn't the whole story.

Pearson's correlation, Kendall's tau, and Spearman's rho are other measurements for quantifying dependence. However, correlation is reserved for linear association and is the derivation of the covariance matrix. The latter two measures, tau and rho, are obtained readily from a copula and provide truer association measures than the covariance matrix. This calls into question why these measures haven't replaced the covariance matrix among asset and risk managers. First, tau and rho aren't easily formulated in a utility function framework, which is the standard approach for most commercial portfolio optimizers. Further, the difficulty is not just including the measures in the utility framework but also developing ways to handle their solutions, which may include nonconvex results that are much more difficult to solve. Second, creating the copula from the estimation universe in the first place is difficult because large multidimensional copulas usually have poor goodness-of-fit statistics compared to covariance estimation. That is, the estimation error is higher under copula formation. Moreover, pension funds may have thousands of securities. If you cannot obtain goodness-of-fit measures for 100-asset portfolios with multidimensional copulas, you can forget about 2,000-asset portfolios. This is a similar problem to multivariate Garch (M-Garch) techniques. The fitting algorithms just often fail to converge.

A FactSet risk vendor commented that from a portfolio manager's perspective of investing, controlling risk isn't the goal; rather, the goal is to produce a return in excess of the risk-free rate generally or to outperform a benchmark. This means that for investing to be a viable exercise, portfolio managers must have some method for forecasting average future returns for each asset. All classical theories of asset pricing (capital asset pricing model [CAPM], arbitrage pricing theory [APT], Fama-French, and so forth) usually assume linearity in the economic relationships for return forecasting, as do most sell-side and buy-side quant alpha models. If returns are forecasted with linear models, then traditional correlation statistics should be sufficient. If you have to use copulas to explain asset behavior, then you need to replace existing asset pricing theory with something else. What exactly is that something else? That is a very good question.

Commercial risk models are used not only to measure the risk of portfolios but also to communicate information about portfolio risks and exposures between managers and clients. Most pension funds and other asset owners don't have personnel with sufficient technical expertise to interpret output from more complex models. At best you could move from a traditional Pearson correlation to a more robust measure like Kendall's tau because you could oversimplify and just call it correlation even though that isn't really the case. It is actually a scalar proxy for nonlinear association.

Additionally, traditional statistics like correlation have well-known forms for the standard error and other diagnostics. Except for a few very well-behaved special cases, the standard errors and sampling statistics for a particular copula are apt to be poorly defined. You can use numerical methods to get there, but it's a lot of work for asset managers who believe their time should be spent on higher economic value prospects for the return forecasting process (i.e., company research).

One famous application of copulas in finance involved the use of the Gaussian copula for calculating expected defaults in mortgage securitizations. Many people believe this was a complete disaster and was a key cause of the 2008 financial crisis.[9] However, the lemmings effect that led to the housing crisis had more to do with continued overconfidence in property appreciation and subsequent lowering of lending standards than because of poor default correlation calculations that used the copula for mortgage risk assessment. The housing bubble and bust had plenty of contributing causes, including government-mandated subprime mortgage sales and overly eager brokers that provided mortgages with little lending oversight and even less documentation. Blaming the Gaussian copula model for the credit crisis that followed the housing bust is akin to blaming an oarsman for the centuries of Vikings pillaging Ireland.

A quote from *Wired* magazine by Nassim Taleb, the hedge fund manager and author of *The Black Swan*, is particularly harsh when it comes to the copula: "People got very excited about the Gaussian copula because of its mathematical elegance, but the thing never worked," he says. "Co-association between securities is not measurable using correlation, because past history can never prepare you for that one day when everything goes south. Anything that relies on correlation is charlatanism." The trouble with this simple diagnosis is that all estimates of the future rely on examining the past, and stationarity is a necessary and sufficient condition for minimizing the difference between forecasted and realized risk, with or without a copula. We've said that before in this book several times. If the covariance (i.e., dependence) structure stays reasonably stable, sans extreme events, then the forecasts are accurate enough and useful for daily risk management.

Taleb does indeed don a raincoat after he looks out the window and we all buy flood insurance if we live next to the Mississippi. But in neither case will the historical record allow us to determine the influence that a large meteor impact will have on the average rainy day or its ability to instigate a deluge. We all make decisions by examining the past frequency of events; the whole insurance industry is predicated on forecasting regular risky events with success most of the time. No good quant claims to be able to forecast extreme event risks, and the Gaussian copula wasn't at fault for not doing so. The classic misinterpretation of what risk forecasting is all about is the chronic error here.

The Gaussian copula was useful and provided a good framework for estimating the relationship between mortgage tranches in collateralized debt obligations (CDOs). What happened in the credit crisis was the banks decided they didn't have to hold mortgages if they could value them and sell them.[10] That, in and of itself, was and is a good idea. That they used a Gaussian copula predicated on data from a period of time in which housing prices were only trending upward and had low correlations across regions to ascertain an estimate of asset concordance wasn't the origin of the problem, either. The problem began when they substituted the results of the copula's dependence calculation for mortgage default against commonsense investing principles of diversification so that a CDO that formerly contained commercial mortgages, student loans, car loans, credit card loans, and residential prime and subprime mortgages would now be stuffed with highly correlated assets since the bankers felt they had a better handle on the dependence estimate. What they failed to consider shouldn't be blamed on the copula. They hadn't stress-tested their model against mercurial environments. It wasn't the use of the copula that made this error; it was the risk managers who were at fault for assuming a perpetually stationary process. This could happen to risk modelers using a covariance matrix for asset correlation estimates as well. You don't need a copula to make that error. If this book teaches anything, it's that covariance and copula risk assessment is for regular environments only, not for extreme event Black Swan risks. For them, one needs stress-testing.

A related but separate observation is that just going further into the tail in a VaR estimate also won't prepare you for risk estimation of an extreme event. It will only estimate large risks in the market environment used to construct the estimate with. You need to use a stressed covariance matrix like in the credit crisis on your current portfolio exposures to estimate Black Swan event risks.

Last, after securitizing and selling mortgages, banks started buying them back. The trouble here was the bank departments selling them were not the same ones buying them. The sellers probably knew a bit more about the riskiness of these products than the groups buying them, but they either didn't know enough or didn't accurately represent the riskiness of the products when they sold them. Of course, the banks buying these assets wrongfully assumed that the sellers and rating agencies had done their proper due diligence when "stuffing" and rating the CDOs, only to be woefully surprised when housing prices reversed course and the bubble burst.

The copula wasn't at fault here, but let's be clear: the interpretation of it was. Likewise, a covariance matrix assessment, whether built from sample returns or from some parsimonious factor risk model, is only as good as the data put into it. The takeaway is: don't conclude that the risk forecast, whether from a good copula assessment or covariance, will hold during extreme events. For risk attribution, portfolio construction, factor exposure analysis, and hedging, assessments from both covariance and copula give good answers. Like any model, though, they have value if you appreciate they are a convenient way to capture the description of a complex interaction under the concordance environment they're modeled with. If they are exploited by unscrupulous agents, however, whether for actual cause or blame, the result can be most unfortunate.

## THE MODEL COVARIANCE MATRIX

The FactSet multi-asset-class (MAC) risk model integrates R-Squared's equity risk model with its own fixed income and commodity risk model factors. Traditionally, model components are all estimated at the same time; however, this is not the case here since the R-Squared equity model is delivered to FactSet with its own covariance matrix. To incorporate our fixed income and commodity factors, we put aside the covariance matrix given to us by R-Squared, and build a new one that incorporates the equity, fixed income, commodity, and derivative factors.

By using the history of factor returns from the R-Squared equity model, along with the history of factor returns from the additional fixed income and commodity factors, we can calculate the new comprehensive covariance matrix that can now cover equities, commodities, fixed income, and their derivatives. Going forward, if coverage is expanded and a new factor is necessary, a history of factor returns for the new factor is needed first, and then the same process is used to calculate and include this new factor in the matrix.

This risk model is designed to be short-term in nature with a forecast horizon that is suitable from one day to two months. The forecast horizon is calibrated with a 0.994 exponential decay rate and two years' worth of daily factor returns.

We have discussed an overview of the issues involved in covariance estimation, when it is appropriate, and under what assumptions it's useful. Though the authors have heard proponents cry since the credit crisis, "The standard deviation used as a risk measure is outdated," it has also been said, "If I could only know one single risk measure, it would be the standard deviation deduced from a well-constructed covariance matrix." We agree.

## NOTES

1. Edward Frees and Emiliano Valdez, "Understanding Relationships Using Copulas," 32nd Annual Actuarial Conference, August 6–8, 1997, University of Calgary, Calgary, Alberta, Canada; Roger Nielsen, *An Introduction to Copulas*, 2nd ed., Springer Series in Statistics (New York: Springer, 2010).
2. Richard O. Michaud, "The Markowitz Optimization Enigma: Is 'Optimized' Optimal?" *Financial Analysts Journal*, January/February 1989.
3. F. Black and R. Litterman, "Global Portfolio Optimization," *Financial Analysts Journal* 48, no. 5 (September/October 1992): 28–43.
4. R. Michaud, "Portfolio Optimization by Means of Resampled Efficient Frontiers," U.S. Patents 6,003,018 (1999), 7,412,414 (2008), and 7,624,060 (2009).
5. Jennifer Bender, Jyh-Huei Lee, Dan Stefak, and Jay Yao, "Forecast Risk Bias in Optimized Portfolios," presented at Denver QWAFAFEW meeting, Denver, CO, March 2011.
6. Sebastian Ceria and Robert Stubbs, "Incorporating Estimation Errors into Portfolio Selection," Axioma Research Paper 003, May 2006.
7. Olivier Ledoit and Michael Wolf, "Honey, I Shrunk the Sample Covariance Matrix," UPF Economics and Business Working Paper 691, June/November 2003.
8. David J. Disatnik and Simon Benninga, "Shrinking the Covariance Matrix," *Journal of Portfolio Management*, Summer 2007.
9. Felix Salmon, "Recipe for Disaster: The Formula That Killed Wall Street," *Wired*, February 23, 2009; David Li, "On Default Correlation: A Copula Function Approach," *Journal of Fixed Income*, March 2000.
10. "In Defense of the Gaussian Copula," *Economist*, April 29, 2009.

CHAPTER 7

# Risk Model Construction

*Steven P. Greiner, PhD; Andrew Geer, CFA, FRM; Jason MacQueen; and Laurence Wormald, PhD*

This chapter focuses on the recipes for constructing your typical risk model; in particular, reference will be made to those models on FactSet. As usual, we'll offer a little history and develop a theme from there. We conclude with an introduction to historical methods, including Arch/Garch methodologies.

> Go to www.wiley.com/go/greiner to see video titled "Multi-Factor Risk Model."

## MULTIFACTOR PRESPECIFIED RISK MODELS

Barra, Inc. was started as a project between Barr Rosenberg and Andrew Rudd in 1975 while at the University of California, Berkeley. The two were specialists in operations research. They began what became an industry standard in risk modeling. Barra used cross-sectional models predicated on factors that were defined from fundamental financial statement data, but deferred to cross-sectional regressions, most likely because of the founders' backgrounds in operations research (decision science), which relies on this method heavily. Later, with the introduction of the Fama-French equations, support for the usage of financial statements as factor exposures grew, and other risk model vendors entered the market, producing variations of risk models that were still mostly constructed the same way, through regressions in cross-section for a given time period, done sequentially to create a time series of factor returns (betas).[1] These models became more flexible and introduced structure to covariance matrix estimations; by their methods they lowered systemic estimation error, but not without model specification error, for each model had a different set of common factors, none being "God's equation" describing returns precisely. However, finding the optimal trade-off by deciding on the kind and number of factors to introduce in a risk model is as much art as it is science, and no one method can claim itself the best method, for each has pros and cons.

Barra had no competitor in the risk space until Dan diBartolomeo incorporated Northfield Information Systems (NIS) in 1985. It was two more years, though, before NIS was launched with its first customer in 1987. As of this writing, the FactSet system has risk models from five vendors numbering over 200 varying types.

Of the various ways of detailing risk, prespecifying the factors was undoubtedly the obvious operation to perform for Barra, simply because we live in a parametric world and the asset management profession grew up associating asset (company) returns to business fundamentals vis-à-vis Graham and Dodd's *Security Analysis* of 1934 and its incarnations since. One of the most important issues a portfolio manager (PM) should use in deciding which risk model to use involves choosing one whose factors most closely follow the PM's decision making process in asset selection. In its simplest sense, risk models are formal statements about the relationships of asset returns in any collection of securities. Any collection, whether index, group, or portfolio of securities, has volatility risk, and a risk model's first responsibilities are to assign those risks to what is common among the assets. It's precisely these common risks that historically were predefined by Barra and others afterward. These fundamental variables are collected first from financial statements such as found on the balance, income, or cash flow accounting sheets. Then, industry, country (region), or currencies factors are usually added to the group of common factors. Sometimes macroeconomic factors are included or substituted, as are trading volume and various momentum (technical) factors as well. At this point of model specification, the raw values these factors can take are termed *exposures*. They are usually winsorized and Z-scored as well before application of any statistics, though ranking the exposures in line with Spearman's correlation conditions is also performed at times, especially when interpretation of the distribution of the exposures is nebulous at best.[2]

For a customized risk model specific for a certain type of portfolio (i.e., U.S. domestic small-cap value or global large-cap growth, for instance) the factors may be decisive, highly granular, and even industry specific. For the risk vendors, however, who are building perhaps a single risk model for an entire market to be used by many clients in that space, risk factors are generally of a higher level and looser granularity. They have to be, to offer exposures to securities that may be less liquid and have less data. Even so, they serve to capture the common risks with sufficient accuracy for any collection of securities drawn from an estimation universe of thousands of securities. This is because the mere operation of reducing (to a model) a full sample of covariance interactions down to a parsimonious few factors (~10,000 securities covariance matrix being reduced to maybe ~120 factors) eliminates noise and deciphers the major themes and trends of the causes of risk. In prespecification of the factors, one is indeed specifying the cause of the risks, but being logical in their selection as economically intrinsic to returns, and is using judicious techniques to adequately apportion each factor's contribution to the risk.

The models can do this because they are derived from the price/return patterns of securities over time. To the extent in regular markets (not driven by extreme events) the past patterns exhibit stationary behavior (meaning that volatility and correlation regimes persist for months), the investor can act upon the forecast appropriately and use the model to minimize or lower risk subject to portfolio constraints and investing mandates. In the overwhelming number of risk models constructed both by vendors and by individual customization, linear regression is the tool of choice to relate asset returns to risk factors. If you realize that all classical asset pricing models have used linear relationships historically, there's no overwhelming pressure to re-create a nonlinear wheel, so to speak.

The type of factors selected preconditions the type of regression chosen also. First, if the exposures are stable through time, it's better to use time-series regressions. If, however, the exposures fluctuate with significant dispersion through time, cross-sectional regressions are chosen. For instance, take equity valuation. It's usually the case that one buys a low-valued stock based on price-to-book (P/B) or price-to-earnings (P/E) ratio and holds that stock long enough for the low-valued stock to become a highly valued stock. This implies, then, that the P/B or valuation factor changes magnitude over time, and this change can be quite large in the numerical value for the exposure. This would mean the beta to valuation would also be more dynamic in its behavior. To the contrary, one might expect that the exposure to an industry lasts a long time with little change. Consider a smaller health care company trading on U.S. exchanges, where its stock is denominated in USD. Chances are that it won't overnight suddenly become an industrial stock with EUR exposure. Even if the company begins selling in Europe, it may take years for sales to increase in Europe enough to acquire EUR exposure and possibly engage in enough manufacturing to gain industrial exposure. Generally, a stock's exposure to an industry and currency is relatively stable through time compared to a valuation estimate, or any fundamental or style variable for that matter.

This defines reasons why one performs cross-sectional regressions on style and fundamental factors and time series on industry, currency, and country. Theoretically, one could simply decompose the common elements of risk to a single beta like the capital asset pricing model (CAPM). However, it's well disregarded as too simple and inappropriate for most applications these days. Few people consider a single CAPM beta (the market beta) as containing enough explanatory power to be useful anymore, though the CAPM beta is still often used for separating alpha from beta for a manager or mutual fund. What it has going for it, however, is enough stability for time-series regressions to be used for its determination. On the other hand, when a parsimonious Barra or Axioma risk model has ~120 factors and resultant betas and is readily available on demand, and when the granularity and clarity of multiple betas allow higher fidelity, clairvoyance, *ex ante* disclosure, and forecasting ability, then frankly, it's silly to refer to CAPM beta anymore. It's very much like comparing the candle with rigid LED driving light bars for luminescence. If you've ever seen these light bars installed on a motorcycle, they're blinding even in bright sunlight! So the analogy fits for illuminating the risks in a portfolio, which leads to the Tarzan definition, "CAPM beta bad, multifactor risk models good!"

The nomenclature has to be reviewed quickly for multifactor models. For cross-sectional regression, in the U.S. factor exposures are the actual numerical values one obtains for a security—the P/B, P/E, accruals, working capital, and so forth. Even after winsorizing and Z-scoring they retain that name (exposures), whereas in the EU these are often called betas. The regression problem is set up with a column of return versus a matrix of exposures for a given date, and the resultant regression coefficients are the betas in the United States, whereas in Europe again, they're called exposures. Additionally, the betas are constant for all assets at a single point in time. That is, a regression of return for 5,000 stocks against 120 factors yields only 120 betas for the particular date of the regression. Hence, regressing daily returns against factors every day for a year results in a year's worth of betas for each factor. All assets have the same beta to P/B, for example, at a single point in time, though each asset has its own exposure (using U.S. nomenclature). Vice versa if using the EU nomenclature. Betas determined through regression are usually called *factor returns* as well (if the topic isn't confusing enough already). Figure 7.1 displays the typical cross-sectional regression methodology for a multifactor risk model in an easy-to-understand cartoon.

In this figure, we show a vector of returns on the far left for each and every day, one day behind another. Then, just to the right of the equal sign, we show a matrix of factor exposures for each day, again one day behind another. Values in this matrix are the prespecified style or common factors for the assets. The returns vector is of length $n$, and the exposure matrix is

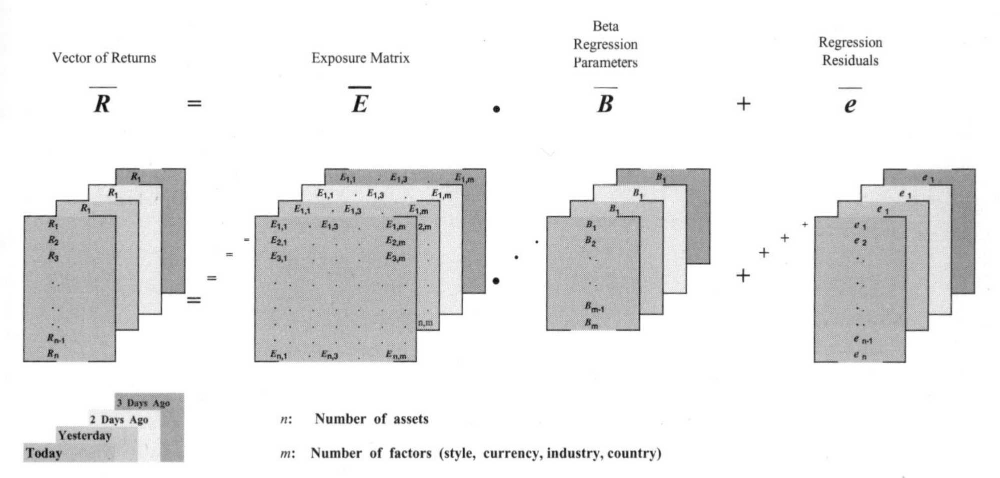


**FIGURE 7.1** A typical cross-sectional multifactor model setup.

of size $n \times m$, where $m$ is the number of factors. There is one regression on each day's set of data. After regression, there is a set of betas of length $m$, one beta for each factor each day, and every regression yields residuals of length $n$. To form the covariance matrix of the common factors, one simply takes the covariance between each of the daily beta vectors one with another. Ultimately, the residuals are assigned as the asset-specific factors and are used to make up the idiosyncratic covariance matrix. We remind the reader that only the idiosyncratic risks are diversifiable; common factor risks are not.

To illustrate this further, multifactor models are predicated on forming linear equations where future-period returns are regressed against the prior-period fundamental factors (B/P, E/P, accruals, size, price momentum, etc.). The resultant solution (the regression coefficients) is the betas or factor returns, while the factors are themselves termed *exposures*. The equation to solve looks like this:

$$R = \beta_1 E_1 + \beta_2 E_2 + " \; " \; " + \beta_m E_m + \acute{\varepsilon} \tag{7.1}$$

where $R$ represents the returns of the stocks, the betas are regression coefficients, and the $E$'s are factor exposures built from financial statement variables of the stocks. The residuals from the regression are assumed to be uncorrelated with each other in time and with the betas.

A typical solution involves first choosing the latest period and regressing returns for that ending date versus exposures obtained from the start date of the return measure, cross-sectionally, meaning not a time-series regression but across all stocks for that specific time. Then, the process moves back one time period and does this again, iteratively, until after, say, 60 time periods

(60 months or five years), one has constructed 60 regressions and obtains 60 betas for each factor, creating a time series of betas for each factor. If it's a daily model there would not be 60 time periods, but either one or two years of daily values typically.

From the results of these regressions of stock returns versus fundamental factors, we can form a covariance matrix by calculating the variance of each factor's betas time series and covariance between betas from differing factors (after applying usually some time-weighting exponential decay to the betas). Here's where modeling the returns via fundamental factor models makes sense. For example, consider if you had a Russell 3000 stock universe and wanted to compute a covariance matrix from historical returns; you'd have to create a covariance matrix of size 3,000 × 3,000. However, in place of this, we could model the returns with, say, 12 fundamental factors and 24 Global Industry Classification Standards (GICS) industry group factors. Then for a single time period we would obtain 36 betas determined by regression of 36 factors on 3,000 stocks. If we did this for 60 months cross-sectionally and iteratively, the factor return (beta) matrix is of size 36 × 60. The covariance matrix computed from that matrix is therefore 36 × 36.

There are other reasons to do this besides the dimensionality reduction with concomitant estimation error reduction, mind you, and some of these include:

- Dealing with initial public offerings (IPOs) or short-history companies in your universe.
- Modeling the returns from fundamental factors your analysts favor.
- Giving better risk predictions than obtained by using historical-return-constructed covariance matrices.
- Avoiding spurious correlations of historical covariance matrices, an artifact of data mining.
- Managing a longer history of data, which increases as the universe grows, to construct the covariance matrix, which is required for robustness.

Drawbacks to this method include retention of correlations between the factors (i.e., exposures) chosen; making sure there is enough data for all the factors for every security; and using Dirac delta functions (1's or 0's) as dummy variables for the industry, currency, and country (region) exposures, which is still often done. Statistical methods using principal component analysis (PCA) overcome the correlation between factors issue, but then we have to attribute the risk after the fact to factors we understand, and this means that the break between cause and effect for the factors may be lost, assuming we seek explanatory risk factors as well as predictive or forecasting models. Some may say that's obvious, but very few of us seek to know the explanatory variables in weather forecasting, and we seek a weather forecast every day. So indeed there are some quant funds that prefer the statistical models even though they have little explanatory power.

For time-series regressions, in the United States the exposures are the regression coefficients, though now the exposure is itself constant for all time for each asset. The betas used in time-series regressions are themselves time series of returns created by grouping a collection of like asset returns in the same industry, for instance, and averaging them through time. Then, one would regress each asset in the estimation universe one at a time against this industry time-series beta. Thus, each asset obtains its own exposure to the industry. It's generally a similar process for currencies, sectors, countries, and regions. So in cross-sectional regressions, one determines betas and is given exposures. In time-series regressions, one determines exposures and is given betas (the opposite using U.S. nomenclature).

When constructing a multifactor risk model, then, you have two decisions to make. First, will you prespecify the factors? If not, then you are going to use a statistical factor model. SunGard APT, Quantal International, and StatPro offer types of models of this ilk. If you say yes to prespecifying the factors, then there is a second question: do you want to specify the exposures or the betas?

If you want to specify the exposures, then Barra, Axioma, and NIS have historically constructed these types of models (all three have statistical models, too, these days). If you'd rather use a model where the betas are specified and exposures determined, then FinAnalytica, UBS, and Quantec have traditionally specialized in using time-series regression models. Nowadays, however, many of these vendors are using many variations of regression and statistical analysis. R-Squared uses both methods along with statistical modeling techniques in a hybrid model. We'll return to the hybrid model after discussing principal component risk models next.

## PRINCIPAL COMPONENT (STATISTICAL) RISK MODELS

Factor risk modeling is designed to express the returns on a stock or portfolio in terms of a linear combination of returns to a set of explanatory factors. The sensitivities representing this linear combination of explanatory factors are often estimated using ordinary least squares (OLS) regression. This estimation procedure will suffice when there is zero or low multicollinearity among the factors, in which case the sensitivities will be estimated with a high level of confidence. In the presence of significant multicollinearity, however, the sensitivities can have large standard errors, leading to results that may be difficult to interpret. Hence, one might resort to statistical methods and practices. Statistical factor models aim to capture the systematic (common) covariation of asset returns and provide robust estimates of market risk without having any prescribed notion of what factors drive returns. The methods are based on principal component analysis.

The risk measures may be the traditional second moment measures (return variance, volatility, tracking error) or downside risk measures (value at risk [VaR], expected tail loss [ETL], CVaR). However, they are still calculated based on the covariance matrix estimate using the model's methodology, but achieve that goal knowing only the asset returns. One chief reason for choosing a PCA model, therefore, is the much smaller demand on data requirements. Consider a daily multifactor risk model of 100 factors and 10,000 assets. Each day one has to determine $10^2 \times 10^5$ or 1,000,000 individual pieces of information, whereas for PCA only 10,000 returns are required. Also, it's only returns that are needed. One doesn't need multiple databases consisting of fundamental data, economic data, trading data, and so forth.

If one does not want to specify factors in the first place, the starting point for a full PCA or statistical model for dimensional reduction is often the construction of a covariance matrix manually from historical returns. This is a sample covariance matrix, and using this matrix directly has been fraught with difficulties in its usage to compute the aforementioned risk measures. In simple terms, it's because often the number of securities in the portfolio is close to if not larger than the number of historical return observations; thus the sample covariance matrix is estimated with a lot of error. It implies that the largest and smallest values in the matrix are extremes; then the estimation error for the extreme values is obviously biased in that direction or they wouldn't be extreme values in the first place. In particular, when using these matrices in mean-variance optimization, these extrema are accentuated, and the biggest bets tend to be on those coefficients.[3] This has led to techniques that "shrink" the sample covariance matrix by various methods to reduce the emphasis on these outlier variance/covariance values; however, the amount of shrinkage to apply is a bone of contention between academic dogs, so to speak. The PCA methodology, however, offers similarities to shrinkage in that it lowers the estimation error akin to using a parametric multifactor fundamental model. Though neither method eliminates the use of shrinkage after the fact completely, they do mitigate the reason for its application somewhat.

To perform a principal component analysis, one needs to solve the eigenvalue problem to reduce the dimensionality of the covariance matrix, say, from 3,000 × 3,000 for the Russell 3000 index constituents, to something representing it, of the order of ~56 × 3,000 through the principal components. In this methodology, one solves for λ in the eigenvalue equation:

$$C\Psi = \lambda\Psi \tag{7.2}$$

where $C$ is the full sample covariance matrix created from returns $R$ of Russell index constituents, $\Psi$ is the eigenvector of like dimension, and $\lambda$ is the eigenvalue vector. Obviously, $C$ could be subject to shrinkage or not beforehand; it doesn't affect the PCA process. There are routine methods for solving this equation, and, after doing so, the eigenvectors can be thought of as linear loadings on the original stocks.

For eigen solutions, it turns out that the first component of the eigenvalue vector explains the largest share of the variance of return, the second eigenvalue explains the next, and by the ~56th eigenvalue (of which there are 3,000 in this example) the majority of the variance can be mostly explained. Hence, the problem can be reduced in size in this hypothetical example (from ~3,000 to something on the order of ~56). In practice one keeps as many eigenvalues and eigenvectors as explains ~70 to 90 percent or more of the variance of the data for later analysis, which could be more or less than 56 (that's a hypothetical number for illustration purposes), totally depending on the $C$ matrix. This is determined by ordering the eigenvalues highest to lowest and computing a rolling sum divided by their total. Typically, this guides the user to select the number of eigenvalues (and hence eigenvectors) that explain most of the variance while reducing the data set considerably, for the fall-off is rather quick in explanatory power of the eigenvalues. In addition, the principal components, which act like exposures, created from the eigenvectors, are completely orthogonal, meaning they have zero correlation between each other, unlike the fundamental factor exposures in the multifactor risk model methodology.

To offer an example of an easy PCA decomposition, consider a portfolio made up from equal weighting the S&P 100 constituents. The data is entered in a matrix consisting of stocks represented on the rows and returns represented on the columns. From this a covariance matrix of the one year's daily returns is constructed simply by taking the variance of each row, which become the diagonals in the covariance matrix, where the off-diagonal components become the covariance between rows (i.e., between stocks). Given this covariance matrix, its eigenvalue equation is solved and we have values for the eigenvector $\Psi$ and eigenvalue $\lambda$. In Figure 7.2 we plot the eigenvalues of the S&P 100's covariance matrix of daily returns from July 2011 to July 2012 in a scree plot on the left and the cumulative distribution of the eigenvalues on the right.

In this plot, one can see that the first eigenvalue explains about 25 percent of the variance of return all by itself. The first 20 eigenvalues explain about 70 percent of the variance, and 50 out of the 100 available are required to explain 90 percent of the variance of the S&P 100's return over the past year (see Table 7.1). After decomposition of the daily returns into their eigenvector components, we essentially completed a rotation of the return matrix

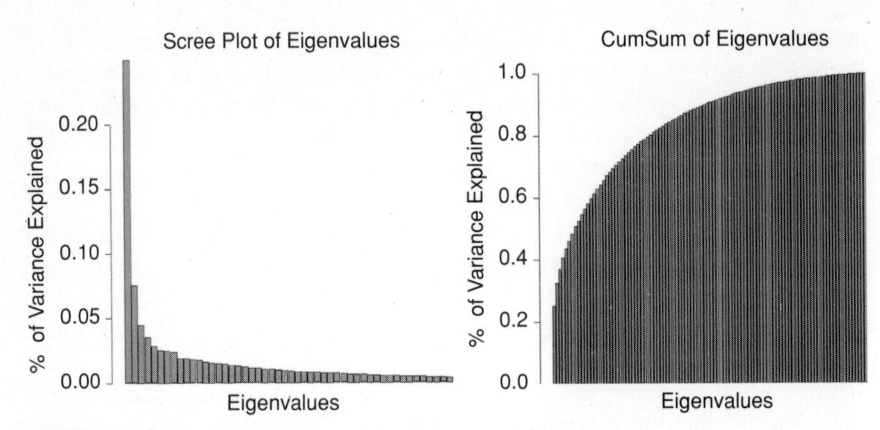


**FIGURE 7.2** The listing of eigenvalues that occur for the PCA analysis of the S&P 100 from July 2011 until July 2012 daily returns. The left chart shows the sequential contribution of the eigen function's percentage of variance explanation while the right chart is the cumulative distribution of the data. About 30 eigenvalues are required to explain 80 percent of the variance of the S&P 100 stocks' returns.

into a coordinate system that makes the original vectors orthogonal, so that there is no correlation between them. Then, the eigenvectors become factors in a return model and form what's known as a complete basis.

Often the mathematics of principal component analysis allows for comparison with the formulation of multifactor risk models. For instance, not specific to any vendor's risk model but to consider if the S&P 100 were our data and we had 250 daily return values (one trading year), then given the eigen solutions, we compute the principal components through the following simple equation:

$$\mathbf{Y} = \Psi^T(\mathbf{R} - \mu) \tag{7.3}$$

where $\Psi^T$ is the transposed eigenvector matrix of size 100 × 100, $\mathbf{R}$ is the returns matrix of size 100 × 250 (for 250 daily returns), and $\mu$ is the mean vector of length 100 (a mean return for the time series of each stock). Matrix $\mathbf{Y}$ therefore is also of size 100 × 250 after matrix multiplication and is termed the principal component matrix.

Next, suppose that the first 10 eigenvalues account for 54 percent of the variance of return. Then, by choosing to use only the first 10 eigenvectors in $\Psi^T$, $\mathbf{Y}$ will be of dimension 10 × 250, and that is precisely where the data reduction comes in, through the matrix $\mathbf{Y}$, whose vectors are the principal components and act like exposures in a multifactor model.

**TABLE 7.1** S&P 100 PCA decomposition example.

| Number of Eigenvectors | Correlation | % Variance Explained |
|---|---|---|
| 10 | 56.9 | 54.6 |
| 30 | 69.9 | 78.8 |
| 50 | 81.3 | 90.3 |
| 70 | 84.1 | 96.5 |
| 90 | 86.4 | 99.4 |
| 100 | 100 | 100 |

Equation (7.3) is invertible and can be used to replicate returns. The replicated return vectors are given by the following equation:

$$\mathbf{R}' = \mu + \Psi' \, \mathbf{Y}' \tag{7.4}$$

This equation has the same form as the fundamental factor risk model, where returns are regressed against exposures to solve for betas. Here, the eigenvectors act like the betas (factor returns) and the factor exposures are equated as the principal components **Y**. This mimics the way multifactor models specify returns; however, keep in mind that they are not actually these components.

If all 100 principal components are used in equation (7.4) after a decomposition of the S&P 100, we get back identically the full **R** matrix we started with and **R** equals **R'**. But, if we use, say, the first 10 principal components, the new returns will not match the original but will only model it. If $\Psi'$ in this equation contains only 10 of the original 100 eigenvectors that **Y'** was computed from, using equation (7.3), then $\mathbf{R}' \neq \mathbf{R}$.

In equation (7.4) the *dimensionality* of **R'** will always equal **R**, regardless of how many principal components are used in $\Psi$ to calculate **Y**. But **R'** will not equal **R** as long as the number of principal components (PCs) used is less than all the eigenvectors. Additionally, there will be correlation between **R** and **R'**, dependent upon the number of eigenvectors used.

To explain this further, the graphs in Figure 7.3 illustrate a return vector in **R** for 3M Corporation drawn from the S&P 100 versus the same vector in the replication matrix **R'**. On top of each chart there is a label for the number of how many eigenvectors in equations (7.3) and (7.4) were used in the matrix multiplication to replicate the **R'** matrix. As the number of eigenvectors increases from 10 to 90 and then toward the full complement (i.e., 100), the **R'** matrix coalesces into the **R** matrix; likewise, the covariance matrix of **R'** coalesces into **R**'s covariance matrix, and the **R'** vector in the plot coalesces into the returns of 3M Corporation. When the line is straight, we have convergence as shown in the bottom right plot.

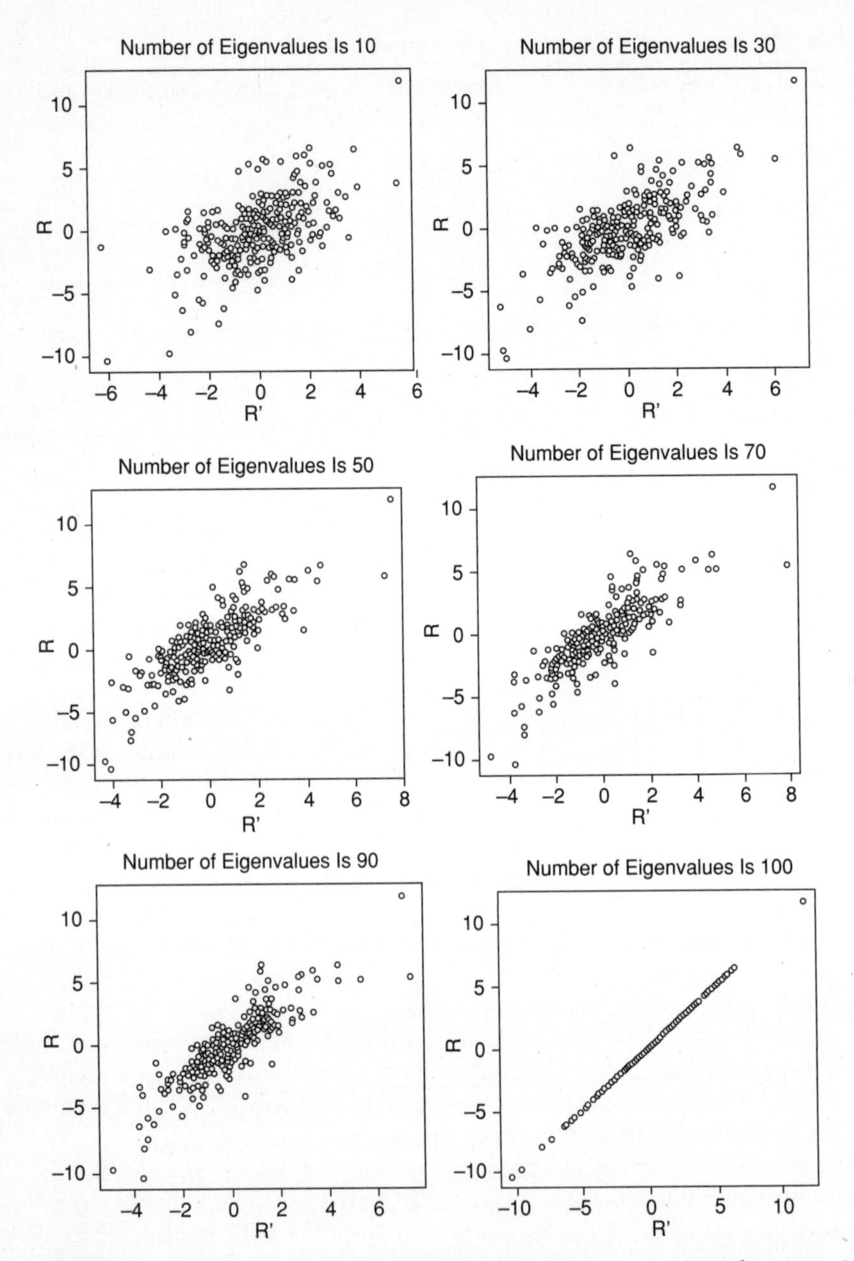


**FIGURE 7.3** Starting in top left, we plot the replicated returns vector R' from equation (7.4) on the *x*-axis and the original vector R on the *y*-axis for 3M Corporation. As the number of eigenvalues used in equation (7.4) increases from 10, 30, 50, 70, 90, to 100, we see the coalescing of replicated returns vector R' into 3M's original return R.

This is the observation we obtain from the first plot to the last, the coalescing of **R'** into **R**. The very last plot illustrates their relationship is 1 to 1 when using all PCs, at which point **R** equals **R'**, and the identical vectors occur for each and every stock and its replicant. These charts serve to illustrate how PCA works in a general fashion and are not representative of any particular vendor's usage. Typically, the number of eigenvectors kept to produce the principal components is determined from the scree plot of Figure 7.2 and is usually much smaller than the total number of PCs available, because one of the method's main purposes is to seek a more parsimonious representation of the data in the first place, and the eigen solution methodology orders the eigenvectors and eigenvalues by their explanatory power, allowing for ease of the numbers of PCs to choose from. Moreover, the parsimonious covariance matrix constructed from the **R'** vector has noise reduction, too, a desired goal for using PCA in the first place.

Table 7.1 demonstrates how the correlation of **R** and **R'** increases as the number of eigen functions is increased in equation (7.4). Along with increasing the number used, the amount of variance of the original returns explained also increases. The goal, however, is not to use so many eigenvalues that you explain 100 percent of the variance, for then you're also explaining the noise of the data. A typical application of PCA would keep enough eigen solutions to cover maybe 80 to 90 percent of the data's variance.

So in constructing PCA risk models, the eigenvector yields all the information necessary to compute the risk measures since it is central to computing a parsimonious covariance matrix from the replicated returns matrix **R'**. It's an important task, however, to select just the right amount of eigenvectors, as too few or too many will bias the estimates of **R'**. In practice one often compares the eigenvalues derived from PCA applied to a *random return matrix* with those from the actual estimation universe. Rules suggest upper and lower bounds on the number of eigenvalues (and eigenvectors therefore) to select.[4]

Given one chooses a small subset of eigenvectors from the whole eigen solution matrix, the total risk then is simply:

$$\text{Total systemic risk variance} = w^t * \mathbf{C'} * w \tag{7.5}$$

Here in this equation, $w$ is the weighting vector of the securities in the portfolio. The covariance matrix **C'** then is that calculated from **R'**, the replicated returns in this implementation.

Alternatively, some PCA applications will regress the original returns against the PCs themselves in a linear factor model as equation (7.1), where the PCs act as exposures through principal component regression as with SunGard APT methodology. Betas are determined in the regression, and the time series of the betas is used to form a covariance matrix used in equation (7.6), which looks surprisingly similar to a multifactor risk model's risk calculation:

$$\text{Total systemic risk variance} = w^t * \text{PC}^t * \text{C} * \text{PC} * w \tag{7.6}$$

for systematic (common) risk calculations. In this method, idiosyncratic risks can be estimated, too, because the linear equation (7.1) allows residual calculations output from the regression and their resultant covariance matrix estimation. Then, the idiosyncratic (security-specific) covariance matrix yields asset-specific risks through equation (7.7):

$$\text{Idiosyncratic risk variance} = w^t \bullet \text{C}^{\text{idio}} \bullet w \tag{7.7}$$

Total risk is the sum of the common factor and idiosyncratic risks in units of variance. To compute relative risk numbers, what is commonly done is to form a relative portfolio by subtracting the benchmark from the original portfolio positions and performing these matrix operations on the result.

For active managers, the lack of definition of factors derived using PCA may be problematic, as one or more factors may be correlated with the manager's stock selection criteria.[5] Often, too, in such a case, efforts to control risk by managing factor exposures would offset the desired exposure to characteristics that the manager believes is alpha additive. This is not a problem, however, if we care only about having exposures strongly similar with an index without any regard to what the criteria for similarity involve. In PCA's favor, however, the method works well and overcomes many of the weaknesses of fundamental factor models.

There are certainly more sophisticated issues, and we highly simplified the art of risk model creation. In addition, the marginal contribution to those risks at the security or factor level can also be displayed through FactSet's attribution system. These are the usual uses for risk models, but there are many variations of usages, including portfolio optimization and the importance to a portfolio manager of highlighting hidden risks, for covariance risks just are not easily identified any other way.

## CUSTOMIZED HYBRID RISK MODELS

Customized hybrid risk models (CHRMs) combine the explanatory power of pure statistical models with the intuitive factor definitions of a prespecified parametric model. This type of risk model combines the most common active factors used in stock selection models with industry and country (or regional) factors, and with statistical factors, to gain the usability and relevance of defined factors with the explanatory power of statistical factors. It usually involves cross-sectional and time-series regressions along with principal component analysis; hence it serves to offer the best of all worlds to the discipline, though the factor specification is still a major consideration in model development. To offer a review of how this type of model is constructed, we illustrate the design of the R-Squared Global Equity Risk model within FactSet.

The R-Squared Short-Term Equity CHRM has four blocks of factors. First are the currency factors, used to capture each stock's significant currency sensitivities. These factors allow for production of currency exposure hedged portfolios alluded to in earlier chapters, and they are constructed in time-series regressions. Then there is a series of country- or region-specific style-like active factors, where the betas are determined from cross-sectional regressions and represent a stock's exposure to the attributes most commonly used in most bottom-up stock selection models. The third involves a double group factor block where each stock's exposures to industry and country (or regional) factors are estimated through time-series regressions. The final block consists of a small number of statistical factors determined through principal component analysis on the residuals left over after the regressions stages.

The way the model is constructed involves running each set of regressions in stages. After the currency block, the currency invariant stock returns, which are the residuals remaining after the currency time-series regressions are performed, are used to derive the active factor returns. Together with each stock's exposures to these active factors, they will explain some portion of each stock's returns in each period. The residuals from the time-series currency regressions are regressed against these active factor returns, and residuals that are left over after this step are called the stock's active factor residual returns.

The country (or regional) and industry factors are built from these active factor residual returns by combining stock returns into capitalization-weighted portfolios of all well-behaved stocks in a particular region or industry. The country (or region) and industry betas for individual stocks are derived by regressing each stock's returns on these factors in time series.

Significantly, this means that, unlike many of the older types of prespecified factor models, the CHRM methodology does not simply assume that a stock will have a beta of 1 on its own industry or country and a beta of 0 on all other industries or countries. That is the default situation for most factor models, which specify these exposures through dummy variables. Instead, it recognizes that not all stocks in an industry or country, or currency for that matter, necessarily have the same exposure to those factors, and that stocks may have significant exposure to other industries, countries, and currencies as well. By exposure we mean beta here.

To recognize that an assigned classification from a source such as Standard & Poor's or MSCI must have some credibility, priors are imposed by first regressing each stock's returns on its assigned currency, country (or region), and industry factor returns as appropriate. Thereafter, all other betas to factors in these groups are checked for statistical significance, to ensure that each stock has only nonzero betas on factors that actually affect its returns.

Finally, the statistical factors are principal components of the residual covariance matrix derived from the stock residual returns to the country and industry factors. It's the last step in risk model construction. The statistical betas for each stock are then estimated by regressing the stock's residual returns on the statistical factors, and again testing for statistical significance.

### Estimation Universe

All calculations are done on daily, exponentially time-weighted, log returns with a historical look-back period of 240 working days (about one year). No attempt is made to fill in for missing data. The time-weighting coefficient is such that the oldest return (one year ago) has about a quarter the weight of the most recent return (yesterday's close), yielding a half-life of around six months. This has the effect of making the model very responsive to recent changes in market volatility by weighting recent data more heavily than historical data. The data comprise is approximately 40,000 global equity securities.

To reduce noise, a well-behaved subset (the screened estimation universe) of all the stocks covered by the CHRM is used to build the factors.

Additionally, two other steps are generally applied to the estimation universe. These include winsorization of extreme values and normalization. For instance, extreme attribute values can distort the attribute distributions and have a large effect on statistical operations. That is not necessarily a good effect in a model. One approach is to change the statistical operations and use robust statistical methods, but these methods often are peculiar and are more difficult to automate. Winsorizing can mean throwing away extreme values, a simple trim, or replacing the extreme values with, say, the 5th and 95th percentile's values. In our case, minimum and maximum sensible values are determined through careful analysis and then used to replace such extreme values.

Last, the raw attributes (i.e., exposures) to each stock are normalized by country and region as appropriate.

### Active Super-Factor Composite Creation

There are many ways to measure the most commonly used exposures, like value or growth. However, including each of them as separate factors could create problems of collinearity and instability in the model. Consider if book-to-price, earnings-to-price, cash-flow-to-price, and sales-to-price were all in a model as distinct style factors. These four factors obviously have high correlation, which means that each explains some identical portion of the return. In a regression with all four variables, the algorithm would typically have difficulty assigning an appropriate amount of variance to each factor, and what would ensue is whatever factor the algorithm gets to first would be assigned the most explanatory power. One would find the regression giving oscillating signs to regression coefficients as well as large values to each like −1.2, +0.96, −1.04, and +0.86 as the regression algorithm tries to accommodate this constraint. In actuality they would all naturally have the same sign on their betas,[6] because if you compute the univariate correlation of each with return, you'd obtain the same sign and probably nearly the same magnitude of correlation, too. A well-constructed model therefore uses composite variables in these cases, and creates a "super-factor" composite factor created from linearizing a sequence of like style factors. For instance, for the growth style factor, it's constructed from three equally weighted factors, which include net income per share along with trailing and forecasted earnings growth. In this way, only the super-factor is placed into the regression algorithm.

### Currency Factors

All stocks are first regressed on their home currency's returns in the base currency, rather than simply assuming that a stock will have a sensitivity of 1 to its home currency. The stock residual from this regression is then regressed on the remaining major currencies, and if there is a statistically significant sensitivity it is kept as an additional currency beta. This methodology allows for later risk attribution analysis to yield an appropriate currency exposure hedge for a portfolio if desired. It cannot be ascertained without dealing with foreign exchange (FX) exposure any other way.

### Active Style Factors

Within each region, a multiple cross-sectional regression (day by day) is done with the stock returns from one day as the dependent variables and the composite or other normalized attributes from the previous day as the independent variables. It's regressing forward returns against past data. The regression coefficients from these 240 regressions are concatenated to give the time series of factor returns to each of the active factors.

The factor returns and the normalized attribute values (or stock betas) are then combined to give a time series of explained return for each stock, and this is then subtracted from the stock's actual returns to give its residual return series.

### Industry and Regional Factors

Only equities in the screened estimation universe are eligible to be constituents of the industry and country or regional factors. The residuals from regressions preceding this point for all acceptable stocks in each industry or region are then combined to form a capitalization-weighted factor returns series. This then creates the industry, country, or regional factors in which stocks are regressed against in time series.

### Priors

Priors are imposed by first regressing the stock's residual returns on the prior factor's returns. Then the stock's residual returns from this regression are regressed on the remaining factors in the block. A stock gets a prior on a factor if its returns were used to build that factor. Stock sensitivities or betas are calculated via a multiple stepwise regression with priors, on a stock-by-stock basis. Note that the model *does not* use dummy variables for country or region sensitivities. As the poets say, "Dummy variables are for dummies."

Most stocks have enough degrees of freedom in their returns history for a full set of factor betas to be estimated by regression. The results for these stocks are then used to help assign betas for stocks with incomplete return histories or missing data. Any prior is applied first. The residuals from this prior regression are then used in a multiple-stepwise regression on the remaining factors in the factor block. All betas generated by the multiple-stepwise regressions are statistically checked for significance (adjusted for the available degrees of freedom). For stocks that do not have enough history to perform full regressions, a peer group average of the betas of stocks in the same industry and same country is used.

For statistical factors, a full correlation matrix is derived from these stocks' residual return time series, and the first three principal components are extracted via eigenvalue decomposition using standard methodology. As the economic meaning of the statistical factors is unknown, no priors are applied to the statistical factors. All stocks with sufficient degrees of freedom are eligible for regression on the statistical factors. As with the previous two blocks, multiple-stepwise regressions are done, again with degrees-of-freedom-adjusted statistical significance checking.

Chapter 19 will detail more specifically what the industry, region, and style factors are for the interested reader for this type of model.

For most stocks, the stock-specific risk is simply the standard deviation of the final residual returns time series. This is not the case for those stocks that at any point in the block regressions had too few degrees of freedom to be regressed, and as a result were assigned averaged peer group betas. For these very short history stocks a similar averaging method is used to determine their stock-specific risk.

What risk models generally do well is capture the risk trend quite appropriately over some time period for the evolution of volatility. However, often the estimation error accumulates in the covariance matrix, leading to an underrealization of the level of volatility, the level of total risk variance. For this reason, scaling is usually applied to raise the forecast level to match the overall market volatility over the past six months or over the past year. The scaling operation then allows for a more accurate forecast, though it is often criticized as some "super fudge factor."

In summary, a hybrid risk model is predicated generally on the same types of factors most prespecified factor models use. However, it combines time-series regressions on currency, country, and industry, which are generally not considered in this fashion under semistandardized risk model construction to date. Additionally, PCA is applied at the final stage, which serves to mop up any residual variance not explained by any preselected factors. A recipe for hybrid risk model development, then, follows a procedure similar to this:

- Form and then screen an estimation universe of securities.
- For a specific base currency, perform *time-series regressions* of daily stock returns against the base/denominated FX rate.
- Take the residuals from the last step and perform time-series regressions against major FX rates; check for statistical significance, removing those without any.
- Form style or common factor exposures for fundamental or financial statement variables (i.e., P/B, P/E, accruals, earnings per share [EPS] growth rates, and so forth).
- Take the residuals of the previous regressions and *regress them cross-sectionally* against the common factor exposures to derive the implied active factor returns.
- Form the current capitalization-weighted industry and country/region time-series factors using the acceptable securities from the estimation universe by grouping the securities residuals together into appropriate

industry and country factors. The data used for grouping are the residuals produced from cross-sectional regressions of the previous step.

- Take the individual stock residuals from the preceding step and run time-series regression against industry and country/regional factors created in that step, using first priors and then statistical significance checking to see if betas are greater or less than zero.
- At this point, the systematic, common factor risks are able to be calculated by forming the common factor covariance matrix from the set of factor returns (i.e., regression betas) obtained to this point, from which total systematic risk can be computed. In matrix algebra notation where $w$ is a weight vector and $E$ and $C$ are matrices, then systematic risks equal:

$$\text{Common variance risk} = w^t \bullet E^t \bullet C^{\text{common}} \bullet E \bullet w$$

- To get the idiosyncratic risks, take the remaining residual return series for all stocks with full histories, form a covariance matrix from them, do eigenvalue decomposition, select three eigen functions associated with sorted eigenvalues, and calculate principal components (PCs) from them.
- Regress residual stock returns on PC factors with statistical significance, checking to obtain betas on PC factors. Then, given these betas, one can form another idiosyncratic (security-specific) covariance matrix and compute idiosyncratic risks through the equation:

$$\text{Idiosyncratic risks} = w^t \bullet C^{\text{idio}} \bullet w$$

Total risk is the sum of the common factor and idiosyncratic risks in units of variance. To compute relative risk numbers, what is commonly done is to form another portfolio by subtracting the benchmark from the portfolio positions and to perform these operations on the result.

Though this recipe is detailed, it still allows room for customization and creativity. It's important to match the process and factors with one's investment process, time horizon, and holding period, and of course what securities go into the model are those available for purchase and sale within the mandate. For FactSet's implementation of the R-Squared Global Equity model, we have only one shoe with which to fit all of our clients, so we're more general and must have factors that one can obtain data for across the planet. Other issues involve exponential time-weighting on the betas, which is usually performed at various steps with half-lives dependent on portfolio mandates and desired risk model sensitivities. Also, the frequency of the data has to be chosen as well. One could use month-ending updating, or weekly, daily, or even Wednesday-to-Wednesday updating. There are many variations on the theme, and one must be aware of the investing mandate, policy statement, benchmark, and investment process for which to customize a CHRM risk model.

### Historical Risk Models

Historical risk models exist primarily for situations in which one only has returns and knows very little about the assets themselves. Funds of funds (FoFs) come to mind, as do private equity, timber, real estate, some exchange-traded funds (ETFs), and many other illiquid assets in which the investor hasn't enough details on the underlying assets to specify factors for a multifactor model. In other words, exposures cannot be calculated. In alternatives generally, the lack of transparency from the manager's perspective is valuable to keep prying competitive eyes off the portfolio. Conventional models for modeling the risk of these assets assume the underlyings are reasonably stable and of similar type if not behavior. For hedge fund holdings, however, the buy-and-hold perspective is outdated a bit for describing risk. Hedge fund strategies can have high frequency, be highly levered, and may demonstrate extravagant kurtosis behavior, with return distributions unlike those of ordinary mutual funds. The same is true for other illiquid assets. This, combined with the lack of standardized reporting for hedge funds, means that using conventional risk models may by difficult if not inaccurate.

Most of the needs in the FoF space are for risk models for internal use, and they want to see risk in explanatory variables (if they're bottom-up), which requires using multifactor models, not statistical models. Taking standard risk models from the mutual fund world isn't going be as useful, however, as one needs to have a deeper understanding of the hedge fund space and create models in full knowledge of it. A drawback with standard predefined factors, for instance, can come about with a model that may assign one FoF investment in a hedge fund that has an Asian long/short strategy to Asian convertibles and produce a beta to it. An incorrectly pre-specified model can find a statistically significant beta with Asian converts, but the fund may not own any convertibles. If the fund managers show this to a consultant or client, it's misleading and they have to explain it away, which is quite awkward. So multifactor models for the alternative space need to have prespecified factors designed for this space. This requires factors that are intelligently designed or economically related to each asset class in some way, as the alternative space isn't similar to long-only equity or fixed income.

As you wouldn't use a standard Barra equity model for risk forecasting in real estate investment trusts (REITs), you shouldn't expect an event driven, fixed income arbitrage, convertible arbitrage, global macro, or managed futures hedge fund to have much to do with the factors in these models, either. Although most alternative investors are absolute return investors, many like to know their betas to hedge fund indexes, too, like Hedge Fund Research Inc. (HFRI), Credit Suisse First Boston (CSFB), and Tass, not the conventional long-only investor suite index sensitivities to FTSE, S&P, Russell, Stoxx, and MSCI. Though it's mostly for reporting purposes (like the CAPM beta), regardless of the index it's less useful than it once was.

One usage that quants, consultants, and FoFs have in common is the goal of separating alpha from beta. The hardest things these people do when analyzing a prospective investment strategy are to determine whether the strategy, hedge fund, or manager really has alpha; find what the beta is; and forecast the volatility. For instance, for a manager holding bonds while hedging with credit default swaps (CDSs), it's extremely hard to separate alpha from beta in this strategy. Some hedge funds actually say, "You cannot separate out the alpha from beta, as our investing process is so complex," and try to hide behind opacity, because it's not in any hedge fund's interest to have the FoF determine its alpha. For the quant developing a new investment strategy, the estimation of the alpha separately from beta is also of concern, and in this exercise, the risk model may also pull double as the alpha model, too.

Other issues that have to be overcome deal with asynchronous data because some return series could be daily, while others are monthly or quarterly in a portfolio. The lowest-frequency data limits the forecast horizon to approximately twice the reporting period via the Nyquist sampling theory. In some cases, however, hole filling through various statistical techniques allows one to form data estimates at higher frequency than the report frequency. Though there are many imaginative ways of achieving this, one general method is to form a model on a longer look-back period (say, on quarterly data for five years); measure its distribution moments (mean, standard deviation, skewness, kurtosis); then, while constraining correlation with other assets and volatility, use the model to interpolate values between quarters. Last, recalibrate the model using the simulated and quarterly empirical data over a shorter look-back period and then forecast the risk. The type of model used to do the interpolation isn't restricted, and there are many ways of accomplishing this whose details are outside the scope of this book, but involve Kalman filters, Savitsky-Golay, Fourier methods, and even simple cubic splines and locally weighted scatterplot smoothing (LOWESS) methods. Anybody skilled in signal processing and computational methodologies can readily deal with the asynchronous data issues in a matter-of-fact way.

One has difficulty, though, in forming the multifactor model exposures even if one prespecifies asset class specific factors acceptable to a client, since the whole point here is to build a risk model where the only data available are returns. Principal component analysis is directly applicable to this situation, as it only needs returns to generate the covariance matrix robustly. Risk estimates would easily be forthcoming, but explanatory variables less so. Combining PCA with principal component regression on the principal components offers the common and idiosyncratic risk contributions, too.

Alternatively, a multifactor model can be constructed from simple factors derived from the price and returns themselves using technical and momentum factors. These would be used in a cross-sectional regression of past values versus forward returns. Additionally, knowing something about the source of returns, there are numerous ETFs and indexes in the portfolio's asset class that may provide fodder for use in time-series regressions in addition to readily forming industry, currency, and country factors. Likewise, time series of true economic factors of investor sentiment, interest rates, inflation, business activity, and so forth can also work as time-series factors. In this way, the model may help investors identify the systematic sources of risk using conventional asset prices and returns they are quite familiar with. This could link common components of alternative asset returns to observable quantities as well,[7] given wisely chosen factors. Last, a hybrid model of cross-sectional regression followed by time-series regressions of cross-sectional residuals with or without PCA on the final residual set, allows a sufficiently accurate portrayal of risk attribution and forecasting.

We comment that of course one can easily construct a covariance matrix from the sample returns but this method is seldom used these days and is fraught with difficulties and errors. At a very minimum if this method is chosen, a high degree of shrinkage must be applied to the covariance matrix before it can be used for risk forecasts.

## Arch/Garch

Depending on the purpose of the model, a generalized autoregressive conditional heteroscedasticity (GARCH) can easily be applied to a portfolio's or asset's return time series to produce a conditional volatility forecast. This is even trivial these days given the availability of R, SAS, Matlab, and other statistical software with these algorithms implemented in code. Garch is of course an extension of autoregressive conditional heteroscedasticity (ARCH), which is basically autoregressive and allows for time-varying volatility. They're modeled allowing a random component that can be drawn from a variety of distributions; in our examples we'll use a Gaussian and t-distribution. The general equation to describe the time evolution of some asset price $S$ with a drift or mean component $\mu_t$, and variance term $\varepsilon_t$ by Garch is:

$$S_t = \in_t + \mu_t \tag{7.8}$$

where:

$$\epsilon_t = \sigma_t Z_t$$

$$\sigma_t^2 = \alpha_0 + \sum_{i=1}^{p} \alpha_i \epsilon_{t-i}^2 + \sum_{j=1}^{q} \beta_j \sigma_{t-j}^2$$

This is the equation for Garch($p$,$q$), but in our use we'll restrict ourselves to $p$ and $q$ equaling 1, yielding the Garch(1,1) nomenclature and process. In this equation, if you restrict the alpha and beta to various constraints, you can create a wide variety of processes: white noise only, with or without higher moments, and so forth.[8] The conditional volatilities given by $\sigma$ are a continually changing function of its previously squared values allowing for the time variation. The innovations, $Z$, are what can be either normally or t-distribution distributed and when fitting a Garch to an asset return (usually using maximum likelihood) one simply chooses the distribution to fit. For t-distributions, the choice is one of unit variance, and the degree of freedom (df) obtained comes from the fit.

To illustrate the effectiveness of the simple Garch methodology for risk computation sans covariance, we took the S&P 100 (OEX) daily time series over the past 10 years and performed a Garch fitting using normal conditional volatilities (called Gaussian innovations). In Figure 7.4, we plot the daily returns and the 95 and 99 percent VaR simply by multiplying the ascertained Garch(1,1) conditional standard deviations by 1.651 for 95 percent and by 2.333 for 99 percent. These multipliers give the proper quantile VaR when multiplied by standard deviations of return, and this is how one uses the parametric risk results of standard multifactor models to compute a parametric VaR number. It depends on believing returns are normally distributed, however, and for many assets that's not a reasonable assumption nor true, especially during stressed environments, as we will see in the next set of numerical experiments. Even with this simple model, however, we see over the 10 years that the 95 percent VaR was breached only 5.38 percent of the time compared to its theoretical value of 5 percent. For 99 percent VaR it was breached 1.85 percent compared to its theoretical value of 1 percent. That's not bad. If one just used the rolling 30-day standard deviation of return times the multipliers, the numbers are 6.21 and 2.69 percent breaching for 95 and 99 percent VaR for comparison, which clearly underestimates the risk.

Knowing that the normal approximation for return is a weak argument, we next computed a series of simulations whereby we created 5,000 random returns drawn from a series of t-distributions with degrees of freedom of

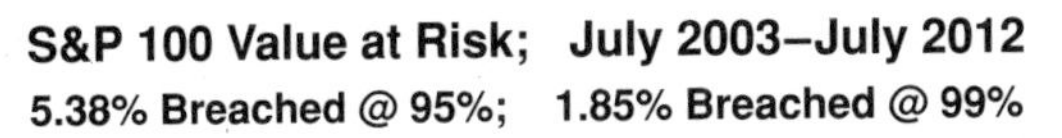


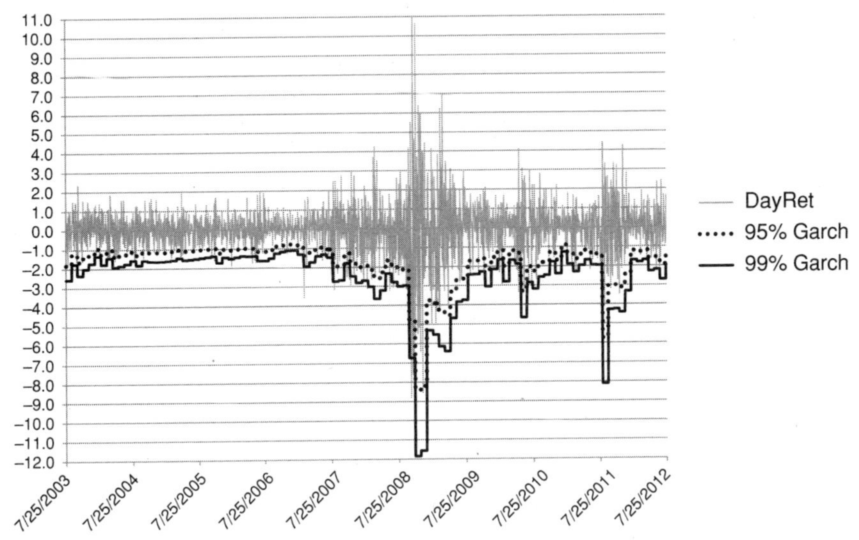


**FIGURE 7.4** This a plot of 10 years of daily returns of the S&P 100 with the daily VaR overlaid, computed at month-ending dates using the normal multiplier times the conditional volatility produced from a Garch(1,1) fitting of the data.

1.5, 2, 3, 4, up to 60 in increments of 1 and then df equaling 400, including a normal draw. Then, for each we computed the standard deviations and the VaR for confidence intervals (CIs) starting at 51 percent and going up to 99.9 percent, creating a VaR surface as a function of confidence intervals and t-distribution degrees of freedom. From this data set, we then divided the VaRs by the standard deviation of the returns to ascertain the multiplier required to compute the VaR as a function of CI and df. In this way, we could then fit the VaR multiplier to a polynomial regression with CI, df, and standard deviation as the independent variables and from then on, given the three variables, instantly compute the multiplier for VaR calculations.

We actually created two models, one for df's greater than 10 at high CI and one for df's less than 10 as the multiplier behaves quite differently for low df's and high CIs than for CIs less than 95 percent and df's greater than 10.

Using these models, then, we took (rolling) one year of daily returns of the S&P 100 and fit it to a t-distribution to determine the best fit, yielding the degree of freedom for the time period. An interesting aside was that the whole 10 years of data yielded a df of about 4.11, demonstrating a much higher kurtosis distribution than a normal would describe. This is well known, however, and not news, but interesting nonetheless because it illustrates that the return-generating process is evidently something quite unlike a random walk. Given we now have the df for the S&P 100's return series for a year of daily returns, we advanced one month and refit it again repetitively. We did this for all months between July 2002 and July 2012 for the index and therefore had monthly df's along with daily conditional standard deviations computed over the same rolling time period using Garch(1,1) but using t-distributions for the conditional volatilities (t-distribution innovations).

In Figure 7.5, we divided the df's by 10 through time to fit them on the same graph as the daily returns. One can see that quiet periods of volatility are more regularly modeled by high df t-distributions (as df's move higher and higher, the distribution more closely approximates the normal distribution) that exist at times. These are the low-volatility environments of 2004 through 2007 and a couple of short time periods since then when you may expect returns to be more normal.

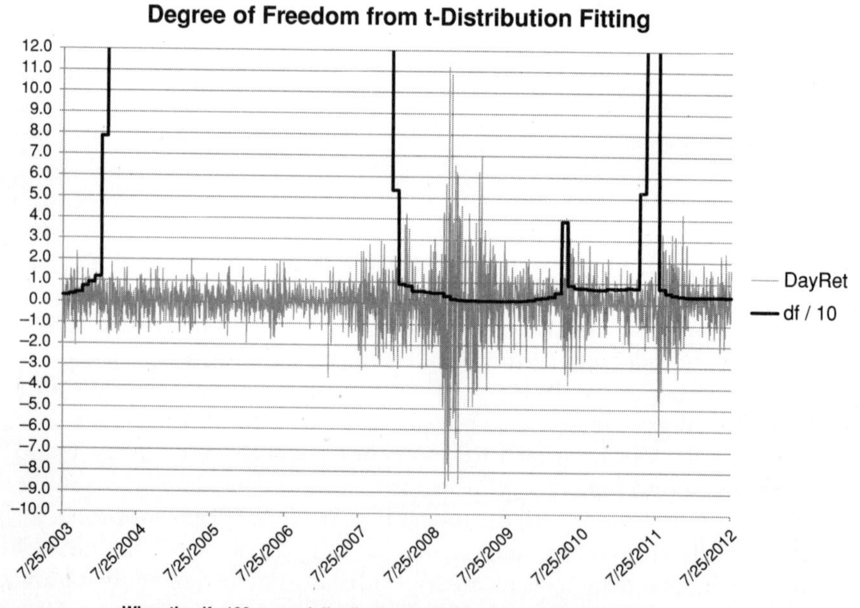


**FIGURE 7.5** One-year rolling periods of daily returns on monthly increments fit to a t-distribution and degrees of freedom extracted (and divided by 10) are plotted along with daily returns. When quiet periods occur, the returns are more approximated by a normal distribution. These are indicated by the highest df (greater than 100 values).

It was straightforward to use the polynomials to compute the 95 percent and 99 percent VaRs as time series given the conditional volatilities (for standard deviations) from the Garch and the df fits, and plot them with the daily returns over the 10 years as seen in Figure 7.6. In this chart, one will notice the wider distance between the returns and the VaRs than when using the normal approximation of Figure 7.4, especially during the turbulent times of 2008. Interestingly, there's a persistence of very low df t-distribution return behavior all through the crisis, moving the VaRs at 99 percent CI, out quite a way from the return series after 2008, which exists even through the summer of 2012, except for two brief periods. This is seen in Figure 7.5 as well. You can observe the VaRs in Figure 7.6 rise significantly after 2008 and stay there due to this effect, whereas in Figure 7.4 the VaRs have receded since 2008. Additionally, the t-distribution calculated VaRs are not breached as much as the normal VaRs (3.88 percent vs. 5.38 and 0.53 vs. 1.85 for 99 and 95 percent VaR, respectively) because they offer a more conservative estimate of the risk. In other words, due to not only the increased volatility during turbulent periods, but also the more kurtotic behavior stressed market environments exert on returns, VaRs calculated based on t-distributions

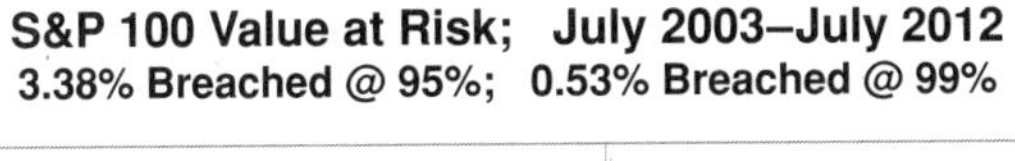


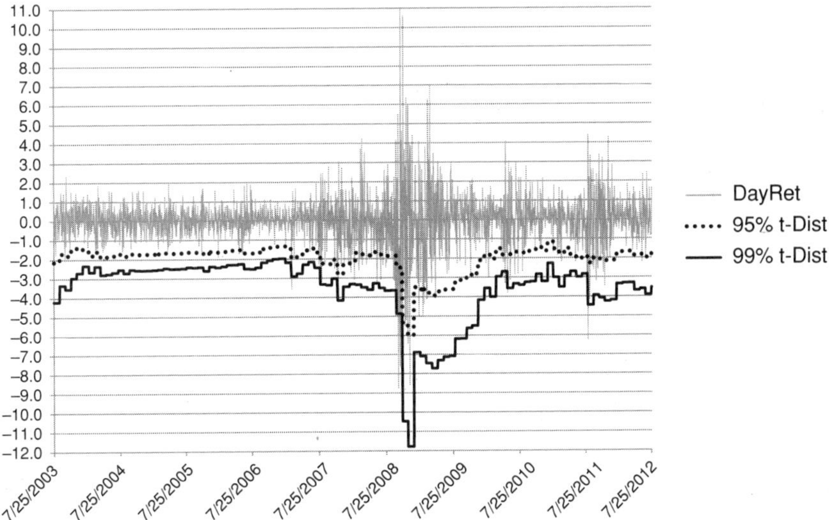


**FIGURE 7.6** This is the same data as in Figure 7.4, but now a rolling one-year period was fit to a t-distribution and optimized to obtain the degrees of freedom (df). Then, given the df, a VaR multiplier optimized for t-distributions was multiplied times the Garch(1,1) conditional volatility to compute the VaR.

capture the tail events more accurately. Then, when you overlay the Garch capabilities on top of that, you model risks quite accurately. Thus the implementation of a Garch model can produce useful risk statistics without any knowledge of the underlying assets for an index or a portfolio (albeit this was an example using linear assets).

If the underlying is a pure option portfolio, it may be quite difficult to use Garch to model its extremely kurtotic nature. However, using Garch methodologies we can also obtain an estimate of the return evolution given the conditional standard deviations. For instance, a plot of one year's daily returns of the S&P 100 superimposed with the conditional volatility over the year, as shown in Figure 7.7, allows for a simple illustration of where the nearest future returns may lie in between, in a probabilistic sense. In this plot, we illustrate visually upper and lower bounds of where the returns can expand to in a year.

If we focus on the latest-period data, the data at the far right, we can then use the conditionally determined volatility from the Garch model as upper and lower bounds for a forecast, as seen in Figure 7.8.

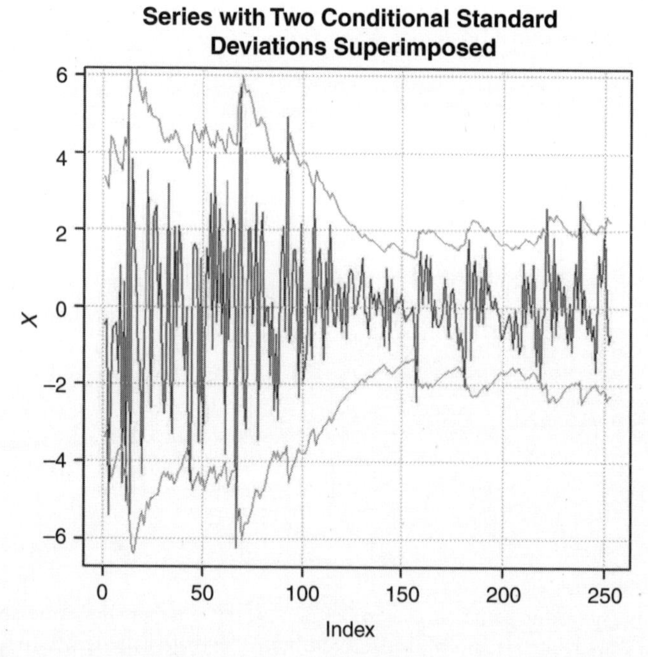


**FIGURE 7.7** One year of daily returns for the S&P 100 with the Garch(1,1) determined conditional volatilities superimposed.

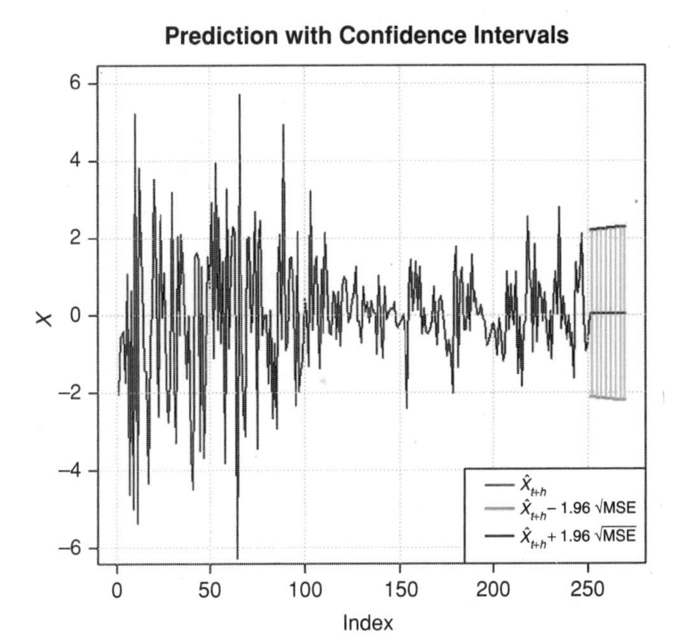


**FIGURE 7.8** Given the conditional volatility, one can say something about the bounds of regular returns in the near future. This plot illustrates how using the forecasted Garch(1,1) volatilities one can create probability limits for future returns, in this case 20 days hence. The multiplier 1.96 would be for 95 percent confidence limits, assuming normally distributed returns.

In this graph we show the evolution of return from a Garch(1,1) with Gaussian innovations for conditional volatility. Then, we determine bounds of return by multiplying 1.96 times the square root of the mean square error (MSE). We show a 20-day forecast, and of course the longer the forecast horizon, the larger the inaccuracies and the larger the estimation error.

We can improve on these forecasts by including a Garch(1,1) using t-distribution innovations for the conditional volatilities, in which case the multipliers move from 1.96 to 1.999 for the mean squared error boundaries. Now, the forecasts are accounting for some element of leptokurtic behavior in returns. Additionally, the forecasts widen faster from one day out to day 20 due to t-distributions having fatter tails than the normal distribution of returns, and this can be observed in the graph of Figure 7.9.

Last, we have to comment that this process of using the historical returns in this fashion is univariate in that we have measured and discussed the risk of a single index's or asset's returns only. For a portfolio of assets, the individual VaR calculations can be processed in this fashion for each asset,

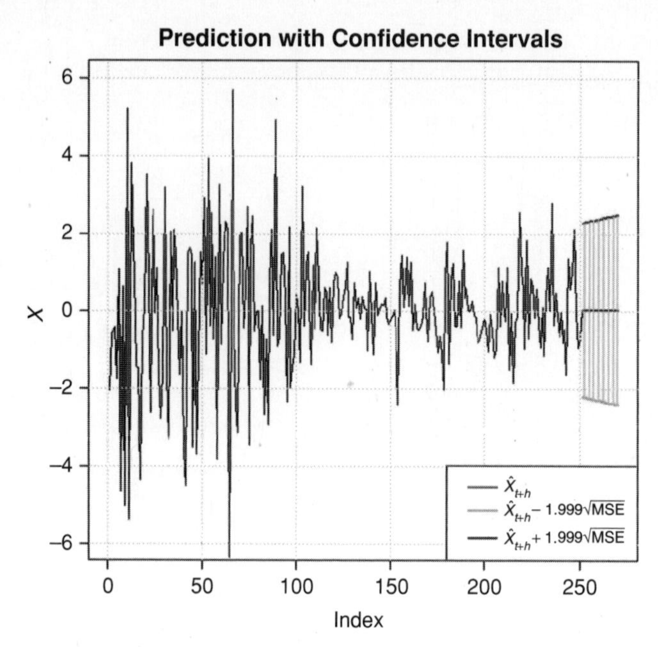


**FIGURE 7.9** If one fits the data to a t-distribution, the multiplier times the conditional volatility changes accordingly from 1.96 to 1.999 depending on the degrees of freedom of the Garch fit. Additionally, the limits diverge more quickly from forecasts out one day to 20, compared to Figure 7.8's normal assumption of returns.

but they do not take into account the diversifying aspects of a collection of assets, which using an APT approach or a multifactor model approach certifies to ascertain the covariance effects. Hence, one might readily calculate individual asset, portfolio, or index VaRs using this methodology as we've shown, but these are not the same as ascertaining the marginal contribution to risk for assets in an index or portfolio VaR.

Multivariate Garch (M-Garch) methodologies are coming of age but are a lot more complicated to implement. The usual routine for solution of the Garch equation (7.8) requires maximum likelihood methods, which for a portfolio with high dimensionality become really time-consuming and may not converge for a large number of assets. Nevertheless, M-Garch in the multivariate framework is becoming increasingly doable. The recent generalized orthogonal Garch (GO-Garch) methodology using method of moments estimation can be computed in several minutes for 100 asset portfolios these days, whereas the older maximum likelihood method can take days on a laptop computer, even if it reaches a solution.[9] The algorithm may get stuck in a local maximum or not converge for portfolios greater than 15 or 20 assets or so, which are most portfolios. There are other M-Garch solutions, but for the most part, practitioners haven't yet caught up with the theoreticians in finding implementations for the wide variety of "Garchy" specifications for a true multivariate framework for more than just a few assets.[10]

Interestingly, even for univariate time series, one study of 330 differing implementations of Arch-type specifications concluded there is no evidence that the Garch(1,1) model is outperformed by other models for foreign exchange examples.[11] For stock returns the study found that Garch(1,1) could be improved on, however, by including a leverage effect. That is, volatility following bad news is found to be higher than following good news, and this is termed the *leverage* effect. The observation of leverage motivated the development of models that allowed for an asymmetric response in volatility to positive and negative shocks.

For Arch/Garch methodologies, one must keep in mind that their usage is considerable for assets that demonstrate relatively uncomplicated return series like stocks and bonds, even with kurtosis and skew. For nonlinear assets such as options, where the distribution of returns can be very atypical, exhibiting very high kurtosis, these numerical methodologies aren't so easily implemented due to the huge jumps that can occur. The Garch framework is still applicable for gauging an estimate of the volatility of the implied volatility and interest rate volatility, but for estimating the risk of an option's pricing volatility it is less useful. For a large, diversified portfolio of options and swaptions, the return distribution of the portfolio still can be modeled readily by Garch but only if the portfolio truly is diversified.

In conclusion, for any type of risk modeling, the crux of the process is to compute a specification of asset association, which usually aims for the covariance matrix rather than a copula. When you only have returns, the methods applicable to decompose the risk are limited. The better methods involve prespecified factor models where the factors are momentum (price or return based) or time-series factors built from other indexes, ETFs, and so forth; Garch-type models; principal component analysis–principal component regression (PCA-PCR) models; or, last, the direct sample covariance method, though with the last named, idiosyncratic risks are not easily identified, and if you choose it, shrinkage methods must be employed.

## NOTES

1. Eugene F. Fama and Kenneth R. French, "Common Risk Factors in the Returns on Stocks and Bonds," *Journal of Financial Economics* 33 (1993): 3–56.
2. For instance, consider two stocks with P/Es of 6 and 7 and two other stocks with P/Es of 37 and 38. Though in both cases they're differentiated by 1, the

meaningfulness of their difference is not interpretable as far as their impact on returns is concerned. Hence, ranking them 1 through 4 may be wiser than Z-scoring their values in a regression.

3. Richard O. Michaud, "The Markowitz Optimization Enigma: Is 'Optimized' Optimal?" *Financial Analysts Journal*, January–February 1989, 31.
4. An APT white paper, "How to Invest More Effectively Using Daily Risk Models: The APT Daily Global Model," SunGard APT, 2011, www.sungard.com/apt/learnmore.
5. There are methods to regress the PCs versus fundamental factors to gauge an interpretation of the major components to risk, and APT's RiskScan technology offers this methodology.
6. S. P. Greiner, *Ben Graham Was a Quant* (Hoboken, NJ: John Wiley & Sons, 2011), chap. 6, 140–148.
7. William Fund and David Hsieh, "Hedge Fund Benchmarks: A Risk Based Approach," *Financial Analysts Journal* 60, no. 5 (2004).
8. Alexander McNeil, Rudiger Frey, and Paul Embrechts, *Quantitative Risk Management* (Princeton, NJ: Princeton University Press, 2005).
9. H. Peter Boswijk and Roy van der Weide, "Method of Moments Estimation of GO-GARCH Models," *Journal of Econometrics* 163, issue 1 (July 2011): 118–126.
10. L. Bauwens, S. Laurent, and J. V. K. Rombouts, "Multivariate GARCH Models: A Survey," *Journal of Applied Econometrics* 21 (2006): 79–109.
11. P. R. Hansen and A. Lunde, "A Forecast Comparison of Volatility Models: Does Anything Beat a GARCH(1,1)?" *Journal of Applied Econometrics* 20, issue 7 (December 2005): 873–889.

# PART Two

# CHAPTER 8

# Fixed Income Issues

*David Mieczkowski, PhD, and William F. McCoy, CFA, PRM*

In prior chapters, we introduced some of the common fixed income (FI) risk measures and put their evolution into a historical perspective. In particular, we introduced the concepts of duration and convexity, and how they provide information on the return profile a bond will enjoy given a movement in interest rates and spreads. We also introduced briefly a few of the bond sectors: government, corporate, and securitized. In this chapter we take a deeper look at how these risk measures can be tied together into a joint estimation of risk for fixed income.

We will start Part Two with a discussion of the issues unique to fixed income that must be dealt with up front in this chapter. The most immediate features of fixed income markets that we must grapple with are their sheer size, variety, and illiquidity. These features present us with very real problems from both a modeling and a physical resource (i.e., computers) perspective. Our approach to overcoming these problems will lay the framework for how we view the individual components of the total risk, specifically the interest rate, rate volatility, spread, bond idiosyncratic, and currency risks. We will introduce a method for linearizing the fix income return equation, and discuss what this means for the concepts of risk exposure and risk factor.

We then discuss each of these risks in detail, starting with interest rate risk. In Chapter 9 we discuss how exposure to the discount curve can be measured and used to measure total interest rate risk. We will review the deep literature on interest rate dynamics. We will contrast the use of key rate duration to principal component durations.

Interest rate optionality is ubiquitous in fixed income, and we use a section in Chapter 11 to discuss how the dynamics of the volatility surface are incorporated into the risk calculus. Since interest rate volatility is intimately linked to the assumptions made in the model used for the dynamics of the interest rate process, we include a discussion of the various flavors of volatility.

In our discussion of spread risk in Chapter 10, we will explore how the fixed income subsector-specific risks are addressed. If interest rate risk is about determining the time value of money risk associated with expected cash flows, spread risk is about determining the risk due to the uncertainty regarding the cash flows themselves. Since fixed income sectors tend to have very different cash flow profiles, spread risk becomes very sector specific. We present two basic approaches to modeling spread risk, and provide detailed descriptions of how to model spreads for mortgage securities and corporates as a backdrop for this.

After systematic spread risk is covered, bond idiosyncratic risk is addressed in Chapter 11. We define idiosyncratic risk in terms of spread residuals, and in so doing discuss what idiosyncratic risk is and is not. The lack of regular return data for many bonds is a big problem, and we present approaches to deal with this based on behavior of bonds contained on an index. What idiosyncratic risk means for corporate bonds is addressed.

As the search for yield knows no borders, we continue with a discussion of currency risk as it applies to fixed income. We detail how currency exposure in bond cash flows themselves means that dollar hedging is insufficient. We will explain how to properly measure true currency exposure, and give examples of how a proper currency exposure hedge is constructed.

Last, we comment that traditional risk models are linear in nature. This assumption influences the impact and study of the factor returns. The factor returns themselves are typically derived from a statistical analysis of the movement of the factor over time, when again linearity is assumed. Don't get us wrong; the linearity assumption has its advantages. Linearity makes the mathematics simpler, which in turn allows the derivation and computation of valuable results about the overall risk to be done quite quickly.

However, statistical (regression) models can sacrifice intuition in the quest for explanation. Little used in risk analysis today are valuation models. Take the case of spread risk in corporate bonds. A respected model for spread valuation is the Merton framework, which explains corporate spreads in an option pricing framework. Such an equation is highly nonlinear, and provides consistent valuation for both stocks and bonds. In addition, unlike statistical models, the Merton model is forward-looking, and will reflect current market expectations. To this end, at FactSet we believe the valuation approach is more robust and accurate in the final risk analysis.

## VARIETY. ILLIQUIDITY. SIZE.

The investable fixed income universe is incredibly varied with regard to the characteristics of its subsectors. From municipal bonds to supranationals, tobacco bonds to Bowie bonds,[1] Yankees to Eurodollar futures, repos to perpetuals, fixed income has something for everyone. All that variety means that there is a cash flow solution for almost every need. It also means that price comparison among securities is difficult. Because of this, fixed income trading is still mainly a specific industry on its own, albeit a very profitable one. With few notable exceptions,[2] fixed income trading is still a highly interpersonal craft, so much so that investment banking titles like managing director, vice president, and associate could easily be replaced with master craftsperson, journeyman, and apprentice with little loss of meaning. Thus, outside of a relatively small fraction of bonds that are covered by a major fixed income benchmark, price discovery for the vast majority of fixed income securities is a dicey exercise at best. In light of this, attempts to estimate individual security exposure to fixed income risk factors similar to the way equity risk models do, or through blind statistical factors, have little chance of success.

Relative to equities, the fixed income universe is enormous. FactSet has terms and conditions on over three million fixed income securities and growing. An investable universe this large presents significant challenges to risk measurement. One such challenge is simply in validating the terms and conditions data that define a security. With so many securities, data scrubbing is a dedicated function at most fixed income asset managers.[3] To be sure, there are data errors in the equity world, but to put it rather bluntly, raw fixed income data is about as sanitary as your average battlefield hospital. In fixed income, reliable data is the result of a lot of hard work; it can't be taken for granted. FactSet has quality assurance programs and data reconciliation services that involve cleaning the data. This is value added for portfolio and risk managers alike.

Yet, for all the high diversity of security type and low market value visibility, there is still hope for meaningful risk measurement. The common element that ties fixed income together as a broad asset class is an inescapable focus on cash flows and their guarantees. At its heart, fixed income is all about the determination and discounting of cash flows, and cash flows are the lens through which any attempt at defining fixed income risk must be viewed. Let equities have their earnings, and let commodities have all that glitters; fixed income will take the cash!

The powerful machinery of risk-neutral valuation was developed to reduce the problem of valuation of a complicated series of uncertain cash flows to a function (hopefully with a simple closed form) of the time value of money and the cash flow risk. We can harness this ability to provide a price from an intrinsic valuation algorithm, rather than through an extrinsic market implied approach, to good effect. With caveats about model dependence, the price of any fixed income security can be expressed as a function of interest rates, interest rate volatility, security-specific spread, and time. We may not have market prices, but a model-driven bond calculator offers us the chance to compute sensitivity measures in a much more direct way than for equities.

The common focus on cash flow is both a curse and a blessing in fixed income valuation and risk management. The conviction that two identical cash flows should be worth the same amount regardless of what security they are embedded in is fundamental for fixed income valuation. It is because of this that fixed income valuation is said to boil down to a mainly mathematical exercise in determining the timing, likelihood, and magnitude of the cash flows associated with a security, and then discounting them by a common discount curve. This is not to suggest that this is an easy task by any means, but as a risk manager, it is tempting to try to avail oneself of a large industry dedicated to building sophisticated valuation models. Let's discuss how this might be done.

In mathematics, the linear dependence of a (smooth) function on an input variable is called the first derivative; it is the rate of change of a function given a change in the input. In fixed income, duration is the name given to the linear dependence of percentage price change to a movement in one of the functional inputs to price. An effective duration is simply the percentage price change associated with a very small parallel shift in the spot curve. Key rate duration and spread duration are analogous. Conversely, convexity measures the linear dependence of duration due to a shift in a functional input, or, equivalently, convexity is a second-order price dependence measure, a second-order derivative in the mathematical sense (not in the financial use of the term).

Mathematically, duration and convexity can be defined in terms of partial derivatives as:

$$D = -\frac{1}{P}\frac{\partial P}{\partial y} \tag{8.1}$$

$$C = \frac{1}{P}\frac{\partial^2 P}{\partial y^2} \tag{8.2}$$

where $y$ is a continuous variable on which price depends (level of the spot curve, value of a key rate, spread, volatility, etc.). In the main, these sensitivities must be estimated numerically.

The preceding therefore suggests that we can define fixed income risk factors as limited to those variables that have a direct functional relationship to price. That is, our bond calculator must recognize it as an input. The spot rate of interest at each cash flow date has a direct functional relationship to price, for example, while other macro variables like gross domestic product (GDP) have an effect only through their relationship to the direct input. Variables that are correlated with functional inputs are coincident risk measures, not direct fixed income risk measures.[4] Fixed income risk factors are determined a priori, through a model-driven bond calculator, rather than a posteriori through statistical back-testing. The question of where model risk fits in, or what constitutes a good bond calculator, is discussed a little later.

Typically, fixed income securities have nonlinear dependencies on risk factors. For the moment, let's assume we are happy with our choice of fixed income bond calculator. The functional approach affords us a boon. Basic calculus provides us with the multivariate Taylor approximation formula, which we can use to linearize the dependence of security price on risk sources.

$$\Delta P \approx \sum_{n_1=0}^{N} \cdots \sum_{n_d=0}^{N} \frac{1}{n_1! \ldots n_d!} \frac{\partial^{n_1+\ldots+n_d} P}{\partial x_{n_1} \ldots \partial x_{n_d}} \Delta x_{n_1} \ldots \Delta x_{n_d} \tag{8.3}$$

where $P(x_1^0, x_2^0, \ldots, x_k^0)$ is the price of a security for some realization of the risk factors, and $\Delta x_i$ is the change in the $i$th risk factor. The use of this approximation provides a very useful framework for fixed income risk measurement, and is the salient concept presented in this chapter and for the FactSet multi-asset-class (MAC) model in general for FI securities.

In terms of durations and convexities (first- and second-order sensitivities only), this becomes:

$$\frac{\Delta P}{P} \approx -\sum_i D_i \cdot \Delta x_i + \frac{1}{2} \sum_i C_i \cdot \Delta x_i^2 + \text{Cross terms} \tag{8.4}$$

Of course, one might ask why we should bother with a linear approximation formula when we have a bond engine that can capture the nonlinearities directly. The answer is that we get a number of useful things out of linearization besides calculation speed.

For one, linearization allows risk forecasting to be neatly separated from the choice of bond calculator. As with equities, the task of risk forecasting for fixed income breaks down into two distinct stages:

1. Determine the sensitivity of each security to each common risk factor.
2. Simulate the change in each risk factor and apply simple linear algebra.

For equities, the sensitivities are determined empirically through multivariate regressions on historical time series of observed returns against factors. This yields betas or factor returns for sensitivities. As discussed earlier, there are serious liquidity issues in fixed income, so time series of price returns are generally not available for bonds. Empirical durations are therefore rarely available. This is where a bond calculator comes into the picture. We can use a bond calculator to determine durations and convexities (and any higher-order sensitivities and cross terms). Sensitivities become model determined. The linearization also allows for easy comparison of different bond calculators by simply swapping out one set of calculator-computed sensitivities for the other. In fact, model risk can essentially be measured as a weighted difference in sensitivities. Linearization also allows for the easy aggregation of risks by type; price-based sensitivities are additive. This makes it very easy to gauge the impact on a risk profile through hedging with other specific securities.

The other major motivation behind the linearization of the fixed income return function is the large computational problem posed by full repricing. Many risk measures, such as value at risk (VaR) or expected tail loss (ETL), are best calculated using Monte Carlo methods. Yet, it is not uncommon for a fixed income asset manager to have hundreds of portfolios that can contain thousands, or tens of thousands, of securities each. The Barclays Capital U.S. Aggregate index, for example, contains roughly 10,000 bonds. For such a portfolio, a Monte Carlo–based VaR calculation with 5,000 scenarios requires 50 million prices to be calculated! Even for a portfolio that consists of fairly basic bonds, this can be a challenge with 2012 computers. Even if the average time to price a bond for a scenario were just a millisecond, 50 million prices would still require a single CPU today, more than 12 hours to complete. For any portfolio that contains mortgage-backed securities (MBSs) or other path-dependent securities, which themselves may require a Monte Carlo simulation to obtain a single price, the computational problem can become intractable. We need CPUs from 2025 or later to realize these calculations in real time for today's problems, let alone problems we'll encounter in 2025!

The typical brute force solution involves a distributed processing grid approach (the use of multiple PCs working in tandem). While this brute force approach can work for smaller portfolios, certain bottlenecks prevent distributed processing from being an infinitely scalable solution. In addition, the monetary cost of setting up and maintaining large CPU grids can be significant. As a result, particularly in the arena of MBS valuation, several shortcut methods for calculating a bond's price, and hence VaR, were developed. McCoy and Ta[5] (2001) compare methods to approximate MBS VaRs and find that a solution based on a multivariable Taylor series approximation provides the best balance between accuracy and computational efficiency.[6] However, their analysis is restricted only to interest rate risk and its effect on prepayment risk. We will shortly provide empirical evidence supporting the efficacy of the Taylor method as it extends to incorporate spread and other risks.

Viewing price as a smooth function of a collection of risk factors and then using the multivariate Taylor formula will be the basis for our further detailed discussion of fixed income risk. Before we can go further, however, we must address the issue of which price we're applying the Taylor formula to. There are usually two prices associated with any fixed income security, corresponding to whether accrued interest is excluded or included. The price excluding accrued interest is referred to as the flat (or clean) price. The price that includes the accrued interest, and therefore represents actual market value, is referred to as the full (or dirty) price.

To aid exposition, for the remainder of this chapter we assume that the flat price of any fixed income security is a smooth function of interest rates, interest rate volatility, spread, currency, and time. Any other variables will be considered coincident to these, their effect on risk being measured through their impact on one of these direct risk factors, possibly through hidden (statistically estimated) processes. We devote a detailed chapter to each of these risk sources later.

The full period returns for fixed income securities can be estimated by decomposing the full return into a return due to a change in the accrual component and a return due to change in the flat price component.

$$\Delta MV = \Delta AI + \Delta P \bullet B(t_1) \tag{8.5}$$

where $\Delta MV$ is the change in the market value, or full price, of the security over the holding period; $\Delta AI$ is the change in the accruals over the holding period; $\Delta P$ is the change in the flat price over the holding period, where the ending price is the estimated flat price; and $B(t_1)$ is the remaining principal balance at the end of the holding period.

Any change in accruals takes into account both the interest and principal components of the cash flows that were scheduled to occur during the holding period. This is a nonstandard definition of accrued interest that captures the expected earnings to the bond over the horizon due to both interest and principal payments.

$$\Delta AI = MV_0 \bullet (R_{PDN} + R_{CPN}) \tag{8.6}$$

where $MV_0$ is the market value or full price of the security at the beginning of the holding period, $R_{PDN}$ is the percentage return due to any principal pay-down component of any cash flows that occur over the holding period (e.g., amortization), and $R_{CPN}$ is the percentage return due to the interest component of any cash flows that occur over the holding period. This is why the change in the flat price gets multiplied by the remaining principal balance and is especially important for amortizing securities such as MBSs when the holding period spans a coupon payment.

Having accounted for accruals thus, we can turn our attention to the question of accuracy of the Taylor approximation, as applied to the clean price change. We won't be able to reap the full benefits of linearization if the Taylor approximation is poor for a tractable order of expansion.

The remainder of this chapter is devoted to presenting the results of an empirical study on how well the Taylor method works when applied to fixed income, as well as some hands-on examples of the Taylor method, and can be viewed as being somewhat tangential to the rest of the book.

The subsequent chapters on interest rate and interest rate volatility risk, bond-specific spread risk, and currency risk will take a deeper look at these risk factors, with an emphasis on describing the practical means of estimating the distributional properties of the changes in these risk factors, and how they can be used in Monte Carlo simulation.

## EMPIRICAL EVIDENCE

In risk management, one of the primary challenges we face is to gain an ability to describe the joint distribution of price movements of securities (i.e., covariance), with a focus on being able to alter that joint distribution for specific portfolios through judicious use of hedging or portfolio construction. Factor analysis is employed, therefore, to reduce this to a problem of estimation of the joint distribution of a set of common risk factors, for which hedging strategies become easily determinable. The Taylor approximation formula provides us with the link we need to employ factor analysis in a tractable manner for fixed income securities. Therefore, what we are after in this chapter is to understand how well we can recover price movements given factor realizations. The issue of estimating the joint distribution properties of those factors is left to later chapters.

To avoid creating a joint test of estimation error along with risk factor distribution estimation error, we conducted our tests using historical market movements and actual market prices. That is, we measure the various risk factors ex post facto, use these ex post facto realizations in the price estimation formula, and then compare to actual market prices to judge how well the method worked.

## TEST PORTFOLIOS AND METHODOLOGY

For our tests we have chosen four sample portfolios. We report both average security-level statistics and portfolio-level statistics for each of the portfolios. There is a portfolio of high yield corporate bonds (with and without call provisions), a portfolio of home equity MBSs, a portfolio of agency interest-only/principal-only (IO/PO) mortgage strips, and an equal-weighted portfolio that combines these three. With the exception of the IO/PO strips, all bonds were listed on a benchmark, which provided the pricing source.[7]

The basic testing setup is as follows:

For a base date:

- Record the market price for each security in the portfolio.
- For each security in the portfolio, given the price, calculate an ordinary least squares (OAS) for each security.
- Record the key interest rates and volatilities for the whole portfolio and OAS for each security; essentially archive these results.
- Calculate the sensitivities.

On the horizon date:

- Record the market price for each security in the portfolio.
- For each security in the portfolio, calculate once from the price to obtain an OAS for each security.
- For each security, calculate the (*ex post*) OAS change from the base date.
- For the whole portfolio, calculate the key interest rate and volatility changes.
- Calculate the estimated price from interest rate, volatility, and OAS changes.
- Calculate the estimated price from interest rate and volatility changes, while holding OAS constant.

We know that the Taylor approximation will be better the smaller the change in the risk factors from the base scenario, by virtue of the properties of smooth functions. When determining repricing accuracy, it suffices to examine the performance of the method out in the tails of the risk factor distribution. We have therefore tested using base days from when the actual one-day interest rate, volatility, or OAS changes were the most dramatic during the period between August 1, 2006, and December 31, 2007. We have also tested the price estimation error across one-day, two-week, one-month, and three-month horizons from the chosen base dates.[8]

Since price is generally a monotonic function of the various risk variables, we are concerned to a large degree with how well the estimation method captures tail risk. Our base interest-rate pricing curve is the U.S. LIBOR curve. We use 12 points along the LIBOR curve as our key rates. The points have tenors of 3, 6, 12, 24, 36, 48, 60, 84, 120, 180, 240, and 300 months. For volatility, we use points from a short volatility curve calibrated using caps and a long volatility curve calibrated using swaptions. We assume a lognormal distribution of interest rates in determining implied volatilities. For OAS, we test the method using actual OAS changes and also test the method with OAS held constant. Our tests utilize FactSet's fixed income analytics engine to produce the relevant bond analytics.

## TEST METRICS

We must define metrics to gauge the accuracy and computational efficiency of the method versus standard full repricing.

Let:

- $P_0$ be the price in the base scenario.
- $P_s$ be the actual full calculated price for a scenario *s*.
- $\tilde{P}_s$ be the estimated price for a scenario *s*.

To determine accuracy, we define the *percentage error* (PE) for a set of scenarios *S* to be:

$$PE = \frac{1}{|S|} \cdot \sum_{s \in S} \frac{|\tilde{P}_s - P_s|}{P_0} \tag{8.7}$$

The *percentage move* (PM) is defined as:

$$PM = \frac{1}{|S|} \cdot \sum_{s \in S} \frac{|\tilde{P}_s - P_s|}{|P_s - P_0|} \tag{8.8}$$

The percentage move gives us the estimation error size relative to the size of the actual price move, averaged over the set of scenarios, while the percentage error gives us the estimation error relative to the base price.

Table 8.1 shows an example of how the Taylor approximation with accruals might come together to estimate the dirty and clean prices for a 30-year agency MBS pass-through (FH30, 5.5, 2009). The table shows the repricing formulas in action over the two-week horizon 8/24/2010 to

**TABLE 8.1** Repricing with accruals.

| | |
|---|---|
| Base dirty price | 107.082 |
| Base clean price | 106.685 |
| Interest rate effect | 0.213 |
| Volatility effect | 0.035 |
| Spread effect | –0.086 |
| Roll-down effect | –0.016 |
| Estimated clean price | 106.831 |
| Actual horizon clean price | 106.839 |
| Horizon pay-down return | –0.071 |
| Horizon coupon return | 0.210 |
| Horizon remaining balance | 0.970 |
| Estimated dirty price | 106.979 |
| Actual horizon dirty price | 106.976 |
| Percentage error | 0.003 |
| Percentage move | 3.046 |

*Sources:* FactSet and BofA Merrill Lynch.

9/7/2010, with comparison to actual market price moves using the accuracy metrics. The bond starts with a clean price of 106.685 on the base date of 8/24/2010. Grouping all the terms in the Taylor approximation that correspond to the interest rate factors, the Taylor approximation ascribes a price move of 0.21 to interest rate movements. Combining this with the combined price move due to volatility movements, spread change, and roll-down produces an estimated horizon clean price of 106.831, compared to the actual horizon clean price of 106.839. Next, the accrual components are factored in to produce an estimated horizon dirty price of 106.979, compared to an actual horizon dirty price of 106.976. Finally, the estimation error from the Taylor approximation with accruals stands at 3 basis points, which represents 3 percent of the price move.

Table 8.2 summarizes the ability of the repricing method to capture the actual price changes of our three security types using the percentage move statistic, ranked from best to worst. Not surprisingly, the combined portfolio containing equal weight in high yield corporate bonds, IO and PO strips, and home equity asset-backed security (ABS) tranches displays the best overall performance in terms of percentage move. Total security count for the combined portfolio was approximately 60 bonds. The obvious trend is that even mild diversification significantly reduces the mean error size and volatility.

The test environment was chosen to approximate the price movement at the tails of the pricing distribution, by choosing base dates over which

**TABLE 8.2** Percentage move.

| Portfolio | 1 Day | 2 Weeks | 1 Month | 3 Months | 1 Year |
|---|---|---|---|---|---|
| Combined | 10.14 | 12.52 | 8.40 | 6.15 | — |
| High yield | 13.79 | 15.10 | 5.32 | 16.95 | 5.15 |
| Home equity | 3.72 | 22.18 | 19.21 | 13.74 | 18.69 |
| PO | 16.48 | 11.80 | 22.14 | 55.57 | — |
| IO | 16.88 | 17.91 | 52.82 | 109.53 | — |
| Security | 19.07 | 54.12 | 55.15 | 43.93 | 35.78 |

*Sources:* FactSet and BofA Merrill Lynch.

the risk factors experienced the largest one-day change. Yet, the method was still able to capture around 90 percent of the price move out to the three-month horizon. The method also showed a remarkable consistency across a range of price moves, with the price moves ranging from 14 basis points (bps) up to 642 bps for the combined portfolio. For the high yield and home equity portfolios, the actual price moves were as large as 20 percent, of which the repricing method was able to capture between 80 and 95 percent of the price move.

There is degradation in the IO and PO portfolios with lengthening horizon. For these highly path-dependent securities, a large portion of this pricing error results from prepayment forecast error. The coupon return, pay-down return, and horizon remaining balance must be forecast at the base date. Even with perfect foreknowledge of the mortgage rate path, prepayment projections are notoriously noisy, even for the best street prepayment models. As IO and PO strips are especially sensitive to prepayments, this means that even with a full repricing of the strips, there would be significant dirty price error. It is also worth pointing out that the pricing errors for an IO and PO tied to the same collateral were of opposite sign but comparable magnitude, which is not surprising. A higher than expected prepayment will be bad for an IO but good for the associated PO. Since if we combine an IO strip and a PO strip written on the same collateral we get a simple pass-through, this means that pass-through MBSs have significantly better performance in this regard.

We compare this to the home equity ABS portfolio, which was composed of mainly senior tranches. While collateral default rates were rising to significantly higher levels than anticipated, at least during the test period, it was the support bonds that were eating most of those early losses. These bonds experienced significant price moves over these horizons, but it was due more to an elevation in the risk of losses, as opposed to an error in forecasting losses over the horizon. As a result, the home equity ABS portfolio performs significantly better, even though the actual price moves for home equity ABSs were significantly larger than those experienced by the IO and PO portfolios.

The percentage move is a good metric for measuring the accuracy of the method, as it simply gives the average ratio of the absolute pricing error to the size of the actual price move. It does not shed any light, however, on the range of price moves the sample encountered. Therefore, we also computed the percentage error, which was defined as the average ratio of the absolute error to the initial base price. We would expect the method to break down over very large price moves, as the Taylor series approach will lose accuracy at a large enough scale. Since the sensitivities are numerically computed, we might also expect the method to break down at very small scales, as those numerical approximation errors become large relative to the price move. The percentage error (PE) metric therefore gives us the ability to decide if a large percentage move (PM) number is the result of an acceptable level of approximation error at very large or small scales.

Table 8.3 presents the results in terms of the percentage error. The error as a percentage of bond prices grows as the time horizon lengthens as expected. The results therefore show that for even mildly diversified portfolios, the repricing method is able to capture most of the price move and that the error scales reasonably well across a range of price moves.

Figures 8.1 and 8.2 contain the plots of predicted versus actual price moves for the combined portfolio across the one-day and three-month horizons for the eight most extreme interest rate movements over our test period. The plots illustrate the ability of the repricing to remain accurate over large factor shocks, and give a sense of the size of the price moves encountered in our tests. The charts contain the regression statistics for the data. The perfect model would have an R-squared of 1 and a regression equation of $y = x$.

**TABLE 8.3** Percentage error.

| Portfolio | 1 Day | 2 Weeks | 1 Month | 3 Months | 1 Year |
|---|---|---|---|---|---|
| Combined | 0.04 | 0.10 | 0.16 | 0.25 | — |
| High yield | 0.04 | 0.16 | 0.07 | 0.06 | 0.39 |
| Home equity | 0.01 | 0.24 | 0.17 | 0.48 | 3.13 |
| PO | 0.14 | 0.32 | 0.82 | 2.38 | — |
| IO | 0.20 | 0.81 | 1.52 | 4.90 | — |
| Security | 0.11 | 0.35 | 0.48 | 1.55 | 4.37 |

*Sources:* FactSet and BofA Merrill Lynch.

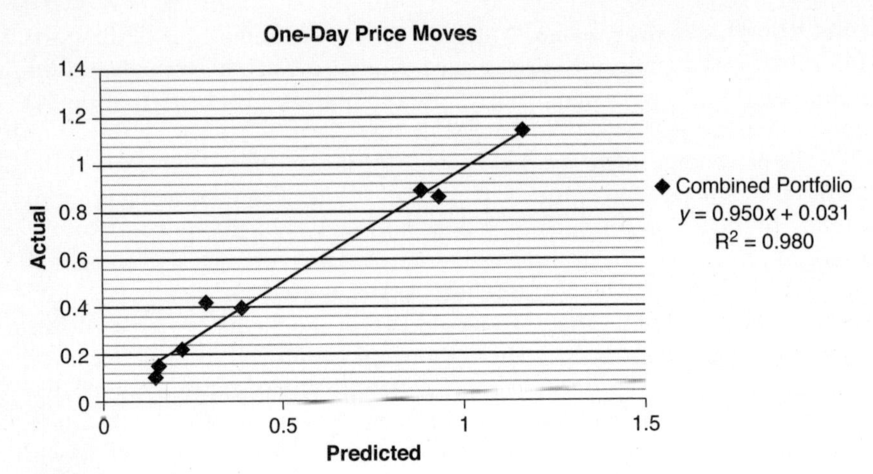


**FIGURE 8.1** Predicted versus actual percentage price moves for the combined portfolio—one-day horizon.
*Sources:* FactSet and BofA Merrill Lynch.

Clearly, the slope coefficient and R-squared statistic are very good and remain very consistent over lengthening time horizons and over a range of price moves. Of particular note is the way that the range of price moves scales with a growing time horizon. This is to be expected, but it's worth pointing out that the base dates were chosen to approximate the tail of the one-day price move distribution and that the scaling of the range of price

**FIGURE 8.2** Predicted versus actual percentage price moves for the combined portfolio—three-month horizon.
*Sources:* FactSet and BofA Merrill Lynch.

moves over longer horizons would indicate that these observations represent a good approximation of tail behavior for horizons up to at least three months.

A particularly important feature of the method is the ability to capture spread change. The second half of 2007 saw a dramatic repricing of risk in the credit markets, and any risk model that a assumed constant spread for VaR purposes would have missed the main driver of price deterioration during that time.

The second half of 2007, therefore, offered a great chance to test the ability of the method to capture large spread changes, since spreads blew out across a number of asset classes (subprime MBSs, municipal bonds, high yield corporates). As might be expected, the home equity portfolio experienced the worst spread changes through this period, with the average spread blowing out by as much as 750 bps across the three-month horizon. This is contrasted against observations taken from the second half of 2006 and first quarter of 2007. Here the three-month spread changes were much smaller, only on the order of 50 to 100 bps. This gave our sample a great variation of price moves across the three-month horizon. In fact, for the home equity portfolio, percentage price changes across all three-month horizons varied from as little as 23 bps to as much as 13.5 percent.[9] Figure 8.3 presents the predicted versus actual chart for the percentage price moves of the home equity portfolio across the three-month horizon.

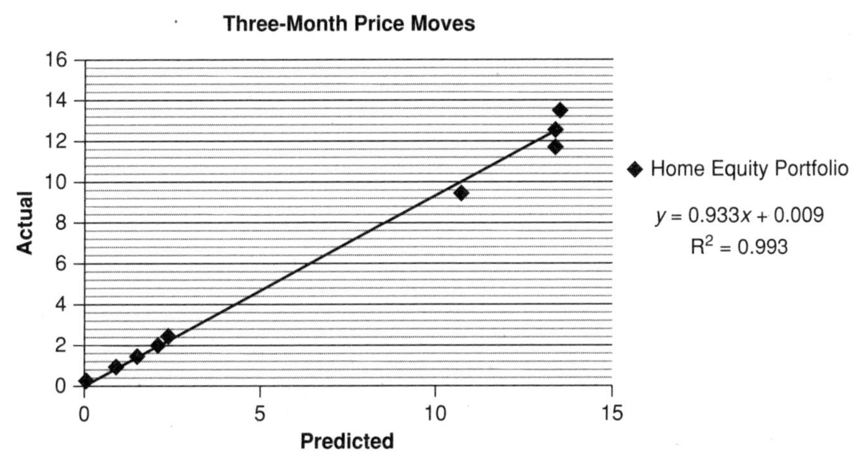


**FIGURE 8.3** Predicted versus actual percentage price moves for the home equity portfolio—three-month horizon.
*Sources:* FactSet and BofA Merrill Lynch.

We tested our model by marking to market, rather than marking to model. It's worth pointing out again that for purposes of the test, the spread change was measured *ex post*. Marking to market then produces realistic spread changes. This was done to test the relevance of our method to real-world risk management. However, the repricing method relies on underlying models to derive the sensitivities. Thus, some of the risk, which manifests as unexplained prediction error, is due to underlying model error as opposed to inaccuracy of the repricing method per se.

This is especially the case with the IO and PO strips, which showed the weakest performance in our tests. Much of the repricing error can be attributed to the failure of the underlying prepay model to correctly capture and allocate prepayment and default risk. That is, the difference between the predicted and actual realized cash flows that occur during the horizon period will be a source of error when measured via mark to market, even for full valuation.

## COMPUTATIONAL EFFICIENCY

As mentioned before, one of the appealing benefits of the Taylor approximation is that, with a set of known sensitivities, the computation of popular risk statistics such as VaR and ETL become significantly more tractable. The linear structure of the Taylor formula produces prices significantly faster for a given scenario than a full bond calculator–based price for all but the simplest bonds. We now discuss to what extent we can measure this rigorously.

Computational savings seem difficult to measure, as there is such a wide array of configurations and variables. The usefulness of any tests using specific hardware or software will likely age quickly as faster chips and more efficient computational methods are created. In computer science, computational efficiency is therefore addressed using complexity classifications. Rather than count physical clock time, time is measured by the number of basic operations that must be performed to do something. For our purposes, we will measure the computational gain of the Taylor approximation over full bond calculator–based pricing in the context of a Monte Carlo–based VaR calculation.

While the linear math of the Taylor formula is appealing, calculation of the sensitivities does not come for free. For most bonds, the sensitivities must be derived numerically. This usually involves using something like the secant method or an analogue. Consider the case of numerically estimating the key rate duration at the 10-year point. The standard approach to numerically calculating this would require a shift up and a shift down of the 10-year rate, and the repricing of the bond in those two scenarios, holding all else constant. The slope of the secant line then provides a good estimate of the first partial derivative of price with respect to a change in the 10-year key rate.

$$\frac{\partial P}{\partial r_{10}} \approx \frac{P_+ - P_-}{2h} \tag{8.9}$$

We get a slightly less accurate estimate of the second partial derivative from this using our knowledge of the base price.

$$\frac{\partial^2 P}{\partial {r_{10}}^2} \approx \frac{P_+ + P_- - 2P_0}{h^2} \tag{8.10}$$

The point of this is that numerical estimation of the sensitivities requires full repricings of the bond using the bond calculator. First-order sensitivities require two full repricings each, and second-order terms like cross partials might require up to four repricings. Higher-order terms improve the accuracy of the Taylor approximation, but require a growing number of repricings to calculate.

The measure of the computational savings is then just the raw number of full repricings that must be done to numerically calculate the sensitivities. For our tests, we required 80 full repricings to compute all of the relevant sensitivities. So the efficient repricing method would compare very favorably against full valuation in a Monte Carlo VaR setting that used significantly more scenarios (500 or more, for example). Since VaR is concerned with behavior in the tails, calculation of VaR using Monte Carlo simulation requires that a lot of scenarios be generated to reduce sample error. So the pricing error of the Taylor approach can be weighed against the sample error imposed by scenario number limitations that full bond calculator repricing might impose for practical implementation. One-day VaR is less useful if it takes a week to calculate it! Simulating a large sample of risk factor scenarios will not add significantly to the overall calculation time because the computational costs of the efficient repricing method are overwhelmingly dominated by the time needed to compute the sensitivities. Therefore, sample error in the tails of the risk factor distribution can largely be eliminated by the Taylor approximation method.

## CONCLUSION

The fixed income universe is large, illiquid, and varied. The familiar approach to defining and measuring risk in equities does not carry over to fixed income. A tractable method for measuring fixed income risk is needed.

Linearization of the price function through Taylor series expansion provides a reasonable approach for formalizing and extending the use of common risk statistics like duration and convexity that have a long history of use in fixed income.

The Taylor method has several appealing features. It allows for a natural separation of risk sensitivities from risk factors. It allows easy comparison of the model risk that comes with using a specific bond price calculator. It allows a risk manager a way to harness the expertise of an evolved industry dedicated to producing ever more sophisticated bond valuation models. The additive property of mathematical derivatives (as opposed to financial derivatives) means that computation of total portfolio exposure and hedges to specific risks are straightforward. Finally, there are significant computational advantages associated with it that make risk forecasting tractable.

While certainly not perfect, the method shows a good level of accuracy for mildly diversified fixed income portfolios in tests meant to approximate the tails of the pricing distribution. The accuracy is generally good across a range of time horizons from one day to three months that includes significant price moves.

## NOTES

1. In 1997, the Prudential Insurance Company bought US$55 million worth of 10-year bonds secured by the royalties from the current and future revenues of the 25 albums that the musician David Bowie had recorded prior to 1990.
2. The agency mortgage to be announced (TBA) market is one notable exception. Daily trading volume in agency TBAs can easily average US$100 billion. It is precisely the uniformity out of heterogeneity of TBA contracts that has afforded this.
3. The FactSet Fixed Income Reconciliation Utility, for example, was created specifically in response to client demand for tools that make the process of creating custom client data QA reports more scalable and cost effective.
4. We can always apply chain rule from calculus if we were to posit a functional relationship between a direct risk factor $y(x)$ and a coincident one $x$.
5. W. McCoy and T. Ta, "Comparing Methods to Approximate Mortgage-Backed Security VaR," *RiskMetrics Journal*, 2001.
6. The other methods they considered were static cash flow analysis, effective duration, ABCD methodology, and quadratic approximation.
7. All prices were sourced from BofA Merrill Lynch.
8. Prices for the IO/PO portfolio were available only on a weekly basis.
9. Of course the performance of subprime ABSs got even worse in the time after our test period. While it would be interesting to reprise our tests to include the worst of the credit crunch, liquidity in these bonds dried up to the extent that price discovery became mostly meaningless.

CHAPTER 9

# Interest Rate Risk

**_David Mieczkowski, PhD, and Mido Shammaa, CFA, FRM_**

Fixed income is all about cash flows and the time value of money. Interest rates are a way of expressing the latter, so interest rate risk is concerned with ways in which the time value of money may change in the future. It's probably not necessary to explain why understanding interest rate risk is such a big deal, but just in case you haven't stared into the abyss in a while, consider this: according to the Bank for International Settlements, notional amount outstanding of interest rate contracts, forward rate agreements (FRAs), swaps, and options totaled over US$550 trillion, with a mark-to-market value of over US$13 trillion, as of June 2011. Given that the U.S. gross domestic product (GDP) is about $15 trillion, that's a lot of money! Now, if you're still wondering what all the fuss regarding interest rate risk is about, you're probably a gold bug who has wandered into the wrong chapter.

With all that interest in interest, you probably wouldn't be surprised at the size of the industry devoted to nothing but understanding interest rate risk. Indeed, it could be said that interest rate risk was the first type of financial risk that people tried to manage. The world didn't get its first stock certificate until the 1600s, whereas the First Council of Nicaea was already setting limits on high yield investments in the year 325, by forbidding the early Catholic Church from lending at rates higher than 13 percent per annum.[1] Money lending, it seems, is the world's second-oldest profession. For all that history and attention focused on it, the trick about discussing interest rate risk is basically, well, where to start?

The problem with interest rates is there's an infinite number of them and twice that many ways to describe them: simple, compound, continuous, floating, fixed, amortizing, back-set, accrued, par, spot, forward, constant maturity, overnight, semiannual, actual, 30/360, real, nominal, risky, risk-free, foreign, domestic, government, LIBOR, tax-exempt, and so forth. If that weren't enough, you also almost need a PhD in mathematics just to understand how to describe their dynamics, not to mention how those dynamics affect the value of different cash flows. As whole books have been written on the subject, we'll limit our focus in this chapter to understanding how interest rate risk is expressed in the context of the Taylor repricing formula alluded to in the preceding chapter.

In this chapter we review the basics of interest rate curves, how to model the evolution of term structures through time, and the different flavors of duration. Since each of these is a very deep subject in its own right, the technical part of our discussion will be limited mostly to defining terms and establishing some notation. Most of our focus will be on providing an economic intuition for the key concepts. We conclude the chapter with a discussion of how these pieces come together to enable computation of some new and old interest rate risk measures.

## THE TERM STRUCTURE

The term structure of interest rates refers to the relationship between the yield to maturity of a set of bonds to their time to maturity; in a sense, it models the time value of money. Additionally, the time value of money in a given currency can be expressed in a lot of different ways. Perhaps the simplest is directly through zero coupon bond prices. A zero coupon bond price (ZCBP) is just the value of a $1 cash flow at some fixed maturity date $T$. Multiplying any certain cash flow by the price of the zero coupon bond with the same maturity provides the present value of that cash flow. Zero coupon bond prices are thus simply discount factors, and the value of any bond with known cash flows can be easily determined once we know these discount factors. Time is infinitely divisible in theory, and thus in theory there is an infinite collection of zero coupon bonds that together determine the time value of money. This term structure of discount factors can be visually expressed as a simple curve of price against time to maturity, as illustrated in Figure 9.1.

While the term structure of discount factors may be the simplest way to express the time value of money, it isn't the most intuitive. In this simple form, it is difficult to decide whether one zero coupon bond represents a better investment than another. Ultimately, investors care about returns, and a more natural way to express the time value of money would be in terms of some type of rate of return. Internal rate of return is a popular way to compare investments, and in fixed income this is just called the yield to maturity.

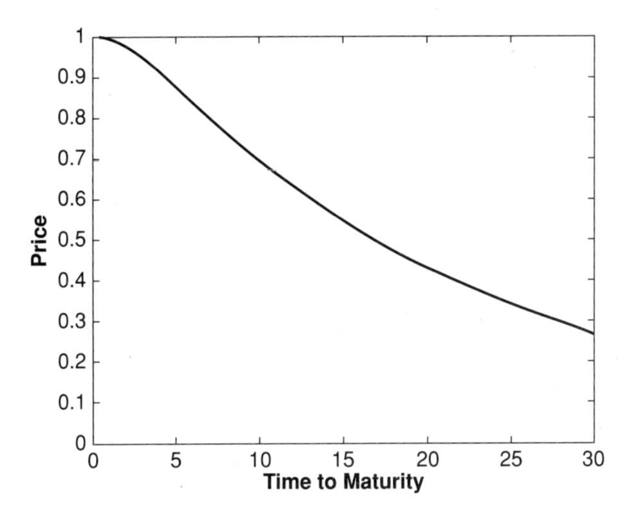


**FIGURE 9.1** The 30-year term structure of discount factors.
*Source:* FactSet.

The $n$ times compounded spot rate of maturity $T$ is the yield to maturity of a zero coupon bond that matures at time $T$. It is the holding period (or internal) return earned by buying the zero coupon bond with time to maturity $T$ and holding it until maturity. At time $t$, we can express this value mathematically as just:

$$r(t,T) = n\left(\left(\frac{1}{P(t,T)}\right)^{\frac{1}{n(T-t)}} - 1\right) \tag{9.1}$$

As with any return calculation, the unit of time and the compounding convention are needed to specify the spot rate fully, with the typical conventions being to express the spot rate on an annualized basis, with either annual or semiannual compounding. In what follows, we assume compounding equal to the time unit, but everything can easily be adjusted to accommodate other compounding conventions.

The *term structure of spot rates* is then just the collection of spot rates that corresponds to the collection of zero coupon bonds for the infinite collection of times to maturity. The spot curve just summarizes this collection in graphical form as a plot of return against time to maturity as in Figure 9.2.

The spot curve therefore provides a compact way to express time value of money as the holding period return of zero coupon bonds and therefore gives the required rate of return on any known cash flow. When we discuss

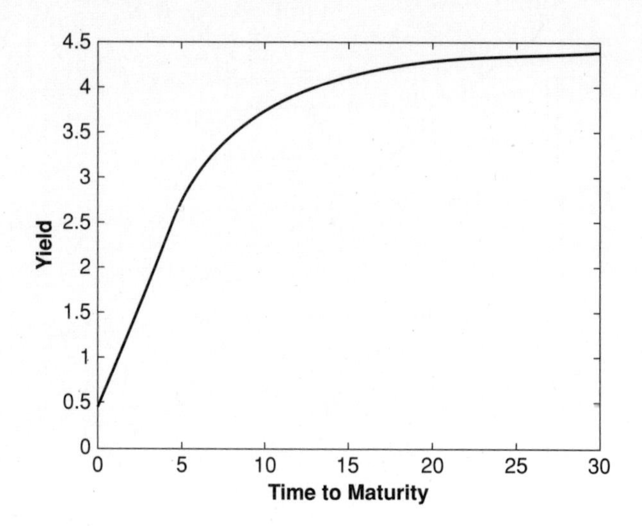


**FIGURE 9.2** The 30-year term structure of spot rates.
*Source:* FactSet.

durations shortly, we will show a preference for using the spot curve for measuring interest rate risk exposure.

Closely related to spot rates are forward rates. Consider a forward contract that delivers at time $T_1$ a zero coupon bond with a later maturity $T_2$ at the *forward price* $F(t, T_1, T_2)$. The forward price of this zero coupon bond can be determined in the same way as the forward price of any commodity, except without warehousing or carry costs. Namely, as there is no warehousing cost, the forward contract can be perfectly hedged through the following cash-and-carry strategy. At time $t$, buy the zero coupon bond with maturity $T_2$ at a price of $P(t,T_2)$ Finance this by selling short $F(t, T_1, T_2)$ shares of the zero coupon bond with maturity $T_1$. This strategy will have a value of $P(T_1, T_2) - F(t, T_1, T_2)$ at time $T_1$. In order for this strategy to provide a hedge against the forward contract, we must have $P(T_1, T_2) - F(t, T_1, T_2) \geq 0$. On the other hand, in order for the forward contract to be a hedge against this strategy, we must have $P(T_1, T_2) - F(t, T_1, T_2) \leq 0$. Combining these and solving forces us to conclude that $(t, T_1, T_2) = \frac{P(t, T_2)}{P(t, T_1)}$. This is summarized in tabular form in Table 9.1.

With this forward contract setup in mind, suppose we entered into a forward contract at time $t$ to buy a zero coupon bond with maturity $T_2$ at time $T_1$. We can ask the question: what will be the holding period

**TABLE 9.1** Forward replication strategy payoff table.

| | |
|---|---|
| Long one share of $T_2$ with maturity zero | $1 \cdot P(T_1, T_2)$ |
| Short $F(t, T_1, T_2)$ shares of $T_1$ with maturity zero | $-F(t, T_1, T_2) \cdot 1$ |
| Long one forward contract | $P(T_1, T_2) - F(t, T_1, T_2)$ |

return that we would realize from time $T_2$ to $T_1$, which we can lock in at time $t$?

Since we know with certainty the price we will pay at time $t$, by definition the holding period return we can lock in at time $t$ is just:

$$f(t, T_1, T_2) = \left( \frac{1}{F(t, T_1, T_2)} \right)^{\frac{1}{(T_2 - T_1)}} - 1 \tag{9.2}$$

This rate of return is known as the time $t$ forward rate with maturity $T_1$ and tenor $T_2 - T_1$.[2] Notice that at time $t = T_1$, the forward contract would be for immediate delivery, so that the forward price of the zero coupon bond is just the spot price of the same, and the locked-in return is just the spot rate of return. This connection with forward contracts on zero coupon bonds is, in fact, how the spot rate gets its name.

In the preceding, we have defined forward rates using strictly positive tenors; that is, we have implicitly assumed that $T_2 - T_1 > 0$. This is in keeping with the intuition that a spot rate and a forward rate are just holding period returns over some strictly positive holding period. This is equivalent to the assumption of discrete compounding and is in keeping with the types of rates that are encountered in actual markets. It should be pointed out, however, that much of the theoretical literature on interest rates posits continuous compounding, which squeezes holding periods down to infinitesimal size. We note that if desired, by taking limits as the tenor goes to zero, we can get a continuous analogue of equation (9.2):

$$f(t, T) = -\frac{\delta \ln\left[P(t, T)\right]}{\delta T} \tag{9.3}$$

The mathematical treatment of interest rates often becomes more elegant through the use of continuous compounding, but some form of discretization is almost always unavoidable in practice. For small tenors (one year or less), simple interest convention is common in the market. If we fix the tenor to be some small time increment $\delta$ (say a quarter of a year), then we can define a forward rate earned from time $T$ to $T+\delta$ to be the holding period return calculated using simple interest convention:

$$f(t,T,T+\delta)=\frac{1}{\delta}\cdot\left[\frac{1}{F(t,T_1,T_2)}-1\right] \tag{9.4}$$

The forward rate calculated in this way is called *forward LIBOR* with tenor $\delta$. When $T=t$ the forward has immediate expiry and we can again link forward LIBOR to spot LIBOR. Spot LIBOR rates with tenors up to a year are common in the market. More importantly, there is a nice connection between interest rate swaps and forward LIBOR.

The time value of money is most accurately expressed using internal rates of return on zero coupon bonds. Unfortunately, except for the shortest maturities, zero coupon bond prices and therefore spot rates are rarely directly observable in fixed income markets.[3] A collection of interest rate swaps and coupon-bearing government bonds is the norm. As noted at the beginning of the chapter, the market for forward rate agreements and interest rate swaps is enormous in both notional and mark-to-market terms. Fortunately, with spot and forward rates defined, a fairly simple relationship between spot and forward rates and rates on coupon-bearing bonds and swaps can be derived, and a link between spot and forward curves and liquid markets can be provided.

Recall that a (payer) interest rate swap can be expressed simply as a long position in a floating rate bond and a short position in a fixed rate bond. If the fixed and floating legs have the same maturity $T$ and pay dates with the same regular frequency $\delta$, then we call the coupon that sets the value of the fixed rate leg equal to par the *swap (or par) rate* with reset frequency $\delta$ and tenor $T$. The value of the floating rate bond at initiation will just be the notional invested, while the value of the fixed rate bond can be expressed as a portfolio of zero coupon bonds with position size equal to the coupon. Assuming a \$1 notional and expressing the swap rate on an annualized basis, we can write this relationship as:

$$1-\left[\sum_{j=1}^{N} S_{1,N}\cdot\delta\cdot P(0,T_j)+P(0,T_N)\right]=0 \tag{9.5}$$

or equivalently, solving for the swap rate, as:

$$S_{1,N}=\frac{1-P(0,T_N)}{\sum_{j=1}^{N}\delta\cdot P(0,T_j)} \tag{9.6}$$

Swap rates are then linked to spot rates through zero coupon bonds, but it is the relationship to forward rates that provides the cleanest link. The swap rate, at time $t$, can be expressed as a weighted average of forward rates if we set weights as:

$$w_j^{1,N}(t) = \frac{\delta \cdot P(t, T_{j+1})}{\sum_{j=1}^{N} \delta \cdot P(t, T_j)} \tag{9.7}$$

so that:

$$S_{1,N}(t) = \sum_{j=1}^{N} w_j(t) \cdot f(t, T_j, T_{j+1}) \tag{9.8}$$

The denominator of the weights is just the annuity factor, and we can use this expression to easily see how to also express forward starting swap rates as a weighted average of the forwards that correspond to the forward starting swap reset dates, where the weights are in terms of the forward starting annuity. We can use this equation to define forward starting swaps as well.

For a fixed reset frequency $\delta$, the *par curve* of reset frequency $\delta$ is the curve that gives the swap rates in terms of swap tenor. For each tenor, we can also construct the associated forward par curves as a function of the forward maturity. To get back to the spot curve from the par curve, we can apply coupon stripping. Stripping is just another way to say we solve equation (9.8) iteratively for the zero coupon bond price that recovers the next swap rate, starting with the shortest-maturity swap.

Whether spot, forward, or par curve, there are finitely liquid market instruments, whereas the curves we have defined describe an infinite continuum. Fitting these infinite dimensional curves to the handful of observable market instruments is therefore something of an art form and has been an object of much study and debate. There are two basic approaches. The first is to take one of the three curves as fundamental and apply interpolation methods. A good survey of interpolation methods popularly in use is Hagan and West.[4] The second approach is to posit a model for the dynamics of the short rate through some stochastic differential equation and to calibrate the parameters of the model to recover the observed market instruments. The prices of plain-vanilla bonds, like zero coupon bonds and swaps, can then be recovered through knowledge of the short rate dynamics, typically through Monte Carlo simulation, short rate trees, or sometimes through closed-form analytic pricing formulas. Term structure dynamics are vitally important for pricing interest rate derivatives and will be discussed next.

## TERM STRUCTURE DYNAMICS

The term structure tells us what the time value of money is today. Term structure dynamics is all about what the time value of money will look like tomorrow. Just as we can express the time value of money using the spot, forward, swap, or zero coupon bond price curve, we could model the evolution of the time value of money through changes to any one of these curves. The models used in practice to describe the evolution of interest rates come in two basic flavors: factor models and stochastic differential equations. To describe the merits of each, we recall that there are two types of probabilities that are important in finance, real-world (or physical) probabilities and risk-neutral probabilities. Real-world probabilities are about trying to describe the world consistent with the rates we're actually likely to see in the newspaper the next morning. We work with real-world probabilities when we do asset-liability matching (ALM), or when we want to calculate an expected default frequency of a corporate bond, or when we're calculating a risk statistic such as VaR. Risk-neutral probabilities are used for valuations, especially when dealing with derivative securities, although any asset can theoretically be valued by computing the risk-neutral expectation of its discounted cash flows. Loosely speaking, we use physical probabilities for accounting and risk-neutral probabilities for valuation.

## FACTOR MODELS

If spot rates are just holding period returns on zero coupon bonds and we're interested in estimating the joint distribution of future returns, we could turn to factor models, as they are fairly simple to use and work reasonably well for defined horizon analysis. One month return equity factor models gained popularity for this reason. We could do the same for zero coupon bond holding period returns (spot rates), or for forward holding period returns on zero coupon bonds, or on swap rates, which are weighted average returns on baskets of forward contracts. We focus mainly on spot rates. When discussing interest rate factor models, the first question invariably is: statistical or fundamental?

Statistical factor models have been the dominant choice in the industry. One reason for this is that curve movements are highly nonnormal, which poses estimation problems for specified factor models. The preferred approach has been to apply principal component analysis (PCA) to curve movements. Studies have been done by a number of authors at different times, for a number of countries. Litterman and Scheinkman (1991)[5] conducted one of the first studies using the blind factor approach to explain changes in the U.S. government spot curve, and found that three factors explain a high proportion of the variation in movements. They also provided interpretations of these factors in terms of level, slope, and curvature (or butterfly) changes to the spot curve. Heidari and Wu (2003)[6] explored the ability of blind factor models to explain the joint movements of both the U.S. swap curve and swaption volatility surface and found that three additional factors are needed. These three volatility factors are also given interpretation in terms of volatility level, slope (or a long maturity/short maturity spread), and volatility surface curvature (or butterfly). They also found high correlation with bullet, barbell, and butterfly type factor-mimicking portfolios. There are numerous other studies that show the same general pattern for other curves in other currencies. Novosyolov and Satchkov (2008)[7] performed a two-stage PCA on a collection of 10 major country curves to determine the common factors between each curve's individual PCs and found that global spot curves share sources of common variation.

The mathematical formulation of the PCA factor model approach was discussed in Chapter 8, but some comments are needed to apply PCA to spot curves. First, we need a choice of a finite collection of spot rates that span the term structure. A time series of observations is then required. For liquid curves, such as U.S. LIBOR, daily time series are often the starting point. More important, however, is whether we apply PCA to rate levels, percent changes, or differences. There is significant autocorrelation in rate levels, and the volatility of spot rates tends to be dependent on the level of rates. When rates are high, the observed association between rate levels and volatilities seems to match an assumption of lognormality. However, when rates get low, the lognormal assumption seems to break down and rates seem to be closer to being normally distributed.

This is important, since spot curves can display large variation in rate levels across the term structure. The upward-sloping spot curve is common. Especially exiting recession, short-term rates may be very low, while the long end of the curve is much higher. This poses a problem for PCA, which is tasked with determining factors in decreasing order of percentage variation explained. Whether we apply PCA to levels or percentage returns or differences, it will affect how we measure variation and therefore how we assign importance to the latent factors. If we only seek to describe the data, PCA on levels or percentage changes is not that important, but if we want to use the PCs as the basis for a blind factor model, the high autocorrelation in the levels of the data will create high autocorrelation in the PCs, making the distributional properties of the factors more difficult to determine. Therefore PCA works best when applied to percentage changes or absolute differences.

When applying PCA to time-series data, it is standard to de-mean the data. When dealing with spot rate percentage changes or differences, it is also wise to normalize the data by the standard deviations. This is especially true for PCA on percentage changes when rates are very low. Finally, central banks often manipulate short rates directly in order to implement monetary policy goals. If the short end of the curve is represented in the PCA, these manipulations can show up as large sources of variation. In order to prevent the dominant PC's loading structure from loading exclusively on the short end of the curve, it can be necessary to remove central bank actions from the data before applying PCA.

To demonstrate the statistical factor approach, we performed principal component analysis on one year of historical daily Z-scored percentage changes of the spot curve as of 4/29/2011. The spot curve here consists of 30 points with annual intervals. In Figure 9.3 we show the percentage of variance explained by the PCs.

Consistent with the findings in the literature, the first three principal components explain roughly 96 percent of the variance in the Z-scored percentage daily moves in the spot curve. The first three factors also display the typical structure that lends itself to the interpretation of the factors representing level, slope, and curvature effects. The factor loadings are displayed in Figure 9.4.

We can see that drivers of movements in the spot (or swap) curve decompose nicely using PCA and that the top PC factors display high correlation

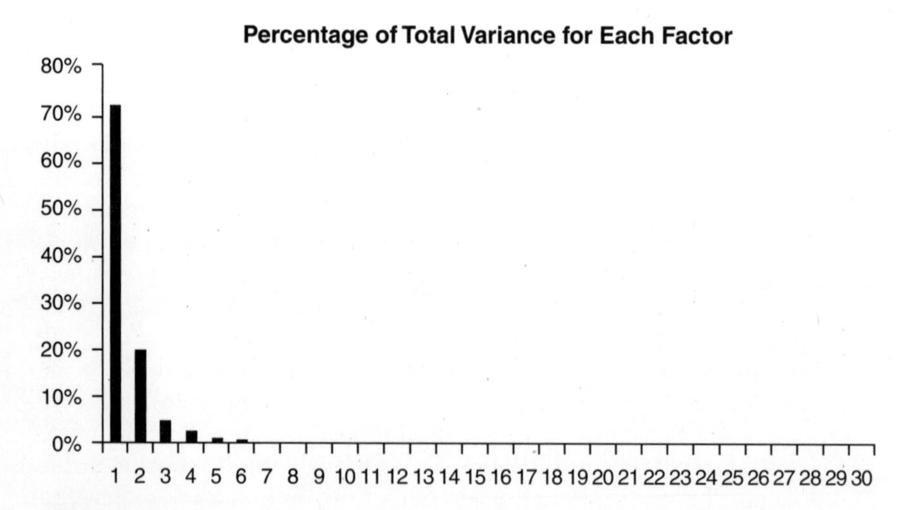


**FIGURE 9.3** PCA percentage of spot rate variance explained from historical data.
*Source:* FactSet.

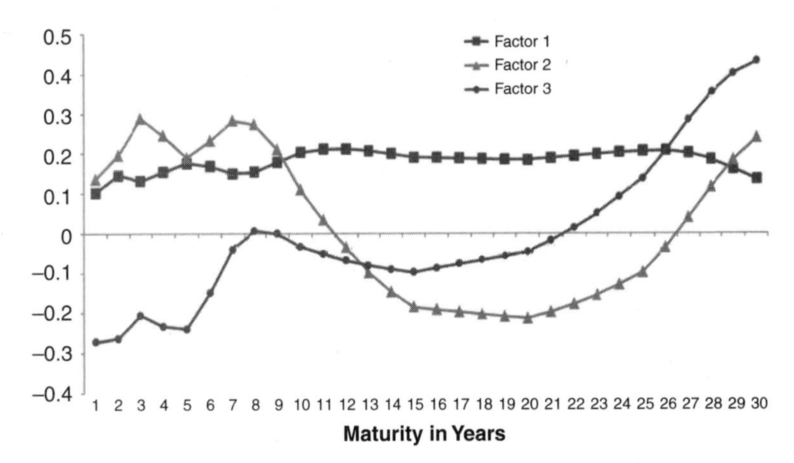


**FIGURE 9.4** PC factor loadings for historical spot curve movements.
*Source:* FactSet.

to level, spread, and butterfly factor-mimicking portfolios. A question we have yet to ask is: are PCA factors economically relevant or a mere statistical artifact?

We now take a more critical look at the PCA decomposition of spot rates. This analysis is based on a paper by Ilias Lekkos.[8] In his paper, Lekkos asks a very simple question. The method involves dividing the forward curve up into a collection of representative forwards and then supposes that there is no correlation between each of these forwards (and hence the forward curve by extension), so that each is driven by an independent factor. If we simulated a bunch of forward curves out of this zero correlation factor structure, built the spot curves associated to each, and then performed a PCA on the spot curves, what would the PC loading (eigenvector) structure look like? Would there be correlation in the derived spot curves even though there was none present in the forward curves from which they were born?

The answer, it turns out, is a resounding yes! We performed an analysis similar to Lekkos's. In addition to replicating his findings, we try to explain why the level, slope, and curvatures are important factors even if they appear to be a statistical construct of the no-arbitrage averaging process that relates spots to forwards.

First we took 251 independent sets of 30 observations drawn from a uniform distribution between 0 and 1 to represent 251 independent one-year forward rates (any distribution would have yielded the same results). Then we created a 30-year spot curve from these forwards for each of the 251 observations and applied principal component analysis to the Z-scored returns of the spot rates. The results are reported in the following figures.

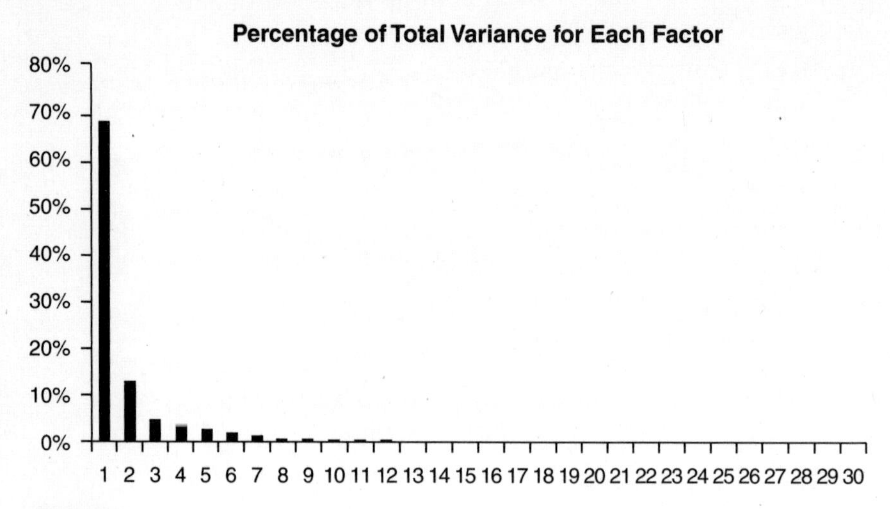


**FIGURE 9.5** PCA percentage of spot rate variance explained from i.i.d. forwards.
*Source:* FactSet.

From Figure 9.5, we see that the first three factors explain about 87 percent of the total variance of the spot curves that are calculated from randomly generated independent and identically distributed (i.i.d.) forwards, and the pattern of the factor loadings looks similar to what we expect the term structure to exhibit as drivers of its covariance based on a historical sample: level, slope, and curvature. The factor loadings are shown in Figure 9.6.

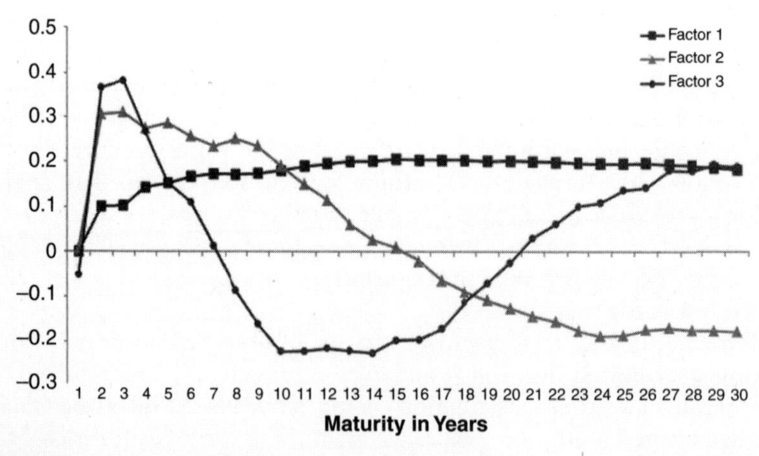


**FIGURE 9.6** PC factor loadings from i.i.d. forwards.
*Source:* FactSet.

The interpretation is almost identical between the spot curves constructed from historical data and the contrived i.i.d. forwards example. In this graph one can see the variation of the three PC factors and what part of the curves each describes. For instance, factor 3 is loaded on the short and long ends of the curve and is negatively loaded on midvalues.

To determine what the real dependence structure on the historical forward curves looks like, we repeated the historical analysis but instead of using the spot curves we transformed the data into forward curves with annual intervals by bootstrapping the spot rates into one-year forward rates. The results of the PCA on the one-year forward rate returns show that the forwards do exhibit a highly correlated structure, as evidenced by the percentage of total variance explained by the first several factors.

As displayed in Figure 9.7, 92 percent of the variation is explained by the first three factors. This is slightly less than for historical spot curves, where the first three factors explained 96 percent of the variation. To get over 95 percent of the variation for the bootstrapped forwards would require one additional factor.

In Figure 9.8, we display the PC factor loading structure. While the first three factors still explain a large part of the variance, the pattern of their loadings is different. The results still exhibit curvature and slope, but the level driver seems to have disappeared (i.e., the equivalent of factor 1 of Figure 9.6).

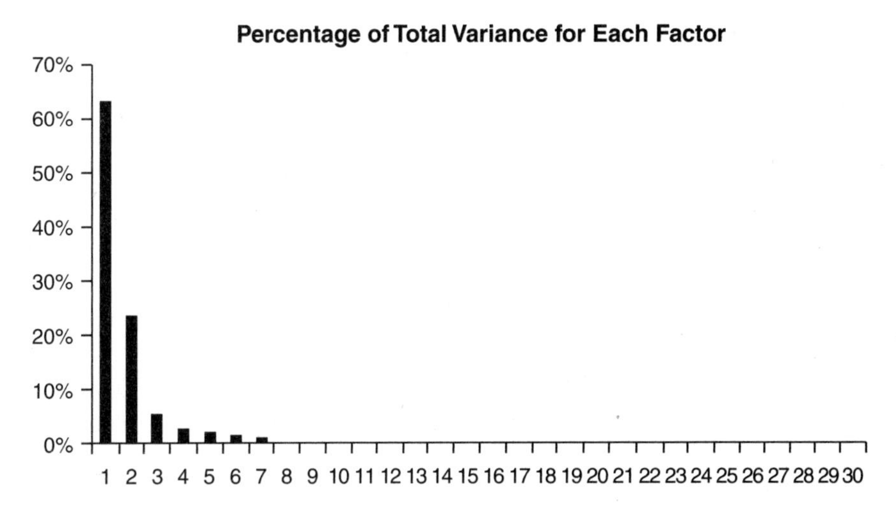


**FIGURE 9.7** Percentage of variance explained by PC factors on bootstrapped historical forward curves.
*Source:* FactSet.

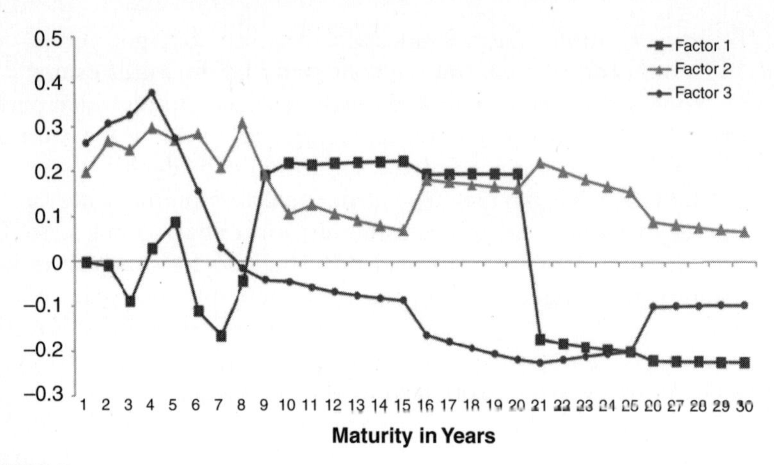


**FIGURE 9.8** PC factor loading structure for historical bootstrapped forward curves. *Source:* FactSet.

What we have shown with this example is that two very different models for what drives changes in the forward curve produce highly similar statistical factor structures when performed on the corresponding spot curves. So while the spot curve is widely known to be driven by level, slope, and curvature factors, it's not terribly clear what those factors really mean economically, in terms of expectations about the time value of money in the future. That's a standard drawback of PCA methods; however, due to high collinearity in the data, PCA is the best method for analysis.

Level and slope do seem to have an economic interpretation, because changes in those drivers for the spot curve imply changes in the forward curve. However, even if the first factor in the spot curve PCA looks like a level shift and explains the most variance, it does not seem to have the biggest impact on the forward curve. Its impact may have been exaggerated by the averaging process that defines the relationship between spots and forwards.

To illustrate this further, take a look at what happens to the spot and forward curves when the factor loadings for the first three factors are shifted. To do this we took the PC loadings matrix we got from the PCA on the spot curve and applied shocks to the first three factors. Each of the factors was shocked by an amount equal to one unit of the explained variance for that factor. We then look at the resulting spot curve and the corresponding forward curve.

Figure 9.9 shows the changes to the spot curve associated with a unit change in each of the first three principal component factors. As expected, the first factor produces an upward level shift, while the second factor

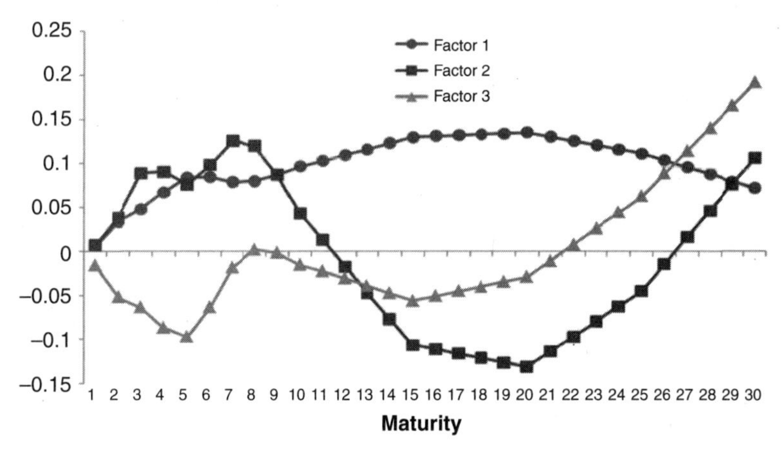


**FIGURE 9.9** Changes to the spot curve from unit shocks to the PC factors.
*Source:* FactSet.

steepens the slope of the curve and the third factor causes a butterfly to lift its wings. The effects of these PC shocks to the bootstrapped forward curve are shown in Figure 9.10.

As we can see, the forward curve responds more to shifts in the second and third factors, which look like a combination of slope and curvature (hump).

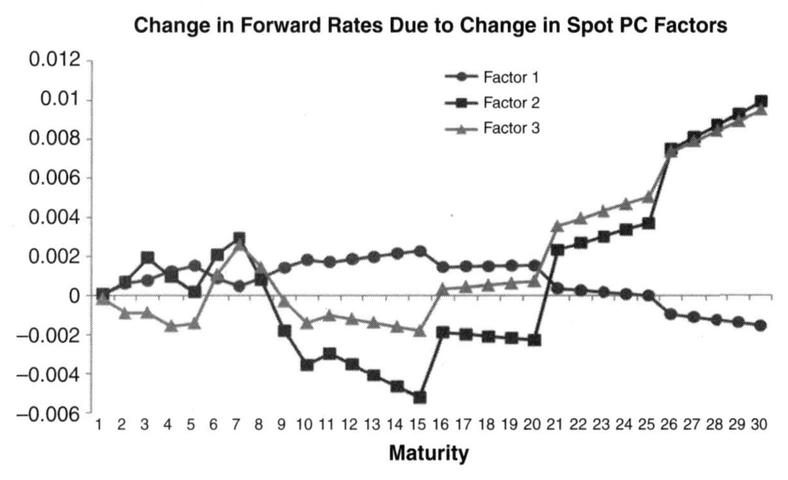


**FIGURE 9.10** Effect on the bootstrapped forward curve from unit shocks in the spot PC factors.
*Source:* FactSet.

To complete the illustration, we take a look at the forward curves generated by shifts to the forward PCA. Here again the results look like changes in slope and curvature. Forward rates are easier to interpret economically because they contain information about future interest rate expectations.[9] As for spot rates, a change in their slope and curvature seem to have a bigger impact on forward rates than a change in their level. Figure 9.11 shows the change in forward rates due to the change in forward PC factors.

While statistical factor models when applied to rate movements have a longer history of study, there has been more recent effort to define fundamental macro-based factor models. Conventional wisdom holds that the level of nominal interest rates is strongly tied to inflation and real economic output expectations over varying time horizons. This wisdom is expressed through the Taylor rule for monetary policy (not to be confused with the Taylor method for linearizing bond price changes presented in the prior chapter), which stipulates how the nominal interest rate should be set based on the equilibrium real interest rate, the inflation gap, and the real economic output gap.

Lildholdt, Panigirtzoglou, and Peacock (2007)[10] studied an affine macro-factor model of the yield curve in the United Kingdom. They provide a three-factor-state space model, where the factors are the (unobserved) inflation target, annual (realized) inflation, and the output gap as measured through Taylor rule residuals. The state space factors are estimated through a Kalman filter model. They then provide the impact to the forward curve for unit deviation shocks to each of the macro factors in their fitted model. There is an interesting similarity with the level, slope, and curvature factors

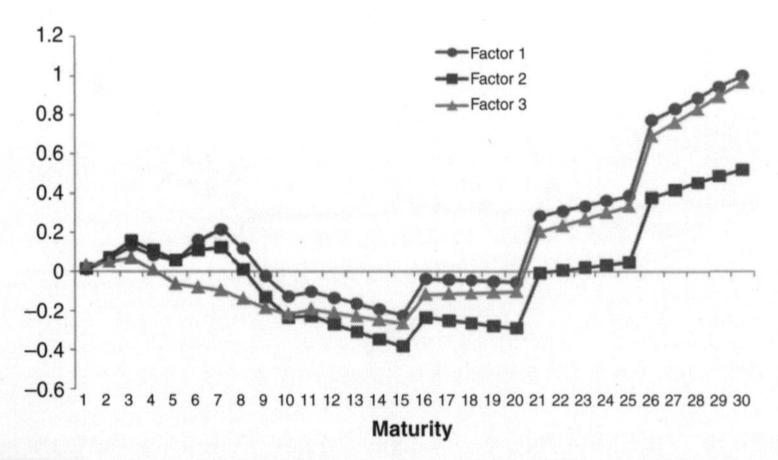


**FIGURE 9.11** Change in forward rates due to the change in forward PC factors.
*Source:* FactSet.

in terms of the type of impact that those factors would produce. The long-run inflation target factor impacts the long end of the curve, providing a level effect; realized annual inflation affects the short end of the curve and creates a slope effect; and the output gap factor creates a bend in the curve that could be interpreted as a curvature effect.

In summary, factor models have been able to explain *how* interest rate curves typically change, but are still struggling to work out the exact economic reason for *why* interest rate curves change. Work is still needed to help risk managers fully understand how precisely their hedges to descriptive risk factors translate into statements about real economic outcomes.

## STOCHASTIC DIFFERENTIAL EQUATIONS

The stochastic differential equation (SDE) approach is used primarily for valuation purposes. These models impact how a bond calculator determines the spread and durations used by the linearized risk model. They are usually calibrated to market prices and so provide a risk-neutral description of rate evolution.

Loosely speaking, an SDE describes the time evolution of a random variable by expressing its rate of change at any point in time through a trend component plus a random shock. If $X$ is any random variable, then by a stochastic differential equation, we mean the following equation on the differential of $X$.

$$dX_t = \mu(X,t)\,dt + \sigma(X,t) \bullet dz_t \tag{9.9}$$

where $\mu(X, t)$ is a drift (or trend) term, $dz_t$ is a Gaussian shock, and $\sigma(X, t)$ is the volatility of that shock. $X$ can be a random vector, in which case the equation is interpreted as being vectorized. This is not dissimilar from the equation used for describing the Garch process for price evolution as shown in Chapter 7, equation (7.8). It's simplified and often referred to as the "Ito equation" also,[11] which we'll revisit in a moment.

The most familiar example comes when we set $X = S$ to be the price of a stock and $\mu(X, t)$ and $\sigma(X, t)$ are constants. This is the basic Black-Scholes setup as well, and for initial option conditions, its solution is the Black-Scholes option pricing model for European options. One of the core results of option pricing theory is that any discounted asset price has zero trend term in the risk-neutral measure, referred to as the martingale condition. The immediate implication of this is that at any time $t$, the expected future value of any discounted asset at time $s > t$ is just the discounted asset value at $t$. So the value of any option on an asset will just be the discounted expected value of its payoff. Slightly less well understood is how the Black-Scholes formula for the price of a European option on a stock is obtained by applying the zero trend condition to the differential of the discounted option value (where we discount by the money market account). Using the Ito formula for taking the differential of a function of a random variable along with the zero trend condition will force the value of the option to satisfy a second-order differential equation with boundary conditions. This can can be recast in terms of the classical heat equation through a transformation of variables.

In fact, if $F(X, t)$ is any twice differentiable function of a random variable and time, then Ito's formula says that the differential of $F$ is:

$$dF(X,t) = \left( \frac{\partial F}{\partial t} + \frac{\partial F}{\partial X} \bullet \mu(X,t) + \frac{1}{2} \frac{\partial^2 F}{\partial X^2} \bullet \sigma(X,t)^2 \right) dt + \sigma(X,t) \bullet \frac{\partial F}{\partial X} \bullet dz_t \quad (9.10)$$

If $F$ is a discounted asset value, then the zero trend condition forces the $dt$ term to be zero and hence forces $F$ to satisfy a second-order partial differential equation (PDE) with boundary condition. This result is known as Feynman-Kac, and most attempts to price more exotic equity options boil down to trying to find tractable solutions to a (potentially multidimensional) Feynman-Kac PDE. This explains, in part, why so many of the bulge bracket banks seem to have a physics department.

We'd like to apply these same techniques to rates, but face a few complications. First, a curve represents an infinite number of rates, so we are forced to consider an infinite system of SDEs, not just a single one. Second and more importantly, rates are not asset values, so the zero trend condition doesn't hold. For example, we might try to write a system of SDEs that governs the movement of the spot curve:

$$dr(t,T) = \mu(r,T,t)dt + \sigma(r,T,t)dz(T)_t \quad (9.11)$$

Basic economic intuition tells us that two very nearby zero coupon bonds should have comparable risk and that market forces should work to keep risk-adjusted returns level with one another. This leads us to expect that there should be some conditions imposed on the system of SDEs to prevent our model from admitting arbitrage opportunities. But without the zero trend condition, it isn't immediately apparent what those conditions should be.

One way to deal with this is to only spell out the dynamics of a single rate. Short rate models are not concerned with the evolution of the full spot curve, but only of a short maturity spot rate. In this case, the SDE simplifies to:

$$dr_t = \mu(r,t)dt + \sigma(r,t)dz_t \quad (9.12)$$

**TABLE 9.2** Popular short rate models.

| Name | $\mu(r,t)$ | $\sigma(r,t)$ |
|---|---|---|
| Ho-Lee | $a(t)$ | $\sigma$ |
| Hull-White | $k(\theta(t)-r)$ | $\sigma(t)$ |
| Vasicek | $k(\theta-r)$ | $\sigma$ |
| Black-Derman-Toy | $-\sigma'(t)\cdot(\ln\theta(t)-\ln r)\cdot r$ | $\sigma(t)\cdot r$ |
| Black-Karasinski | $k(t)\cdot(\ln\theta(t)-\ln r)\cdot r$ | $\sigma(t)\cdot r$ |
| Cox-Ingersoll-Ross | $k(\theta-r)$ | $\sigma\cdot\sqrt{r}$ |
| Lognormal | $a(t)\cdot r$ | $\sigma\cdot r$ |
| Mean-reverting constant elasticity of variance (CEV) | $k(\theta-r)$ | $\sigma\cdot r^{\beta}$ |

The short rate model is then fully specified once a formula for the trend and stochastic volatility term are determined. A number of short rate models have been proposed. In Table 9.2 we list a few of the more popular ones.

In practice, these models are nice because they often admit analytic formulas relating zero coupon bond prices in terms of their parameters, making calibration to market instruments easy. Also, option pricing using a binomial tree or Monte Carlo simulation can be more computationally tractable in these models. Unfortunately, they typically cannot fully recover observed term structures, so potentially wide pricing error must be tolerated. Also, a priori there is still no theoretical guarantee that the models avoid arbitrage.[12]

The key insight of Heath, Jarrow, and Morton (1992)[13] was to use the relationship between zero coupon bonds and forward rates as a bridge that allowed the zero trend condition to be applied and hence no arbitrage conditions would be derived. The HJM setup involves the continuously compounded forward rates, which we recall can be expressed in terms of a partial derivative of the log of the zero coupon bond prices:

$$f(t,T) = -\frac{\partial \ln(P(t,T))}{\partial T} \tag{9.13}$$

The HJM framework then seeks conditions that must be satisfied by the system of SDEs that govern the forward curve evolution:

$$df(t,T) = \mu(T,t)\,dt + \sigma(T,t)\,dz(T)_t \tag{9.14}$$

In a nutshell, Heath, Jarrow, and Morton arrive at the no-arbitrage conditions by applying the Ito formula to the differential of the log of the zero coupon bond prices, switching the order of derivatives, collecting terms, and then applying the fact that the discounted zero coupon bond price process must have zero trend. When finished, they end up with the HJM no-arbitrage conditions:

$$\mu(T,t) = \sigma(t,T) \cdot \left(\int_t^T \sigma(t,s)ds\right) \tag{9.15}$$

The no-arbitrage conditions still leave a lot of room for choosing the volatility process. Looking back to the short rate models, there was a lot of interest in working with a time-homogeneous lognormal volatility process, $\sigma(t,T) = \sigma(T-t) \cdot f(t,T)$. Unfortunately, such a volatility process is not admissible for continuously compounded forward rates, as such a form leads to explosive drift terms.

This leads us to the LIBOR market model, which provides a system of SDEs for the forward LIBOR curve and is very popular in the industry. In the typical implementation of this model, one starts by choosing a fixed tenor $\delta$ and then evolving the forward LIBOR rates that correspond to fixed maturity dates $\{T_1,\ldots T_N\}$, where $T_i - T_{i-1} = \delta$, according to the SDEs:

$$\frac{df_i}{f_i} = \mu_i(t)dt + \sigma_i(t)dz_t^i \tag{9.16}$$

Here, $\sigma_i(t) = \sigma(T_i - t)$ is chosen to be a nonrandom function of time to maturity. Before proceeding, it is worth pointing out that this functional form implies that the forwards will share the same volatility in the sense that as longer-maturity forwards get closer to their maturity dates, they will experience the same volatility that shorter-maturity forwards experience now. For example, a forward with maturity in 10 years will have the same volatility in nine years as a forward with maturity in one year will have today. Thus a key feature of the LIBOR market model is that the volatility of the forward curve is self-similar.

The forward rates are not assets, but similar to the HJM setting, the drift terms can be calculated through their relationship to zero coupon bond prices. Recall that we can write forward LIBOR as:

$$f(t,T,T+\delta) = \frac{P(t,T) - P(t,T+\delta)}{\delta \cdot P(t,T+\delta)} \tag{9.17}$$

Forward LIBOR is then just the value of a portfolio long a zero coupon bond and short a longer-maturity zero coupon bond, denominated in shares of that zero coupon bond. We already know that discounted asset prices have zero trend when expressed using risk-neutral probabilities. Another commonly used tool when dealing with SDEs is the change of variable. When we talk about solutions to differential equations (stochastic or otherwise), we are really talking about integrals. Integrals are often easier to deal with if we change variables. For example, many ordinary differential equations are solved by changing to polar coordinates. We change coordinates in ordinary differential equations by applying chain rule from calculus. Ito calculus provides us a chain rule for stochastic differentials. Changing variables doesn't change value, just the way we express it. A zero coupon bond will ultimately have the same value whether expressed in dollars or troy ounces of gold. In finance, this is called change of numeraire.

If we fix a maturity $T_i$, then when we change variables to be shares of the zero coupon bond with maturity $T_i$, the SDE for the forward rate with maturity $T_i$, becomes driftless.

$$\frac{df_i}{f_i} = \sigma_i(t)\,dz_t^i \tag{9.18}$$

This SDE has a familiar solution:

$$f(T_i, T_i, T_i + \delta) = f(0, T_i, T_i + \delta)\exp\{-\hat{\sigma}(T_i)\sqrt{T_i}Z - \frac{1}{2}T_i\hat{\sigma}^2(T_i)\} \tag{9.19}$$

where $Z$ is a standard normal Gaussian random variable and $\hat{\sigma}(T) = \sqrt{\frac{1}{T}\int_0^T \sigma^2(s)\,ds}$. Put another way, the value of the forward LIBOR rate at maturity is determined by its value today times a lognormally distributed random variable whose log variance is just the average of the variance of the forward LIBOR rate along its time-dependent volatility curve. This puts us firmly in the Black-Scholes option pricing framework, which can be applied to price simple interest rate caps and floors. As with equity options, caps and caplets display volatility skews and the Black implied volatility is used as a quoting mechanism in cap markets. We call this root mean squared volatility the spot volatility. We can apply similar methods to swap rates and price swaptions using the Black formula.

We cannot make the drift term of all forward rates zero simultaneously, but we can solve for the drift term for all other forward LIBOR rates in the coordinates defined by our fixed zero coupon bond. These drift terms do not become explosive in the LIBOR market model and so provide a way to impose time homogeneity of volatility.

While the lognormal time homogeneous volatility assumption has some appeal, it is not always consistent with observed cap volatility term structures. In a stressed market, for example, the spot volatility term structure can decay so quickly that no strictly positive forward volatility can recover it. In Figure 9.12, we show the three-month Black caplet implied volatility term structure, along with the corresponding time-homogeneous lognormal forward volatility curve for 10/17/2008, at the beginning of the credit crisis.

To review quickly, an interest rate cap is a derivative in which the buyer receives payments at the end of each period in which the interest rate exceeds the agreed-upon strike price. In an interest rate floor, the buyer receives payments at the end of each period in which the interest rate is below the agreed-upon strike. "Agreed upon" is essential because these are over-the-counter derivatives. They're often used to hedge against interest rate fluctuations. Hence caplets and floorlets are call and put options on interest rates.

So, in Figure 9.12, we see the spot volatility term structure decay so quickly that the implied forward volatility curve cannot keep up and stay strictly positive. Mathematically, the time-homogeneous relationship would force forward variance to become negative. Economically, what this suggests is that there are market environments in which expectations about future short-maturity forward volatility do not match today's short-maturity volatility.

There are two ways to deal with this. One is to introduce mean reversion into the model; the other is to allow forward volatility to be stochastic

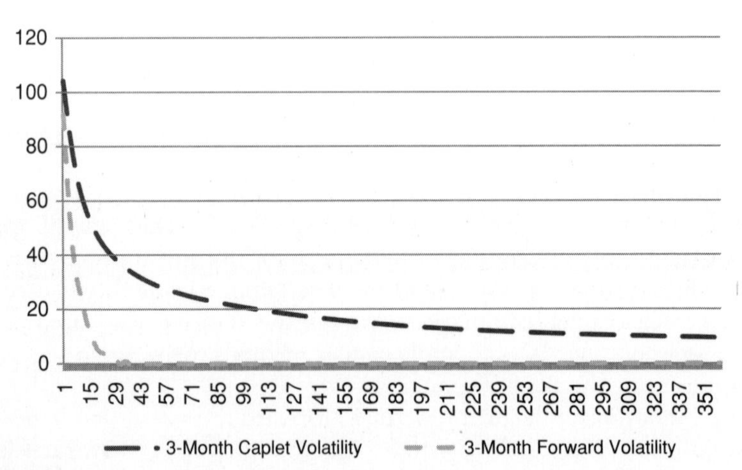


**FIGURE 9.12** Three-month Black caplet and three-month forward volatility on 10/17/2008.
*Source:* FactSet.

and therefore forward maturity dependent. We will discuss the stochastic volatility extension of the LIBOR market model in the section on interest rate volatility risk in Chapter 11.

The stochastic differential equation approach is used for valuation and for determination of interest rate exposures. We discuss those exposures next.

## INTEREST RATE RISK EXPOSURES

Spot rates are yields on zero coupon bonds, but bond prices and hence returns are inversely related to yields. The Taylor formula linearizes the bond returns through derivatives of return with respect to the risk factors. The degree of nonlinearity dictates how high an order of derivatives is needed. In fixed income, the first and second derivatives get called duration and convexity. When we talk about interest rate risk exposures, we're mainly talking about duration and convexity. We can form a few different types of durations, and in this section we focus on the two main options and how to decide which is better for risk management.

Effective duration is defined to be the percentage price change with respect to a parallel shift in the spot curve. In reality, the spot curve changes in more complicated ways than just parallel shifts, so risk measurement through effective duration and convexity alone is clearly not sufficient. In addition, bonds are often only exposed to specific points along the curve. A two-year swap is not sensitive at all to changes in the curve beyond two years, while a 30-year swap most definitely is.

One way to deal with this is to measure exposure to specific regions of the spot curve separately. The resultant exposures are called key rate durations and convexities. Calculation of the key rate durations and convexities is fairly straightforward. For illustrative purposes, suppose that the key rates that represent the interest rate risk have tenors of 1, 5, 10, 15, 20, 25, and 30 years. Then the key rate duration with respect to the 10-year key rate, at a given base scenario, is obtained by calculating the full price of the security for a shift up and a shift down in the 10-year rate, holding all other variables constant, which in particular means holding the spread constant.

$$P_+ = P(\ldots, r_{10} + h, \ldots) \tag{9.20}$$

$$P_- = P(\ldots, r_{10} - h, \ldots) \tag{9.21}$$

Here $h$ represents some positive increment (say 50 bps).

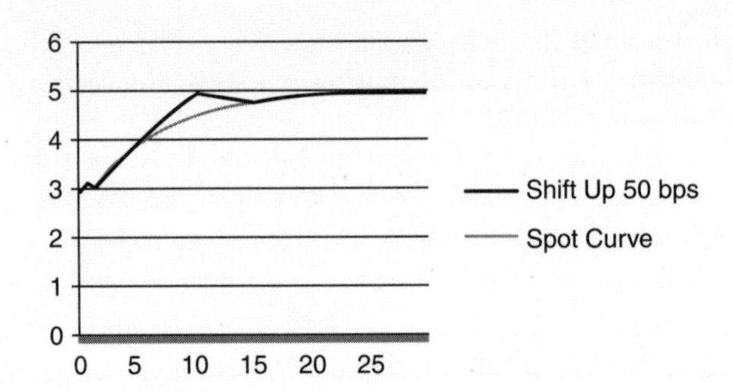


**FIGURE 9.13** Spot curve for a 50 bps shift up at the 10-year key tenor.
*Source:* FactSet.

One of our assumptions was that the full term structure of spot rates could be recovered from knowledge of the key rates. So for our example, if we assumed that the term structure were interpolated from the key rates, then the curve used for pricing resulting from a 50 bps shift up in the 10-year rate is shown in Figure 9.13.

The curve used for pricing for a 50 bps shift up in the 10-year spot rate is obtained as follows:

- Spots five years and prior: shift 0 bps.
- Spots five years to 10 years: interpolated shift.
- Spots 10 years: 50 bps shift.
- Spots 10 years to 15 years: interpolated shift.
- Spots 15 years and after: shift 0 bps.

The slope of the secant line then provides a good estimate of the first partial derivative of price with respect to a change in the 10-year key rate.

$$\frac{\delta P}{\delta r_{10}} \approx \frac{P_+ - P_-}{2h} \tag{9.22}$$

Using our knowledge of the base price allows us to compute the second partial and first cross partial derivative as well.

$$\frac{\delta^2 P}{\delta {r_{10}}^2} \approx \frac{P_+ + P_- - 2P_0}{h^2} \tag{9.23}$$

We can obtain even higher-order derivatives by generating more upshifts and downshifts and using numerical stencils to produce estimates of the derivatives. Knowing how to calculate key rate durations, the next question is: at how many key rates should exposure to be calculated? There clearly is no right answer, but common implementations will select anywhere from seven to 20 key rates. A realistic implementation might choose 1 month, 3 months, 6 months, 1 year, 2 years, 3 years, 4 years, 5 years, 6 years, 7 years, 8 years, 9 years, 10 years, 15 years, 20 years, 25 years, and 30 years. The finer the collection of key rates, the more specific the duration and convexity hedge ratios will become.

In the introductory section of this chapter, we presented results on the ability of the linearized pricing formula to capture sufficient amounts of real price changes given movements in key rates and spreads. The study showed that key rate durations and spread durations do reasonably well at capturing real price moves based on *ex post* measurement of risk factor moves. With this in hand, we might be tempted to claim victory and move on. The use of key rate durations is not the only option, however.

While key rate durations measure exposure to specific regions of the spot curve and therefore provide a means for determining hedges to those regions, they do not tell us anything about whether a change to the curve in that region is likely to occur. While the numerical calculation is straightforward, it is also commonly claimed to produce potentially unnatural shapes in the implied forward curve, especially when applied to key rates at the long end of the curve.

In Figure 9.14, we show the implied forward curve that results when we do an isolated 50 bps shock up to a portion of the spot curve. While 50 bps may be larger than would be used in practice to emphasize a point, what is clear is that whatever size shift we choose, it will be amplified in the way it shows up in the implied forward curve. Using forward rates as a proxy for expected future short spot rates, the implied forward curve associated with a shock up at the 15-year point indicates an expectation that rates will be

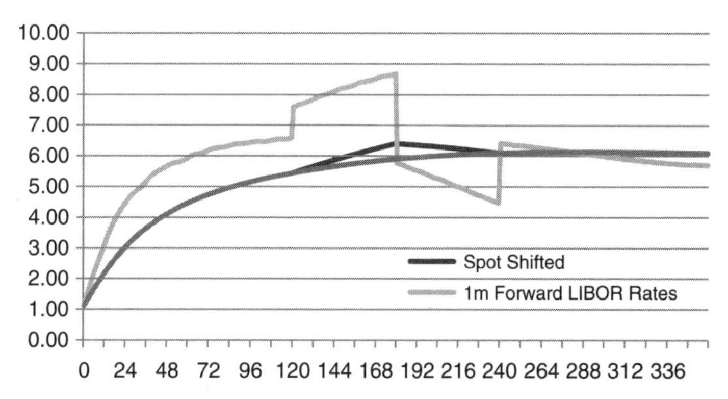


**FIGURE 9.14** Key rate shock at the 15-year point with implied forward curve.
*Source:* FactSet.

significantly higher starting 10 years from now, then sharply lower starting 15 years from now, until returning to equilibrium in 20 years.

The immediate question should be: is such a scenario really likely?

Interestingly, if we compare this impact to the forward curve to the PC factors we obtained from the PCA on historical bootstrapped forward curves (Figure 9.8), we do see some similarity. If we had chosen our key rates to include only the 10-, 20-, and 30-year points in the tail, the first PC on the forward curve would produce something similar to a shift in the 20-year point of the curve relative to the 10- and 30-year points. We also see that the first three PCs on forwards display step-function-like characteristics. That said, the factors imply that those step functions do not occur in isolation and it's clear that arbitrary choice of key rates can easily be in conflict with observed movements in forward curves. If our swap curve is constructed using a spline, for example, then we should choose our key rates to be a subset of our knot points.

Interest rates tend to be highly correlated, whether we are talking about swap, spot, or forward. Determination of key rate durations with respect to a robust set of key rates may provide us the means to calculate hedges to specific scenarios, but we have to wonder if we might be overhedging, unnecessarily sacrificing yield. Just as importantly, throwing lots of highly correlated risk factors into a risk model has serious model estimation implications. Thus, even if we prefer to think of our interest rate risk exposures in terms of key rates, the high correlation between key rates demands some form of further factor reduction. In contrast to the highly correlated key rates, the statistical factors that are produced using principal component analysis are uncorrelated with each other by construction and therefore might provide a better alternative for risk measurement and forecasting.

In our discussion of statistical factor models, we saw that the spot curve is driven primarily by level, slope, and curvature factors. We call the first- and second-order exposures obtained by computing the sensitivity of bond price to a change in the spot curve implied by a shift in these statistical factors principal component durations and convexities. In addition to having the desirable characteristic of being uncorrelated, these factors tend to have high correlations with factor-mimicking portfolios that are constructed out of the most liquid maturity market instruments, such as the three-month, two-year, 10-year, and 30-year bonds. This should mean that any hedges we compute can be executed fairly efficiently. The big question, though, is how well the PC durations and convexities stack up against the key rate durations and convexities as a hedge. The way we will measure this is through the linearized Taylor pricing formula.

When comparing key rate–based exposures to principal component–based exposures, there are two important areas to focus on, *ex post* risk measurement (e.g., risk attribution) and *ex ante* risk forecasting (e.g., VaR).

For *ex post* risk measurement, we would like to compare how well the two exposure types are able to capture actual price movements using historical curve movements. For *ex ante* risk forecasting, we would like to compare how well the two exposure types are able to capture price movements using *in-sample* curve movements. From a risk forecasting perspective, parametric methods quickly become impractical for fixed income. Especially when there is need to incorporate spread risk, or in any multi-asset-class risk forecasts, the preferred strategy is to use Monte Carlo–based techniques. In this situation, the need to further factor reduce the key rates leaves us with two options. In the first option, in every Monte Carlo simulation we reconstruct the key rates from some realization of the principal component factors and then use the key rate changes in conjunction with key rate durations and convexities through the Taylor formula. In the second option, we use the principal component factor realizations directly with the principal component durations and convexities. In either case, we decompose the key rate factors into principal component factors and conduct risk forecasting out of this common factor structure. This is what we mean by *in-sample*: compare repricing accuracy using only scenarios generated by the PC factor structure, since this is all that matters for risk forecasting. This gives the PC exposures a bit of a home field advantage, but nobody said it was supposed to be a fair fight.

Before we move to the empirical tests, we take a moment to point out the theoretical relationship between key rate durations (KRDs) and principal component durations (PCDs). We recall that principal component analysis is simply a change of coordinates. Mathematically, this relationship between the vector of key rates $X$ and the vector of PCs $Y$ is expressed similarly to equation (7.3), using the PC loading (eigenvector) matrix $\Psi$, as:

$$Y = X \bullet \Psi \tag{9.24}$$

Since PCA is a linear coordinate transformation, it is associative with respect to the derivative operation, and we can use the PC loading matrix to relate key rate durations to principal component durations similarly:

$$\text{PCD} = \text{KRD} \bullet \Psi \tag{9.25}$$

If our PC factor analysis has full rank—that is, if we preserve as many PC-based factors as we have key rates—then we can invert the loading matrix similar to equation (7.4) to obtain the reverse relationship.

$$\text{KRD} = \text{PCD} \bullet \Psi^{-1} \tag{9.26}$$

One question we would also like to explore in our empirical tests is: how well does this relationship hold if we restrict ourselves to the first three or four PCs?

## RISK FORECASTING

We start with the in-sample comparisons for risk forecasting. To illustrate the test procedure, consider a portfolio composed of corporate, government, agency, and mortgage securities and with prices from 05/11/2009. First, we generate key rate durations, convexities, and off-diagonals for 17 key rate points at 1-, 3-, 6-, 12-, 24-, 36-, 48-, 60-, 72-, 84-, 96-, 108-, 120-, 180-, 240-, 300-, and 360-month maturities. One of the advantages of using PC-based exposures is that, since there are fewer of them to compute, we can compute higher-order terms for the same computational expense as computing more key rates, but lower-order derivative terms.

Corporates and mortgages are analyzed using the LIBOR curve, and U.S. Treasuries and agencies are analyzed using the UST curve. We then run the same principal component analysis (PCA) used in the calculation of the derivatives (a PCA of Z-scored interest rate returns over 250 trading days) for both the UST and the LIBOR curves.

Now we draw four independent random numbers to simulate a set of PC shocks. The shocks are adjusted by the amount of variance explained by each principal component so as to make the effect of a one-unit shift in each PC comparable. The result is a column vector of PC shifts that is multiplied by the PC loading matrix for the UST and LIBOR curves. That vector, when multiplied by the PCA matrix for each of the curves, results in a set of Z-scored spot curve returns that we then transform into a new spot curve.

Applying the vector of PC shocks to the PCA matrix results in the change to the UST spot curve shown in Figure 9.15 (note that the direction and shape of the shift depend on the signs of the principal components vectors).

Applying the vector of PC shocks to the PCA matrix will result in the change to the LIBOR spot curve shown in Figure 9.16 (note that the direction and shape of the shift depend on the signs of the principal components vectors).

For each of these curves, we calculate the changes in the spot rates at the key rate points and use this in the Taylor repricing formulas with the key rate durations, convexities, and off-diagonals, to get the change in price due to the changes in the key rates. We also take the PC shocks for each curve, apply them to the derivatives, and use the Taylor series approximation to calculate a price change for the securities.

To compare the performance of the repricing methods, we need a full price to compare the Taylor formula one to. To get a full price, we take the spot curves that were generated by the shocks and use simple interpolation to calculate a 360-point spot curve, which is used to calculate the prices of these securities by discounting their cash flows by the OAS calculated from the original price over the corresponding discount curve. That is, we

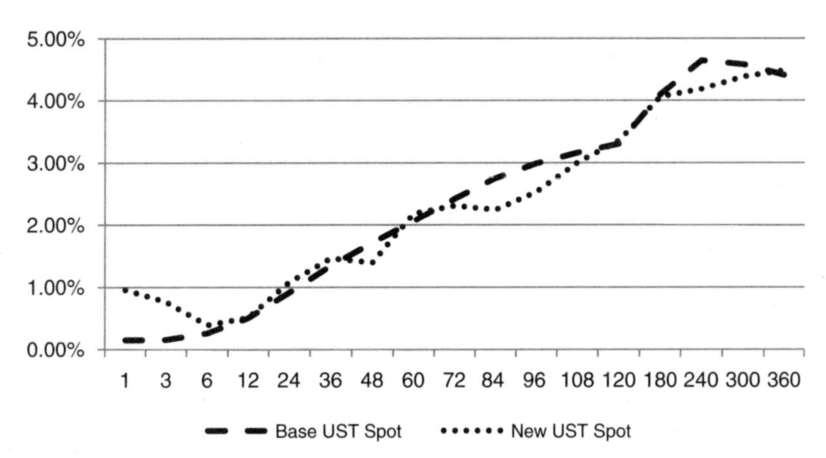


**FIGURE 9.15** Base and scenario realized spot curves from factor model for UST curve.
*Source:* FactSet.

produce a full price in the shocked interest rate scenario, holding OAS constant using our bond calculator. We use these prices to measure the accuracy of the KRD method versus the PCD method.

In Table 9.3, we show the results of this process for our sample portfolio. We see that PC-based exposures and key rate–based exposures perform exactly the same for Treasury securities, and on average the PC method does better than the key rate method.

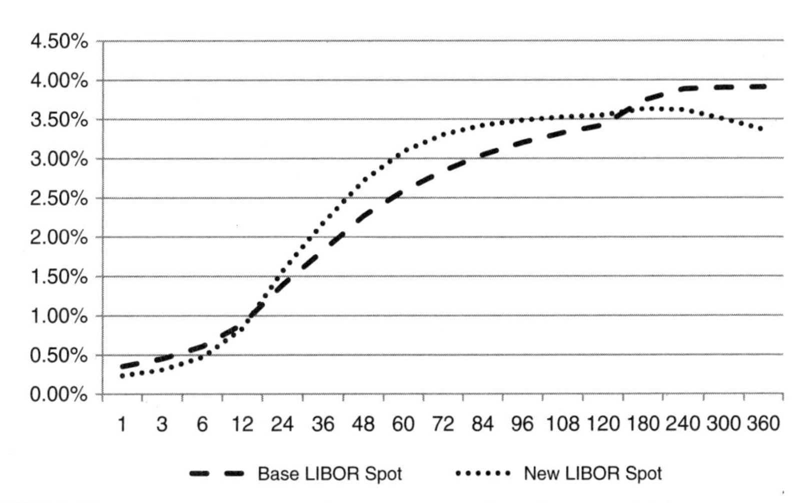


**FIGURE 9.16** Base and scenario realized spot curves from factor model for LIBOR curve.
*Source:* FactSet.

**TABLE 9.3** Sample portfolio KRD-versus PCD-based repricing.

| Sector | CUSIP | Original Price | OAS | Discount Curve | KRD-Based Price | PCD-Based Price | Discounted CFs Price | KRD Absolute Error | PCD Absolute Error |
|---|---|---|---|---|---|---|---|---|---|
| Corporate | 020002AC | 102.81 | 4.48 | LIBOR | 103.89 | 102.80 | 101.32 | 2.57 | 1.48 |
| Corporate | 760759AF | 71.47 | 5.36 | LIBOR | 72.33 | 71.48 | 72.61 | 0.28 | 1.12 |
| Corporate | 828807CA | 111.89 | 5.40 | LIBOR | 113.63 | 111.88 | 110.42 | 3.21 | 1.46 |
| Corporate | 837004BX | 90.80 | 2.35 | LIBOR | 91.83 | 90.83 | 93.13 | 1.30 | 2.30 |
| Corporate | 29078EAC | 98.00 | 5.10 | LIBOR | 99.03 | 97.99 | 96.57 | 2.46 | 1.41 |
| U.S. Gov't | 3133XGVF | 111.38 | 0.56 | UST | 111.38 | 111.38 | 112.17 | 0.79 | 0.79 |
| U.S. Gov't | 912810EN | 138.77 | 0.41 | UST | 138.77 | 138.77 | 139.38 | 0.61 | 0.61 |
| U.S. Gov't | 31398AFD | 109.19 | 0.90 | UST | 109.21 | 109.21 | 110.89 | 1.67 | 1.68 |
| Mortgage | GN300651999 | 106.63 | 1.76 | LIBOR | 107.54 | 106.62 | 106.22 | 1.32 | 0.40 |
| Mortgage | FN200452003 | 104.30 | 0.85 | LIBOR | 105.44 | 104.29 | 102.44 | 3.00 | 1.85 |
| Mortgage | FN150552002 | 105.06 | 0.08 | LIBOR | 105.52 | 105.06 | 107.49 | 1.97 | 2.42 |
| Mortgage | FHH5L1Y525IO0542008 | 103.61 | 1.83 | LIBOR | 104.46 | 103.60 | 102.91 | 1.55 | 0.69 |
| Mortgage | FHH5L1Y525IO0542007 | 103.97 | 1.70 | LIBOR | 104.66 | 103.96 | 103.72 | 0.94 | 0.24 |
| Mortgage | G2300452009 | 102.14 | 0.81 | LIBOR | 103.30 | 102.13 | 101.56 | 1.74 | 0.57 |

*Sources:* FactSet and BofA Merrill Lynch.

## CONDITIONAL DURATION AND EXPECTED TAIL DURATION

Typically, in risk forecasting, the forecasts are limited to return-based risk measures (VaR, tracking error [TE], etc.). The risk exposures themselves are assumed not to change. In fixed income, we know that durations and convexities are themselves functions of the same risk factors as price—not unlike equity valuation changing as a stock's price changes, in effect changing the beta to valuation slightly. Thus, in a risk forecast, as price changes, so must these exposures. Indeed, we include convexity and higher-order terms in the Taylor repricing formula precisely to correct for the fact that the duration can change significantly even over moderate movements in the underlying risk factors.

The Taylor method, however, not only provides us a chance to estimate price for a given scenario, but it can also be used to estimate the change to the exposures as well. This is because the second derivative of the price with respect to the risk factors is just the first derivative of the first derivative. Therefore, if we have a Taylor expansion of price, we also have a Taylor expansion of the first derivative of price, and so forth. Since we are using expansions in terms of a finite number of derivatives, any expansion of exposures will lose an order of accuracy for each order of exposure we try to estimate. Thus, if we are using a second-order expansion of price in terms of durations and convexities, we can obtain a first-order expansion of duration in terms of convexity.

Since the number of terms needed for a Taylor expansion grows exponentially with the order of the expansion, computational tractability limits how far we can take this and what order our estimates will be good to. This is one way in which using principal component exposures proves to be useful. With principal component–based exposures, we can spend precious computational resources calculating higher-order terms for use in the Taylor expansion, rather than spending those resources calculating redundant risk exposures. For example, if we had 17 key rates and four PC factors, we could calculate PC-based derivatives out to fourth order for a lower computational cost than calculating key rate derivatives out to second order. If pressed, we can also use the linear relationship to estimate the KRDs from the PCDs.

This means that in a Monte Carlo–based VaR simulation, we can have an estimate of not only price and return but also of duration and convexity for each scenario. This is especially appealing if duration thresholds are used as a risk control measure or as a fund-prospectus-proscribed investment style. If we can estimate our durations, we can answer the question of what the VaR and ETL would be if the portfolio was subject to duration constraints. We can also reverse the situation to provide an estimate of the expected duration profile of an unconstrained portfolio at the VaR threshold. Similarly, we could compute the expected duration profile in the tail of the return distribution. This is extremely useful for risk managers who want to make sure their risk management controls are neither too strong nor too weak.

The formal definition of value at risk and expected tail loss are given in the chapter on risk measures. Assuming those definitions, we formalize the conditional duration metrics as follows.

Define the *unconstrained duration at VaR* (DVaR) to be the expected duration given a loss exactly equal to the VaR for some confidence level:

$$\mathrm{DVaR}_\alpha = E\{\mathrm{Duration} | \mathrm{Loss} = VaR_\alpha\} \tag{9.27}$$

Define the *unconstrained conditional expected tail duration* (ETD) to be the expected duration given that the loss is greater than or equal to the VaR for some confidence level:

$$\mathrm{ETD}_\alpha = E\{\mathrm{Duration} | \mathrm{Loss} \geq VaR_\alpha\} \tag{9.28}$$

Define the *duration-constrained value at risk* (VaRD) to be the value at risk subject to duration threshold constraints:

$$\mathrm{VaRD}\{\alpha, \mathrm{C}\} = inf\{L | P(\mathrm{Loss} > L | \mathrm{C}) < 1 - \alpha\} \tag{9.29}$$

Define the *duration-constrained expected tail loss* (ETLD) to be the expected loss given that the loss exceeds the duration-constrained value at risk:

$$\mathrm{ETLD}\{\alpha, \mathrm{C}\} = E\{L | L \geq \mathrm{VaRD}\{\alpha, \mathrm{C}\}\} \tag{9.30}$$

This allows us to calculate a reasonable estimate of conditional duration at VaR (DVaR) and an expected tail duration (ETD) in a tractable computational manner.

We can expand these definitions to include spread duration constraints, which we will discuss in Chapter 10 on spread risk.

## CONCLUSION

Interest rates are compensation for bearing the time value of money risk. The time value of money can be expressed using either spot, forward, or par curves. The spot curve expresses the time value of money as a holding period return on zero coupon bonds of lengthening maturity, and represents the best curve for discounting cash flows generally. Since bond price is a function of the spot curve, interest rate exposure can be measured by altering the spot curve to see how bond price changes. The two main methods are to measure exposure by altering isolated regions of the spot curve associated with contiguous time-to-maturity regions, or to shift, twist, and butterfly the spot curve in reflection of the dominant ways that the spot curve is observed to move in reality. This gives rise to key rate durations and principal component durations (and higher-order terms). Interest rate factors are then expressed as either key rates along the spot curve or independent principal components of the curve movements.

Whether exposures are measured through key rate durations or through principal component durations, forecasting factor changes is still primarily accomplished through principal component analysis (statistical factor models). The shift, twist, and curvature factors that drive spot or par curves that are commonly cited in literature may ultimately derive explanatory power from the averaging relationship between forward rates and spot rates. Combining this with the lack of research into fundamental curve factor models means that there is still difficulty in connecting the model that explains how the curve moves with why the curve moves. Stochastic differential equations were introduced that focus on the former.

The Taylor formula allows us to potentially estimate how first-order exposures themselves change as the spot curve changes. This provides a way to incorporate the effect of duration constraints when calculating certain risk metrics, like VaR. As many funds have duration targets or frequently engage in duration hedging, this allows us to better gauge how stable those hedges will be when our portfolio is under stress.

## NOTES

1. Usury—the act of charging excessively high interest rates—has been the subject of religious and moral debate for thousands of years.
2. A forward contract is typically said to have a maturity or expiry date. Since a forward rate is a holding period return on an underlying zero coupon bond, we say that the forward matures on the reset date to be consistent with its relationship to the forward contract that defines it. The tenor is then the holding period.
3. In 1985, the U.S. Treasury began to issue zero coupon bonds called STRIPS. Prior to that, there were sponsored investment bank intermediary programs with feline acronyms like CATS, COUGRs, LIONs, and TIGRs that provided investors with zero coupon bond options backed by the full faith and credit of the U.S. government. Liquidity in these bonds is not nearly as robust as ordinary coupon-bearing Treasuries or interest rate swaps, however.
4. P. Hagan and G. West, "Interpolation Methods for Curve Construction," *Applied Mathematical Finance* 13, no. 2 (2006).

5. R. Litterman and J. Scheinkman, "Common Factors Affecting Bond Returns," *Journal of Fixed Income*, June 1991.
6. M. Heidari and L. Wu, "Are Interest Rate Derivatives Spanned by the Term Structure of Interest Rates?" *Journal of Fixed Income*, June 2003.
7. A. Novosyolov and D. Satchkov, "Global Term Structure Modeling Using Principal Component Analysis," FactSet white paper, 2008.
8. Ilias Lekkos, "A Critique of Factor Analysis of Interest Rates," *Journal of Derivatives*, Fall 2000, 72–83.
9. It has been commonly asserted that forward rates represent expectations of future short spot rates. A collection of such assertions is known as the forward expectations hypothesis. Jarrow et al. have shown that there is a convexity adjustment that represents the risk premium associated with hedging forwards that must be accounted for, implying that forward rates are not pure expectations of future short rates. That said, forward rates still carry meaningful information about future short rate expectations.
10. P. Lildholdt, N. Panigirtzoglou, and C. Peacock, "An Affine Macro-Factor Model of the UK Yield Curve," Working Paper 322, Bank of England, 2007.
11. S. P. Greiner, *Ben Graham Was a Quant* (Hoboken, NJ: John Wiley & Sons, 2011), chap. 9, 270.
12. The HJM no-arbitrage conditions have since been recast to show that short rate models do remain arbitrage free.
13. D. Heath, R. Jarrow, and A. Morton, "Bond Pricing and Term Strucutre of Interest Rates: A New Methodology," *Econometrica*, 1992.

CHAPTER 10

# Spread Risk

*David Mieczkowski, PhD, and Sameer R. Patel*

Fixed income is all about cash flows and the time value of money. Interest rates are a way of expressing the time value of money, and interest rate risk describes the present value risk associated with known, hedgeable cash flows given changes in the time value of money. Bond spreads, on the other hand, capture the value of cash flow uncertainty and lack of complete hedgeability, and spread risk describes the present value risk associated with uncertain cash flows, given changes in that uncertainty or hedgeability.

Cash flow uncertainty breaks into two major categories: uncertainty regarding timing of cash flows and uncertainty regarding the realized amount of cash flows. The dominant forms of cash flow uncertainty for fixed income revolve around prepayments, defaults, and loss severity. Prepayment and default risk deals with uncertainty regarding the timing of scheduled cash flows, while loss severity risk deals with the uncertainty regarding the realized amount of scheduled cash flows. A bond's spread, then, is the excess rate of return over the internal rate of return on known, hedgeable cash flows, required to compensate for the combination of prepayment, default, loss severity, and liquidity risks.

We begin this chapter with a more concrete definition of spread. Bond spread is very dependent on the nature of that bond's cash flows, and we will touch on the approaches to computing bond spread taken by the major fixed income sectors, such as corporate and sovereign debt and structured products. We then discuss how exposure to spread risk is measured in the context of the Taylor linearization method. We conclude with a discussion of how to model changes in bond spreads, which we can then use together with the spread exposures to generate risk forecasts.

## SPREAD BASICS

A spot rate is the required internal rate of return on a zero coupon bond, and any bond with certain, hedgeable cash flows can be valued by discounting each cash flow by the required internal rate of return. When cash flows become uncertain, discounting becomes more challenging. Being uncertain does not mean we know nothing, however. Usually we know, or can form an estimate of, the range of outcomes, and can assign probabilities to them. Having an estimate of the probability distribution of a cash flow, however accurate, provides a means for valuation. A fundamental result of modern finance is that, if we know the joint distribution of *any* random cash flow with the money market account and the market is complete, we can value it according to the risk-neutral measure by taking the discounted (risk-neutral) expectation of that cash flow. This is easier said than done, of course.

To start simply and motivate definitions, suppose we had a simple defaultable corporate bond. The holder of this bond can be thought to be long a straight government bond and short a put option on the recovery value. The defaultable nature of the bond means that we may not get all the scheduled cash flows. What should be the excess rate of return that should be associated to these uncertain cash flows?

We know that the value of the straight bond can be written in terms of the spot rates and the known cash flows as:

$$\text{Straight bond}(t) = \sum_{i=1}^{N} \frac{CF(T_i)}{(1 + r(t, T_i))^{(T_i - t)}} \tag{10.1}$$

One simple question we could ask is: how much more do we need to discount each cash flow in order to recover the price of the defaultable bond?

The value of a known cash flow is independent of which bond it belongs to, but the value of a cash flow that is part of the defaultable bond depends on the bond to which it belongs. This is because the likelihood that the cash flow will be paid depends on the likelihood that the put will be exercised, which depends on the value of the straight bond in relation to the recovery value. Since defaultable cash flows can't be stripped out of the bonds they belong to, it makes sense to look for a sort of average excess rate of return that is required to compensate for the embedded option. This motivates the definition of the *static spread* to be the constant that needs to be added to each spot rate in order to equate the discounted scheduled cash flows to the value of the defaultable bond.

$$\text{Defaultable bond }(t) = \sum_{i=1}^{N} \frac{CF(T_i)}{(1 + r(t, T_i) + \text{Spread}(t))^{(T_i - t)}} \tag{10.2}$$

Spread is then just a type of quoting mechanism that gives us a way to compare the non-interest-rate-related risks inherent in two different defaultable bonds in terms of excess return. Spread risk is then simply the impact to the value of the defaultable bond, given that the spread changes.

Now suppose we had a simple (nondefaultable) callable government bond. The holder of this bond can be thought to be long a straight government bond and short a European call option. In a perfectly efficient market (where everyone is using the same option pricing calculator), we can value the bond by discounting the cash flows, and value the option by standard option pricing theory by computing the risk-neutral expected discounted payoff.

$$PV(t) = B(t) \bullet \tilde{E}\left\{ \frac{V(T)}{B(T)} \middle| F_t \right\} \tag{10.3}$$

where $F_t$ represents information about interest rates available at time $t$, $V(T)$ is the value of the option at maturity, and $B(t)$ is the value of the money market account at time $t$. The callable nature of the bond means that we may not get all the scheduled cash flows. What should be the excess rate of return that should be associated to these uncertain cash flows?

Again, the value of a cash flow that is part of a callable bond depends on the bond to which it belongs. This is because the likelihood that the cash flow will be paid depends on the likelihood that the call will be exercised, which depends on the straight bond value. So again, it makes sense to look for an average excess rate of return that is required to compensate for the embedded option. Using the same definition we used for the defaultable bond spread, we can determine the spread of a callable (nondefaultable) bond as:

$$\text{Callable bond}(t) = \sum_{i=1}^{N} \frac{CF(T_i)}{(1 + r(t,T_i) + \text{Spread}(t))^{(T_i - t)}} \tag{10.4}$$

This is a second type of spread, but we don't need a separate risk section devoted to it. This spread arises purely from interest rate and interest rate volatility risk, which we have already covered in detail. There is uncertainty in the cash flows, but that uncertainty is due solely to the uncertainty regarding interest rates and volatilities, so this spread is not as interesting as the spread of a defaultable bond. What would be more interesting is if we computed the value of the call option (whose valuation only requires interest rate and interest rate volatility inputs), added it to the market value of the callable bond (so that we essentially created a synthetic straight bond), and found that this value did not match the value of the straight bond determined by discounting the known cash flows using the spot curve. We call the spread formed in this way the *option-adjusted spread* (OAS). In this way the OAS represents a risk premium present after we have taken out what is known about interest rates and interest rate volatilities.

The option-adjusted spread might reflect market inefficiency and indicate that the option was rich or cheap, depending on the sign of the spread. Alternatively, it might reflect incompleteness in the market, and thus give the required excess return needed to bear imperfect hedging risk. Since we need to specify a model for the option pricing, an option-adjusted spread may also be due to model risk. Simple callable government bonds may not exhibit large option-adjusted spreads, as the option is not that complicated, but complex path-dependent options can have significant OAS, and since those spreads arise for reasons beyond interest rates (e.g., imperfect option pricing models), they represent exposure to risk sources that are outside of interest rates.

One important such bond that has a complex embedded option is a prepayable mortgage. In the United States, substantially all mortgages originated have an embedded prepayment option, and are not assignable. This means that whenever someone decides to relocate or trade up, there will be a prepayment that is not purely a function of interest rates. In addition, there are significant transaction costs associated with refinancing a mortgage, borrowers often lack the ability to determine optimal exercise strategy, and investors in mortgage-backed securities (MBSs) face informational asymmetry in determining what the incentive to refinance actually is for a given pool of borrowers. Finally, borrowers can default. On the other hand, from a purely financial point of view, a mortgage is just an amortizing bond with an embedded call option on the mortgage rate. The value of a mortgage-backed security is therefore highly model dependent. The deviation between the model-driven value of the MBS and its market value will then be reflected through OAS.

For path-dependent securities, the option-adjusted spread calculation is a little more involved than for a straight European callable government bond. Because of the path dependency, MBSs are usually valued using a Monte Carlo simulation. MBSs have monthly cash flows, corresponding to the monthly payments made by the mortgage holders. Along each interest rate path for each month, cash flows are generated using a prepayment/loss model that predicts what portion of the collateral backing the MBS will prepay and what portion will default in that month, with corresponding loss severities being generated. Most of these models do take into account the paths that interest rates have taken as part of this determination. Once a prepayment and loss rate for a month has been generated, it is fed into a cash flow engine that deals with how raw collateral payments get divided up to the MBS bondholders (for collateralized debt obligations [CMOs], this includes taking the cash waterfall rules into account). We then end up with a series of cash flows and discount rates (via money market account evolution) along each path. We can then discount these cash flows by the discount rates, and take the average over all paths to get the present value. If this present value does not match the market value, we can look for the single spread that we would need to add to all of the discount rates in order to get the present value to match the input price. This is the OAS of the mortgage-backed security. Mathematically, it is:

$$\mathrm{MBS} = \frac{1}{|S|}\sum_{p \in S}\sum_{i=1}^{N}\frac{CF(p,i)}{\prod_{j=1}^{i}(1+r(p,j,j+1)+OAS)} \tag{10.5}$$

where $S$ represents the sample space of interest rate paths, $r(p,j,j+1)$ is the short rate between month $j$ and month $j+1$, and $CF(p,i)$ is the cash flow at time $i$, along path $p$.

The option-adjusted spread represents an average excess return required by MBS investors to compensate for risks not explained by interest rates. The OAS is *not* compensation for prepayments or losses; it is compensation for the uncertainties in prepayments and losses that remain *even after interest rates and volatilities are known*. That is, conditional on knowledge of interest rates, interest rate volatility, home prices, unemployment, and other observable background information, whether a borrower will prepay or default in any month is still essentially random. The prepayment modeler may have information about regional home prices, employment statistics, and so on, but information about an individual borrower's job status, house price, and the like is not available. This means that, conditional on macroeconomic data, the best a prepayment modeler can do is to assign a probability to the individual prepayment or loss event. Spread arises from that probability, and spread risk arises from how that probability is likely to change.

The idea that the arrival time of a mortgage prepayment, conditional on knowledge of some background macroeconomic variables, is essentially a random event is not unique to the mortgage sector. The same assumptions are often applied to the modeling of corporate bond spreads and corporate credit default swap (CDS) premiums.

If $F_t$ represents information about interest rates and other background macroeconomic variables, $H_t$ represents information about an uncertain cash flow, and $B(t)$ is the value of the money market account at time $t$, then we can express the value of that cash flow as:

$$PV(t) = B(t) \bullet E\left\{\frac{CF(T)}{B(T)}\middle| F_t \vee H_t\right\} \tag{10.6}$$

Of course, there is no easy single approach to computing this expectation, as it is highly dependent on the type of uncertainty surrounding the cash flow. On the other hand, the evolution dynamics of the interest rate environment can be specified using one of a number of well-understood stochastic differential equations, as discussed in the chapters on interest rate and interest rate volatility risk. We might view the other macroeconomic variables germane to the cash flow as being similarly well understood.

When trying to describe a joint probability between two (possibly multidimensional) random variables, we can always write that joint probability down as the product of a marginal distribution and a conditional distribution, which in calculus just says we can change the order of integration of a double integral.[1] If we applied this to the preceding expectation, we'd get:

$$PV(t) = B(t) \bullet E\left\{ E\left\{ \frac{CF(\tau)}{B(\tau)} \middle| H_t \right\} \middle| F_t \right\} \tag{10.7}$$

We are now at a crossroads. The decomposition in equation (10.7) doesn't get us much unless we are willing to make a decision. What we need to decide is whether $H_t$ contains information not available in $F_t$. That is, even after we know what interest rates are and what other macroeconomic variables are, do we believe that the timing of the cash flow is still essentially random, or do we believe that the cash flow is completely predictable once all those other observable macroeconomic variables are known?

Models that are built around the former are called *reduced form*, while models built around the latter are called *structural*. What spread means depends entirely upon which assumption we are making. Again, the literature encompassing each is extensive, so we restrict our focus in what follows to providing some intuition into each area within the context of properly understanding spread risk.

## REDUCED FORM APPROACH

The reduced form approach is most commonly associated with corporate credit models, but as we mentioned, the basic concepts were already being implemented in mortgage prepayment models long before the approach was put on more theoretically rigorous footing. In the reduced form approach, knowledge of the observable macroeconomic variables is not sufficient to predict the timing of a cash flow; there is randomness in the timing of the cash flow not explained by anything that we can directly observe. We can observe when the cash flow occurs, of course, but like Schrodinger's cat, we have to check on it directly to know whether it's alive. Ultimately, the informational asymmetry between the payer and the receiver of the cash flow is such that there will always be residual uncertainty regarding the payment of the cash flow from the point of view of the cash flow receiver.

Consider first a defaultable \$1 cash flow. Economically, we want a model that allows us to value the defaultable \$1 cash flow by discounting by the interest rate plus a (time-varying) short spread, which we can then view as just the (instantaneous) conditional probability of default. To accomplish this, in the reduced form approach, we impose the assumption that the $F_t$-conditional probability of default is not too wild. That is, if we set:

$$\Gamma(t) = -\ln\left(1 - P\left(\tau \leq t | F_t\right)\right) \tag{10.8}$$

then we assume that we can write:

$$\Gamma(t) = \int_0^t \gamma(s)ds \tag{10.9}$$

With this assumption in hand, we can evaluate the inner expectation in the present value formula above as:

$$E\left\{\frac{1_{\{\tau>t\}}}{B(\tau)}\middle| H_t\right\} = 1_{\{\tau>t\}} \bullet \exp\left\{-\int_t^T (r_s + \gamma_s)ds\right\} \tag{10.10}$$

where $\tau$ is the arrival time of the cash flow, $1_{\{\tau>t\}}$ is the indicator function that takes value 1 if the cash flow has occurred and 0 if it has not, $r_s$ is the short spot interest rate, and $\gamma_s$ is the conditional hazard rate.

We can generalize from the \$1 defaultable cash flow rather immediately to credit default swaps, corporate bonds, mortgages, and other securities with $F_t$-dependent cash flows. We can value the two legs of a CDS, for example, as:

$$\begin{aligned} V^{\text{premium}}(t) = {} & \text{Spread} \bullet \sum_{k=1}^{N} (T_k - T_{k-1}) \\ & \bullet E\left\{\exp\left\{-\int_t^{T_k} (r_s + \gamma_s)ds\right\} \middle| F_t\right\} \end{aligned} \tag{10.11}$$

$$V^{\text{default}}(t) = E\left\{\int_t^{T_N} \delta_u \gamma_u \exp\left\{-\int_t^u (r_s + \gamma_s)ds\right\} du \middle| F_t\right\} \tag{10.12}$$

where $\delta_u$ is the loss given default.

Practical implementation requires further simplifying assumptions about the form of the hazard process (e.g., Poisson, Cox, affine) and about the recovery value. We get formula (10.5) for mortgage-backed securities, for example, by setting the hazard process equal to the constant OAS and working with discrete discount factors instead of continuous ones. The $F_t$-conditional cash flows are specified through the prepayment and loss model, meaning MBS valuation follows the reduced form approach. The OAS is then fit to the market observable MBS price, given the prepayment model.

For corporate bonds, determining an $F_t$-conditional formula for the cash flows is harder, as corporate defaults are much less frequent. In this case, hazard rates are assumed to be nonconstant, and CDS data of multiple tenors is consumed to calibrate a parametric form for the conditional hazard rate process. Affine and Cox processes, in particular, are favored, but no direct information about firm balance sheet data is used by these models. Also note that the hazard process gives the conditional *risk-neutral* probability of default. It says nothing about the *physical* probability of default, and so cannot be used to generate real-world expected default frequencies. On the other hand, an upshot of formulas (10.11) and (10.12) is that if we assume the hazard rate and the loss given default to be constant, then we can approximate the CDS spread in terms of the risk-neutral hazard rate as:

$$\text{CDS spread} \approx \gamma \cdot \delta \tag{10.13}$$

Corporate credit models that use firm balance sheet information and can be used to calculate expected default frequencies typically fall under the structural approach.

## STRUCTURAL APPROACH

The structural approach is probably best embodied by the Merton model for corporate credit. In the Merton model, corporate debt is modeled as a defaultable zero coupon bond. Firm asset value is modeled as a geometric Brownian motion, and firm equity is modeled as a European call option on the value of the assets, where the barrier (strike) is the notional $D = D_0$ on the outstanding debt. Because assets equal debt plus equity, owning the debt is equivalent to being long a default-free zero coupon bond and short a put option on the assets of the firm. Although this model is highly simplified in its assumptions about a firm's capital structure, the appeal of the model is that it provides a direct tractable link, in the form of the Black-Scholes option pricing, between the debt, the assets, and the equity.

In the Merton model, the assets are financed through a single zero coupon bond and equity, so the value of the assets is related to the equity and risky debt simply as:

$$A_t = D_t + E_t \tag{10.14}$$

The defaultable debt is equivalent to a long position in a risk-free bond and a short put option on the assets of the firm. If the assets are not worth the notional value of the debt at maturity, the owners for the firm (equity) can default and put the assets on the bond holds. However, if at maturity the assets are worth more than the notional value of debt, then the equity holders can pay the notional debt off, sell the assets, and get a payoff equal to $A_T - D$. This makes equity a call on the value of the assets of the firm.

Mathematically, the Merton model provides us with two nonlinear equations that we can attempt to solve for the asset value and the asset volatility:

$$\sigma_E \bullet E = \frac{\partial}{\partial A}(C(A, D, \sigma_A, r, T)) \bullet \sigma_A \bullet A \qquad (10.15)$$

$$E = C(A, D, \sigma_A, r, T) \qquad (10.16)$$

where the $A$ is the value of the assets, $D$ the notional on the debt, $E$ the value of the equity, $C$ is the value of the European call option, and the $\sigma$'s represent the volatility of the assets and equity, respectively.

Asset value and asset volatility are generally not observable, but the equity value and equity volatility are. The two equations above give us a means for solving for asset value and asset volatility once equity value and equity volatility are known. Once we have solved this system, standard Black-Scholes option pricing theory can be applied to determine the value of the debt, the spread, and the probability of default.

Bond valuation in the Merton model is done by applying the Black-Scholes option pricing formula to value the short put option, and the term structure to value the long default-free bond. In terms of equation (10.10), the default event is completely predictable given conditional knowledge of the asset value. If the asset value is known to be below the value of the notional debt at maturity, the put option will be exercised, and a default will occur with 100 percent certainty. This is in contrast to the reduced form approach, where the default event is uncertain, even given conditional information about the asset value.

Mathematically, the value of the defaultable bond is:

$$PV(t) = D \bullet e^{-r(T-t)}\Phi(d_t^2) + A_t\Phi(-d_t^1) \qquad (10.17)$$

where $d_t^1 = \dfrac{\ln\left(\dfrac{D}{A_0}\right) - \left(r - \dfrac{1}{2}\sigma_A^2\right)(T-t)}{\sigma_A\sqrt{T-t}}$ and $d_t^2 = d_t^1 - \sigma_A\sqrt{T-t}$.

The spread to the continuously compounded spot curve is then:

$$\text{Spread}(t) = \frac{-1}{T-t}\ln\left(\Phi(d_t^2) + \frac{A_t}{D\cdot e^{-r(T-t)}}\Phi(-d_t^1)\right) \tag{10.18}$$

The spread of the defaultable corporate bond is similar in nature to the spread of a (nondefaultable) European callable bond, in that the spread arises from uncertainty about the cash flows, but in a way that is entirely contained in the dynamics of observable variables. In each case, the spread comes from being short an option whose value we have the information to compute. If we add back this option value to the bond, we should get the value of the straight bond. When we use a structural model to quantify spread, we are trying to attribute the risk of cash flow uncertainty to sources we believe we effectively can model and, more importantly, hedge. In the case of the Merton model, spreads arise due to uncertainty in whether the asset value will be sufficient to pay off the debt at maturity, and asset value dynamics can be determined from equity price dynamics. Interest rates are also an input, but the risk-free discount rate contributes only a small amount to the overall spread. The Merton-derived spread already has the effect of interest rates taken out, in that they are a nominal contribution to the spread to begin with.

Finally, in the Merton model, and the structural approach generally, the conditional probability of default does not admit a nontrivial conditional default intensity. The probability of default is just the probability that the asset value will end below the notional value of debt, which can easily be expressed in terms of the cumulative normal distribution and the asset value process as:

$$P(A_T \le D) = \Phi\left(\frac{\ln\left(\frac{D}{A_0}\right) - \left(\mu_A - \frac{1}{2}\sigma_A^2\right)T}{\sigma_A\sqrt{T}}\right) \tag{10.19}$$

If the asset drift $\mu_A$ comes from the physical probability, then this gives us the physical probability of default. If the drift $\mu_A$ comes from the risk-neutral probability (so that it is just the risk-free rate $r$), then we get the risk-neutral probability of default. In the Merton model, the physical probability of default is then related to the risk-neutral probability of default via the Sharpe ratio.

$$Q(A_T \le D) = \Phi\left(\Phi^{-1}\left(P(A_T \le D)\right) + \frac{(\mu_A - r)}{\sigma_A}\sqrt{T}\right) \tag{10.20}$$

## SPREAD EXPOSURE

We started the measurement of risk for fixed income securities by applying the Taylor formula to the clean bond price or return. Fixed income is about cash flows and all cash flows have an associated time value of money component, so all bonds have some interest rate risk. Therefore, the first risk we examined was interest rate risk. Next, we want to measure risk that comes from non-interest-rate-related sources. Spread represents the total premium for this broad set of risks. Spreads, we saw, can be static or adjusted. We saw that the static spread of a nondefaultable callable bond probably doesn't have risk other than interest rate and interest rate volatility risk, and any residual risk that it might have should be expressed not through a static spread, but through an option-adjusted spread. This is because the interest rate and interest rate volatility exposures already contain the risk to the option due to interest rate and volatility moves. Therefore, to the extent that we have already measured interest rate and volatility risk through key rate durations and vegas, and their associated key rates and volatilities, we want to adjust spreads for interest rate and interest rate volatility risk, so that we do not double count risks. This is illustrated best in the example of mortgage-backed securities.

For a mortgage-backed security, there is significant optionality that arises from interest rates. An MBS is therefore exposed to both interest rate and interest rate volatility risk. By specifying a prepayment model and computing an option-adjusted spread based on discounting expected cash flows, we are trying to remove from the spread the exposure to interest rates and interest rate volatility. Thus, when we compute spread exposure, we have to realize we have already measured the sensitivity to an interest rate move and the sensitivity to a volatility of interest rate move. The OAS is not compensation for bearing interest rate and interest rate volatility risk. It is compensation for bearing prepayment model risk.

Many commercially available prepayment models consume additional macroeconomic variables, like house price appreciation, in addition to mortgage rate forecasts as part of the information that is conditionally available when making the prepayment forecast. For an MBS, the OAS would not reflect the uncertainty in cash flows due to any of these inputs; it reflects the residual uncertainty in the cash flows due to prepayment model prediction error. For the example of house prices, the better the prepayment model is at capturing the effect of house price appreciation on prepayment speeds, the less the OAS will reflect a premium due to uncertainty in future house prices. We would need to measure exposure to house prices, or any other observable background variable, separately. The other alternative is to not try to take out what is known, except as it ultimately depends on interest rates, so that the OAS will reflect it. For a simple fixed or floating coupon corporate bond, there is no interest rate optionality; hence to capture default risk within the spread, we would use a static spread.

The bond exposure to the spread is measured using spread durations and convexities, and possibly higher-order terms. Spread duration is measured in practice numerically by holding the spot curve and expected cash flows fixed, and then calculating price given a shift in spread up and down. This is different from an interest rate exposure measure like effective duration. With an effective duration calculation, we hold the option-adjusted spread constant and perform a parallel shift in the spot curve. This parallel shift may cause a change in the cash flows if they are dependent on interest rates, as with an MBS.

## SPREAD VOLATILITY

The option-adjusted spread is compensation for cash flow uncertainty not related to uncertainty about interest rates and potentially other macroeconomic variables. Spread risk is concerned with the change in that uncertainty and the compensation required for bearing it. Spread risk exposure is measured through spread duration, convexity, and higher-order derivatives, and the Taylor formula prescribes how to use these to combine a change in spread with the spread exposure. All that remains to do is to model the (option-adjusted) spread changes, which is highly dependent on the bond sector and whether the spread is of structural or reduced form.

Consequently, we will focus on two approaches to modeling spread change. In the structural approach, spreads are derived from more fundamental observable econometric variables. The principal example of this type of model is the Merton model, and we will discuss how the derived spread change models can be used to model spread changes for corporate and sovereign bonds. The primary advantage of derived spread change models is that they capture the often significant nonlinearities that exist in the relationships between spreads and the fundamental variables of import. When spread cannot be derived in terms of other observable variables, nonlinearity is not as much of a concern, so it is reasonable to assume that spread change can be reduced via a factor model. Our primary example of how to implement a factor model approach will be in describing mortgage-backed securities, specifically U.S. agency collateralized mortgage obligations (CMOs) and pass-through structures.

## DERIVED SPREAD APPROACH

The derived spread approach is best illustrated through the Merton model, and how it can be applied to model spread changes for corporate and sovereign bonds. First, the Merton model is simplistic in its assumptions, so the first problem we face when applying the Merton model is how to condense a complex capital structure into a single zero coupon bond representation. If all of the outstanding debt of an obligor is available, one way to condense would be to compute the duration of a notional weighted portfolio of all the outstanding. The notional of the bullet bond then becomes the sum of all outstanding bonds' notional values. The maturity of the bullet is then just set equal to the duration of notional weighted portfolio. Effectively, we are then using a duration-matched bullet bond to represent a more complex bond portfolio. The spread of this bullet bond has been given in equation (10.18), and is a function of only the volatility of the assets and the discounted leverage of the firm:

$$L_t = \frac{De^{-rt}}{A_t} \tag{10.21}$$

If we want to know how the spread of this bullet changed over some time period, all we need to know is how the volatility of the assets changed and how the discounted leverage changed. If we were to assume that the notional debt did not change over this time period, then a knowledge of how the equity value and the equity volatility level changed over the time period would allow us to solve the system of equations (10.15) and (10.16) for the asset value and volatility at both the start and end of the time period. This would give us the asset value change, and hence the leverage change, and finally the spread change. If we assume the asset and equity volatility is constant over the period, up to first-order approximation, then assets are proportional to equity, so equity returns can provide an approximation of asset returns, provided they are not too extreme, which can be useful for practical implementation.

The main drawback of the Merton model is its simplistic assumptions regarding capital structure of obligors. This will lead to some error in modeling the obligor probability of default. However, one of the main advantages of using the Merton model is that it gives us a tractable way to model default correlation. We now discuss why being able to model default correlation matters so much.

Consider obligors $A$ and $B$, and a time horizon $T$. Let's denote the probability of default of $A$ before $T$ by $p_A$ and similarly the probability of default of $B$ before $T$ by $p_B$. Now for a little pop quiz.

**Question:** With knowledge of $p_A$ and $p_B$ you can determine which of the following?

**a.** $p_{A|B}$ The conditional probability that $A$ defaults given $B$ has defaulted.
**b.** $p_{AB}$ The joint probability that both $A$ and $B$ default.
**c.** $\rho_{AB}$ The linear correlation coefficient between the default indicator events $1_A$ and $1_B$.
**d.** None of the above.

Unfortunately, knowledge of the marginal probabilities of default is insufficient to determine the conditional probabilities of default, the joint probability, or the linear correlation. So the answer is (d), none of the above. Knowledge of the marginal distributions and the linear correlation of default is, however, enough to determine the conditional default probabilities and the joint probability of default. The relationships between these quantities are given by:

$$p_{AB} = p_A p_B + \rho_{AB}\sqrt{p_A(1-p_A)p_B(1-p_B)} \tag{10.22}$$

$$p_{A|B} = p_A + \rho_{AB}\sqrt{\frac{p_A}{p_B}(1-p_A)(1-p_B)} \tag{10.23}$$

$$p_{A|B} = \frac{p_{AB}}{p_B} \tag{10.24}$$

Before discussing how one might go about estimating the linear correlation of default, let's just take a moment to see just how important this number is for credit risk. Let's suppose that the individual default probability for each obligor is 2 percent, so that $p_A = p_B = 2\%$. In Figures 10.1 and 10.2 we plot the joint probability of default, and the (identical) conditional probability of default.

It is important to note that the linear default correlation completely dominates both the conditional and joint probabilities of default. The joint probability of default, for example, is roughly 10 times as large under a correlation of 20 percent as under 0 percent, and the magnitude of this effect increases as the individual probabilities decrease. This is different from our experience with correlation as it applies to equity return variance, where the marginal effect of a lower average correlation is constant on a relative basis. Thus the relative value of proper diversification increases as the risk decreases for credit-sensitive portfolios. Given that historical analysis by the ratings agencies suggests that the five-year default probability of the majority of investment grade rated bonds is below 2 percent, this suggests that for

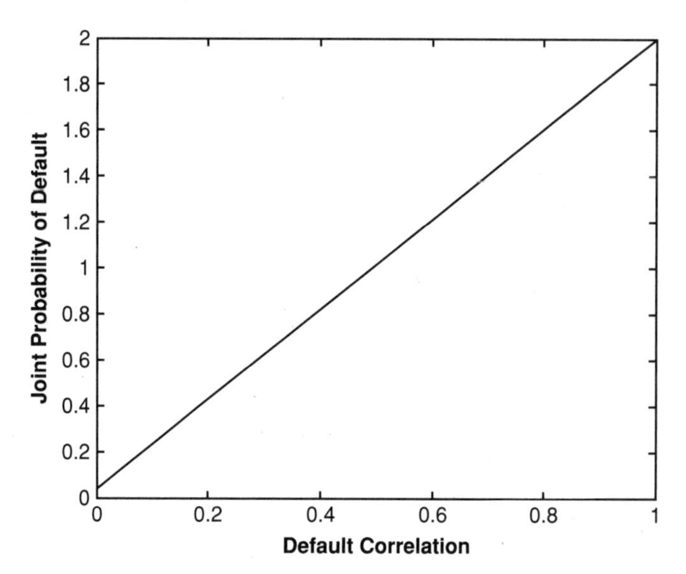


**FIGURE 10.1** Linear default correlation versus joint probability of default.

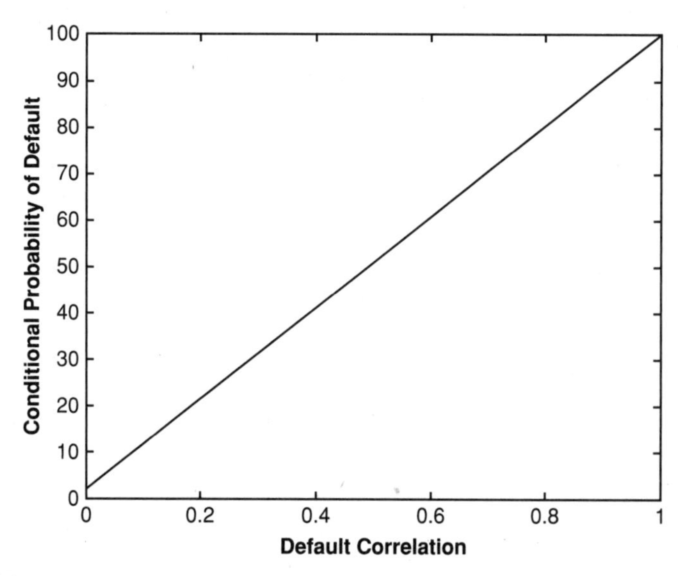


**FIGURE 10.2** Linear default correlation versus conditional probability of default.

a typical investment grade portfolio of credits, default correlation should dominate the risk calculus. In particular, the use of average credit rating by some bond funds to summarize credit risk is inappropriate, not because it hides a few lower-quality bonds, which may skew the loss risk, but because it provides absolutely no information about the dominant risk, the default correlation.

To illustrate the impact of default correlation on the portfolio VaR, consider the case of an equally weighted portfolio of 100 obligors with identical independent individual probabilities of default of $p = 5\%$ over a horizon $T$, and zero recovery. Neglecting the interest rate component, the VaR over the horizon of this portfolio is characterized simply by the number of defaults over that horizon. In this example, we can compute the probability of there being $k$ or fewer defaults using the cumulative binomial distribution function.

$$p(x \le k) = \sum_{k=0}^{N} \binom{N}{k} p^k (1-p)^{N-k} \tag{10.25}$$

In Figure 10.3 we display the 99 percent VaR for this stylized portfolio.

As with equities, to fully determine the joint probability of default would require us to estimate all the pairwise correlations within a portfolio. Even for a portfolio of 100 obligors, this would require the specification of 4,950 pairwise correlations, which would in turn require obtaining at a minimum 4,950 default events. This is simply not feasible. Even for an equity

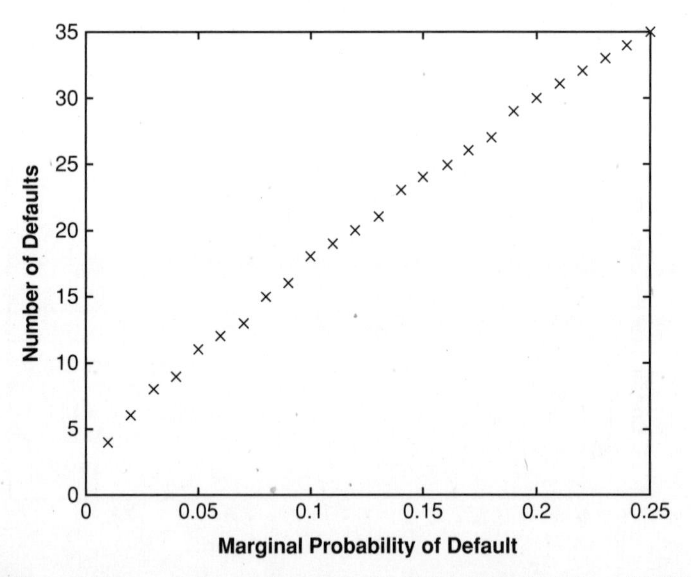


**FIGURE 10.3** 99 percent VaR as a function of individual probability of default.

world, where there is ample return data, a factor structure is employed to make the correlation problem tractable. The solution for corporate bonds is twofold. First, we employ a factor model structure on the equity returns to dimension reduce the problem. Second, we will apply the Merton model in order to link equity return correlation to asset return correlation, and asset return correlation to default correlation.

To keep things simple for now, let's just consider a one-factor model of the firm assets directly. Specifically, let's assume that all assets are driven by a single, common factor with a standard normal distribution.

$$A_k = \sqrt{\rho} \cdot F + \sqrt{1-\rho} \bullet \varepsilon_k \tag{10.26}$$

Because the idiosyncratic components are assumed to be uncorrelated, the covariance between the assets will just be $\rho$. If we normalize the asset values first, then we can view $\rho$ as an asset correlation. For the structural model part, we will assume a simple barrier model. Namely, an obligor defaults if its asset value at the horizon $T$ falls below some critical level $K$.

If we assume that all obligors in an equally weighted portfolio have the same barrier $K$, then having uncorrelated idiosyncratic components means that, conditional on a realization of F, the probability of having $k$ or fewer defaults in an $N$-obligor portfolio is given by the binomial cumulative distribution function in equation (10.26). Since the common factor has standard normal distribution, the VaR is given by further integrating the binomial against the Gaussian density function. In Figure 10.4 is the plot of the 99 percent VaR for a 100-obligor portfolio for different choices of $\rho$, where the barrier $K$ is set so that zero correlation corresponds to a marginal probability of default of 2 percent.

We can immediately see two things from the figure. First, the VaR converges to the independent binomially distributed case as correlation goes to zero (compare to Figure 10.3). Second, a 2 percent individual probability of default with a 20 percent asset correlation has a 99 percent VaR of 14. We would get the same VaR by having a 7.5 percent individual probability of default, with a zero percent asset correlation. To put this in context, this is like saying that an average BBB-rated portfolio would bear the same credit risk (as measured by the 99 percent VaR) as a BB-rated portfolio. Three guesses on which portfolio would have a higher yield.

In this example, we highlighted the importance of default correlation through a simple factor model,[2] showing how asset correlation dominates the risk equation for a portfolio of investment grade credits. Now let's go into more detail as to how an equity factor model can be harnessed to estimate the credit risk, and how correlation stress-testing can be leveraged, by looking at some real-world examples.

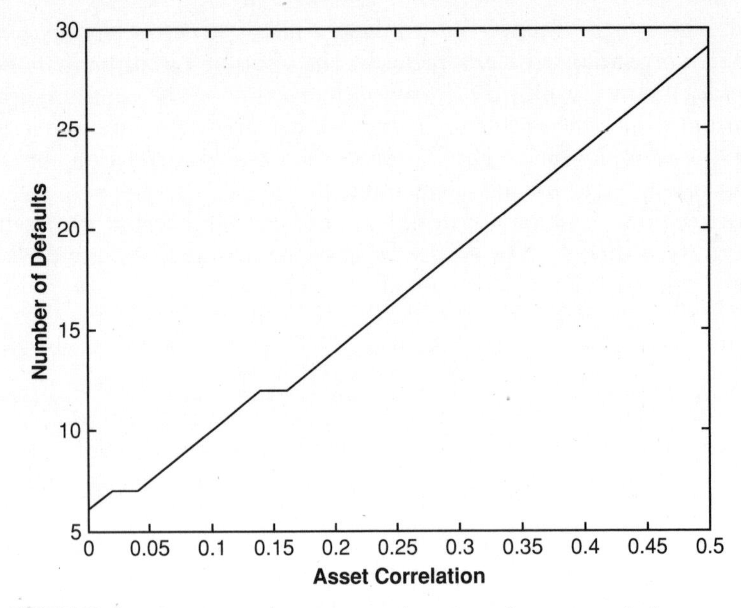


**FIGURE 10.4** The 99 percent VaR as a function of asset correlation.

Turning to factor models, we recall that in a factor model, the goal is to express the $N$ individual returns in terms of a linear combination of common factors as:

$$R_i = \alpha_i + \sum_{k=1}^{M} \beta_{ik} F_k + \epsilon_i \tag{10.27}$$

where:

$$E(\epsilon_i) = 0, \quad E(\epsilon_i\ F_k) = 0, \quad E(\epsilon_i \epsilon_j) = 0 \tag{10.28}$$

The main benefit of this is that the covariance (and therefore correlation) structure is highly simplified, and determined by the covariance of the common factors. If those factors are orthogonal (and we can always perform some form of factor rotation to make this so), then the variance and covariance structure is simply given by:

$$\operatorname{var}(R_i) = \sum_{k=1}^{M} \beta_{ik}^2 \operatorname{var}(F_k) + \operatorname{var}(\varepsilon_i) \tag{10.29}$$

$$\operatorname{cov}(R_i, R_j) = \sum_{k=1}^{M} \beta_{ik} \beta_{jk} \operatorname{var}(F_k) \tag{10.30}$$

In the next example, we want to take a closer look at how sensitive the VaR of a real-life portfolio is to changes in the correlation matrix when we apply a more realistic factor model structure. For our test portfolio, we use the BofA Merrill Lynch U.S. Corporates Large Cap/Industrials (5- to 10-year) index, which has a weighted average rating of A3. For the equity factor model, we perform a simple principal component analysis (PCA) on the daily equity returns of the issuers for the prior 250 days, and retain the top 10 principal components. We use PCA for the factor model, for example, because the principal components are already orthogonal (uncorrelated), and hence provide a simple way to alter the correlation structure while preserving the individual variances within a Monte Carlo–based simulation. This lets us examine the effect on the 99 percent VaR of a correlation shift for a real-life portfolio, while at the same time not altering any of the marginal probabilities of default.

The scree plot for this is shown in Figure 10.5. Effectively the first 10 PCs explain roughly 58 percent of the daily variation in returns, with the first component accounting for more than 40 percent of the variation alone. It is worth pausing for a moment to compare this to the simple one-factor asset value model. The scree plot indicates that such a simple model may not be terribly inappropriate.

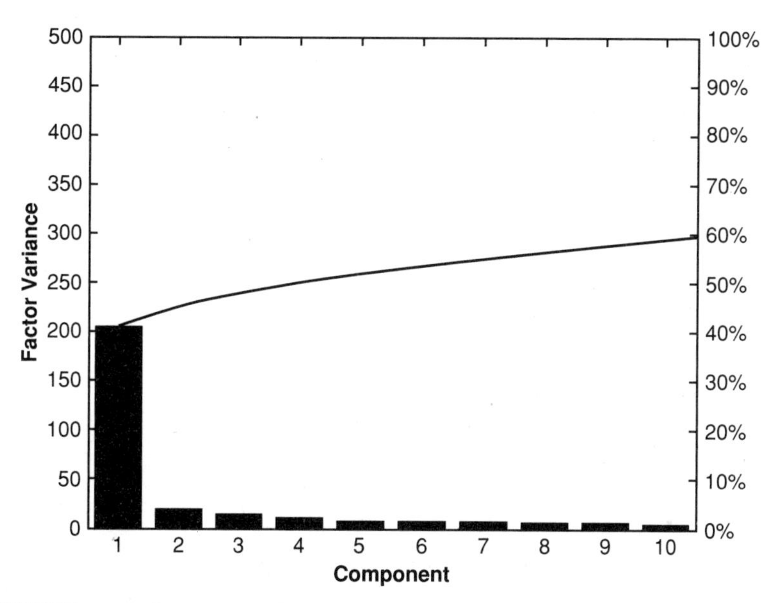


**FIGURE 10.5** U.S. large-cap industrials principal component scree bar chart.
*Sources:* FactSet and BofA Merrill Lynch.

The equity factor and Merton model frameworks come together to generate a VaR number in the following four steps:

1. Given the observable equity value, equity volatility, and outstanding firm debt, calculate the asset value and asset volatility by solving equations (10.15) and (10.16).
2. With the equity factor model in hand, run simulated returns of the common and idiosyncratic factors to generate equity return scenarios. Assume debt is unchanged, and then calculate asset value changes as $A(\text{sim}) = A(\text{base}) + E(\text{sim}) - E(\text{base})$.
3. Hold the asset volatility constant and use the asset value changes to compute new probabilities of default, and then compute a spread change.
4. Use the simulated spread changes to compute the portfolio weighted average returns (due solely to spread moves), and calculate VaR.

To see the effect of an equity return correlation change on our real-life portfolio of credits, we do two tests. First, we do a Monte Carlo simulation where we randomly perturb the issuer equity factor loadings while leaving the percentage of variation due to idiosyncratic risk unchanged. In general, this spreads the systematic risk out across the factors more evenly and, as a result, lowers the average pairwise equity return correlations. The results of this are presented in Figure 10.6. As expected, the VaR is a function of the average correlation. Recall that the equity factor model is using daily returns, so the analysis effectively shows the impact on one-day VaR on our portfolio, in basis points.

Comparing the trend line to the single-factor model, the impact of increasing the correlation from 0.3 to 0.4 is roughly 10 bps, which represents an increase of 25 percent to the VaR. This compares to a 20 percent increase in VaR when going from a correlation of 0.3 to 0.4 for the simple single-factor model.

The second test is to shift variance from the idiosyncratic components to the systematic components in a relatively uniform way. Figure 10.7 confirms that shifting risk from uncorrelated idiosyncratic components to the systematic factors increases average correlation and the VaR. Slightly different than in the stylized single-factor model, the magnitude of the effect declines with rising correlation. This is mostly due to the fact that the idiosyncratic exposures are heterogeneous in our real-life portfolio.

Finally, to emphasize the point that correlation dominates, we examine the effect of holding the correlation structure constant, but simply increasing the individual risk-neutral probabilities of default (achieved by raising the equity volatilities). This is presented in Figure 10.8. The base case weighted

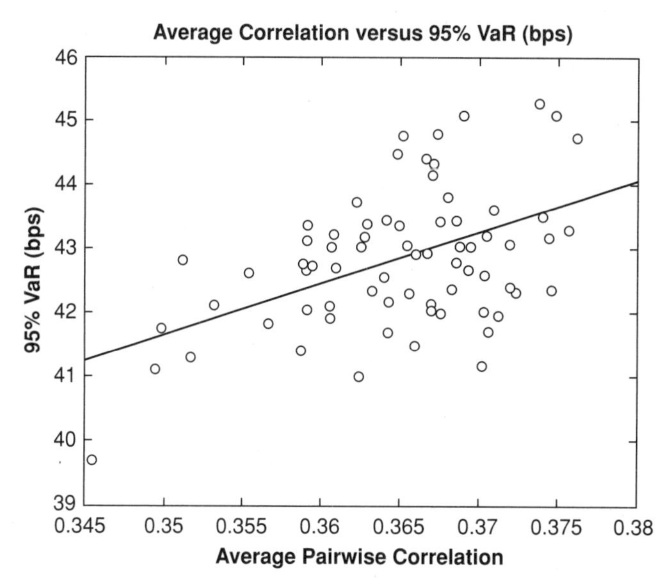


**FIGURE 10.6** Portfolio VaR as a function of average pairwise correlation for U.S. large-cap industrials.
*Sources:* FactSet and BofA Merrill Lynch.

average probability of default was roughly 4 percent. The 95 percent VaR level for the base case was 44 bps.

There are a few really interesting aspects of the graph to note. First, there is a clear pivot point in the risk at about 9 percent. In a real-life portfolio, the linear increase in marginal risk of the stylized example does break down at some point. The second aspect to note is how flat the VaR profile is below 6 percent. There is very little to be gained VaR-wise from decreasing the individual probabilities of default. The same probably cannot be said of the portfolio yield. Last, the probabilities are risk neutral, not physical, so they do not directly translate to empirical default frequencies as measured by the rating agencies without knowledge of investor's risk aversion. That said, if the pivot point corresponds to a point just beyond the investment grade/high yield break point, a manager might be able to add significant extra yield by selectively crossing the divide. For the sake of comparison, the yield on our test portfolio is 3.84 with an average rating of A3, while the yield on the BofA Merrill Lynch U.S. High Yield Master II is 8.47, with an average rating of B1.

The structural approach via the Merton model then provides a good way to model default correlation through equity return correlations, which in practice comes from specification of a robust equity return factor model. As an additional boon, the joint risk profile of a corporate bond/equity

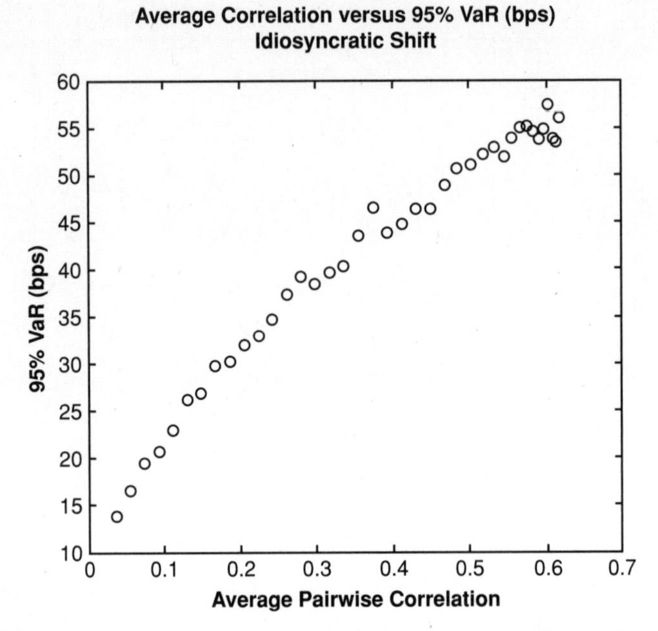


**FIGURE 10.7** Portfolio VaR as a function of pairwise correlation for a shift in idiosyncratic risk contribution for U.S. large-cap industrials.
*Sources:* FactSet and BofA Merrill Lynch.

balanced portfolio can be modeled in a way that takes into account the nonlinear dependence between bond returns and equity returns. Idiosyncratic firm risk is also consistently distributed to both the equity and the bond in this joint framework. The major drawback, however, is simplicity of the Merton model assumptions regarding capital structure. We can explain how the spread of a duration-matched bullet bond changes with changes in the equity, which gives us a sort of average spread change, but how do we apply this to individual bonds within the capital structure? Also, we have measured the total debt using publicly issued debt, and a very real criticism of the Merton model is that it does not reflect any off-balance-sheet liabilities.

One way to adjust the model is to appeal to a reduced form relationship between the spread, the risk neutral probability of default, and the loss given default.

$$S = \frac{-\ln(1-Q)}{T}(1-R) \tag{10.31}$$

Recall that in the Merton model, the risk-neutral probability of default depends on the leverage and the asset volatility. If we hold asset volatility

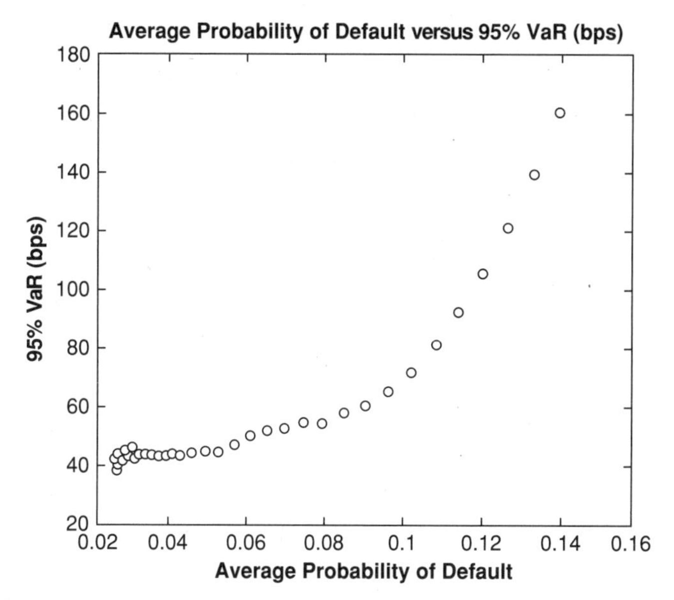


**FIGURE 10.8** The 95 percent VaR as a function of average probability of default under constant correlation.
*Source:* FactSet.

fixed, we can use this relationship on any bond in the capital structure to determine the leverage that would set the model spread equal to the observed spread. Each bond would have a different calibrated leverage, providing a way to incorporate differing exposure to total liabilities for different bonds in the capital structure. Alternatively, we could fix leverage and calibrate an implied asset volatility for each bond, which is not so different from what is done with deep in- and out-of-the-money equity options.

In FactSet's Monte Carlo–based multi-asset-class risk model, we use the approach as roughly outlined earlier. In Figure 10.9 and Figure 10.10, we plot one year's worth of the 95 percent one-day VaR for using the model against the empirical (historical) VaR based on trailing 250 trading days for both the BofA Merrill Lynch U.S. Corporate Master index and the S&P 500, to illustrate how spread risk is driven through a derived process that ultimately links equity and corporate bonds together, and reasonably captures the joint risk profile within each sector separately.

Having discussed the structural approach for corporate credit, we now show how the framework can also be applied to sovereign debt by examining the credit spreads of Eurozone countries over the euro benchmark curve, demonstrating how the Merton model generalizes.

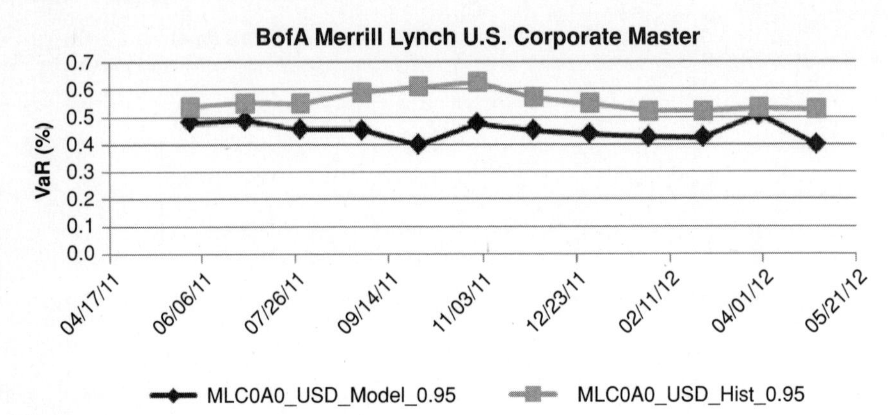


**FIGURE 10.9** Empirical versus model 95 percent one-day VaR for broad corporate portfolio.
*Sources:* FactSet and BofA Merrill Lynch.

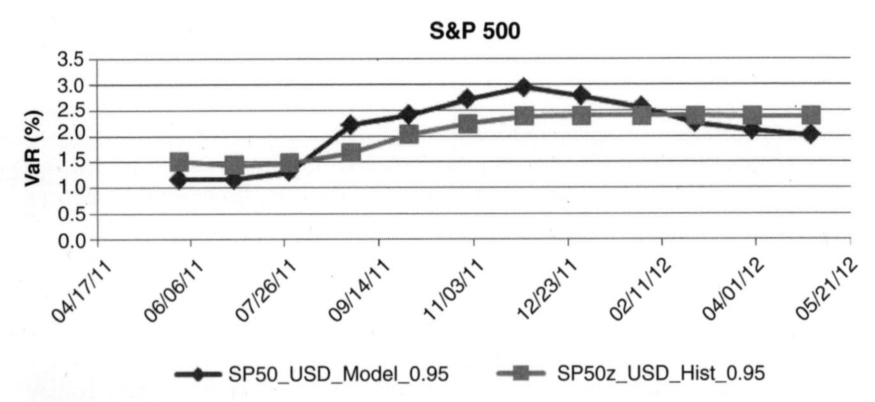


**FIGURE 10.10** Empirical versus model 95 percent one-day VaR for broad equity portfolio.
*Sources:* FactSet and BofA Merrill Lynch.

## EURO-SOVEREIGN SPREADS

The model uses the basic contingent claims framework that underlies the Merton model. To use this balance-sheet-centric model, we will need to determine suitable values for six items:

1. The market value of the junior liability claim (equity).
2. The volatility of the junior liability returns.

3. The notional amount of the senior liability claim (bond) or debt-to-equity ratio.
4. The duration on the senior claim.
5. The risk-free rate.
6. The recovery rate upon default.

We will call this collection of values the *Merton inputs*, and with them we can determine the asset value, the asset volatility, and then the market value of the senior liability claim (bond price).

Obtaining these inputs in the corporate model is straightforward. For the Euro-Sovereign model, we use the following six items as proxies:

1. FactSet Country Aggregate index value (in euros).
2. Implied volatility of the FactSet Country Aggregate index returns, determined by taking the 60-day trailing historical volatility multiplied by an implied volatility factor. The implied volatility factor is derived by computing the ratio of the VStoxx implied volatility level over the 60-day trailing volatility of the Euro Stoxx 50.
3. Global Insight's three-year-ahead forecasted debt-to-GDP ratio, reset on a yearly frequency.
4. Average life of the scheduled principal and interest (P&I) on all outstanding sovereign debt.
5. Rate on the euro benchmark with equivalent duration as before.
6. Country-dependent recovery that ranges from 35 percent for Greece to 85 percent for France.

In Figures 10.11 and 10.12 we present the time-series plots of the actual and model-predicted spreads for the major Eurozone members.[3]

Overall, the model-predicted spreads track the actual spreads fairly well, although there is some divergence for some of the GIIPS countries (Greece, Ireland, Italy, Portugal, Spain). One explanation for this is that the implied volatility for the GIIPS is, in fact, higher than the proxy derived using the VStoxx.

Now that we've looked at performance of the model on a country-by-country basis, let's turn to measuring the joint predictive power. Let's start by taking a look at the historical correlations. Figure 10.13 presents some empirical correlations. In the first panel we see that pairwise spread correlations are fairly high among the 10 major Eurozone countries in general, but the GIIPS and non-GIIPS subgroups have higher correlations in group than out of group.

Also, in the second panel we see that each country's daily spread changes are negatively correlated with their FactSet country aggregate equity index

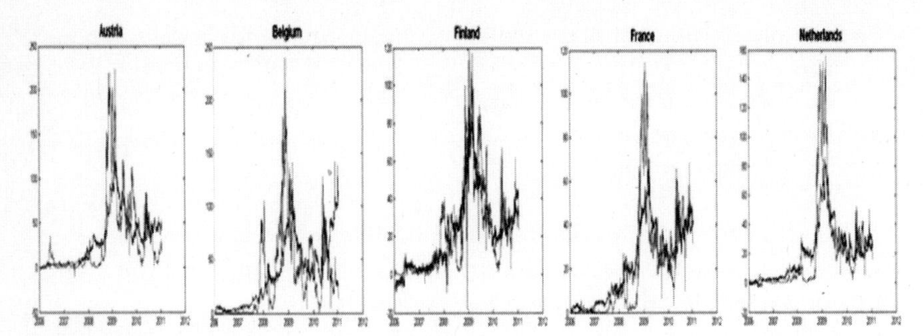


**FIGURE 10.11** Model versus actual spreads for Austria, Belgium, Finland, France, Netherlands (2006–2012).
*Sources:* FactSet and BofA Merrill Lynch.

returns, while being positively correlated with daily equity index volatility, as in the third panel. In particular, spread/return and spread/volatility correlations differ from zero more significantly among the GIIPS than the non-GIIPS. In Figure 10.14, we show the same three sets of correlations using model-predicted spreads.

On the whole, the correlation structure is reasonably well preserved. The better the predicted spreads for a country match the actual spreads, the more closely the correlations match. It's worth noting that a significant amount of the correlation structure is preserved even for the countries that are the least accurate. For corporate credits, we showed that the VaR of a portfolio of investment grade credits was dominated by the default correlation, and that significantly more yield could be achieved at the same risk through careful portfolio construction that gave full consideration to the

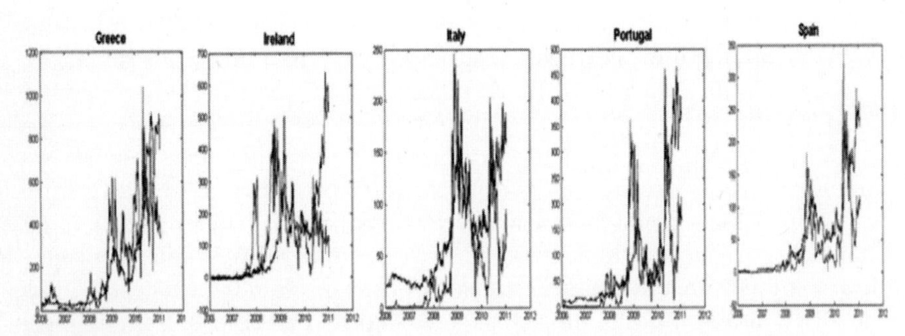


**FIGURE 10.12** Model versus actual spreads for Greece, Ireland, Italy, Portugal, Spain (2006–2011).
*Sources:* FactSet and BofA Merrill Lynch.

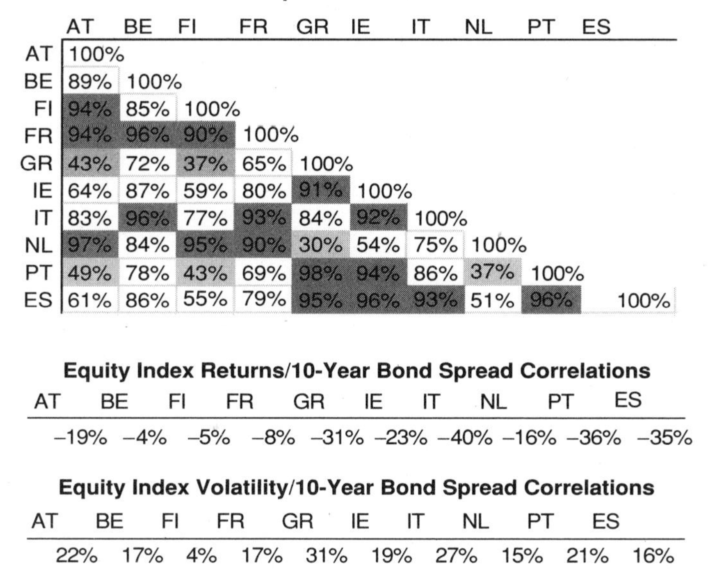

**Empirical Correlations**

| | AT | BE | FI | FR | GR | IE | IT | NL | PT | ES |
|---|---|---|---|---|---|---|---|---|---|---|
| AT | 100% | | | | | | | | | |
| BE | 89% | 100% | | | | | | | | |
| FI | 94% | 85% | 100% | | | | | | | |
| FR | 94% | 96% | 90% | 100% | | | | | | |
| GR | 43% | 72% | 37% | 65% | 100% | | | | | |
| IE | 64% | 87% | 59% | 80% | 91% | 100% | | | | |
| IT | 83% | 96% | 77% | 93% | 84% | 92% | 100% | | | |
| NL | 97% | 84% | 95% | 90% | 30% | 54% | 75% | 100% | | |
| PT | 49% | 78% | 43% | 69% | 98% | 94% | 86% | 37% | 100% | |
| ES | 61% | 86% | 55% | 79% | 95% | 96% | 93% | 51% | 96% | 100% |

**Equity Index Returns/10-Year Bond Spread Correlations**

| AT | BE | FI | FR | GR | IE | IT | NL | PT | ES |
|---|---|---|---|---|---|---|---|---|---|
| –19% | –4% | –5% | –8% | –31% | –23% | –40% | –16% | –36% | –35% |

**Equity Index Volatility/10-Year Bond Spread Correlations**

| AT | BE | FI | FR | GR | IE | IT | NL | PT | ES |
|---|---|---|---|---|---|---|---|---|---|
| 22% | 17% | 4% | 17% | 31% | 19% | 27% | 15% | 21% | 16% |

**FIGURE 10.13** Empirical correlations of 10-year Eurozone government bond spreads.
*Sources:* FactSet and BofA Merrill Lynch.

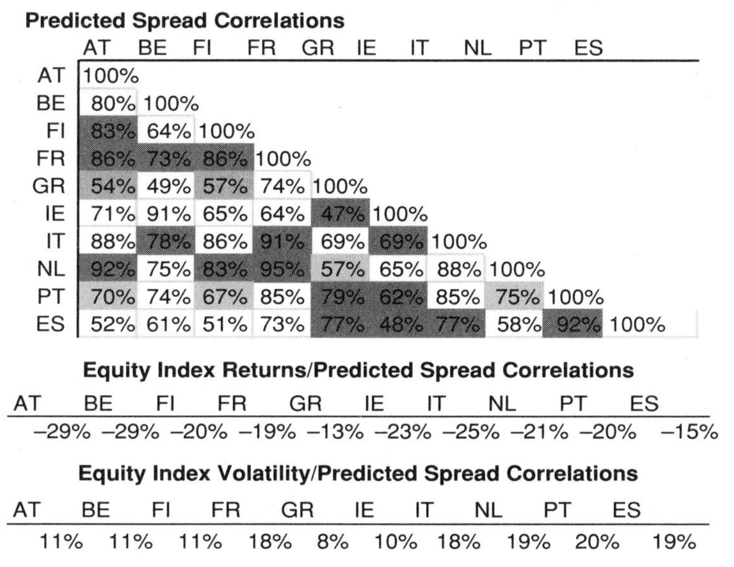

**Predicted Spread Correlations**

| | AT | BE | FI | FR | GR | IE | IT | NL | PT | ES |
|---|---|---|---|---|---|---|---|---|---|---|
| AT | 100% | | | | | | | | | |
| BE | 80% | 100% | | | | | | | | |
| FI | 83% | 64% | 100% | | | | | | | |
| FR | 86% | 73% | 86% | 100% | | | | | | |
| GR | 54% | 49% | 57% | 74% | 100% | | | | | |
| IE | 71% | 91% | 65% | 64% | 47% | 100% | | | | |
| IT | 88% | 78% | 86% | 91% | 69% | 69% | 100% | | | |
| NL | 92% | 75% | 83% | 95% | 57% | 65% | 88% | 100% | | |
| PT | 70% | 74% | 67% | 85% | 79% | 62% | 85% | 75% | 100% | |
| ES | 52% | 61% | 51% | 73% | 77% | 48% | 77% | 58% | 92% | 100% |

**Equity Index Returns/Predicted Spread Correlations**

| AT | BE | FI | FR | GR | IE | IT | NL | PT | ES |
|---|---|---|---|---|---|---|---|---|---|
| –29% | –29% | –20% | –19% | –13% | –23% | –25% | –21% | –20% | –15% |

**Equity Index Volatility/Predicted Spread Correlations**

| AT | BE | FI | FR | GR | IE | IT | NL | PT | ES |
|---|---|---|---|---|---|---|---|---|---|
| 11% | 11% | 11% | 18% | 8% | 10% | 18% | 19% | 20% | 19% |

**FIGURE 10.14** Model correlations of 10-year Eurozone government bond spreads.
*Source:* FactSet.

correlations. Contingent claims analysis shows that the same holds for the Euro-sovereign debt. Since changes in the country aggregate equity index can be obtained through an equity risk factor model, this allows correlation information in equity markets to proxy correlation information between Euro-sovereigns.

An identical approach can be taken to deal with sovereign bonds that issue in a currency other than their own. These hard currency bonds will have spread risk when measured relative to the spot curve of the hard currency. To deal with these, we again just need to specify the Merton inputs. Following the work of Gray, Merton, and Bodie,[4] we briefly summarize how this can be done.

The liabilities of a sovereign nation consist of foreign-denominated debt, local currency money supply, and debt denominated in the local currency. We can divide these liabilities into senior and junior claims. The sum of the local currency debt and the local currency money supply becomes the junior claim (expressed in foreign currency terms it can be thought of as sovereign equity in the Merton model), while the foreign currency debt in foreign currency terms becomes the senior claim and can be thought of as the bond in the Merton model. The volatility of the junior claim can then be extracted from the volatility of local currency debt and the foreign exchange (FX) market.

In summary, the derived approach using structural models can provide us a means to effectively take out what is known about spreads. Since equity markets are far more liquid than debt markets and are commonly believed to be more efficient, it makes sense to draw as much information out of those markets as we can, just as we take out interest rate risk using option-adjusted spreads. Next we explore how to deal with spread risk in the event we cannot derive it from something else.

## FACTOR MODEL APPROACH

To motivate the factor model approach, we will consider in detail the problem of explaining what gives rise to the option-adjusted spread of an agency mortgage-backed security. Earlier, we described how the OAS of a mortgage-backed security arises by taking out what is known via specification of a mortgage prepayment-and-loss model. For agency MBSs, losses are fully insured by the government-sponsored entities (GSEs), so only the impact of prepayments needs to be considered. Due to the information asymmetry inherent in MBSs, even the best prepayment models are not capable of perfectly predicting prepayments in all interest rate and housing market environments. Conceptually, therefore, the OAS exists due to the demand for

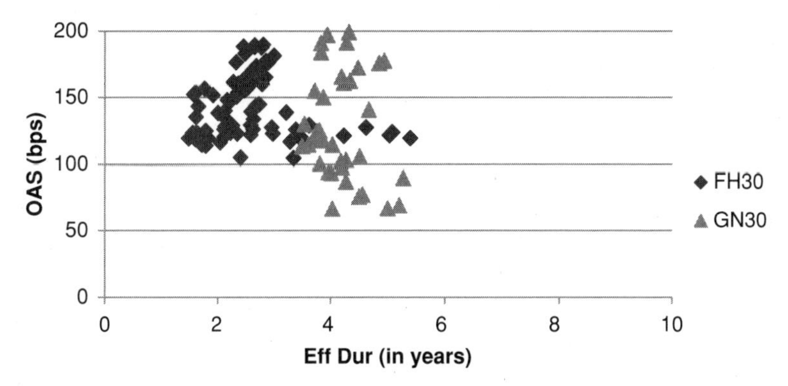


**FIGURE 10.15** OAS versus effective duration for agency 30-year MBS generics.
*Source:* FactSet.

compensation for bearing the uncertainty in prepayments that remain even after interest rates and interest rate volatilities are known.

In Figure 10.15, we plot the OAS versus the effective duration for a set of agency 30-year MBS generics, using FactSet's agency prepayment model to determine the analytics. We see that there is a negative relationship between effective duration and OAS, which conforms to the general intuition about OAS we discussed. Higher effective duration indicates a lower amount of optionality in the MBS, a lower exposure to prepayment risk, and thus a lower OAS.

A simple linear regression of OAS on effective duration produces an R-squared of 25 percent. The convexity of a straight bond is typically positive; however, the short prepayment option embedded in the MBS leads to negative effective convexity. The more negative the effective convexity, the more exposed to the option an MBS is, and when we regress OAS on both duration and convexity, the explained variance in the data rises. This quick analysis on agency generics confirms our intuition that differences in prepayment risk are what drive OAS. While duration and convexity have moderate success explaining OAS variation on a cross section of agency MBS generics, these are simple pass-through structures. For more complicated cash waterfalls, like interest-only (IO) and principal-only (PO) strips, we will need to do better, since these structures greatly amplify the exposure of the bond to the prepayment model, and hence to prepayment risk.

Ideally, we would like to be able to explain a much higher percentage of the variation in OAS. Duration and convexity do not differentiate between the sources of the prepayment risk; prepayments can occur for a number of reasons: a rate-term refinance, a sale of the home due to relocation, an equity take-out driven refinance, foreclosure, or curtailment. If we can measure the sensitivity of the OAS to the individual components of the total prepayment risk, we might achieve better results.

Prepayments come, broadly, in two flavors: rate sensitive and rate insensitive. Rate-sensitive prepayments are mainly due to rate-term refinancing, which just means they are motivated by a desire to save on interest expense due to a fall in rates or a favorable spread in rates due to amortization type. To the extent that home price appreciation is linked to changes in affordability caused by falling interest rates, equity take-out refinances can also fall into this category.[5] Rate-insensitive prepayments are primarily driven by housing turnover.

To compute the sensitivity of OAS to each of these components of the total prepayment rate, we introduce refinance and turnover durations. A refi (or rate-sensitive) duration measures the sensitivity of percentage price change to a change in the intensity in the refinance component. There are many ways to measure this, but the simplest is to just multiply the refi component of the prepayment function by a multiplier, and to measure duration numerically by shifting the multiplier up and down from a base of 1.[6] We treat turnover duration in the same manner. Now, to capture the full spectrum of prepayments sensitivies,[7] we perform a breakeven regression analysis of cross-sectional OAS using IO/PO strips. As IO and PO strips represent the opposite ends of prepayment sensitivity (as shown in Figure 10.16), fitting

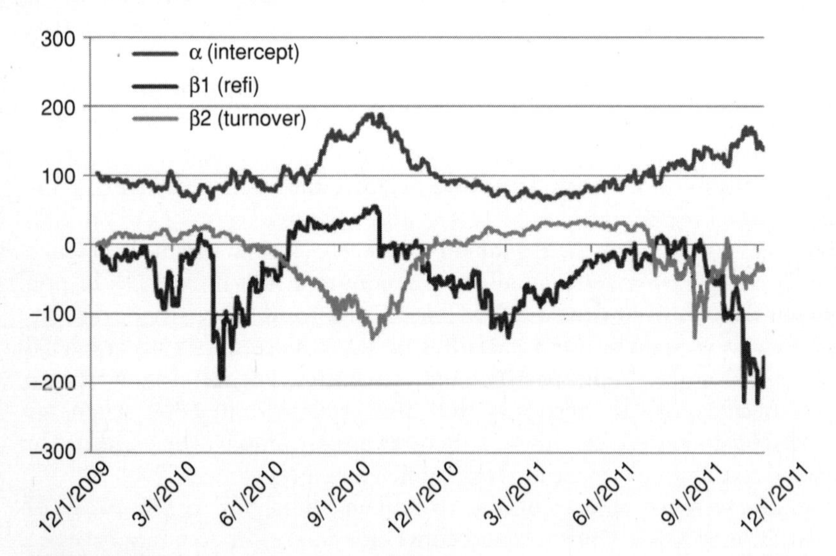


**FIGURE 10.16** CMO factors through time.
*Source:* FactSet.

to this breakeven level allows the flexibility to determine spread risk for a wide range of MBS and mortgage-related ABS assets.

In Table 10.1, we show the regression R-squared for the cross-sectional linear regression using refinance and turnover durations for the more prepayment risk leveraged IO/PO strip index. Note that the regression improves considerably as we limit the data set to IO/PO strips with pool factors greater than

**TABLE 10.1** Agency MBS spread model regression fit for IO/PO index.

| | Adjusted R-Squared (Factor > 0.25) | Adjusted R-Squared (Factor > 0.01) |
|---|---|---|
| 12/15/2009 | 1.34% | 3.35% |
| 1/15/2010 | 13.90% | –0.88% |
| 2/15/2010 | 16.67% | 4.00% |
| 3/15/2010 | 8.73% | –0.10% |
| 4/15/2010 | 36.39% | 13.65% |
| 5/15/2010 | 34.10% | 14.82% |
| 6/15/2010 | 18.91% | 14.92% |
| 7/15/2010 | 31.76% | 33.27% |
| 8/15/2010 | 47.67% | 42.86% |
| 9/15/2010 | 59.03% | 47.31% |
| 10/15/2010 | 85.87% | 57.58% |
| 11/15/2010 | 56.98% | 32.23% |
| 12/15/2010 | 33.77% | 9.18% |
| 1/15/2011 | 45.35% | 14.70% |
| 2/15/2011 | 43.06% | 5.07% |
| 3/15/2011 | 40.82% | 7.60% |
| 4/15/2011 | 41.11% | –0.63% |
| 5/15/2011 | 40.78% | 0.04% |
| 6/15/2011 | 53.90% | 9.08% |
| 7/15/2011 | 45.60% | 7.31% |
| 8/15/2011 | 33.50% | 19.70% |
| 9/15/2011 | 53.78% | 46.49% |
| 10/15/2011 | 70.73% | 65.38% |
| 11/15/2011 | 84.00% | 78.72% |

25 percent. Low pool factors indicate bonds with low unpaid notional remaining, which makes their market prices, and hence observed spreads, less reliable. After exclusion, however, the spread model captures a significant amount of the cross-sectional variation, even on a notoriously difficult class of bonds to handle. But the R-squared varies considerably over time, which may indicate limitations of this model during some time periods. We will show later that the ability to capture spread risk using this regression is still preserved.

Building factor models to explain bond spreads is entirely analogous to building factor models to explain equity returns. In an equity factor model, we first try to explain cross-sectional returns through a linear regression, and then we attempt to estimate the distributional properties of the factors through time. For our agency MBS example, we have shown how to explain OAS cross-sectional variation on agency CMOs using regressions of OAS on refinances, and turnover durations on agency IO and PO strips, which also explains significant cross-sectional variation on simple pass-through MBSs out of sample. The alphas and betas from our regression form the basis for our daily factor realizations. Next we turn to characterizing the time series behavior of our MBS factors.

Figure 10.16 shows the fitted factors for 2010 and 2011. The factors are the refi duration, the turnover duration, and the intercept of the regression. The factors were fit using agency IO and PO strips. Generally the intercept tracks the OAS of the agency MBS pass-through index, and therefore is analogous to the average total prepay exposure, so that the refi and turnover durations represent sources of deviation from that overall prepayment risk exposure. The refi duration contributes mainly with a negative sign, which tells us that bonds with higher exposure to refinance response shifts have lower OAS than bonds with less refinance exposure. In this market environment, this makes sense, since bonds with the lowest OAS are the bonds that the mortgage holders have the least ability to refinance. Many mortgages in these pools are upside down on their loans, and are effectively locked out of refinance opportunities. So while mortgage rates were setting new all-time lows in the second half of 2011, these rates were not available to all pools equally. In this market, having a high refi duration is an indication of loan impairment.

We recall that ultimately we are trying to determine what drives spread change. The daily factors are the direct output of the daily breakeven regression, but in order to determine spread risk, we use the daily differences as shown in Figure 10.17. There is significant autocorrelation in the factors, and so we must de-trend them in some manner. The simplest approach is to work with first differences. For agency MBSs, first differenced factors have much cleaner distributional properties.

Examining the daily differences is an important part of the CMO model to properly estimate the spread risk. Figure 10.17 also shows select days

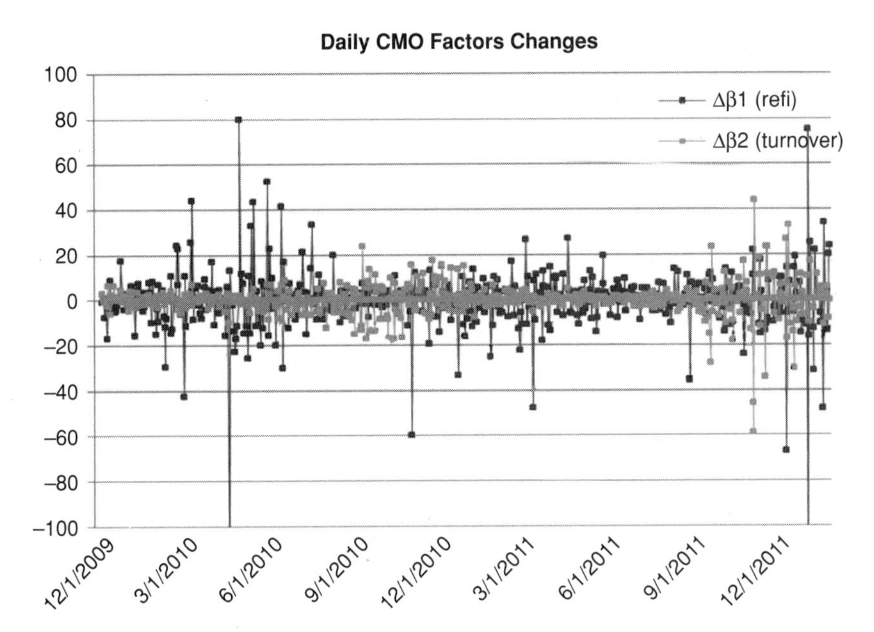


**FIGURE 10.17** CMO daily spread factor changes.
*Source:* FactSet.

with large swings in factor changes. These large swings illustrate the need for a factor smoothing process. On certain days, factor changes can be large due to prepayment model misspecification or update and breakeven regression data issues, among other phenomena.[8] The development of a smoothing algorithm is critical at this point to ensure that spread risk is not drastically over- or underestimated. In the context of spread risk, what is a valid factor change that properly estimates risk? If the underlying prepayment model calculating the refi and turnover durations was updated or calibrated on a date, a large swing would be observed on that date. Essentially this would overestimate risk once fed back into our repricing formula. However, if factor changes are observed due to the breakeven regression results, that may indicate a drastic shift in market sentiment while refi and turnover durations may show little change. Thus in this case, risk may actually be higher due to these factor changes, and smoothing such changes could underestimate risk.

On our way to estimating spread risk, so far we have used the breakeven methodology whereby OAS for IO/PO strips are regressed with their refi and turnover durations to capture the full range of prepayment sensitivities. Figures 10.18 and 10.19 show the OAS as calculated from a prepayment model versus the OAS as estimated from the CMO breakeven methodology

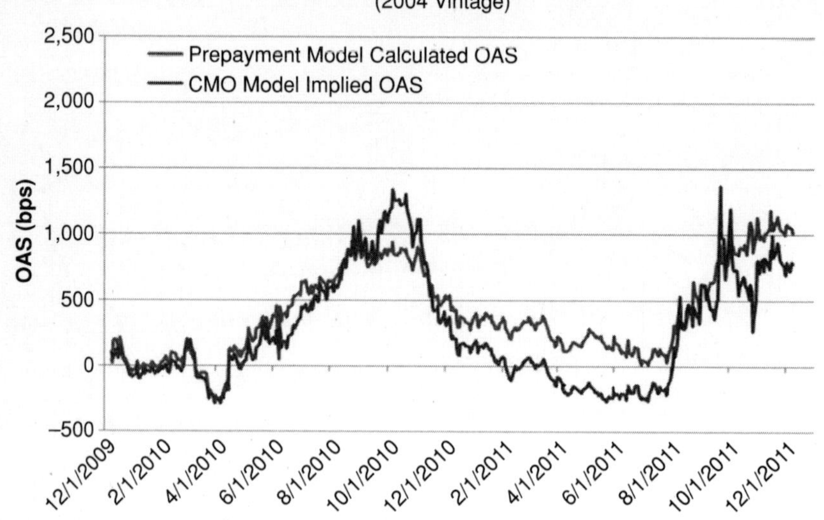


**FIGURE 10.18** IO OAS comparisons over time.
*Source:* FactSet.

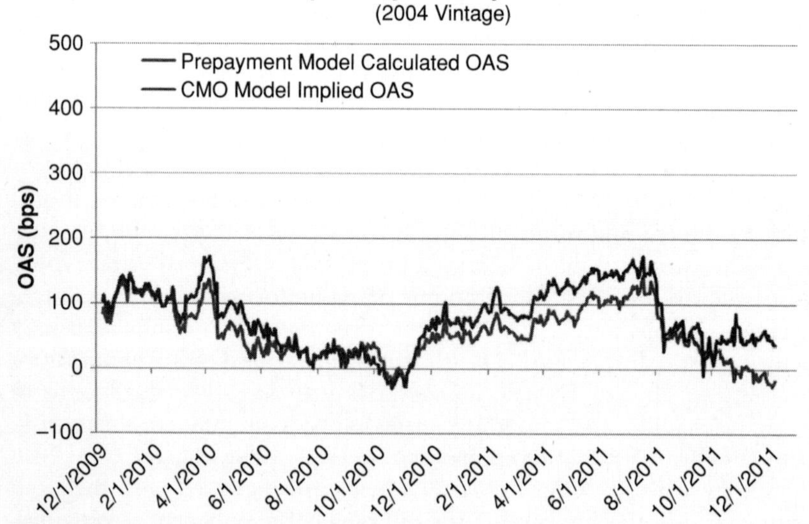


**FIGURE 10.19** PO OAS comparisons over time.
*Source:* FactSet.

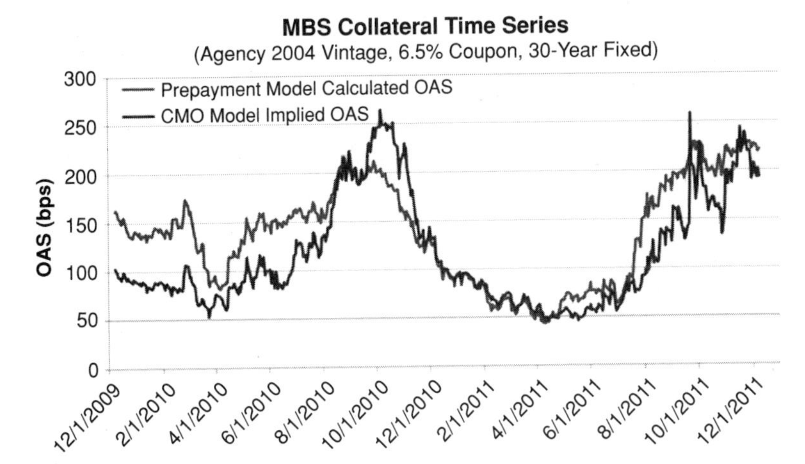


**FIGURE 10.20** MBS collateral OAS comparisons over time, Fannie Mae 30-year, 6.5 percent, 2004.
*Source:* FactSet.

for a typical 2004 vintage IO and PO strip. The graphs clearly show that the OASs track fairly well through the test period, even during periods where the breakeven regression fit exhibited extremely low R-squared.

For Figures 10.20 and 10.21, we illustrate the CMO model estimation of OAS for agency MBSs. Both a Fannie Mae and a Ginnie Mae

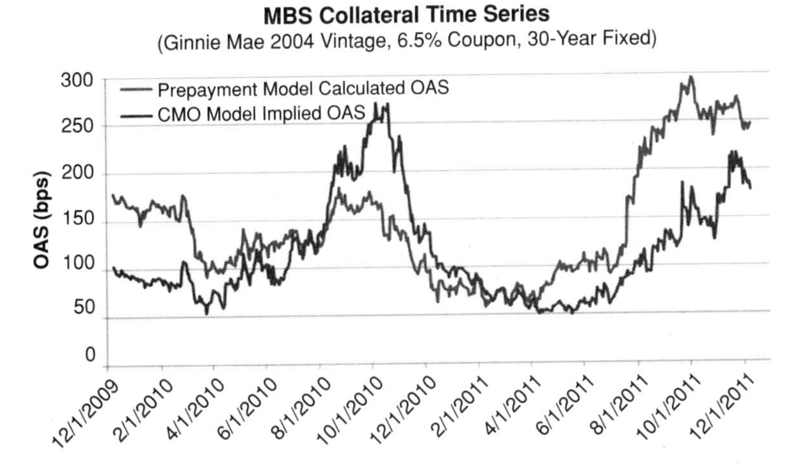


**FIGURE 10.21** MBS collateral OAS comparisons over time, Ginnie Mae 30-year, 6.5 percent, 2004.
*Source:* FactSet.

2004 Vintage 30-year fixed 6.5 percent coupon generic pass-throughs are shown.

Before we continue, let's pause to recap. The goal of the CMO model is to estimate the spread risk, which we can then feed into the Taylor repricing formula (and eventually allow for portfolio VaR calculations, etc.). As an initial input, IO/PO strip prices (market sentiment) are input to calculate OAS, refi duration, and turnover duration using a prepayment model. The breakeven regression across the cross section of IO/PO strips is conducted daily to determine the factors that predict OAS. Using these factors, we can then predict OAS (and more importantly OAS changes) using refi and turnover durations for a host of MBS and MBS-related collateral, no matter how illiquid the specific security.

Now let's check whether the CMO model can indeed predict returns, not using the Taylor repricing formula, but using the full bond calculator to get price from OAS.

$$\textit{IO/PO strip price} \rightarrow \textit{Durations} \rightarrow \textit{Factors} \rightarrow$$
$$\textit{OAS implied by factors} \rightarrow \textit{Price from implied OAS}$$

First we start with the IO/PO strip portfolio and their prices.[9] Then after the breakeven regression, the CMO model implied OAS can be calculated. To complete the round-trip back to prices, prices for each strip are calculated from CMO model implied OAS.[10] Figures 10.22 and 10.23

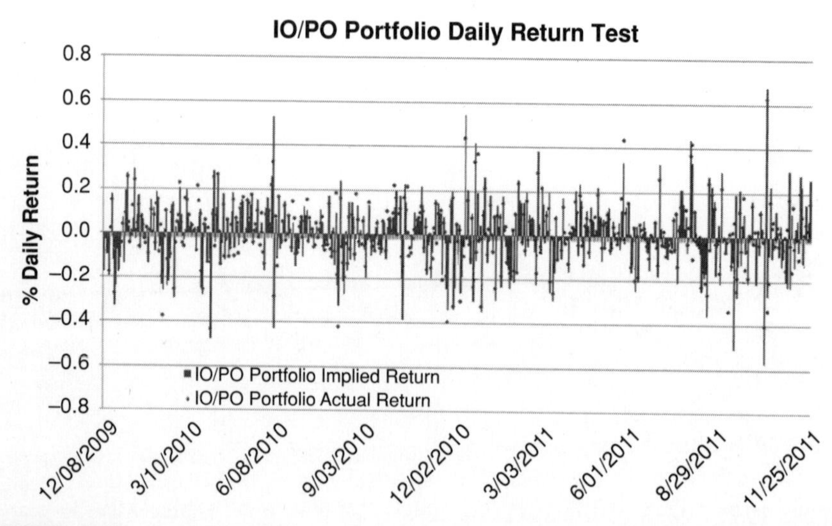


**FIGURE 10.22** IO/PO portfolio model implied returns and actual returns.
*Source:* FactSet.

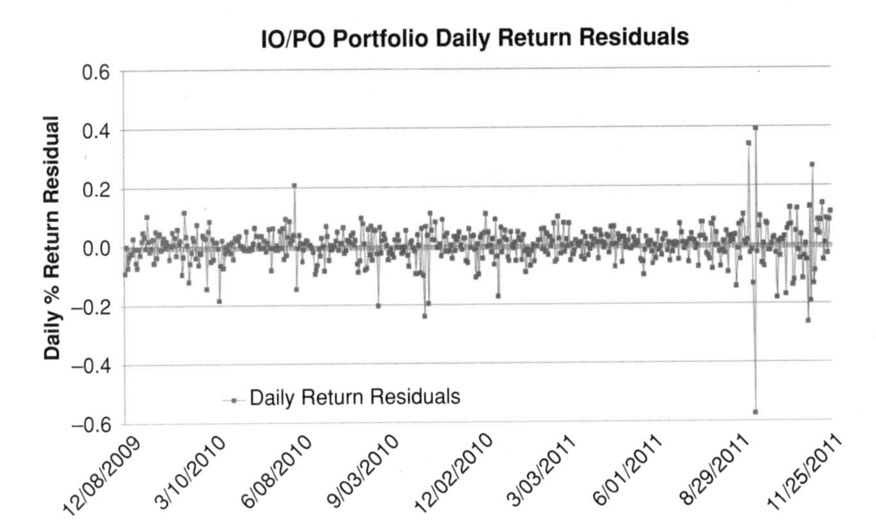


**FIGURE 10.23** IO/PO portfolio return residuals.
*Source:* FactSet.

show the comparison of daily returns from the price source and from the CMO model implied prices (as calculated from CMO model implied OAS). Returns that are implied by the CMO model at the portfolio level for the IO/PO strips resemble the returns from the actual prices. This result is significant, as we use the same portfolio's prices to create the factors and then predict returns for it. The return mismatches here show the importance of prepayment model selection. A sophisticated prepayment model allows for robust duration calculations resulting in closer returns to actual returns. However, no prepayment model is perfect, no matter how sophisticated, and will still require market sentiment inputs to track OAS.

In summary, whether we take a derived approach or a factor model approach to modeling spread change, we use the spread change in the same way. We apply the spread change to the spread sensitivities within the Taylor repricing formula, along with the interest rate and volatility changes and their Taylor sensitivities. We sum this to get a clean price return for the Monte Carlo draw. We then incorporate any expected accrued interest effects to get a full price return.

We have used this detailed analysis of mortgage-backed securities to illustrate the factor model approach to spread risk. The spread factor model approach is fairly generic in that it can be applied to pretty much any class of bonds, provided we can estimate the cross section of spreads reasonably well. We look for variables that explain cross-sectional variation in spreads

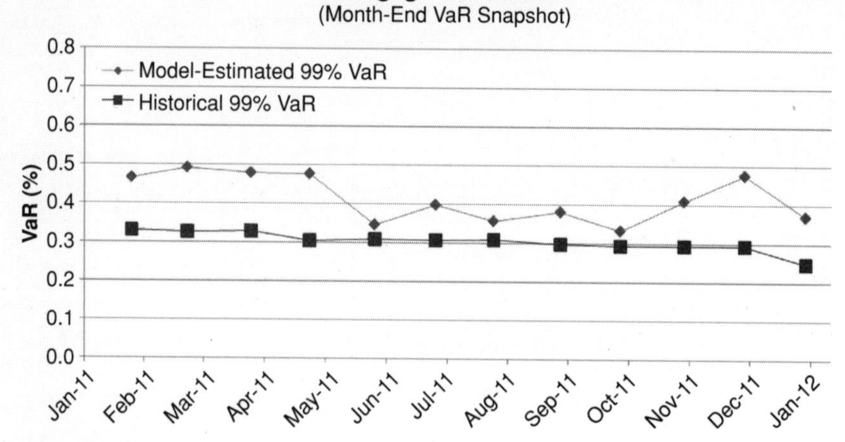


**FIGURE 10.24** Model-predicted versus historical 99 percent VaR for mortgage benchmark.
*Source:* FactSet.

(and, as with mortgage-backed securities, this may require a sophisticated prepayment or credit model to properly measure). These become our factor exposures. Then we estimate the factors using linear regression, which are just the regression coefficients on the independent variables. We remove autocorrelation by first differencing the factor levels. We jointly estimate the covariance of these first differenced spread factors with the other global risk factors, including the statistical interest rate factors. We can then do a Monte Carlo simulation out of that joint covariance structure, and use the spread factor structure to determine a spread change for each Monte Carlo draw. This is in contrast to the derived approach, where we do not need to estimate additional spread factors to add to the joint covariance structure.

Finally, in Figure 10.24 we show the results of a Monte Carlo VaR simulation for the agency mortgage benchmark. This figure illustrates the process of capturing the full spectrum of prepayment risk through IO/PO strip duration factors and applying them to estimate risk for agency MBSs.

## CONCLUSION

Spread is excess return that represents compensation for cash flow uncertainty. When the uncertainty in cash flows is due to uncertainty in interest rates or interest rate volatility, it is standard to extract what is known about the way the cash flows depend on interest rates and volatilities by conditioning on this information. The conditional cash flows then can be discounted by an option-adjusted spread to match market value. The option-adjusted spread then represents the residual risk remaining after interest rate and volatility risk have been taken out.

The major decision that must be made to define spread, then, is how much information about interest rates, interest rate volatility, and other macroeconomic variables can and should be taken out. This brings about two basic approaches, reduced form and structural. In either case, spread risk exposure is measured by shifting the spread and holding all else constant. The next concern is how to measure spread change.

In reduced form approaches, there is a limit to how much can be taken out. This is because there is imperfect information, so that even after basic macroeconomic information is known, the timing and the magnitude of cash flows are still essentially random. Knowledge of this background information may improve the estimate of the distribution of the random cash flows, but they will never be completely predictable. Two prototypical examples of this are hazard rate models that are popular to model credit default swaps, and mortgage-backed securities that involve prepayment model risk. We chose to highlight the reduced form approach through the example of mortgage-backed securities. For these, we defined spread as an option-adjusted spread, and showed how to build a spread factor model in terms of exposures to the components of the prepayment model itself (refi and turnover durations) in order to predict spread movements.

We did not focus much on the reduced form approach for corporate credit, instead choosing to use it to highlight the second basic approach, the structural approach to spread risk. In the structural approach, observable macroeconomic variables completely determine cash flow timing and magnitude. For corporates, this is accomplished most simply through the Merton model. Cash flow uncertainty for corporates is driven mostly by uncertainty over asset value relative to firm leverage, and interest rates play a small role. In this way the bond spread can be considered option adjusted simply through the lack of interest rate optionality. The majority of the cash flow uncertainty comes from the uncertainty over the evolution of the value of the firm assets. Contingent on knowing the value of firm assets, the default event is predictable. The calculation of spread does not involve taking out what is known about the macroeconomic variables. Their influence is felt through the Merton framework when we attempt to predict spread change. We showed how equity factor models can be used to predict spread change. This has the advantage of incorporating equity market information about correlations to get an estimate of asset value correlations, and hence default correlations. We showed why this is important, as default correlation is a dominant risk source for corporate and sovereign credits.

## NOTES

1. Mathematicians call this Fubini's theorem.
2. While this might seem highly stylized, it is worth pointing out that this setup is essentially the mechanism that is used to quote CDO tranches in terms of base correlation.
3. Germany, Cyprus, Estonia, Luxembourg, Malta, Slovakia, and Slovenia are not displayed. Germany effectively is the euro benchmark, and the others do not have reliably liquid spread or equity index data.
4. Dale F. Gray, Robert C. Merton, and Zvi Bodie, "Contingent Claims Approach to Measuring and Managing Sovereign Credit Risk," *Journal of Investment Management* 5, no. 4 (2007).
5. This distinction will depend entirely on how the prepayment model in question treats equity take-out. Some models view it as rate insensitive, while others view it as being mainly rate driven. In FactSet's first-generation agency prepayment model, equity take-out is primarily rate insensitive, while the second-generation model is equipped with a more sophisticated house price appreciation model that allows equity take-out to have significant interest rate exposure.
6. In FactSet's prepayment model, this is defined as a price change sensitivity to a +/–20 percent shift in the refinance portion of prepayment. The single-monthly mortality (SMM, which is the principal paid in excess of scheduled principal for each month) attributable to the refinance component is shifted up and down while recalculating the price using constant OAS for each shift. The duration is then simply: (Price at downshift in refinance SMM – Price at upshift in refinance SMM)/2.
7. As described in Appendix A (by Jeffrey D. Biby and Srinivas Modukuri) of Vikas Reddy and Andrew Miller, "An Introduction to Floating Rate CMOs," *Lehman Brothers Fixed-Income Research*, August 23, 2004.
8. In the breakeven regression, IO/PO strip prices are provided by a price source. It is possible to see inconsistencies in the data or a high number of securities screened due to low pool factor. Additionally, refi and turnover durations are calculated by a prepayment model, which may go through periodic updates and calibration. So for these days, factors would respond with large day-over-day factor changes.
9. Price discovery of MBSs can be problematic. Price providers are inherently necessary for this approach but also will introduce further error into the model to some extent.
10. Recall that OAS is the spread to the spot curve for bond cash flows that account for the optionality. In MBSs, a prepayment model will determine the cash flows for each rate path and then calculate the OAS with respect to the spot curve to match the given price. Or to calculate price from OAS, the same cash flows are discounted at the *given* OAS with respect to spot curve to get the resulting price.

CHAPTER 11

# Fixed Income Interest Rate Volatility, Idiosyncratic Risk, and Currency Risk

*David Mieczkowski, PhD, and Steven P. Greiner, PhD*

## FIXED INCOME INTEREST RATE RISK

Interest rates are just a way to express the time value of money in terms of holding period returns. Spot rates, which are the holding period returns of zero coupon bonds, also provide a term structure of holding period returns in terms of the length of the holding period. Interest rate risk is then concerned with the uncertainty or volatility of the holding period returns through time. If the spot curve were constant through time, there would be no interest rate risk. The spot curve needn't be flat, since we could determine with full certainty the future value of any known cash flow over a horizon if we know what the term structure will be.

When thinking about interest rate volatility risk, we are led to ask two questions: Is interest rate volatility constant? For which securities does it even matter?

Let's start with the second question. Consider a 10-year swap and a one-month investment horizon. Suppose we know the one-month volatility of the spot curve; then even if the volatility of the spot curve is itself volatile, it will not matter for determining the one-month risk. Over a particular horizon, once we know what the volatility of the spot curve is over that horizon, we do not care what future interest rate volatility will be. This might seem odd at first, but consider an overnight money market account. For a one-day investment horizon, there is no interest rate risk associated with an overnight money market account. We will know with certainty what our return will be tomorrow, no matter what tomorrow's overnight rate is. The same goes for a one-month certificate of deposit (CD) and a one-month investment horizon. There is no interest rate risk because at the horizon, the cash flows are no longer exposed to interest rates, because they have matured. Investment horizons longer or shorter than one month will retain interest rate exposure, but on that day at least, we have cash in hand, and we don't need to know what interest rates are to value it. Measuring risk over a defined horizon does not involve calculation of reinvestment risk.

For a bond to be exposed to interest rate risk over a horizon, that bond needs to be exposed to interest rates at the horizon date. A 10-year swap remains exposed to interest rates at a one-month horizon, but it is not exposed directly to interest rate volatility at a one-month horizon. This is because all we need to know to value the swap at the one-month horizon is the spot curve at the one-month horizon; volatility is not an input we need to price a swap at the horizon. Therefore it has no direct interest rate volatility risk exposure. The term structure of interest rates depends on future interest rate volatility, not concurrent interest rate volatility, so swaps are indirectly exposed to interest rate volatility changes through their effect on interest rates. Interest rate options do have a direct exposure to current interest rate volatility, however. A two-year option on a 10-year swap is exposed to what interest rate volatility will be in one month, and so has an interest rate volatility exposure; volatility is an input we must have to price the swaption at the horizon. If interest rate volatility is not random, then a volatility risk exposure is moot, because we will know with certainty how to value the swaption once interest rates are known; a swaption will have interest rate risk, but no interest rate volatility risk. So the answer to the second question is that interest rate volatility risk matters only for securities that require interest rate volatility as an input to get a price.

To answer the first question, we have to get a little more precise about what we mean by interest rate volatility. Practical experience tells us that the higher rates get, the larger we expect level changes to be. So if we define interest rate volatility as something like the standard deviation of level changes, we expect interest rate volatility to have randomness driven in part by the level of rates. This is very similar to stock price volatility. In that case, we deal with this by defining volatility in terms of percentage changes. A key question is whether volatility defined in terms of percentage changes removes the randomness.

In the remainder of this section, we first define the term structure of volatility using the stochastic differential equation (SDE) approach to describing interest rate term structure dynamics. We then review evidence that suggests that interest rate volatility defined using (fractional) percentage changes is indeed random, so that interest rate volatility risk is a real source of risk for volatility-dependent securities. We then discuss how to measure interest rate volatility risk exposure. We conclude with how to put everything together for risk forecasting.

### Term Structure of Volatility

To discuss the term structure of interest rate volatility, we need to decide what interest rates we are referring to. We have discussed spot, forward, and par curves in Chapters 3 and 8 and we can define volatility for any one; and, just as there are relationships between forward, spot, and par rates, there are relationships between forward, spot, and par volatility.

Volatility is just a statistic used to describe a probability distribution; it is the second moment. In the context of interest rates, volatility is important for the pricing of interest rate derivatives. Just as interest rates are really just an alternative way to express the value of a bond in terms of holding period returns, volatility is just an alternative way of expressing the value of an interest rate option. As with any type of derivative security, volatility is essentially a model-dependent construct. The most basic types of interest rate derivatives are interest rate caps and options on interest rate swaps (swaptions), and the most basic model is Black-Scholes.

We will start with interest rate caps. To reiterate from earlier chapters, an *interest rate cap* is a contract that pays the difference between a variable interest rate and a fixed interest rate whenever the variable rate exceeds the fixed interest rate cap. In real markets, the variable interest rate is a simple interest rate with a short-term tenor, and the cap payments are subject to a discrete reset schedule that generally corresponds to the tenor of the simple interest rate. A two-year quarter reset LIBOR 2.5 percent cap is then a contract that pays the maximum of the difference between the spot three-month LIBOR rate and 2.5 percent, and zero, on a quarterly payment or reset schedule.

Cap payments can be replicated using the payouts of simple call options on the simple interest rate with the same tenor as the cap payment frequency (e.g., quarterly).

$$(f(T_i, T_i, T_i + \delta) - K)^+ \tag{11.1}$$

A standard market cap can then be replicated using a portfolio of these simple call options, which are called *caplets*. To price this option, we need to posit dynamics for the forward LIBOR rate. The LIBOR market model (LMM) was developed for this purpose. The starting point for the LIBOR market model is the stochastic differential equation:

$$\frac{df(t,T,T+\delta)}{f(t,T,T+\delta)} = \mu(T,T+\delta,t)\,dt + \sigma(T,T+\delta,t)\,dz(T)_t \tag{11.2}$$

Here the term $\sigma(T,T+\delta,t)$ is called the *forward volatility* of maturity $T$ and tenor $\delta$. It is the instantaneous volatility function that applies to the forward rate of maturity $T$ and tenor $\delta$. This formulation puts the concept of volatility as a measure of the standard deviation of percentage changes in the interest rate level into precise mathematical terms.

In the LMM framework, the forward volatilities are nonrandom functions of time, and commonly assumed to be a function only of the time to maturity $\tau = T - t$, which means that the volatilities of the various maturity forward rates all share a common volatility function, and differ only in terms of how much time to maturity they have left at any moment.

If the forward volatility is nonrandom, for a fixed maturity $T$, this SDE has a familiar solution:

$$f(T,T,T+\delta) = f(0,T,T+\delta)\exp\{-\hat{\sigma}(T)\sqrt{T}Z - \frac{1}{2}T_i\hat{\sigma}^2(T)\} \tag{11.3}$$

where $z$ is a standard normal Gaussian random variable, and $\hat{\sigma}(T) = \sqrt{\frac{1}{T}\int_0^T \sigma^2(T,T+\delta,s)\,ds}$. That is, the forward LIBOR rate is lognormally distributed and represents the value of a traded asset in terms of shares of a zero coupon bond. The price of a call option on such a lognormally distributed variable can be determined using the Black-Scholes option pricing formula. The volatility $\hat{\sigma}(T)$ is called the spot volatility of maturity $T$. The spot volatility is the root mean square of the forward volatility.

If the forward volatility function is time homogeneous, so that $\sigma(T,T+\delta,s=\sigma(T-s))$, then as with interest rates, this relationship allows us to derive the forward volatilities in terms of the spot volatilities, and vice versa. We have mentioned before that this is a very strong assumption, but if we accept it, then the spot and forward volatilities as functions of maturity can be grouped together to create a curve or term structure of volatilities that are linked together through an integral. Just as with spot and forward interest rates, the term structure of volatility has observed shape tendencies. In nonstressed markets, there is typically a hump shape to the implied volatility curves, and volatility curves can be broken into what they imply about short, intermediate, and long-term views on rates. In Figure 11.1, we show a typical hump-shaped spot and associated forward implied volatility curves derived using the Black formula from the prices of at-the-money caplets.

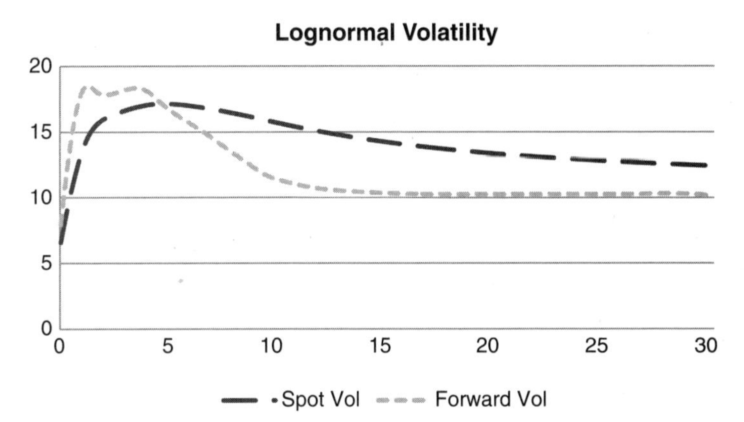


**FIGURE 11.1** Term structure of market implied ATM spot and forward volatility curves on 6/11/2006.
*Source:* FactSet.

The next question is: is this a reasonable model in the sense that it captures all the information needed to price derivatives sensitive to forward rate evolution?

To see that the answer is no, we don't need to look past the cap market itself. One immediate problem is the presence of a volatility smile or skew according to moneyness of the caplet. Several authors have documented the presence of skews in implied volatility cap data.[1] The LMM is not able to reproduce this skewed implied volatility surface. What is needed is a refinement to the LMM model that governs forward rate dynamics. One could introduce a jump process into the stochastic differential equations that govern forward rate evolution, as in Jarrow, Li, and Zhao[2] (2007). Another approach is to relax the lognormality assumption and adopt dynamics based on fractional percentage changes (fractional lognormality), which are the so-called constant elasticity of variance (CEV) models. Because the LIBOR market model can be extended to include the class of CEV models, which are much easier than models based on jump processes, practitioners were quicker to adopt them.

In the CEV-LMM, a fractional parameter $0 \leq \beta\ 1 \leq$ is introduced into the stochastic equations:

$$\frac{df(t,T)}{f(t,T)^{\beta}} = \mu(T,t)dt + \sigma(T,t)dz(T)_t \tag{11.4}$$

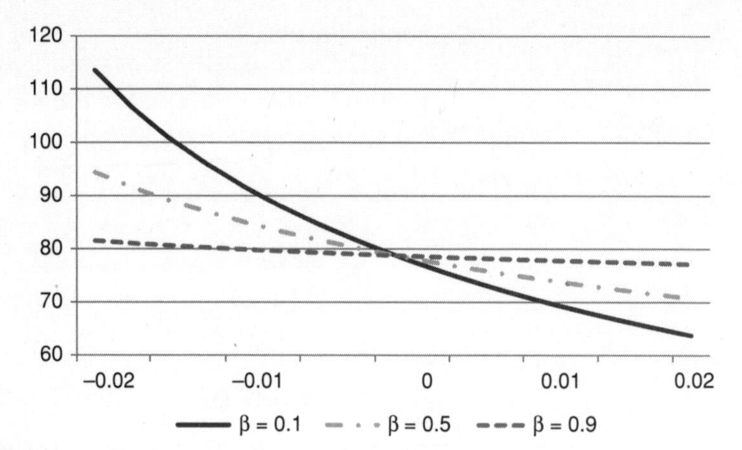


**FIGURE 11.2** Black volatility skew dependence on CEV parameter.
*Source:* FactSet.

The residual forward volatility function is then assumed to be deterministic. The CEV parameter β provides a fractional proportionality between rate level and volatility. Figure 11.2 shows how decreasing the parameter from 1 to 0 increases the volatility skew across moneyness.

The CEV extension of the LIBOR market model creates skew in the Black (lognormal) volatilities, but it still assumes that spot volatilities are root mean squared forward volatilities.

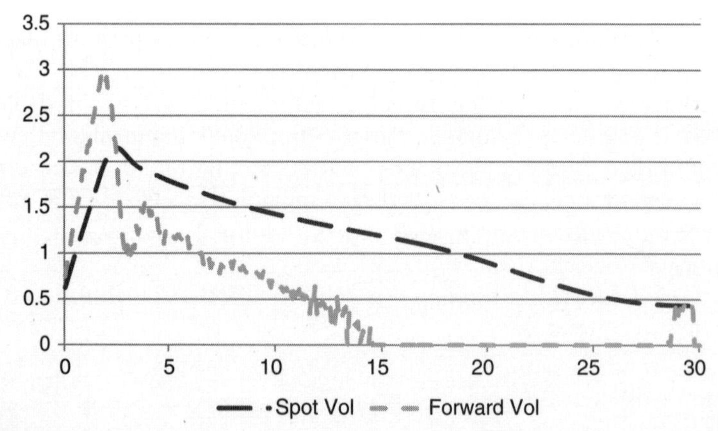


**FIGURE 11.3** Violation of forward volatility under time-homogeneous assumption.
*Source:* FactSet.

In Figure 11.3, we show the spot and forward volatility curves for forward rates from a stressed market environment date of 3/16/2010 using a CEV parameter of $\beta = 0.1$. The spot curve still shows a classic hump shape, but the spot curve still decays too quickly to maintain the integral relationship between the spot variance and the forward variance curves. In particular, the implied forward volatility curve crashes to zero, which is clearly nonsensical.

The assumption that forward volatility is time homogeneous is the problem. This functional form implies that the forwards will share the same volatility in the sense that as longer-maturity forwards get closer to their maturity date, they will experience the same volatility that shorter-maturity forwards experience now. For example, a forward with maturity in 10 years will have the same volatility in nine years as a forward with maturity in one year will have today. This is evidence that deterministic, time-homogeneous forward volatility is not consistent with market implied volatility.

One solution is to allow forward volatility to be stochastic. There is support for a stochastic volatility if we estimate volatility using historical rate moves. In Figure 11.4, we estimate forward rate volatility by computing annualized rolling standard deviations of daily fractional percentage changes in the one-year forward rate using a fractional parameter of $\beta = 0.1$. The historically estimated one-year forward volatility is fairly constant before the credit crisis, but clearly rises substantially during the period of market stress.

In Figure 11.5, we look at the historical volatility of volatility, calculated by computing the rolling standard deviation of percentage changes in the historical volatility levels. We see that the volatility of volatility estimate is fairly range-bound around 20 percent. Given the noise inherent in using

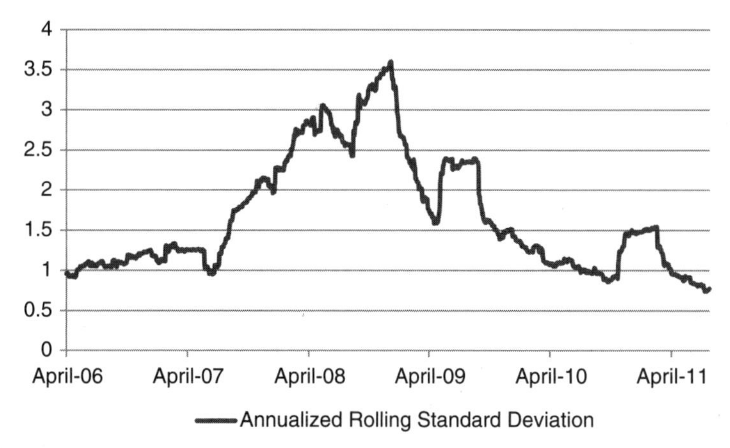


**FIGURE 11.4** Historical one-year forward volatility.
*Source:* FactSet.

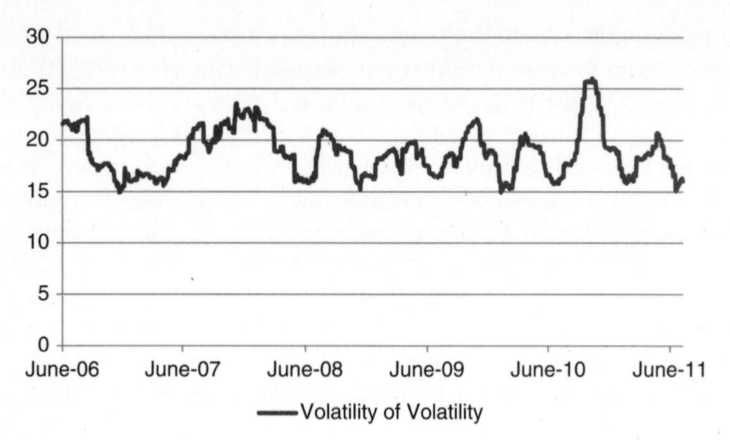


**FIGURE 11.5** Volatility of the historical one-year forward volatility.
*Source:* FactSet.

rolling standard deviation to estimate volatility historically, this supports the hypothesis that volatility is indeed random, and that the forward volatility itself is truly a lognormally distributed random variable, with constant volatility of volatility. This suggests that we extend the CEV-LMM to allow for a stochastic volatility term that is lognormally distributed with constant volatility of volatility. Allowing the forward volatility to be stochastic will require us to specify not only a volatility of volatility term (vanna), but also a correlation between the stochastic volatility and the forward rate. The extension of the LIBOR market model that does this is known as the SABR-LMM model. A good introduction to the SABR-LMM can be found in Rebonato, McKay, and White[3] (2009).

The dynamics of the SABR-LMM are written as:

$$df_i = \mu_i \, dt + (f_i)^{\beta} \sigma_i \, dz_i \tag{11.5}$$

$$d\sigma_i = g(T - t_i) dk_i \tag{11.6}$$

$$\frac{dk_i}{k_i} = \eta_i \, dt + v_i \, dw_i \tag{11.7}$$

$$E\left[dz_i dz_j\right] = \rho_{ij} dt \quad E\left[dz_i dw\right] = R_{ij} dt \quad E\left[dw_i dw_j\right] = r_{ij} dt \tag{11.8}$$

In the SABR-LMM, the forward volatility is decomposed first into a fractional proportionality component $(f_i)^{\beta}$, and a stochastic volatility component $\sigma_t$. This first decomposition pulls out as much of the randomness in forward volatility that is due to forward rate levels as possible. This is represented by equation (11.5). Next, the stochastic volatility component is expressed as a deterministic time-homogeneous function, times some stochastic multiplicative residual. FactSet's data shows that in calm markets, the distribution of forward rates does seem to be consistent with fractional lognormality and time-homogeneous forward volatility functions. Even in stressed markets where there is deviation from this, it still makes sense to extract as much of the time homogeneity in forward volatilities as possible. This is accomplished by the decomposition of the stochastic forward volatility into a product of a deterministic time-homogeneous function (deterministic component) and a stochastic multiplicative residual, as in equation (11.6). The stochastic multiplicative residual is a lognormally distributed random variable, as in equation (11.7). The various correlations between the forward rates and forward volatilities are then given by equation (11.8).

In calm markets, we expect the corrective multiplication terms to be very near unity, so that the model is fairly consistent with the observations that suggest volatility to be nearly self-similar during these calm periods. During periods of market stress, the stochastic multiplicative terms can grow to allow forward volatilities of different maturities to follow different volatility term structures. In Figure 11.6 we show the SABR spot volatility as implied by the cap market and the deterministic component of that curve for a calm market day (1/2/2007), using a fractional lognormality parameter of $\beta=0.1$.

The time-homogeneous component of the spot curve and the market implied spot curve are fairly similar, indicating that a fractional lognormality assumption for forward rate evolution is a good one for the calm market environment, and that the stochastic volatility component is muted. In the second panel of Figure 11.6, we present the stochastic multiplicative residual for this calm market example.

As expected, the multiplicative correction term is fairly close to unity, indicating little need for a large contribution from a stochastic volatility component in the calm market environment.

Next we look at a date that is more representative of a stressed market environment. In Figure 11.7 we show the same graphs for 10/08/09, a year into the U.S. credit crisis.

As the panels in the figure show, in the stressed market, a significant portion of the shape of the term structure is contained in the stochastic volatility component. When comparing the calm market and stressed market figures, we also see that the time-homogeneous forward volatility curve is nearly the same in the two environments, indicating that there is indeed a time-homogeneous component, and that it is fairly stable through the cycle.

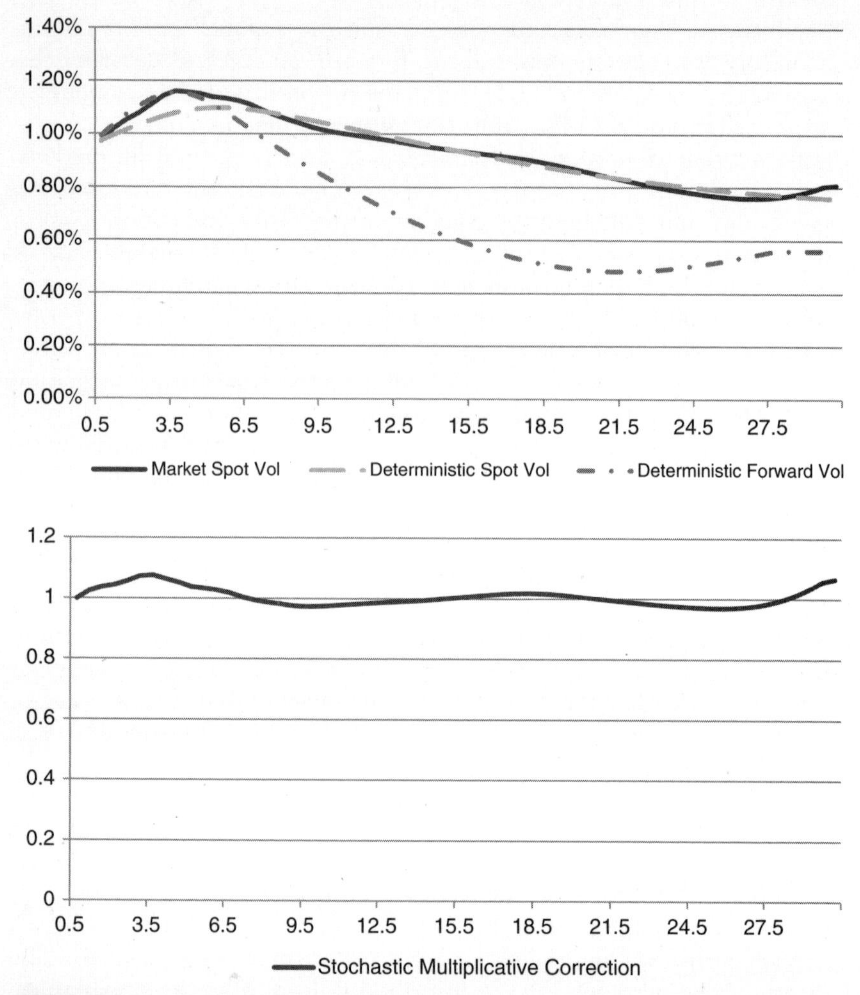


**FIGURE 11.6** Cap implied spot volatilities, deterministic forward volatilities, derived deterministic spot volatility term structures, and stochastic multiplicative residuals for 1/2/2007.
*Source:* FactSet.

The SABR-LMM has the advantages that it can recover almost any cap volatility skew, and, as we have shown, it has good properties through the cycle. The time-homogeneous component of forward volatility is reasonably stable, and the lognormality assumption of the forward volatility seems supported by the fact that the lognormal volatility of volatility is also reasonably stable when estimating historically. All of this would indicate that the

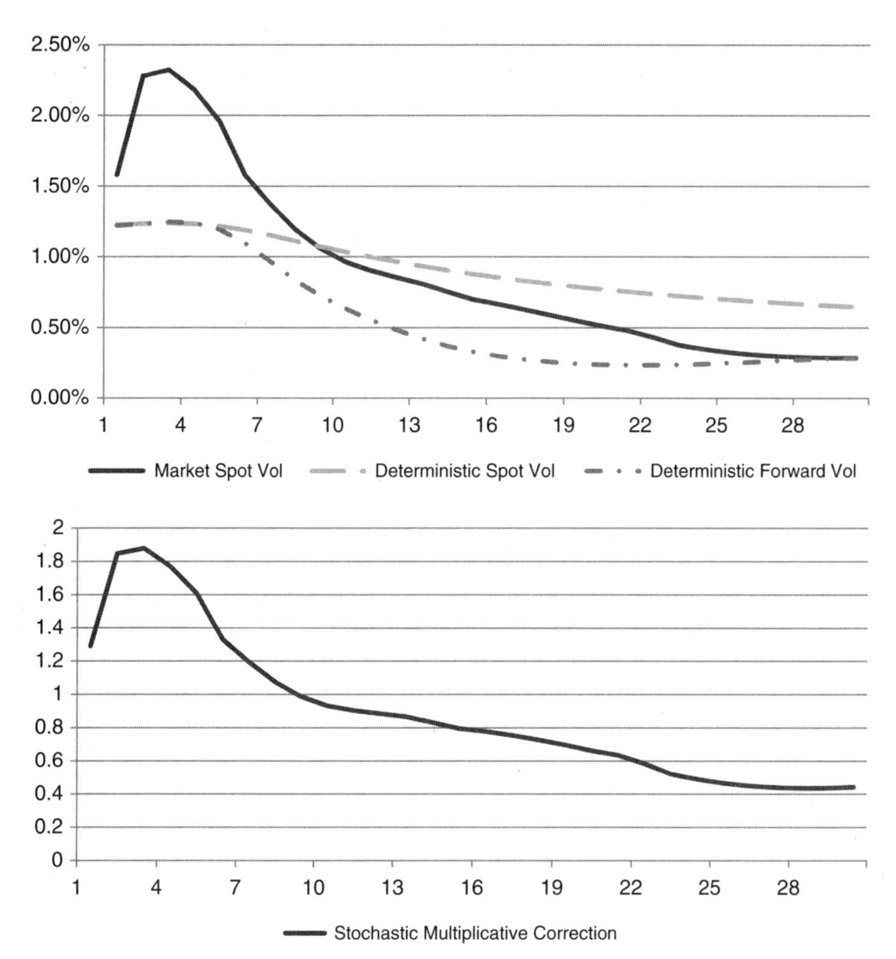


**FIGURE 11.7** Cap implied spot volatilities, time homogeneous forward volatilities, derived time homogeneous spot volatility term structures, and stochastic multiplicative residuals for 10/08/2009.
*Source:* FactSet.

SABR-LMM is capable of capturing all of the relevant dynamics of forward rates in a framework consistent with both observed market prices and historical analysis.

We now have a meaningful way to talk about term structure of volatility for forward rates. We require three fundamental curves: the market implied SABR spot volatility curve, the time-homogeneous component of the forward (or spot) volatility curve, and the volatility of volatility curve. With forward rate dynamics and the cap market addressed, we can now move on to swap rate dynamics and the swaptions market.

For the major currencies, interest rate swaps provide the deepest and most liquid market for trading interest rates, so it is not surprising that there is an active market for options on swap rates. Call options on swap rates come in flavors defined by the tenor of the swap rate, the expiration date of the call, and the moneyness (strike) of the option. The price of swaptions will vary greatly depending on these, but if we restrict our attention to a fixed tenor, maturity, and moneyness, we can use the Black-Scholes option pricing formula to convert price to an implied volatility. This will leave us with a three-dimensional volatility cube, with dimensions for swaption expiry, swap tenor, and swaption moneyness. Similar to cap volatilities, the Black volatilities are just an intuitive quoting convention, but what we need is to determine how swaption volatility is related to forward rate volatilities.

Recall that the swap rate can be expressed as a weighted average of forward rates with tenor equal to the reset frequency of the swap, $S_{1,N}(t) = \sum_{j=1}^{N} w_j(t) f(t, Tj, Tj+1)$, where the weights were functions of all the forward rates with maturity up to the maturity of the swap. This means that swap rate dynamics are determined fully by forward rate dynamics; we can express swap volatility in terms of forward rate volatility (though mathematically this not trivial). In a complete market, arbitrage opportunities would keep the cap market and the swaption market from disagreeing about the volatility structure. Unfortunately, the lack of a liquid market for serial options means that the cap and swaption markets are to some extent disjointed.

We have two ways to deal with this. The first is to pick a market and calibrate the SABR-LMM to it. In the case of swaption volatilities, numerically efficient ways to estimate swaption volatility from forward volatility have been developed by Rebonato and White.[4] We could also specify swap curve dynamics directly. A version of the LIBOR market model that is expressed using swap rates rather than forward rates has been developed by Jamshidian.[5] This model can be extended to CEV and SABR variants. In the swap-based models, one uses annuities instead of zero coupon bonds as numeraires.

### Interest Rate Volatility Forecasting

Now that we know how to define interest rate volatility in a way that isolates the non-interest-rate-dependent randomness in the volatility, we can turn to how to forecast the way the stochastic volatility component will change over some time horizon.

Interest rate volatility is model dependent. The SABR-LMM was introduced in order to reduce the relationship between interest rates and volatility of those interest rates to its most fundamental form. We measured the interest rate volatility risk exposure using durations to changes in the SABR-LMM stochastic volatility curve. This model needs to be calibrated to recover market observables, the Black implied swaption, and cap volatility surfaces. From the standpoint of the end results, then, we really don't have a preference if we back out the SABR-LMM volatility from today's market observables and then forecast the SABR-LMM volatility directly, or if we forecast the Black implied swaption and cap surfaces and then back out the SABR-LMM volatility. From a practical point of view, however, it makes much more sense to extract the SABR-LMM stochastic volatility up front, and then build a model to forecast the SABR-LMM stochastic volatility curve directly. This would be true whether we use the SABR-LMM model to govern the dynamics of the forward curve or another stochastic volatility model.[6] The important point is that any model that is built on a deterministic volatility assumption is a model that is using the wrong numbers in the wrong model to get the right answer, which is a common criticism leveled at the original Black model. If we honestly believe that interest rate volatility is deterministic, then tomorrow's volatility does not need forecasting; it is known, and there is no need to worry about volatility risk.

The natural starting point for stochastic volatility forecasting is simple statistical analysis using principal components. We have devoted a lot of attention to the importance of taking out what is known in order to settle on a definition of what we mean by the random component of interest rate volatility. This starts with extracting information about interest rate volatility that is contained in the level of interest rates. We have provided evidence that there is still residual randomness even after we account for the level of interest rates. One thing we should be interested in is to what degree there is remaining correlation between interest rates and the residual stochastic volatility, and whether there should even be correlation between interest rates and the residual stochastic volatility. For this reason, when doing principal component analysis, we want to include interest rates and the derived residual volatilities in the same factor rotation, so we can see not only the common drivers of interest rates, but the common drivers of the derived stochastic volatilities, and whether the factors load on forward rates and stochastic volatilities independently.

First, we make the distinction between the correlations between interest rate levels and stochastic volatility levels, and the correlations between the changes in interest rate levels and changes in stochastic volatility levels. For forecasting purposes, we are not really concerned with correlations between levels. The correlations we are concerned with are the correlations in the changes, since this is how we cast the equations that govern the evolution dynamics in the first place.

In Figures 11.8 through 11.10 we graph the interest rate and volatility correlations. Using six-month forward rates as of 1/2/2007, we show the correlations of the daily fractional percentage changes ($\beta = 0.1$) in the forward rates in the first graph. These are the SABR-LMM correlation inputs $E[dz_i dz_j] = \rho_{ij}dt$ in equation (11.7). Next we show the correlations of the daily percentage changes in the stochastic forward volatility, which are the SABR-LMM correlation inputs $E[dz_i dz_j] = r_{ij}dt$ in that equation. Finally, we show the correlations between the daily fractional percentage changes in the forward rates and the daily percentage changes in the stochastic forward volatilities, which are the SABR-LMM correlation inputs $E[dz_i dz_j] = R_{ij}dt$ in equation (11.7). The correlations are based on historical data, and are not calibrated to market instruments.

The forward rate/forward rate correlations are high, even on a daily (fractional) percentage change basis. This says that the changes to the forward curve are not isolated, that the curve moves as an object. This confirms the expectations that we formed when we performed PCA on the spot and forward curves in Chapter 9. The forward curve is driven by a few factors that can be described as shift, twist, and curvature. We see a similar correlation structure in the forward volatility/forward volatility correlations, indicating that the forward volatility curve is also a connected object. In Figure 11.11,

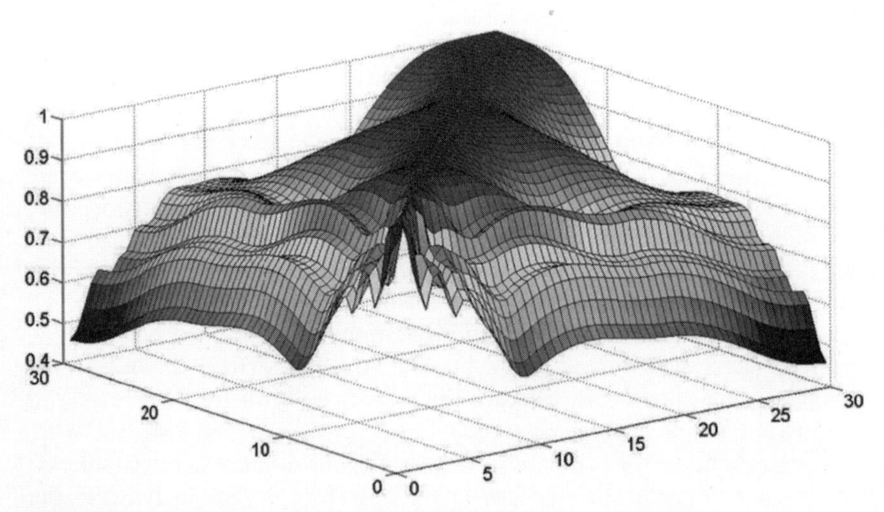


**FIGURE 11.8** Forward rate/forward rate correlations for 1/2/2007.
*Source:* FactSet.

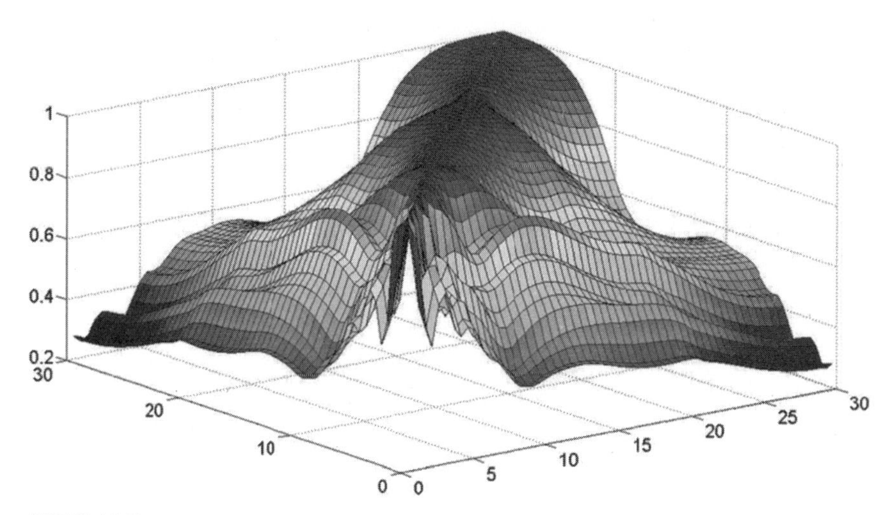


**FIGURE 11.9** Forward volatility/forward volatility correlations for 1/2/2007.
*Source:* FactSet.

we show the percentage of variance explained by the PC factors when factor rotation is restricted to the forward volatility/forward volatility correlation matrix.

As expected from the correlation matrix, the principal component decomposition of the forward volatility curve shows that a high percentage of the daily variation in the curve can be attributed to a few factors, and

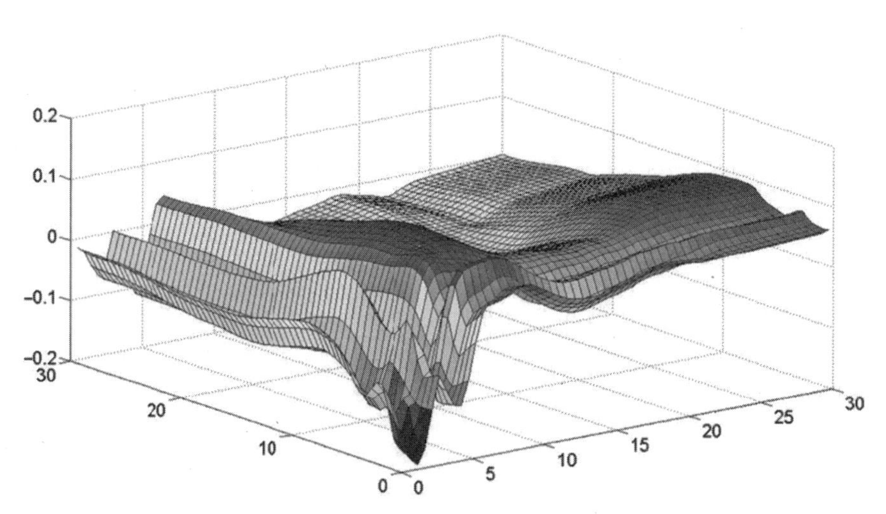


**FIGURE 11.10** Forward rate/forward volatility correlations for 1/2/2007.
*Source:* FactSet.

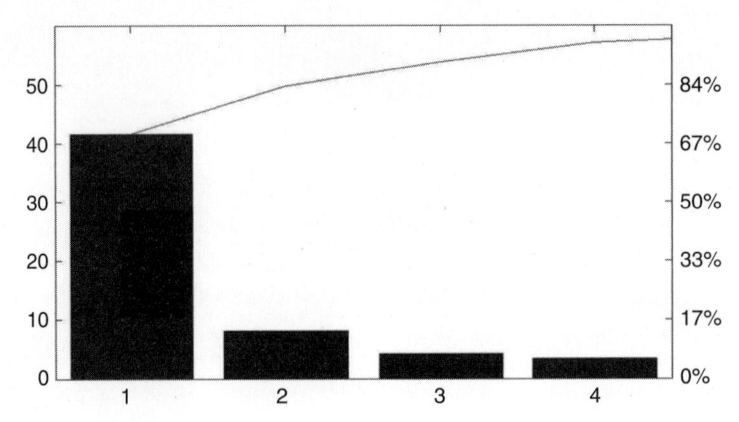


**FIGURE 11.11** Forward volatility principal component percentage of variance.
*Source:* FactSet.

the first three factors have high similarity with level, slope, and curvature effects. The next question is how the forward volatility curve factors interact with the forward curve factors. Figure 11.10 shows that the correlation between the forward curve and the forward volatility curve is small, and basically centered around zero (except for the shortest maturities, correlations range between –10 percent and 10 percent). Based on historical rate and volatility moves, this suggests that at least for the real-world probabilities, there is little interaction between the forward curve factors and the forward volatility curve factors.

In Figure 11.12, we show the loadings of the first four principal components on the forward curve and the forward volatility curve. The top panel shows the PC loadings on the 30-year forward curve, while the bottom panel shows the loadings of the same PCs on the 30-year forward volatility curve. What we see is that the first and the fourth PC have loadings on the forward curve that fit with interpretations as level and slope factors; the first PC has high, flat loading on the forwards (the negative sign of the loadings doesn't matter), while the fourth PC has a sloping loading structure. On the other hand, those same PCs have relatively small loadings on the forward volatility curve. The forward volatility curve is independent of forward curve level and slope factors. Similarly, the second and third PCs have essentially no loading on the forward curve, but loadings on the forward volatility curve that support level and slope factor interpretations there. This supports the claim that the factors driving the majority of the joint dynamics between both curves are really two sets of independent factors driving each curve independently.

For risk forecasting purposes (VaR, ETL, etc.) we are most concerned with the evolution of risk factors according to real-world probabilities; the risk factor exposures contain the risk-neutral valuation information. The previous discussion then shows how stochastic volatility forecasting can be done in terms of a statistical factor model employing stochastic forward volatility level, shift, and curvature factors. It also suggests a modification to the statistical factor model that should be employed to forecast interest rate risk to be consistent with the volatility statistical factor model. In Chapter 9, we discussed PCA on spot and forward curves using either absolute differences or percentage changes. With the description of the SABR-LMM now in hand, we can extend that to PCA on the fractional percentage changes, which then put absolute differences ($\beta = 0$) and percentage changes (($\beta = 1$) on opposite ends of the fractional parameter scale, and include volatility into the mix.

We have estimated our correlations using simple rolling standard deviations, but the SABR-LMM is naturally equipped with a sense of volatility clustering. Our estimators of the volatilities of the PC factors therefore may benefit from more sophisticated volatility estimation tools, such as Garch. The stochastic volatility assumption makes the interest rate process a mixture model, in fact. This means that interest rate movements, when estimated from a distribution that assumes deterministic volatility, will look as though they have skew and kurtosis (so-called fat-tailed behavior). This is

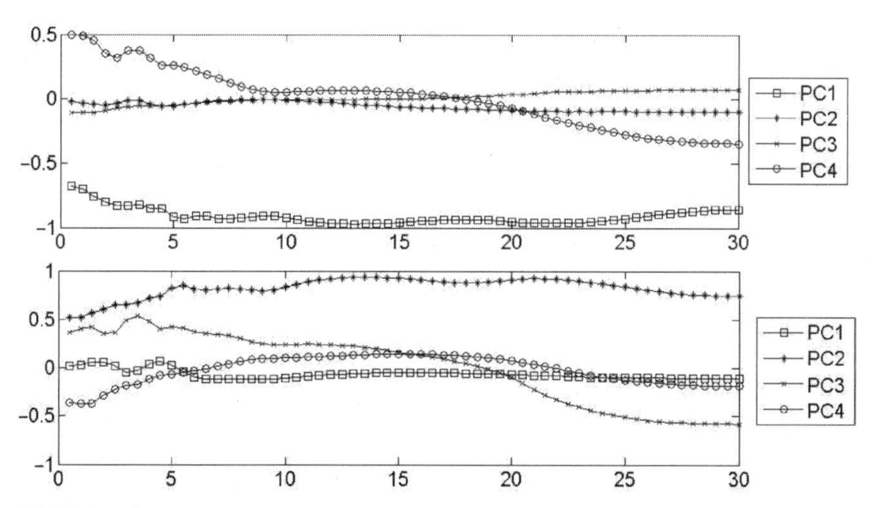


**FIGURE 11.12** Joint principal component loadings on the forward and on the forward volatility curve.
*Source:* FactSet.

a more practical way to treat the appearance of higher moments, since the vast literature on interest rate (and equity) derivative valuation models is skewed toward mixture models (geometric Brownian motion in particular), and not Pareto-type distributions.

Principal component estimation does not put too many restrictions on the distributional assumptions of the PC factors. That said, the way we have constructed them means we cannot scale the volatility of the factors the way we might be used to doing. The constant volatility of volatility assumption of the SABR-LMM means we can scale those factors according to quadratic variation law, but this is not the case with the forward curve factors. The volatility of the forward curve factors is directly dependent on the factor realizations of the stochastic volatility factors, and when the volatility of volatility happens is important; there is path dependence. This means that while there is low covariance between the forward curve and the forward volatility curve, the variance of the forward curve itself depends on the realized forward volatilities. This effect is small over shorter horizons (one day to three months), but must be dealt with for longer-horizon analysis.

### Interest Rate Volatility Risk Exposures

For interest rate risk exposures, we computed either key rate durations or principal component durations to measure the sensitivity of bond returns to changes in the spot curve. We did this because the spot curve was a random object. If the spot curve were an eternal static object, there would be no such thing as interest rate risk, since we would know with certainty what the value of any certain cash flow would be over any time horizon. There might be risk due to the uncertainty in cash flows that did not stem from interest rates, but no risk that discount rates would change, so no interest rate risk. Of course, interest rates are random, and interest rate risk is real.

The same logic applies to interest rate volatility. If tomorrow's interest rate volatility will look like today's volatility, there is no risk due to interest rate volatility. In the lognormal and CEV versions of the LIBOR market model, the forward volatility curve is nonrandom. The randomness in the volatility of the level of forward rates is (fractionally) proportional to the forward rates themselves, so that uncertainty in interest rate volatility is due only to uncertainty in the forward rates themselves. This risk is already captured in the interest rate risk exposures, so we do not want to double count it. This is why we decompose forward volatility into a (fractional) level component and a pure volatility component. In the CEV-LMM, this pure volatility component is deterministic, so there is no volatility risk by definition.

If we stick to the deterministic forward volatility assumption, we cannot still insist that tomorrow's volatility may not look like today's, without admitting that our model of forward volatility is wrong (and so to any complex option pricing models that are based off the deterministic volatility assumption). We can take a practitioner's view and compute a sensitivity to changes in the volatility anyway and then hope to model the changes in the volatility through some process. This can be thought of similar to the way we think of Black volatility of a stock price. The basic Black-Scholes model is the wrong model and the Black volatility is the wrong volatility, but we can compute an option's vega anyway, and then model the supposedly deterministic Black volatility as if it were a random variable (possibly through some Garch method, for example). This would be reasonable if we had no real idea how to create a better option pricing model. If we have a stochastic volatility option pricing model, however, it is always better to use it to compute the option vega than to use Black-Scholes. The same goes for interest rate volatility. Fortunately, we have a true stochastic volatility model for forward rates.

In the SABR-LMM, the deterministic component of the forward volatility and the volatility of volatility are nonrandom, so there is risk of them changing. We presented evidence that supports that this is a decent reflection of reality, since the deterministic component of volatility was shown to be very similar in both calm and stressed market environments, and the volatility of volatility was shown to be tightly range-bound, even when estimating with noisy historical estimators. Since the model assumptions are seemingly consistent with reality, we only need to treat the risk posed by the change in the portion of the volatility that the model treats as random, the stochastic multiplicative correction.

Since the deterministic, time-homogeneous portion of the forward volatility and the volatility of the volatility are nonrandom and do not depend on time, knowledge of the stochastic forward volatility is equivalent to knowledge of the stochastic multiplicative correction. We can determine one from the other. The stochastic volatility is represented by a curve with forward maturity being the independent variable. As with spot rates, we can divide that curve up into key maturities. The full volatility curve is then represented by some finite collection of maturity/forward volatility pairs, with the full curve being recovered through some interpolation scheme. We can then compute a sensitivity to that portion of the volatility curve by shifting the volatility at the key maturity up and down (e.g., through tent-shaped shifts to the curve), recomputing bond price in each scenario, and then computing a numerical duration and convexity using these price/shift pairs. Alternatively, as with interest rate risk exposures, we can compute stochastic volatility risk exposures using either key rate or principal component durations and convexities.

Interest rate volatility risk is measured through exposure to this single stochastic volatility curve. This provides significant dimension reduction, as we can formulate impact to any swap-dependent option through an impact to this single curve. That said, we did mention that cap and swaption markets are not perfectly tied together because of incompleteness of the two markets. To the extent that cap and swaption markets do disagree about the stochastic forward volatility curve, it may be worthwhile to determine sensitivities to the swaption- and/or cap-calibrated stochastic forward volatility curve, depending on which rate type an option is most exposed to. Alternatively, if we use the swap formulation to infer dynamics of the swap rates, we may choose to measure exposure to the forward- or swap-based stochastic volatility curves, depending on which rate type an option is most exposed to. The cap market deals with short tenor rates, while the swaption market deals with long tenured rates. We could then measure a short volatility exposure and a long volatility exposure for each security to fully capture volatility exposure. If we did this, we would need to account for the joint dynamics of both short and long tenured rate volatility.

Now that we know what curve we would like to measure exposure to (the stochastic volatility curve), we can measure that exposure by computing key rate vegas and convexities in a manner similar to how we compute key rate durations and convexities. We isolate a portion of the stochastic volatility curve associated with a given key rate, then we shift the curve up and down by some amount (the curve tenting shown in Figure 10.16), and then we price the volatility-sensitive security under these two scenarios and compute the numerical estimate of first and second derivatives. Alternatively, as we have shown that the stochastic volatility curve is driven by a small collection of common factors, we can compute principal component vegas and convexities.

### Risk Forecasting

For risk forecasting, we can follow the discussion in Chapter 9 on interest rate risk. Interest rate derivatives will have both interest rate and interest rate volatility risk exposures. We combined these in the Taylor repricing formula with the interest rate and stochastic volatility factors, either through correlated key rate and key volatility factors derived from the PC loading structure or directly to the PC factors themselves, depending on whether we are using key rate–based exposures or principal component–based exposures. Since we have taken out (essentially) all interest rate dependence in the way we defined stochastic volatility via the SABR-LMM, we have ensured by construction that the cross-sensitivities are independent. This means that in application of the Taylor approximation formula, we can ignore the effect of cross-partial derivatives. That is, there is no exposure to factors of the form interest rate factor times volatility factor.

It is important to point out what our construction of volatility exposure means for risk forecasting. Interest rate options, like equity options, have a much larger delta than a vega. That is, the risk exposure to a move in the underlying generally dominates the risk exposure to a move in the volatility of the underlying. We have constructed the interest rate volatility exposure in such a way as to try to remove as much of an option's exposure to the underlying (the spot and derived rate curves) as possible first, and to then measure the exposure to the volatility of the underlying after we have taken out what is known first. This is a theme of Chapter 10 on spread risk when we talked about measuring the non-interest-rate-related risk of mortgage-backed securities, among others. The consequence of this is that we will be in a better position when we perform risk attribution or risk budgeting. For attribution, we will know that our volatility bets were really volatility bets, and not volatility bets mixed with residual interest rate bets. For risk budgeting, we will know that a strategic risk budget that allocates a portion of total risk to interest rate volatility strategies is actually capable of measuring marginal contribution to total risk from volatility correctly, without introducing residual interest rate volatility risk. Since an interest rate derivative (IRD) fund/strategy will contain both exposure to interest rate and interest rate volatility risk, this is important, as we can better identify whether a manager is really good at using IRDs to create interest-rate-related alpha or interest rate volatility alpha.

In a quick summary, we have pointed out that a financial risk factor like interest rate volatility can arise only due to uncertainty (i.e., randomness) in that factor, and that if there is no randomness in a price input, there is no risk that can arise from it. This is important for interest rate and equity volatility because many popular option pricing models make deterministic (i.e., nonrandom) volatility assumptions. The easiest example of this is the Black-Scholes option pricing model for equities (equivalently, the Black model for caplets and swaptions). If our deterministic (constant) volatility acts as though it is actually a random variable in practice, then we have to admit that our option pricing model is misspecified. This may be unavoidable, but when possible it is clearly better to remove this misspecification risk and eschew deterministic volatility models.

In the context of interest rate volatility, we have shown how this misspecification arises, and when it is important. In calm markets, the standard LIBOR market model, or its CEV extension, can often be sufficient. In these markets, the stochastic volatility contribution is low, and a mild misspecification between model and the assumption of volatility risk may be tolerated. In stressed markets, this approximation breaks down, and proper treatment of stochastic interest rate volatility becomes important. To prove this we highlighted how in a stressed market environment it is possible to produce deterministic forward volatility curves that admit arbitrage. Indeed, the LMM cannot avoid producing them.

To model stochastic interest rate volatility, we introduced the SABR extension of the LIBOR market model. While this model does a better job of fitting volatility skews than deterministic volatility models, the real value of it is that only through a stochastic volatility model is it possible to truly identify what interest rate volatility risk actually means. We showed that the SABR-LMM has good properties in that it allows us to properly take out what is known. Specifically, it tells us how to take out the portion of volatility that is actually due to interest rate levels and how to take out any time-homogeneous tendencies, before it leaves us with a residual that contains the real source of randomness that interest rate volatility risk is concerned with. Without a stochastic volatility model, we're contradicting ourselves when we attempt to measure volatility risk.

## FIXED INCOME IDIOSYNCRATIC BOND RISK

Bonds are all about cash flows, and fixed income is diverse in its offerings regarding the structure and timing of those cash flows. Grouping bonds together according to similarities in the cash flow structure and the collateral backing them allows us to determine common sources of risk through exposures to interest rates, volatility, and spread. Even within a narrowly defined class, bonds can have idiosyncratic features. Differences in the timing of cash flows, the nature of the collateral, or the market for a bond's particular terms can create a source of risk that needs to be addressed.

The first thing to consider is whether idiosyncratic risk is part of spread risk or separate from it. The one-to-one relationship between spread and price means that spread contains compensation not only for the systematic sources of risk common to all bonds within a class, but also for any bond-specific compensation. One approach to measuring idiosyncratic risk would be to measure spread residuals. On the other hand, the Taylor approximation we have been using gives us a means of producing bond clean-price-based returns given realizations of the factors, and we could try to describe idiosyncratic risk through return residuals directly. Adopting the latter potentially could provide a means of correcting for the linearization error introduced by the use of the Taylor formula. This would most certainly introduce autocorrelation into our residuals, however, so care must be taken if we decide to go this route.

In this section, we discuss methods to estimate idiosyncratic bond risk using spread residuals. The basic concepts we will introduce using a spread approach translate readily to return residuals, so we won't make much further reference to it.

Since we are going to be measuring idiosyncratic bond risk though spread residuals, we need to view every bond as having the potential to have a spread; otherwise there will be no residual to measure. We also need to decide if residual spread is due to spread model misspecification or to true idiosyncratic features. This might seem somewhat obvious, but it's easy to overlook these simple statements. Consider the situation of U.S. Treasuries. Should U.S. Treasuries, discounted to the U.S. Treasury curve, have a spread?

For some investors, the answer is no. Treasuries carry only interest rate risk and liquidity risk, but not spread risk. This is mainly just a matter of terminology, of course, but it's worth pointing out. For our purposes, liquidity risk falls under the heading of spread risk, and so we do allow for Treasuries to have spreads to the Treasury curve.

In Figure 11.13, we plot Treasury spreads as a function of maturity. We see that the spreads are not large, and vary between positive and negative 5 basis points. While the spreads are not very large, there is clearly some structure to them, just based on maturity. One possibility is that the spot curve construction process is responsible for this. Any parametric representation of the infinite dimensional spot curve that is fit to a finite collection of observable market instruments is going to have some error. In this case, a cubic spline with 13-knot points was used to build the curve. This would then make spread an artifact of the curve construction.

It is well known that on-the-run Treasury bonds have a price premium relative to off-the-run Treasuries. Simple supply-and-demand forces can offer a more fundamental explanation for Treasury spreads. Demand for exposure to specific portions of the curve and the relative supply at or near that specific maturity can be a source of relative premium or discount.

If the spreads have predictability in terms of common characteristics, then we need to build a spread model to include them, and measure the spread residuals. For Treasuries, we might posit a spread factor model that includes seasoning (time outstanding), depth of the issue (amount outstanding), and maturity (average life), for example. Only when the remaining residuals are uncorrelated can we call them idiosyncratic.

Assuming the spread residuals from our simple Treasury spread factor model were uncorrelated, our spread factor model estimation would then produce factors and residuals for each day. When we discussed spread risk, we focused on the time-series properties of the common spread factors. Now we focus on the time-series properties of the residuals. Because the spread factors tend to have high autocorrelation in the levels, we applied first differences to the common factors to estimate covariance structure for use in risk forecasts. We must do the same with the spread residuals.

For each Treasury bond on the index, we have daily pricing, and hence can compute a time series of observable spreads. We can estimate the spread fac-

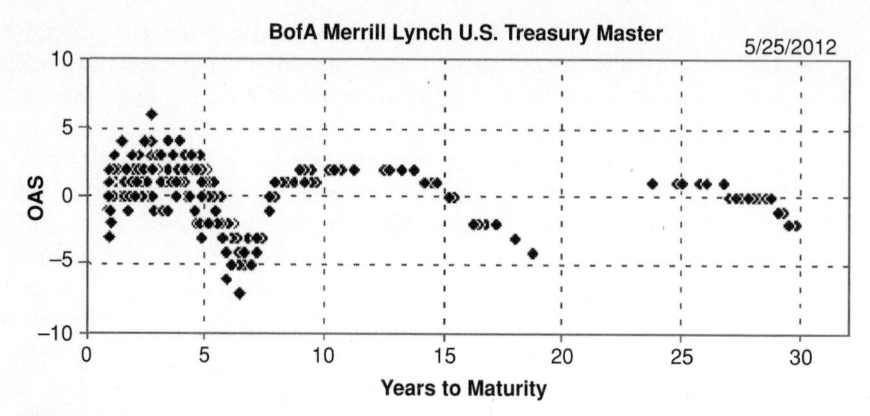


**FIGURE 11.13** U.S. Treasury spreads.
*Sources:* FactSet and BofA Merrill Lynch.

tors and daily spread residuals for each bond on the index. We can then form the daily spread residual change and estimate a (perhaps time-weighted) rolling standard deviation. We could do the same for the mean of the daily residual changes, but it makes sense to assume that they are zero, and not expose our residuals to undue sample estimator error. The mean of the daily changes is assumed to be zero. In the context of a Monte Carlo VaR simulation, we would draw from the factor covariance matrix to determine the interest rate, volatility, and common spread factor realizations. The predicted spread change from the factors would be modified to include a draw from independent, bond-specific distributions to provide the bond idiosyncratic effects. On the individual bond level, for each bond our simulated spread change would be the starting spread level, plus the simulated spread change due to statistical factors, plus the simulated change in spread residual. Mathematically, this is just:

$$OAS_i = BaseOAS_i + \Delta OAS_i + \varepsilon_i \tag{11.9}$$

This would involve one idiosyncratic draw for each bond, per scenario. This could obviously start to add up. Since the idiosyncratic terms are independent and normally distributed by definition, we could also choose to compute idiosyncratic contribution on the group level to lessen the computational burden. For example, we could draw a single MBS sector idiosyncratic term by computing the group weighted average standard deviation of the individual bond idiosyncratic terms.

In Figure 11.14 we see how this would look for an agency MBS generic. The agency CMO spreads were calibrated using a cross-sectional fit to a benchmark of IO and PO strips using the spread model based on the refinance and turnover durations, as discussed in Chapter 10. Using the factor realizations, and the computed refinance and turnover durations for an agency MBS generic (FH30, 2006, 5.5 percent), we see the spread model residuals for this generic. The time-series properties of the residuals of a sufficiently large sample of bonds represented by the model will indicate if the spread model is well specified or is missing sources of systematic risk.

If there is lingering correlation in the residual data, we might be tempted to deal with it using pure statistical factors. While this would be a reasonable approach for bonds on an index, most bonds do not have a robust daily pricing source that would allow for a determination of the exposure to such latent factors. This is one reason that statistical factors do not work well for fixed income. If our residuals are independent, then we can feel confident that our spread model is reasonably well specified. This imbues the bonds on the index we use for spread factor model calibration with idiosyncratic components, but what do we do about bonds not on the index?

If a bond not on an index has a reliable daily pricing source, we could use the index calibrated factors to measure a spread residual and then estimate rolling standard deviation of the first differences in the same way as we do for bonds on the index. Unfortunately, much of the fixed income universe lacks such liquid pricing. In the more commonly encountered case

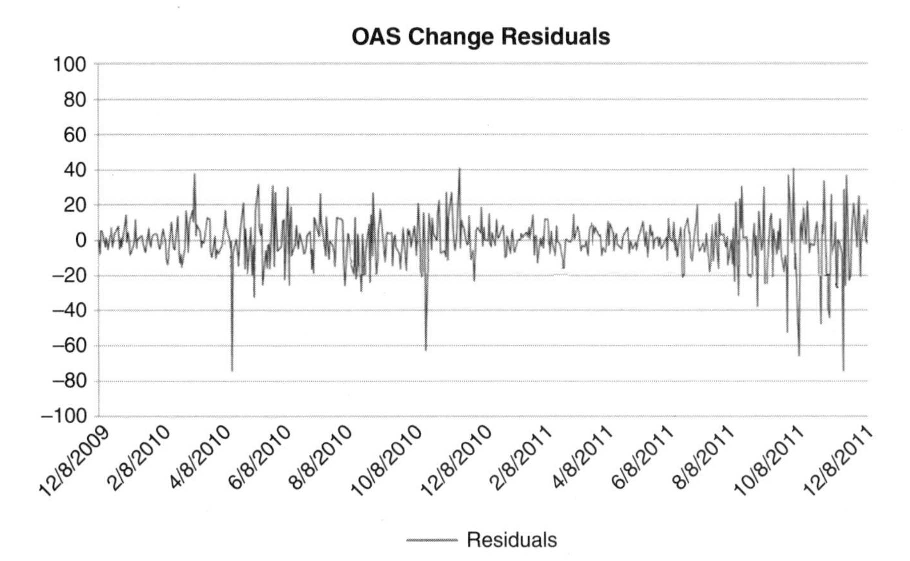


**FIGURE 11.14** Spread model residuals for a sample agency MBS generic.
*Source:* FactSet.

that the bond is not on an index and we do not have a time-series record of observable spreads, a practical approach would be to assign such a bond idiosyncratic characteristics that are in some way average. Since we trusted our index enough to estimate the spread factors, we could use the residuals of each bond on the index as a basis for defining average residual. Since we assumed the means of the residual changes were zero and that residuals are all uncorrelated, we just need to specify the standard deviation of the idiosyncratic terms. The standard deviations for the benchmark bonds are formed from rolling standard deviations of the residuals, and we could simply average those standard deviations to get an expected standard deviation for the idiosyncratic components of bonds not belonging to the index, but for which the index is considered representative. We could also choose to average the variances, so that the expectation for the idiosyncratic term has root mean squared–like features. We could also group residuals by type if our index was too broad. For example, if we calibrated our MBS spread model to IO/PO prices, we could calculate average idiosyncratic terms by IO or PO type. Then when we encountered a specific CMO tranche, we would have to decide if it was more IO- or PO-like.

This gives us a way to include bond idiosyncratic features for bonds whose spread risk is modeled through a spread factor model. For bonds that have spreads derived from other sources, we need some other way to measure spread residual. For credit sensitive bonds like corporates that use the Merton model, there is no spread residual. Recall that in our implementation of the Merton model described in Chapter 10 on spread risk, we used the spread to calibrate the firm leverage so as to fully recover the spread. Unless this calibration fails, there will be no spread residual by definition. But corporates clearly are exposed to firm idiosyncratic risk, so how does the Merton model capture that?

The Merton model applied to corporate bonds allowed us to derive changes in corporate spreads from changes in the equity price. The systematic drivers of spread change among corporates then arise from the systematic drivers of equity returns. It follows then that issuer-specific idiosyncratic drivers of spread change arise from the idiosyncratic drivers of equity returns. This is true if the Merton model were a perfect representation of the capital structure. Since it is not, some mention is made of how to impart idiosyncratic risk to different bonds on the same issuer. Using calibrated leverage to tune the Merton model for individual issues within the same corporate capital structure allows each bond in the capital structure to have a different sense of firm leverage that it is exposed to. While this gives a very practical way to incorporate individual issue differences into the spread, the main implication is that it assumes that all issues tied to a given issuer are perfectly correlated. Issues will have different variances, but still have the direction of spread changes driven by the same underlying equity model. For risk calculations that are primarily interested in tail behavior, such as a 95 percent VaR, issue-specific idiosyncratic contribution is likely to be very small relative to issuer-generic contribution. That is, it is highly likely that if the spreads of one corporate issue blow out, the spreads of all the other issues outstanding on that issuer will blow out, with the size of the blowout depending mainly on the issue-specific loss given default rate. Since we can ascribe a different recovery rate for bonds based on where in the capital structure they fall, differences in bond risk based on issue-specific features are still captured. For these types of risk calculations, calibrating an implied leverage is probably sufficient.

We have covered how the Merton model captures firm-specific idiosyncratic risk. If we want to include an issue-specific idiosyncratic component that can admit nonperfectly correlated issue spread moves, we have to make some choices. We could relax the calibrated leverage per bond assumption and only calculate a single implied leverage per issuer. This would then give rise to spread residuals across a single issuer credit term structure. Using the previous comments, we could then estimate firm-specific or industry-level issuer idiosyncratic terms to determine capital-structure-specific idiosyncratic effects.

At this point, it's worth a reminder about what idiosyncratic bond risk is not. It is not risk that can be captured using any sort of spread factor model. That is, if we can explain some of the cross section of spreads using some fundamental or statistical factor, then the risk that emanates from that factor is not idiosyncratic bond risk by definition. For example, if it is observed that off-the-run Treasuries trade with a spread to a Treasury curve constructed using on-the-run bonds, then a model that can predict spread based on time since issuance (recent off-the-run) or depth of issue is not a model of idiosyncratic bond risk; it is a model of systematic bond spread risk. It is only the residuals that exist after all systematic explanatory terms have been taken out that can be ascribed to idiosyncratic risk. If our spread model leaves correlated spread residuals, we need to improve the spread model.

Returning to corporate bonds and variation in spreads of the bonds associated with a particular issuer, we have to be careful to make sure that we have built a spread model that has extracted all systematic sources of spread before we try to characterize the individual bond on the capital structure's idiosyncratic risk. If we use a single leverage for a firm in the Merton model so that we generate spread residuals, we then might want to add a further spread model that focuses on market structure factors similar to the Treasury bond example. Seasoning, depth of issue, differential in tax treatment, and issue-specific rating are among the possible sources of systematic variation in spread, and it is perfectly rational to try to capture them. They cannot be classified as idiosyncratic sources of risk, however.

No spread model is likely ever the final word, as models always can be improved, but practical considerations mean that at some point we have to stop and assign residual spread variation to idiosyncratic sources. As modelers (and risk managers), we can feel better about deciding we've reached that point if the spread residuals are uncorrelated, or at least have acceptably low correlation. Otherwise we need to put more work into our spread model. Idiosyncratic bond risk is then what happens after our best efforts at creating a spread model have been exhausted. We can capture this through spread residuals or return residuals. Spread residuals may be preferable since we will eventually have to deal with bonds that rarely trade, and assigning a variance to the idiosyncratic term of off-index bonds is potentially easier through spread residuals. However, idiosyncratic risk at the issuer level is captured well by structural credit models such as the Merton model.

## FIXED INCOME CURRENCY RISK

Consider a 10-year Japanese government bond (JGB) issued in yen paying a 1.5 percent coupon. From the point of view a EUR-based investor, what is the risk of owning this bond?

We have discussed interest rate risk, interest rate volatility risk, spread risk, and residual bond idiosyncratic risk. In all of this we have emphasized the central role of understanding these risks in terms of cash flows to the point of sounding like a broken record, repeating the same statements with little variation. While far from trivial to implement, the road map up to now has been clear for measuring fixed income risk. Discount cash flows to assign a present value measure risk exposure by determining how sensitive bond value is to changes in bond price inputs, specify dynamics for bond price input changes, and then combine these using the linear repricing formula. The discount curve is broken into a risk-free component, a systematic bond sector spread component, and a bond-specific idiosyncratic spread residual component. How we describe the dynamics of each component has been discussed at length, including how to incorporate volatility and volatility dynamics for derivative securities that depend on those inputs.

In all of this, we have implicitly assumed that the present value of the cash flows being discounted and the cash flows themselves are expressed in the same currency as the discount curve. In this section, we discuss how to measure the risk posed by holding a fixed income security whose cash flows are in a currency other than the one we want to measure the risk in. We start with a discussion of how to measure currency risk exposure (warning:

it's more than just your foreign currency position size) by discussing dollar hedging and currency exposure hedging. We provide concrete examples that show how dollar hedges can be highly misspecified relative to true currency-exposure-based hedges. We then discuss the relationship between interest rates and FX rates and how it applies to understanding currency unions. We conclude with an example of how you can use interest rate parity to construct hypothetical stress tests involving the exit of a sovereign from the Eurozone.

Turning to our JGB 10-year, we could first discount the bond by the Japanese (yen-based) spot curve to get a yen-denominated present value and then multiply that value by the spot euro/yen exchange rate to get the present value of the bond in euros. Risk exposures and hedges are the same thing, so to understand how exposed we are to currency risk, we just need to determine the proper hedge. For a given risk horizon, sell forward the euro/yen FX with notional equal to the horizon present value of our JGB (in yen) over the horizon.

Even if interest rates are constant over a horizon, we expect that a bond will accrue interest, and there will be a cash flow roll-down effect as coupon payments move closer to payment dates. In a deterministic interest rate environment, these effects can be calculated with certainty.

If the Japanese interest rates do not change, the value of the JGB will be exactly equal to the horizon present value. We can then convert it at the locked-in exchange rate, and the euro-based value will not depend on how FX spot rates evolved over the horizon. Even if the Japanese spot curve does change, the euro-based value of our position at the risk horizon date will be dependent on how the present value of the JGB changed due to interest rate movements. The currency forward is not a perfect hedge, however. The forward will allow us to lock in the exchange rate, but we must choose the notional amount to exchange before we will know exactly what the yen-based present value of the JGB will be. This will leave us with a yen surplus or shortfall relative to the currency forward. While a surplus or shortfall will be due to Japanese interest rate risk, changes in the spot FX will factor in to confound that from the perspective of a euro-based investor.

Shrinking the risk horizon down to an instantaneous horizon, we see that on a return basis the first-order currency exposure is equal to minus 1 over the exchange rate; one might say that it is the currency duration for the foreign currency bond from the perspective of the local currency investor. The spot FX rate is then like a currency factor for the foreign currency bond from the perspective of a local currency investor. The return-based exposure to the currency factor duration is not sufficient to cover all of the currency risk, however, as there are interacting effects. This exposure is often referred to as the dollar exposure, and the hedge that involves shorting the currency in equal proportion to the position size is called a dollar hedge. For a fixed coupon bond like a JGB, this dollar hedge does represent the currency exposure, but in general is not sufficient to act as a true currency hedge. If the cash flow itself depends on the exchange rate, we will need to dig deeper to measure the true currency exposure for the security. We will return to this shortly, but for now continue our discussion assuming that the cash flows are independent of exchange rates.

If we choose to not linearize the currency effect, we can incorporate it into a Monte Carlo VaR calculation fairly simply with the machinery we've developed so far. For a given Monte Carlo scenario, we would use the linearized bond price/return formula to compute the clean price return in the foreign currency. We would then add in any accrual component in the foreign currency, to get the bond return in the foreign currency. The new foreign currency bond market value is then multiplied by the simulated exchange rate. Then, simply divide by the starting market value of the foreign bond in the report currency to get a 1 plus percentage based return. For the JGB held by a euro-based investor, the euro-based return on the yen-denominated bond for a given Monte Carlo scenario would be calculated as:

$$1 + ret_{EUR} = \frac{(BaseFullPrice_{JPY} + ret)\,FX_{EUR/JPY}}{BaseFullPrice_{EUR}} \tag{11.10}$$

The interest rate, interest rate volatility, spread, and bond idiosyncratic risk factor contributions all get multiplied by the FX, so that the factor contributions stay confounded with the exchange rate risk. Depending on the needs of the risk manager, this may be an acceptable approach. The prime benefit of doing this is that the nonlinear dependency between the foreign currency risk factors and the exchange risk itself are perfectly captured.

While the preceding approach does fully capture the currency effect, it does not attempt to isolate the contribution in a way that is consistent with the bond return linearization formula in general. If we are willing to accept some estimation error, we could include the currency effect within the linearized return formula directly.

Ignore the currency effect on the accrual component for the moment. Returning to the Taylor formula for clean price change, up through second-order effects, we have:

$$\Delta P_{Loc} \approx \sum_i \frac{\partial P_{Loc}}{\partial x_i} \cdot \Delta x_i + \sum_i \sum_j \frac{\partial^2 P_{Loc}}{\partial x_i \partial x_j} \cdot \Delta x_i \cdot \Delta x_j \tag{11.11}$$

Here and in what follows, the $x_i$'s represent the risk factor bond price inputs (key rates, volatilities, spread, etc.). In the local reporting currency, the risk exposures are determined by the derivatives of local currency price with respect to a change in the risk factors (such as foreign yield curve). Using the relationship between the local currency price and the foreign currency price, the rules of basic calculus can be used to compute the first-order and second-order derivatives of the local price in terms of the derivatives of the foreign price. The price relationship between the local currency price and the foreign currency price is just:

$$P_{Loc} = FX_{Loc,For} \cdot P_{For} \tag{11.12}$$

In the case where the cash flows and discount rates are independent of the exchange rate, we can compute the exposures easily in terms of the foreign-currency-based exposures directly. This will break down into the exposures to the currency factor, and the exposures to the interest rate factors, the interest rate volatility factors, and the spread factor (we modeled idiosyncratic risk within the spread; otherwise we would have an idiosyncratic price residual to contend with as well). The local currency price sensitivity to a change in a foreign-currency-measured risk factor is simply the exchange rate times the foreign currency price exposure:

$$\frac{\partial P_{Loc}}{\partial x_i} = FX_{Loc,For} \cdot \frac{\partial P_{For}}{\partial x_i} \tag{11.13}$$

In terms of durations, this is just:

$$D_{i,Loc} = \frac{-1}{P_{Loc}} \frac{\partial P_{Loc}}{\partial x_i} = \frac{-FX_{Loc,For}}{FX_{Loc,For} \cdot \cdot P_{For}} \cdot \frac{\partial P_{For}}{\partial x_i} = \frac{-1}{P_{For}} \frac{\partial P_{For}}{\partial x_i} = D_{i,For} \tag{11.14}$$

The formula for convexities and cross-convexities is analogous. The first-order local currency price sensitivity to the exchange rate is:

$$\frac{\partial P_{Loc}}{\partial FX} = P_{For} \tag{11.15}$$

And in terms of duration is:

$$D_{FX,Loc} = \frac{-1}{FX_{Loc,For} \cdot P_{For}} \cdot \frac{\partial P_{Loc}}{\partial FX} = \frac{-1}{FX_{Loc,For} \cdot P_{For}} \cdot P_{For} = \frac{-1}{FX_{Loc,For}} \tag{11.16}$$

This just says that the return-based FX exposure of the foreign bond in local currency terms is just the foriegn/local exchange rate, so that returns due to currency will be just the percentage change in the FX rate. Note that we maintain the negative sign in the definition of duration to be consistent with the treatment for other risk factors where it's customary to define it so, so that minus that duration is the FX exposure. There is no pure FX convexity term, since the first derivative of local price to the FX rate is just the foreign currency price. If that price is independent of the FX rate (because the discount curve and the cash flows are independent of the FX rate), the second derivative of the local currency price with respect to FX will be zero. There will be a cross-partial term, however. The cross-convexity of the local currency price with respect to the FX rate and a foreign currency measured risk factor is:

$$C_{FX,i,Loc} = \frac{1}{FX_{Loc,For} \cdot P_{For}} \cdot \frac{\partial^2 P_{Loc}}{\partial FX \partial x_i} = \frac{1}{FX_{Loc,For} \cdot P_{For}} \cdot \frac{\partial P_{For}}{\partial x_i} = \frac{-1}{FX_{Loc,For}} \cdot D_{i,For} \tag{11.17}$$

These cross-convexities cannot be ignored in general, and will provide the means to measure the residual FX risk even after a currency forward hedge is put on. Indeed, the cross-convexities show why a forward- or futures-based currency hedge will not be complete, as foreign cash has no duration with which to cancel out the FX cross-convexity. It's also important to point out that these cross-convexities represent joint exposures, and to remind us that the presence of nonlinearity in the price formula puts limits on how we interpret risk factor exposures. It's easy to think in terms of equity risk models and assume that there are no higher-order effects and interactions. Alternatively, we have to remember to ask about interacting and higher-order effect factors, as they are common and important for fixed income.

This provides a complete description of how to measure the contribution of the currency risk in the case that the cash flows and discount rates of the foreign bond do not depend on the exchange rate with the local reporting currency. This is a fairly safe assumption in the case of foreign government bonds (though we may change our minds later when we discuss interest rate parity), but is not so safe in general. One good example is foreign corporate bonds. The cash flows of the corporate bond depend on the revenues of the firm (default risk). The revenues of the firm can be subject directly to currency risk (the firm may generate revenue directly in a foreign currency) or indirectly by being part of a supply chain that draws revenue from exports. Either way, a firm can have significant exposure to foreign currency in ways that materially affect the firm's financial health. This is obvious for some of the bigger multinational companies like General Electric, IBM, Ford, Sony, BP, Hyundai, and so on, but even companies with supposedly purely domestic operations can have significant exposure to foreign currency exchange rates, as the economy has become truly global.

This exposure to currency risk creates uncertainty in the firm's ability to pay bondholders in the local currency, which adds to the bond's spread. Also, demand among foreign investors for the debt in a given currency (due to attractive relative yields) can influence the spread at which a bond is discounted. This means that the value of the average corporate bond, in its own currency, is partially dependent on exchange rates. This is similar to the observation that firms have multiple industry exposures, even if they are best classified by agencies within a particular one. Finally, as we will discuss later, interest rate parity suggests that relative spot curve changes will induce FX changes due to financial flows. Therefore the assumption that the cash flows and the discount rates of foreign bonds do not depend on exchange rates (both the local/foreign, but also foreign/foreign) is too strong and needs to be relaxed. We do this next.

For a domestic investor who invests in a foreign bond whose value is dependent on the exchange rate between the domestic and foreign currency, equation (11.15) will not hold. Instead, we have the following relationship between the derivative of the local currency price with respect to the (foreign-currency-based) risk factors:

$$\frac{\partial P_{Loc}}{\partial FX} = P_{Loc} + FX_{Loc,For} \cdot \frac{\partial P_{For}}{\partial FX} \tag{11.18}$$

In terms of duration this is:

$$D_{FX,Loc} = \frac{-1}{FX_{Loc,For}} + D_{FX,For} \tag{11.19}$$

Depending on the sign (both positive and negative exposures are possible) and magnitude of the foreign-currency-based FX duration term, the dollar-based hedge (that uses currency forwards equal to the foreign currency position value) will be too large or too small, and the dollar hedged portfolio will be over- or underhedged. Also, since the value of the foreign corporate bond could depend on multiple exchange rates, we need to determine the exposure to exchange rate risk between currencies other than just the local currency of the investor and the foreign currency that the payment of the bond's coupons are in. To measure the exposure to the risk due to the exchange rate between the foreign currency that the bond coupon payments are in and a second foreign currency that the bond cash flows (and hence spread) are sensitive to, we use basic calculus again to measure the local currency price sensitivity as:

$$\frac{\partial P_{Loc}}{\partial} = FX_{Loc,For} \cdot \frac{\partial P_{For}}{\partial FX_i} + \frac{\partial FX_{Loc,For}}{\partial FX_i} \cdot P_{For} \tag{11.20}$$

And in terms of durations this is:

$$D_{FX_i,Loc} = D_{FX_i,For} + \frac{-1}{FX_{Loc,For}} \cdot \frac{\partial FX_{Loc,For}}{\partial FX_i} \tag{11.21}$$

This says that the local currency return exposure to a foreign/foreign currency exchange rate is going to be equal to the foreign currency return exposure to that FX rate plus a term that depends on the correlation between the local/foreign and foreign/foreign exchange rates. Thus the local currency exposure to a second foreign exchange will be magnified or mollified based on whether the local currency is positively or negative correlated to it. This dependency of the foreign currency bond price on various global FX rates will show up in the higher-order and cross-order sensitivities as well. In particular, the local currency FX pure convexity will not be zero in general.

Thus to form a true (up to first order) currency hedge, we must use exchange rate forwards or futures not only between the local report currency and the currency that the bond coupons pay in, but also between the local currency and all currencies to which the foreign bond is exposed. The magnitude will depend on how exposed the foreign bond's foreign value is to each FX, as well as how correlated the local report currency is to each FX.

While this section has been devoted to currency risk as it relates to fixed income, it's worth pointing out that the preceding logic flows through directly to equity-only portfolios. In the equity risk management space, linear factor models that are regressed on equity returns are the norm. The Taylor framework still applies; we just estimate the currency durations from historical return data rather than through direct appeal to a pricing function. There are no messy higher-order terms to deal with, but the relationship between the equity return local currency exposures and foreign currency exposures holds. In particular, the dollar hedge will almost never be the correct one. Since we have favored using equity factor models to help drive corporate bond spreads through the Merton model framework (structural approach), it is worth presenting how this works for a global equity portfolio.

In Table 11.1, we compare the dollar hedged and currency exposure hedged positions for a sample portfolio of a few global large-cap equities. The currency of the investor, or report currency, is the U.S. dollar. The hedges are implemented by buying or selling foreign currencies. In the first panel, we show the portfolio positions by USD market value. In the second panel, we show the portfolio positions and the corresponding standard dollar hedges. In the third panel, we show the currency-exposure-based hedges using the equity factor model determined factor exposures to each currency. It is important to point out that this equity factor model allows each stock to have exposure to currencies beyond the clear exposure to its home currency. After controlling for home currency, residuals of the first-stage regression are subjected to further currency regressions against the dollar, yen, euro, and other global currencies, and only statistically significant betas are retained. Thus, betas to home currency and foreign currencies can occur, and they can be different from 1, even for the home currency. In particular, a stock can have negative beta to its home currency (UK-based mining companies, all of whose operations are outside of the United Kingdom and for whom the United Kingdom is a mere home office domicile, provide a good example of this). As can be seen, the hedges are very different between the two, with the UK pound hedge being twice the magnitude in the exposure hedge compared to the dollar hedge. In addition, the exposure-hedged portfolio includes hedges to the Canadian dollar, the Australian dollar, and the euro, which don't even appear in the dollar-hedged panel.

## Currency Unions and Interest Rate Parity

Finally, we discuss the relationship between currency risk and interest rate risk in currency unions or generally between any two currencies that are tied through a (government-supported) fixed exchange rate. Our prime example would be a hypothetical departure of one of the GIIPS countries (Greece, Italy, Ireland, Portugal, Spain) from the Eurozone, and a reintroduction of the pre-euro local currency, which would then float to the euro. With seemingly no historical exchange rate data to draw from, how could we measure the covariance of a reintroduced currency (e.g., new drachma) to the euro and other currencies so that we could stress-test a reintroduction and immediate devaluation of this hypothetical currency on a portfolio (even if that portfolio has no GIIPS domicile-based investments)?

**TABLE 11.1** Dollar hedge/currency exposure hedge example.

| | Portfolio | | | Dollar Hedged | | | Exposure Hedged | | |
|---|---|---|---|---|---|---|---|---|---|
| Grouped by Currency | Portfolio Shares | Portfolio Weight | Portfolio Ending Market Value | Portfolio Shares | Portfolio Weight | Portfolio Ending Market Value | Portfolio Shares | Portfolio Weight | Portfolio Ending Market Value |
| Total | | 100.000 | 3,764,091 | | 100.000 | 3,764,091 | | 100.000 | 3,764,089 |
| **British Pounds** | | 33.102 | 1,245,977 | | 33.102 | 1,245,977 | | 33.102 | 1,245,977 |
| Rio Tinto PLC | 10,000 | 18.213 | 685,549 | 10,000 | 18.213 | 685,549 | 10,000 | 18.213 | 685,549 |
| Standard Chartered PLC | 10,000 | 6.932 | 260,925 | 10,000 | 6.932 | 260,925 | 10,000 | 6.932 | 260,925 |
| Xstrata PLC | 10,000 | 5.894 | 221,842 | 10,000 | 5.894 | 221,842 | 10,000 | 5.894 | 221,842 |
| BP PLC | 10,000 | 2.063 | 77,661 | 10,000 | 2.063 | 77,661 | 10,000 | 2.063 | 77,661 |
| **Japanese Yen** | | 15.727 | 591,969 | | 15.727 | 591,969 | | 15.727 | 591,969 |
| Toshiba Corp. | 100,000 | 15.727 | 591,969 | 100,000 | 15.727 | 591,969 | 100,000 | 15.727 | 591,969 |
| **Swiss Franc** | | 7.745 | 291,545 | | 7.745 | 291,545 | | 7.745 | 291,545 |
| ABB Ltd. | 10,000 | 6.302 | 237,216 | 10,000 | 6.302 | 237,216 | 10,000 | 6.302 | 237,216 |
| Nestle S.A. | 1,000 | 1.443 | 54,329 | 1,000 | 1.443 | 64,329 | 1,000 | 1.443 | 54,329 |
| **U.S. Dollar** | | 43.426 | 1,634,600 | | 43.426 | 1,634,600 | | 43.426 | 1,634,600 |

| | | | | | | | | | |
|---|---|---|---|---|---|---|---|---|---|
| General Electric Co. | 20,000 | 10.701 | 402,800 | 20,000 | 10.701 | 402,800 | 20,000 | 10.701 | 402,800 |
| PowerShares DB Precious Metals Fund | 10,000 | 12.763 | 480,400 | 10,000 | 12.763 | 480,400 | 10,000 | 12.763 | 480,400 |
| PowerShares DB Gold Fund | 10,000 | 12.449 | 468,600 | 10,000 | 12.449 | 468,600 | 10,000 | 12.449 | 468,600 |
| PowerShares DB Energy Fund | 10,000 | 7.513 | 282,800 | 10,000 | 7.513 | 282,800 | 10,000 | 7.513 | 282,800 |
| **[Cash Dollar Hedged]** | | | | | — | 0 | | | |
| Buy U.S. Dollar | | | | 2,129,491 | 57 | 2,129,491 | | | |
| Sell Swiss Franc | | | | –273,950 | –7.745 | –291,545 | | | |
| Sell Japanese Yen | | | | 48,499,999 | –15.727 | –591,969 | | | |
| Sell British Pounds | | | | –777,885 | –33.102 | –1,245,977 | | | |
| **[Cash** Exposure Hedged] | | | | | | | | 0 | –1 |

*(Continued)*

**TABLE 11.1** (*Continued*)

| | Portfolio | | | Dollar Hedged | | | Exposure Hedged | | |
|---|---|---|---|---|---|---|---|---|---|
| Grouped by Currency | Portfolio Shares | Portfolio Weight | Portfolio Ending Market Value | Portfolio Shares | Portfolio Weight | Portfolio Ending Market Value | Portfolio Shares | Portfolio Weight | Portfolio Ending Market Value |
| Buy U.S. Dollar | | | | | | | 4,106,543 | 109.098 | 4,106,543 |
| Buy Canadian Dollar | | | | | | | 119,480 | 3.173 | 119,450 |
| Sell Australian Dollar | | | | | | | –124,371 | –3.294 | –123,998 |
| Sell Swiss Franc | | | | | | | –294,663 | –8.331 | –313,588 |
| Sell Japanese Yen | | | | | | | –47,907,650 | –15.635 | –584,738 |
| Sell Euro | | | | | | | –562,158 | –20.476 | –770,719 |
| Sell British Pounds | | | | | | | –1,518,934 | –64.636 | –2,432,953 |

*Source:* FactSet.

First, recall the (covered) interest rate parity formula that relates the interest rates and forward exchange rates between two sovereign countries:

$$(1 + r_{Loc}(T)) = \frac{FX(T, Loc, For)}{FX(0, Loc, For)} \cdot (1 + r_{For}(T)) \tag{11.22}$$

where $r_{Loc}(T)$ is the spot interest rate in some sovereign local currency with a maturity $T$, $r_{For}(T)$ is the spot interest rate of a foreign sovereign with maturity $T$, and $FX(T, Loc, For)$ is the maturity $T$ forward exchange rate giving the value of a unit of foreign currency in local currency. Note that the immediate-maturity forward $FX(0, Loc, For)$ is just the spot exchange rate. In the uncovered interest rate parity formula, the forward exchange rate is replaced by the FX futures value.

If we restrict our attention to short maturities, interest rate parity says that the short-horizon expected FX rate is largely determined by relative differences in the two sovereign's interest rates. It is a short leap to then say that short-term spot FX changes are driven primarily by relative interest rate movements. Over longer horizons, the drivers of the spot FX rate are more complicated and involve relative interest rate movements and relative long-range inflation movements. Since long-run inflation changes slowly relative to short-term interest rates, in the short term we can view spot FX rates as being primarily driven by financial flows, rather than trade flows.

A sovereign, through its central bank, can choose to control its short-term interest rate through open market operations. A sovereign also has control over its currency, and can choose to manage or fully peg its currency to that of another sovereign. If Greece had not joined the Eurozone, it still could have pegged the drachma to the euro, effectively adopting the euro as its own. Interest rate parity just says that a sovereign can choose to do one or the other, but not both.

There are two exceptions to this. First, for a short time, a country can use its foreign currency reserves to preserve a currency peg and an interest rate policy simultaneously, but this will last only as long as the reserves do. The second exception is when a country does not have free markets, so that foreign investment in domestic assets and domestic investment in foreign assets are regulated. In this case market forces cannot work to enforce parity. China is an example that has both—a regulated domestic market and vast USD reserves—allowing it to sustain a USD peg while still controlling domestic interest rates.

With that in mind, and using the euro as the main example of a currency union, there is very little practical difference between viewing the creation of the Eurozone and the euro in the following two ways:

1. On January 1, 1999, all Eurozone countries adopt a brand-new joint currency called the euro, which is issued by a new central bank called the European Central Bank (ECB) that is a holding bank for all formerly independent national central banks. Prior sovereign currencies cease to exist.
2. On January 1, 1999, all Eurozone countries decide to peg their currencies to the deutsche mark (DM) in a $N$:1 exchange rate, effectively outsourcing their central banks to Germany. Germany decided to rename the deutsche mark the euro in appreciation of this honor.

There are few meaningful differences between these two versions of reality. Since the sovereign debt of each Eurozone country is still subject to that country's law, there is no effective difference between a Greek bond issued in euros and a Greek bond issued in drachmas that contained a promise to keep the drachma pegged to the euro for the term of the bond. When it comes to risk management, we can adopt the view that there never really was a euro; there was a simultaneous pegging of 16 European sovereign currencies to the DM, and an abolition of any costs to exchange local money for German money as it flowed across national borders. The fact that you can't get your hands on a physical franc, peseta, or drachma banknote is irrelevant.

When discussing interest rate volatility risk, we made a point of emphasizing that if interest rate volatility were deterministic (i.e., nonrandom), then there is no interest rate volatility risk. Similarly, if interest rates were constant, there would be no interest rate risk. In a currency union (or whenever a sovereign pegs its currency to another) there is no individual sovereign currency risk, because the currencies are effectively pegged (i.e., the exchange rates are constant). Notice, however, that interest rate parity says that that risk does not simply vanish; it just gets transformed into interest rate and inflation risk. This is exactly what we have seen develop in the Eurozone. Once the credit crisis hit and erased the wave of global prosperity, the very real risks of owning Greek or Spanish or Irish debt started to grow. The prices of those government bonds had to fall relative to the bonds of the stronger countries like Germany. There are two alternatives for sovereigns in this situation generally; either yields rise or currencies depreciate. Since the currency had been pegged, this forced the risk to be expressed through a rise in bond yields. The European banking crisis is a direct result of the fact that Basel Accords allowed European banks to treat all Eurozone sovereign debt as if it had the same risk profile as German debt, and in particular allow it to have zero risk weighting toward regulatory capital. European banks naturally loaded up on the higher-yielding riskless debt. Interest rate parity says (and proved) that this was an error. In summary, interest rate parity tells us that sovereign government bond risk can neither be created nor destroyed through adoption or abandonment of a currency peg; it can only change its form.

We can use this to ask the question: what happens if one of the GIIPS member countries abandons the euro?

The first thing that would happen is the formerly constant exchange ratio between the euro (DM) and the relisted GIIPS sovereign currency would become random (i.e., float) again. This randomness creates currency risk. Since total risk should be preserved, it will also reduce interest rate risk. Indeed, a prime motivation for abandoning the euro for a GIIPS country would be precisely in order to lower borrowing costs. Interest rate parity tells us how interest rate risk and currency risk are related, but it does not tell us how low domestic interest rates would go in the event a GIIPS country abandoned the euro. Let's assume for the moment that the sovereign decides to peg its interest rate to the euro (German) benchmark.

Let's take Greece as an example. Assume that Greece abandons the euro and revalues all of its euro-based debt in reissued drachmas. It then uses open market operations of its repatriated central bank to set interest rates to align with the euro benchmark curve. Regardless of whether the outstanding debt had high coupons, the yields on these bonds will fall in line with new issues whose coupons are set to price them at par. Alternatively, the Greek government could choose to haircut coupons on former euro issues to rates consistent with the par yields it is striving to obtain. The result of this is that the Greek drachma would quickly devalue relative to the euro. We can determine how much by just solving the interest rate parity equation. If we assumed that the new Greece yield curve and the euro benchmark curve were identical, then the spot FX rate would have to be the ratio of the old Greece yield to the new Greece yield. Assuming that the 10-year Greek spot rate was 22 percent and the euro benchmark 10-year spot rate was 1.5 percent, the drachma/euro FX rate would have to devalue by roughly 20 percent.

With this in hand, we would like to stress-test our portfolio to see how a 20 percent devaluation of the new drachma would impact it. This poses some problems. To conduct the most robust stress test, we need to alter our exposures to interest rates, interest rate volatility, spreads, and other currencies to make room for the new drachma and the new drachma-based yield curve. We also need to reestimate spread and interest rate factors themselves, and then reestimate the factor covariance matrix.

This is a tall order just to test a hypothetical Eurozone departure. If Greece did abandon the euro, we wouldn't have a choice, but given the level of effort involved, a less costly alternative is to treat the new drachma as a latent factor and to determine how the factors of our current multi-asset-class risk model covary with this latent new currency factor. In doing this, we would feel confident that our measure of the total risk would be reasonable, but that our contributions from specific risk factors would be misspecified. The benefit is that this leaves us with only the more manageable problem of finding a good proxy for the new currency factor that we could use to create a historical time series that we could use to estimate covariances with. That is, we would like to create a sort of "ether" currency that has the same properties that the drachma would have had, if Greece had never adopted the euro in the first place. Not surprisingly, we use interest rate parity to create such an ether drachma.

We assumed that Greece would have set its interest rate policy so that its government curve would have matched the euro benchmark curve to determine that the size of the drachma devaluation would be around 20 percent. We can create an alternate reality where Greece had maintained a rate peg to the euro benchmark rather than a currency peg to the euro to construct our ether drachma. There is nothing unique about Greece, of course, and we could have done this with any of the GIIPS or other Eurozone countries. In Figure 11.15 we show what the ether currency exchange rate would have looked like for several other Eurozone countries to demonstrate how interest rate parity can be used to construct ether currencies in general.

With the ether drachma defined and a historical exchange rate established, we can perform latent factor stress tests to a hypothetical 20 percent devaluation on the drachma. In Figure 11.16 we show the results of such a stress test on a global equity portfolio. We show the effect on an unhedged global equity portfolio, along with the exposure hedged and dollar hedged portfolios. We also show the S&P Global 100 and the MSCI EAFE for comparison.

As expected, the global portfolio has a bad day. What is interesting is that while the dollar hedged portfolio does significantly better than the unhedged portfolio, the exposure hedged portfolio outperforms the dollar hedge by a wide margin, –3 percent exposure hedge to –9 percent dollar hedge. Finally, even for the currency exposure hedged portfolio there is still an unavoidable loss. This is partly because of the interaction effects that even the exposure hedge does not take into account. Unfortunately, these interaction effects are very difficult to fully hedge, as investment vehicles that isolate them are not easy to find. Nontheless, the exposure hedged portfolio cannot officially be hedged against the drachma, simply because the drachma doesn't exist. You cannot buy or sell drachma forwards! It's the

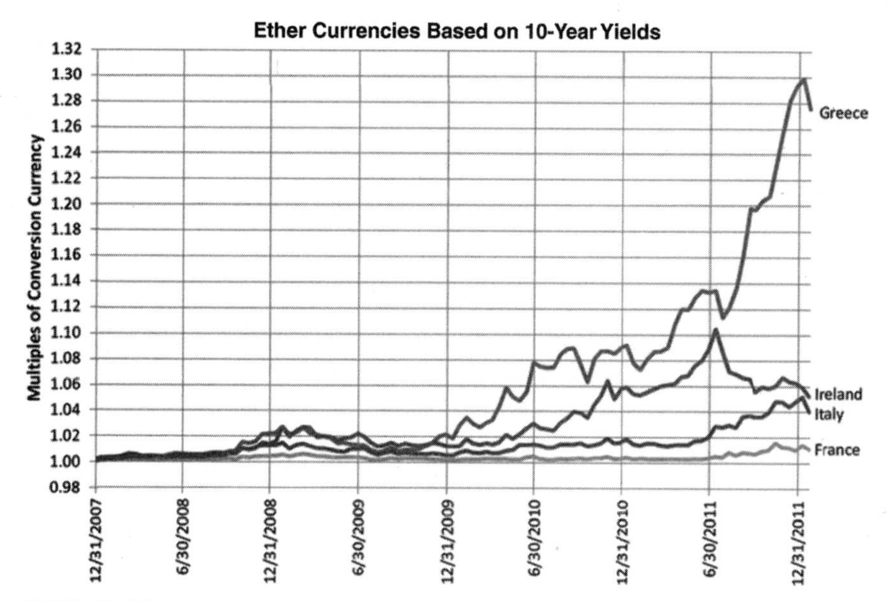


**FIGURE 11.15** Some ether currency FX multipliers for some Eurozone sovereigns.
*Source:* FactSet.

resultant covariance between currencies in general that performs the hedging operation that is still present.

## CONCLUSION

We discussed the contribution from interest rates and idiosyncratic effects to risk and how currency risk can be included in the Taylor framework to make our fixed income risk discussion truly globally aware. Of the three, idiosyncratic risks are the hardest to pin down simply because the price itself is, well, a moving target and usually not marked to market for most bonds due to illiquidity. We showed how the full nonlinearity of the FX risk can be computed to measure a total risk exposure (e.g., VaR). We have also shown how the FX conversion formula can be differentiated to measure the contribution of currency risk specifically through the standard Taylor linearization. We mentioned how the higher-order and interaction effects can appear and be measured. In doing this, we pointed out that when the cash flows of our security (be it bond or equity) are themselves dependent on exchange rates, a plain dollar hedge will be insufficient to truly capture all of the risk. With equities being the most exposed asset class to this phenomenon,

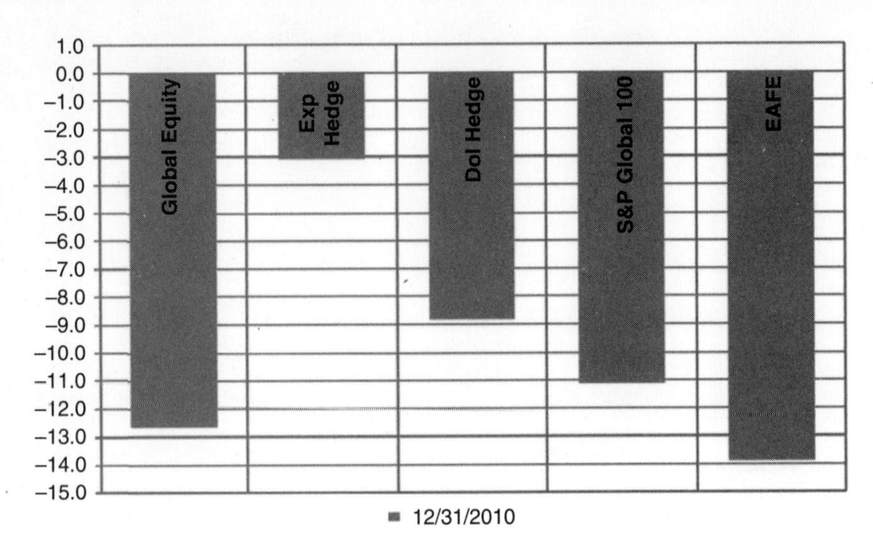


**FIGURE 11.16** Unhedged, exposure hedged, and dollar hedged portfolios in a 20 percent ether drachma devaluation stress test.
*Source:* FactSet.

we highlighted the concept using an equity portfolio and equity risk model as an example. Finally, we discussed how to measure the currency risk for a currency union breakup by outlining the effective implications of a currency peg. We showed how interest rate parity can be used to create "ether" currencies and how we can use those ether currencies to perform stress tests of hypothetical abandonment of a currency peg.

## NOTES

1. R. Jarrow, H. Li, and F. Zhao, "Interest Rate Caps Smile Too! But Can the LIBOR Market Models Capture the Smile?" *Journal of Finance*, February 2007.
2. Ibid.
3. R. Rebonato, K. McKay, and R. White, *The SABR/LIBOR Market Model: Pricing, Calibration and Hedging for Complex Interest-Rate Derivatives* (Hoboken, NJ: John Wiley & Sons, 2009).
4. R. Rebonato and R. White, "Linking Caplets and Swaptions Prices in the LMM-SABR Model," *Journal of Computational Finance*, 2009.
5. V. Jamshidian, "LIBOR and Swap Market Models and Measures," *Financial Stochastics*, 1990.
6. Jarrow, Li, and Zhao consider a Heston model for the stochastic volatility, with and without a jump component.

CHAPTER 12

# Portfolio Risk Measures

*William F. McCoy, CFA, PRM, and Steven P. Greiner, PhD*

At this point, we've discussed risk either as a concept or as it relates to a particular asset class. In upcoming chapters, we will discuss risk models in greater detail. However, it is a good idea to spend some time discussing risk measures themselves as they relate to the total portfolio. This chapter reviews the attributes of any good risk measure and discusses some commonly used risk measures.

Variance, tracking error (TE), and value at risk (VaR) are all commonly used risk measures. Each of these measures answers a specific question regarding the variability of a portfolio, but no measure answers all questions. Depending on the assumptions used, each of these measures can be translated into the others.

A secondary issue relates to the underlying mathematics of risk. Expected return is a linear function, with its associated ease of computation. In the classic Markowitz framework, risk is a quadratic function, based on an individual security's variance and its covariance with other securities, simply because of the squared term in the definition of variance. There are two important implications of the last sentence. First is the nonlinear nature of a risk calculation. Whether risk is quadratic or some other formula, the calculation of risk is more difficult and requires more complex mathematics than the calculation of return. Additionally, it is the interaction of each security with the other that relates to covariance. No security is an island unto itself, simply because it has vendors and customers that force some covariation with them, especially while in a portfolio. Last, risk measures dispersion. The focus is on the change in return, not on the known levels, and of course risk is relative to your objective. In an absolute return portfolio, risk is the variation of the portfolio itself. However, once a benchmark is introduced, risk is the variation of the portfolio versus its benchmark.

## COHERENT RISK MEASURES

Coherent risk measures became a topic in the late 1990s with the appearance of two papers.[1] These papers went on to help risk managers for the first time define statistical properties that revealed risk in the most sensible and usable manner. Some people go so far as to say that if a common risk statistic isn't coherent, it's not a risk measure at all.[2] While we won't go that far, we do believe attention to the definition of coherence can be useful.

There are four properties for a risk measure to be coherent: subadditivity, monotonicity, homogeneity, and translation invariance.

Subadditivity is the property that a portfolio can only risk an amount no larger than the sum of the risks of the individual assets. Usually, however, due to diversification in a portfolio, the portfolio risk is less than the sum of the parts, which are the assets' risks. Subadditivity is useful in that diversification only helps you, and your risk measure is not explosive.

Monotonicity is the property that if some portfolio under all scenarios has less risk than some other portfolio, then the risk of the first must be less than the risk of the second. Obviously, "all" scenarios is infinitely difficult to estimate, but the intent of this property makes sense. Monotonicity is useful in that a lower risk measure implies a lower risk in all states of the world.

Homogeneity implies that if you double the size of the portfolio, you double the risk. Risk has to be linearly related to the size of the portfolio with a zero intercept, because the risk of holding no assets must be zero, too.

Translation invariance implies that if you add a riskless asset to the portfolio, the risks of the new portfolio cannot be greater than the risks of the original portfolio. In fact, if the asset is an insurance-like asset (a true hedge), the risk of the new portfolio must be less than the risk of the original. Unfortunately, though not widely known, coherent risk measures are inconsistent with utility theory. If security X is preferred over Y by some risk-averse investor maximizing $X > Y$, it may happen that X carries a greater risk as specified by some coherent risk measure.[3] This led to an additional axiom being added to monotonicity, called isotonicity, which marries the investor preferences into the criteria.

Taken together, these criteria would imply useful standards for any risk measure. The sad truth is that many commonly used risk measures fall short on at least one of these criteria. For that reason, it is important to be aware of the strengths and weaknesses of each risk measure.

## COMMONLY USED RISK MEASURES

Go to www.wiley.com/go/greiner to watch video titled "Risk Measures."

For an absolute return manager, possibly the most commonly used risk measure is the total *ex ante* forecasted risk of the portfolio. In the classic Markowitz framework, the total risk was captured by the variance of the portfolio. If returns are assumed to be normally distributed, variance is sufficient to describe the distribution of possible returns. Even given the nonlinearity of the variance calculation, assuming normality made the analytics easier to work with as opposed to one of Markowitz's original recommendations using semivariance. As an interesting aside, in Harry Markowitz's keynote lecture for the shared Nobel Prize in 1990, we read:

> *But perhaps there is an alternative. Perhaps some other measure of portfolio risk will serve in a two parameter analysis for some of the utility functions which are a problem to variance. For example, in Chapter 9 of Markowitz (1959) I propose the "semi-variance" S as a measure of risk.*[4] *Semi-variance seems more plausible than variance as a measure of risk, since it is concerned only with adverse deviations. But, as far as I know, to date no one has determined whether there is a substantial class of utility functions for which mean-semi-variance succeeds while mean-variance fails to provide an adequate approximation to expected utility.*

However, as has been discussed several times in this book, returns are not normally distributed. Variance can understate the likelihood of extreme events if the underlying data has fat tails. Moreover, variance is not coherent. It fails a variation of the monotonicity attribute. Still, used properly, variance can be a useful measure of the dispersion about the mean of the distribution.

If the portfolio is managed versus a benchmark, then tracking error is the most commonly used statistic. Tracking error is simply the standard deviation of the active return of the portfolio versus the benchmark. Like variance, it reflects the dispersion about the mean of the excess return distribution, but does not capture any fat tail behaviors. Moreover, tracking error fails the homogeneity test of coherence. For instance, doubling the size of the portfolio still implies the same relative mismatch.

Total risk can also be decomposed into systematic and idiosyncratic risk. Systematic risk is the risk due to common factors of the portfolio, while idiosyncratic risk is that portion of total risk not attributed to any common factors, usually thought of as independent and identically distributed (i.i.d.) for each asset and noncorrelated with common factors or idiosyncratic risks of other assets. In essence, specific risks are what are left over in the returns distribution after one removes all common components of correlation between the assets. Most models of systematic risk are linear and uncorrelated by construction, so the portfolio total risks are linear as a result. Systematic risk analysis is used by performance analysts in the search for cheap providers of market exposure. Idiosyncratic risk, in contrast, is very messy. While financial theory dictates that idiosyncratic risk can be diversified away, and therefore not compensated, in practice, alpha is usually discovered in idiosyncratic risk. In practice, idiosyncratic risk is highly skewed, fat-tailed, nonlinear, and not uncorrelated.

In their original form, most of the risk measures discussed so far describe normally distributed events and risks about the central tendency of the return distribution. Value at risk (VaR) was proposed in the 1980s as a risk measure to address these and other shortcomings. VaR is the probability the minimum loss will be of this magnitude over the given horizon and confidence limit. The original form of VaR is parametric, in that it assumes a normal distribution. To calculate parametric VaR, all that is needed are security exposures, standard deviations, and correlations. The parametric VaR could then be derived using the normal distribution at any desired confidence limit.

To truly overcome the nonnormality of returns, Monte Carlo (MC) VaR must be used. The nonnormality of returns can occur for two reasons. First, the linear asset could be subject to a nonnormal distribution, have fat tails, and exhibit kurtosis, especially during crisis. Monte Carlo VaR can overcome this via use of nonnormal sampling distributions for the asset returns (i.e., t-distribution, for instance). The second reason is that the payoff function of the security can be nonlinear like in an option. However, it is possible to overcome this situation by using a pricing function to derive the new security value in the simulated market environment. That is, the price of the underlying for a derivative can be linear, while the derivative's price is a nonlinear function of the underlying, and of course one knows the formula.

All of these benefits come at the price of increased complexity and computation time. VaR may also be difficult to derive supporting analytics for. Essentially, each security in the portfolio in each environment is revalued and summed, the portfolio returns are sorted, and the confidence limit is retrieved. This process is very different from a smooth and continuous formula, such as variance. The consequence is that some variance-based risk statistics are not easily computed for VaR-based measures, and are difficult in portfolio optimization. Finally, one last nuance of VaR should be mentioned. Earlier, we noted that risk is focused on change or fluctuation and can ignore known or mean return. Since VaR is an absolute level (a quantile) at some point on the distribution, the known return shifts the distribution left or right, though the relative ranking of each security's returns remains the same.

Additionally, however, VaR has some problems as a coherent risk measure.[5] VaR violates subadditivity, though simulations have shown it's not as bad in this regard as was first thought. That the VaR of a portfolio can be higher than the sum of the VaRs of the individual assets in the portfolio is the reason for the violation. There are two areas where the violation is most likely to occur: when the underlying assets have *huge* fat tails and when events that normally are extremely rare occur in the middle of the historical return distribution.[6] For instance, consider two 10-year bonds where each bond has an independent default probability of 3 percent over the next year. Individually, the annual 95 percent VaR is zero for a 3 percent probable loss that is less than 5 percent, meaning over the next year, the 5 percent probable minimum loss is zero owning just one bond. In an equal-weighted portfolio, however, there are three outcomes, either both default with a probability of $(0.03)^2$, neither defaults with a probability of $(0.97)^2$, or either bond defaults with a probability of $2 * 0.03 * 0.97$ since there are two bonds. This latter probability evaluates to 5.82 percent, meaning that collectively the 95 percent VaR is greater for the portfolio than for the individual assets. You can view the risks here as largely fat-tailed for the portfolio return, which is a small cash flow with some interest rate risk overlaid, so that regular volatility of return is low (unless there's default, in which case the volatility jumps by multiples of daily standard deviation of return). Or you can interpret it as a large event risk happening. Either way, the VaR is shown to be in violation of nonadditivity.

The nonadditivity violation has to do with the probability of a loss equal to the VaR not having any bearing on the actual value of the VaR. So, for the subadditivity violation to kick in, so to speak, the distribution of returns has to be so fat that the second moment, the standard deviation of return, is so large that it approaches infinity, or, more appropriately, it is not a naturally arising economic scale parameter, nor recurring. It also would yield a return distribution under this scenario, described more accurately by a Cauchy or Lorentzian distribution rather than a t-distribution with, say, 4 degrees of freedom (as, for example, in Chapter 7, where we report that 10 years of daily returns of the S&P 100 fit a t-distribution with 4.11 degrees of freedom). We would add that if returns are normally distributed (conflicting all empirical evidence), then VaR would indeed be coherent. Violations occur, for the most part, only during a Black Swan or when an extinction-level event happens. The majority of time cataclysmic events aren't happening, giving credence that VaR isn't such a bad measure.

Subadditivity violations can occur, for instance, when some currency pegged to the dollar suddenly becomes unpegged. Consider the jump that could occur in the euro if Germany left the Eurozone and let the euro devalue abruptly. These kinds of stochastic jumps could lead to a VaR violation of subadditivity. In contrast, a portfolio of equity securities and corporate bonds numbering in the hundreds most likely wouldn't entertain a large, sudden move in prices leading to a VaR violation of the rule. They certainly could move enough to breach the VaR, but that's not the same thing as a violation of the subadditivity rule. Option portfolios can be constructed in such a way as to give super-fat tails, and certainly holding a concentrated portfolio of high-yield bonds (where the return is coupon mostly) where several bonds suddenly default could lead to subadditivity violations as well. So one must be a little careful when managing a portfolio based on VaR, but for most applications VaR is an acceptable risk measure. Certainly being aware of the VaR value is helpful at a minimum, but being mindful where higher VaR values come from within a less risky portfolio is also important. Again, we reiterate that major covariance/correlation disruptions due to event risk aren't modeled by simply computing a VaR and moving further out into the tail to 99.9 percent confidence interval (CI), for instance, and losses during these events that breach the VaR may not involve subadditivity violations.

Last, for relative VaR, the odds of a subadditivity violation decrease dramatically. Given a portfolio whose VaR violates subadditivity, we can always create a benchmark similar enough such that relative or active VaR will not violate subadditivity. Given that in general benchmarks are similar enough to the portfolio that the inherent asset types that lead to the violation are included in each, relative VaR can be a more meaningful descriptor of risk. Consider the gedankenexperiment of the two bonds mentioned earlier, each with 3 percent default probabilities, where a benchmark exists that holds these two bonds plus two more bonds of similar but different default probabilities, equally weighted. The relative VaR would not violate subadditivity under these conditions.

FactSet has the capabilities of offering Monte Carlo VaR for multiple asset classes in its Balanced Risk product. This solution is a global multi-asset-class (MAC) platform for performing this type of risk analysis. It provides estimates of the entire distribution of the portfolio returns and allows for calculation of various risk statistics such as tracking error, value at risk (VaR), expected tail loss, kurtosis, skewness, and others. The system consists of the following:

- A FactSet Balanced Risk multi-asset-class factor model, which unites equity, currency, and fixed income risks across global markets.
- A Monte Carlo simulation algorithm, which uses multi-asset-class models to create numerous scenarios from which a distribution of returns is calculated.
- An extensive asset-pricing algorithm for fixed income and derivatives, which uses the output of Monte Carlo simulation and repricing algorithms to ultimately compute returns whose covarying risks are calculated.

- FactSet's flexible reporting platform, which allows for calculation of portfolio risk statistics and their asset contributions to these risks, as well as easy porting of portfolios and data to other modules of FactSet.

To produce VaR in a separate and distinct calculation, Monte Carlo–generated numbers are run to simulate factor returns for equities, commodities, interest rates, and spreads for fixed income, and hypothetical exchange rates for currencies. These MC-generated numbers, which proxy for interest rates, spreads, and equity factor returns, are then combined and multiplied by a Cholesky matrix to generate a set of data that has a covariance matrix similar to the starting one. The resultant interest rates and spreads are then used in the repricing algorithms to generate fixed income prices and ultimately returns, while the equity and commodity factors are multiplied by exposures to calculate returns. In this way, numerous generated returns are produced, and the VaR is calculated from their return distribution at a chosen level of confidence: 68, 90, 95, or 99 percent, for example. Conditional value at risk (CVaR), the expected tail loss (ETL), is also available, as are marginal contributions to VaR.

With a VaR estimate at a chosen confidence level, there is still estimation error. To assess a confidence limit on the VaR, FactSet simply takes the 5,000 returns calculated under MC-VaR from security-level analytics and performs bootstrap resampling with replacement 1,000 times with them. For each of the 1,000 bootstraps, one calculates the VaR at the same CI as the original VaR the user has chosen. Then, the distribution of the 1,000 VaRs will lead to robust nonparametric estimates of the VaR and give statistics on its error. For instance, some raw results of just such a calculation are:

| sample.var95 | better.var95 | lowerCI95 | upperCI95 |
|---|---|---|---|
| –2.017444 | –2.020867 | –2.128 | –1.913733 |

One should never report these values out to this significance in practice, however. Nevertheless, the sample VaR at 95 percent CI is –2.017, and the mean of the 95 percent VaR from the 1,000 bootstraps is a negative –2.021. The mean of the 1,000 VaRs from the bootstrap offers a better estimate of the VaR than using the original data. Additionally, we can state with 95 percent confidence that the real VaR is somewhere between –1.914 and –2.128 based on the results of the bootstrap. So yes, confidence intervals on confidence intervals can be performed appropriately.

## MARGINAL CONTRIBUTION

Once a manager has the portfolio risk statistics available, the next step is to manage that risk. One key statistic is how each security contributes to the overall risk of the portfolio. These statistics are the marginal contributions of risk. For the marginal contributions to risk, one could have these in the numeraire of the base currency or in percentages of the portfolio.

The *marginals* represent the derivative of risk with respect to the weight of the assets in a mathematical sense. They can be interpreted more broadly in an economic sense to be directives of whether risk is increasing or decreasing should the asset's weight in the portfolio be increased or decreased, depending on the sign of that derivative. It holds for small changes in asset weights, however. If you increase the weight of an asset from 25 bps to 10 percent of the portfolio, the marginal contribution won't accurately predict what will happen to the portfolio risk for that large a change. The marginals give one a direct connection between whether the asset is diversifying or concentrating risk. Additionally, their relative magnitude offers some information about the asset's approximate importance in the portfolio as compared to the other assets, with the caveat that one shouldn't rely too much on that comparison. Too often investors will misinterpret as meaningful the contributions to risk from two securities where the values are 2.1 percent and 1.9 percent. One must understand that the estimation error can be half a percentage point or so, such that distinguishing contributions to risk between two securities of 1 and 3 percent is estimable, but not between 2.1 and 1.9 percent. We revisit this topic in great detail in Chapter 17. Investors' own tolerances they place on their alpha estimates are too large to distinguish between return estimates of individual securities, too (mostly). Investors should practice this application when considering risk estimates as well.

An explicit calculation of the marginal contribution to any risk factor involves computing the risk measure with and without the asset in the portfolio. Alternatively, producing the risk measure by increasing the weight of an asset by 1 percent while prorating the remaining weights so they sum correctly across all other assets and then comparing with the original calculation also allows marginal determination. This latter method allows one to interpret the measure by stating, "A 1 percent increase in weight moves the risk so and so," whereas the former method changes the definition slightly because the derivative of risk with respect to weight then pivots on a weight of zero, which means it's ill-defined and a singularity in the risk equation. Obviously, however, the difference between the risk measure with and without the asset is a sufficient proxy to allow determination of whether the risk is increasing or decreasing with the asset weight. These are technical points, but the interpretation of the marginal contribution is dependent on how you calculate it.

We are confident that risk measures related to deviation are close relatives of coherent measures so that the standard deviations of risk calculated from any of the vendor risk models are substantially risk measures.[7] The following illustrates the parametric risk measures we have on the FactSet system, in general for any risk model.

- Total risk, the *ex ante* forecast of the volatility of the portfolio (or asset) in variance or standard deviation units.
- Systematic (systemic, factor, or common) risk, that portion of total risk attributed to the common factors of the risk model. These can be in variance units or standard deviations.
- Stock (asset)-specific or idiosyncratic risks, that portion of total risk not attributed to any common factors, usually thought of as independent and identically distributed for each asset and noncorrelated with common factors or idiosyncratic risks of other assets. These can be in variance units or standard deviations. In essence, specific risks are what are left over in the returns distribution after one removes all common components of correlation between the assets.
- Value at risk, the probability that the minimum loss will be of this magnitude over the given horizon and confidence limit.
- Conditional value at risk (CVaR) or expected tail loss (ETL).
- Tracking error, the standard deviation of the excess return distribution for any horizon between a portfolio and its benchmark.

These measures can be either in absolute measures or relative (active) to any benchmark.

This short section might have confused more than it explained, and that is intentional. It discussed the theoretical aspects of a good risk measure, and covered several commonly used risk measures. We then proceeded to show the uses and shortcomings of each of these measures. In short, all risk measures have deficiencies, and the wise risk analyst will use multiple measures to build his or her intuition of the portfolio's potential variability.

## STRESS-TESTING

Go to www.wiley.com/go/greiner to see video titled "Stress Testing."

Given any risk estimate, there is a close cousin related to calculating risk measures, and that is doing it under a stressed portfolio situation or in a stressed market environment. In particular, Undertakings for Collective Investment in Transferable Securities (UCITS) regulations list criteria required for acceptance of their validation that involve stress-testing. Their stress-testing requirements to obtain UCITS eligibility include:

- Cover all major risks.
- Test risks not captured by a VaR model (used for primary UCITS requirement).
- Look for risks driving portfolio or fund net asset value (NAV) below zero.
- Focus on risks that would be expected to be significant when the portfolio is stressed.
- Carry out stress-testing minimally at monthly frequency.
- Implement clear procedures related to design and ongoing considerations and testing (i.e., document the process).

These stress-testing criteria from UCITS, though extensive, do not issue specificity as to how to perform them. It's left to the portfolio, risk manager, or fund compliance department to design the tests and carry them out. You can be sure the UCITS oversight committee will examine all supporting reasoning justifying carrying out the stress test.

To assist with this task, we have on the FactSet system several methods for calculating risk measures given stresses applied to the portfolio and a wide capability of reporting the results. This solution lets users perform both historical stress tests and hypothetical factor shocks using any of FactSet's extensive data libraries. The first of these methods calculates the beta between some stress and vendor risk model factors; hence it's called Factor Stress Tests. All one needs to perform this function is a time series of returns to model the chosen stress.

For example, suppose you're interested in examining the impact that rising oil prices have on your portfolio, specifically a 30 percent rise in oil price. Given the return to oil price time series, one first calculates the beta between each and every factor return in the user's chosen risk model. Given this new beta, compute new factor returns by multiplying it times the size of the shock applied to the stress, in this case +30. To finish the calculation and compute a portfolio return estimate due to the shock, we simply multiply each new factor return times the current exposure for that factor and compute their sum. The default is to use all available data to compute the beta, so whichever has the shorter history, the stress or risk model determines the length of time used to compute the betas.

Figure 12.1 depicts a bunch of preselected factors within the Risk in Portfolio Attribution (PA) product. There are sector indexes falling and rising, currency foreign exchange, and ordinary benchmarks already set up; however, it's quite easy to create your own as well.

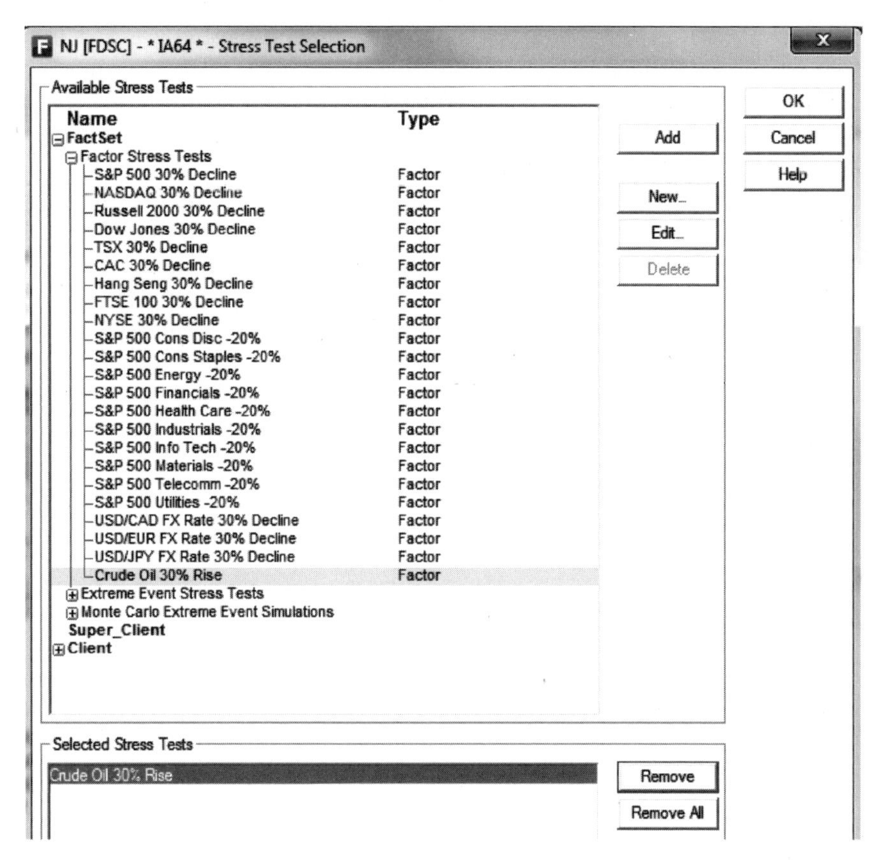


**FIGURE 12.1** The FactSet predefined factor stress tests with the system.

There are two choices available in addition: whether one would like to use time weighting or event weighting. Time weighting is the conventional method described earlier whereby one has a time series of the stress and of the risk factor returns synchronous in time as they actually happened (chronological). The beta calculated, then, is a historical beta between the pair. *Event weighting* simply re-sorts the stress time-series data, realigning the largest values whenever they occurred. The stress is no longer chronological in this method. In this way, one is able to emphasize the size of the stress more closely in time to the current situation. It mimics a larger event occurring than the time weighting would depict.

To emphasize an advantage of event weighting, remember Chapter 7, where we discussed exponential decay rates applied to the data when you form the covariance matrix. Typically half-lives are of the order of a year or so for a daily updating risk model. Well, we commented that most market participants remember events, not history, in a decaying exponential fashion. Hence a covariance matrix weighted by events is still waiting to be created. In event weighting a shock in a stress test, in essence one is sorting the shock such that the major events in its time series are frontmost and prominent, thus electrifying the result of the stress and putting the events in the order humans probably remember them. The shock is sorted by how market participants remember it.

To offer an example output for stress-testing, we have in Table 12.1 a large-cap value portfolio and we show the output using the R-Squared Global Equity Risk model for two stresses, one for oil increasing 30 percent and one for precious metals falling by 30 percent. The energy sector is expanded in the attribution report, so one can see the return estimates as of the report date, 6/30/2011, for the individual stocks. We computed time-weighting as well as event-weighting stress tests. Interestingly, most of the energy stocks have a positive performance estimate for oil rising, but have losses for precious metals falling. Likewise the effect is more pronounced in time weighting for oil rising, but larger in magnitude for precious metals falling on average. The top-level numbers for the portfolio illustrate that the gains are larger for the portfolio versus its benchmark (S&P 500) if oil rises, while the losses are greater for the portfolio for falling metals prices. Hence a conclusion here might be that given both scenarios, the riskier situation is metals falling. However, if you're a believer that event weighting more appropriately captures market participants' reactions to the event, then the oil shock is hardly a gain in comparison to the losses of metals falling.

The R-Squared risk model is a short-horizon model good for two-day to two-month risk horizons, but we can change the risk model to a longer-horizon model if we substitute with the Northfield Information Systems (NIS) U.S. Fundamental model. This is a monthly risk model with monthly updates and five years' look-back. Table 12.2 offers the longer-horizon view and looks very similar to Table 12.1, even after the risk model was changed to Northfield's. The qualitative results are similar, suggesting the robustness of calculating the beta between stresses and risk model factor returns. Moreover, the gains are still greater for the portfolio should oil rise, and the losses are greater should precious metals fall versus the benchmark, so the story is consistent.

Currently, at this writing FactSet can do stress tests only for fundamental equity risk models with fixed income stress-testing on the operations plan. We're also working on an improvement to the factor stress test whereby we take into account the correlation between the stress and the factor returns. For instance, currently, the new factor return is simply the beta between the stress with the old factor return, multiplied by the size of the stress.

**TABLE 12.1** Using the R-Squared Daily Global Risk model, we computed stress tests of two shocks for a large-cap U.S. domestic portfolio for oil rising 30 percent and precious metals falling 30 percent.

**Percent of Total Holdings**
**LC-VALUE vs. S&P 500**
**6/30/2011**
**U.S. Dollar**

| | | | R-Squared Daily Global Equity Model (USD) | | | | | | | |
|---|---|---|---|---|---|---|---|---|---|---|
| | | | Crude Oil 30% Rise | | | | Precious Metals – 30% Loss | | | |
| Economic Sector | Portfolio Weight | Benchmark Weight | Percent Return (Time Wght) | Benchmark Percent Return (Time Wght) | Percent Returnt (Event Wght) | Benchmark Percent Return (Event Wght) | Percent Return (Time Wght) | Benchmark Percent Return (Time Wght) | Percent Return (Event Wght) | Benchmark Percent Return (Event Wght) |
| **Total** | **100.00** | **100.00** | **6.546** | **5.242** | **2.549** | **1.850** | **–7.329** | **–6.615** | **–12.207** | **–9.335** |
| **Consumer Discretionary** | 25.32 | 10.53 | 1.122 | 0.450 | 0.490 | 0.187 | –0.873 | –0.450 | –2.405 | –0.927 |
| **Consumer Staples** | 6.02 | 10.68 | 0.225 | 0.275 | 0.090 | 0.082 | –0.197 | –0.419 | –0.460 | –0.375 |
| **Energy** | **13.63** | **12.63** | **1.889** | **1.401** | **0.670** | **0.513** | **–2.547** | **–2.002** | **–2.933** | **–2.016** |
| CARBO Ceramics Inc. | 1.21 | — | 0.124 | | 0.039 | | –0.189 | | –0.213 | |
| RPC Inc. | 1.19 | — | 0.184 | | 0.070 | | –0.270 | | –0.345 | |
| Holly Corp. | 1.16 | — | 0.176 | | 0.058 | | –0.183 | | –0.256 | |
| Range Resources Corp. | 1.08 | 0.07 | 0.156 | 0.011 | 0.063 | 0.004 | –0.210 | –0.014 | –0.206 | –0.014 |

*(continued)*

**TABLE 12.1** *(Continued)*

| | | | R-Squared Daily Global Equity Model (USD) | | | | | | | |
|---|---|---|---|---|---|---|---|---|---|---|
| | | | Crude Oil 30% Rise | | | | Precious Metals – 30% Loss | | | |
| Economic Sector | Portfolio Weight | Benchmark Weight | Percent Return (Time Wght) | Benchmark Percent Return (Time Wght) | Percent Returnt (Event Wght) | Benchmark Percent Return (Event Wght) | Percent Return (Time Wght) | Benchmark Percent Return (Time Wght) | Percent Return (Event Wght) | Benchmark Percent Return (Event Wght) |
| Frontier Oil | 1.04 | — | 0.118 | | 0.036 | | –0.113 | | –0.214 | |
| Patterson-UTI Energy Inc. | 1.00 | — | 0.161 | | 0.062 | | –0.254 | | –0.251 | |
| Helmerich & Payne Inc. | 0.99 | 0.06 | 0.136 | 0.008 | 0.055 | 0.003 | –0.191 | –0.011 | –0.202 | –0.012 |
| SM Energy Co. | 0.95 | — | 0.163 | | 0.068 | | –0.219 | | –0.245 | |
| Concho Resources Inc. | 0.81 | — | 0.128 | | 0.037 | | –0.198 | | –0.152 | |
| Cabot Oil & Gas Corp. | 0.79 | 0.06 | 0.127 | 0.009 | 0.041 | 0.003 | –0.159 | –0.012 | –0.205 | –0.015 |
| Oil States International Inc. | 0.76 | — | 0.096 | | 0.039 | | –0.139 | | –0.159 | |

| | | | | | | | | | | |
|---|---|---|---|---|---|---|---|---|---|---|
| El Paso Corp. | 0.71 | 0.13 | 0.077 | 0.014 | 0.034 | 0.006 | –0.112 | –0.020 | –0.113 | –0.020 |
| Core Laboratories N.V. | 0.66 | — | 0.059 | | 0.011 | | –0.084 | | –0.082 | |
| Tesoro Corp. | 0.65 | 0.03 | 0.094 | 0.004 | 0.029 | 0.001 | –0.104 | –0.004 | –0.128 | –0.005 |
| Halliburton Co. | 0.63 | 0.39 | 0.089 | 0.055 | 0.030 | 0.018 | –0.121 | –0.075 | –0.162 | –0.100 |
| **Health Care** | 12.21 | 11.67 | 0.615 | 0.448 | 0.176 | 0.129 | –0.670 | –0.584 | –1.081 | –0.755 |
| **Industrials** | **20.54** | **11.59** | **1.143** | **0.628** | **0.398** | **0.198** | **–1.422** | **–0.819** | **–2.398** | **–1.262** |
| **Information Technology** | 15.61 | 17.72 | 0.956 | 0.827 | 0.538 | 0.390 | –0.720 | –0.799 | –1.919 | –1.682 |
| **Materials** | **3.28** | **3.65** | **0.287** | **0.302** | **0.078** | **0.099** | **–0.389** | **–0.420** | **–0.547** | **–0.560** |
| **Telecommunication Services** | 0.89 | 2.91 | 0.048 | 0.090 | 0.016 | 0.029 | –0.046 | –0.107 | –0.084 | –0.199 |
| [Unassigned] | 2.50 | — | 0.257 | — | 0.094 | — | –0.465 | — | –0.380 | — |

Holdings Data As Of
LC-VALUE 6/30/2011
S&P 500 6/30/2011
Risk Model As Of
R-Squared Daily Global Equity Model (USD) 6/30/2011
NIS US Fundamental Model 6/30/2011
Hidden: Benchmark-Only Securities and Groups

**TABLE 12.2** Using the Northfield U.S. Fundamental risk model, we computed stress tests of two shocks for a large-cap U.S. domestic portfolio for oil rising 30 percent and precious metals falling 30 percent. Results are similar and consistent with using the R-Squared risk model of Table 12.1.

**Percent of Total Holdings**
**LC-VALUE vs. S&P 500**
**6/30/2011**
**U.S. Dollar**

| | | | NIS U.S. Fundamental Model | | | | | | | |
|---|---|---|---|---|---|---|---|---|---|---|
| | | | Crude Oil 30% Rise | | | | Precious Metals – 30%Loss | | | |
| **Economic Sector** | **Portfolio Weight** | **Benchmark Weight** | **Percent Return (Time Weight)** | **Benchmark Percent Return (Time Weight)** | **Percent Return (Event Weight)** | **Benchmark Percent Return (Event Weight)** | **Percent Return (Time Weight)** | **Benchmark Percent Return (Time Weight)** | **Percent Return (Event Weight)** | **Benchmark Percent Return (Event Weight)** |
| **Total** | **100.00** | **100.00** | **11.223** | **8.698** | **3.225** | **1.344** | **–5.986** | **–4.925** | **–11.047** | **–10.067** |
| **Consumer Discretionary** | 25.32 | 10.53 | 2.580 | 0.915 | 0.381 | 0.002 | –1.058 | –0.394 | –2.336 | –1.094 |
| **Consumer Staples** | 6.02 | 10.68 | 0.595 | 0.532 | 0.163 | –0.067 | –0.402 | –0.542 | –0.571 | –0.474 |
| **Energy** | **13.63** | **12.63** | **2.732** | **1.929** | **1.558** | **1.099** | **–1.528** | **–1.221** | **–2.797** | **–1.604** |
| CARBO Ceramics Inc. | 1.21 | — | 0.137 | | 0.033 | | –0.094 | | –0.195 | |
| RPC Inc. | 1.19 | — | 0.305 | | 0.205 | | –0.195 | | –0.318 | |
| Holly Corp. | 1.16 | — | 0.215 | | 0.154 | | –0.087 | | –0.185 | |
| Range Resources Corp. | 1.08 | 0.07 | 0.201 | 0.014 | 0.114 | 0.008 | –0.130 | –0.009 | –0.189 | –0.013 |

| | | | | | | | | | | |
|---|---|---|---|---|---|---|---|---|---|---|
| Frontier Oil | 1.04 | — | 0.283 | | 0.177 | | –0.127 | | –0.315 | |
| Patterson-UTI Energy Inc. | 1.00 | — | 0.233 | | 0.165 | | –0.156 | | –0.212 | |
| Helmerich & Payne Inc. | 0.99 | 0.06 | 0.215 | 0.013 | 0.129 | 0.008 | –0.111 | –0.007 | –0.245 | –0.014 |
| SM Energy Co. | 0.95 | — | 0.200 | | 0.126 | | –0.123 | | –0.184 | |
| Concho Resources Inc. | 0.81 | — | 0.123 | | 0.040 | | –0.069 | | –0.092 | |
| Cabot Oil & Gas Corp. | 0.79 | 0.06 | 0.179 | 0.013 | 0.116 | 0.008 | –0.111 | –0.008 | –0.170 | –0.012 |
| Oil States International Inc. | 0.76 | — | 0.134 | | 0.020 | | –0.078 | | –0.191 | |
| El Paso Corp. | 0.71 | 0.13 | 0.131 | 0.023 | 0.046 | 0.008 | –0.059 | –0.011 | –0.134 | –0.024 |
| Core Laboratories N.V. | 0.66 | — | 0.097 | | 0.066 | | –0.056 | | –0.078 | |
| Tesoro Corp. | 0.65 | 0.03 | 0.129 | 0.005 | 0.074 | 0.003 | –0.050 | –0.002 | –0.119 | –0.005 |
| Halliburton Co. | 0.63 | 0.39 | 0.149 | 0.091 | 0.091 | 0.056 | –0.081 | –0.050 | –0.169 | –0.103 |
| **Health Care** | 12.21 | 11.67 | 0.904 | 0.650 | 0.205 | 0.137 | –0.850 | –0.694 | –1.064 | –0.831 |
| **Industrials** | **20.54** | **11.59** | **1.869** | **1.125** | **0.117** | **0.065** | **–0.864** | **–0.561** | **–2.026** | **–1.507** |
| **Information Technology** | 15.61 | 17.72 | 1.750 | 1.258 | 0.487 | –0.127 | –0.663 | –0.323 | –1.366 | –0.621 |
| **Materials** | **3.28** | **3.65** | **0.490** | **0.504** | **0.165** | **0.111** | **–0.439** | **–0.421** | **–0.588** | **–0.775** |

*(continued)*

**TABLE 12.2** (*Continued*)

| | | | NIS U.S. Fundamental Model | | | | | | | |
|---|---|---|---|---|---|---|---|---|---|---|
| | | | Crude Oil 30% Rise | | | | Precious Metals – 30%Loss | | | |
| Economic Sector | Portfolio Weight | Benchmark Weight | Percent Return (Time Weight) | Benchmark Percent Return (Time Weight) | Percent Return (Event Weight) | Benchmark Percent Return (Event Weight) | Percent Return (Time Weight) | Benchmark Percent Return (Time Weight) | Percent Return (Event Weight) | Benchmark Percent Return (Event Weight) |
| Telecommunication Services | 0.89 | 2.91 | 0.089 | 0.128 | 0.023 | 0.021 | –0.060 | –0.163 | –0.090 | –0.151 |
| [Unassigned] | 2.50 | — | 0.214 | — | 0.126 | — | –0.120 | — | –0.208 | — |

Holdings Data As Of
LC-VALUE 6/30/2011
S&P 500 6/30/2011 Risk Model As Of
R-Squared Daily Global Equity Model (USD) 6/30/2011
NIS U.S. Fundamental Model 6/30/2011 Hidden: Benchmark-Only Securities and Groups

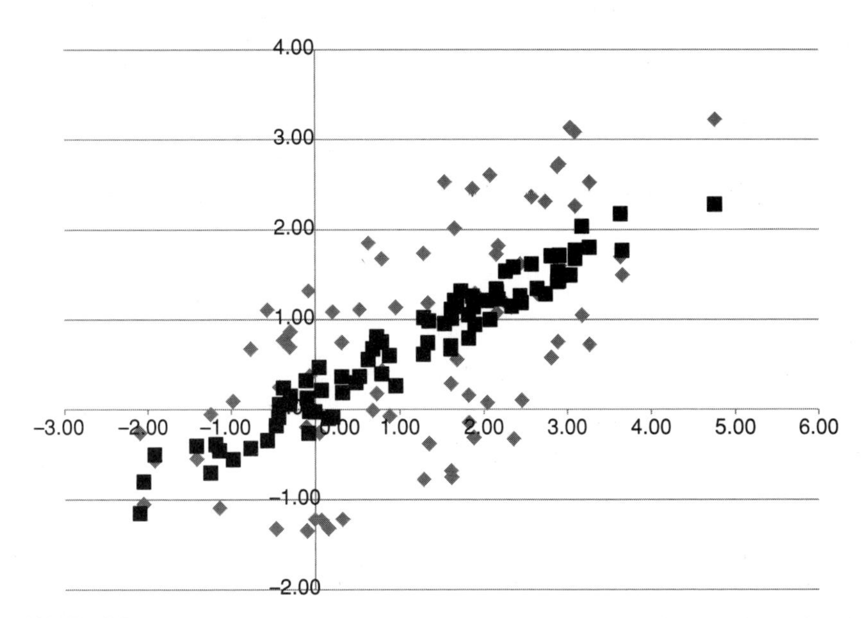


**FIGURE 12.2** A plot of two stresses' time series versus a single hypothetical risk model factor return on the *x*-axis. They have nearly identical betas, one of 0.491 and the other of 0.494, with respective correlations with the risk model factor return of 0.63 and 0.97. Which would be expected to offer a better estimate of return?

An alternative stress test involves consideration of the correlation between the stress time series and the risk model factor returns. Consider the plot in Figure 12.2.

In this plot we simulate two different stresses in which we need to compute their betas for stress-testing and plot them versus a single hypothetical risk model factor return. The lighter one a wider dispersion and a correlation with the risk model factor return of 63 percent, while the more narrowly distributed stress has a correlation of 97 percent. However, their betas are identical out to two decimal places, both with a value of 0.49. Given these betas, the standard formula for factor stress-testing would return the identical result. However, if one considers the impact of correlation, one would conclude the narrow distribution would offer a more resilient return forecast.

In Table 12.3 we show the data for a portion of the time series plotted in Figure 12.2 for the hypothetical factor return and the two stresses. We also show summary statistics above it where we give parameters for a regression through the data. Clearly, two stresses with identical betas can have more or less statistically significant interaction with a risk model. The beta doesn't determine this. It's agnostic about whether its value is useful, which has led

**TABLE 12.3** The data for a portion of the time series plotted in Figure 12.2 for the hypothetical factor return and the two stresses.

| | Intercept | 0.142 | 0.138 |
|---|---|---|---|
| | Slope | 0.497 | 0.500 |
| | Variance | 1.424 | 0.609 |
| | Beta | 0.491 | 0.494 |
| | R-Squared | 0.399 | 0.944 |
| | Correl | 0.631 | 0.971 |
| | | | |
| | **Factor Return** | **Stress 1** | **Stress 2** |
| 1 | 1.82 | –0.15 | 0.79 |
| 2 | 2.16 | 1.07 | 1.31 |
| 3 | 0.31 | 0.75 | 0.36 |
| 4 | –1.24 | –0.05 | –0.70 |
| 5 | –0.46 | –1.32 | –0.18 |
| 6 | 0.21 | 1.08 | –0.08 |
| 7 | 0.53 | 1.11 | 0.37 |
| 8 | –1.41 | –0.55 | –0.41 |
| 9 | 0.73 | 0.17 | 0.81 |
| 10 | 1.29 | –0.77 | 1.02 |
| 11 | 0.79 | 1.67 | 0.75 |
| 12 | 3.10 | 3.08 | 1.76 |
| 13 | 2.74 | 2.31 | 1.28 |
| 14 | 1.87 | 2.45 | 1.26 |

some to declare, "Beta Is Not 'Sharpe' Enough."[8] You can always calculate a beta, but just knowing it doesn't determine whether a forecast made from it is good or bad.

Thus we can modify the calculation for computing the new factor returns given a stress with its shock from the existing formula:

$$\text{New factor return} = \text{Beta} \times \text{Shock amount}$$

to a new formula incorporating correlation:

$$\begin{aligned}\text{New factor return} = {} & [1 - \text{abs(cor)}] \times \text{Current factor return} \\ & + \text{abs(cor)} \times \text{Beta} \times \text{Shock amount}\end{aligned}$$

where cor is the correlation between the stress time series and the risk model factor returns. We perform this operation for all available risk model factor returns. This interpretation means if the correlation is large and +/-1, the first term drops out leaving the old definition. And if it's weak, it has little effect and the return forecast is more similar to an estimate under no stress.

For example, if the correlation is very weak, one would assume the stress isn't coupled to the portfolio in any way and the return estimate is as if the stress wasn't applied in the first place. So if the stress is a time series of the mean monthly temperatures of Chicago, it won't produce an impact on the portfolio, whereas without incorporating correlation, it might. One needs the absolute value of correlation in the equation, too, because if the correlation is negative—for instance, the beta will be negative and on the right side of this equation the two negatives would multiply and produce a positive result—this would ultimately lead to an incorrect direction for the return estimate.

There is another stress test available whereby we use historical factor returns from a risk model and multiply them by current exposures. We call this Extreme Event stress testing. In an ordinary return estimate, one simply multiplies the latest available factor returns times one's current exposures, summing the result, and presto, voilà, and eureka, one has a return estimate! If, however, you'd like to go back in time to perhaps a period when markets were stressed as in the credit crisis (CC) of 2008, grab the risk model factor returns that were operative at that time, and use these for a return estimate, then one is modeling an extreme event in a stress test. The risk model chosen for this kind of stress test is still up to the user to decide, but it must have history residing within FactSet for the time period that factor returns are chosen from.

There also resides a Monte Carlo Extreme Event risk stress test within the Balanced Risk product on FactSet's PA system. This type of stress test involves a unique combination of Extreme Event stress-testing and Monte Carlo VaR. In this example, one is allowed to choose some historical period again as in Extreme Event, but instead of selecting factor returns, one selects the whole covariance matrix. Coupling this technology with a multi-asset-class risk model allows us to compute VaR and other risk measures at any confidence interval, using historical variance/covariances with current exposures.

Like ordinary Balanced Risk MC-VaR, where a sophisticated fixed income pricing model is merged with an equity risk model, commodities risk model, and derivative pricing algorithms, this extension for extreme event analysis allows for using the covariance matrix from some crazy Black Swan event in an MC return simulation to compute risk.

An example of the results one can obtain from this type of stress test can be seen with a global portfolio of equities, fixed income, options, and small cash positions as seen in Table 12.4.

**TABLE 12.4** An example global multi-asset-class portfolio used in the Monte Carlo Extreme Event risk stress test. It contains global equities and fixed income, some equity options, and several small cash positions.

**Percent of Total Holdings**
**GLOB_BAL_MAND vs. MSCI EAFE**
**9/23/2010**
**U.S. Dollar Report**

| Asset Class | Portfolio Weight | Benchmark Weight | Difference |
|---|---|---|---|
| **Total** | **100.00** | **100.00** | **—** |
| **Equity** | **73.60** | **100.00** | **-26.40** |
| United States | 25.15 | — | 25.15 |
| Japan | 13.10 | 21.62 | -8.52 |
| France | 9.34 | 9.52 | -0.18 |
| Germany | 7.34 | 7.75 | -0.41 |
| Australia | 4.38 | 8.59 | -4.21 |
| Canada | 3.48 | — | 3.48 |
| United Kingdom | 2.81 | 21.72 | -18.91 |
| Sweden | 1.60 | 3.02 | -1.42 |
| Hong Kong | 1.59 | 2.66 | -1.07 |
| Hutchison Whampoa Ltd. | 0.48 | 0.18 | 0.31 |
| Sun Hung Kai Properties Ltd. | 0.31 | 0.22 | 0.09 |
| Hang Seng Bank Ltd. | 0.28 | 0.11 | 0.17 |
| Swire Pacific Ltd. | 0.26 | 0.10 | 0.16 |
| China Mobile Ltd. | 0.20 | — | 0.20 |
| Lenovo Group Ltd. | 0.06 | — | 0.06 |
| Netherlands | 1.32 | 2.75 | -1.43 |
| Finland | 0.95 | 1.08 | -0.14 |
| Switzerland | 0.84 | 7.85 | -7.01 |
| Italy | 0.73 | 2.70 | -1.97 |
| Singapore | 0.38 | 1.64 | -1.26 |
| United Overseas Bank Ltd. | 0.26 | 0.16 | 0.10 |
| Singapore Telecommunications Ltd. | 0.11 | 0.18 | -0.07 |
| Ireland | 0.32 | 0.23 | 0.09 |
| Israel | 0.28 | 0.84 | -0.56 |

**TABLE 12.4** *(Continued)*

| Asset Class | Portfolio Weight | Benchmark Weight | Difference |
|---|---|---|---|
| **Fixed Income** | 20.69 | — | 20.69 |
| Corporate | 14.05 | — | 14.05 |
| Canada | 4.60 | — | 4.60 |
| South Korea | 2.18 | — | 2.18 |
| Australia | 2.12 | — | 2.12 |
| France | 2.01 | — | 2.01 |
| United States | 1.95 | — | 1.95 |
| United Kingdom | 1.04 | — | 1.04 |
| Italy | 0.12 | — | 0.12 |
| Spain | 0.02 | — | 0.02 |
| Hungary | 0.02 | — | 0.02 |
| Japan | 0.02 | — | 0.02 |
| Honda Bank Gmbh 0.0% 12-oct-2010 | 0.01 | — | 0.01 |
| Toyota Motor Credit Corp. 0.0% 04-jan-2011 | 0.01 | — | 0.01 |
| Toyota Finance Australia Ltd. 4.12% 31-jul-2017 | 0.01 | — | 0.01 |
| Toyota Capital Malaysia Sdn. Bhd. 4.2% 02-jul-2014 | 0.01 | — | 0.01 |
| Government Related | 5.08 | — | 5.08 |
| United States | 1.07 | — | 1.07 |
| Sovereign | 0.48 | — | 0.48 |
| United States | 0.48 | — | 0.48 |
| **Derivatives** | **5.39** | — | **5.39** |
| Metlife Inc Call Dec 10 36 | 1.71 | — | 1.71 |
| FactSet Research S Call Dec 10 80 | 1.57 | — | 1.57 |
| State Street Corp Put Jan 11 32 | 1.02 | — | 1.02 |
| Bank Of Ny Mellon Put Dec 10 22.5 | 0.40 | — | 0.40 |
| Costo Whsl Corp N Put Jan 11 65 | 0.25 | — | 0.25 |

*(continued)*

**TABLE 12.4** (*Continued*)

| Asset Class | Portfolio Weight | Benchmark Weight | Difference |
|---|---|---|---|
| Kraft Foods Inc Put Dec 10 28 | 0.25 | — | 0.25 |
| Bristol-Myers Squi Put Dec 10 23 | 0.15 | — | 0.15 |
| Astrazenec a Plc Put Oct 10 28 | 0.02 | — | 0.02 |
| Standard Chartered Plc Put Oct 10 14 | 0.01 | — | 0.01 |
| **[Cash]** | **0.32** | — | **0.32** |
| U.S. Dollar | 0.10 | — | 0.10 |
| British Pounds | 0.09 | — | 0.09 |
| Euro | 0.08 | — | 0.08 |
| Japanese Yen | 0.06 | — | 0.06 |

Holding Data As Of
GLOB_BAL_MAND 12/31/2009
MSCI EAFE 9/23/2010
Hidden: Benchmark-Only Securities and Groups

The crux of this product is FactSet's multi-asset-class (MAC) risk model, though it works for several other vendors' risk models, too, specifically SunGard APT and NIS EE. For an example, we're going to use the MAC covariance matrix from November 2008, chosen from the midst of the worst part of the crisis. Then, we'll compute the MC-VaR for the portfolio using exposures from September 2010 and then from the mini-crisis of September 2011, all for the portfolio of Table 12.4.

To begin, we illustrate the return distribution that is computed under MC-VaR by taking the covariance matrix, forming a Cholesky decomposition, generating normal random variables, and multiplying them times the Cholesky matrix. These then form equity factor returns and/or are fed back into the Balanced Risk FI fast repricing algorithm. For equity, these become new exposures, whereas for fixed income (FI) they result in recomputed new prices, both of which ultimately yield returns after more computing.

Figure 12.3 demonstrates what the return distributions look like for the two covariance matrices. The darker bars are from using the CC matrix and form a fat tail to the right. The lighter distribution was created by using the covariance matrix of September 2010. In both cases, exposures are from September 2010. The higher density to the right for the CC simulation is due to returns in that period falling so much due to covariance being so tight that the option puts went deeply into-the-money, whereas using the

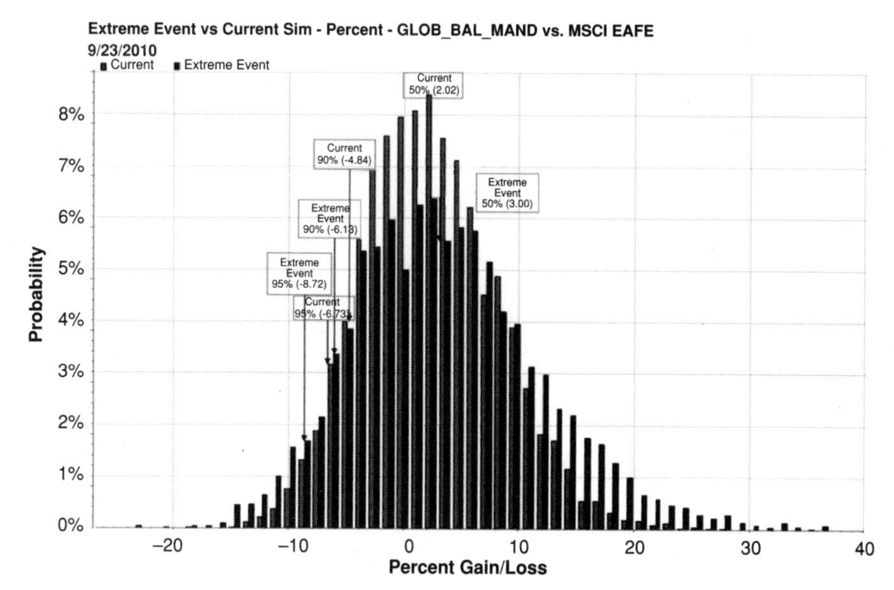


**FIGURE 12.3** The return histogram involved in the MC-VaR calculation using two covariance matrices. The darker distribution with the right fat tail is from the credit crisis (CC), while the narrow lighter distribution is from September 2010. The right tail using the CC covariance structure means that returns were so bad due to high correlation among assets that all the put options went deeply into-the-money, ultimately giving positive portfolio returns.

covariance matrix of 9/2010, the simulation doesn't yield such underlying negative returns that the options, which were out-of-the-money to start with, went strongly in-the-money.

We can examine the actual one-month, 95 percent VaR generated from these data in a screen shot from FactSet's Risk in PA module. In Table 12.5, we illustrate attribution with VaR for the portfolio where we group by asset class: equity, fixed income, derivatives, and cash. There are two columns under the "Credit Crisis" heading. The left one is the ordinary portfolio VaR, and the right one is the stand-alone VaR. In the stand-alone VaR column, the reported numbers represent VaR if the group was its own portfolio, independent of the other assets. In essence the stand-alone VaRs are higher than the regular VaRs to the left simply because of the impact of diversification, which isn't accessible in the stand-alone computation. The three columns to the right show the VaR results using the covariance matrix of September 2010 for regular, marginal, and stand-alone risk measures.

We draw your attention to the CC portfolio VaR being 878 bps, while using the 9/2010 covariance matrix it is 688 bps. Equity is about a 50 percent

**TABLE 12.5** The FactSet MC-VaR calculation results grouped by asset class. The middle columns show 95 percent confidence, one-month (22 trading days) VaR for the portfolio and for the stand-alone numbers using the CC matrix. The three columns on the right show the VaR portfolio, marginal VaR, and stand-alone VaR using the September 2010 covariance matrix for the portfolio of Figure 12.3.

**Percent of Total Holdings**
**GLOB_BAL_MAND vs. MSCI EAFE**
**9/23/2010**
**FactSet/R-Squared Daily Global Multi-Asset-Class Model (USD)**
**U.S. Dollar**

| | | | | Credit Crisis | | | | |
|---|---|---|---|---|---|---|---|---|
| Asset Class | Portfolio Weight | Benchmark Weight | Difference | ST% Value at Risk 22 Day, 95% | ST% Stand-Alone Value at Risk 22 Day, 95% | MC% Marginal Value at Risk 22 Day, 95% | MC% Stand-Alone Value at Risk 22 Day, 95% | MC% Stand-Alone Value at Risk 22 Day, 95% |
| Total | 100.00 | 100.00 | — | 8.78 | 8.78 | 6.88 | | 6.88 |
| Equity | 73.60 | 100.00 | –26.40 | 8.78 | 14.05 | 5.89 | 0.07 | 8.76 |
| Fixed Income | 20.69 | — | 20.69 | 0.63 | 7.29 | 0.23 | 0.02 | 3.35 |
| Derivatives | 5.39 | — | 5.39 | –0.62 | 42.31 | 0.73 | 0.12 | 48.48 |
| [Cash] | 0.32 | — | 0.32 | 0.01 | 259 | 0.00 | 0.01 | 2.11 |
| U.S. Ddlar | 0.10 | — | 0.10 | –0.00 | –01 | –0.00 | –0.00 | –0.01 |
| British Pounds | 0.09 | — | 0.09 | 0.00 | 6.04 | 0.00 | 0.02 | 3.94 |
| Euro | 0.08 | — | 0.08 | 0.00 | 5.38 | 0.00 | 0.03 | 4.32 |
| Japanese Yen | 0.06 | — | 0.06 | -0.00 | 5.91 | –0.00 | –0.00 | 4.32 |

increase in VaR using the CC matrix, while fixed income risks as measured by VaR go up by almost a factor of three (23 bps to 63 bps). In our labeling a positive VaR value means a probable loss, a negative VaR a probable gain. Due to the volatility of equities being so much higher than fixed income, they dominate the risk in the portfolio; however, the fixed income risk is significantly increased above and beyond the equity risks as a percentage of the position size alone, an increase by almost a factor of three, 63 bps versus 23 bps. Derivatives, on the other hand, actually were diversifying in this case (–62 bps) due to those being mostly option puts that go deeply into-the-money under a stressed scenario (when equity returns are strongly negative). Under the 9/2010 simulation (like we saw examining the return distribution) there wasn't enough correlation among assets to lead to large losses, pushing the option values way above cost (73 bps). However, they still had risk in this more benign situation.

If the options were their own portfolio as seen in the stand-alone VaR numbers, the risks were huge (42.31 and 48.48 percent) for a one-month horizon. Luckily, owning the other assets seriously lowered the risk of the portfolio due to diversification.

We now move one year forward in the simulation to September 2011. This month offered a period of large losses in the equity markets. Figure 12.4 shows the return distributions again for the two simulations using the CC and 9/2011 covariance matrices. They almost overlap, insinuating how similar the

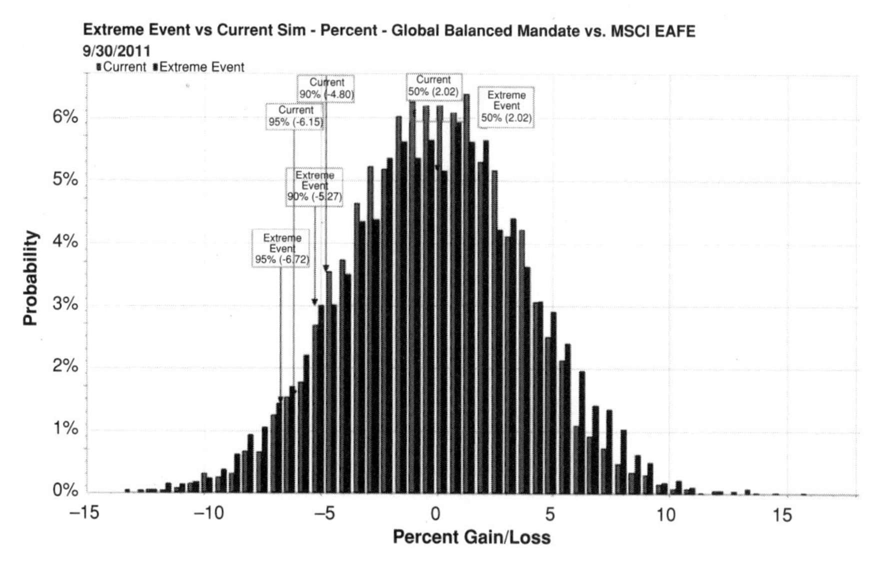


**FIGURE 12.4** Return distributions involved for MC-VaR for CC matrix and September 2011.

**TABLE 12.6** MC-VaR for the portfolio of Figure 12.4 grouped by asset class. The middle three columns are one-month 99 percent VaR for the portfolio, stand-alone, and relative to the benchmark, the MSCI-EAFE index using the CC matrix. The three rightmost columns are the same data but for computing VaR using the covariance matrix of September 2011.

Percent of Total Holdings
Global Balanced Mandate vs. MSCI EAFE 9/30/2011
FactSet/R-Squared Daily Global Multi-Asset-Class Model (USD)

| | | | | Credit Crisis (10/2008) | | | | | |
|---|---|---|---|---|---|---|---|---|---|
| Asset Class | Portfolio Weight | Benchmark Weight | Difference | ST% Value at Risk 22 Day, 99% | ST% Stand-Alone Value at Risk 22 Day, 99% | ST% Port. vs Bench. Difference Value at Risk 22 Day, 99% | MC% Value at Risk 22 Day, 99% | MC% Stand-Alone Value at Risk 22 Day, 99% | MC% Port. vs Bench. Difference Value at Risk 22 Day, 99% |
| Total | 100.00 | 100.00 | — | 9.375 | 9.375 | –7.491 | 8.806 | 8.806 | –6.379 |
| Equity | 70.81 | 100.00 | –29.19 | 10.666 | 14.803 | –6.457 | 10.417 | 14.367 | 4.783 |
| Fixed Income | 20.14 | — | 20.14 | 0.598 | 6.354 | 0.598 | 0.177 | 2.778 | 0.177 |
| Derivatives | 8.71 | — | 8.71 | –1.760 | 23.325 | –1.760 | –1.713 | 19.538 | –1.713 |
| Exxon Mobil Corp Put Oct11 115 | 4.16 | — | 4.16 | –1.090 | 34.841 | –1.090 | –0.905 | 25.583 | –0.905 |
| Deutsche Bank Ag Put Dec11 83.949997 | 3.87 | — | 3.87 | –0.374 | 12.953 | –0.374 | –0.475 | 12.891 | –0.475 |

| | | | | | | | | | |
|---|---|---|---|---|---|---|---|---|---|
| Hsbc Holdings Pic Put Dec11 7.2 | 0.36 | — | 0.36 | –0.135 | 46.147 | –0.135 | –0.134 | 38.889 | –0.134 |
| Costco Whsl Corp N Put Oct1180 | 0.21 | | 0.21 | –0.161 | 100.000 | –0.161 | –0.199 | 100.000 | –0.199 |
| [Cash] | 0.34 | | 0.34 | 0.007 | 3.426 | 0.007 | 0.009 | 3.188 | 0.009 |

Holdings Data As Of
Global Balanced Mandate 12/31/2009
MSCI EAFE 9/30/2011
Risk Model As Of
FactSet/R-Squared Daily Global Multi-Asset-Class Model (USD) 9/30/2011
MarketPortfblio: MSCI EAFE
Hidden: Benchmark-Only Securities and Groups

risks in 9/2011 were to those during the credit crisis. In Table 12.6 we document the VaR values for the portfolio, this time for a one-month (22 trading days) 99 percent confidence interval.

In this last table, we show the regular, stand-alone, and relative VaR values for two calculations, one using the CC matrix on the middle three columns. The last three columns use the September 2011 covariance matrix. Here now the overall portfolio VaR is 9.37 versus 8.80 percent of the portfolio's value. The equity risks are essentially equivalent (10.66 vs. 10.41). But notice the fixed income risks. Here the covariance matrix of the credit crisis results in fixed income risks again three times as large as in September 2011. So though 9/2011 was a risky market environment, its impact was mostly on equity, not on fixed income. Likewise, this equity risk translated into equivalent increased diversification in the derivatives, where VaR is –176 bps and –171 bps for the CC and 9/2011 matrix calculations, respectively.

If one compares the fourth column from the right and the last column on the right to see the relative VaR values, the CC environment across assets does result in less risk for the portfolio relative to its benchmark if covariance and correlations tighten up due to a CC-like structure (event risk) happening across assets. The negative relative VaR of –7.49 percent versus –6.38 percent means the portfolio would be subject to less risk should the risk across assets enter a market like the credit crisis versus one like the one that existed in September 2011.

In summary, the only effective way to attempt to get ahead of extreme event risk is to perform iterative what-ifs to your portfolio under stress-testing environments. FactSet offers the risk and portfolio manager the tools to flexibly create various stresses and estimate the impact a stress may (or may not) have on the portfolio. The question the prudent investor must ask is simply: what is my fear? Given that question can be proxied with a time-series stress or a period in historical time for which one has risk model factors or covariances, it should lead the way to investigate many scenarios along these lines.

## NOTES

1. P. Artzner, F. Delbaen, J.-M. Eber, and D. Heath, "Thinking Coherently," *Risk* 10, no. 11 (1997); P. Artzner, F. Delbaen, J.-M. Eber, and D. Heath, "Coherent Measures of Risk," *Mathematical Finance* 9, no. 3 (1999): 203–228.
2. Carlo Acerbi and Dirk Tasche, "Expected Shortfall: A Natural Coherent Alternative to Value at Risk," Abaxbank working paper at arXiv:condmat/0105191 (2001).

3. P. Krokhmal, M. Zararankin, and S. Uryasev, "Modeling and Optimization of Risk," *Surveys in Operations Research and Management Science* 16 (2011): 49–66.
4. H. M. Markowitz, *Portfolio Selection: Efficient Diversification of Investments* (New York: John Wiley & Sons, 1959; New Haven, CT: Yale University Press, 1970; Malden, MA: Blackwell Publishers, 1991).
5. Its cousin, conditional value at risk (CVaR), expected tail loss, or expected shortfall by its other names, is coherent.
6. Jon Danielsson, Bjorn N. Jorgensen, Sarma Mandira, Gennady Samorodnitsky, and C. G. de Vries, "Subadditivity Re-Examined: The Case for Value-at-Risk," Discussion Paper 549, Financial Markets Group, London School of Economics and Political Science, London, 2005.
7. Tyrrell R. Rockafellar, Stanislav P. Uryasev, and Michael Zabarankin, "Generalized Deviations in Risk Analysis," University of Florida Department of Industrial and Systems Engineering Working Paper 2004-4, September 3, 2004; Pavlo Krokhmal, "Higher Moment Coherent Risk Measures," *Quantitative Finance* 7 (2007): 373–387.
8. S. P. Greiner, *Ben Graham Was a Quant* (Hoboken, NJ: John Wiley & Sons, 2011), chap. 3.

# CHAPTER 13

# Risk for the Fundamental Investor

*Richard Barrett, CFA, FRM; Roberto Isch, CFA, FRM; and Steven P. Greiner, PhD*

We've all heard the expression, especially in recent years, that *risk* is a four-letter word. It is often viewed as something unwanted that needs to be completely managed out of a process. We've talked throughout previous chapters of the book about different ways to manage risk for investment portfolios and the merits of doing so, but for some investors, *risk* is a four-letter word for an entirely different reason. Managers employing a purely fundamental style of investing often do not believe in using standard risk controls in their investment process. Some are pure stock pickers who build models to determine the values of companies and then purchase those stocks that are viewed as undervalued and sell or short those that are thought to be overvalued. This chapter provides an overview of fundamental investing and compares it to other investment approaches. We talk about why fundamental investors should consider integrating risk models into their process and how they can actually increase performance while lowering portfolio volatility. Finally, we talk about how a fundamental shop can overlay a risk management process onto its existing strategy.

## FUNDAMENTAL INVESTING VERSUS OTHER APPROACHES

There are many different investment styles that asset managers use to manage money. Three main types are fundamental analysis, technical analysis, and quantitative analysis. We'll provide a brief introduction of all three and then return our focus to the namesake of this chapter.

With fundamental analysis, investors analyze not only quantitative measures of a firm's financial statements but also such qualitative aspects as the strength of the company's management team and product line. They use valuation models such as a dividend discount model to calculate the present value of future cash flows to the investor. They look at ratios such as price-earnings (P/E) and return on equity (ROE) relative to a firm's own history as well as relative to other companies in the sector. They talk to suppliers, customers, and company management, and read research reports produced by sell-side firms. They traditionally get to know their smaller subset of stocks and companies much better than their counterparts using other investment approaches. They compile their data and create models to determine if they believe a stock is worth more or worth less than its current trading price. Most times, a lot of intuition that is gained through years of experience is used in this approach. Portfolios are constructed on a stock-by-stock basis based on where the largest perceived upside lies. Some portfolios may be very concentrated if there is a particularly high level of strength in the manager's convictions.

Two other investment styles are technical analysis and quantitative analysis. Technical analysis looks at the movements of the markets to forecast future price trends. Most often, price and volume charts are analyzed for patterns. This nomenclature was developed before the advent of the microprocessor for the most part, but technical analysis and momentum investing are quite similar and many consider them to be the same thing, though this is often denied by true chartists. Unlike fundamental analysts, technicians believe that everything that can affect the price of a stock or other security is already reflected in its market price. As such, they don't pore over historical fundamental data very much nor spend time talking to company management. They analyze the stock charts and make decisions on the future direction of the market based on the effect that supply and demand for the stock will have, along with examining what previous historical price patterns evolved into for the stock. It should be noted that investors do not have to be 100 percent in one camp or the other. Investing is seldom a binary practice. Many technicians will incorporate some fundamental analysis into their models, while many fundamental analysts will also analyze price and volume charts as part of their analysis as well.

The third style of investing is quantitative investing. This approach uses historical data in mathematical models to value companies. Unlike fundamental analysts, quantitative analysts usually do not meet with company management or talk to customers and suppliers. They build computer models using financial statement data, economic data, estimate data, and pricing data, and the model chooses which stocks to buy and sell. There are many different types of models and procedures, but it is important to note that the intuition and gut feeling that play a large role in fundamental investing have no place in quantitative investing; in fact, this is a motivation for using models, because they take the emotion of investing out of the equation (pun intended).

Risk systems are often built into these models. Quantitative analysis is used extensively by asset managers, and most large firms rely on it to some extent.

In addition, many portfolios are managed using a hybrid approach in which two strategies are combined into one conveniently called *quantamental* investing. It may be as simple as a small-cap manager first using a quantitative screen to narrow down the list of securities to a more manageable number before starting to analyze those stocks individually. Or different teams within a firm may perform separate quantitative and fundamental analysis and look for the overlap in the best names from each model. These quantamental approaches make sense to those managers since the data being used in both models are often very similar. Quant models and fundamental models both may utilize free cash flow analysis, evaluate earnings per share (EPS) and sales growth rates, and compare valuation ratios to the industry averages. Different components of the hybrid model may perform better during different market conditions, so model weights can be adjusted accordingly or even dynamically in an automated fashion. Finally, asset allocation in a quantitative or quantamental process most often utilizes intelligent optimization to set asset weights.

## TYPICAL RISK CONTROLS FOR FUNDAMENTAL INVESTORS

Now that we've covered a basic overview of different investment approaches, we'll focus our attention on fundamental investing for the remainder of this chapter. I am sure you can guess from the title of this book that we are going to cover how fundamental analysis relates to investment risk. Traditional fundamental analysts may simply evaluate their position weights as a means of risk control. They will look at the weights of the securities in the portfolio relative to the benchmark. They will do the same for sector and country weights and, if any position is too big, the manager will look to trim it. A portfolio manager may even consider the volatility of the individual stock returns and may conclude that being overweight stocks whose daily returns have a low standard deviation over the past year will ensure that the portfolio's risk will be within reasonable limits. Much of fundamental asset allocation is heuristic in practice and follows the intuition of the manager. The liability in this process is that asset weights often have little methodology for establishing their values.

The fundamental manager may also aggregate many of the same company fundamentals used to decide which stocks to buy and sell. Computing weighted average P/Es, ROEs, and market values for a portfolio and benchmark is easy with software that is currently available. The fundamental manager will compare these aggregate metrics of the portfolio to those of the benchmark, and will also look at trends of the portfolio and market through time. If too high an exposure to a given metric exists, the portfolio manager may execute trades to minimize that exposure.

The critical missing element of solely employing these methods to control risk is that they don't account for the impact of linear correlations or covariance in the market, let alone nonlinear associations that would be captured by a multidimensional copula. Correlation only provides a single number to describe the relationship between two variables such as the return series of two factors (P/E and market value, for example) or between two stocks, but it yields more information than ignoring covariance altogether. Taking a large exposure in one factor has unintended consequences, as that factor is sure to be significantly correlated to at least one other factor. Building a portfolio piecemeal, one stock at a time, using only active exposures as the main risk constraint without considering the part correlations play is a recipe for disaster. It assumes the securities are independent of each other. There are many cases, even over the past 15 years, that bring to mind the tremendous adverse consequences that ignored or underestimated correlations (or possible increases in correlations) can have on a portfolio and on the market.

In the case of Long Term Capital Management (LTCM), the Russian default in 1998 had a much greater impact on the portfolio than anticipated. The resulting worldwide flight to quality also brought down values of LTCM's European and Japanese government bonds. Combined with its leverage, LTCM was on a downward spiral it could not escape. In these circumstances, Russian debt was much more highly correlated with many other assets than managers had modeled. Another example is the 2008 credit crisis, where correlations of credit default swaps to other instruments, including the underlying bonds, were misunderstood. When correlations are high, fundamental managers perform very poorly on average since stock-picking skill becomes less and less relevant. Pairwise correlations remained very high during 2011, during which time fundamental managers had their worst year in over a decade. At the same time, quant funds using factor strategies performed quite well. This is partially because the portfolio optimization process will tend toward diversifying factors to build a minimally correlated portfolio in a quant strategy. For fundamentally constructed portfolios, there's no way to do this, as the covariance matrix is not an observable quantity.

These examples involved major blowups. It is not just the possibility of these types of major events with which one should be concerned, however. Thinking that your portfolio is more diversified than it really is will have an impact on the performance and volatility of that portfolio. It may not always blow up, but nearly a hundred basis points in losses a year can compound rather quickly.

For a fundamental investment manager whose portfolio was primarily built based on picking stocks, we'll show how a quantitative risk management process can be employed and can successfully coexist with the fundamental process, without making dramatic changes to the way the portfolio is managed. Unintended exposures are the number one problem with picking stocks from a bottom-up mandate. A simple example of such an incidental exposure is a low-P/E strategy that also leads to an overweight of energy stocks and an underweight of technology stocks. A more complete look at all factor exposures and a more accurate view of correlations can highlight the impact that adding or decreasing position weights can have on the portfolio. We'll now work through misperceptions and hesitations one may have with overlaying a risk process on a fundamental portfolio.

Managers often feel that they live and breathe the companies they invest in and understand better than anyone what they are worth. Overweighting those that are undervalued and underweighting those that are overvalued are core parts of their strategies. Some have an absolute return strategy and don't manage against a traditional benchmark. Others have very few trading restrictions or simply don't believe in risk models or optimizers at all. We'll show that the view you gain with access to *ex ante* risk techniques can add so much to the understanding of a portfolio that any hesitations regarding implementing a risk process should be trumped by the benefits of doing so. Coupling *ex ante* analysis with *ex post* analysis will paint an even clearer picture. While client mandates or compliance requirements may necessitate the use of risk overlay strategies, at the very least managers may want to integrate a risk overlay simply as a means to cover themselves (CYA) while supplementing their fiduciary duties. If the portfolio underperforms dramatically, the manager will be able to explain the risk controls to the chief investment officer (CIO) and to investors. We're not suggesting a major investment strategy overhaul; even just a few tweaks to the weights of existing positions can substantially lower risk without changing the objective of the portfolio.

## IMPLEMENTING RISK MANAGEMENT STRATEGIES INTO A FUNDAMENTAL PROCESS

We've discussed different types of risk models and their construction in prior chapters, so we won't cover those base topics here. Instead, we'll focus on implementing risk models into a fundamental process. Our focus will be on analyzing risk and return contributions on the basis of managing the portfolio more efficiently. We'll look at the common outputs of risk reports and consider if the exposures stated in those results are in line with our expectations or if they are cause for alarm.

A good place to start is to look at a top-level view of portfolio risk alongside fundamental characteristics of the portfolio compared to the benchmark. What is the predicted tracking error (TE)? Is this in line with the manager's expectations? Other top-level statistics to analyze include value at risk, predicted beta, and exposures to and risk contributions of style and industry factors. Depending on the type of model being used, other factors related to countries and currencies should also be evaluated. The sample portfolio we will use throughout this chapter is the concentrated 35-stock U.S. portfolio shown in Table 13.1.

**TABLE 13.1** Stocks and weights in large-cap focused portfolio.

**Percent of Total Holdings**

**Large-Cap Focused Fund vs. S&P 500**

**12/31/2010**

**U.S. Dollar**

| *Economic Sector* | *Portfolio Weight* | *Benchmark Weight* | *Difference* | | *Port folio Weight* | *Bench mark Weight* | *Difference* |
|---|---|---|---|---|---|---|---|
| **Total** | 100.00 | 100.00 | — | | | | |
| **Consumer Discretionary** | **11.13** | **10.42** | **0.71** | **Health Care** | **17.08** | **10.87** | **6.21** |
| Amazon.com Inc. | 3.44 | 0.56 | 2.89 | Allergan Inc. | 3.42 | 0.18 | 3.23 |
| Dollar Tree Inc. | 3.19 | — | 3.19 | Amgen Inc. | 3.53 | 0.45 | 3.08 |
| Target Corp. | 1.66 | 0.37 | 1.29 | Merck & Co. Inc. | 4.40 | 0.97 | 3.43 |
| Walt Disney Co. | 2.84 | 0.62 | 2.22 | Pfizer Inc. | 2.65 | 1.22 | 1.42 |
| **Consumer Staples** | **8.48** | **10.68** | **-2.19** | UnitedHealth Group Inc. | 3.09 | 0.35 | 2.74 |
| CVS Caremark Corp. | 3.78 | 0.41 | 3.37 | **Industrials** | **8.23** | **11.36** | **-3.13** |
| Philip Morris International Inc. | 4.70 | 0.93 | 3.78 | Ametek Inc. | 2.15 | — | 2.15 |

**TABLE 13.1** (*continued*)

| *Economic Sector* | *Port-folio Weight* | *Bench-mark Weight* | *Difference* | | *Port folio Weight* | *Bench mark Weight* | *Difference* |
|---|---|---|---|---|---|---|---|
| **Energy** | **12.52** | **11.99** | **0.53** | Boeing Co. | 3.05 | 0.42 | 2.63 |
| Chevron Corp. | 3.11 | 1.60 | 1.51 | Cintas Corp. | 3.03 | 0.03 | 2.99 |
| Exxon Mobil Corp. | 1.41 | 3.21 | −1.81 | **Information Technology** | **15.05** | **18.58** | **−3.53** |
| Occidental Petroleum Corp. | 3.17 | 0.69 | 2.48 | Apple Inc. | 3.31 | 2.58 | 0.73 |
| Schlumberger Ltd. | 2.54 | 0.99 | 1.54 | Google Inc. Cl A | 2.13 | 1.29 | 0.83 |
| Unit Corp. | 2.29 | — | 2.29 | Hewlett-Packard Co. | 1.65 | 0.83 | 0.82 |
| **Financials** | **21.09** | **16.18** | **4.91** | Microsoft Corp. | 2.73 | 1.83 | 0.90 |
| Bank of America Corp. | 3.29 | 1.17 | 2.12 | Novellus Systems Inc. | 3.08 | 0.03 | 3.05 |
| Camden Property Trust | 2.65 | — | 2.65 | Oracle Corp. | 2.16 | 1.06 | 1.10 |
| Citigroup Inc. | 3.15 | 1.20 | 1.96 | **Materials** | **6.42** | **3.73** | **2.70** |
| City National Corp. | 1.97 | — | 1.97 | Carpenter Technology Corp. | 2.17 | — | 2.17 |
| Goldman Sachs Group Inc. | 2.71 | 0.75 | 1.96 | FMC Corp. | 2.49 | 0.05 | 2.44 |
| JPMorgan Chase & Co. | 4.00 | 1.45 | 2.55 | Royal Gold Inc. | 1.76 | — | 1.76 |
| Wells Fargo & Co. | 3.32 | 1.42 | 1.90 | | | | |

Holdings Data As Of
Large-Cap Focused Fund 12/31/2010
S&P 500 12/31/2010
Hidden: Benchmark-Only Securities and Groups

We benchmark to the S&P 500 and use Axioma's U.S. Mid-Horizon (MH) fundamental model for the risk analysis. Running the analysis produces a top-level risk report shown in Table 13.2 that can start shedding some light on the risk of our portfolio and the sources of that risk.

From the report, you can see that the active risk or tracking error (TE) of our sample portfolio is 2.70 percent. That's representative of a one standard deviation event, which is usually misinterpreted to mean that 67 percent of the time, the portfolio is expected to perform within 2.7 percent of how the benchmark performs. That's not true, however. Tracking error is the standard deviation about the excess return, not the benchmark's return. Thus it is centered about the return given by the difference between the portfolio and the benchmark, not the benchmark alone. So a TE of 2.7 percent means that

**TABLE 13.2** Top-level portfolio risk summary.

| Portfolio Summary | Large-Cap | |
|---|---|---|
| Large Cap-Focused Fund vs. S&P 500<br>12/31/2010<br>Axioma U.S. 2 MH Fundamental | Focused Fund<br>*Data* | S&P 500<br>*Data* |
| U.S. Dollar | | |
| # of Securities | 35 | 500 |
| Portfolio Ending Market Value | 93,754,727 | 11,469,940 |
| Market Capitalization | 91,652 | 88,094 |
| Dividend Yield | 1.33 | 2.00 |
| Price to Earnings using FY1 Est. | 14.32 | 13.00 |
| ROE | 14.25 | 19.55 |
| Risk | | |
| Total Risk | 17.70 | 16.66 |
| Predicted Beta | 1.05 | — |
| Total Return at Risk (%) (5%) | 29.12 | 27.41 |
| Total Value at Risk ($) (5%) | 27,297,251 | 3,143,694 |
| Active Risk | | |
| Active Risk | 2.70 | |
| Active Specific Risk | 2.16 | |
| Axioma—Active Factor Risk | 1.61 | |

**TABLE 13.2** (*continued*)

| Axioma—Factors | Axioma—Std. Dev. | Axioma Active Exp. |
|---|---|---|
| Liquidity | 0.04 | -0.01 |
| Volatility | 1.44 | 0.30 |
| Market Sensitivity | 0.06 | -0.02 |
| Leverage | 0.04 | 0.03 |
| Medium-Term Momentum | 0.04 | 0.02 |
| Short-Term Momentum | 0.10 | 0.05 |
| Size | 0.09 | -0.03 |
| Value | 0.06 | 0.05 |
| Growth | 0.04 | 0.05 |
| Exchange Rate Sensitivity | 0.05 | -0.04 |
| Industries | 1.05 | 0.00 |

67 percent of the time, the portfolio minus the benchmark will be found between –2.7 percent and +2.7 percent of the mean excess return, not the mean benchmark return.

The data in Table 13.3 generated in a simulation dramatizes this more clearly. In this simulation, we generated 5,000 normally distributed random returns, with targeted means of 2 and –1 and a standard deviation of 4 and 2, respectively, for a hypothetical portfolio and benchmark. After generating the data, the numerical means were calculated to be 2.026 and –0.997, while the standard deviations were 3.974 and 2.004 for the portfolio and benchmark, respectively. Then, we computed the excess return (XS) time series. Its mean was 3.023, while its standard deviation, which is the tracking error (TE), was 4.443.

Next, we compute two sets of lower and upper boundaries. One set takes the excess return mean and adds and subtracts the TE. The other takes the benchmark's mean return of –0.997 and adds and subtracts the TE. Then we go through the excess return data and calculate what percentage of the time the excess return is found between the two sets of limits and what percentage of time it's found between plus and minus the TE of the benchmark's return. We find that ~67 percent of the time, the excess return is found between the limits of the mean excess return and plus and minus one tracking error. On the other hand, we find that only ~61 percent of the time is the portfolio found within plus and minus one TE of the benchmark in this example.

**TABLE 13.3** The data here are 5,000 normally distributed random returns, with targeted means of 2 and –1 and a standard deviation of 4 and 2, respectively, for a hypothetical portfolio and benchmark. After generating the data, the numerical means were calculated to be 2.026 and –0.997, while the standard deviations were 3.974 and 2.004 for the portfolio and benchmark, respectively. Then, we computed the excess return (XS) time series. Its mean was 3.023 while its standard deviation, which is the tracking error (TE), was 4.443. The result demonstrates that TE does mean the portfolio will be found within plus/minus the TE about the benchmark's return.

| | Portfolio | Benchmark | | | | XS +/–TE | Benchmark +/– TE |
|---|---|---|---|---|---|---|---|
| Std. = | 3.974 | 2.004 | TE = | 4.443 | Lower Limit = | –1.42 | –5.44 |
| Avg. Ret. = | 2.026 | –0.997 | Mean XS = | 3.023 | Upper Limit = | 7.466 | 3.446 |
| Percentage of time returns found between upper and lower limit = | | | | | | 67.66% | 61.24% |
| Number of times returns found between upper and lower limit = | | | | | | 3,383 | 3,062 |

| | Portfolio | Benchmark | XS | XS +/– TE | Benchmark +/– TE |
|---|---|---|---|---|---|
| 1 | –2.959 | –5.623 | 2.66 | 1 | 1 |
| 2 | 2.240 | –0.392 | 2.63 | 1 | 1 |
| 3 | 0.440 | –0.510 | 0.95 | 1 | 1 |
| 4 | 3.193 | –1.378 | 4.57 | 1 | 1 |
| 5 | –1.416 | –0.294 | –1.12 | 1 | 1 |
| 6 | 9.087 | –1.168 | 10.26 | 0 | 0 |
| 7 | 3.779 | –1.508 | 5.29 | 1 | 0 |
| .. | .. | .. | .. | .. | .. |
| .. | .. | .. | .. | .. | .. |
| .. | .. | .. | .. | .. | .. |
| 4,994 | 0.980 | 1.533 | –0.55 | 1 | 1 |
| 4,995 | –3.021 | –2.277 | –0.74 | 1 | 1 |
| 4,996 | 2.097 | –2.362 | 4.46 | 1 | 1 |

**TABLE 13.3** (*continued*)

| | Portfolio | Benchmark | XS | XS +/– TE | Benchmark +/– TE |
|---|---|---|---|---|---|
| 4,997 | 1.721 | –3.016 | 4.74 | 1 | 1 |
| 4,998 | 9.193 | –0.301 | 9.49 | 0 | 0 |
| 4,999 | –2.787 | –0.245 | –2.54 | 0 | 1 |
| 5,000 | 10.572 | –0.723 | 11.30 | 0 | 0 |

Tracking error is generally misinterpreted by the investment community. It's a useful yardstick still, however, and since returns are never normally distributed, but usually fat-tailed and exhibiting kurtosis, one can expect that the portfolio's return will be found within the vicinity of its benchmark's (plus/minus one TE unit) return a higher percentage of the time than given by the normal distribution anyway, though it will vary. For selected portfolios, the percentage could be as low as 60 but is usually higher and could be as high as 80 over the course of a year with daily returns.

Not surprisingly, stock-specific risk is a larger contributor to active risk than factor risk is. This corresponds to the bottom-up nature of the way this portfolio is constructed. However, the manager may wish to have even a larger percentage of risk come from stock-specific risk and may even want to increase tracking error in search of more alpha. The goals all depend on what the portfolio manager is trying to accomplish and what the guidelines of the portfolio dictate. It's not simply the case that risk measurement and analysis are used to minimize risk. Risk measurement and monitoring are just tools to help analyze the portfolio's current makeup so that appropriate position adjustments can be made.

The active exposures in the chart represent the portfolio's over- or underweight of each factor relative to the benchmark in standard deviation terms. For example, the 0.05 corresponding to short-term momentum signifies that the portfolio's exposure to short-term momentum is 0.05 standard deviations higher than the benchmark's exposure to that same factor. Looking at all units in terms of standard deviations makes analysis of different factors comparable. In this case, most exposures are actually held pretty tightly around the benchmark. The one that stands out is the 0.30 active exposure to the volatility factor. Axioma uses a three-month horizon for its volatility calculation, so we know that our portfolio's volatility is a bit higher than that of the benchmark over the prior three months. If this exposure was unintended, it's important to be aware of it so that adjustments to the portfolio can be made.

Looking at the contributions to risk of each factor shows that the positive active exposure to volatility contributed almost half the factor risk of the portfolio. Note that it is not just the level of exposures and risk that are important. Performing time-series analysis of these measures provides additional insights. You can detect changes in management style or changing thoughts on market direction. You can also determine the timing of when constraints were initiated at points of high exposure. Performing time-series analysis will also highlight a manager's drift in style. For example, when growth stocks were significantly outperforming in the late 1990s, some value managers chased returns and positioned their portfolios more toward a growth orientation than they should have. Many who did got burned by the tech bubble whereas they should not even have been invested in those stocks at all. A time-series risk chart would highlight a style drift like this very clearly and also generally more quickly than *ex post* analysis due to the common use of daily data with most risk vendors. There are a lot of data that can be analyzed, but in this section, we'll focus on the data that are most relevant to the fundamental manager.

One piece of information shown in Table 13.4 that may be of particular interest to the fundamental manager is the implied alpha. This number, provided for each stock, shows what each stock's alpha must be for the portfolio's current positions to be optimally weighted. In essence, implied alpha is the minimum expected active return needed to justify the position size. This is sometimes referred to as *reverse optimization*. This takes into account the weights of each stock as well as the contribution to risk from each stock and from each factor. It is critical to understand that the risk model accounts for the correlations across the market so that all risks are considered in the implied alpha values. Portfolio managers may simply want to sort in order of implied alpha the combined list of stocks they own in the portfolio as well as those they are eligible to own but do not. Not owning a stock in the benchmark is just as active a decision as owning a stock since you are making the choice to underweight that stock.

When sorting by implied alpha, there are sure to be many surprises. Even a modest overweight in a particularly risky stock will result in a large implied alpha. Managers must ask themselves if the implied alphas are in line with their expectations. The portfolio manager's conviction on that stock may not be so strong, so she may decide to pull back the weight. Similarly, she may not own or be extremely underweight a stock that provides tremendous diversification benefits to the portfolio. That will be reflected in a positive implied alpha on the underweight stock. Oftentimes, the most overweight stocks, particularly in concentrated portfolios, will yield very high implied alphas. When the portfolio manager considers whether these stocks will actually outperform to the level specified in the implied alpha, she may decide to take action. She may lower the active weight on some of those stocks and reinvest the proceeds in stocks whose implied alphas are less than her own modeled alphas. Sorting by the difference in the manager's expectation of alpha and the implied alpha is a useful exercise that may lead to several trades that can provide the portfolio with more return and lower risk. Two stocks with identical active weights may have very different implied alphas based on the different expected contributions to risk and diversification benefits of each. A manager may assume that equal active weights equates to equal feelings about each stock and comparable impacts on the portfolio, but this mistaken belief can have severe consequences. The implied alpha of a stock is a better indicator of a manager's convictions than active weight.

Performing marginal analysis is another way to look at the risk of a portfolio to get an understanding of what trades to make to control risk. The marginal contribution to active risk is a measure provided both at the individual security level and at the factor level. It's an indication of the risk that will be added or removed from the portfolio should you increase your position size by 1 percent. For example, in Table 13.4, at an active weight of 2.55 percent, JPMorgan Chase shows a marginal tracking error of 0.115 percent. Since the marginal risk is positive, if we increase our weight in this stock, we'll increase the risk of the portfolio. On the flip side, if we decrease the weight of this stock, we will decrease the risk of our portfolio. In this particular case, if we trim this position by 1 percent, we will reduce the tracking error of our portfolio by 0.115 percent. Sorting stocks by marginal contribution to risk will provide an indication of positions you can add to or reduce in order to bring down the risk of the portfolio.

Another interesting analysis to perform is shown in the scatter plot of Figure 13.1. This graphs the marginal tracking error on the $x$-axis versus the active weight on the $y$-axis for each company. The size of each company's bubble represents the magnitude of the implied alpha, with larger bubbles representing larger implied alphas. In the case of the bubble on the far right representing Bank of America Corporation, the size of the bubble indicates that the manager believes this stock will significantly outperform. The security also has the largest marginal tracking error, indicating that decreasing the position in the stock will reduce the portfolio risk more than decreasing an equivalent weight in any other security.

The same analysis can be performed at the factor level. In our case, at 0.022 percent we can see in Table 13.5 that volatility has by far the highest marginal standard deviation of all factors. This shows that if we lower our exposure to the volatility factor, we will lower the overall risk of the portfolio.

Just like the evaluation of implied alphas, marginal analysis at the stock and factor levels can be used by a fundamental manager to get ideas

**TABLE 13.4** Analysis of implied alpha and marginal tracking error.

**Percent of Total Holdings**

**Large-Cap Focused Fund vs. S&P 500**

**12/31/2010**

**Axioma U.S. 2 MH Fundamental**

| Security Name | Portfolio Weight | Benchmark Weight | Difference | Implied Alpha | Marginal Tracking Error | Security Name | Portfolio Weight | Benchmark Weight | Difference | Implied Alpha | Marginal Tracking Error |
|---|---|---|---|---|---|---|---|---|---|---|---|
| Total | 100 | 100 | — | 0.43 | — | | 100 | 100 | — | 0.43 | — |
| Philip Morris International Inc. | 4.70 | 0.93 | 3.78 | 0.22 | 4.16 | Ametek Inc. | 2.15 | — | 2.15 | 0.41 | 7.58 |
| Merck & Co. Inc. | 4.40 | 0.97 | 3.43 | 0.23 | 4.28 | Bank of America Corp. | 3.29 | 1.17 | 2.12 | 0.85 | 15.79 |
| CVS Caremark Corp. | 3.78 | 0.41 | 3.37 | 0.39 | 7.31 | City National Corp. | 1.97 | — | 1.97 | 0.53 | 9.75 |
| Allergan Inc. | 3.42 | 0.18 | 3.23 | 0.38 | 6.97 | Goldman Sachs Group Inc. | 2.71 | 0.75 | 1.96 | 0.45 | 8.34 |
| Dollar Tree Inc. | 3.19 | — | 3.19 | 0.42 | 7.71 | Citigroup Inc. | 3.15 | 1.20 | 1.96 | 0.64 | 11.77 |
| Amgen Inc. | 3.53 | 0.45 | 3.08 | 0.29 | 5.37 | Wells Fargo & Co. | 3.32 | 1.42 | 1.90 | 0.68 | 12.57 |
| Novellus Systems Inc. | 3.08 | 0.03 | 3.05 | 0.45 | 8.31 | Royal Gold Inc. | 1.76 | — | 1.76 | 0.49 | 9.06 |
| Cintas Corp. | 3.03 | 0.03 | 2.99 | 0.39 | 7.29 | Schlumberger Ltd. | 2.54 | 0.99 | 1.54 | 0.44 | 8.10 |

| | | | | | | | | | | |
|---|---|---|---|---|---|---|---|---|---|---|
| Amazon.com Inc. | 3.44 | 0.56 | 2.89 | 0.61 | 11.30 | Chevron Corp. | 3.11 | 1.60 | 1.51 | 0.29 | 5.31 |
| UnitedHealth Group Inc. | 3.09 | 0.35 | 2.74 | 0.44 | 8.23 | Pfizer Inc. | 2.65 | 1.22 | 1.42 | 0.25 | 4.56 |
| Camden Property Trust | 2.65 | — | 2.65 | 0.42 | 7.77 | Target Corp. | 1.66 | 0.37 | 1.29 | 0.27 | 4.95 |
| Boeing Co. | 3.05 | 0.42 | 2.63 | 0.44 | 8.07 | Oracle Corp. | 2.16 | 1.06 | 1.10 | 0.39 | 7.23 |
| JPMorgan Chase & Co. | 4.00 | 1.45 | 2.55 | 0.62 | 11.50 | Microsoft Corp. | 2.73 | 1.83 | 0.90 | 0.29 | 5.42 |
| Occidental Petroleum Corp. | 3.17 | 0.69 | 2.48 | 0.43 | 7.91 | Google Inc. Cl A | 2.13 | 1.29 | 0.83 | 0.40 | 7.44 |
| FMC Corp. | 2.49 | 0.05 | 2.44 | 0.38 | 6.98 | Hewlett-Packard Co. | 1.65 | 0.83 | 0.82 | 0.38 | 6.97 |
| Unit Corp. | 2.29 | — | 2.29 | 0.62 | 11.51 | Apple Inc. | 3.31 | 2.58 | 0.73 | 0.29 | 5.46 |
| Walt Disney Co. | 2.84 | 0.62 | 2.22 | 0.31 | 5.79 | Exxon Mobil Corp. | 1.41 | 3.21 | –1.81 | 0.15 | 2.85 |
| Carpenter Technology Corp. | 2.17 | — | 2.17 | 0.80 | 14.80 | | 2.17 | — | 2.17 | 0.80 | 14.80 |

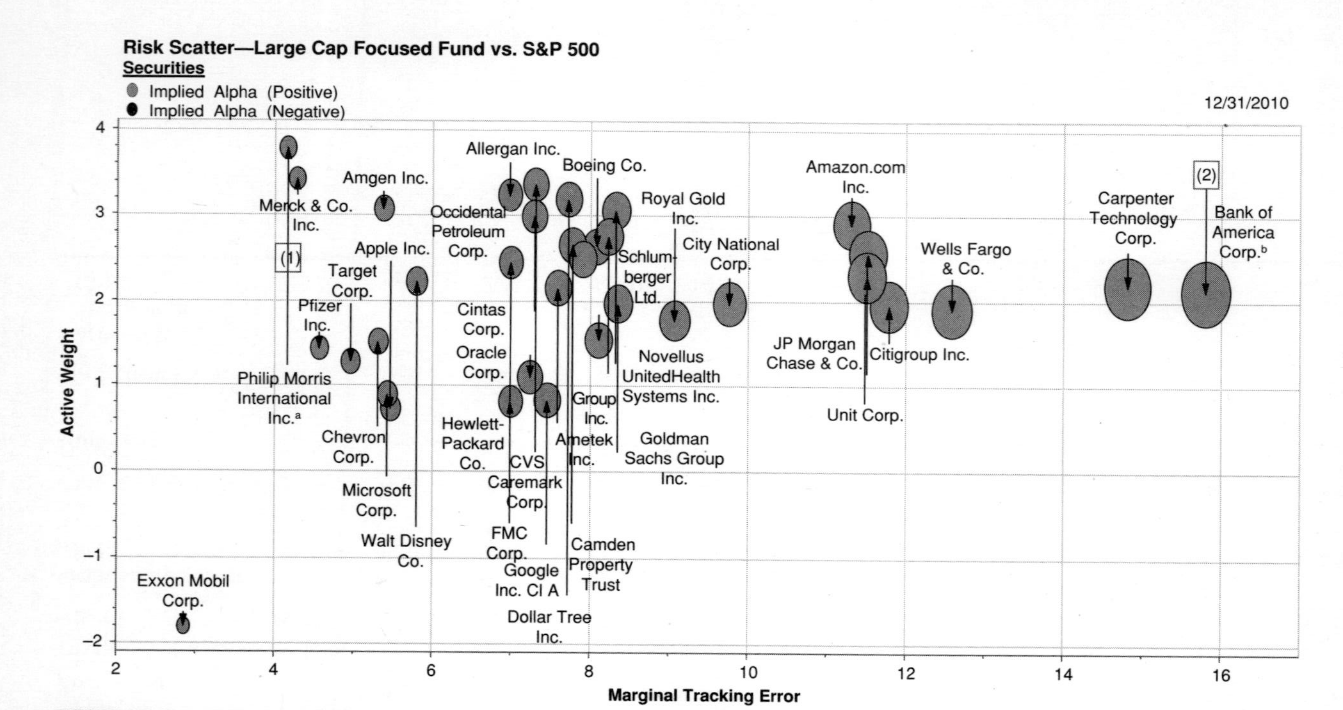


**FIGURE 13.1** This graphs the marginal tracking error on the *x*-axis versus the active weight on the *y*-axis for each company. The size of each company's bubble represents the magnitude of the implied alpha, with larger bubbles representing larger implied alphas.

[a]Philip Morris International Inc. active weight of 3.78; high marginal tracking error (4.17); high implied alpha.
[b]Bank of America Corp. active weight of 2.12; high marginal tracking error (15.81); high implied alpha (0.85).

**TABLE 13.5** Factor risk decomposition, including market capitalization at risk (MCaR).

| Risk Decomposition | | | | | | | |
|---|---|---|---|---|---|---|---|
| Large-Cap Focused Fund vs. S&P 500<br>12/31/2010<br>Axioma U.S. 2 MH Fundamental<br>U.S. Dollar | | | | | | | |
| Risk | | | | Standard Deviation | | Contribution to Variance | |
| Factor Names | Factor Volatility (%) | Active Exposure | Factor MCAR | Standard Deviation | Percent of Variance | Contribution to Variance | Percent of Variance |
| Total | | | | 1.62 | 35.86 | 2.61 | 35.86 |
| Exchange Rate Sensitivity | 1.13 | –0.04 | –0.0004 | 0.05 | 0.03 | 0.00 | 0.06 |
| Growth | 0.83 | 0.05 | –0.0005 | 0.04 | 0.02 | –0.01 | –0.09 |
| Leverage | 1.55 | 0.03 | 0.0007 | 0.04 | 0.02 | 0.00 | 0.07 |
| Liquidity | 2.97 | –0.01 | 0.0024 | 0.04 | 0.03 | –0.01 | –0.13 |
| Market Sensitivity | 3.51 | –0.02 | 0.0074 | 0.06 | 0.05 | –0.03 | –0.47 |
| Medium-Term Momentum | 1.94 | 0.02 | –0.001 | 0.04 | 0.02 | 0.00 | –0.07 |
| Short-Term Momentum | 1.92 | 0.05 | –0.0016 | 0.10 | 0.13 | –0.02 | –0.29 |
| Size | 2.86 | –0.03 | 0.0012 | 0.08 | 0.10 | –0.01 | –0.13 |
| Value | 1.21 | 0.05 | 0.001 | 0.06 | 0.05 | 0.01 | 0.17 |
| Volatility | 4.79 | 0.30 | 0.0219 | 1.44 | 28.45 | 1.77 | 24.32 |

for a handful of trades to make to bring the portfolio more in line with expectations. The trades don't have to be very numerous or dramatic in order to have an impact on the portfolio.

We've discussed many different risk measures one can analyze in order to get a better understanding of a portfolio as well as to gather information to make trades. Next, we can focus on analyzing the performance attribution of the portfolio to determine whether the asset and factor exposures of the portfolio have paid off historically. The two primary methodologies that managers use to analyze performance are Brinson attribution and risk-based performance attribution.

Brinson attribution breaks down the portfolio's excess return relative to the benchmark into several different categories. In the case of a fundamental manager, the most common practice would be to analyze the allocation effect, selection effect, and total effect at some group level, most often sector. Flexible grouping options exist so one may use country, industry, market cap quintiles, or any other type of grouping the manager can think of. In our case, we'll use GICS sectors and analyze the impact of each sector on performance as well as break out the effect of that performance into allocation and selection components.

The allocation effect tells us the performance impact of the portfolio based on our active sector weights. If we overweight a sector that outperforms the benchmark, we have a positive allocation effect. In contrast, if we overweight a sector that underperforms the benchmark, we're left with a negative allocation effect. The selection effect details how good a job we did at choosing stocks within each sector. A positive selection effect indicates that the sector performance of our portfolio beat the benchmark's performance for that sector. A negative selection effect indicates the exact opposite. A stock picker with a concentrated portfolio such as in the example we are using would most likely see the larger impact come from the selection effect. A positive number would mean that, as a whole, he was in fact a good stock picker. Brinson attribution is fairly commonly performed by most portfolio managers.

A different type of attribution that may be more eye-opening for the fundamental manager is risk-based performance attribution. Rather than the breakdown performance by sector allocation and stock picking ability, risk-based attribution breaks down performance by the factors in the risk model. An overweight to a given factor that has a positive return over the time horizon will have a positive impact on the performance of the portfolio. An overweight to a factor with a negative return will have a negative impact. Similar to analyzing risk in these terms, analyzing performance in these terms will shed a different light on the portfolio than what the manager is used to seeing. In our 11-year example shown in Tables 13.6 and 13.7, the portfolio underperformed the benchmark by 12.6 percent, represented by the –12.61 percent

**TABLE 13.6** Risk-based performance attribution and Brinson attribution.

**Risk-Based Performance Attribution**

**Large-Cap Focused Fund vs. S&P 500**
**12/31/1999 to 12/31/2010**
**Axioma U.S. 2 MH Fundamental**
**U.S. Dollar**

| | | | | Risk-Based Performance Attribution | | | Brinson Attribution | | |
|---|---|---|---|---|---|---|---|---|---|
| Economic Sector | Portfolio Average Weight | Benchmark Average Weight | Variation Average Weight | Risk Factors Effect | Stock-Specific Effect | Total Effect | Allocation Effect | Selection | Total Effect |
| Total | 100.00 | 100.00 | — | -50.00 | 37.39 | -12.61 | -1.50 | -11.11 | -12.61 |
| Consumer Discretionary | 11.30 | 10.86 | 0.43 | -9.88 | -0.54 | -10.43 | -0.10 | -9.04 | -9.13 |
| Consumer Staples | 10.02 | 9.94 | 0.08 | 3.16 | 3.01 | 6.17 | 1.26 | 3.51 | 4.77 |
| Energy | 10.18 | 8.91 | 1.27 | -5.80 | 16.25 | 10.45 | 1.66 | 12.68 | 14.34 |
| Financials | 17.68 | 18.11 | -0.43 | -5.68 | 8.20 | 2.52 | -0.36 | -2.52 | -2.87 |
| Health Care | 14.68 | 13.00 | 1.68 | -6.32 | 3.18 | -3.14 | -1.49 | -1.74 | -3.23 |
| Industrials | 7.77 | 11.15 | -3.38 | -11.93 | 3.56 | -8.37 | -1.23 | -7.36 | -8.59 |

(*Continued*)

**TABLE 13.6** (*Continued*)

| | | | | Risk-Based Performance Attribution | | | Brinson Attribution | | |
|---|---|---|---|---|---|---|---|---|---|
| Economic Sector | Portfolio Average Weight | Benchmark Average Weight | Variation Average Weight | Risk Factors Effect | Stock-Specific Effect | Total Effect | Allocation Effect | Selection | Total Effect |
| Information Technology | 18.25 | 17.75 | 0.50 | −7.31 | 3.72 | −3.59 | −0.86 | −2.31 | −3.17 |
| Materials | 2.68 | 2.93 | −0.25 | −2.78 | −1.73 | −4.51 | −1.73 | −2.87 | −4.60 |
| Telecommunication Services | 4.39 | 4.01 | 0.38 | 0.27 | −1.65 | −1.38 | −0.08 | −3.30 | −3.38 |
| Utilities | 3.01 | 3.32 | −0.31 | −3.85 | 3.57 | −0.28 | 0.68 | 2.24 | 2.92 |

Holdings Data As Of
 Large-Cap Focused Fund 12/31/1999 through 11/30/2010
 S&P 500 12/31/1999 through 11/30/2010
Risk Model As Of
 Axioma U.S. 2 MH Fundamental 12/31/1999

total effect on the top line. The risk factors effect was –50.0 percent, while the remaining effect was stock specific at 37.4 percent. Controlling exposure to the factors in the model can help reduce losses coming from the factor level and lead to enhanced performance. In this case, even over the 11-year period, the return of all factors except for one had a negligible impact on the portfolio. The one factor, volatility, had a –51.97 percent impact on the performance of the portfolio during this time. That's a tremendous impact for a single factor and one that should be examined more closely.

## OPTIMIZATION

One method we discussed earlier is to evaluate the marginal contributions to the volatility factor at the stock level and execute trades that will reduce the risk from that factor in the portfolio. Another methodology is to use an optimizer to produce a new portfolio based on a manager's predicted alphas, tolerance for risk, and portfolio and asset constraints. Common constraint inputs available in most optimizers include controlling for asset weights, sector weights, factor exposures, number of assets, and custom constraints such as constraining the weighted average portfolio P/E. In our example, using the optimizer to simply reduce our exposure to the volatility factor may be the best first step. We can do this for a single date and also run this historically using FactSet's Portfolio Simulation application. We can take each portfolio from every month over those 11 years and set our volatility exposure range from –0.1 to +0.1. As the initial portfolio had an exposure of 0.30, this constraint will cut that exposure down substantially. Doing so will also cut down the risk of that factor, as well as minimize the return impact this factor can have on the portfolio. This factor had by far the largest negative impact on the performance of the portfolio, so this should be the first factor to constrain.

Another consideration is the number of assets in the portfolio. The initial portfolio had 35 names and we may want to keep it at that level, so we'll set a constraint to do so. We may also want to control the tracking error of the overall portfolio. In this case, we'll set the maximum to 3.5 percent. Finally, we can add constraints around the GICS sectors and keep each sector of our portfolio within 10 percent of the corresponding benchmark sector weight.

These simple inputs can produce fairly remarkable results. As shown in Table 13.8, with volatility constrained, we move from a portfolio in which volatility detracted almost 52 percent from return during the 11-year period to one in which our exposure to volatility contributes only 6.2 percent to return. Overall portfolio performance increases from –12.6 percent to +3.5, as shown in Table 13.9.

**TABLE 13.7** Factor attribution.

**Factor Attribution**

**Large-Cap Focused Fund vs. S&P 500**
**12/31/1999 to 12/31/2010**
**Axioma U.S. 2 MH Fundamental**
**U.S. Dollar**

| | Ending Factor Exposures | | | Factor Performance Attribution | | | |
|---|---|---|---|---|---|---|---|
| Standard | Portfolio Exposure | Benchmark Exposure | Active Exposure | Average Active Exposure | Factor Return | Compounded Factor Impact | Factor Impact T-Stat |
| **Industries** | **1.00** | **1.00** | **0.00** | **0.00** | | **1.36** | **0.01** |
| **Style** | **1.75** | **1.19** | **0.55** | **0.41** | | **-51.37** | **-8.24** |
| Exchange Rate Sensitivity | 0.26 | 0.21 | 0.05 | 0.00 | −0.03 | −0.12 | −0.15 |
| Growth | 0.27 | 0.22 | 0.05 | 0.03 | 0.31 | 1.30 | 3.41 |
| Leverage | −0.24 | −0.19 | −0.05 | 0.00 | −0.18 | −0.31 | −0.70 |
| Liquidity | 0.26 | 0.21 | 0.05 | 0.03 | 0.33 | 1.46 | 1.60 |
| Market Sensitivity | 0.10 | 0.05 | 0.05 | 0.02 | −0.10 | −1.02 | −0.60 |

| | | | | | | | |
|---|---|---|---|---|---|---|---|
| Medium-Term Momentum | 0.16 | 0.12 | 0.04 | 0.01 | 0.41 | 1.17 | 1.87 |
| Short-Term Momentum | -0.06 | -0.06 | 0.00 | 0.01 | -1.18 | -2.34 | -3.90 |
| Size | 1.37 | 1.32 | 0.05 | 0.01 | -0.34 | -0.04 | -0.09 |
| Value | -0.32 | -0.33 | 0.01 | 0.00 | 0.22 | 0.50 | 1.42 |
| Volatility | -0.06 | -0.36 | 0.30 | 0.30 | -1.20 | -51.97 | -8.70 |
| **Total** | 2.75 | 2.19 | 0.55 | 0.41 | | -50.00 | -6.56 |

Holdings Data As Of
Large-Cap Focused Fund 12/31/1999 through 11/30/2010
S&P 500 12/31/1999 through 11/30/2010
Risk Model As Of
Axioma U.S. 2 MH Fundamental 12/31/1999

**TABLE 13.8** Factor attribution of optimized portfolio.

**Factor Attribution**

**Large-Cap Focused Fund Opt. vs. S&P 500**
**12/31/1999 to 12/31/2010**
**Axioma U.S. 2 MH Fundamental**
**U.S. Dollar**

| | Ending Factor Exposures | | | Factor Performance Attribution | | | |
|---|---|---|---|---|---|---|---|
| **Standard** | **Portfolio Exposure** | **Benchmark Exposure** | **Active Exposure** | **Average Active Exposure** | **Factor Return** | **Compounded Factor Impact** | **Factor Impact T-Stat** |
| **Style** | **1.31** | **1.19** | **0.12** | **0.01** | | **1.47** | **0.80** |
| Exchange Rate Sensitivity | 0.20 | 0.21 | –0.01 | 0.00 | –0.03 | 0.18 | 0.45 |
| Growth | 0.24 | 0.22 | 0.01 | 0.00 | 0.31 | 0.34 | 1.08 |
| Leverage | –0.14 | –0.19 | 0.05 | 0.00 | –0.18 | 0.46 | 0.84 |
| Liquidity | 0.16 | 0.21 | –0.05 | –0.03 | 0.33 | –1.47 | -3.12 |
| Market Sensitivity | 0.09 | 0.05 | 0.04 | 0.01 | –0.10 | –0.43 | –0.47 |
| Medium-Term Momentum | 0.17 | 0.12 | 0.05 | 0.01 | 0.41 | 0.05 | -0.01 |
| Short-Term Momentum | –0.07 | –0.06 | –0.01 | 0.00 | –1.18 | –2.07 | -3.06 |
| Size | 1.37 | 1.32 | 0.05 | 0.05 | –0.34 | –2.40 | -3.72 |

| | | | | | | | |
|---|---|---|---|---|---|---|---|
| Value | −0.28 | −0.33 | 0.05 | 0.01 | 0.22 | 0.62 | 1.79 |
| Volatility | −0.41 | −0.36 | −0.05 | −0.04 | −1.20 | 6.19 | 5.91 |
| **Industries** | **1.00** | **1.00** | **0.00** | **0.00** | | **−15.42** | **−1.65** |
| **Total** | 2.31 | 2.19 | 0.12 | 0.01 | | −13.95 | −1.50 |

Holdings Data As Of
Large-Cap Focused Fund Opt. 12/31/1999 through 11/30/2010
S&P 500 12/31/1999 through 11/30/2010
Risk Model As Of
Axioma U.S. 2 MH Fundamental 12/31/1999 through 11/30/2010

**TABLE 13.9** Risk-based performance attribution and Brinson attribution of optimal portfolio.

**Risk-Based Performance Attribution**

**Large-Cap Focused Fund Opt. vs. S&P 500**
**12/31/1999 to 12/31/2010**
**Axioma U.S. 2 MH Fundamental**
**U.S. Dollar**

| | | | | Risk-Based Performance Attribution | | | Brinson Attribution | | |
|---|---|---|---|---|---|---|---|---|---|
| Economic Sector | Portfolio Average Weight | Benchmark Average Weight | Variation Average Weight | Risk Factors Effect | Stock-Specific Effect | Total Effect | Allocation Effect | Selection | Total Effect |
| Total | 100.00 | 100.00 | — | −13.95 | 17.49 | 3.54 | −17.40 | 20.94 | 3.54 |
| Consumer Discretionary | 10.99 | 10.86 | 0.13 | −7.37 | −0.73 | −8.11 | −3.72 | −6.49 | −10.21 |
| Consumer Staples | 6.78 | 9.94 | −3.16 | 6.22 | −3.06 | 3.15 | 1.97 | 6.79 | 8.77 |
| Energy | 7.68 | 8.91 | −1.23 | −13.78 | 4.46 | −9.32 | −7.50 | −0.99 | −8.50 |
| Financials | 21.16 | 18.11 | 3.05 | 8.22 | 3.72 | 11.95 | 2.71 | 3.40 | 6.11 |
| Health Care | 14.40 | 13.00 | 1.40 | −12.68 | 4.62 | −8.06 | −1.42 | −1.77 | −3.19 |
| Industrials | 12.94 | 11.15 | 1.79 | 4.15 | −7.67 | −3.52 | −2.53 | −4.24 | −6.77 |

| | | | | | | | | | |
|---|---|---|---|---|---|---|---|---|---|
| Information Technology | 18.64 | 17.75 | 0.89 | –2.09 | 14.58 | 12.49 | –1.74 | 15.00 | 13.27 |
| Materials | 1.09 | 2.93 | –1.84 | 2.76 | 3.23 | 5.99 | –0.22 | 7.19 | 6.97 |
| Telecommunication Services | 4.98 | 4.01 | 0.97 | –2.72 | 1.04 | –1.68 | –2.75 | –1.93 | –4.68 |
| Utilities | 1.34 | 3.32 | –1.98 | 3.20 | –2.50 | 0.70 | –1.91 | 3.97 | 2.06 |

Holdings Data As Of
Large-Cap Focused Fund Opt. 12/31/1999 through 11/30/2010
S&P 500 12/31/1999 through 11/30/2010
Risk Model As Of
Axioma U.S. 2 MH Fundamental 12/31/1999 through 11/30/2010

In practice, a fundamental manager can use an optimizer to control some exposures and apply constraints, and then merely use the resulting trades as suggestions. He may want to execute some of the trades and ignore others. The main point is that the optimizer can become a tool for the fundamental manager to help construct the portfolio without changing the overall strategy. Using an optimizer should be secondary to first performing the risk and return decomposition on the existing portfolio and making trades based on that analysis.

We have now come full circle since discussing hybrid strategies earlier in this chapter. Incorporating risk techniques such as these into a fundamental management style may not exactly make the management style a hybrid approach, but it certainly could be categorized as fundamental with a risk overlay strategy.

## CONCLUSION

This chapter introduced you to how fundamental managers can integrate risk management practices into their approach. We covered the differences between fundamental investing and other investment approaches as well as the typical risk controls that fundamental managers employ. The crux of the chapter was a discussion of how traditional risk management strategies can be implemented into a fundamental process. Analyzing factor exposures and the associated risk from those factors, looking at implied alphas side by side with active asset weights, and performing marginal analysis are all ways of incorporating some risk management approaches into a fundamental style. Comparing risk-based performance attribution to Brinson attribution will show the sources of under- and overperformance of the portfolio at the factor level. Optimization may also be performed, the results of which can be used to any degree with which the manager feels comfortable.

The key point is that there are options. Portfolio managers do not need to abandon their investment approaches; they may simply wish to add some of these tools to their process to more thoroughly evaluate the risk and performance of the portfolio. Doing so will surely lead to new insights and may help the manager better understand and control different sources of risk while improving the performance of the portfolio. Last, availing oneself of the enormous benefit of combining stress-testing into the fundamental process for evaluation of risky events is within the usual expectations of fundamental analysts' thought processes.

CHAPTER 14

# Portfolio Optimization

***Sebastian Ceria, PhD, and Kartik Sivaramakrishnan, PhD***

Every portfolio manager faces the challenge of building portfolios that achieve an optimal trade-off between risk and return. Harry Markowitz[1] was the first to develop a mathematical framework to solve this problem in the 1950s. The Markowitz model, as it is known in the literature, considers the first two moments of the asset returns, namely the mean and the variance, to measure the return and the risk of the portfolio, respectively. The model is known as Markowitz's MVO (mean-variance optimization) in the financial world.

Let the weight of an asset in a portfolio be the proportion of the total funds invested in this asset. The portfolio return is modeled as a linear function of the weights, representing the portfolio's expected return; and the portfolio risk is modeled as a quadratic function in the weights, representing the variance of the portfolio. The trade-off between risk and return is obtained by solving a simple quadratic program (QP) of the form:

$$\max_w (\alpha^T w - \lambda w^T Q w) \tag{14.1}$$

where $\alpha$ is the vector of expected returns, $Q$ is the covariance matrix of returns, and $\lambda > 0$ is the portfolio manager's risk aversion parameter that represents the investor's preference as how to trade-off risk and return. The solution to the QP determines the asset weights in an *efficient* portfolio—the portfolio with the minimum risk for a given level of expected return or (equivalently) the one with the largest expected return for a given level of allowed risk. The Markowitz model has had a profound impact on the investing world and is now widely used for asset allocation, tactical portfolio construction, hedging, and other portfolio construction problems. From a computational perspective, MVO is an *easily solvable* optimization problem; it is a convex quadratic program that can be efficiently handled by state-of-the-art optimizers even in the case where there are tens of thousands of assets in the investable universe.

When $\lambda$ is small, the contribution of the portfolio risk to the overall objective is small, leading to higher risk portfolios with larger returns. Conversely, when $\lambda$ is large, less risky portfolios with lower returns are generated. In fact, one can solve the MVO model with different values of $\lambda$ starting from zero to design portfolios with different risk and return profiles. The set of all these portfolios determines the *efficient frontier*. Investors can then choose a portfolio from the efficient frontier based on their return or risk mandates and appetites. It is worth reiterating that the MVO approach does not return a single optimal portfolio but rather a family of them that lie on the efficient frontier. For a given target return, a portfolio on the efficient frontier gives the least risky portfolio. Similarly, for a given target risk, a portfolio on the efficient frontier gives the portfolio with the greatest return.

Consider a simple MVO model where we have a budget constraint and nonnegativity requirements on the asset weights. We will highlight the importance of these constraints later. The efficient frontier for this model is shown in Figure 14.1. Note that this frontier is a hyperbola. Let us briefly explain how this frontier was obtained. First, we minimize the risk of the portfolio over these constraints to find the minimum risk value. We then choose 100 risk values between the minimum risk value and the maximum risk threshold (50 percent). For each risk value, we solve an MVO model where we maximize the expected return of the portfolio subject to the portfolio constraints and the requirement that the risk of the portfolio be less than or equal to the aforementioned risk value. We then plot these 100 portfolios in the (standard deviation of portfolio return, expected return) space to generate the efficient frontier. Note that portfolios that are below the efficient frontier can be improved; that is, for a given risk threshold one can get a larger return by choosing the portfolio on the efficient frontier instead. Moreover, since the frontier is efficient, there cannot be any portfolios satisfying the constraints that are above the frontier.

The Markowitz MVO model contains two critical parameters that must be estimated: the expected return vector $\alpha$ and the covariance matrix $Q$. Both these parameters are estimated with a variety of statistical techniques that rely on historical and forward-looking information, such as analysts' estimates of future earnings. Estimating expected returns is a far more difficult task, and is what most believe differentiates portfolio managers. While estimating the covariance matrix $Q$ is also nontrivial, the structure of the asset covariances and volatilities is more stable over time, somewhat simplifying the task. $Q$ is commonly estimated by *dimensionality reduction*

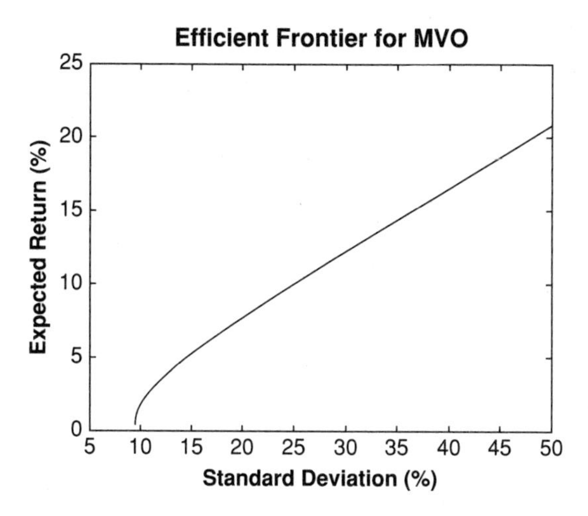


**FIGURE 14.1** Note that this efficient frontier is a hyperbola and is created by minimizing the risk of the portfolio over constraints to find the minimum risk value. It's created by choosing 100 risk values between the minimum risk value and the maximum risk threshold. For each risk value, solve an MVO model where expected portfolio return is maximized subject to portfolio constraints and the requirement that the risk of the portfolio be less than or equal to the aforementioned risk value. The 100 portfolios are simply plotted in the (standard deviation of portfolio return, expected return) space to generate the efficient frontier.

*techniques* that decompose this matrix into a *factor model* (see Grinold and Kahn[2] and Zangari[3]).

This chapter is organized as follows: It begins with a description of the *enhanced MVO* (EMVO) model with objectives and constraints. Then it describes the commonly used objectives and constraints in the EMVO model along with a classification that indicates the complexity of the mathematical functions that are used to model them. We will also cover new techniques based on *robust optimization* and *Bayesian approaches* that improve the EMVO model by addressing the issue of estimation errors in the expected returns. Then you'll find a description of the *factor alignment problems* (FAPs) that arise due to natural disparities in the information that is used to construct EMVO models, together with techniques that address them. Later sections describe *constraint attribution* that is commonly used by portfolio managers to quantify the impact of each individual constraint in the EMVO model as well as specially structured EMVO models arising in *multiportfolio* and *trade scheduling* problems. *Extreme tail loss* (ETL) models and *downside risk* measures, where the return distributions have long left tails, are covered in addition to methods for incorporating *nonlinear* instruments, such as *options* in the EMVO model. We then cover the common algorithms that are used to solve EMVO models. Finally, the last section of the chapter describes the important features that portfolio managers should consider when they shop for a *portfolio optimizer* that best meets their needs.

Go to www.wiley.com/go/greiner to see video titled "Portfolio Optimization."

## THE ENHANCED MVO MODEL

In addition to trading off risk and return, portfolio managers must often make investment decisions that satisfy a set of constraints imposed by asset owners, regulators, risk managers, and trading desks alike. In addition, portfolio managers may implement some of their insights and investment views in the form of additional constraints. Constraints have also been used historically to address some of the well-known deficiencies of the MVO model, especially those concerning the impact of estimation errors in the optimal portfolio; see DeMiguel et al.[4] and Jagannathan and Ma.[5]

We briefly describe the enhanced MVO model with various constraints and objectives in this section. First, we must introduce some notation. Consider a portfolio manager with an investment universe of $n$ assets. Let $w_i$ denote the weight (proportion of total funds) invested in the $i$th asset. Let $\alpha_i$ denote the manager's estimate of the expected return for the $i$th asset. The portfolio return is given by:

$$r_p = \sum_{\{i=1\}}^{n} \alpha_i w_i \tag{14.2}$$

The covariance matrix of the asset returns is generally obtained from a factor-risk model. The factors represent macroeconomic or fundamental entities or the different industries of the economy. An asset's return is decomposed into a portion driven by these factors (common factor return) and a residual component (specific return). Let us assume that there are $k$ factors in the model. The decomposition of the asset returns can be expressed as $r = Bf + u$ where $r$ is the asset returns vector of size $n$, $f$ is the factor returns vector of size $k$, $u$ is the specific returns vector of size $n$, and $B$ is the $n \times k$ exposure matrix. Each row of the exposure matrix denotes an asset's exposure to the $k$ factors. Each asset-specific return is uncorrelated with the other asset-specific returns; moreover, each specific return is also uncorrelated with the factor returns. The covariance matrix of the asset returns is given by:

$$Q = B\,\Sigma B + \Delta^2 \tag{14.3}$$

where $B$ is the factor covariance matrix of size $k$ and $\Delta^2$ is a diagonal matrix containing the specific variances. The risk of the portfolio is given by:

$$\text{Portfolio risk} = w^T(B\Sigma B^T + \Delta^2)w \tag{14.4}$$

The original Markowitz MVO model used the variance of the returns to measure the portfolio risk. This gives rise to a quadratic program (QP) for which an algorithm based on the simplex method for linear programming was available in Markowitz's time. One can also use the standard deviation of the returns to measure the risk of the portfolio; the resulting EMVO is now a convex program that we discuss in a later section. Let $\Omega$ denote the set of *admissible portfolios*. The *enhanced* MVO model is given by:

$$\begin{aligned} \max\ & \alpha^T w - \lambda w^T(B\Sigma B^T + \Delta^2)w \\ s.t.\ & \quad w \in \Omega \end{aligned} \tag{14.5}$$

where $\lambda > 0$ determines the trade-off between return and risk.

Let us illustrate the utility of constraints that define the set of admissible portfolios by considering the following MVO model:

$$\begin{aligned} \max\ & \alpha^T w - \lambda\, w^T Q w \\ s.t.\ & 0 \le w_i \le u_i,\ \ i = 1, \ldots, n \end{aligned} \tag{14.6}$$

with simple bounds on the asset weights. In this case, it is possible to find an equivalent unconstrained portfolio optimization problem. In fact, the portfolio manager is actually solving the following unconstrained MVO model:

$$\max_w\ (\alpha + \gamma - \pi)^T w - \lambda w^T Q w \tag{14.7}$$

where $\gamma \ge 0$ and $\pi \ge 0$ contain the optimal dual (Lagrangian) multipliers for the lower and upper bounds on the asset variables, respectively. When the lower bound constraint on asset $i$ is binding (i.e., $w_i = 0$), we have $\gamma_i > 0$ and $\pi_i = 0$. This is likely to be the case when $\alpha_i$ is small. In this case, the expected return for the $i$th asset is increased from $\alpha_i$ to $(\alpha_i + \gamma_i)$. Conversely, when the upper bound on asset $i$ is binding (i.e., $w_i = u_i$), we have $\gamma_i = 0$ and $\pi_i > 0$. This is likely to be the case when $\alpha_i$ is large. In this case, the expected return for the $i$th asset is reduced from $\alpha_i$ to $(\alpha_i - \pi_i)$. So, imposing these constraints in the optimization problem is equivalent to *shrinking* the expected return vector toward the average of the expected returns in this vector. This, in turn, will prevent the optimizer from taking large bets on the assets with small and large alpha components.

Although constraints change the structure of the MVO model, most of the commonly used constraints can still be modeled within what we term the *enhanced MVO* (EMVO) model, and the resulting problem can still be solved efficiently by modern optimizers. In the next section, we enumerate the most typical constraints and classify them according to how they can be modeled mathematically. In fact, the true test of a good optimizer is found in its ability to handle these disparate constraints and to produce accurate solutions in reasonable amounts of time, regardless of the type (or number) of constraints that are used.

## CONSTRAINTS AND OBJECTIVES IN EMVO

Portfolio managers use constraints to model a variety of business rules that are imposed to the optimal portfolios. (See Table 14.1.) We classify constraints in the following four categories:

1. **Holding constraints:** These are constraints that are imposed on the individual portfolio holdings, or in any linearly weighted combination of the holdings:
   - *Bounds on individual holdings:* These are general lower and upper bounds on the holdings in an individual asset or a group of assets, such as an industry, sector, country, or region. The simplest such constraint is the long-only constraint on an asset holding.
   - *Bounds on active holdings:* The active holding for an asset is the difference in investment in the asset between the portfolio and the benchmark. Active holding constraints allow the portfolio manager to directly limit the active bet with respect to any asset in the benchmark. One can also impose bounds on the active holdings on a group of assets in the portfolio, such as those in an industry.
   - *Budget constraint:* The budget constraint limits the total dollar holding in the portfolio to the budget available to the manager.
   - *Bounds on the expected return:* This constraint imposes a lower bound on the expected return of the portfolio.

**TABLE 14.1** Classification of commonly used constraints and objectives in MVO.

| Strategy | Classification |
|---|---|
| Bounds on holdings | LIN |
| Minimum threshold holdings | COMB |
| Limiting the long/short ratio | NLC |
| Names constraint | COMB |
| Turnover constraint | NLC |
| RMCTR | COMB (risk parity case is NLC) |
| Budget constraint | LIN |
| Dollar-neutral (fully invested) | COMB |
| Risk constraint/objective | NLC |
| Variance constraint/objective | QUAD |
| Expected return constraint | LIN |
| Portfolio beta constraint | LIN |
| Factor exposure constraint | LIN |
| Round lot constraint | COMB |
| Issuer holding constraint | COMB |
| Transaction objective | LIN or NLC |
| Market-impact objective | QUAD or NLC |
| Tax liability objective | COMB |
| Sharpe ratio objective | NLC |

- *Limits on the portfolio beta:* The beta of the portfolio measures how its returns move with respect to the market. One can impose lower and upper limits on the beta of the portfolio.
- *Limiting the factor exposure:* Factor exposure measures how a portfolio is exposed to particular factors in the risk model. Portfolio managers can add factor exposure constraints either to get greater exposure or to limit their exposure to the factors in their risk models.
- *Round lot constraint:* In the real world, assets can be bought or sold in multiples of round lots (for example, 50 or 100 shares). Round lot constraints can be added for the relevant assets in the portfolio to ensure that an asset transaction is a multiple of its round lot size.
- *Issuer holding constraint:* Portfolio managers and exchange-traded fund (ETF) providers who track a benchmark often must satisfy

regulatory issuer holdings constraints, such as the 5–50 constraint that prescribes that the sum of all the asset weights that are greater than 5 percent should be less than 50 percent.

- *Limiting the long/short ratio:* Legal or institutional guidelines often require a portfolio manager to limit the ratio of the long to the short holdings of a portfolio. This constraint is used, for example, to create 130/30 portfolios.
- *Minimum threshold holdings:* This constraint models the restriction that if an asset is held, then the position must be at least some threshold (minimum) amount (either long or short). This constraint is used to ensure that the optimal portfolio does not contain positions that are *too small.*

2. **Names constraints:** These are limits that are set on the number of positions held in the optimal portfolio, the number of trades executed, or the maximum number of holdings for any particular group of assets.
   - *Limit the number of names held:* This constraint limits the number of assets that are held in the portfolio. One can also impose this constraint over a subset of the portfolio; for example, one can limit the number of assets that are held in a specific industry in the portfolio.
   - *Limit the number of transactions:* This constraint limits the number of assets traded in a portfolio or a subset of a portfolio, such as an industry in the portfolio. This is another way to control the transaction costs associated with a portfolio.
3. **Risk constraints:** Although the MVO model allows the portfolio manager to control risk via the risk aversion parameter, an alternative approach is to limit risk directly by imposing an explicit constraint that the portfolio risk be less than a target value. There are various types of risk that can be controlled in this manner:
   - *Limit absolute risk:* This constraint limits the standard deviation of the portfolio returns over the rebalancing time horizon.
   - *Limit active risk:* The active risk of a portfolio is the standard deviation of the difference of the portfolio and benchmark returns over the rebalancing time horizon. This constraint limits the portfolio risk relative to the benchmark. This constraint is commonly known as a *tracking error* constraint, and it is sometimes imposed on the active variance of the portfolio.
   - *Limit the relative marginal contribution to total risk or active risk:* These constraints impose lower or upper bounds on the total or active risk that can be attributed to a specific asset or group of assets. One special case of the constraint is used in the construction of *risk-parity* portfolios (see Maillard, Roncalli, and Jerome;[6] Axioma Advisor;[7] and Asness, Frazzini, and Pedersen[8]), where the objective is to equalize

the total risk over all the assets in a long-only portfolio. This can be done by adding a relative marginal contribution to total risk constraint on each asset in the portfolio with a lower bound of $(1/n)$, where $n$ is the number of assets in the portfolio.

4. **Trading constraints:** Most of the time, a portfolio manager is using the MVO model not to generate a portfolio from scratch (all-cash position), but to rebalance an existing portfolio. We define an asset transaction as the amount of the asset that is either bought or sold in the rebalancing. Here are some of the popular constraints on transactions:
   - *Bounds on transactions:* These are general lower and upper bounds on the transactions in an individual asset or a set of assets.
   - *Minimum threshold transactions:* These constraints impose a minimum transaction size for assets; they ensure that if there is a transaction (buy/sell) on an asset, the transaction is at least for the minimum threshold amount.
   - *Limit turnover:* The turnover of an asset is the total amount of the asset that is either bought or sold. A portfolio manager can impose a turnover constraint on an asset or a group of assets in order to put an upper limit on the turnover of the portfolio, industry, or even an individual asset in the portfolio. This is commonly done to reduce the transaction costs associated with a portfolio rebalancing.

The constraints just described can be mathematically modeled by using either linear (LIN), quadratic (QUAD), nonlinear-convex (NLC), or combinatorial (COMB) functions of the portfolio weights. Linear constraints can be easily added to the EMVO model without affecting its complexity. In fact, the original Markowitz model had a budget constraint and nonnegativity (no-shorting) constraints on the weights of the portfolio. Adding quadratic constraints to the EMVO model destroys the quadratic programming structure. These constraints are typically added to limit the deviation of the optimized portfolio from one or more benchmarks, such as the Russell 1000. Quadratic constraints can be added to the objective term of the MVO model with weights that quantitatively indicate their importance in the optimization. However, it is a challenging task to calibrate a weight parameter for each constraint that is added to the objective function of the EMVO model. Some of the constraints that have been recently proposed by practitioners can be modeled with nonlinear but convex functions, while others require the use of combinatorial and nonconvex functions. A popular portfolio constraint is the names constraint that limits the number of assets held in the portfolio; this is very helpful in keeping the underlying portfolio as simple as possible. Unfortunately, the names constraint is a difficult combinatorial constraint to handle in practice. Constraints play an important role in the enhanced MVO model; they greatly align the portfolio weights with the desires of the portfolio manager. We will classify constraints by the complexity of the mathematical functions that are required to model them. These are linear, quadratic, nonlinear convex, and combinatorial.

Some portfolio managers are also allowed to short assets in the portfolio. The short positions allow the manager to achieve leverage (i.e., the ability to finance the portfolio with more than the available budget by investing the proceeds from the assets that are held short). A dollar-neutral portfolio has zero net investment; that is, the long positions are entirely financed by the short positions. Suppose that we require in addition that the portfolio is fully invested in these long positions. This strategy is said to be leveraged 2:1. The constraints that model this strategy are combinatorial in nature. Contrast this with the equality budget constraint in the long-only case that can be modeled as a simple linear constraint. This discussion highlights that a simple constraint (LIN) can become complicated (COMB) due to the presence of both long and short assets in the portfolio. This, in turn, increases the complexity of an EMVO model.

An important distinction is between *hard* and *soft* constraints in the portfolio. Hard constraints must be exactly satisfied in the model. Soft constraints can be violated by a user-specific amount but there is a penalty imposed for violating these constraints. Sometimes, the portfolio manager is interested only in finding a portfolio that best satisfies a set of constraints and also has a ranking of constraints that are layered in their order of importance. In this case, the EMVO model is solved in a hierarchical fashion, where the constraints are sequentially added in their order of importance. If the resulting problem is infeasible, an auxiliary problem that minimizes the constraint violation is solved. The solution to this auxiliary problem is used to correct the right-hand side of the violated constraint, and the procedure continues through all the levels that the portfolio manager has considered in the hierarchy.

Portfolio managers may also consider other goals in addition to the trade-off between risk and return. Some of the commonly used objectives in the MVO model are the following:

1. *Minimize active risk:* Minimizing active risk is a common *passive* investment strategy, where the aim is to stay close to a benchmark.
2. *Minimize active variance:* One can also minimize the active variance to ensure that the portfolio tracks a benchmark.
3. *Minimize transaction costs:* Transaction costs model explicit costs, such as fees and commissions. They are typically modeled by linear or piecewise-linear functions of the asset transactions.

4. *Minimize market-impact costs:* Market-impact costs are important for large institutional investors. They model implicit costs associated with trading assets that are difficult to measure in practice. Market-impact costs are typically modeled by quadratic, three-halves, or five-thirds power functions of the asset transactions, and they serve to discourage large transactions.
5. *Minimize tax liability:* The U.S. tax code specifies that short-term and long-term capital gains are taxed at different rates. For a tax-sensitive investor, the difference in the rates can have a significant impact on the after-tax return of the portfolio. One of the primary objectives of the *tax-sensitive* portfolio manager is to minimize the tax liability of the portfolio. The tax liability objective, however, is a combinatorial function of the individual tax lots of the transactions.
6. *Maximize the Sharpe ratio:* The Sharpe ratio is a common performance measure that evaluates the excess portfolio return (portfolio return above the risk-free rate) per unit of risk. In the Sharpe ratio, the risk in the denominator is measured as the standard deviation of the portfolio returns. Although the Sharpe ratio by itself is a nonconvex function of the asset holdings, one can model the problem of maximizing the Sharpe ratio of an EMVO problem with an equality budget constraint as a convex optimization problem (see Cornuejols and Tutuncu[9]). An additional assumption required in this convex reformulation is that the optimal portfolio has an expected return that is greater than the risk-free rate so that the Sharpe ratio of the optimal portfolio is positive. The reformulation exploits the *scale-invariance* property of the Sharpe ratio.

When using multiple objectives, the portfolio manager has the additional challenge of assigning appropriate weights (aversion) to the various objectives terms that are used in the EMVO model. On the other hand, the portfolio manager typically has a ranking of objectives that are layered in their order of importance. In addition, each objective has a tolerance that specifies the maximum degradation in the objective value that can be tolerated. In this case, the portfolio manager can solve the EMVO model in a hierarchical manner, where a different (chosen) objective is optimized in each level of the hierarchy, subject to constraints that ensure that the objectives in the preceding levels get no worse than their maximum degradation values. Let us illustrate this approach on a simple example. A portfolio manager wants to track a benchmark as closely as possible and is willing to tolerate a degradation of 1 percent from the minimum tracking error. The secondary objective is to minimize the tax liability. In the first level of the hierarchical approach, an EMVO model with only the tracking error objective is solved. Suppose that the optimal portfolio to this EMVO model has a

3 percent tracking error. In the second level, the EMVO model with only the tax objective is solved. This EMVO model has an additional tracking error constraint that limits the deviation from the benchmark to be 4 percent. The optimal portfolio to the EMVO model in the second level of the hierarchy is the required portfolio for the manager. The success of this approach hinges on a portfolio optimizer's ability to interchange objectives with their corresponding constraints and to solve the sequence of EMVO models at the different levels of the hierarchy quickly.

We conclude this section with the concept of *implied alpha* that we will use later in this chapter. Effectively, constraints can be thought of as distorting the holdings in the unconstrained MVO model. Implied alpha is the vector of expected returns that when used in the unconstrained setting (no constraints in the EMVO model) has the same optimal solution (in terms of portfolio weights) as the constrained EMVO model. Let us illustrate the concept of the implied alpha with the following EMVO model:

$$\max \alpha^T w - \frac{\lambda}{2} w^T Q w$$

$$s.t. \quad Aw \leq b \tag{14.8}$$

where $Aw \leq b$ includes a set of linear inequality constraints on the portfolio weights.

The first-order optimality conditions for this model can be written as:

$$\alpha - \lambda Q w - A^T \pi = 0,$$

$$\pi^T (Aw - b) = 0, \quad \pi \geq 0 \tag{14.9}$$

where $\pi$ is the vector of dual multipliers for the inequality constraints $Aw \leq b$. Let $\alpha^i$ represent the implied alpha of the portfolio. From the optimality conditions for the unconstrained case, we have $\alpha^i = \lambda Q w$.Plugging this expression in the first-order optimality conditions, we obtain:

$$\alpha^i = \alpha - A^T \pi \tag{14.10}$$

This shows that the implied alpha is obtained by tilting the portfolio manager's alpha in the direction of the constraints as determined by the optimal dual weights. Note that only the active (binding) constraints with positive dual multipliers affect the $\alpha$ vector.

## FURTHER IMPROVEMENTS TO THE ENHANCED MVO MODEL

A common complaint from practitioners regarding the EMVO (and MVO) model is that the efficient frontiers are often *error-maximized* and *investment-irrelevant* portfolios. This is due to the fact, they argue, that the solution to the EMVO model is highly sensitive to perturbations in the data parameters. Typically, the mean and the variance estimates are obtained from historical information, and these estimation processes are subject to statistical errors. Furthermore, it is believed that most of the estimation error sensitivity of optimal portfolios is due to errors in the estimated expected returns, rather than in errors in the estimation of the covariance matrix. Michaud[10] also argues that EMVO overweights assets with a large ratio of estimated expected returns to estimated variances, and these are precisely the assets with large estimation errors. Michaud proposes using a Monte Carlo approach by sampling repeatedly from the return distribution and averaging the portfolios that are generated in the EMVO model. Michaud calls his approach *portfolio resampling* and advocates it as a solution to the estimation problem. While the resampling approach may indeed reduce the effect of estimation errors in the (resampled) optimal portfolio, the solution to this problem involves the solution of an EMVO problem for each return sample that is drawn, which may be time-consuming for large portfolios. In addition, the resampled average portfolio generated with this method need not satisfy all the constraints that are imposed in each individual EMVO model, especially the constraints that are nonconvex or combinatorial in nature.

One method to address estimation errors in the expected returns in EMVO is to use a technique called *robust optimization* (see Ben-Tal, El Ghaoui, and Nemirovskii[11]). The robust optimization approach assumes that, although the asset returns are unknown, they are confined to an uncertainty set $\Psi$. One popular uncertainty set is an ellipsoidal uncertainty set that is constructed from the mean and the covariance of the asset returns. This set is of the form:

$$\Psi = \{r : \ (r-\alpha)^T \ Q^{-1} (r-\alpha) \leq \ \kappa^2\} \tag{14.11}$$

where $\alpha$ is the investor's estimate of the mean return and $Q$ is the covariance matrix. These are also the inputs to the EMVO model. Also, $\kappa > 0$ is the radius of this ellipsoid; a larger value for $\kappa$ results in a larger uncertainty set. The robust portfolio optimization approach is then set in the following game theoretic setting. The investor has a highly intelligent and rational opponent. The investor chooses the portfolio weights $w$ from the set of all admissible portfolios $\Omega$ and the opponent chooses the worst return vector $r$ in the uncertainty set $\Psi$ for this set of portfolio weights. So, the objective of the investor is to choose portfolio weights $w$ in a way that maximizes the worst possible objective value. This problem can be formulated as:

$$\max_{\{w \in \Omega\}} \min_{\{\alpha \in \Psi\}} w^T \alpha - \lambda w^T Q w \tag{14.12}$$

At the outset, the robust portfolio problem appears daunting since the inner minimization is over an infinite number of returns in the uncertainty set $\Psi$. However, one can show that for the choice of the ellipsoidal uncertainty set, the robust portfolio problem can be reformulated as:

$$\max_{\{w \in \Omega\}} \alpha^T w - \lambda w^T Q w - \kappa \sqrt{w^T Q w} \tag{14.13}$$

Note that the robust optimization problem has an additional risk term with the $\kappa$ multiplier in the objective function. We can interpret this term as the penalty for estimation errors in the returns $\alpha$. The resulting problem can be formulated as second-order cone program and solved to optimality in about the same time as a regular EMVO model (with the same constraints in $\Omega$) by a state-of-the-art optimizer. Different uncertainty sets are considered in Ceria and Stubbs,[12] Goldfarb and Iyengar,[13] and Tutuncu and Koenig.[14] Although the robust EMVO model is more conservative in its choice of optimal portfolio weights, the resulting weights are less sensitive to errors in the estimated returns.

Another approach to dealing with estimation errors is to use Bayesian adjustment techniques. For example, it is possible to use stable estimators for the returns. James-Stein estimators take a weighted average of the expected return and another estimator called the *shrinkage target*. Jorion[15] uses the return from the minimum variance portfolio as the shrinkage target. In some cases (but not always!), optimized portfolios utilizing shrinkage estimates lead to improved realized performance. The Black-Litterman approach[16] uses two sources of information to compute the expected return vector in the EMVO model. The first is a *prior* belief that the expected returns can be expressed as:

$$\alpha = \pi + \epsilon_\pi \tag{14.14}$$

where $\pi$ is the market equilibrium return (i.e., the return in the EMVO model that gives the market portfolio), and $\epsilon_\pi$ is normally distributed with zero mean and covariance $\tau\Omega$. The $\tau$ parameter reflects the level of belief in the equilibrium returns; more weight is given to the equilibrium return if $\tau$ is small. The market provides a second source of views on the expected return vector. Suppose we have $k$ views that can be expressed in matrix notation as:

$$P\alpha = q + \epsilon_q \tag{14.15}$$

where $P$ is a $k \times n$ views matrix, $q$ is a $k$ dimensional views vector, and $\epsilon_q$ is normally distributed with zero mean and covariance matrix $\Gamma$. These two sources are combined in the Black-Litterman approach to give the following expression:

$$\alpha = \left( \tau^{-1}\Omega^{-1} + P^T\Gamma^{-1}P \right)^{-1} (\tau^{-1}\Omega^{-1}\pi + P^T\Gamma^{-1}q) \tag{14.16}$$

for the expected return. This estimate is then used in the MVO model. An important feature of the Black-Litterman model is that in addition to absolute views on the returns, *relative* views, such as "The return of Oracle will exceed the return of IBM by 5 percent," can also be incorporated into the model. Good overviews of the Black-Litterman model can be found in Litterman,[17] Idzorek,[18] and Meucci.[19]

## FACTOR ALIGNMENT PROBLEMS

As we discussed in the previous sections, there are three sources of information that are used to build portfolios with the EMVO model, namely, (1) the expected return (alphas), (2) a factor-based risk model that is used to measure the predicted risk of the admissible portfolios, and (3) constraints or additional objective terms that are used to model portfolio preferences or the set of admissible portfolios. Since all can be generated by disparate and sometimes independent estimation processes, there are natural disparities between these three *entities*. The problems that arise due to these disparities are called *factor alignment problems* (FAPs) in the literature; see Ceria, Saxena, and Stubbs.[20] FAPs result in optimal portfolios that suffer from risk underestimation, undesired exposures to factors with hidden systematic risk, a consistent failure of the portfolio manager in achieving *ex ante* performance targets, and an intrinsic inability to transform a competitive advantage in terms of alphas into outperforming portfolios. FAPs have recently received considerable attention in the financial literature (see note 20; Lee and Stefek;[21] Bender, Lee, and Stefek;[22] and Saxena and Stubbs[23]).

We illustrate the FAP that arises due to the misalignment between the alpha and the risk factors by considering a simple EMVO model where there are no portfolio constraints (i.e., where the portfolio manager only considers the trade-off between risk and return). Let's also assume that the covariance matrix $Q$ is given by a factor risk model. For simplicity, we will assume that all the assets in the risk model have the same specific risk $\sigma$ (i.e., the specific covariance matrix is given by $\Delta^2 = \sigma^2 I$, where $I$ is the identity matrix). The portfolio manager's $\alpha$ can be broken into the following components:

$$\alpha = \alpha_B + \alpha_{\{B^{\{\perp\}}\}} \tag{14.17}$$

where $\alpha_B = B(B^T B)^{\{-1\}} B^T \alpha$ is the projection of $\alpha$ that is spanned by the exposures in the risk model and $\alpha_{\{B^{\{\perp\}}\}} = \alpha - \alpha_B$ is the portion of $\alpha$ that is orthogonal to the risk exposures. By definition $B^T \alpha_{\{B^{\{\perp\}}\}} = 0$. The optimal portfolio is given by:

$$w = \frac{1}{\lambda} Q^{\{-1\}} \alpha = \frac{1}{\lambda\sigma^2} \alpha_{\{B^{\{\perp\}}\}} + \frac{1}{\lambda\sigma^2} \left( I - B\left(B^T B + \sigma^2 \sum{}^{\{-1\}}\right)^{\{-1\}} B^T \right) \alpha_B. \tag{14.18}$$

The optimal portfolio is given by the sum of two terms that are based on the decomposition of the portfolio manager's alpha. The first term is the $\alpha_{\{B^{\{\perp\}}\}}$ component scaled to adjust for the specific risk. The second is the $\alpha_B$ term that is also scaled to adjust for the specific risk; this component is also attenuated in the optimal portfolio to minimize the systematic risk that it bears. In other words, the optimizer does not perceive any systematic risk in $\alpha_{\{B^{\{\perp\}}\}}$ and it overweights this component relative to $\alpha_B$. In doing so, the optimizer takes excessive exposure to factors that are missing from the risk model that is used to construct the optimal portfolio. The risk underestimation phenomenon was verified empirically in A. Saxena and R. Stubbs's work. The presence of constraints introduces additional sources of misalignment. In this case, it is possible to perform an equivalent analysis if we use the *implied alpha* that we introduced earlier in the chapter. The alignment issues are then expressed in terms of the component of the implied alpha that is spanned by the exposures in the risk model and the component that is orthogonal to the risk exposures.

Some novel techniques have been proposed to correctly account for the systematic risk for the *hidden* factors that are not part of the risk model. Axioma's patented Alpha Alignment Factor (AAF) (see Renshaw et al.[24]) dynamically constructs a new factor during the solution of the EMVO by penalizing the portion of the portfolio that is not spanned by the factors in the risk model. This is done by solving the following optimization problem:

$$\max_{\{w \in \Omega\}} \alpha^T w - \lambda(w^T Q w + \gamma\, w^T_{\{B^{\{\perp\}}\}} w_{\{B^{\{\perp\}}\}}) \tag{14.19}$$

where $Q = (B^T \Omega B + \Delta^2)$ is a factor risk model, $\gamma > 0$ is a suitable weight, $w_{\{B^{[\perp]}\}}$ is the portion of $w$ that is orthogonal to the exposures in the risk model, and $\Omega$ is the set of admissible portfolios. This optimization problem has two important features: (1) it can be set up as a convex problem and solved to optimality, and (2) it improves the accuracy of risk prediction and also the *ex post* performance of the optimal portfolio.

Saxena and Stubbs consider an EMVO model where one maximizes the expected return subject to a risk constraint and other user specified constraints. The risk constraint is of the form:

$$w^T \left(B^T \Omega B + \Delta^2\right) w \leq \sigma \tag{14.20}$$

where $\sigma > 0$ is an appropriate risk threshold. The EMVO model is solved for different values of the risk threshold to generate several portfolios. The realized risk for these portfolios is plotted against the true expected returns for these portfolios to generate the *ex post* traditional risk-return frontier. Saxena and Stubbs then generate the AAF portfolios by solving the EMVO model where the factor risk model is also augmented with the AAF. This model is generated by replacing the earlier risk constraint with the following constraint:

$$w^T \left(B^T \Omega B + \Delta^2\right) w + \gamma\, w^T_{\{B^{[\perp]}\}} w_{\{B^{[\perp]}\}} \leq \sigma \tag{14.21}$$

where $\gamma > 0$ can be effectively calibrated. The *ex post* AAF frontier is then generated similarly. They show that the realized risk of the portfolios on the AAF frontier is much closer to the risk predicted by the EMVO model with the AAF. Augmenting the user factor risk model with the AAF addresses the risk underestimation problem. Moreover, Saxena and Stubbs also show that the *ex post* AAF frontier is above the *ex post* traditional risk-return frontier. In other words, for a given risk threshold, the optimal portfolio generated by augmenting the user risk model with the AAF gives a larger return than the optimal portfolio that is generated by the user risk model alone. This, in turn, allows portfolio managers to access portfolios that are above the efficient frontiers generated by their risk models alone.

## CONSTRAINT ATTRIBUTION

We have discussed the importance of constraints in the EMVO model. Since constraints are used theoretically to improve the qualities of the optimal portfolio, the portfolio manager is often interested in the impact of the individual constraints on the overall performance of the portfolio. In other words, the portfolio manager wants to decompose the optimal portfolio by assigning a portion of the optimal portfolio holdings to each of the constraints that affect the optimal portfolio, with the understanding that the constraint with a larger portion of the optimal holdings plays an important role in the design of the optimal portfolio. Different decomposition schemes are discussed in Grinold,[25] Scherer and Xu,[26] and Stubbs and Vandenbussche.[27] One popular decomposition scheme is called *holdings decomposition* and it works as follows: Assume that all the constraints and the objectives in the portfolio problem are convex. We will refer to the problem without any constraints as the MVO model, and the one with constraints as the EMVO model. The holdings decomposition scheme decomposes the difference in the optimal portfolio weights between the EMVO model and the MVO model into components corresponding to the different constraints. This decomposition is based on the first-order optimality conditions for convex optimization problems (see Boyd and Vandenberghe[28]). We illustrate this decomposition on the following EMVO problem:

$$\max (\alpha^T w - \lambda w^T Qw)$$
$$s.t. \sum_{\{i=1\}}^{n} w_i = 1$$
$$w_i \geq 0, \quad i = 1, \ldots, n \tag{14.22}$$

where the constraints include an equality budget constraint and nonnegativity (no-shorting) requirements on the asset weights. The optimality constraints to this problem can be written as:

$$\alpha - \lambda Qw - \mu e + \sum_{\{i=1\}}^{n} \gamma_i e_i = 0 \qquad (OPT) \tag{14.23}$$

where $e$ is the all-1's vector of size $n$ and $e_i$ is the vector with 1 in the $i$th position and zeros elsewhere. In addition, one has the following constraints on the $\gamma_i$ variables:

$$\gamma_i w_i = 0, \quad \gamma_i \geq 0, \quad i = 1, \ldots, n \tag{14.24}$$

These constraints indicate that dual multipliers on the nonnegativity constraints are nonnegative and positive for those assets that have zero holding (these represent the active inequality constraints in the model). Since the covariance matrix $Q$ is nonsingular, one can solve for $w$ in $(OPT)$ to get:

$$w = \frac{1}{\lambda} Q^{\{-1\}}\alpha - \frac{\mu}{\lambda} Q^{\{-1\}}e + \sum_{\{i=1\}}^{n} \frac{\gamma_i}{\lambda} Q^{\{-1\}}e_i \quad (HD) \tag{14.25}$$

Note that $w^{\{MVO\}} = \frac{1}{\lambda} Q^{\{-1\}} \alpha$ contains the optimal weights for the MVO model; this is the first term in the right-hand side of (*HD*). The second and the third terms on the right-hand side of (*HD*) represent the contributions from the equality budget constraint and the various no-shorting constraints. If a no-shorting constraint is not binding (i.e., $w_i > 0$), then $\gamma_i = 0$ and the constraint does not contribute anything in (*HD*). One can regard each of the contributions as a separate portfolio to get the following holdings decomposition:

$$w^{\{opt\}} = w^{\{MVO\}} + w^{\{budget\}} + \sum_{\{i=1\}}^{n} w^{\{binding\ no\text{-}short\}} \qquad (14.26)$$

for the managed portfolio. In other words, the EMVO optimal portfolio is the aggregation of a *pure MVO portfolio*, a *budget portfolio* corresponding to the budget constraint, and *no-short portfolios* corresponding to the binding no-shorting constraints. The portfolio manager requires three sources of information to construct the portfolios corresponding to the different constraints in the holdings decomposition: optimal portfolio weights, the gradient of the constraint evaluated at the optimal portfolio weights if this constraint is differentiable, and the Lagrangian multipliers in the first-order optimality conditions. A good portfolio optimizer should be able to give the manager this information, which can be used to construct the holdings decomposition. The situation is complicated when the underlying constraint is not differentiable. Consider the following turnover constraint:

$$\sum_{\{i=1\}}^{n} | x_i - h_i | \leq T \qquad (14.27)$$

where $h_i$ is the initial holding of the *i*th asset. This constraint is not differentiable at the optimal weights if $x_i = h_i$ for any of the assets in the portfolio. In this case, one has to work with the subdifferential of this constraint that is the combination of intervals (of the form [–1, 1]) on the real line. Finding the correct subgradient from this subdifferential that satisfies the first optimality conditions is a challenging job, and often requires the solution to an auxiliary problem that resembles an MVO model.

Other decompositions, such as implied-alpha decomposition, expected-returns decomposition, and utility decomposition, are also considered in the literature, and we refer the interested reader to Scherer and Xu (2007) and Stubbs and Vandenbussche (2010) for more details.

## SPECIALLY STRUCTURED MVO MODELS

In this section we discuss specially structured EMVO models arising in multiportfolio and multiperiod settings. These models can be interpreted as individual EMVO models that are loosely *coupled* together. Special state-of-the-art parallel algorithms are available to solve these specially structured models.

Let us first consider multiportfolio optimization. Consider a portfolio manager who handles multiple accounts for various clients. Clients have their own preferences and constraints, which can be expressed in an individual EMVO model and optimized separately. However, assume that the trades for the different accounts are pooled and executed together (which is commonly the case in practice). Moreover, the portfolio manager is generally not allowed to *cross* trades among the various accounts. For a large institutional portfolio manager, the combined market impact of the trading on the various accounts can be very large and scales nonlinearly with the size of the trade. This, in turn, affects the portfolio weights obtained by optimizing each account separately. Hence, in order to solve this problem, the portfolio manager actually needs to solve a *multiportfolio* EMVO model that accounts for the fair allocation of the transaction costs among the individual accounts; see O'Cinneide, Scherer, and Xu[29] and Stubbs and Vandenbussche.[30] Different multiportfolio EMVO models are discussed in the latter work. In this section we limit the discussion to the *collusive* multiportfolio EMVO model. In this model, the total utility maximized by the portfolio manager is the sum of the individual account utilities that is subtracted by the total market-impact cost across all the accounts.

Consider the following collusive multiportfolio EMVO model:

$$\max_{\{w^i \in C_i\}} \sum_{\{i=1\}}^{k} \left( \left(\alpha^i\right)^T w^i - \lambda_i \left(w^i\right)^T Q^i w^i \right)$$

$$-\theta \; i = 1kwiT\Delta \; i = 1kwi \qquad (14.28)$$

over $k$ accounts, where $w^i$, $C_i$ denote the portfolio weights and the set of admissible portfolios for the $i$th account, respectively. The first term in the objective function represents the usual trade-off between return and risk across all the individual accounts. For simplicity, we assume that we are starting from an all-cash position and so the asset holding variables also represent the asset transactions. The combined market-impact cost over all the accounts is included in the second term in the objective function, where $\Delta$ is a diagonal matrix with positive market-impact costs. Note that the second term links the individual accounts together. This term is not separable across the various accounts; if this were the case, then one could optimize the $k$ accounts separately to find the optimal trades for each account.

To emphasize this point, we rewrite the multi-account model as:

$$\max_{\{w^i \in C_i,\ y\}} \sum_{\{i=1\}}^{k} \left( \left(\alpha^i\right)^T w^i - \lambda_i \left(w^i\right)^T Q^i w^i \right) - \theta y^T \Delta y$$

$$s.t.\ \sum_{\{i=1\}}^{k} w^i - y = 0 \tag{14.29}$$

Note that the only constraints that link the accounts together are the $y$ variables and the equality constraints in the holding and $y$ variables. One can adopt a Lagrangian dual approach (see Hiriart-Urruty and Lemarechal[31]), where these linking constraints are added to the objective using appropriate Lagrangian multipliers to give a min-max saddle point problem. This saddle point problem is solved in an iterative fashion between a master problem that is over the Lagrangian multipliers and $k$ separable subproblems that can be solved in parallel. The solution to the $i$th subproblem gives the holdings for the $i$th account. The special structure of these MVO models can also be used to parallelize interior point methods that solve the entire EMVO multiportfolio model; see Gondzio and Grothey.[32]

A second source of specially structured EMVO models arises in a multiperiod MVO model called *trade scheduling*, where a portfolio manager wants to liquidate an existing portfolio over $k$ time periods. The objective in this case is to trade-off the risk of the portfolio versus the market impact that will occur from trading the portfolio. We will assume a quadratic model for the market-impact costs. The trade scheduling problem can be modeled as:

$$\min \sum_{\{i=1\}}^{k} \lambda_i \left(w^i\right)^T Q^i w^i + \theta_i \delta_i \left(t^i\right)^2$$

$$s.t.\ w^{\{i+1\}} - t^i - w^i = 0,$$

$$\left(w^i,\ t^i\right) \in C_i, \quad i = 1,\ldots,k-1$$

$$w^k = 0 \tag{14.30}$$

where $w^i$ and $t^i$ denote the portfolio holdings and transactions in the $i$th period. The first set of constraints expresses the relationship between the holding and transaction variables in two successive time periods. Note that these are the only constraints that link the time periods together. Moreover, each time period is only linked at most to its preceding and successive time periods, and the linking constraints have a *staircase* structure. The second sets of constraints represent the portfolio manager's constraints over the individual time periods. The last set of constraints models the liquidation requirement; that is, the holdings of all the assets in the final period should be zero. This EMVO model can also be solved using a decomposition algorithm that can be parallelized in practice. Moreover, one can also parallelize interior point methods to speed up the solution of the trade scheduling problem.

## EXTREME TAIL LOSS OPTIMIZATION

The MVO model uses the variance of the returns to quantify the risk of the portfolio. Variance considers both positive and negative deviations from the mean and treats both of these variations as equally risky. However, in general, the portfolio manager should only be concerned with *underperformance* relative to the mean. Secondly, a portfolio manager may have in her portfolio nonlinear assets, such as options, that have asymmetric return distributions. In this case, the aim of the portfolio manager should be to maximize the probability that the portfolio loss is less than a maximum acceptable level. These requirements have led to the development of various *downside* risk measures in finance.

The best-known downside risk measure is *value at risk* (VaR) (see Jorion[33]), first developed by JPMorgan in 1994. The 1998 Basel Accord further popularized VaR by stipulating exposures and minimum capital requirements for banks in terms of the 10-day 95 percent VaR.

Let $\in > 0$ denote the confidence level. For a given portfolio, confidence level, and time horizon, VaR is defined as the threshold value, such that the probability that the portfolio loss exceeds this threshold value is the given confidence level. For example, a 10-day 95 percent VaR of $100 million for a portfolio indicates that there is a 95 percent probability that the portfolio will not fall in value by more than $100 million over a 10-day period. In other words, there is a 5 percent probability that the portfolio will lose more than $100 million over this period. VaR, however, has three shortcomings:

1. It is shown in Artzner et al.[34] that VaR is not a subadditive risk measure as we stated in Chapter 12; that is, the VaR of a portfolio can be greater than the sum of the VaR of the individual assets of a portfolio. Using VaR as a risk measure (say in the MVO model) would lead to concentrated (less diversified) portfolios that the VaR measure considers less risky.
2. It is challenging to minimize VaR as a risk measure in the MVO model. The resulting MVO model is a nonconvex optimization problem, and one has to resort to mixed-integer programming techniques to solve it to optimality.

3. VaR only measures a percentile of the portfolio loss distribution; it does not measure the length of the tail of the portfolio loss distribution. The VaR value can be much smaller than the worst-case loss, which, in turn, could mean absolute ruin for the investor.

There is another downside risk measure, called conditional value at risk (CVaR), that is closely related to VaR and addresses some of its shortcomings. CVaR measures the expected value of the loss that exceeds VaR. It is larger than VaR since it measures the losses that can occur in the tail of the loss distribution. Let $CVaR(w,\in)$ and $VaR(w,\in)$ denote the CVaR and VaR measures for a portfolio with weights $w$ and confidence level $\in$. We will assume that there are $k$ equally likely scenarios for the asset returns, and let $r_i$ denote the asset return vector for the $i$th scenario. So, $-r_i^T w$ denotes the loss suffered by the portfolio in the $i$th scenario. We can express CVaR in terms of VaR as follows:

$$CVaR(w,\in) = VaR(w,\in) + \frac{\frac{1}{k}\sum_{\{i=1\}}^{k} \max[-VaR(w,\in) - r_i^T w, 0]}{\in} \quad (14.31)$$

Note that the numerator of the fraction on the right-hand side of the equation measures the average excess loss over VaR, and the denominator measures the probability of this loss. Using this expression for CVaR, Rockafellar and Uryasev[35] show that the MVO model where the risk is measured in terms of CVaR (rather than variance) can be written as a linear programming problem. Setting up the linear program, however, requires a scenario-based approach where one has to draw samples from the portfolio return distribution. For large portfolios, more samples have to be drawn, and the solution time grows quickly.

El Ghaoui, Oks, and Oustry[36] consider a robust downside risk measure called the *worst-case value at risk* (WCVaR). Consider the asset returns to be random variables with mean $\mu$ and covariance matrix $Q$. The WCVaR for a confidence level $\in$ is the worst VaR obtained over all probability distributions with mean $\mu$ and covariance matrix $Q$ (some of these distributions can conceivably have long tails). At the outset, this appears to be a hopeless quantity to estimate, since one needs to run through an infinite number of probability distributions, compute the VaR for each distribution, and choose the largest VaR that is obtained. However, in their landmark paper, El Ghaoui et al. show that for a portfolio with holdings $w$ and confidence level $\in$,

$$WCVaR_{\{\in\}}(w) = \max_r \{-w^T r : (r-\mu)^T Q^{\{-1\}} (r-\mu) \le \kappa^2\} \quad (14.32)$$

where $\kappa^2 = \frac{(1-\epsilon)}{\epsilon}$. In other words, the WCVaR for a portfolio can be obtained by solving a convex optimization problem, where WCVaR measures the worst-case loss suffered by the portfolio when the asset returns are unknown and can take any values in the ellipsoidal uncertainty set. This is also the uncertainty set that we consider in the section on robust optimization. Moreover, one can also easily minimize WCVaR (as a downside risk measure) in an MVO model by solving a convex optimization problem as well. This is again a surprising result since minimizing VaR is a difficult non-convex problem. Also, unlike CVaR, minimizing WCVaR does not require a scenario-based optimization approach. One complaint against WCVaR is that it is a conservative downside risk measure. In fact, the WCVaR measure is more conservative for larger values of $\kappa$ (that determines the radius of the ellipsoidal uncertainty set). If the portfolio manager is optimistic that the return distribution does not have very long tails, one could conceivably choose a smaller value for this parameter.

## INCORPORATING NONLINEAR INSTRUMENTS IN THE EMVO MODEL

There has been recent work to incorporate nonlinear instruments, such as options, in an EMVO model; see Zymler, Kuhn, and Rustem[37] and Sivaramakrishnan, Stubbs, and Vandenbussche.[38] Consider a portfolio manager who wants to protect the optimal portfolio from adverse market movements, such as in the financial crisis of 2008. To do so, the portfolio manager can purchase American and European call and put options on the underlying assets in the portfolio. Options are *leveraged* instruments and so they offer better downside protection for a given investment. Note that an option is a *nonlinear* instrument; that is, its return is a nonlinear function of the return of the underlying asset. This function is, however, a convex function if we go long on (purchase) the option. The options can have varying times to expiration. The only requirement is that the time to expiration is at least equal to the portfolio manager's rebalancing time horizon, to ensure that all the options have value during the rebalancing period. Sivaramakrishnan et al. derive the following convex return function:

$$r_j^0 = \max\{-1, f(r_{\{uj\}})\} \tag{14.33}$$

for the $j$th option in the portfolio, where $uj$ denotes the underlying asset for this option. The convex function is derived from an appropriate option pricing formula, such as the Black-Scholes model for a European option and the Cox-Ross-Rubinstein binomial asset pricing model for an American option. This return function is incorporated in the WCVaR risk measure (that we considered in the previous section) to obtain a downside risk measure for thc portfolio containing equities as well as options. This risk measure can be represented as:

$$WCVaR_{\{\epsilon\}}\left(w,\ w^0\right) = \max_{\{r,\ r^0\}} -\left(w^T r + \left(w^0\right)^T r^0\right)$$

$$s.t.\ \ (r-\mu)^T Q^{\{-1\}}(r-\mu) \le \kappa^2$$

$$r_j^0 = \max\{-1,\ f\left(r_{\{uj\}}\right)\},\ j \in 0 \tag{14.34}$$

where O is the set of options in the portfolio. For a portfolio with equity and long option holdings, the WCVaR measure for the portfolio can be obtained by solving a convex optimization problem. The problem of minimizing the downside risk of the portfolio containing equities and options can then be written as:

$$\min_{\{w,\ w^0\}} WCVaR_{\{\epsilon\}}(w,\ w^0)$$

$$s.t.\ \ w^0 \ge 0,\ \left(w,\ w^0\right) \in \Omega \tag{14.35}$$

where $w^0 \ge 0$ represents the no-shorting requirements on options and the set $\Omega$ contains the portfolio manager's other constraints on the asset and option variables. One specific constraint in $\Omega$ is a budget constraint on the option variables. This optimization problem is convex if the set $\Omega$ is also convex (i.e., when there are no combinatorial constraints on the asset and option variables). State-of-the-art optimization solvers can solve this problem to optimality in the same time as a typical EMVO problem. Sivaramakrishnan et al. compare this approach with the delta and delta-gamma hedging strategies (see Hull[39]), that are commonly used in practice. They show that the WCVaR-based hedging strategy offers better downside protection for a wider range of option budgets than the delta and delta-gamma hedging strategies.

## ALGORITHMS FOR SOLVING MVO MODELS

We briefly describe algorithms for solving MVO models in this section. The basic MVO model that trades off risk versus return can be modeled as a QP. This is no longer the case once constraints (quadratic, NLC, and combinatorial) or objectives (NLC, combinatorial) are added to the EMVO model.

Recently, there has been considerable interest in using second-order cone programming (SOCP) models in portfolio optimization. SOCP deals with a special case of convex optimization problems that can be written as linear conic problems over the second-order (ice cream) cone; see Boyd and Vandenberghe (note 28), Alizadeh and Goldfarb,[40] and Ben-Tal and Nemirovski.[41] There are two major reasons for this interest:

1. A variety of LIN, QUAD, NLC portfolio objectives and constraints can be modeled via SOCP. In fact, the QP model is itself a special case of SOCP. Here are some prominent examples that can be modeled via SOCP but not as QPs:
   - *Risk objective or constraint that uses the standard deviation of returns:* Most portfolio managers measure risk using the standard deviation (rather than the variance) of returns, since the standard deviation of the returns has the same unit as the expected returns.
   - *Market-impact terms with the $^3/_2$ and $^5/_3$ powers:* Almgren et al.[42] show that the market cost of trading an asset is best approximated by a function that is a five-thirds power of the trade size of the asset.
   - *Robust portfolio problems:* Most robust EMVO problems where the expected returns lie in well-known uncertainty sets described in Ceria and Stubbs, Goldfarb and Iyengar, and Tutuncu and Koenig.
2. Interior point algorithms that were originally developed for solving linear and quadratic programs (LPs and QPs) have recently been extended to solve second-order cone programs; see Boyd and Vandenberghe, Alizadeh and Goldfarb, and Ben-Tal and Nemirovski. Moreover, with the development of efficient numerical linear algebra techniques and the availability of good software, one can now solve SOCPs with tens of thousands of variables and constraints efficiently, and in times that are comparable to that for LP and QP.

We will briefly highlight how the EMVO model

$$\max \alpha^T w - \lambda \sqrt{w^T Q w} \tag{14.36}$$

with risk measured as the standard deviation of returns can be modeled as an SOCP. For simplicity, we will consider the case when the covariance matrix $Q$ is positive-definite. Let $t = Q^{\left\{\frac{1}{2}\right\}} w$, where $Q^{\left\{\frac{1}{2}\right\}}$ (the square root of $Q$) is obtained via an eigenvalue decomposition. Note that $t$ is an $n$ dimensional vector with components $t_1,\ldots,t_n$, where $n$ is the number of assets in the EMVO model. The EMVO problem can be equivalently written as:

$$\max_{\{w,\bar{t},t\}} \alpha^T w - \lambda \bar{t}$$

$$s.t. \; t - Q^{\left\{\frac{1}{2}\right\}} w = 0$$

$$\bar{t} \geq \sqrt{t_1^2 + \ldots + t_n^2} \qquad (14.37)$$

where $\bar{t}$ is a new scalar variable. The resulting formulation is an SOCP. Observe that the objective function in the SOCP is a linear function in the $w$ and $\bar{t}$ variables. Moreover, the constraints that express the relationship between the $t$ and $w$ variables are also linear. The only source of nonlinearity in the SOCP is the requirement that the vector $(\bar{t}, t_1, \ldots, t_n)$ lies in a second-order cone of size $(n + 1)$.

Combinatorial constraints, such as the names constraint, further complicate the EMVO model. In this case, the resulting EMVO model becomes a mixed-integer problem (MIP); see Wolsey.[43] MIPs are notoriously difficult to solve to optimality. One reason for this difficulty is that MIPs have variables that take discrete rather than continuous values, and the feasible set for the admissible portfolios is no longer convex. In most cases, one can use heuristic approaches to find a good solution but it is hard to verify that the solution found is indeed the best possible, or even close to the best. There exist exact approaches called *branch and cut* techniques (see Wolsey) to solve MIPs to optimality, but these approaches lead to solution times that are not practical. Therefore, a portfolio manager often has to be satisfied with a good (while not the best) solution. The branch and cut technique also provides a provable upper bound that indicates how far this solution is from the best one possible. We will illustrate MIP modeling by modeling the names constraint. Assume that the portfolio weights have the following lower and upper bounds:

$$0 \leq w_i \leq u_i, \quad i = 1, \ldots, n \qquad (14.38)$$

We want to model the requirement that no more than $K$ assets can be held in the portfolio, where $K$ is much smaller than the number of assets $n$ in the investable universe. Consider the binary vector $z$ in the portfolio problem, where $z_i = 1$ if asset $i$ is held in the portfolio and 0 otherwise. The names constraint can be modeled using the following constraints:

$$w_i \geq 0, \quad w_i - u_i z_i \leq 0,$$

$$\sum_{\{i=1\}}^{n} z_i \leq K,$$

$$z_i \in \{0, 1\}, \quad i = 1, \ldots, n \tag{14.39}$$

Note that if $z_i = 0$, the first set of constraints ensure that $w_i = 0$. Conversely, if $z_i = 1$, these constraints ensure that the weight of the $i$th asset is between its permissible bounds. The names constraint is then modeled as a linear inequality constraint in the binary $z$ variables.

## HOW TO CHOOSE AN OPTIMIZER

Consider a portfolio manager who manages a 130/30 international portfolio with about 200 assets and a large-cap growth mandate. Assume that the portfolio manager's factor risk model uses the fundamental factors in the Fama-French three-factor model (see Fama and French[44]). Two of the fundamental factors in this model are the *size* and *value* factors. The size factor measures the additional returns that investors have generated by investing in small companies. The value factor measures the additional returns that investors have generated by investing in companies with high book-to-price ratios. Since the manager wants to invest primarily in large-cap growth companies, the alpha is constructed from negative linear combinations of the asset exposures to the size and value factors. Alternatively, one can short the size and value factor exposures in the constraints in order to get large negative exposures to these factors. We will describe the EMVO model that represents the portfolio manager's strategy:

- *Maximize expected return:* The manager uses custom *alphas* that are generated from negative linear combinations of the asset exposures to the size and value factors. This ensures that the optimizer takes larger bets on large-cap growth companies that have small book-to-price ratios. This is a linear objective function.
- *Tracking error constraint:* The benchmark is the MSCI EAFE growth index with a tracking error of 8 percent. Assume the portfolio manager uses the standard deviation of the returns as a measure of risk. The TE constraint is then an NLC constraint that can be modeled as an SOCP constraint.

- *130/30 requirement:* Short 30 percent of the portfolio that the manager believes to be overvalued. Invest the proceeds from the short sale in the long assets. Assume that the long position is fully invested; that is, there is no cash in the portfolio. This is a combinatorial constraint with the full investment requirement. Moreover, one has to create separate long and short variables for each asset that represents the amount held long and short, respectively.
- *Short the* size *and* value *factor exposures:* This is to get a large negative exposure to these factors, thereby satisfying the large-cap growth mandate. These are linear inequality constraints in the factor exposure variables. There are also two linear equality constraints that link the factor exposure variables with the portfolio weights.
- *Limit on the number of names:* Do not hold more than 100 assets in the portfolio. This is a combinatorial constraint.
- *Threshold holdings on positions:* If an asset is held, hold at least 20 basis points. This is a combinatorial constraint.
- *Liquidity constraints:* Limit the holding in each asset to 10 percent of the average daily volume (ADV). These are linear inequality constraints.
- *Minimize transaction costs:* Limit the turnover to 5 percent of the portfolio value. This is a linear inequality constraint.
- *Minimize market impact:* Use the three-halves market-impact function. This is an NLC objective function that can be modeled using SOCP.

We will describe how one chooses a good portfolio optimizer to solve this EMVO model:

- A good portfolio optimizer should be able to handle constraints directly rather than choosing a set of weights (or preferences) for each constraint and then adding it to the objective function. It is a challenging task to calibrate the weights for the constraints that are added to the objective function so that the resulting problem is equivalent to the portfolio manager's original problem. Moreover, since the aforementioned EMVO model has combinatorial constraints, the portfolio manager cannot adopt a dual Lagrangian approach to compute the correct set of weights for each constraint that is added to the objective. The dual problem is no longer equivalent to the original problem. In optimization terminology, there is a *duality gap* (see Boyd and Vandenberghe) between the two problems, and solving the dual problem does not give the best solution to the original problem.
- The three-halves market-impact objective and the tracking error constraint in the EMVO model can be modeled exactly via SOCP functions. A good portfolio optimizer should be able to handle SOCP constraints

and objectives. Besides, there exist efficient algorithms to solve SOCPs in about the same time as a QP model.

- The EMVO model has three different combinatorial functions: (1) the fully invested 130/30 requirement, (2) the names constraint, and (3) minimum threshold holdings constraint. These constraints model different objectives of the manager that can potentially be in conflict with each other. Some portfolio managers use an ad hoc manner to handle combinatorial constraints; they simply solve the convex model without these constraints, and in a postprocessing phase try to round the resulting solution to satisfy the combinatorial constraints. This is not a good strategy as it is hard to find a heuristic solution in this manner that satisfies the other combinatorial constraints in the problem. Moreover, there is no guarantee that the solution found in this manner will be close to an optimal solution to the original problem. A good portfolio optimizer should have a good branch and bound algorithm to find provably good solutions (i.e., good solutions that also come with certificates on how close the purported solution is from a global optimal solution).
- A good portfolio optimizer should ideally use a *primal-dual interior point method* (IPM) to solve the EMVO model. Interior point algorithms are extremely versatile; they can be used to solve linear, quadratic, and second-order cone-based EMVO models. This is unlike simplex and active-set-based algorithms to solve linear and quadratic programs. An active-set algorithm cannot be used for the EMVO model due to the presence of the nonlinear tracking error constraint. Interior point algorithms can also be easily embedded in a branch and bound algorithm to solve portfolio models with combinatorial constraints. IPMs have proven worst-case complexity estimates; see Ben-Tal and Nemirovski. Moreover, with recent advances in numerical linear algebra algorithms and software, IPMs can routinely solve convex portfolio problems with tens of thousands of assets reliably in a few seconds of computing time.
- Suppose the portfolio manager follows a *value-momentum* mandate instead. Let the risk model continue to be the Fama-French three-factor model, which does not contain the momentum factor. In this case, a factor alignment problem would ensue, since the optimizer would overload on the momentum factor where it does not perceive a systematic risk. The FAP issue can be mitigated by dynamically incorporating the AAF in the tracking error constraint. The resulting portfolio problem can still be formulated as an SOCP and solved efficiently with an interior point optimizer. This shows that a good interior point optimizer handling SOCP objectives and constraints can potentially also address the FAP issue.

## NOTES

1. H. Markowitz, "Portfolio Selection," *Journal of Finance* 7 (1952): 77–91; H. Markowitz, *Portfolio Selection: Efficient Diversification of Investments*, 2nd ed. (New York: John Wiley & Sons, 1991).
2. R. Grinold and R. Kahn, *Active Portfolio Management: A Quantitative Approach for Producing Superior Returns and Controlling Risk* (New York: McGraw-Hill, 1999).
3. P. Zangari, "Equity Risk Factor Models," in *Modern Investment Management: An Equilibrium Approach* (Hoboken, NJ: John Wiley & Sons, 2003), 297–333.
4. V. DeMiguel, L. Garlappi, F. Nogales, and R. Uppal, "A Generalized Approach to Portfolio Optimization: Improving Performance by Constraining Portfolio Norms," *Management Science* 55, no. 5 (2009): 798–812.
5. R. Jagannathan and T. Ma, "Risk Reduction in Large Portfolios: Why Imposing the Wrong Constraints Helps," *Journal of Finance*, no. 58 (2003): 1651–1684.
6. S. Maillard, T. Roncalli, and T. Jerome, "The Properties of Equally Weighted Risk Contribution Portfolios," *Journal of Portfolio Management* 36, no. 4 (2010): 60–70.
7. "Risk Parity: Applying the Concept to Equity Strategies," *Axioma Advisor: The eNewsletter from Axioma*, March 2012.
8. C. Asness, A. Frazzini, and L. Pedersen, "Leverage Aversion and Risk Parity," *Financial Analysts Journal* 68, no. 1 (2012): 47–59.
9. G. Cornuejols and R. Tutuncu, *Optimization Methods in Finance* (Cambridge: Cambridge University Press, 2007).
10. R. Michaud, *Efficient Asset Management: A Practical Guide to Stock Portfolio Management and Asset Allocation* (Boston: Harvard Business School Press, 1998).
11. A. Ben-Tal, L. El Ghaoui, and A. Nemirovskii, *Robust Optimization* (Princeton, NJ: Princeton University Press, 2009).
12. S. Ceria and R. Stubbs, "Incorporating Estimation Errors into Portfolio Selection: Robust Portfolio Construction," *Journal of Asset Management* 7, no. 2 (2006): 109–127.
13. D. Goldfarb and G. Iyengar, "Robust Portfolio Selection Problems," *Mathematics of Operations Research* 28 (2003): 1–38.
14. R. Tutuncu and M. Koenig, "Robust Asset Allocation," *Annals of Operations Research* 132 (2004): 157–187.
15. P. Jorion, "International Portfolio Diversification with Estimation Risk," *Journal of Business* 58, no. 3 (1985): 259–278.
16. F. Black and R. Litterman, "Asset Allocation: Combining Investor Views with Market Equilibrium," *Goldman Sachs Fixed Income Research*, 1990; F. Black and R. Litterman, "Global Portfolio Optimization," *Financial Analysts Journal* 48, no. 5 (September/October 1992): 28–43.
17. R. Litterman, "Beyond Equilibrium, the Black-Litterman Approach," in *Modern Investment Management: An Equilibrium Approach* (Hoboken, NJ: John Wiley & Sons, 2003), 76–88.

18. T. Idzorek, "A Step-by-Step Guide to the Black-Litterman Model," Duke University, 2002.
19. A. Meucci, *Risk and Asset Allocation*, Springer Finance (New York: Springer, 2009).
20. S. Ceria, A. Saxena, and R. Stubbs, "Factor Alignment Problems and Quantitative Portfolio Management," *Journal of Portfolio Management* 38, no. 2 (2012): 29–43.
21. J. Lee and D. Stefek, "Do Risk Factors Eat Alpha?" *Journal of Portfolio Management* 34, no. 4 (2008): 12–25.
22. J. Bender, J. Lee, and D. Stefek, "Refining Portfolio Construction When Alphas and Risk Factors Are Misaligned," *MSCI Barra Research Insights*, 2009.
23. A. Saxena and R. Stubbs, "Alpha Alignment Factor: A Solution to the Underestimation of Risk for Optimized Active Portfolios," Axioma Research Paper 15, 2010 (to appear in the *Journal of Risk*); A. Saxena and R. Stubbs, "Pushing the Frontier (Literally) with the Alpha Alignment Factor," Axioma Research Paper 22, 2010.
24. A. Renshaw, R. Stubbs, S. Schmieta, and S. Ceria, "Axioma Alpha Factor Method: Improving Risk Estimation by Reducing Risk Model Portfolio Selection Bias," Axioma Research Paper 6, 2006.
25. R. Grinold, "Implementation Efficiency," *Financial Analysts Journal* 61 (2005): 52–64.
26. B. Scherer and X. Xu, "The Impact of Constraints on Value-Added," *Journal of Portfolio Management* 33, no. 4 (2007): 45–54.
27. R. Stubbs and D. Vandenbussche, "Constraint Attribution," *Journal of Portfolio Management* 36, no. 4 (2010): 48–59.
28. S. Boyd and L. Vandenberghe, *Convex Optimization* (Cambridge: Cambridge University Press, 2004).
29. C. O'Cinneide, B. Scherer, and X. Xu, "Pooling Trades in Quantitative Investment Process," *Journal of Portfolio Management* 32, no. 4 (2006): 33–43.
30. R. Stubbs and D. Vandenbussche, "Multi-Portfolio Optimization and Fairness in Allocation of Trades," Axioma Research Paper No. 13, 2009.
31. J. Hiriart-Urruty and C. Lemarechal, *Convex Analysis and Minimization Algorithms: Advanced Theory and Bundle Methods*, vol. 2 (New York: Springer, 1993).
32. J. Gondzio and A. Grothey, "Parallel Interior Point Solver for Structured Linear Programs," *Mathematical Programming* 96 (2003): 561–584; J. Gondzio and A. Grothey, "Parallel Interior Point Solver for Structured Quadratic Programs: Applications to Financial Planning Problems," *Annals of Operations Research* 152, no. 1 (2007): 319–339; J. Gondzio and A. Grothey, "Exploiting Structure in Parallel Implementation of Interior Point Methods for Optimization," *Computational Management Science* 6 (2009): 135–160.
33. P. Jorion, *Value at Risk: The New Benchmark for Managing Financial Risk*, 3rd ed. (New York: McGraw-Hill, 2006).
34. P. Artzner, F. Delbean, J. Eber, and D. Heath, "Coherent Measures of Risk," *Mathematical Finance* 9, no. 3 (1999): 203–228.

35. R. Rockafellar and S. Uryasev, "Optimization of Conditional Value-at-Risk," *Journal of Risk* 2 (2000): 493–517.
36. L. El Ghaoui, M. Oks, and F. Oustry, "Worst-Case Value at Risk and Robust Portfolio Optimization: A Conic Programming Approach," *Operations Research* 51 (2003): 543–556.
37. S. Zymler, D. Kuhn, and B. Rustem, "Worst-Case-Value-at-Risk for Nonlinear Portfolios," *European Journal of Operational Research* 210 (2011): 410–424.
38. K. Sivaramakrishnan, R. Stubbs, and D. Vandenbussche, "Minimizing Downside Risk in Axioma Portfolio with Options," Axioma Research Paper 32, 2011.
39. J. Hull, *Options, Futures, and Other Derivatives*, 8th ed. (Upper Saddle River, NJ: Prentice Hall, 2011).
40. F. Alizadeh and D. Goldfarb, "Second Order Cone Programming," *Mathematical Programming* 95 (2003): 3–51.
41. A. Ben-Tal and A. Nemirovski, *Lectures on Modern Convex Optimization: Analysis, Algorithms, and Engineering Applications*, MPS-SIAM Series on Optimization (Philadelphia: Society for Industrial and Applied Mathematics [SIAM], 2001).
42. R. Almgren, C. Thum, F. Hauptmann, and H. Li, "Equity Market Impact," *Risk* 18 (2005): 21–28.
43. L. Wolsey, *Integer Programming* (New York: Wiley-Interscience, 1998).
44. E. Fama and K. French, "Common Risk Factors in the Returns of Stocks and Bonds," *Journal of Financial Economics* 33 (1993): 3–56; E. Fama and K. French, "The Cross-Section of Expected Stock Returns," *Journal of Finance* 47, no. 2 (1992): 427–465.

# PART Three

CHAPTER 15

# The SunGard APT Risk Management System

*Laurence Wormald, PhD*

Go to www.wiley.com/go/greiner to see video titled "Laurence Wormald."

Risk is the energy that drives markets. A robust model of market risk must take account of the comovement of asset returns both in normal times and when markets are stressed. SunGard APT provides a risk management solution based on the concept of "three pillars of risk management": risk measurement, risk attribution, and scenario analysis. Flexibility in both attribution and scenario analysis is the key to effective risk management. To achieve that flexibility, APT constructs statistical factor models of risky asset markets and then allows users to select the explanatory factors that match their own investment process when carrying out attribution and scenario analysis; this approach based on explanatory factors is called RiskScan. However, for robust risk measurement, APT has always relied on statistical factor modeling methodologies.

## INTRODUCTION TO STATISTICAL FACTOR MODELS

Statistical factor models are economically motivated and consistent with asset pricing theory and the observed effects of arbitrage across markets. Theoretical work on arbitrage pricing theory was pioneered by Ross[1] and Roll and Ross,[2] and extended by Connor and Korajczyk;[3] early applications to risk management for investment were documented by Blin, Bender, and

Guerard.[4] Recent evidence for the robustness of the approach for optimized strategies is provided by Wormald and van der Merwe.[5]

Because statistical factor models based on arbitrage approaches to pricing theory make fewer assumptions about the systematic risk factors that drive markets, there is a better chance of capturing the effects of these factors. If we attempt to prespecify (and likely misspecify) those factors when estimating a model from historical data, we cannot capture their effects as completely. Hence there is a much higher likelihood of building a genuinely robust risk model when using a statistical methodology such as principal components modeling.

In the multi-asset-class (MAC) case this advantage is vital, since the estimation of cross-asset-class correlations is quite natural within statistical models, whereas it is an ad hoc process based on a separate methodology for prespecified models. Thus the statistical factor modeling process generates a more coherent risk model than other approaches, and is less likely to create unreliable risk measures for portfolios containing assets across different classes.

### Why Use a Statistical Factor Model for a Single Asset Class?

The first factor risk models were built for equities, and included industry factors only. It quickly became apparent that for these simple multivariant regression models, adding style factors would improve the explanatory and forecast power of these models. But how many truly independent styles are there? When we build global equity models, is it better to include all country factors (say 40 factors or more) or to rely on regional factors? How many independent currency risk factors do we need? How much would the addition of commodity or macroeconomic factors (such as oil, inflation, interest rates, credit spreads) improve a global equities model?

These are difficult questions for risk modelers to answer, because all the obvious explanatory factors are correlated with one another, and there may be other important risk factors that are not obvious. In addition, there are transitory factors that can affect equities markets strongly during some periods but are much less influential during other times. So building an equities risk model with prespecified factors is always based on judgment rather than objective methods, and the results are often far from robust. It is this difficulty that has led some prespecified risk modelers to include principal components factors alongside fundamental factors in their models to capture the structure that prespecified factors cannot capture. Whether the regression model for estimating betas is implemented on time series or cross-sectionally, ultimately this approach provides little confidence that the systematic part of the risk is correctly estimated. Many surprises in realized risk compared to forecasts from prespecified models have been observed because of market risk factors that were identified only with the benefit of hindsight.

Similar problems occur with other asset classes such as bonds. The risk factors associated with yield curves (e.g., shift, twist, butterfly factors) are very highly correlated across currencies (for example, euro and Swiss franc), and the total number of factors to include in a global bond model is far from obvious.

We think that it is much more sensible to start with a methodology that is theory-based and objectively defined, so as to avoid misspecification of the risk factors and to provide a robust measure of the systematic part of the risk on any portfolio. The method of principal components, applied to the historical correlation matrix of a carefully selected "estimation core" of the assets within a single class such as equities, can be shown to provide a stable and robust set of systematic factors without the problems of collinearity and arbitrary selection. By reestimating the model factors every month, the problems associated with transitory factors are much reduced. Users can then overlay the explanatory factors of their choice within the portfolio analysis to provide intuitive attribution and scenario analysis.

It is also quite straightforward to create long-term and short-term risk models by applying an appropriate influence function to the historical data, and the statistical factor methodology does not require that we make arbitrary judgments about which factors may or may not be most strongly affected when changing the effective time horizon of the risk model.

### Why Use a Statistical Factor Model for Multiple Asset Classes?

The problems of prespecified factor models are multiplied when trying to create MAC models. The lack of robustness associated with the judgmental approach to factor selection in each asset class becomes compounded when attempting to model the cross-asset-class correlations. A number of MAC risk modelers use only index-level correlation estimates between asset classes since their methods do not allow security-level estimation of these correlations. The estimation of factor correlations across asset classes is a judgmental exercise since there is no objective measure of how many factors are really required to explain cross-asset-class behavior.

In contrast, the statistical factor model methodology provides a coherent approach to MAC modeling, in which macroeconomic factors (whose influence extends across all asset classes) may be properly included within the estimation core. By including these macro factors and carefully selecting the assets within the estimation core, we create a set of principal component factors that capture not only the systematic risks associated with equity/credit, rates, foreign exchange (FX), and commodity markets, but simultaneously all the cross-asset-class effects observed in the historical data.

The most complete MAC model from APT contains 96 factors: 30 associated with rates, 20 associated with equity and credit, 26 associated with FX, and 20 associated with commodities (to which all assets may be exposed). This we believe is an economically sensible number of factors to represent the truly independent risk drivers of the global marketplace.

In the sections that follow we describe in some detail how APT builds statistical factor models for a single asset class (equities) and for multiple asset classes (equities, FX, and bonds).

## APT FACTOR MODEL ESTIMATION—EQUITIES MODELS

A linear factor model is an attempt to explain the relationships among a set of securities in terms of their exposure to a set of common factors. The intuition behind this is that stocks with similar characteristics should behave similarly and therefore be influenced by the same subset of factors. For example, stocks that belong to the banking sector should be affected by a factor that is common to all banking stocks.

As discussed earlier, there are several ways to model this relationship. The APT approach is to use statistical factor analysis to uncover the underlying unobservable constructs that affect or explain the behavior of a collection of variables. In the context of equities, we seek to use factor analysis to uncover the underlying systematic factors that drive equity prices. The application for extracting the systematic factors from a core universe of asset returns is known as factorization, which is a proprietary technique developed by APT. The basic details of the process, however, are that the application takes in a set of asset returns and extracts a set of returns on uncorrelated systematic factors (known as the APT component returns) that maximally explain the common comovement of asset returns in the core universe.

The three key stages involved in the estimation of the APT equity factor models are:

1. Selection of assets and explanatory factors from the estimation universe to create the core universe.
2. Factorization of the core universe asset returns to extract a set of systematic factors known as the APT component returns.
3. Estimation of the component loadings and specific risks of the assets and explanatory factors.

### Estimation Window

A key consideration in risk modeling is choosing the appropriate length of historical data series to use. Choosing too short a window may result in large sampling errors, while choosing too long a window may result in a shortage of stocks with sufficiently long history.

APT currently provides short-term and medium-term volatility models. Both use weekly Wednesday closing prices, with estimation windows given as follows:

- *Medium-term volatility (MTV) models:* Medium-term volatility models calculate risk profiles based on the weekly price returns for a period of 3.5 years (180 weeks). Each weekly return takes on equal significance in the calculation, so the volatility figures generated by the model are medium-term estimates of average volatility for horizons between three months and two years out. Medium-term models are typically available for monthly delivery.
- *Short-term volatility (STV) models:* Short-term volatility models are also based on weekly prices for a period of 3.5 years; however, the returns are exponentially weighted with a half-life of approximately 13 weeks. This means that the more recent price history takes on a greater significance in the calculation, so the volatility figures generated by the model are short-term estimates of average volatility for horizons between one and nine months out.

## SELECTION OF THE CORE UNIVERSE FOR FACTOR MODELING

There are hundreds of thousands of assets that are traded on the various stock exchanges around the world. A factor analysis of this huge universe of assets is therefore computationally intensive and most probably infeasible. A crucial step in the model estimation process is therefore to narrow down this universe by selecting a much smaller representative group of assets while at the same time ensuring that important drivers of the economy are still captured; we refer to this process as core selection.

Rather than going into the intricate details of core selection, we will focus on its main features. The process of core selection starts with the enumeration of the common shares listed on the various exchanges across the world. For domestic models, we will restrict our enumeration to the region of interest. For example, in building a U.S. equity model, we restrict our interest to the common shares whose parent companies are domiciled in the United States. Economy-wide factors such as interest rates, energy prices, commodity prices, credit spreads, and FX rates also drive equity prices. We therefore include a considerable number of these factors, which we call explanatory factors, in the core universe for every APT model.

Invariably we will encounter assets such as shares that have only started trading recently or shares that have been suspended in the recent past. Such shares will not have the desired full weekly returns history over the estimation window of 180 weeks used in our regular factor models. These shares are therefore removed from the core universe. This is done because initial public offerings (IPOs) often trade erratically for several months after issue and therefore cannot contribute to the common variation of asset prices, so their inclusion in the core universe is unnecessary.

Illiquidity is a major concern in model estimation, resulting in long periods of stale pricing, where the previous day's price is used as an estimate of today's price. Stale pricing causes an underestimation of the asset return covariances and we therefore exclude illiquid shares from the core universe by placing a threshold on the number of zero weekly returns.

Another potential problem is data errors, sometimes causing major jumps in share price from one week to the next. To guard against data errors, we exclude all shares whose returns series contain an outlier, defined as a value exceeding a threshold of 0.5. The only exception to this rule is if the asset is included in the model as an explanatory factor, when the data is manually verified and included for risk attribution purposes.

Having obtained the core universe, we convert the returns data into a common base currency before subjecting them to factor analysis. An exception is our multiple numeraire models, where the asset returns are expressed in their local currency units and a postfactorization transformation is used to convert the asset factor profiles into a common base currency.

### Estimating Component Returns

The aim of factor analysis is to uncover the underlying unobservable innovations that affect or explain the behavior of a collection of variables. For our equity models based on weekly returns data, the number of factors extracted is 20, a number that has been shown to perform well in back-tests. In the global daily model, recently developed by APT, the number of factors retained (50 factors) has been determined using the results of random matrix theory.

## CHOOSING THE NUMBER OF APT FACTORS

Choosing the best number of components in a statistical factor model is an important part of the modeling process. The historical explanatory power of the model will tend to increase as more factors are included, but there will come a point where the forecast power will start to decline. We expect that the most suitable number of components will be less than the number of factors used within comparable prespecified factor models, and this is borne out by our testing.

The most useful tool for determining the number of components to use is provided by the component factorization, effectively an eigenvalue decomposition process. The eigenvalues can be ranked from greatest to least, and the eigenvectors corresponding to the larger eigenvalues are selected to form the model components.

Out-of-sample back-testing to validate the forecast power of the model is then used to confirm the choice of number of components. In this way the value of 20 components for APT's standard weekly equity factor models was established, and has been maintained since the development of the first models.

For multi-asset-class models (including bonds, commodities, credit instruments) and the daily global equities models, the preferred number of components is higher. Extensive testing of these models has established a value of 50 components as a reasonable parameter in these cases. Clearly this number cannot be taken as a rigorous optimum value under all circumstances, but rather as an economically sensible choice that has been confirmed by eigenvalue analysis and back-testing. In addition, the methods of random matrix theory have been applied to the multi-asset-class and daily models to test the significance of the components within these models. This random matrix theory methodology provides support for the inclusion of 50 components in the extended models.

## ESTIMATING THE RISK PROFILES IN AN APT FACTOR MODEL

Within a linear factor model framework, the returns of an asset are expressed as a linear combination of common factors and a factor that is specific to the asset; that is,

$$r_t = \alpha + F_t\beta + \varepsilon_t \tag{15.1}$$

with the condition that $E[F.\varepsilon_t] = 0$. Writing $y_t = \alpha + F_{t\beta} + \varepsilon_t$, the risk of the asset may be decomposed into the sum of two parts:

$$\text{var}[r_t] = \text{var}[y_t] + \text{var}[\varepsilon_t] \tag{15.2}$$

where $\text{var}[x] = E[x^2] - (E[x^2])$.

Equation (15.1) is often estimated using time-series regression, where sample values of $r_t$ are regressed against sample values of $F_t$, yielding estimates $\hat{\alpha}$, $\hat{\beta}$, and $\hat{\varepsilon}$, or equivalently, $\hat{r}_t = \hat{\alpha} + F_t\hat{\beta}$ and $\hat{\varepsilon}_t = r_t - \hat{r}_t$. Under ordinary least squares (OLS) regression, the coefficients are estimated such that the summation of the squared errors is minimized. We therefore need to find $\hat{\alpha}$ and $\hat{\beta}$ such that $\sum_{t-1}^{T}(r_t - \hat{r}_t)^2$ is minimized.

It can be shown that the preceding minimization procedure leads to sample residuals $\hat{\epsilon}_t$ that are uncorrelated with those of $\hat{r}_t$, in the sense that their sample correlation with each other is zero; that is,

$$p\left(\hat{r}_t, \hat{\varepsilon}_t\right) = \frac{\sum_{t=1}^{T}(\hat{r}_t - \hat{\alpha})\hat{\varepsilon}_t}{\sqrt{\sum_{t=1}^{T}(\hat{r}_t - \hat{\alpha})^2}\sqrt{\sum_{t=1}^{T}\hat{\varepsilon}_t^2}} = 0 \qquad (15.3)$$

Therefore an estimate of the total risk of the asset may be decomposed as:

$$\hat{\sigma}^2 = \hat{s}^2 + \hat{e}^2 \qquad (15.4)$$

where:

$$\hat{s}^2 = \frac{1}{T-1}\sum_{t=1}^{T}(\hat{r}_t - \hat{a})^2 \qquad (15.5)$$

$$\hat{e}^2 = \frac{1}{T-1}\sum_{t=1}^{T}\hat{\varepsilon}_t^2 \qquad (15.6)$$

Thus under OLS regression, the decomposition of risk is in accordance, by construction, with the properties of the linear factor model. It should be noted at the outset that the use of regression analysis is not about decomposing the return of the asset into the sum of two uncorrelated parts but about finding the best linear unbiased estimator (BLUE) estimates of the regression coefficients. Indeed, the coefficients estimated under OLS meet this requirement only under certain conditions, such as the error being homoscedastic. In practice, however, the error may be heteroscedastic, due, for example, to outlying observations in the data set. Under such situations, we may still obtain BLUE estimates of the regression coefficients by suitably transforming the data. One such method of transformation is weighted least squares regression, where the weighted sum of squares of errors is minimized. Hence, find $\hat{\alpha}$ and $\hat{\beta}$ such that $\sum_{t=1}^{T} W_t\left(r_t - \hat{r}_t\right)^2$ is minimized.

Under this minimization scheme, the realized residuals $\hat{\varepsilon}_t$ may be correlated with those of $\hat{r}_t$, resulting in the difficulty of expressing the total risk of the asset as the sum of two independent parts. In the next section, we describe how we address this problem.

## Scaling to Historical Volatility

We have noted that under a regression scheme other than OLS, the realized residuals $\hat{\varepsilon}_t$ may in general be correlated with those of the expected returns $\hat{r}_t$. Thus the total risk of the asset can no longer be expressed as:

$$\hat{\sigma}^2 = \hat{s}^2 + \hat{e}^2 \tag{15.7}$$

but is instead given by:

$$\hat{\sigma}^2 = \hat{s}^2 + \hat{e}^2 + 2\mathrm{cov}(\hat{s}, \hat{e}) \tag{15.8}$$

where $\mathrm{cov}(\hat{s},\hat{e})$ represents the sample covariance between $\hat{s}$ and $\hat{e}$.

In order to force the risk to be expressed as the sum of two parts, we define scaled systematic and specific risk terms:

$$\tilde{s} = \gamma^2 \hat{s}^2,\ \tilde{e}^2 = \gamma^2 \hat{e}^2,\ \text{where } \gamma^2 = \frac{\hat{\sigma}^2}{\hat{s}^2 + \hat{e}^2} \tag{15.9}$$

so:

$$\tilde{s}^2 + \tilde{e}^2 = \hat{\sigma}^2 \tag{15.10}$$

## Cohesion

In general, the APT factor model assumes that the residual returns of assets are uncorrelated. In some situations there are economic reasons why this assumption may not hold. For example, in the case where a company has *A* and *B* lines of equity that trade under different International Securities Identification Numbers (ISINs), these have slightly different risk due to liquidity or different voting rights, but the return series are likely to exhibit strong residual correlation. The cohesion estimate in the APT factor model is used to ensure that the residual correlation between such pairs of assets is taken into account in the calculation of portfolio risk.

The (de-meaned) residual return on date $t$ for asset $i$ is calculated as:

$$\varepsilon_i(t) = r_i(t) - r_i^{sys}(t) - \left(\beta_{i,0} + \sum_{k=1}^{K} \beta_{i,k} f_k(t)\right). \qquad (15.11)$$

where:

$r_i(t)$ = the total return
$r_i^{sys}(t)$ = the systematic return
$\beta_{i,0}$ = the average return of asset $i$
$K$ = the number of statistical components in the model
$\beta_{i,k}$ = the loading of asset $i$ on component $k$
$f_k(t)$ = the return of component $k$ on date $t$

The cohesion between assets $A$ and $B$ is then simply the correlation between the residual returns:

$$Cohesion_{A,B} = Cor(\varepsilon_A, \varepsilon_B) \qquad (15.12)$$

If there are missing data points in the returns series, cohesion is calculated over the subset of valid data points only.

### Correlated Residuals

The main limitation of the cohesion functionality in APT models is that it can take into account only residual correlations between disjoint pairs of assets. A more general modeling of correlated residuals is used for funds in some APT factor models, and for user-defined assets (in any APT factor model).

In order to take into account correlated residuals for assets in a factor model, the time series of residual returns are used to calculate a residual correlation matrix for assets. For the calculation of the portfolio variance, this residual correlation matrix is used instead of the usual diagonal residual correlation matrix that is used when residuals are modeled as independent. Missing (de-meaned) returns for an asset are treated as zero when calculating the residual correlation matrix, ensuring that the correlation matrix is positive semidefinite. The APT system supports the correlated residuals functionality for multiple disjoint groups of assets.

## APT MULTI-ASSET-CLASS FACTOR MODEL ESTIMATION

APT balanced (equities plus bonds) models allow the estimation of risk for portfolios containing equities as well as fixed income securities. The models follow a local factor approach in which APT's equity model is augmented with the inclusion of additional bonds components, estimated from bond price series calculated from a yield model.

The use of constant-maturity bond return series ensures the risk analysis is based on the fixed income securities as they stand at the model estimation date, while offering ease of integration with other asset classes.

### Balanced Model Overview

Fixed income modeling in the APT framework is based on risky yield curve time series estimated from quoted prices for plain-vanilla fixed coupon bonds. Yield curve time series are constructed for combinations of currency, rating, and sector (borrower classification), as well as for individual issuers (including sovereigns) for which sufficient data is available. As most issuers do not have a sufficient number of liquid bond issues with different maturities for a term structure of interest rates to be estimated, the yield curves are constructed at a constant Z-spread or option-adjusted spread to the term structure of interbank interest rates for the currency. The yield curve time series are then used to value bonds included in the risk model.

For every bond, a price series is calculated based on the yield curve history, employing the terms and conditions of the bond as they stand today. For example, a bond maturing one year from the model estimation date is priced on each historical date as if it has one year to maturity. The constant-maturity return series obtained for core fixed income securities are then used in the estimation of two sets of statistical components, the first set shared with the core stocks in the model, the second set specific to fixed income. These statistical components represent the systematic or shared behavior of the assets in the model.

As the global and regional balanced models contain many different assets in different currencies, very similar assets frequently have correlated residual or unexplained behavior. The systematic components in APT balanced models are derived statistically, so a risk factor is systematic to the extent that it characterizes the shared behavior of the model estimation universe. In general, every APT model is optimized for analyzing portfolios with similar compositions to the model estimation universe, and produces accurate risk estimates for portfolios diversified over the assets included in the model. Risk forecasts for portfolios that are concentrated in a specific market segment are likely to be less accurate, and using a more specific risk model is recommended for accurate risk estimates in such cases. For example, to analyze a portfolio concentrated within one country, a country-specific model is recommended, and to analyze a pure money market portfolio, the use of a specialized money market model is recommended.

Several methods are available for attributing risk to fixed income factors in balanced portfolios. As for equities, position-based attribution and return-based attribution using the RiskScan methodology are available for balanced portfolios. In addition, the APT Bond Scenario Analysis methodology allows the exposures of a portfolio to yield curve movements and spread changes to be calculated. Finally, an intuitive approach based on yield curve factors (called Credit FIRA) is also provided.

### Yield Curve Construction

APT balanced models use proprietary sector-rating-level and issuer-level yield curves, calculated from plain-vanilla bond prices at a constant Z-spreads to the interbank rate curve. The yield estimation system is designed to robustly estimate yield curves from pricing time series, which are, in their unprocessed form, highly unreliable. Due to gaps, errors, liquidity, or abrupt changes in the amount of notional outstanding for given issues, the spread time series for individual assets sometimes exhibit less than optimal coverage as well as some level of pricing noise. In order to remove the noise, aggregate issuer and sector (borrower classification) spread series are calculated. Data quality is ensured by requiring that a minimum number of quotes is used for the creation of yield curves. Where coverage is sufficient, issuer-level yield curves are constructed. The most specific proxy data available is then used to fill the missing issuer and sector spread quotes with realistic values.

For every combination of currency, rating, and sector, we first calculate the median bond spread change on each date. We similarly estimate the median spread level for the sector spread series at the beginning and end of the model estimation window. (We add a constant long-term trend to the spread change time series to make it consistent with the two spread-level estimates.) Because spread changes are the important quantity for risk estimation, this method produces more robust results than working directly with spread estimates for each date, especially when the number of bonds contributing to a yield curve varies significantly from date to date.

The APT yield database contains yield curve histories for many issuers. If no exactly matching issuer yield curve is found, a fixed income security is mapped to the most closely matching sector curve. The mapping of a bond to a yield curve uses the currency, rating, borrower classification, and issuer.

For a user-defined bond, specifying the currency, rating, and borrower classification is required and specifying the issuer is optional. All bonds implemented in the APT factor model have a currency for which the model contains a risk-free curve (usually an interbank curve), but the rating, borrower classification, and issuer may not be known. The APT model uses Moody's ratings and APT's proprietary borrower classification. If the issuer of a bond is known but the bond is not rated by Moody's or the APT borrower classification is not available, then the bond mapping process attempts to use the most common rating or borrower classification for that issuer.

First, the mapping process tries to map the bond to an issuer curve with the correct currency, rating, and issuer. Second, the process tries to map the bond to the nearest sector curve based on the currency, rating, and borrower classification.

For each date in the model estimation period, a bond can then be valued by discounting its future cash flows using the chosen yield curve, in order to obtain a constant-maturity return series reflecting the terms and conditions of the bond as they stand today. The constant-maturity return series of a bond can then be regressed against the APT components, giving component loadings and a residual term. When building global APT models that cover both equities and bonds, an extra 30 APT components are estimated to capture the systematic effects of interest rates and credit factors. To capture the systematic effects of FX rate factors, 26 additional APT components are included. Thus a global equities, FX, and bonds model will be based on a total of 76 APT components. When commodities are included in the multi-asset-class models, the total number of APT components rises to 96.

## MODELING DERIVATIVES AND OTHER NONUNDERLYING SECURITIES

We have described the method by which underlying securities (stocks, FX, commodities, and synthetic constant-maturity bond products) are modeled (assigned risk profiles) within the APT statistical factor models. Many other financial securities that are traded and used for investments can also be modeled within this framework—these we describe as synthetic securities or derivatives. The most common examples are futures, swaps, options, and forward-starting products. All these securities have the feature that their future payoffs, until the contract expires, are contingent upon the level or return of one or more underlying securities (plus other variables such as realized inflation or volatility in some cases).

The simplest derivatives (described as "delta 1" products) are futures and swaps, in which two cash flow streams are swapped by the parties to the derivative contract. In some cases, each of the two cash flows are essentially based on the return to an underlying asset already described in the APT factor model, so the swap can simply be described as a *synthetic* security—that is, a security with two legs, one held long and one held short. Thus an interest rate swap can be described as a synthetic in which the *pay floating* investor is long a risk-free fixed coupon bond, and short a risk-free floating-rate coupon bond with the same terms and maturity. The exposure or delta to the underlying assets can be described in terms of a notional cash value, and does not vary significantly over the course of the contract.

Derivatives with optionality are more complicated and require a different treatment within APT. We support both a parametric (delta approximation) and Monte Carlo (full repricing) approach within the software, and users can choose to use either for risk measurement, attribution, or scenario analysis of portfolios containing derivatives. Consider a simple European-style put option on the S&P 500 as an example: such a contract (whether exchange-listed or over-the-counter [OTC]) will be defined by a strike price and an expiry date. The cost (premium) of this contract will be negotiated between buyer and seller but is likely to be based on a Black-Scholes formula involving discount rates, expected dividends, and estimated volatility of the underlying in addition to today's S&P 500 level, the strike, and the maturity.

At a given S&P 500 level, we may calculate the put option delta as the equivalent holding in the underlying that will reproduce the expected return of the option (for some short period from the present). It is that delta that typically captures the most important risk feature of the put option (its exposure to the underlying S&P 500 level), so as a crude approximation we may represent the investor's position in the put option as a delta-equivalent position in the underlying asset. This is the basis of the parametric approach in APT. It has the advantage of requiring very little calculation effort and allowing the risk to be attributed very simply to the underlying asset (in this case the S&P 500 index). However, it cannot be relied upon to provide robust downside risk measures such as value at risk (VaR) and conditional value at risk (CVaR), and it does not take into account other sensitivities of the option price such as vega (sensitivity to changes in volatility), theta (sensitivity to time to expiry), rho (sensitivity to changes in the discount rate), and, most importantly, gamma (sensitivity of delta to the level of the underlying).

To model optionality correctly requires a completely different way of estimating the risk measures associated with a portfolio, one based on simulation of future paths rather than an algebraic calculation of statistics such as variance (the second moment of the distribution of expected returns). This simulation approach is achieved by Monte Carlo methods, in which options are fully repriced in terms of the levels of their underlying assets within the simulation via standard pricing functions such as Black-Scholes (for European options), Garman-Kohlhagen (for currency options), and Barone-Adesi Whaley (for American options). In the APT system, the Monte Carlo process is based on the principal components of the risk model, which provides a very efficient method for simulating the future paths of all underlying assets and thus for creating the pricing factor inputs for the revaluation of derivatives within the simulations.

APT supports multi-time-step Monte Carlo simulations (e.g., using 13 separate weekly time steps to estimate a distribution after one quarter) with full repricing of derivatives at each time step. In addition, the underlying distribution of the APT factors is not assumed to be Gaussian—sampling may be carried out from a fat-tailed distribution itself estimated from the historical returns to the APT factors. In this way the nonlinear payoffs of derivatives with optionality are properly accounted for, taking into account the empirically observed non-Gaussian nature of securities returns. Thus APT provides a robust framework for the estimation of downside risk measures such as value at risk, making it suitable for use in regulated investment firms where this is a legal requirement.

## USER-DEFINED ASSETS WITHIN APT MODELS

APT software supports residual correlations for user-defined assets. For certain types of user-defined asset, by default, the APT system creates residual correlation groups consisting of instruments driven by the same risk factors. This ensures that similar instruments hedge correctly. More generally, residual correlation groups may be defined by the user in addition to (or instead of) the default ones.

By default, fixed income derivatives within each currency form a residual correlation group. Specifically, the residuals of short-term interest rate futures, swaptions, and the legs of interest rate, inflation, and currency swaps are grouped by currency. This ensures that swap positions in the same currency hedge perfectly. For example, the residual correlation between an interest rate swap in euros (EUR) and an inflation swap linked to the French consumer price index (CPI) in EUR is taken into account. On the other hand, the residuals of an interest rate swap in EUR and an interest rate swap in USD are modeled as independent. Modeling residual correlations for fixed income derivatives allows a more accurate estimation of specific risk. This is particularly important when a portfolio or benchmark contains very similar interest rate derivatives, for example when a liability profile is defined synthetically in terms of swaps.

By default, credit default swaps with a known issuer (reference entity) are grouped by issuer, ensuring that no diversification occurs between multiple credit default swap (CDS) positions on the same reference entity. Finally, supported user-defined assets may be assigned to any existing or new residual correlation group. For example, a time series representing an interest rate derivative can be added to the group of interest rate derivatives in that currency. Another application would be the creation of a residual correlation group for time-series assets belonging to an asset class that is not explicitly supported by the factor model. Although the correlations between such assets may not be accurately captured by the APT components, they can be modeled exactly using the functionality of correlated residuals.

A limitation of the correlated residuals functionality for user-defined time series is the modeling of missing returns as zero. In situations where missing returns are a significant issue, employing data-engineering techniques to fill missing data may produce more realistic results.

### Perpetual Futures (Continuous Front-Month) Series

When a futures contract (e.g., on an equity index) is represented directly from its historical price history rather than as a synthetic index, a time series may be constructed to represent the behavior of all currently traded contracts. This time series (sometimes called a continuous front-month series) is perpetual and maintained by periodically switching (rolling over) to the most liquid contract for the security. This time series may be regressed onto the statistical components in the same way as any other security in order to represent that future in the model.

Unlike individual futures contracts, this series does not expire, so it allows for the previous trading history to be used to represent newer contracts when they have a short history, giving all contracts a full data series for their estimation within the APT models.

## CONCLUSION

The focus of this introduction to APT's risk management system has been on the methodology by which the APT family of risk models are estimated. The most important feature of this methodology for users of our products is that while explanatory factors and asset returns are both used within the statistical factorization process, the user has the flexibility to select the most appropriate set of explanatory factors when carrying out both portfolio risk attribution and scenario analysis. In this way we aim to provide a robust method for estimation of both systematic and specific risk measures associated with any portfolio (without prespecifying the risk factors that are used within the regressions that drive the model estimation), as well as offering a choice of conventional attribution factors for each asset class and a macro attribution and scenario analysis framework across the multi-asset-class universe that APT supports.

## NOTES

1. Stephen A. Ross, "The Arbitrage Theory of Capital Asset Pricing," *Journal of Economic Theory* 13 (1976): 341–360.
2. Richard W. Roll and Stephen A. Ross, "An Empirical Investigation of the Arbitrage Pricing Theory," *Journal of Finance* 35 (1980): 1073–1103.
3. Gregory Connor and Robert A. Korajczyk, "Risk and Return in an Equilibrium APT: Application of a New Test Methodology," *Journal of Financial Economics* 21 (1988): 255–289; Gregory Connor and Robert A. Korajczyk, "A Test for the Number of Factors in an Approximate Factor Model," *Journal of Finance* 48 (1993): 1263–1291; Gregory Connor and Robert A. Korajczyk, "The Arbitrage Pricing Theory and Multifactor Models of Asset Returns," chap. 4 in *Finance*, Handbooks in Operations Research and Management Science, vol. 9, ed. Robert A. Jarrow, Vojislav Maksimovic, and William T. Ziemba (Amsterdam: North Holland, 1995), 87–144.
4. John Blin, Stephen Bender, and John Guerard, "Earnings Forecasts, Revisions and Momentum in the Estimation of Efficient Market-Neutral Japanese and US Portfolios," *Research in Finance* 15 (1997).
5. Laurence Wormald and Elmarie van der Merwe, "Constrained Optimization for Portfolio Construction," *Journal of Investing* 21, no. 1 (2012): 44–59.

# CHAPTER 16

# Axioma Risk Models

***Bill Wynne; Melissa Brown, CFA; and Sebastian Ceria, PhD***

Go to www.wiley.com/go/greiner to see video titled "Sebastian Ceria."

This chapter identifies the advantages of Axioma risk models and exemplifies the use of the Axioma optimizer and risk models in portfolio construction. It is divided into the following sections: first, background information is conveyed including a description of the types of industry participants who employ risk models and the advantages they gain. Applications of the models and beliefs of practitioners that influence these applications are considered next. Then Axioma core organizational competencies and advantages of multiple risk models delivered daily are discussed; and finally, Axioma niche innovations of importance to specific clients are outlined, and we give an example highlighting the benefits of daily and multiple risk models.

## BACKGROUND

Risk models are critical tools for investors, enabling them to fully understand the risks in their portfolios. Endowments, pension funds, foundations, family offices, consultants, risk management departments of investment banks, private wealth managers, traders, and investment managers face many complex decisions and reporting requirements. These industry practitioners employ risk models to both facilitate decisions and to simplify communication via standardized reports. In the past, risk models may have been viewed as tools mainly for quantitatively driven managers. More recently, fundamental managers have come to appreciate the advantages of using risk models (especially since the 2008 credit crisis) to communicate their value to prospective investors, meet reporting requirements, and understand sources of portfolio risk and return. Risk models can provide useful reality checks and answer questions such as: "Am I meeting the contractual terms of the mandate?" "Am I taking any unintended bets? If so, how have they impacted my performance?" and "What are the sources of my outperformance?" Risk analysis and factor-based performance attribution can also help managers and asset owners speak the same language. For asset owners, risk models facilitate manager comparisons and analysis of strategy consistency through time.

As will be seen later in this chapter, individual beliefs and the types of risk model applications drive significant differences in desirable risk model properties.

## RISK MODEL–BASED REPORTING

Asset owners and their representatives frequently analyze the risk profiles and past performance of a multitude of portfolios. Investment managers who present to these asset owners face the daunting task of clearly communicating the value that they add under extreme time constraints. Factor-based performance attribution and risk analysis reports simplify communication between these parties. These reports also enable investment managers and traders to distill the value that they have added in the past effectively and efficiently. In addition, they empower asset owners and their delegates to screen candidate portfolios for desired characteristics, compare their risk and return profiles, and monitor the adherence of previously selected funds to their mandates.

One of the primary components of a mandate is often a requirement for investment managers to target or stay within a certain level of realized active risk. Investment managers use risk analysis reports in at least two capacities to communicate with consultants and asset owners. First, they can decompose the sources of risk at the time they make the investment decision. These reports typically forecast volatility and indicate the manager took steps to control risk at the beginning of the investment period. In addition, they can detail bets the portfolio manager has taken, such as industry, style, or country tilts, and help the manager ensure he or she is only exposing the portfolio to intended sources of risk. For example, the manager who does not have a view about whether high- or low-momentum stocks will outperform over the next few months would most likely not want an extreme active tilt toward low-momentum stocks. Second, risk reports can also estimate realized volatility during the period under examination. This shows whether portfolio performance complied with the risk mandate. In both of these capacities, risk reports act as a type of control to enforce compliance but also help the manager and asset owner to better understand the portfolio. Risk model estimates are analogous to financial ratios from accounting data. Risk models expose sources of portfolio profitability and risk, whereas financial ratios do the same for companies. To extend the analogy, while asset owners employ risk models to ensure compliance with a mandate, bondholders may use ratios to evaluate whether companies have violated loan covenants.

Given the importance of communicating with asset owners, many investment management organizations employ professionals whose main objective is to explain allocation decisions and subsequent performance. To relay information efficiently, these individuals frequently prioritize standardization of presentation, model transparency, and intuitiveness of factors and construction. They frequently show reports that highlight the stock selection, sector allocation, or intentional style bets made by the portfolio manager. While the ability of the model to explain the data is important, it is not the sole objective. Continuing with the previous analogy, consider construction of risk models to be analogous to writing generally accepted accounting principles (GAAP) standards. GAAP accounting standards are not only designed to be accurate; they also prioritize clarity, understandability, and standardization of presentation, while allowing some flexibility of use.

## ROLE OF RISK MODELS IN INVESTMENT DECISIONS

Risk models may play multiple differentiated roles when applied to investment decisions. The type of application and manager beliefs both play crucial roles in determining the desired characteristics of the model and software employed. For example, some quantitative investment managers believe human intervention corrupts investment decisions. Suppose a quantitative manager takes a data-driven approach to investing and employs statistical and computational algorithms, including risk models, to select and weight portfolio holdings. To research and implement the strategy, the quant may run historical simulations, conduct stress tests, analyze the risk profile of current or hypothetical holdings, rebalance a portfolio, and assess compliance with certain objectives and constraints. Many of these tasks require the use of a risk model. The quant seeks to answer the question: "Given the current environment, history, and my views, how should I allocate funds?" Her strategy requires enterprise systems that input alpha and risk model parameters to drive investment decisions and report the results. If the firm invests only the funds of its partners and their sole consideration is risk-adjusted returns, then the partners may not require the manager to produce any reports beyond profit and loss statements. In this case, the manager may be concerned only with the statistical accuracy of the risk model. However, suppose a fund of funds allocates capital to this manager. The decision makers at the fund of funds may be concerned about diversification. They may require the manager to attribute performance and risk according to standard risk factors that are completely irrelevant to her strategy. These reports help them to ensure that they are not betting on the same risk factors with multiple strategies. Therefore, the manager may employ one type of risk model for the strategy and another for reporting.

On the opposite end of the spectrum, some fundamental investors do not believe standard deviation or variance risk to be a meaningful risk metric (similar to Warren Buffett or Ben Graham). A fundamental manager has a high level of knowledge regarding the business, risks, and profit drivers of individual holdings. This leads to an intuitive understanding of correlations between stocks. A risk model will help the manager understand unintuitive exposures, risks, and correlations between industries, countries, currencies, and styles inherent in the portfolio. Unintended bets can lead to unexpected and undesirable portfolio performance. In addition, some fundamental managers create reports to generate new business and satisfy requirements of asset owners and their consultants. While the managers may pick stocks based on fundamental research, they need to be able to explain these decisions using standardized reports. If they have difficulty explaining a security choice in light of the risk and attribution reports, then they may have to allocate funds elsewhere. Thus, reporting requirements may affect decision making even when the practitioners do not fully embrace the validity of the models.

## AXIOMA VALUE AT A HIGH LEVEL

Since beliefs based on experience or dogma are often intertwined with investment decisions and reporting criteria, software vendors face the difficult goal of attempting to meet the highly specialized needs of prospects and clients while minimizing the complexity of their systems. When analytics providers design excellent software, clients make efficient and effective investment decisions and minimize time spent creating reports and presentations.

Axioma is a recognized leader in designing flexible and transparent decision-support and reporting tools. The corporate motto of "Flexible is better" directly addresses industry needs. Over more than a decade, the company hired pioneers in optimization and risk modeling techniques from academia and industry, highly experienced product specialists, and buy-side technology gurus. As a result, Axioma efficiently and effectively innovates new decision-support algorithms, modeling techniques, and computational methods to meet and exceed the unique specifications of prospects and clients. Through the flexibility of its platform and the skill set of its employees, Axioma has been able to innovate in two critical areas: daily risk models delivered daily and multiple risk models. As will be shown in later sections, Axioma continuously innovates to meet or exceed specific demands of prospects or clients. This attention to detail is important within the industry.

## DAILY RISK MODELS, DELIVERED DAILY

Many investment systems were built in the 1980s and have archaic system architecture. When combined with exoduses of crucial employees who manage technology and data infrastructure, some vendors still need to perform non-value-added, manual activities to support their decaying platforms. Since these processes are time-consuming and sometimes produce errors, these providers have difficulty supplying data more frequently than once a month. Data delivered less frequently results in two separate but related problems. First, all clients receive updated data simultaneously. Therefore, if they customize their strategies to invest based on the freshest data available from the vendor, then they are likely to rebalance on the same day and with the same data as many other market participants. In times of turbulence, this can lead to a simultaneous rush for the exits in certain names. Alternatively, if they wait, the data becomes stale and irrelevant. Additionally, they risk making the same trades as others but later, which effectively results in other market participants front-running their trades. Last, market environments may change dramatically in the middle of a month. In contrast, data delivered daily gives the manager an option to rebalance using the latest risk information to inform investment decisions. The Nyquist sampling theory outlined in Chapter 2 comes into play for monthly updating models, meaning cyclicality in risk may be missed.

As a relatively new entrant into the investment industry, Axioma distinguished itself through integrating cutting-edge technology into its products, automating nonvalued functions, and hiring top-notch data experts who specialize in providing the highest-quality data possible to clients. These investments yielded the following distinguishing innovation: Axioma was the first risk analytics provider to supply daily data delivered daily. Therefore, stale data is a nonissue with Axioma risk models. In addition, clients rebalance according to *their* schedule with data that is likely to be different from the data used by their competitors, at least some of whom are likely to rebalance on alternative days.

## MULTIPLE RISK MODELS

As described previously, different practitioners and applications require unique risk models. For example, some providers offer statistical models, which employ statistical methods to extract accurate risk forecasts from a large data set of security returns. This type of model sometimes might be ideal for the quant without reporting requirements introduced earlier. Other vendors create only fundamental models, whose factors are meant to be transparent and intuitive, for we live in a parametric world and factors that are predefined make sense to fundamental managers. Investment management marketing departments frequently use these to facilitate communication between asset owners and managers. The predefined factor type of model would likely be ideal for the previously introduced hypothetical fundamental manager. Finally, some vendors build hybrids that contain some fundamental factors and also employ statistical techniques to enhance forecast accuracy. They attempt to provide the best of both worlds: standardization, intuition, and transparency with a high degree of statistical accuracy.

When risk modeling was still in its infancy, companies differentiated themselves based on the types of models they developed. Certain analytics vendors became renowned for their fundamental models, others for statistical models, and a final small group for hybrids. Fundamental models became the most common, and investment managers typically employ them for reporting and strategy construction. Statistical models became popular among quantitative managers but had limited success outside of this area. Hybrid models never really caught on. As time passed, problems with a single product approach began to manifest themselves. In addition, the quant meltdown of August 2007 led managers to desire more strongly ways to differentiate themselves. Since standardization, intuition, and transparency do not necessarily lend themselves to innovation in risk modeling techniques, fundamental providers attempted to compete on the accuracy of their forecasts and introduced increasing complex features that did not necessarily correspond to the needs of their customers. For example, some analytics vendors employ many unintuitive descriptors when calculating exposures to factors such as volatility. In addition, the weighting of each descriptor may be intentionally opaque, changes over time, and makes one question whether the vendor tweaks weights with a hindsight bias to give the appearance of enhanced historical ability to forecast risk. This overzealous pursuit of accuracy and focus on a single type of model at the expense of transparency, intuition, and standardization is likely to lead to confusion if the volatility exposure takes an unexpected magnitude or sign and an analyst needs to decompose it into descriptors. Similarly, certain products incorporate proprietary industry classification schemes with the same trade-off between accuracy and communicability.

Axioma recognizes that statistical accuracy, although extremely important, is not the only consideration when choosing a risk model. In certain applications, standardization of presentation, intuitiveness, and transparency provide immense value. Axioma entered the industry later than many other vendors and has built its name upon providing flexible technology that enables practitioners to model decisions according to their specifications. Its core competency as an organization is to supply technology that helps the practitioner make the best decisions possible. To this end, Axioma provides both fundamental and statistical risk models that clients may use simultaneously for both decisions and reporting requirements. This advantage allows Axioma to avoid compromising the accuracy of statistical models to enhance their stability, transparency, and intuition. Axioma researchers define fundamental exposures in a transparent, standardized, and intuitive manner that also explains the data well. Many clients integrate features and forecasts from both models into their strategies. The final section illustrates the use of both statistical and fundamental models to make investment decisions.

## EMPIRICAL RESULTS

To assist the investment manager, analyst, and researcher in validating the wide applicability of the Axioma models, some empirical results are in order. This next section will serve to convey some practical considerations when using or selecting a risk model.

### Accuracy of Model Forecasts

Figures 16.1 and 16.2 illustrate the accuracy of Axioma risk models. The graphs represent the returns of the Russell 1000 in black. The 95 percent confidence intervals (CIs) are calculated using the risk forecasts from the Axioma US2 Short and Medium Horizon Fundamental models. If the model forecasts risk perfectly, then 95 percent of all observations would fall between the two bands. Visually, the confidence interval lines should track the edges of the black zigzags. Both models superbly estimate risk, as most of the data falls within the 95 percent CI. It's understood that only 5 percent of the returns should fall outside these bands, effectively modeling the 95 percent value at risk. Though visually the data looks like a decent representation of the risk variance, numerically it is true as well.

Short-horizon models are estimated with a shorter history than medium-horizon models, and more weight is placed on recent observations. In risk model construction, there is usually a trade-off between responsiveness and stability. Figures 16.1 and 16.2 illustrate that while the short-horizon

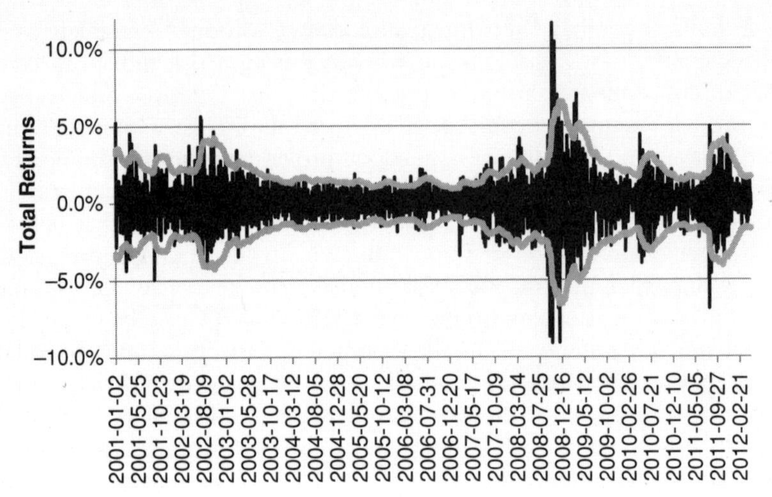


**FIGURE 16.1** Russell 1000 total returns (black) plotted with Axioma US2 Short Horizon Fundamental model 95 percent confidence intervals (gray) from January 2, 2001, to May 1, 2012.

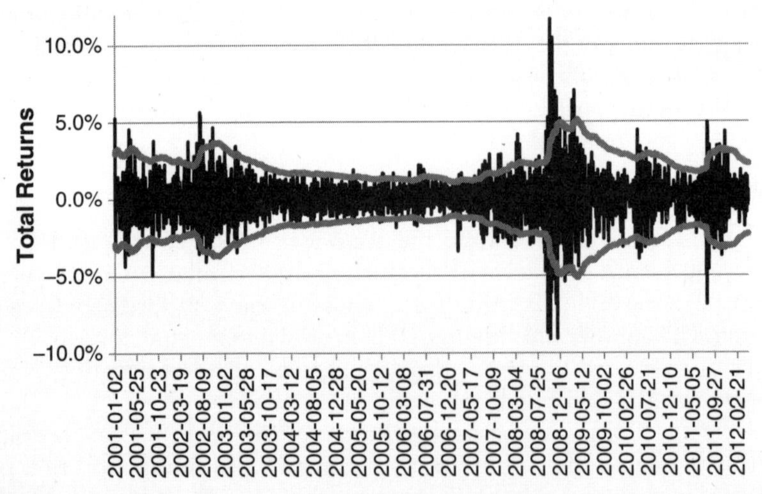


**FIGURE 16.2** Russell 1000 total returns (black) plotted with Axioma US2 Medium Horizon Fundamental model 95 percent confidence intervals (gray) from January 2, 2001, to May 1, 2012.

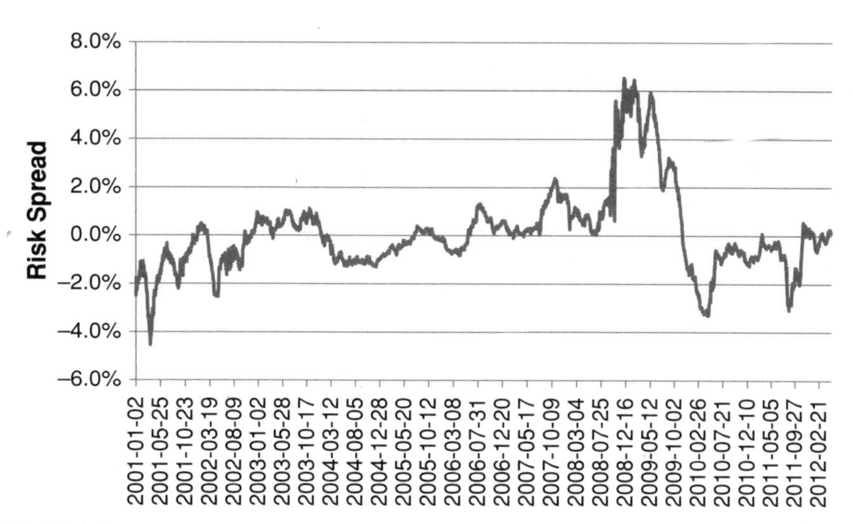


**FIGURE 16.3** Axioma US2 statistical and fundamental risk spread from January 2, 2001, to May 1, 2012.

estimates closely track the dispersion of returns, they are also more volatile than medium-horizon numbers. Short-horizon estimates may be more interesting to investors who have high portfolio turnover and frequently rebalance. Medium-horizon models ensure that risk estimates are stable and may be more appropriate for long-term investors.

### Multiple Risk Perspectives

During certain periods, fundamental and statistical models provide different views of risk. This was especially apparent during the credit crisis of 2008 when statistical models picked up systemic risk that was not captured with fundamental models. Figure 16.3 shows the average difference, or spread, between the risk estimates of the Axioma US2 statistical and fundamental models as applied to the Russell 1000. The large hump in the spread during 2008 highlights the period during the credit crisis when statistical estimates significantly exceeded fundamental ones. One interpretation of this result is that statistical models captured additional systemic risk factors not included in the prespecified fundamental model.

Similarly, Figure 16.4 displays an adjusted spread between the World-Wide 2.1 short-horizon statistical (SHS) and medium-horizon (MH) fundamental risk estimates of the Russell Developed Index. The spread was adjusted such that each cumulative minimum over time is set to be zero and subsequent data points are measured relative to the minima. The graph

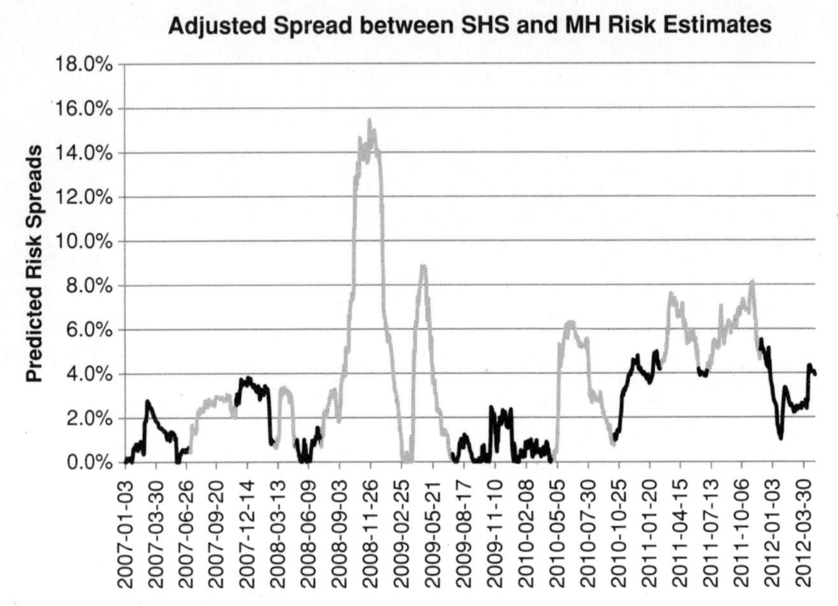


**FIGURE 16.4** Axioma WW2.1 short-horizon statistical (SHS) and medium-horizon (MH) fundamental risk spread from January 2, 2001, to May 1, 2012. Financial events in chronological order (light gray): quant crisis of 2007, Bear Stearns collapse, credit crisis, first Eurozone panic, Fukushima reactor meltdown, U.S. debt stalemate.

highlights various financial crises. In summary, differences between statistical and fundamental risk estimates may provide information regarding international as well as domestic financial crises.

Differences between risk model estimates may also signal changes in the volatility environment and forecast market adjustments. The black line in Figure 16.5 shows the cumulative value of $1 invested in the Russell 1000 index in January 2, 2001, through May 1, 2012. The dark gray line is the average difference between the Axioma short- and medium-horizon model estimates. Spikes in volatility and corresponding market declines are highlighted in light gray. Vertical dotted lines signal the beginning of the volatility spikes. In many cases, sharp increases in risk spread anticipate additional market turbulence and pullbacks of the index.

## DETAILS OF AXIOMA INNOVATIONS

In addition to pioneering daily delivery of multiple risk models, Axioma has made other major advances, such as delivering a platform to develop

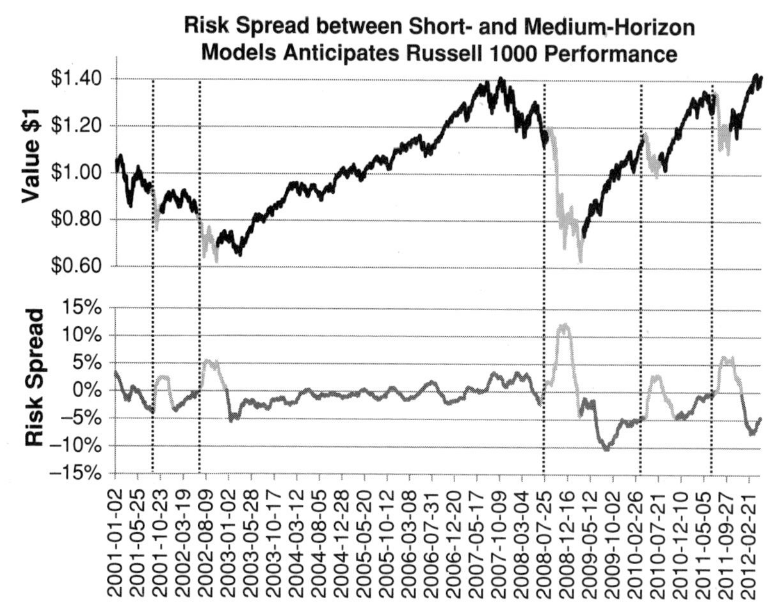


**FIGURE 16.5** The top line shows the cumulative value of $1 invested in the Russell 1000 on January 2, 2001, through May 1, 2012. The bottom line plots the risk spread between the average short- and medium-horizon risk estimates over the same period. Light gray periods indicate spikes in the spread and corresponding market declines. Vertical dotted lines demonstrate the beginning of sharp increases in the risk spread.

custom risk models, although only some of these innovations are currently available through FactSet. However, Axioma has integrated many other features based on internal research and client input into the standard risk models. While it is beyond the scope of this chapter to discuss these in detail, many of these features solve important niche problems. A summary follows.

- *Dynamic volatility adjustment:* Any risk model estimates constructed using historical data will lag the actual volatility of the market. Axioma has developed a technique known as the dynamic volatility adjustment to address this issue. This algorithm determines when volatility regimes have changed and adjusts the risk estimate accordingly.
- *Returns timing adjustment:* Frequently, U.S. news today drives Asian markets tomorrow. For example, suppose that the United States releases exceptional gross domestic product (GDP) numbers on Tuesday. The U.S. market might respond favorably on Tuesday, whereas this information will influence Hong Kong on Wednesday. Axioma models explicitly

account for this phenomenon, resulting in more accurate risk estimates for international portfolios.

- *Issuer-specific risk:* When adjusted for currency differences, the price series for depositary receipts (DRs) and local issues tend to track each other closely. Typical correlation estimates between a DR and its underlying are biased low. This leads to overestimating the active risk of a portfolio with a DR against a benchmark containing the underlying. Axioma incorporates the concept of cointegration of prices, based on the Nobel Prize–winning work of Robert Engel and Clive Granger,[1] through a unique concept called issuer-specific covariance. This results in an unbiased estimate of correlations between securities from the same issuer.
- *Robust regression:* Data errors, illiquidity, or corporate actions may result in returns of very large magnitude. These outliers can potentially have undesirable effects on risk estimates. Axioma implements robust regression, which underweights outlier securities, when calculating factor returns. Therefore, clients can be confident that risk factors capture systemic sources of risk as opposed to unduly reflecting the noisy influence of any individual security.
- *Autocorrelation:* Certain risk factors exhibit dependence in their returns through time. For example, a positive factor return today may increase the likelihood of factor outperformance tomorrow. This type of dependence is known as *autocorrelation* and increases the risk associated with the factor. Axioma incorporates autocorrelation into risk estimates using the Newey-West[2] adjustment. This estimator is used to overcome autocorrelation and heteroscedasticity in the errors of a model.
- *Thin industries:* Sometimes a few corporations account for a large proportion of the total market capitalization of companies within an industry. In this case, it is likely for a small number of stocks to have an abnormally large influence on the magnitude of industry factor risk. Therefore, high concentration reduces the reliability of the factor risk estimates. To combat this problem, Axioma introduces a dummy asset with the return of the market into the industry and weights this asset proportionally to industry concentration. Therefore, less accurate risk estimates are adjusted to be closer to the risk of the market factor.
- *Constrained regression:* Many clients want to be able to distinguish market, country, and industry sources of risk. A typical regression cannot reliably extract sources of return associated with each of these factor groups. To separate these sources of risk and return, Axioma estimates factor returns via constrained regression.
- *Currency modeling:* Some currencies are liquid and others are pegged to some hard currency. A risk model estimated with these types of raw

currency returns is likely to be inaccurate, in our opinion. Axioma risk models employ a proprietary currency model to distill the relationships between difficult-to-model currencies and ones that are more common. The result is stable and realistic currency risk estimates.

To exemplify the advantages of daily and multiple risk models in strategy construction and reporting, we have several innovations. To demonstrate their effectiveness, we have some examples to show.

## Setup

In an effort to show the key benefits of Axioma risk models and exemplify performance attribution and risk analysis, the following scenario constructs two hypothetical international portfolios containing JPMorgan and Sanofi and a market-cap-weighted benchmark containing these securities plus BHP Billiton. Both portfolios are optimized and long-only. One is rebalanced quarterly and the other daily starting on December 30, 2011. The strategy for both is to maximize the difference between alpha and active risk while limiting total factor risk to be less than or equal to 32 percent.

## Strategy Construction

Suppose a hypothetical manager wants to rebalance a portfolio consisting of just these two stocks. Each stock will have an alpha score based on the manager's alpha expectations. A fundamental manager might intuitively judge a company based on its growth prospects, expected multiple expansion, and strength of the management team. A quantitative manager might combine various descriptors to arrive at alpha forecasts typically created from financial statement variables.

Assume the hypothetical manager decides alpha is one-third of the active exposure to the volatility factor and forecasts active risk using the Axioma World-Wide 2.1 medium-horizon fundamental model. In normal market environments, the manager might equally value a 1 percent increase and decrease in expected return and active risk, respectively. Therefore, the manager is willing to tolerate a 2 percent increase in active risk if alpha increases by an equal amount. Suppose he decides to implement a medium-horizon fundamental risk model for three reasons. First, these volatility estimates of the medium-horizon model are smooth over time, which limits portfolio turnover during rebalancing. Second, he plans to present to consultants and wants the active risk estimate to be the same for both portfolio construction and reporting. Last, fundamental factors' intuitiveness and transparency should facilitate communication with the consultants and client.

Figure 16.6 indicates the Axioma optimizer settings that correspond with this scenario. It should be noted that the Axioma optimizer is flexible enough to build strategies (i.e., portfolios) according to the specifications of any type of manager and address any constraints clients or regulators impose. For example, the Axioma optimizer handles taxable and long/short strategies. In contrast, some optimizers require clients to specify their strategies in a mean-variance framework and cannot handle risk constraints properly.

Suppose the hypothetical manager believes capital preservation to be paramount. When markets are turbulent and securities are highly correlated, he might want to enhance portfolio diversification. Therefore, he might constrain factor risk to be below a certain threshold. Imagine he picks 32 percent based on historical research. Sometimes markets become turbulent quickly, and medium-horizon model estimates may lag the volatility environment. In some cases, difficult-to-measure risk factors may drive returns. To mitigate these possibilities, the manager might want the risk model to be as responsive and as statistically accurate as possible. Therefore, he would pick the

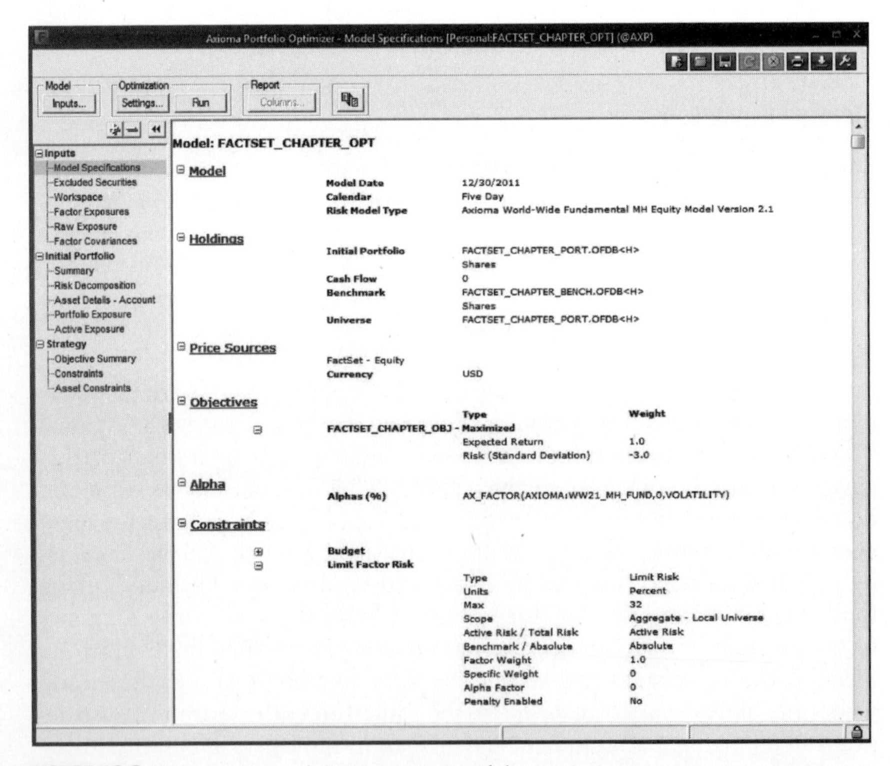


**FIGURE 16.6** Screen shot of the Axioma portfolio optimizer strategy parameters.

Axioma World-Wide 2.1 short-term statistical model to be used for the risk constraints. As can be seen in Figure 16.6, factor weight equals 1 while specific weight is zero. This ensures that the constraint applies only to the factor component of risk (systematic or market risk) and not idiosyncratic (stock-specific) risk.

## Risk Decomposition

The hypothetical manager would most likely want to decompose risk into its components, to ensure that the portfolio takes only intended bets and satisfies all the constraints. Even though this manager invested in only two companies, there are multiple categories of risk associated with both total and active returns. The Axioma World-Wide 2.1 fundamental models decompose risk into several sources. These are market, currency, country, industry, and style. The manager can then analyze both active and total factor exposures and risk. The following section describes and interprets FactSet risk decomposition reports using Axioma risk models.

Figure 16.7 decomposes active risk of 10.99 percent into its constituents. Active specific and factor contributions to risk are 7.45 percent and 8.07 percent. As a result, the percentage of variance contributed by specific and factor risk are 46.01 percent and 53.99 percent, respectively. Therefore, stock selection and factor bets each account for approximately half of active risk.

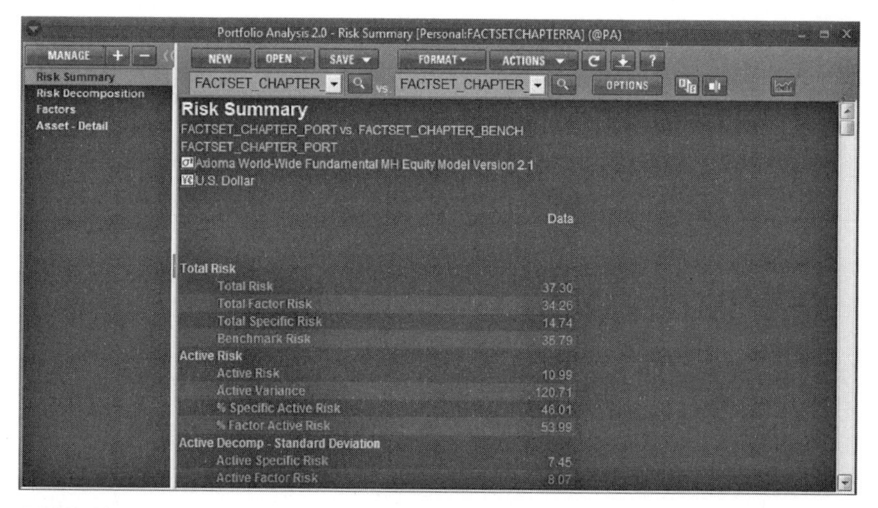


**FIGURE 16.7** Active risk decomposition using Axioma World-Wide 2.1 medium-horizon fundamental model screen shot within FactSet.

Figure 16.8 shows two alternative ways of decomposing factor risk. The "Standard Deviation" columns segregate contributions from variance and covariance. For example, currency factors as a group contribute 5.28 percent to active risk and account for 23.05 percent of variance when considered in isolation. However, other factors may diversify currency risk. Suppose the Australian dollar tends to fluctuate with commodity prices and correlates with the health of aggregate global economies, whereas investors may consider pharmaceuticals to be noncyclical and typically overweight them during times of crisis. Then, it is possible for the Australian dollar to correlate negatively with pharmaceuticals. The "Contribution to Variance" columns allocate half of the contribution from the covariance terms to groups of factors. This accounts for the diversification benefits between factors. For example, currency percentage of variance is only 15.22 percent when correlations are included. This indicates that country, industry, and styles diversify currency risk.

The manager may analyze the risk decomposition to determine whether the portfolio has any undesirable properties in two different ways. First, he can examine active differences. Typically active exposures are thought of, and for currencies, countries, and industries they are the sum of the active weights of the securities corresponding to those categories. Therefore, the

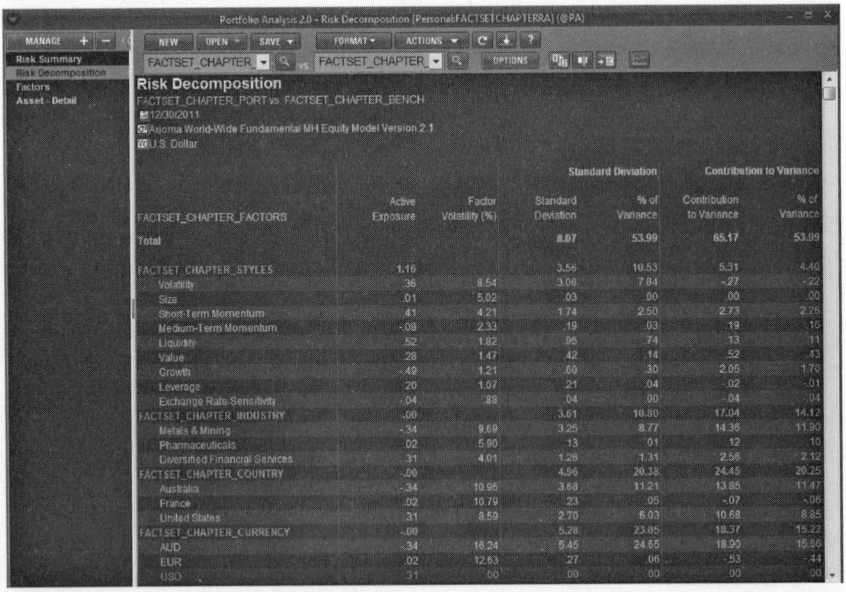

Portfolio Analysis 2.0 - Risk Decomposition [Personal:FACTSETCHAPTERRA] (@PA)

MANAGE | NEW | OPEN | SAVE | FORMAT | ACTIONS | OPTIONS

Risk Summary
Risk Decomposition
Factors
Asset - Detail

FACTSET_CHAPTER_ vs. FACTSET_CHAPTER_

**Risk Decomposition**

FACTSET_CHAPTER_PORT vs. FACTSET_CHAPTER_BENCH
12/30/2011
Axioma World-Wide Fundamental MH Equity Model Version 2.1
U.S. Dollar

| | | | Standard Deviation | | Contribution to Variance | |
|---|---|---|---|---|---|---|
| FACTSET_CHAPTER_FACTORS | Active Exposure | Factor Volatility (%) | Standard Deviation | % of Variance | Contribution to Variance | % of Variance |
| **Total** | | | **8.07** | **53.99** | **65.17** | 53.99 |
| FACTSET_CHAPTER_STYLES | 1.16 | | 3.56 | 10.53 | 5.31 | 4.40 |
| Volatility | .36 | 8.54 | 3.08 | 7.84 | -.27 | -.22 |
| Size | .01 | 5.02 | .03 | .00 | .00 | .00 |
| Short-Term Momentum | .41 | 4.21 | 1.74 | 2.50 | 2.73 | 2.26 |
| Medium-Term Momentum | -.08 | 2.33 | .19 | .03 | .19 | .16 |
| Liquidity | .52 | 1.82 | .95 | .74 | .13 | .11 |
| Value | .28 | 1.47 | .42 | .14 | .52 | .43 |
| Growth | -.49 | 1.21 | .60 | .30 | 2.05 | 1.70 |
| Leverage | .20 | 1.07 | .21 | .04 | -.02 | -.01 |
| Exchange Rate Sensitivity | -.04 | .88 | .04 | .00 | -.04 | -.04 |
| FACTSET_CHAPTER_INDUSTRY | .00 | | 3.61 | 10.80 | 17.04 | 14.12 |
| Metals & Mining | -.34 | 9.69 | 3.25 | 8.77 | 14.36 | 11.90 |
| Pharmaceuticals | .02 | 5.90 | .13 | .01 | .12 | .10 |
| Diversified Financial Services | .31 | 4.01 | 1.26 | 1.31 | 2.56 | 2.12 |
| FACTSET_CHAPTER_COUNTRY | -.00 | | 4.96 | 20.38 | 24.45 | 20.25 |
| Australia | -.34 | 10.95 | 3.68 | 11.21 | 13.85 | 11.47 |
| France | .02 | 10.79 | .23 | .05 | -.07 | -.06 |
| United States | .31 | 8.59 | 2.70 | 6.03 | 10.68 | 8.85 |
| FACTSET_CHAPTER_CURRENCY | -.00 | | 5.28 | 23.05 | 18.37 | 15.22 |
| AUD | -.34 | 16.24 | 5.45 | 24.65 | 18.90 | 15.66 |
| EUR | .02 | 12.63 | .27 | .06 | -.53 | -.44 |
| USD | .31 | .00 | .00 | .00 | .00 | .00 |

**FIGURE 16.8** Screen shot of factor risk decomposition using Axioma World-Wide 2.1 medium-horizon fundamental model.

manager can confirm allocations to these categories through analyzing the exposure column on the decomposition report. If he decides any of the weights are undesirable, he can set a constraint to limit individual exposures or groups of industry, country, or currency exposures to the appropriate level. In actuality, exposures are not active weights, but are used in this sense here just for ease of communication.

Since style exposures are normalized, they are not comparable with the other types. Suppose a mandate requires the manager to have tilts to or away from certain exposures. For example, a growth manager may need to have a minimum tilt toward a growth factor and a negative exposure to value. The manager can select constraints such that the optimized portfolio satisfies these conditions.

In this case, the risk decomposition report indicates that volatility has a high active exposure (0.3604) and contributes significantly to portfolio risk (7.84 percent of variance) when considered in isolation. This is to be expected since alpha is equal to one-third of the volatility exposure and is maximized in the strategy. In other words, it is an intended bet. Interestingly, other factors diversify this risk, resulting in –0.27 contribution to variance when including correlations.

Sometimes a manager is unable to determine whether inappropriate bets are made solely through exposure analysis. Such cases arise when there is a large difference between factor volatilities and diversification benefits. In Figure 16.8, the factor risk of short-term momentum is smaller than that of volatility. Even though portfolio exposure to short-term momentum is higher, the volatility factor has a larger contribution to variance when considered in isolation. However, volatility provides diversification with respect to the other factors. In the distributed covariance columns, percentage of variance is negative, indicating this factor detracts from active risk when considered in combination with other factors. Short-term momentum does not achieve the same diversification benefits and contributes significantly to active risk when correlations are included. This information would not be considered if the manager solely reviewed exposures.

If the manager decides a factor contributes an undesirable amount to portfolio risk, he can implement constraints on contributions to risk from individual factors or groups of factors with the Axioma optimizer. In addition, the optimizer has the ability to ensure equal contributions to risk from all factors, known as *risk parity*.

The manager might also analyze risk decomposition reports to ensure that the strategy was implemented correctly. For example, factor risk was constrained to be less than 32 percent. In Figure 16.9, total portfolio risk is decomposed. Notice the factor risk constraint is binding.

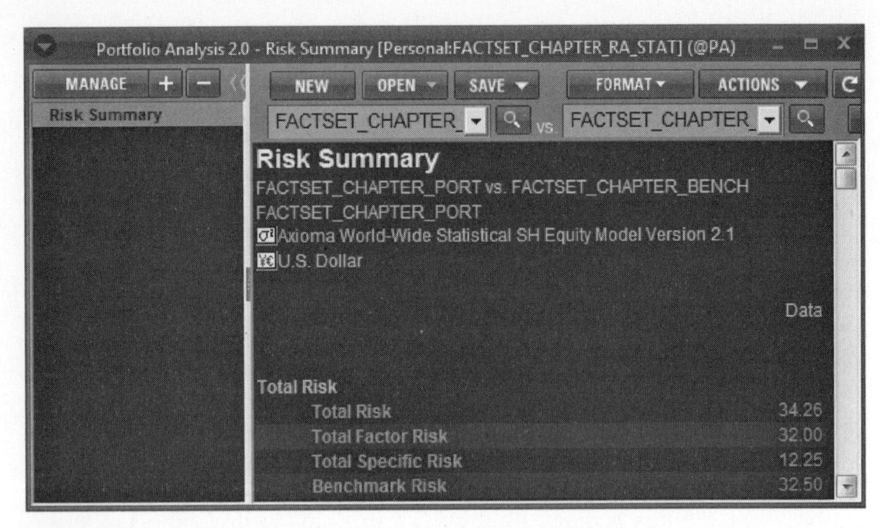


**FIGURE 16.9** Total risk decomposition using Axioma short-horizon statistical model.

To decompose active and total specific risk, the manager can look at the asset details page shown in Figure 16.10. Only weights and the specific risk for each holding determine portfolio-level specific risk. JPMorgan accounts for the highest percentage of active specific risk even though BHP Billiton exhibits the largest magnitude of active weight. Therefore, the specific risk of JPMorgan must be higher than that of BHP Billiton.

The manager might diversify individual security risk through constraining asset weights to be below a certain threshold. For example, if all asset weights of securities within a portfolio are constrained to be less than 1 percent, then the portfolio must hold at least 100 securities to satisfy the constraint. However, it is possible for the specific volatility of one security to be significantly larger than that of other portfolio holdings. In this case, a seemingly well-diversified portfolio might have an undesirable amount of specific risk. To avoid this, the manager could introduce a constraint on aggregate specific risk or the contribution to specific risk from each security within the portfolio.

### Performance Attribution

After the quarter is over, the manager would implement attribution to ensure that portfolio performance complies with the risk analysis forecasts and help the asset owner understand the sources of active return. This analysis assumes the portfolio was rebalanced at the beginning of the quarter and then held without any further changes until the end of the quarter.

**Asset - Detail**

FACTSET_CHAPTER_PORT vs. FACTSET_CHAPTER_BENCH
12/30/2011
Axioma World-Wide Fundamental MH Equity Model Version 2.1
U.S. Dollar

| Security Name | Active Weight | Axioma-Active Specific Risk | Axioma-% Specific Active Risk |
|---|---|---|---|
| Total | .00 | 7.45 | 46.01 |
| Sanofi ADS | 2.17 | .36 | .11 |
| JPMorgan Chase & Co. | 31.42 | 6.30 | 32.93 |
| BHP Billiton Ltd. ADS | -33.58 | 3.96 | 12.98 |

Holdings Data As Of
FACTSET_CHAPTER_PORT 12/30/2011
FACTSET_CHAPTER_BENCH 12/30/2011
Risk Model As Of
Axioma World-Wide Fundamental MH Equity Model Version 2.1 12/30/2011

**FIGURE 16.10** Active specific risk decomposition using Axioma World-Wide 2.1 medium-horizon fundamental model.

In Figure 16.11 we show that the portfolio outperformed the benchmark by 11.08 percent. Active return is then decomposed into contributions from stock selection and risk factors. Stock selection and risk factors contribute 5.37 percent and 5.72 percent to outperformance, respectively. In other words, 48 percent of outperformance came from stock selection, which is in keeping with the 46 percent specific percentage of risk estimate.

Similar to risk decomposition, factor attribution, shown in Figure 16.12, separates sources of active return into style, industry, currency, and country contributions. Style contributes 1.5 percent to compounded factor impact. Since the strategy intentionally tilts toward volatility, it is perhaps not surprising that volatility contributed the most to outperformance of all the styles. As noted in the risk decomposition, short-term momentum has a larger exposure than volatility. While the volatility factor performed well and contributed 89 basis points to performance, short-term momentum performed poorly over the quarter. The large 0.34 average exposure to an underperforming factor detracted 79 basis points from performance. In the

**Factor Attribution**

Factor Performance Attribution

FACTSET_CHAPTER_PORT vs. FACTSET_CHAPTER_BENCH

12/30/2011 to 3/30/2012

Axioma World-Wide Fundamental MH Equity Model Version 2.1

U.S. Dollar

| Active | Risk Factors Effect | Risk Stock Specific Effect | Risk Total Effect |
|---|---|---|---|
| Active | 5.72 | 5.37 | 11.08 |
| **Total** | | | **11.08** |

Holdings Data As Of

FACTSET_CHAPTER_PORT 12/30/2011 through 12/30/2011

FACTSET_CHAPTER_BENCH 12/30/2011 through 12/30/2011

Risk Model As Of

Axioma World-Wide Fundamental MH Equity Model Version 2.1 12/30/2011 through 3/29/2012

**FIGURE 16.11** Active performance attribution using Axioma World-Wide 2.1 medium-horizon fundamental model.

future, the manager might consider adding a short-term momentum exposure constraint to the strategy to avoid this tilt.

Figure 16.13 decomposes active specific return into its constituents. An average overweight of 31.69 percent combined with positive specific returns results in a 5.19 percent specific return contribution for JPMorgan, which is almost the entire active specific return. As shown in Figure 16.10, JPMorgan active specific risk accounts for 32.93 percent of portfolio variance. Therefore, the active specific return outperformance justifies the large active bet the manager placed on JPMorgan at the start of the quarter.

### Time-Series Analysis

Simulated portfolios were constructed using the preceding strategy with both quarterly portfolio and daily portfolio rebalancing frequencies. Figures 16.14a to 16.14d demonstrate that a manager is able to bet more heavily on alpha, take more active and total risk, and realize a higher return if the simulated portfolio had been rebalanced more frequently

**Factor Report**
FACTSET_CHAPTER_PORT vs. FACTSET_CHAPTER_BENCH
12/30/2011 to 3/30/2012
Axioma World-Wide Fundamental MH Equity Model Version 2.1
U.S. Dollar

| FACTSET_CHAPTER_FACTORS | Average Portfolio Exposure | Average Benchmark Exposure | Average Active Exposure | Compounded Factor Return | Compounded Factor Impact |
|---|---|---|---|---|---|
| FACTSET_CHAPTER_STYLES | 2.88 | 1.77 | 1.11 | | 1.50 |
| Exchange Rate Sensitivity | .40 | .15 | .25 | .45 | .08 |
| Growth | -.19 | .31 | -.50 | .09 | -.07 |
| Leverage | -.10 | -.24 | .14 | .56 | .09 |
| Liquidity | .48 | .11 | .36 | 1.16 | .66 |
| Medium-Term Momentum | -.29 | -.29 | -.00 | -2.01 | .23 |
| Size | .61 | .60 | .01 | -.40 | -.01 |
| Short-Term Momentum | .47 | .14 | .34 | -2.65 | -.79 |
| Value | 1.20 | .90 | .30 | 1.08 | .41 |
| Volatility | .30 | .09 | .22 | 1.56 | .89 |
| FACTSET_CHAPTER_INDUSTRY | 1.00 | 1.00 | -.00 | | 4.16 |
| Diversified Financial Services | .72 | .40 | .32 | 3.36 | 1.25 |
| Metals & Mining | – | .33 | -.33 | -7.29 | 2.99 |
| Pharmaceuticals | .28 | .27 | .01 | -3.11 | -.08 |
| FACTSET_CHAPTER_COUNTRY | 1.00 | 1.00 | -.00 | | .34 |
| Australia | – | .33 | -.33 | -.47 | .10 |
| France | .28 | .27 | .01 | .63 | .03 |
| United States | .72 | .40 | .32 | .68 | .21 |
| FACTSET_CHAPTER_CURRENCY | 1.00 | 1.00 | -.00 | | -.28 |
| AUD | – | .33 | -.33 | .62 | -.27 |
| EUR | .28 | .27 | .01 | 1.16 | -.00 |
| USD | .72 | .40 | .32 | – | – |
| **Total** | | | | | 5.72 |

Holdings Data As Of
FACTSET_CHAPTER_PORT 12/30/2011 through 12/30/2011
FACTSET_CHAPTER_BENCH 12/30/2011 through 12/30/2011

**FIGURE 16.12** Active factor attribution using Axioma World-Wide 2.1 medium-horizon fundamental model.

than quarterly. Daily optimization may not be feasible or desirable due to operational constraints, transaction costs, and taxes. However, the ability to rebalance with fresh data gives a manager the option to modify alpha exposure and stay compliant with the mandates of the strategy when market volatility changes. If the increase in predicted alpha is higher than the expected costs of rebalancing, then daily risk model data may also lead to higher active returns. Figure 16.14a illustrates that the difference between daily and quarterly expected active returns is greater than 14 percent less than one month after the initial rebalancing. A manager who received only monthly data would not see the benefits of increasing bets until he received updated risk model data at the end of the month.

Figure 16.14b indicates that the market environment is initially volatile, resulting in a binding total factor risk constraint. Afterward, the market calms and the factor risk constraint becomes nonbinding. Therefore, the manager is able to increase alpha exposure and factor risk while

**Performance Attribution**

FACTSET_CHAPTER_PORT vs. FACTSET_CHAPTER_BENCH

12/30/2011 to 3/30/2012

Axioma World-Wide Fundamental MH Equity Model Version 2.1

U.S. Dollar

| Security Name | Port. Average Weight | Bench. Average Weight | Variation in Average Weight | Risk Stock Specific Effect |
|---|---|---|---|---|
| **Total** | **100.00** | **100.00** | -- | **5.37** |
| BHP Billiton Ltd. ADS | -- | 32.97 | -32.97 | .15 |
| JPMorgan Chase & Co. | 71.80 | 40.11 | 31.69 | 5.19 |
| Sanofi ADS | 28.20 | 26.92 | 1.29 | .03 |

Holdings Data As Of
FACTSET_CHAPTER_PORT 12/30/2011 through 12/30/2011
FACTSET_CHAPTER_BENCH 12/30/2011 through 12/30/2011
Risk Model As Of
Axioma World-Wide Fundamental MH Equity Model Version 2.1 12/30/2011 through 3/29/2012

**FIGURE 16.13** Active specific attribution using Axioma World-Wide 2.1 medium-horizon fundamental model.

maintaining compliance with the mandate. In Figure 16.14c, the quarterly portfolio achieves only 61 percent of optimal active risk after 15 trading days. If the manager has an effective alpha strategy, the ability to take risk when desired should result in outperformance. Figure 16.14d reveals that the option to rebalance daily has the ability to add 7 percent to cumulative active returns. Additionally, a static portfolio may violate its risk constraints when market volatility increases. In Figure 16.14b, the quarterly portfolio

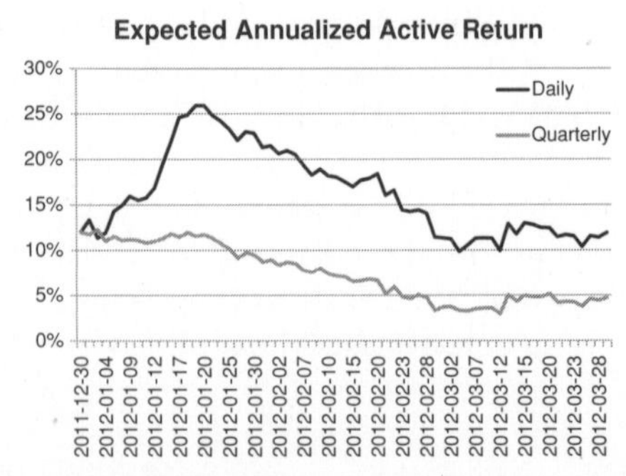


**FIGURE 16.14a** The daily portfolio adjusts to the changing risk environment through increasing its bet on alpha, while expected active return of the quarterly portfolio declines over time.

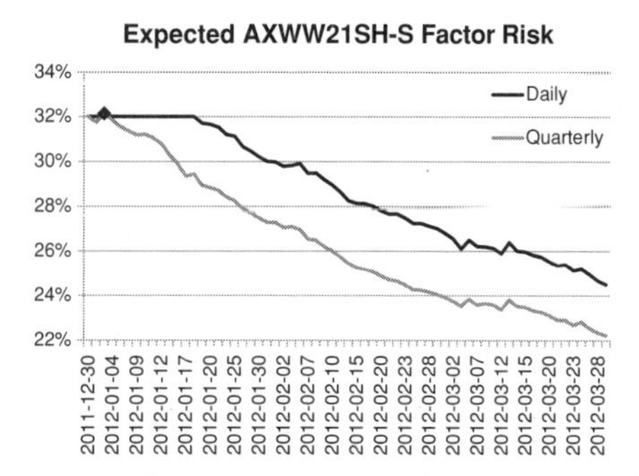


**FIGURE 16.14b** The factor risk constraint is initially binding for both daily and quarterly portfolios. A black diamond indicates the violation of the risk constraint by the quarterly portfolio. As the risk environment changes, the daily portfolio maintains its factor risk levels while the quarterly portfolio diverges from the constraint after a few days. After a few weeks, the calm market environment leads to the constraint becoming nonbinding for both strategies.

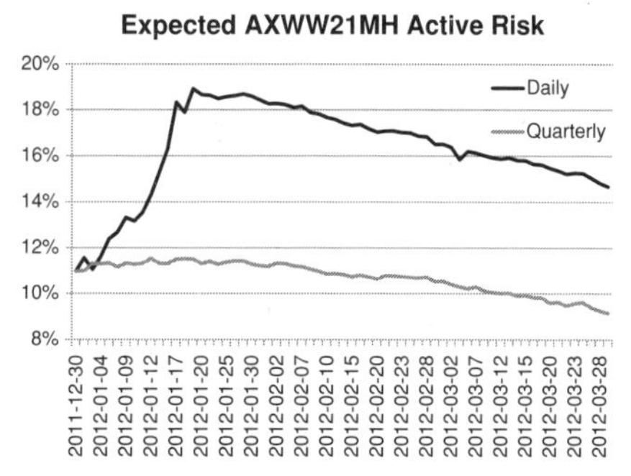


**FIGURE 16.14c** As the daily portfolio increases alpha exposure, its active risk increases. The quarterly portfolio does not take advantage of the ability to increase alpha or active risk.

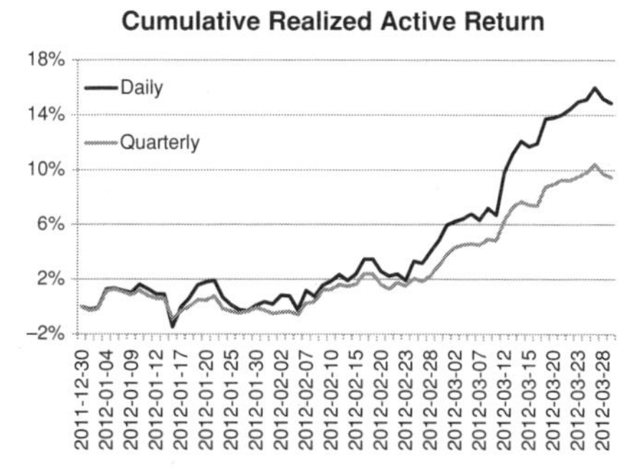


**FIGURE 16.14d** Increased alpha exposure of the daily portfolio leads to realized outperformance of this strategy versus the quarterly portfolio.

breaches the factor risk constraint a couple of days after rebalancing. Daily data enables the manager to evaluate whether such violations are acceptable and provides the option to rebalance when nonconformance exceeds the desired threshold.

## CONCLUSION

This chapter has outlined some of the features and benefits of using Axioma risk models and optimizer on FactSet. The availability of multiple types of daily risk models adds significant value to industry practitioners who construct and analyze portfolios. These capabilities and others are manifestations of the flexibility, innovation, and client-centric culture of the Axioma organization.

## NOTES

1. Robert F. Engle and Clive W. J. Granger, "Co-Integration and Error Correction: Representation, Estimation and Testing," *Econometrica* 55, no. 2 (1987): 251–276.
2. Whitney K. Newey and Kenneth D. West, "A Simple, Positive Semi-Definite, Heteroskedasticity and Autocorrelation Consistent Covariance Matrix," *Econometrica* 55, no. 3 (1987): 703–708.

# CHAPTER 17

# Distinguishing Risk Models

*Steven P. Greiner, PhD, and Richard Barrett, CFA, FRM*

In this chapter we discuss distinguishing some popular risk models. We begin by tracing the background of the company and model that historically has been the most popular, MSCI-Barra, then offer a general review and analysis of reporting capabilities on FactSet for any risk model. We demonstrate an analysis through an example portfolio risk attribution report. Additionally, we'll spend some time illustrating that though level calculations can vary somewhat, risk model to risk model, they all tend to capture the trends of risk well, and, importantly, the differences between level estimates of risk models can be used to derive rules of thumb for estimation error estimates.

## HISTORY

The history of Barra is pretty interesting and can be found detailed by John Guerard Jr.[1] Barra was the first organization to bring quantitative techniques to bear for risk management; hence a review of their beginnings is a great story. In 1973 Barr Rosenberg and Walt McKibben of the Universities of Berkeley and Western Ontario, respectively, published a landmark paper on the prediction of systematic and specific risk in common stocks.[2] They went on to show that these predictions can be based on simple firm accounting data. These data were:

- The quick ratio, those assets that can be quickly converted to cash as needed, defined by:

$$QR = (\text{Cash and equivalents} + \text{Marketable securities} + \text{Accounts receivable})/(\text{Current liabilities})$$

- Leverage (total debt to total assets).
- Growth in earnings per share.
- Variance of the preceding, the earnings per share growth.
- Latest annual change in earnings per share.
- Book-to-price ratio.
- Historical capital asset pricing model (CAPM) beta to its appropriate index.
- Log of stock price, a type of momentum factor.
- Property, plant, and equipment percentage of total assets.
- Share turnover.

From this study (and of course a bit of evolution after its publication) Barr Rosenberg with Andrew Rudd produced in 1975 the U.S. fundamental risk model called US-E1, and Barra was born. It was and for the most part still is proprietary to some extent. The amount of information MSCI-Barra shares about factor specifics is guarded somewhat, but its representatives are some of the best and brightest in the business and will offer complete consulting if requested. Some factors are actually composite factors and may consist of up to nine individual factors. It was Barra's strong opinion historically that fundamental multifactor models outperform multifactor models based on gross economic variables and/or statistical arbitrage pricing theory (APT)-like models. Recently, however, Barra has tempered that opinion a bit and now produces statistical models as well as daily updating models.

## RISK MODEL DETAILS

The first step in estimating the risk for a model similar to a Barra fundamental multifactor model involves selecting, acquiring, and cleaning the data. Market prices as well as fundamental company-specific data are used, with special attention to capital restructuring, earnings restatements, and market action.

Factor selection and construction comprise the next step. Correlations between factors with forward returns and statistical significance testing are thoroughly applied to allow determination of which factors partition risk in the most effective and efficient way. This also necessitates studying which factors go with which and seeking combinations that minimize collinearity in super-factor constructs. Though judgment plays a major role, it's not applied independent of the quantitative analytics. Cluster analysis is often applied in this step to elucidate characteristics common between factors. These risk "descriptors," as they call them, are usually winsorized and Z-scored, as with most multifactor models' factor constructs.

The next step involves industry and country assignment for each security. Usually a single industry assignment occurs for each stock in most Barra models, but for the largest of stocks and conglomerates an assignment between multiple industries can occur.

The last step involves performing the cross-sectional regressions of forward returns of a period as long as the model's update frequency to gauge factor returns (i.e., betas) and use them for covariance matrix construction. Time decay to emphasize the more recent data is employed in addition. Garch(1,1) models are used to estimate the conditional volatility of the portfolio's time series, and to produce a scaling factor that is applied to the model's forecast to allow better estimates of the level of risk, applicable only on the systemic risks. To clarify that procedure a bit, the model's volatility forecast comes from a bottom-up association between fundamental factors and forward returns at the individual asset level, whereas the Garch method is applied at the portfolio level on the time series of portfolio (or estimation universe) return. The differences between the magnitudes of the conditional volatilities for the portfolio then are used to set a scaling that is multiplied by the model's volatility forecast to raise the level of the estimate toward the most recent time period's Garch estimate. There are intricacies involved in this scaling process, however, that make this a nontrivial procedure. This is not a universal application across all risk models, either.

The residuals of the regressions used to create the data for specific (idiosyncratic) risks come from the regressions on the factors (descriptors). The greater the asset's specific risk, the larger the proportion of its return that is attributed to the stock itself. These residuals are examined for the usual suspects of a bad model, heteroscedacity, and the like, and the appropriate feedback goes into factor description recipes.

There are a large set of quality assurance tests run on a model before it's released to clients, involving *ex ante* forecasts in history with *ex post* realizations and comparison with other model constructs. The final result is a robust risk model ready for deployment in real risk management situations. Since the Barra US-E1 model released in 1975, there have been several updates, and US-E3 (FactSet notation USE3) has been significantly improved. Many of these advances involve better industry classification, larger estimation universe, the addition of size, better Garch modeling, real estate investment trust (REIT) risk indexes, improved model diagnostics, and so forth.[3] These days, there are the US-E3L and US-E4S for long-term and short-term model forecasting in the Barra suite.

In Figure 17.1, we illustrate the selection of available risk models on the FactSet system that are chosen simply by menu selection. The data for each model is uploaded at each model's update frequency, establishing an ease of use unavailable elsewhere. All the data handling is done for the client,

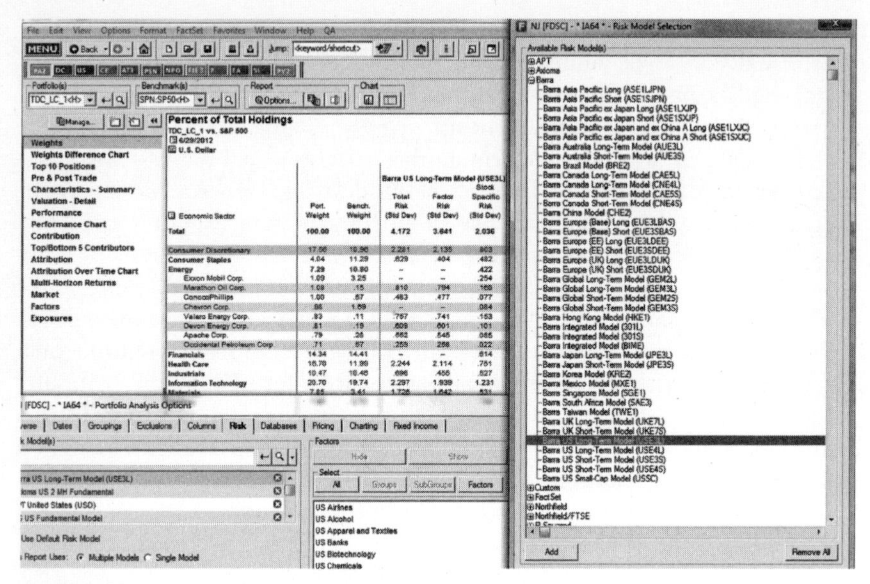


**FIGURE 17.1** A screen shot of the MSCI-Barra risk models available on FactSet.

mitigating maintenance of factor returns, covariance matrix, and so forth. Combining this with the client portfolio holdings uploaded to the cloud servers each night, risk reporting is facile, is quick, and offers many variations of grouping, slicing and dicing for monitoring/reporting purposes.

## RISK MODEL–BASED REPORTING

There are several objectives for reporting risk and they are dependent on who the user is for the most part. Portfolio managers (PMs), for instance, will often prefer a description of risk broken down into the respective factors that go into the forecast. Their need is to see how much exposure the portfolio has to various factors to gauge whether the intentions and leanings in the portfolio are appropriate and of the right magnitude. In particular, if managers are using the Barra models, they've already decided that the explanatory variables in their risk model are those they want to see attribution to. Subsequently, the top-level portfolio risk measures are important for PMs as well as total risk, and its two addends, systematic and specific risk, can elucidate the direction in which to position the portfolio. If systematic risks are increasing, for instance, tightening tracking error may be the better part of valor because stock picking generally loses efficacy when common risks are increasing. This would mean that correlations across assets are increasing, making securities less distinguishable and squashing alpha expectations. Alternatively, if specific risks are increasing—as when coming out of a market crisis, for instance—then widening tracking error to take advantage of active risk may be more beneficial and appropriate. This would be the case when stock specificity matters more, and where alpha expectations are more likely fulfilled.

Thus the PM has two overarching viewpoints: One is hindsight, as PMs definitely want to know if their portfolio leanings have paid off and want to decompose the risk/reward payoffs. The second, however, is *ex ante* forecasts. Given that one has formed the portfolio just this morning, for instance, what is the prediction of risks over the next time horizon? If it's too much in aggregate or concentrated in specific groups, industries, currencies, or assets, the PM needs to be aware and have a sense of the magnitude of these risks. An example of the top-level risks for a portfolio can be seen in Table 17.1.

In this table, we illustrate the relative total risks, relative factor (common), and stock-specific risks for a U.S. domestic portfolio versus the S&P 500 for five different risk models. The total relative risks vary from a low of 2.93 for R-Squared's estimate to 5.54 for the Northfield Information Systems (NIS) fundamental model. Considering that each model is constructed differently from a variety of factors, methods, and update frequencies, it's quite ordinary for the level forecasts to yield separate solutions. Appropriately, a time series of the forecasts is usually trend following, however. We comment that the factor risks and the specific risks needn't sum to the total in this chart, because we're showing the results in standard deviations units. If we displayed risks in variance units, then the contributions would sum to the total. This can be seen more clearly in Table 17.2.

In this table we illustrate the relative risk measures in variance terms, and beneath the totals we show the percentage contributions the factor risks and stock-specific risks make to the total risks for the five models. One can interpret these values in this fashion: The extent the factor contribution to total risk is larger than the idiosyncratic piece from one model to the next means that the explanatory variables in that model explain more of the common relative risks. In this fashion, therefore, the Barra model explains 76.2 percent of the common risks whereas the R-Squared daily model explains 45 percent. This would be expected if you knew much about these two models and this particular portfolio. For a U.S. domestic portfolio, one would anticipate the many years of factor construction and deep detail Barra has invested in the US-E3L model's fundamental factors would have high explanatory power, whereas the R-Squared daily global model has simpler factors for style and fundamental variables designed to be sure these types of factors exist for global assets. For a global model, one has

**TABLE 17.1** A FactSet portfolio attribution report on a U.S. large-cap value portfolio, displaying the total risk, common factor risk, and specific risks for five popular risk models—one each from of MSCI-Barra, SunGard APT, Axioma, NIS, and R-Squared—versus the S&P 500.

Percent of Total Holdings
TDC_LC_lvs. S&P 500
6/29/2012
U.S. Dollar

| | | | Barra U.S. Long-Term Model (USE3L) | | | APT United States (USD) | | | Axioma U.S. 2 MH Fundamental | | | NIS U.S. Fundamental Model | | | R-Squared Daily Global Equity Model | | |
|---|---|---|---|---|---|---|---|---|---|---|---|---|---|---|---|---|---|
| Economic Sector | Port. Weight | Bench. Weight | Total Risk (Std Dev) | Factor Risk (Std Dev) | Stock-Specific Risk (Std Dev) | Total Risk (Std Dev) | Factor Risk (Std Dev) | Stock-Specific Risk (Std Dev) | Total Risk (Std Dev) | Factor Risk (Std Dev) | Stock-Specific Risk (Std Dev) | Total Risk (Std Dev) | Factor Risk (Std Dev) | Stock-Specific Risk (Std Dev) | Total Risk (Std Dev) | Factor Risk (Std Dev) | Stock-Specific Risk (Std Dev) |
| Total | 100.00 | 100.00 | 4,172 | 3.641 | 2.036 | 3.231 | 2.371 | 2.194 | 3.033 | 2.153 | 2.135 | 5.539 | 4,202 | 3.608 | 2.930 | 1.966 | 2.173 |
| Consumer Discretionary | 17.56 | 10.96 | 2.281 | 2.135 | 0.803 | 1.791 | 1.546 | 0.903 | 1.549 | 1.312 | 0.824 | 2.611 | 2.159 | 1.469 | 1.856 | 1.652 | 0.846 |
| Consumer Staples | 4.04 | 11.29 | 0.629 | 0.404 | 0.482 | — | — | 0.520 | 0.530 | — | 0.588 | 0.890 | 0.581 | 0.674 | — | — | 0.576 |
| Energy | 7.29 | 10.80 | — | — | 0.422 | — | — | 0.459 | — | — | 0.449 | — | — | 0.706 | — | — | 0.469 |
| Exxon Mobil Corp. | 1.09 | 3.25 | — | — | 0.254 | — | — | 0.277 | — | — | 0.277 | — | — | 0.372 | — | — | 0.229 |
| Marathon Oil Corp. | 1.08 | 0.15 | 0.810 | 0.794 | 0.160 | 0.492 | 0.463 | 0.168 | 0.478 | 0.452 | 0.155 | 0.975 | 0.914 | 0.337 | 0.644 | 0.617 | 0.182 |
| Conoco Phillips | 1.00 | 0.57 | 0.483 | 0.477 | 0.077 | 0.255 | 0.246 | 0.066 | 0.226 | 0.218 | 0.057 | 0.472 | 0.467 | 0.065 | 0.339 | 0.330 | 0.077 |
| Chevron Corp. | 0.98 | 1.69 | — | — | 0.084 | — | — | 0.085 | — | — | 0.084 | — | — | 0.098 | — | — | 0.082 |

| | | | | | | | | | | | | | | | | | |
|---|---|---|---|---|---|---|---|---|---|---|---|---|---|---|---|---|---|
| Valero Energy Corp. | 0.83 | 0.11 | 0.757 | 0.741 | 0.153 | 0.532 | 0.499 | 0.186 | 0.444 | 0.396 | 0.201 | 0.785 | 0.747 | 0.240 | 0.602 | 0.560 | 0.221 |
| Devon Energy Corp. | 0.81 | 0.19 | 0.609 | 0.601 | 0.101 | 0.300 | 0.283 | 0.100 | 0.351 | 0.331 | 0.118 | 0.693 | 0.668 | 0.187 | 0.480 | 0.465 | 0.117 |
| Apache Corp. | 0.79 | 0.28 | 0.552 | 0.545 | 0.085 | 0.320 | 0.311 | 0.077 | 0.323 | 0.314 | 0.073 | 0.606 | 0.580 | 0.174 | 0.438 | 0.430 | 0.084 |
| Occidental Petroleum Corp. | 0.71 | 0.57 | 0.259 | 0.258 | 0.022 | 0.146 | 0.144 | 0.023 | 0.161 | 0.160 | 0.022 | 0.262 | 0.259 | 0.042 | 0.243 | 0.242 | 0.023 |
| Financials | 14.34 | 14.41 | — | — | 0.614 | 1.152 | 0.880 | 0.744 | 0.326 | — | 0.505 | 0.698 | — | 1.042 | — | — | 0.654 |
| Health Care | 16.70 | 11.99 | 2.244 | 2.114 | 0.751 | 1.680 | 1.471 | 0.811 | 1.407 | 1.199 | 0.736 | 2.440 | 2.222 | 1.006 | 1.642 | 1.443 | 0.783 |
| Industrials | 10.47 | 10.46 | 0.696 | 0.455 | 0.527 | 0.772 | 0.528 | 0.563 | 0.635 | 0.428 | 0.469 | 1.239 | 0.903 | 0.849 | 0.448 | — | 0.534 |
| Information Technology | 20.70 | 19.74 | 2.297 | 1.939 | 1.231 | 1.468 | 0.766 | 1.253 | 1.708 | 0.940 | 1.426 | 3.389 | 2.311 | 2.478 | 1.458 | 0.671 | 1.295 |
| Materials | 7.85 | 3.41 | 1.726 | 1.642 | 0.531 | 1.223 | 1.079 | 0.577 | 1.205 | 1.102 | 0.486 | 2.091 | 1.887 | 0.903 | 1.610 | 1.487 | 0.618 |
| Utilities | 1.05 | 3.73 | — | — | 0.134 | — | — | 0.136 | — | — | 0.090 | — | — | 0.203 | — | — | 0.132 |

Holdings Data As Of
TDC_LC_1 4/02/2012
S&P 500 6/29/2012
Risk Model As Of
Barra U.S. Long-Term Model (USE3L) 7/01/2012
APT United States (USD) 6/27/2012
Axioma U.S. 2 MH Fundamental 6/29/2012
NIS U.S. Fundamental Model 6/30/2012
R-Squared Daily Global Equity Model USD V2 6/29/2012
Hidden: Benchmark-Only Securities and Groups

**TABLE 17.2** This is the same data as in Table 17.1, but showing risk in units of variance, where the constituent contributions of risk sum to the total.

Percent of Total Holdings
TDC_LC_1 vs. S&P 500
6/29/2012
U.S. Dollar

| | | | Barra U.S. Long-Term Model (USE3L) | | | APT United States (USD) | | |
|---|---|---|---|---|---|---|---|---|
| Economic Sector | Port. Weight | Bench. Weight | Total Risk (Variance) | Factor Risk (Variance) | Stock-Specific Risk (Variance) | Total Risk (Variance) | Factor Risk (Variance) | Stock-Specific Risk (Variance) |
| **Total** | **100.00** | **100.00** | **17.405** | **13.260** | **4.144** | **10.439** | **5.623** | **4.816** |
| | | | 100.0% | 76.2% | 23.8% | 100.0% | 53.9% | 46.1% |
| Consumer Discretionary | 17.56 | 10.96 | 5.202 | 4.557 | 0.645 | 3.207 | 2.391 | 0.815 |
| Consumer Staples | 4.04 | 11.29 | 0.396 | 0.163 | 0.233 | −0.416 | −0.686 | 0.271 |
| Energy | 7.29 | 10.80 | −0.781 | −0.959 | 0.178 | −0.161 | −0.371 | 0.210 |
| Exxon Mobil Corp. | 1.09 | 3.25 | −0.461 | −0.525 | 0.064 | −0.231 | −0.307 | 0.077 |
| Marathon Oil Corp. | 1.08 | 0.15 | 0.657 | 0.631 | 0.026 | 0.243 | 0.214 | 0.028 |
| Conoco Phillips | 1.00 | 0.57 | 0.233 | 0.227 | 0.006 | 0.065 | 0.061 | 0.004 |
| Chevron Corp. | 0.98 | 1.69 | −0.191 | −0.198 | 0.007 | −0.084 | −0.091 | 0.007 |
| Valero Energy Corp. | 0.83 | 0.11 | 0.573 | 0.550 | 0.023 | 0.283 | 0.249 | 0.034 |
| Devon Energy Corp. | 0.81 | 0.19 | 0.371 | 0.361 | 0.010 | 0.090 | 0.080 | 0.010 |
| Apache Corp. | 0.79 | 0.28 | 0.305 | 0.297 | 0.007 | 0.103 | 0.097 | 0.006 |
| Occidental Petroleum Corp. | 0.71 | 0.57 | 0.067 | 0.067 | 0.000 | 0.021 | 0.021 | 0.001 |
| Financials | 14.34 | 14.41 | −0.326 | -0.703 | 0.376 | 1.328 | 0.774 | 0.554 |
| Health Care | 16.70 | 11.99 | 5.033 | 4.470 | 0.564 | 2.823 | 2.164 | 0.658 |
| Industrials | 10.47 | 10.46 | 0.485 | 0.207 | 0.278 | 0.596 | 0.279 | 0.317 |
| Information Technology | 20.70 | 19.74 | 5.274 | 3.760 | 1.515 | 2.156 | 0.587 | 1.569 |
| Materials | 7.85 | 3.41 | 2.978 | 2.696 | 0.282 | 1.496 | 1.164 | 0.333 |
| Utilities | 1.05 | 3.73 | −0.346 | −0.364 | 0.018 | −0.333 | −0.352 | 0.019 |

Holdings Data As Of
TDC_LC_1 4/02/2012
S&P 500 6/29/2012
Risk Model As Of
Barra U.S. Long-Term Model (USE3L) 7/01/2012
APT United States (USD) 6/27/2012
Axioma U.S. 2 MH Fundamental 6/29/2012
NIS U.S. Fundamental Model 6/30/2012
R-Squared Daily Global Equity Model USD V2 6/29/2012
Hidden: Benchmark-Only Securities and Groups

| Axioma U.S. 2 MH Fundamental | | | NIS U.S. Fundamental Model | | | R-Squared Daily Global Equity Model | | |
|---|---|---|---|---|---|---|---|---|
| Total Risk (Variance) | Factor Risk (Variance) | Stock-Specific Risk (Variance) | Total Risk (Variance) | Factor Risk (Variance) | Stock-Specific Risk (Variance) | Total Risk (Variance) | Factor Risk (Variance) | Stock-Specific Risk (Variance) |
| **9.197** | **4.637** | **4.560** | **30.678** | **17.657** | **13.021** | **8.584** | **3.864** | **4.721** |
| 100.0% | 50.4% | 49.6% | 100.0% | 57.6% | 42.4% | 100.0% | 45.0% | 55.0% |
| 2.401 | 1.721 | 0.680 | 6.820 | 4.662 | 2.157 | 3.444 | 2.728 | 0.716 |
| 0.281 | –0.065 | 0.346 | 0.792 | 0.338 | 0.454 | –0.546 | –0.878 | 0.331 |
| –0.228 | –0.429 | 0.201 | –0.240 | –0.739 | 0.498 | –0.926 | –1.146 | 0.220 |
| –0.038 | –0.115 | 0.077 | –0.267 | –0.406 | 0.139 | –0.515 | –0.567 | 0.052 |
| 0.229 | 0.205 | 0.024 | 0.950 | 0.836 | 0.114 | 0.414 | 0.381 | 0.033 |
| 0.051 | 0.048 | 0.003 | 0.222 | 0.218 | 0.004 | 0.115 | 0.109 | 0.006 |
| –0.060 | –0.067 | 0.007 | –0.126 | –0.135 | 0.010 | –0.204 | –0.211 | 0.007 |
| 0.197 | 0.157 | 0.040 | 0.616 | 0.558 | 0.058 | 0.363 | 0.314 | 0.049 |
| 0.124 | 0.110 | 0.014 | 0.481 | 0.446 | 0.035 | 0.230 | 0.216 | 0.014 |
| 0.104 | 0.099 | 0.005 | 0.367 | 0.336 | 0.030 | 0.192 | 0.185 | 0.007 |
| 0.026 | 0.025 | 0.000 | 0.069 | 0.067 | 0.002 | 0.059 | 0.059 | 0.001 |
| 0.106 | –0.149 | 0.255 | 0.488 | –0.597 | 1.085 | –0.276 | –0.703 | 0.428 |
| 1.979 | 1.437 | 0.542 | 5.951 | 4.940 | 1.012 | 2.695 | 2.081 | 0.614 |
| 0.403 | 0.183 | 0.220 | 1.535 | 0.815 | 0.720 | 0.200 | –0.085 | 0.285 |
| 2.918 | 0.883 | 2.035 | 11.484 | 5.342 | 6.143 | 2.126 | 0.450 | 1.676 |
| 1.451 | 1.215 | 0.236 | 4.374 | 3.559 | 0.815 | 2.593 | 2.211 | 0.382 |
| –0.071 | –0.079 | 0.008 | –0.265 | –0.306 | 0.041 | –0.273 | –0.290 | 0.017 |

to design simpler fundamental factors, because so often for many global securities there just isn't enough data. Hence you have to design a model to offer some level of style/fundamental risk decomposition while assuring that there aren't many factors "NA" for any model that is operating on low-density security data.

Now we remind the reader that these are relative risks and the explanatory part of common factors is accentuated in these circumstances because we're looking at relative differences. This may lead the reader to believe that models other than Barra are weaker. We need to see a breakout of total risk decomposition on an absolute basis to examine this question. To do so, simply choose a benchmark of cash (or LIBOR) from the menu of indexes FactSet provides. The next table (Table 17.3) illustrates this.

In this table we now can see a better picture of how much of the common risks are determined from the suite of factors in each model. They all provide explanatory variables that account for about 99 percent of the observed variance of return. In absolute risks, the Axioma model has the lowest estimate, while for relative risks it is the R-Squared model. Northfield's U.S. Fundamental model still has the highest estimate, however, both relative and absolute. All the idiosyncratic specific risks are on the order of 1 percent or so.

From all of these tables, one can see the risks for the assets and the groups, in this case the S&P GICS sectors. The rule holds that the estimation errors are largest for the assets, followed by the groupings, followed by the portfolios.

It's helpful to examine the risk forecasts for the energy sector to outline the discrimination or lack thereof on asset risk numbers. In Figure 17.2, we show the five total absolute risk measures for each of eight stocks in the portfolio on this date along with the average value, sorted by the average. Starting on the left of the bar chart, Occidental has the lowest average risk. As we move left to right, we see the risks increasing on average until finally we arrive at Marathon. It appears that all the models are reporting risks in a relative sense, one stock to another. To gauge whether this is true, Figure 17.3 shows the average risk per stock with the minimum and maximum risk measures superimposed.

Here again, we have the data sorted for the stocks by average risk from all five models. Clearly Marathon stands out. It alone is readily deciphered as the riskiest asset among the portfolio's holdings. However, would you conclude that ConocoPhillips is less risky than Devon Energy or Apache? Barra ranks these completely in reverse order for riskiness, whereas APT and R-Squared ranks them precisely that way. Axioma and NIS are mixed. Who's right? Well, the average difference among these three securities for all five models is ~0.5, which, to offer a "chi-by-eye" statistic, one should

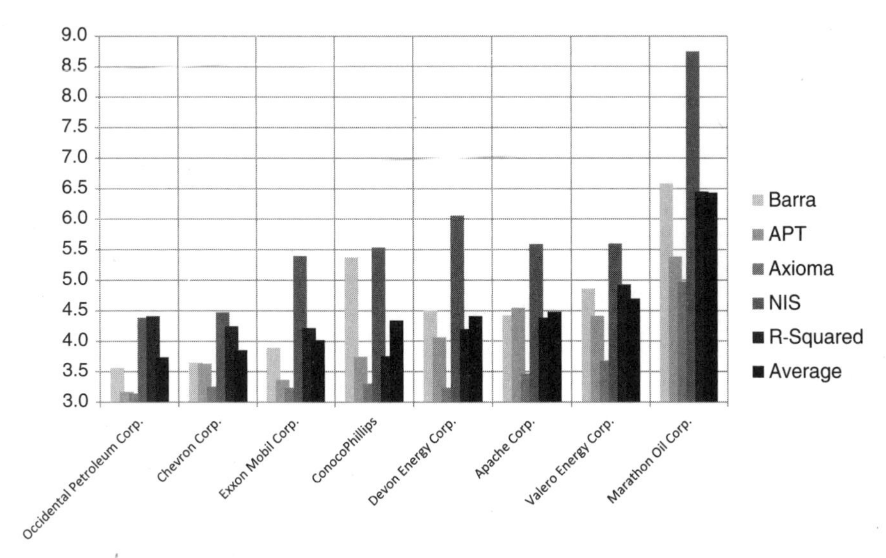


**FIGURE 17.2** The energy sector stocks in the portfolio, sorted by the average total risk from five popular risk models.

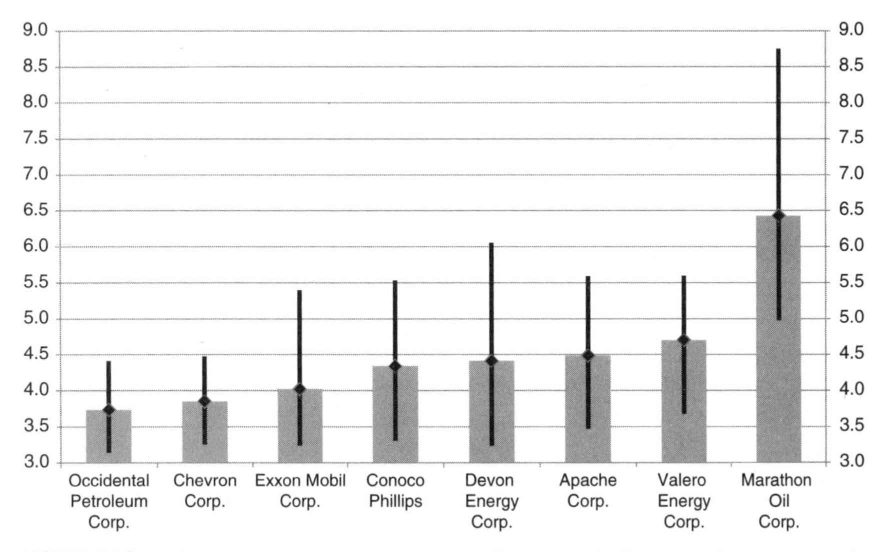


**FIGURE 17.3** The same data as in Figure 17.2, but now the bars are the average risk only and the error bars are the highest and lowest reported risk chosen among the five vendor risk models.

**TABLE 17.3** The same portfolio as before, but with the benchmark exchanged for LIBOR, allowing the absolute risk measures to be observed from five vendors.

**Percent of Total Holdings**
**TDC_LC_1 vs. 1 Week LIBOR USD**
**6/29/2012**
**U.S. Dollar**

| | | | Barra U.S. Long-Term Model (USE3L) | | | APT United States (USD) | | |
|---|---|---|---|---|---|---|---|---|
| Economic Sector | Port. Weight | Bench Weight | Total Risk (Variance) | Factor Risk (Variance) | Stock-Specific Risk (Variance) | Total Risk (Variance) | Factor Risk (Variance) | Stock-Specific Risk (Variance) |
| **Total** | **100.00** | **100.00** | **445.196** | **442.033** | **3.163** | **421.806** | **417.922** | **3.884** |
| | | | 100.0% | 99.3% | 0.7% | 100.0% | 99.1% | 0.9% |
| Consumer Discretionary | 17.56 | — | 81.030 | 80.304 | 0.726 | 79.446 | 78.547 | 0.899 |
| Consumer Staples | 4.04 | — | 17.253 | 17.117 | 0.136 | 12.499 | 12.331 | 0.168 |
| Energy | 7.29 | — | 36.859 | 36.685 | 0.175 | 32.321 | 32.136 | 0.185 |
| Exxon Mobil Corp. | 1.09 | — | 3.892 | 3.876 | 0.017 | 3.366 | 3.346 | 0.020 |
| Marathon Oil Corp. | 1.08 | — | 6.583 | 6.548 | 0.034 | 5.385 | 5.347 | 0.038 |
| ConocoPhillips | 1.00 | — | 5.374 | 5.341 | 0.033 | 3.742 | 3.718 | 0.024 |
| Chevron Corp. | 0.98 | — | 3.649 | 3.636 | 0.013 | 3.630 | 3.616 | 0.014 |
| Valero Energy Corp. | 0.83 | — | 4.864 | 4.833 | 0.031 | 4.417 | 4.372 | 0.046 |
| Devon Energy Corp. | 0.81 | — | 4.508 | 4.491 | 0.017 | 4.065 | 4.047 | 0.017 |
| Apache Corp. | 0.79 | — | 4.424 | 4.407 | 0.017 | 4.547 | 4.533 | 0.014 |
| Occidental Petroleum Corp. | 0.71 | — | 3.565 | 3.553 | 0.012 | 3.170 | 3.157 | 0.013 |
| Financials | 14.34 | — | 66.322 | 65.993 | 0.329 | 83.443 | 82.955 | 0.489 |
| Health Care | 16.70 | — | 62.637 | 62.050 | 0.587 | 57.369 | 56.643 | 0.727 |
| Industrials | 10.47 | — | 47.965 | 47.747 | 0.218 | 42.486 | 42.242 | 0.244 |
| Information Technology | 20.70 | — | 90.529 | 89.848 | 0.681 | 74.210 | 73.402 | 0.807 |
| Materials | 7.85 | — | 40.311 | 40.012 | 0.299 | 36.934 | 36.582 | 0.352 |
| Utilities | 1.05 | — | 2.290 | 2.278 | 0.012 | 3.097 | 3.084 | 0.012 |

Holdings Data As Of
TDC_LC_1 4/02/2012
1 Week LIBOR USD 6/29/2012
Risk Model As Of
Barra U.S. Long-Term Model (USE3L) 7/01/2012
APT United States (USD) 6/27/2012
Axioma U.S. 2 MH Fundamental 6/29/2012
NIS U.S. Fundamental Model 6/30/2012
R-Squared Daily Global Equity Model USD V2 6/29/2012
Hidden: Benchmark-Only Securities and Groups

| Axioma U.S. 2 MH Fundamental | | | NIS U.S. Fundamental Model | | | R-Squared Daily Global Equity Model | | |
|---|---|---|---|---|---|---|---|---|
| Total Risk (Variance) | Factor Risk (Variance) | Stock-Specific Risk (Variance) | Total Risk (Variance) | Factor Risk (Variance) | Stock-Specific Risk (Variance) | Total Risk (Variance) | Factor Risk (Variance) | Stock-Specific Risk (Variance) |
| **330.253** | **327.056** | **3.196** | **653.336** | **644.520** | **8.816** | **449.188** | **445.423** | **3.765** |
| 100.0% | 99.0% | 1.0% | 100.0% | 98.7% | 1.3% | 100.0% | 99.2% | 0.8% |
| 60.575 | 59.850 | 0.725 | 125.031 | 122.452 | 2.579 | 80.161 | 79.385 | 0.776 |
| 10.353 | 10.075 | 0.278 | 22.023 | 21.751 | 0.272 | 13.038 | 12.815 | 0.223 |
| 28.300 | 28.114 | 0.185 | 45.783 | 45.299 | 0.484 | 36.603 | 36.381 | 0.222 |
| 3.238 | 3.218 | 0.020 | 5.399 | 5.363 | 0.035 | 4.218 | 4.204 | 0.013 |
| 4.978 | 4.946 | 0.032 | 8.748 | 8.596 | 0.152 | 6.454 | 6.410 | 0.045 |
| 3.305 | 3.287 | 0.018 | 5.534 | 5.511 | 0.023 | 3.753 | 3.720 | 0.033 |
| 3.254 | 3.241 | 0.014 | 4.473 | 4.455 | 0.018 | 4.248 | 4.235 | 0.013 |
| 3.680 | 3.626 | 0.054 | 5.597 | 5.521 | 0.076 | 4.930 | 4.866 | 0.065 |
| 3.236 | 3.212 | 0.024 | 6.055 | 5.995 | 0.060 | 4.202 | 4.178 | 0.024 |
| 3.468 | 3.455 | 0.013 | 5.591 | 5.518 | 0.073 | 4.385 | 4.368 | 0.017 |
| 3.142 | 3.130 | 0.012 | 4.385 | 4.340 | 0.045 | 4.413 | 4.399 | 0.014 |
| 46.670 | 46.420 | 0.250 | 105.851 | 104.812 | 1.039 | 70.344 | 69.931 | 0.413 |
| 41.341 | 40.746 | 0.595 | 83.216 | 82.107 | 1.109 | 57.730 | 57.067 | 0.663 |
| 38.155 | 37.966 | 0.189 | 72.348 | 71.680 | 0.668 | 49.631 | 49.381 | 0.250 |
| 70.358 | 69.637 | 0.721 | 132.019 | 130.241 | 1.778 | 94.188 | 93.394 | 0.794 |
| 32.703 | 32.454 | 0.249 | 63.376 | 62.521 | 0.855 | 45.034 | 44.621 | 0.413 |
| 1.799 | 1.795 | 0.004 | 3.689 | 3.657 | 0.033 | 2.459 | 2.449 | 0.010 |

consider the relative error in the security-level total risk values to be about of that magnitude, in which case the riskiness of these three assets isn't distinguishable from any of these risk models. From the data in Figure 17.3, we should conclude that Occidental is probably riskier than Conoco, Devon, and Apache, and certainly less risky than Marathon.

This idea has ramifications when optimizing a portfolio, then, as well, as the optimizer isn't usually considering the error in the risk (or alpha) estimate that is part of the flat-file input. The level of risk estimate is interpreted by the magnitude of the risk measure from the risk model and orders the securities accordingly. It's precisely this effect that is the reason portfolio optimization has been said to be an error-maximization process, as discussed in previous chapters.

For risk managers, on the other hand, the top-level risk numbers usually are often their entire focus. In Europe where UCITS and regulatory considerations have higher levels of priority among asset managers than in the United States, risk managers have veto power over portfolio positions, leanings, and tilts. They are empowered to force a risk-reducing allocation among assets and their classes if needed. For this reason, they pay attention to overall portfolio measures of risk to ensure that the risks are not higher than the investing mandate and guidelines suggest. If the value at risk (VaR) measure supersedes threshold levels, the PM may be forced to rebalance the portfolio. Then, the question might be what positions should be adjusted, ejected, or exchanged. The guiding risk measures assisting this decision come from the marginal contributions to risk and, in this example, the marginal contributions to VaR, with the caveat that security-level risk numbers have large errors.

## CONCLUSION

Last, but not least important, risk reporting for the consultant, client, or asset owner must also be recognized. They want to see the value the manager has provided and, regardless of whether they mention it, they have a vested interested in separating alpha from beta. They want to see the risk levels relative to a prespecified benchmark, so active risk measures are most appropriate for their analysis. Even for hedge funds or funds of funds, the clients' perspective will always compare those results, appropriate or not, to what a classic beta investment (i.e., passive index) would have achieved during the same time period. Though with any risk model the absolute risk levels and benchmark relative risk levels (active risk) are readily computed, active risk is the primary concern for this class of participants in the process. Additionally, for asset owners, the screening of managers through the lens of a risk model's deconstruct enables them to compare possible investment manager candidates in terms of risk, characteristics, and return potential, yielding confidence that a selection will meet either mandate or strategy requirements.

Within the FactSet system, the ease of report construction and the flexibility, standardization, and automation of reporting make the process for all three users transparent, easy, and consistent.

This chapter has outlined some basics of the risk models and methodologies. It's not meant to be comprehensive, but merely to be a survey providing an introduction for risk models bundled on FactSet. Readers should reference the numerous MSCI-Barra, Axioma, Northfield, R-Squared, and APT white papers and handbooks for a more detailed exposition. You can easily speak at length with their on-staff professionals for more information and assistance.

## NOTES

1. John B. Guerard Jr., *Handbook of Portfolio Construction: Contemporary Applications of Markowitz Techniques* (New York: Springer, 2010).
2. B. Rosenberg and W. McKibben, "The Prediction of the Systematic and Specific Risks in Common Stocks," *Journal of Financial and Quantitative Analysis* 8:317–333.
3. *MSCI-Barra Handbook*, available on request from MSCI-Barra.

CHAPTER 18

# Northfield's Integration of Risk Assessments across Multiple Asset Classes

***Dan diBartolomeo, PRM, and Joseph J. Importico, CFA, FRM***

Risk management for investment portfolios is in strong contrast to the concepts of risk management that are common for banks and other financial intermediaries who operate with at-call liabilities (i.e., borrowed money where the lender such as a bank's depositors can demand repayment at any time). *For a bank or highly leveraged hedge fund, solvency is the key aspect of risk management.* If the risk of the asset portfolio is high, the entity must reduce gearing by either increasing capital or decreasing assets. Rather than being concerned about the probability distribution of cumulative returns over long periods, the emphasis here is controlling risks on a day-to-day basis so as to ensure that the entity has a positive net accounting worth at all times and remains viable under the applicable regulatory scheme. For financial intermediaries, *risk measures such as value at risk (VaR) and expected shortfall are denominated in wealth units* (e.g., dollars) so as to highlight the need for the entity to *maintain a positive net worth in the face of the potential range of immediate losses in asset values.*

To manage risk, we first must assess the magnitude of the risk and then must decompose the risks into a set of cause-and-effect relationships that we call factors. Just as a chef knows how changing the amount of an ingredient changes the taste of a dish, we must understand the nature of the risks we take, and whether our expectations of reward justify those risks. For financial intermediaries who often address risk management as an exercise in complying with regulations, a factor representation is of less importance. For asset managers who are seeking to make intelligent trade-offs between returns and risks, just seeing one or more representations of the magnitude of risk is a necessary but not sufficient condition to carrying out their mandates. *There must be an understanding of the root causes of risk.*

When investors make investments, they recognize that in almost all cases there is significant potential for the financial outcomes to be less favorable than expected. The ability of investors (and their agents, such as consultants and asset managers) to control unfavorable investment outcomes within acceptable limits is what risk assessment and management are all about.

We begin by drawing a sharp semantic distinction between *risk* and *uncertainty*. Let's define *risk* as the precisely known probability of unfavorable outcomes from an investment. Let's define *uncertainty* as our inability to precisely define the probability of a bad outcome. For illustration, consider two gamblers in a casino. The first gambler is playing roulette, where the odds and economic payoffs associated with winning or losing any particular bet are precisely known and do not change over time. This gambler is facing risk only. Our second gambler is playing poker with both a dealer and several other players participating. This gambler is facing both risk and uncertainty. While there is certainly some probability of losing your bet on a given hand of poker, this gambler does not know what those odds are because the odds depend on the cards as well as the skills and financial resources of the other players, which are unknowns to the poker-playing gambler.

Financial risk experts often further categorize uncertainty into *parameter estimation error* and *model risk*. For example, assume we have estimated the return volatility (standard deviation) of a particular investment portfolio to be 20 percent per annum. If our estimate of 20 percent volatility is an incorrect value, we have a case of parameter estimation error. If the portfolio consists of a single call option that has a highly skewed return distribution, the use of standard deviation as a measure of risk is conceptually inappropriate, so we have an instance of model risk.

## A UNIFIED FRAMEWORK

Estimating the risk of a portfolio that spans multiple asset classes represents a complex problem for large financial institutions. To achieve coherent risk estimates, disparate assets must be analyzed under consistent underlying assumptions. In addition, some asset classes may represent particular difficulties. Some assets such as convertible bonds and many derivatives have highly nonlinear properties with skewed return distributions. Other asset classes such as direct-owned real estate or private equity have no readily observable pricing, returns, or risk information.

One approach is to model risk for each portfolio separately and aggregate the risks, which might be called the bottom-up approach. It might be thought of as akin to a patchwork quilt, where each panel represents the risk analysis of an asset class. The advantage is a certain degree of internal consistency. You are using the same model to measure the risk of each asset class as part of the whole as you use for measuring the risk of that asset class as a stand-alone portfolio. However, there are serious limitations to this methodology. As each asset class would be modeled with the set of factors most relevant to that asset, factor exposures will not be additive across the many disparate models that are used within the aggregate portfolio. For example, we might know that our private equity portfolio has a large exposure to the technology sector. We might also have an assessment of the risk of owning a shopping mall in Palo Alto, California. But we are unlikely to be able to observe the linkage (i.e., correlation) existing between these two asset classes, because the local economy of Palo Alto is highly concentrated in technology firms. There is also a technical limitation in such an approach. The large number of factors arising from having many models stitched together may result in the aggregate factor covariance matrix not having the property of being positive semidefinite. To have a good estimate of factor covariance, we need to have many more observations than factors. If we have hundreds of factors in our models, we need a number of observations to estimate the relationships that is impractically large.

The alternative approach is to use a unified and parsimonious model for all asset classes everywhere, as suggested by Chaumeton, Connor, and Curds (1996). In such an approach, all assets in the world are related to the same consistent set of factors, so interrelationships are easily observed and understood, and the limited number of factors allows for stable estimation of factor relationships. In such a model, the complexity arises in determining how to represent the returns and risks of many different asset classes as functions of the same tractable set of underlying factors. The caveat associated with this approach is that the model is necessarily a compromise across asset classes and geography. As such, this type of model should not replace asset-class-specific models for day-to-day portfolio management.

There are some important considerations in formulating the factor structure of a unified model. In the absence of leverage, some asset classes such as equities are much more risky than other classes such as government bonds. Additionally, most long-term investors have a greater fraction of their wealth investing in equities and related assets than in assets related to fixed income. This means that the predominant sources of risk for most large investors will be associated with equity rather than fixed income assets.

The assertion that long-term investors have a greater percentage of wealth invested in equity-related assets may be unintuitive given the fact that on a global basis fixed income markets are notionally much larger. The apparent conflict is resolved by making a careful distinction between assets held by investors and assets held by financial intermediaries such as banks. Consider the situation of a bank that issues $1 billion in bonds, which are bought by an investor. The bank then lends the $1 billion out as home mortgages, 90 percent of which are repackaged into mortgage-backed securities (MBSs). Of the $900 million worth of MBSs, let's assume $500 million worth are securitized as collateralized mortgage obligations (CMOs). The market value of all the securities is $2.4 billion, but there is only $1 billion in actual investment by an investor. Some of the extra $1.4 billion might be held by long-term investors, but in reality most of those additional securities will be held by other financial intermediaries as assets financed by short-term deposits or commercial paper. A related issue here is that the bond markets in many countries such as Brazil and Australia are theoretically traded markets, but trading is so illiquid that they really should be thought of as syndicated loans between borrowers and groups of private parties, which are not normally thought of as securities.

## INTEREST RATE RISK

The general structure of factor models and some of the considerations of factor selection for equity risk modeling have been well explored in the financial literature. We will therefore consider factor representation of the risks of other asset classes here.

Within the realm of fixed income securities there are three basic types of risk to which investors are exposed. Of course, *the single most important risk is changes in the interest rate environment*, as described by a yield curve (coupon bond yields) or term structure (zero coupon bond yields). To the extent that interest rates rise or fall, the present value of any stream of cash flows is impacted. When interest rates vary differently across maturities rather than rising or falling in a simple parallel fashion, multiple factors are required to represent this process. One popular approach is to define a three-factor representation of the yield curve:

$$Y(x) = (a) + (b \cdot x) + [c \cdot (x)^{0.5}] \tag{18.1}$$

where:

$x$ = the time to maturity of the bond
$a$ = represents the average level of interest rates
$b$ = represents the slope of the yield curve (i.e., long rates minus short rates)
$c$ = represents the degree of curvature of the yield curve

In this approach, the interest rate factors are the time series of changes in the values of coefficients *a*, *b*, and *c*. By modeling the covariance of the changes in these values and estimating how each fixed income security is exposed to these factors, we can describe the interest rate portion of fixed income risk in a factor model. The three factors are often respectively termed *shift*, *twist*, and *butterfly* by fixed income investors.

The second risk that fixed income investors run is prepayment risk. Every fixed income security has some schedule over which the principal value of a loan or bond is to be repaid to the investor. In most cases, the borrowers have the option to repay the loans early if their financial circumstances allow. Early repayment is undesirable to the lender if interest rates have fallen, as the principal received will now have to be reinvested at the new lower interest rates. Many types of fixed income instruments have prepayment penalties (i.e., call premiums) that are intended to discourage borrowers from early repayment. To the extent that a fixed income security has a prepayment option for the borrower, the economic value of this option varies with the volatility of interest rates. In periods when interest rates are still, there is little benefit to borrowers to refinance old debts with new ones. In periods when interest rates are volatile, there exists greater potential for interest rates to fall, making it advantageous for borrowers to refinance their existing debt. We can think of a bond with prepayment risk as a portfolio consisting of a prepayment-free bond and being short the prepayment option. Both of these assets can be modeled in our factor framework, and their respective factor exposures are roughly additive. Alternatively, we can add an interest rate volatility factor to our basic model.

## CREDIT RISK

The third form of risk for fixed income investors is credit risk, which is also shared by derivative investors. The traditional approach to managing credit risk has involved the use of credit ratings that are assigned for a fee by credit rating agencies such as Standard & Poor's, Moody's, and Fitch. Such ratings have been widely criticized during the recent financial crisis years as biased in favor of the borrower, highly unreliable in actually measuring credit risk, and being inconsistent to the extent that the same rating may imply different probabilities of default when applied to two different types of fixed income security. Credit risks associated with derivative trading are often referred to as counterparty risks.

A more quantitative approach to the use of credit ratings has been to segment the universe of fixed income securities into buckets (i.e., groups) and calculate the option-adjusted yield spread (OAS) for each security within a group over a series of dates. The OAS represents the portions of bond yield that can be attributed to credit and liquidity risk. We can then estimate the central tendency of the OAS for each group (average or median) at each date. The changes in the central tendency over time can then be used as factors in a risk model, or the time series of OAS changes can be further modeled as a function of equity factors, thereby connecting credit risk and equity risk. Obviously, the bankruptcy of a firm involves both default on debts and the equity of the firm losing all value in a concurrent fashion.

## EQUITY FACTOR REPRESENTATION OF CORPORATE CREDIT RISK

Another approach to credit risk is the use of structural models (i.e., contingent claims models). In many ways it is intuitive to think of a corporate bond as being a combination of a riskless bond and the equity of the issuing firm. Low-credit-quality bonds (i.e., high yield or so-called junk bonds) are often treated by investors as a sort of middle ground between owning a bond and owning the stock of the issuing firm. Other securities such as convertible bonds and preferred stocks obviously also share some of the properties of both equity and debt. As such, it is often useful to know the equity factor exposure of a corporate bond.

Since Merton (1974) the *contingent claims* framework for bond default has provided a conceptual linkage between corporate bonds and the equity of the issuer. The classic Merton process is based on the idea that stockholders of a limited liability company hold two options. The first option is a call option on the assets of the firm, with a strike price of the value of the firm's debt and an expiration date of the maturity of the debt. The shareholders can choose to own the assets of the firm outright by paying off the debt.

The second option is a put option on the firm's assets, with a strike price of the value of the firm's debt and an expiration date of the maturity of the debt. If the value of the assets of the firm falls below the value of the debt, the stockholders can simply walk away and give the lenders (bondholders) the assets of the firm in lieu of payment. The bondholders are short this put option. In the original Merton formulation, the options are assumed to be European options expiring at the maturity date of the bond. Subsequent papers by Black and Cox (1976) and Leland and Toft (1996) extend practicality of the method to allow for bond default before maturity, multiple bond issues from the same issuer, the potential for technical defaults (e.g., violating a covenant with respect to a balance sheet ratio), and the frictional costs of bankruptcy proceedings. To the extent that a company can issue new bonds, these options may be treated as a perpetual American option. A computational framework for evaluating perpetual American options is provided in Yaksick (1998).

The general context for combining equity factor models and contingent claims models of bond default is provided in diBartolomeo (2010). This paper also turns the problem around to estimate the expected lives of firms, as the framework of the European option with an expiration date of the maturity of the debt is a less than conceptually perfect fit.

Depending on the willingness to endure technical complexity, a variety of pricing models can be used to value the options, allowing for inclusion of stochastic processes for volatility and interest rates. If we make the simplifying assumptions that interest rates are fixed for the option term (consistent with Black-Scholes) and we also assume that the equity dividend payments of the firm are inconsequentially small, the approximate equity factor exposures of a corporate bond are given by equation (18.2). Essentially, the equity factor exposure of the bond is given as the factor and residual exposures of the equity itself (the last of the three portions) times two scaling coefficients. The first scaling coefficient represents the approximate return on the bond per unit change in the value of the options. The second scalar is just the ratio of the delta values for the shareholder put and call options. To the extent that the value of the bond, the value of the riskless bond, and the delta of the call are strictly nonnegative, and the delta of the put is strictly nonpositive, we obtain the intuitive result that the bond's exposure to equity factors is always nonnegative.

$$\%R_{bt} \sim [-(T - B)/B] * (\delta_p / \delta_c) * [(\delta_{j = 1 \text{ to } n} B_j F_{jt}) + e_t] \qquad (18.2)$$

where:

$R_{bt}$ = the return on bond $b$ during period $t$
$T$ = the value of the bond if it were riskless
$B$ = the market value of the bond
$\delta_p$ = the delta of the shareholder put option
$\delta_c$ = the delta of the shareholder call option

It should be noted that while the contingent claims approach was originally developed to deal with corporate credit risk, the concept has been extended to sovereign (government) bond credit risk in Bodie, Gray, and Merton (2007). An alternative analytical procedure for dealing with sovereign risk is provided in Johnson, Srinivasan, and Bolster (1990.

## DEFAULT CORRELATION

As with corporate bankruptcies, bond defaults are rare, generally singular events, so it is impossible to directly observe the pairwise correlations of default among a set of firms. When we talk about default correlation, we are either describing the variations in the frequency of events within large samples of firms or describing the time-series variation in some measure of the likelihood of default, such as yield spread or bond rating. In some semantic sense, we might describe default correlation as the degree of dependence between two firms such that the joint likelihood of both firms defaulting within a defined time interval is correctly specified.

Papers by Hull and White (2001) and Overbeck and Schmidt (2005) illustrate that you can estimate default correlation if you know the true (but generally unobservable) dependence between firms. The analytical framework of structural models provides the ability to estimate default correlation, given the correlation between the asset values of firms, as described in Zhou (2001). Two papers by Giesecke (2003, 2006) try to improve the estimation of default correlation by including the correlation of changes to default boundaries, such as the tightening of bond covenants during periods of tight credit conditions.

We can also make the simplifying assumption that asset correlations are equal to equity return correlations. The book value of firm assets is a very incomplete measure of firm assets, so observing asset volatility and asset correlations across firms from financial statement data provides only very weak statistical estimates. Conversely, equity return volatility and correlation are readily observable for publicly traded firms. This approach is followed in Hull, Nelkin, and White (2004), and apparently in the commercial service CreditMetrics.

The assumption that asset correlation equals equity return correlation is intuitive for situations where firm financial leverage is low and time horizons are short. However, Zeng and Zhang (2001) show that the asset correlations must be inferred from the correlations of both the equity and debt components of the firm's balance sheet. A paper by de Servigny and Renault (2002) also presents negative empirical results regarding this assumption.

Given that almost all large asset managers have access to a commercial equity factor risk model, those same firms can estimate firm asset value correlations. From such an equity risk model, one can estimate the numerically equivalent full covariance matrix among any set of included stocks, as described in diBartolomeo (1998). Qi, Xie, Liu, and Wu (2009) provide a complex analytical derivation of asset correlations given equity return correlations and data on the firm's balance sheet.

We can think of the equity of a firm as being a portfolio that is long the assets of the firm and short the debt of the firm. If we have a multi-asset-class risk model that includes both equity and fixed income securities, we can use the fundamental accounting identity to get a direct factor representation of asset volatility and equity as Assets = Liabilities + Equity. Asset volatility is just equity volatility delevered, adjusted for covariance with the market value of debt. When interest rates rise, equity values usually drop. However, the market value of debt definitely declines, so leverage is sometimes reduced. Current accounting standards recognize this situation by allowing firms to show a profit by buying back their own debt below par value in the secondary market. Using the same algebra as before, we can convert the factor representation to pairwise asset correlation values across firms.

## COMPLEX INSTRUMENTS AND DERIVATIVES

In order to have a tractable number of factors in a model that spans the entire universe of investable assets, we need to be clever. The first technique we can employ to reduce the required number of factors is to rescale factor exposures. Consider bond duration (price sensitivity to changes in bond interest rates) as a factor. If I have two bonds in two different countries, I can use duration as a factor exposure only if I have two interest rate volatility factors to describe the differing rate volatility in the two countries, so we need four factors in total. Alternatively, we can have one global measure of rate volatility as a factor and rescale the factor exposures to be a direct expression of interest rate risk (i.e., the product of duration and the ratio of local/global interest rate volatility). Similar scaling relationships can be used to address differences in volatility between long-term and short-term bond yields.

The second method we can employ to keep a unified model manageable is to take complex assets and decompose them into portfolios of "atomic" (simple) securities that the model already understands. A few examples:

- A risky bond is like being long a riskless bond and short a credit swap.
- A convertible bond is being long a riskless bond, short a credit swap, and long an equity warrant.
- Real estate assets can be approximated as a combination of bondlike securities, with coupons that are adjustable and inflation related.

The key to making this portfolio approach work is that the underlying assumptions that impact the analysis of each of the simple securities must be uniform. For example, we cannot simultaneously assume that interest rates have volatility for analyzing a bond, but also assume that interest rates are fixed for analyzing an option embedded within the bond structure.

One good example of a complex instrument is a convertible bond. To effectively analyze this type of instrument, we must consider a portfolio that contains a default-free bond that is subject only to interest rate risk, a credit default swap, and an equity warrant (long-term call option). The analysis becomes particularly complex because the strike price of the equity option is the market value of the bond, and hence is variable, unlike the fixed strike price of a conventional option. To carry out such an analysis in the context of a factor model, we can represent the variability of interest rates as occurring by a process of paths through a binomial tree that represents the passage of time. At each branching of the tree, we can allow the interest rate to rise or fall. The probability of the interest rate rising or falling at each branching can be calibrated to the current yield curve as in Black, Derman, and Toy (1990). We can then build another binomial tree to represent the potential price movements of the equity into which the bond is convertible. The two trees are structured on the same periodicity, so there is a one to one correspondence between nodes. The covariance matrix of the factors is then used to intertwine the two binomial trees to represent the correlation of the interest rate process and the equity prices process as in Margrabe (1978). Having the correspondence between the two processes allows us to coherently evaluate the factor exposures and risk of all three components of the convertible bond.

Factor models are often critiqued as being unsuitable for evaluation of many derivative instruments because the return distribution from such instruments often has extreme degrees of skew. While some complex derivatives are best evaluated by a "factor within Monte Carlo" methodology, most can be satisfactorily described by taking account of a fact that we know whether our portfolio holds a long position or a short position in the derivative. For example, let us assume we are short a stock index call option. In this case, our potential loss is large (theoretically unlimited), while our potential profit is limited to the amount of the call premium received. If we are long the same option, our potential profit is large whereas our potential loss is limited to the 100 percent of the option premium paid. Since the delta and gamma of the option are easily obtained, we can use Cornish-Fisher to calculate the volatility value that best represents the loss potential for each of the two skewed distributions to any desired confidence interval (i.e., 99 percent). To assess risk satisfactorily while retaining the mathematical convenience of a parametric framework, we can treat a long position and a short position in the derivative as having two different volatilities. Care must be taken that any factor representation of combinations of derivatives with the same underlying asset appropriately handles the lack of independence between the asset-specific portions of risk as described in diBartolomeo (1998).

## PRIVATE EQUITY

Historically, the unobservable volatility of illiquid investments such as direct real estate, private equity (PE), and venture capital (VC) has been essentially ignored by institutional investors. At most, they would use a volatility of a private equity or venture capital index (e.g., Venture Economics) as a proxy for these risks in asset allocation exercises. For many large investors, such as sovereign wealth funds, large pension funds, and life insurance companies, inclusion of such assets in formal enterprise-wide risk assessments has been simply beyond their capabilities.

During the recent global financial crisis it was amply demonstrated that having formal risk management systems and practices that ignore significant portions of the overall portfolio is a disaster waiting to happen. Every commercial bank and investment bank that failed or required rescue had a formal risk system in place. In some cases those risk systems successfully measured the extreme risks being taken, but bank executives chose to proceed anyway. In many other cases, the high risk levels were poorly estimated because exotic and often illiquid portions of the overall asset portfolios were simply omitted from the risk analysis.

There have been a few attempts to quantify private equity fund risks. Kaplan and Schoar (2005) use CAPM-type analysis of returns against a chosen market portfolio as a way to describe the risk-adjusted returns of PE/VC funds. The weakness of these processes is that the return of an illiquid fund up to the point of liquidation is largely subjective. Fund operators typically have very lax processes for marking to market similar to real estate appraisals. There is a large literature in both PE/VC and real estate confirming that the appraisal biases dramatically reduce the apparent volatility of such investments. Of course, the relevance of the beta of an investment arises from the CAPM, which itself assumes that investments are fully liquid. One recent paper, by Bitsch, Buchner, and Kaserer (2010), suggests that the idiosyncratic risk, not the beta risk, is what is relevant for asset pricing in illiquid markets.

Phalippou and Gottschalg (2007) provide two different suggestions. The first approach is to assume that the beta of a given private investment is equal to the central tendency of the beta value for public firms in the same industry. This same paper also proposes to use the observed risk characteristics of firms just after they have gone public via an initial public offering (IPO) to infer risk characteristics of the firm when it was private. Another related paper, Driessen, Lin, and Phalippou (2007), uses a factor model approach on fund partnership returns. Loadings to factors such as size and value as defined by Fama and French (1992) are estimated via a generalized method of moments approach.

The European Private Equity and Venture Capital Association has circulated draft guidelines suggesting ways to estimate risks for PE and VC portfolios. One suggestion is to use discounted cash flow analysis to examine each of the underlying company investments within a PE/VC fund portfolio.

This approach as described will be insufficient. To understand how the changes in net present value of each investment are correlated to the changes in the net present value of other investments, a detailed analytical model is required. A second suggestion is to simply observe the time series of returns based on fund net asset values provided by general partners, similar to the academic papers described previously. An objection to this suggestion is that only a very small fraction of general partners create return estimates based on valuations consistent with the Financial Accounting Standards Board's FASB 157 (mark to market) accounting standard. A second objection is that even when marking to market is done, the valuations are based largely on appraisals rather than transaction values. There is an extensive academic literature showing that such appraisal-based processes tend to smooth volatility and artificially induce seasonality in the return time series. The draft guidelines also have brief suggestions as to the issues of liquidity risk and funding risk in that investors might sustain losses under partnership rules if they are unable to meet a commitment for a future cash infusion into a fund.

One way to handle PE/VC risk that is viable would be to do the firm by firm discounted cash flow analysis within the context of a Monte Carlo simulation wherein the parameters of the valuation of each firm such as expected firm growth rates, the discount rate (interest rate plus an uncertain risk premium), and the timing and valuation at liquidation could all operate as random variables. By coordinating the various simulation analyses across the portfolios firms, we would also be able to estimate the correlation of the unobservable returns of each portfolio company. A framework similar to this was proposed by Cheung, Howley and Kapoor, (2007) for rating credit default obligations on bonds issued by PE funds in order to leverage their portfolios. However, we should keep in mind the rather poor track record of the rating agencies with respect to collateralized debt obligations (CDOs) during the recent financial crisis.

We believe the best way to handle PE/VC risk is with a *matched pair* analysis. This analysis takes advantage of the fact that the predominant exit strategy for PE/VC funds is to sell the company in which they have invested to a public company or undertake an initial public offering (IPO). For each investment within the PE/VC fund, we first select a publicly traded company that is the most similar to the private portfolio company. For example, if our PE portfolio company is a supermarket chain in Europe, we identify the most comparable public company. The risk characteristics of the matched public company are immediately accessible within our risk models to act as a baseline risk estimate for the private firm. *The factor structure of the model allows for immediate analysis of the unobservable correlation between private firms.* Use of a "public market equivalent" index has been widely proposed as a way of doing performance measurement for PE/VC portfolios.

Our next step is to adjust the risk exposures of the private firm away from those of the public firm given any specific information we have relating to the structure of the private firm. For example, if we know that the private firm has a debt-to-equity ratio of 3, while the matched public company has no debt, we need to make appropriate changes. Given the very large number of public firms available in our equity risk models, the cross-sectional relationships between key fundamental variables and factor exposures are readily statistically estimated.

The third step in the process is to adjust the estimated beta and firm-specific risk of the private entity to compensate for the particular sensitivity to the IPO market. We know that the IPO market is largely inactive during stock market declines, removing this mechanism as a potential exit strategy. The estimated beta of the private firm must be increased to reflect the high sensitivity of the IPO market to general stock market performance. We also assume that the firm-specific risk is comparable to the highest specific risk value observed in our models within a country/sector cohort, as the transition from private to public firm often involves extensive internal stress on company operations.

The fourth and final step is to adjust each private firm-level risk estimate within the portfolio both for the illiquidity of investing in private firms and for any special liquidity constraints arising from the PE/VC partnership structure (e.g., lockup provisions). At the firm level, we accomplish this by including a potential fire-sale scenario in the risk process (e.g., there is a 1 percent per month chance that the firm would have to be sold at two-thirds of current estimated value). There is an extensive literature relating to fire sales of other illiquid assets such as houses. At the fund level, we recognize that even if we choose to express risk in annual volatility units, a typical PE/VC partnership may have lockup provisions that require investors to keep their money in the fund for five years or longer. Over such an extended period, the potential for a fund to have a large drawdown for at least one moment of time will accumulate. In essence, we have to worry about first-passage rather than end-of-period risk. The risk of future funding commitments can be modeled, as well as a long/short portfolio that is long generic equity and short a bond. In essence, the investor has made a promise of future cash to the partnership in return for additional participation in the equity partnership. To the extent that the future firm-level investments of the partnership are unknown at present, we can only use a generic representation.

Once each firm-level investment within a PE/VC fund has been evaluated, we construct a composite asset to represent the fund and all of its constituents within the risk model framework. At this point, any risk analysis or optimization task can be performed on the investor's entire portfolio (multi-asset-class) inclusive of the PE/VC fund components.

## DIRECT REAL ESTATE AND GEOGRAPHICALLY LOCALIZED ASSETS

The financial crisis of recent years has had many causes and has been manifested in a variety of ways. While the effect in residential property prices has been widely recognized, the immense effects on commercial real estate are now just beginning to become more visible. For example, during November 2009, the *Wall Street Journal* reported that the real estate investments of CalPERS, the largest pension fund in the United States, had had a return of negative 48 percent in the prior fiscal year. This is a stunning result given that many financial market participants assume that the volatility of real estate returns is less than 5 percent per year.

Large asset owners such as pension funds and insurance companies have always invested in illiquid assets such as directly owned property to a substantial degree. It has been widely argued that since large pension funds can predict their needs for outgoing benefit cash flows quite accurately, their need for liquidity is low and they can earn additional returns by intentionally investing in illiquid assets such as property, private equity, and the financing of public infrastructure projects such as airports, power plants, and toll roads. Some large investors, such as Australian defined contribution pension plans known as superannuation funds, often have a third or more of their total assets in such funds.

There are four obvious aspects of property and infrastructure investment that make managing risks much more difficult than for traditionally traded financial assets such as stocks and bonds. The first is that being illiquid (very rarely traded), changes in asset value from day to day or even year to year are not observable. One cannot simply look at the financial page of the newspaper for a quote on the value of the local shopping mall or airport. Valuations are limited to periodic appraisals that are optimistically biased and seasonally dependent, substantially reducing expected volatility and expected correlation to other asset classes.

One very troubling aspect of financial markets is that *some financial service firms represent illiquid assets as investments guaranteed to be low in risk, on the explicit basis that the price movements are not observable.* In essence, investors are encouraged to take a head-in-the-sand attitude to the risks of investments such as tracts of timber, assuming that since we can't readily observe changes in value, we may as well assume that no such changes in value are taking place. Recently, FASB 157 has loosened the requirements on some financial institutions with regard to valuations, but simply assuming no value changes are taking place seems to be the height of folly for investors.

The second aspect of these investments that complicates the risk management task is leverage. To the extent that most real estate and infrastructure investments are perceived as having relatively predictable future cash flows, leverage is often employed through various debt structures such as mortgages on property. In many countries, the use of such debt financing also represents a tax benefit to investors, although institutional investors in most countries are tax exempt and therefore do not enjoy this advantage. While in a conceptual sense, leverage in a real estate investment is no different than leverage employed to boost expected returns on a hedge fund, there are important distinctions. In most hedge funds, the assets held for investment are marked to market on a regular basis (admittedly with less than perfect accuracy), so the potential for a margin call requiring that the debt be reduced is a day-to-day fact of life. Equity investors in direct property and infrastructure projects typically assume that the probability of foreclosure is so slight as to be insignificant, which often turns out to be an extremely poor assumption.

The third aspect of these investments that clouds the risk management picture is the lack of divisibility. If an asset owner owns shares of stock in a traded company, it can choose to sell any portion of that position without having to make a decision to sell it all. If the position is large enough, limitations on market liquidity may require that the selling process be stretched over a significant time period, but it can still be done without protracted negotiations with buyers. On the other hand, one cannot sell one floor of an office tower or half a power plant.

The fourth aspect of these investments that make risk management difficult is the frequent reliance on regional rather than national economic conditions for financial success. Large investors are very accustomed to investing in companies that sell goods and services to a geographically dispersed, often global customer base. In contrast, the financial viability of an office building, shopping complex, or port facility will often be dominated by local conditions about which far less objective data is available. While every major investment bank around the world can provide economic forecasts for major countries at the national level, few are able to provide meaningful information about the conditions in and likely futures of specific cities or regions. In addition, real estate investors normally operate without the broad diversification institutional investors enjoy in their stock portfolios. In the vocabulary of equity managers, real estate portfolios have large tracking errors.

One might consider various approaches to the problem. Estimating the risk of property investing as an asset class by observing index returns is problematic because of the volatility-dampening effects of the appraisal process.

A good economic explanation of these effects is presented in Getmansky, Lo, and Makarov (2004) with respect to illiquid securities. Returns of illiquid securities exhibit strong positive serial correlation, which invalidates the assumption of independent observations that is explicit in estimation of the usual statistical risk measures. After correcting for serial correlation the estimated volatility of broad real estate indexes, we find the volatility of U.S. real estate in recent years (as measured by the NCREIF index) to be close to 18 percent annually, which is at least double traditional estimates. This is consistent with results in a recent paper by Cheng, Lin, and Liu (2011) in which they used bootstrap simulations to avoid the peak-to-trough issues associated with the long-term cyclical behavior of real estate returns.

One approach to resolving this problem, which has been used for residential real estate, are the repeated-sale indexes where index returns are estimated from repeated sales of the same house. If enough houses in a given area are transacted per period of time, one can statistically infer returns on the index portfolio. Unfortunately, the number of transactions on large commercial properties or infrastructure projects is far too few for this approach to be viable. Finally, there are some academic studies suggesting that real estate volatility can be observed by taking a portfolio of traded property companies (e.g., REITs in the United States) and hedging out the influence of the general stock market on the sector returns. However, the very local nature of real estate returns limits the usefulness of this approach to portfolios.

The most promising approach to address these issues is to use existing protocols that allow us to include geographically defined assets within a unified framework spanning all asset classes. Rather than trying to observe variations in appraised values, we choose to construct proxy portfolios of marketable securities, using our unified risk model. We assume that the true, if unobservable, volatility of the illiquid asset is comparable to the proxy portfolio. *The financial instruments in these portfolios are selected and weighted such that the economic payoffs and economic risks of the portfolio mirror those of the illiquid asset.* Cash flow streams arising from property leases are treated like corporate bonds that are extendable with a higher coupon (i.e., a rent increase), mortgage debt is handled as short positions in mortgage securities, and the long-term inflation effects on property returns are modeled using inflation-linked bonds such as Treasury Inflation-Protected Securities (TIPS).

Fluctuations in property rents arising from supply and demand are modeled as lagged functions of the relative participation of various economic sectors in the local economy, as compared to the national average. A city like New York or London that has a large concentration of financial services firms would be perceived as overweighted in the financial sector, while Houston might be perceived as overweighted in energy compared to the rest of the

United States. For each region, a long/short portfolio of stock market exposures is used to characterize the economic makeup of the area. The key benefit of this approach is that once a proxy portfolio has been created for a specific property, the full range of analytical risk information is available, such as the correlation with other assets and the marginal contribution of the property asset to the overall enterprise risk level. As property assets are considered as not being divisible for trading, special reports should be constructed that report incremental (whole position) rather than marginal contributions to risk. The full details of how real estate may be included into a unified model are provided in Baldwin, Belev, diBartolomeo, and Gold (2005).

Regional economic models may be to another important purpose. Given the broad declines in asset values that has been experienced during the recent financial crisis, the pension funds of many local and state governments now have negative actuarial surpluses. Until asset values recover, the viability of these retirement systems depends on the promise of additional future inward funding from the concerned local government. In the United States, these promises of future funding from a state or local government are essentially an unrecorded form of municipal bond. For example, if a county pension fund is 25 percent underfunded, the asset portfolio fund now consists of 75 percent of the recognized set of assets and implicitly 25 percent a municipal bond from that county. Having 25 percent of a fund's assets in a single municipal bond issue has dramatic impact on the diversification of the portfolio and on the effective asset allocation.

Using regional economic models, we can understand the underlying economic drivers of tax revenues for a given city or state. Through this structure, we can observe how the economic fortunes of a given area are likely to be correlated with various sectors of financial markets, and select investment assets that jointly diversify the asset portfolio with the local tax revenue stream. This is similar to our earlier example where we considered an investor with a large exposure to the technology sector through a private equity portfolio. In this context a shopping mall in Palo Alto, California, might be considered more risky than an identical property in another city where the technology sector plays a smaller role in the regional economy.

Recently, we have extended this methodology for property risk assessment to a broad range of infrastructure projects such as airports, power plants, and toll roads. For example, one might think of the risk of a modern airport being something similar to a shopping mall, where part of the property is rented out to conventional merchants, but a large part of the facility is rented out to a specialty firm called an airline. So our airport becomes a combination of fixed cash flow leases, plus exposures to inflation, plus some exposure to the regional and national economy. The predominant exposure is to a portfolio of the airlines that service that particular airport. In turn, the exposures of the airlines to things like interest rates and energy costs are accounted for, and may be aggregated across all assets of the entity.

## CONCLUDING EXAMPLE

The model from Northfield that has embedded in it the details discussed to this point is a multi-asset-class risk model on the FactSet system called Everything Everywhere. The NIS-EE model is a global model covering equities, fixed income securities, and currencies and has the ability to model more exotic assets, as we'll show in the analysis to follow. There are a variety of risk factors included in this model that are designed to help provide an accurate barometer of portfolio risk. These factors include regions or countries, sectors, economic variables (for instance, interest rates and oil prices), fundamental characteristics (style), statistical factors, currencies, and Treasury curve factor sensitivities.

In the ensuing text we'll analyze the risk profile of a multi-asset-class portfolio. The balanced portfolio portion created for this example is comprised of many different assets, which include equities, fixed income instruments, credit default swaps, interest rate derivatives, and investments in direct real estate. Accommodating such a diverse mix of assets requires robust analytics. To satisfy such a request, we'll be utilizing FactSet's portfolio analysis software along with the NIS-EE risk model. Broadly speaking, FactSet's platform offers end users a robust, yet intuitive, set of tools for analyzing portfolios for any risk model.

In Figure 18.1, we show a screen shot from the FactSet system that describes the multi-asset-class portfolio, which has allocation of 70 percent comprised of equities and fixed income instruments, 12.09 percent in various derivatives, and 30 percent in direct real estate. The "offset" refers to the cash balance accompanying the derivatives in the portfolio. This fund has long positions in futures and a few other similar instruments, so it lumps cash balance into that category for accounting purposes. We also tabulate the percentage of risk from each asset class determined by the NIS-EE model in this figure. Even though the largest allocation is to the category of "balanced" product (exchange-tradable assets), more of the fund's risk is attributed to the direct real estate investments.

We further decompose the risk with a high-level review as depicted in Figure 18.2, which is another screen shot captured from the FactSet system. In this figure we decompose risk into its components. We show the total risk of 13.2 percent (annualized) as the first line item for the MAC portfolio. That is the *ex ante* forecast of the expected volatility over the next one-year risk horizon with the usual assumptions. The risk is further decomposed

**Asset Detail**

Balanced Portfolio vs. U.S. Dollar Index
4/30/2012
NIS EE Model (+)
U.S. Dollar

| | Weights | Risk |
|---|---|---|
| Asset Class | Port. Weight | % of Risk |
| **Total** | **100.00** | **100.00** |
| BALANCED | 70.00 | 41.19 |
| DERIVATIVES | 12.09 | 15.48 |
| DIRECT REAL ESTATE | 30.00 | 43.33 |
| OFFSET | -12.09 | -- |

**FIGURE 18.1** Portfolio asset types and the asset risk.

into "asset selection," which is specific or idiosyncratic risk that is usually the smallest contribution to risks. As we said in previous chapters, specific risks are all risks not common. The risk model's purpose is to determine the common risks, and all residuals from the regressions and/or principal component analysis (PCA) used to produce the model are subsequently categorized as specific. Common factor risks account for 12.34 percent out of the 13.2 percent of volatility for this portfolio on this date, so it's certainly the majority of the risk. Further down the list, we see that common factor risk is 93.43 percent of the risk, much of which is attributable to super-sector allocations that account for nearly 37 percent of the fund's risk. The exposure to the Treasury curve factors, however, is the majority of the common factor contribution, contributing another 55.3 percent. From this data we can see that blind factors (statistical) and fundamental factors are actually diversifying, as their contributions are negative.

Figure 18.3 depicts the partitioning of the sources of risk by asset class for the portfolio in a pie chart. In this picture, it becomes very clear the majority of the risks are due to common factors versus specific risks, and the

| Risk Decomposition | |
|---|---|
| Balanced Portfolio vs. U.S. Dollar Index | |
| 4/30/2012 | |
| NIS EE Model (+) | |
| U.S. Dollar | |
| | Data |
| Summary | |
| Total Risk | 13.20 |
| Risk Decomp. | |
| Asset Selection | .87 |
| Common Factor | 12.34 |
| Factor Contribution | |
| Region | .34 |
| Super Sectors | 4.88 |
| Economic | .20 |
| Fundamental | -.17 |
| Blind Factors | -.21 |
| Currency | .00 |
| Curve | 7.30 |
| Risk Decomp. (%) | |
| %Asset Selection | 6.57 |
| %Common Factor | 93.43 |
| %Factor Contribution | |
| Region | 2.54 |
| Super Sectors | 36.94 |
| Economic | 1.49 |
| Fundamental | -1.30 |
| Blind Factors | -1.55 |
| Currency | .03 |
| Curve | 55.29 |

**FIGURE 18.2** Risk decomposition.

size of their contributions is more easily ascertained and communicated by an analyst. Clearly, common factor risks dominate.

Finally, in Figure 18.4 we further depict the relative contributions of the factor types to the common risks. This chart collects the factors into their top-level designation and graphs their apportioned risks, allowing a greater perspective on contributions. One can also drill down to a more

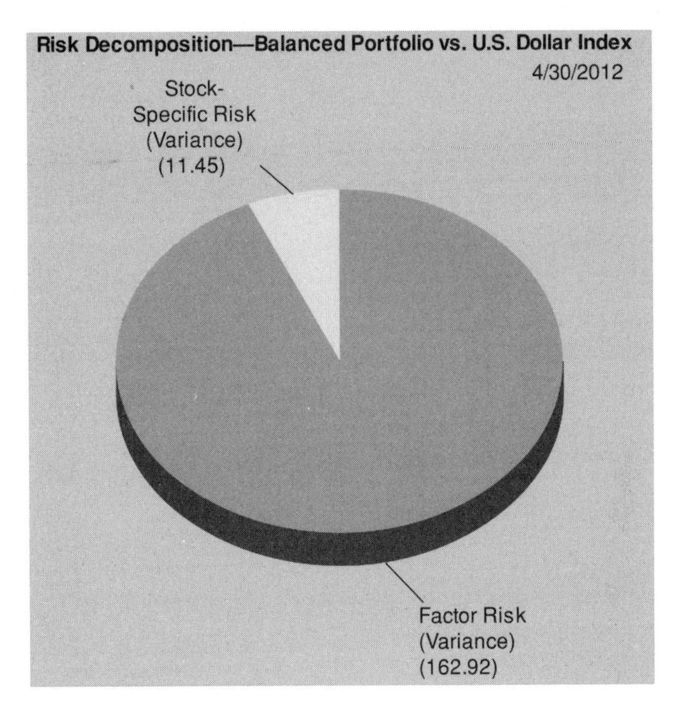


**FIGURE 18.3** Portfolio variance, Part 1.
*Source:* FactSet.

granular level and see the risk on a per-factor basis as well. Additionally, since we chose a benchmark that is just a U.S. dollar index, these particular risks are in a sense absolute risks. Had we chosen an equity or fixed income benchmark, or better yet a composite benchmark of each, which the FactSet system easily allows for construction of, relative risks could be measured and presented in this fashion as well.

In short, the application of Northfield's Everything Everywhere risk model not only empowers one to accurately calculate risk estimates for a multi-asset-class portfolio, but also enables one to uncover inherent relationships among the positions within the fund. All the regular risk measures are readily determined from the output of the risk model, too.

## CONCLUSION

While pursuing a unified approach to risk assessment across all asset classes is a complex task, it is one that the industry has recognized as the best approach to sound risk management (see Tasman 2011). The global financial

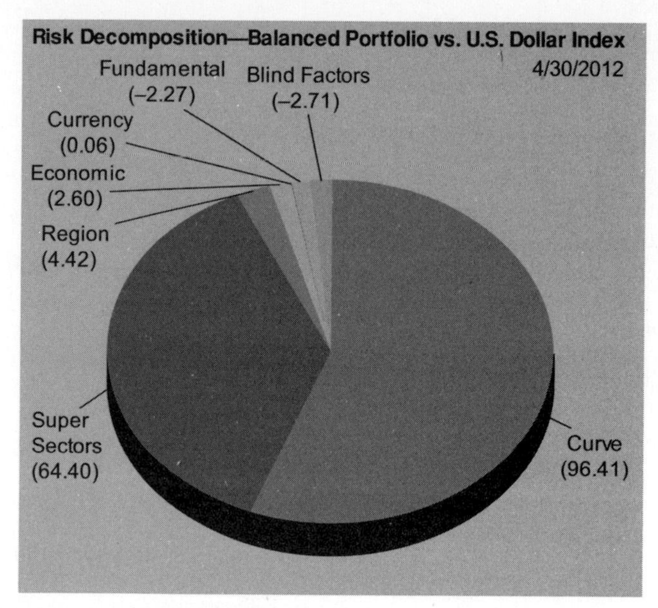


**FIGURE 18.4** Portfolio variance, Part 2.
*Source:* FactSet.

crisis of recent years has underscored the economic linkages between asset classes when a dramatic decline in the value of thinly traded fixed income mortgage securities forced many investors such as leveraged hedge funds to very rapidly sell more liquid instruments such as large-capitalization equities. The resultant decline in both equity and fixed income markets contributed to a global economic recession.

A unified approach also allows for the inclusion of illiquid assets such as real estate and private equity in the risk framework. Such inclusion means that the underlying economic drivers of potential investment success or potential investment failure are being correctly evaluated both in whole and at the margin across the entire spectrum of assets.

## REFERENCES

Baldwin, Ken, Emilian Belev, Dan diBartolomeo, and Richard Gold. 2005. "A New Approach to Real Estate Risk." Northfield Working Paper.

Bitsch, Florian, Axel Buchner, and Christoph Kaserer. 2010. "*Risk, Return and Cash Flow Characteristics of Infrastructure Fund Investments*," *EIB Papers* 15, no.1: 106–136.

Black, Fischer, and John C. Cox. 1976. "Valuing Corporate Securities: Some Effects of Bond Indenture Provisions." *Journal of Finance* 31:351–367.

Black, Fischer, Emanuel Derman, and William Toy. 1990. "A One-Factor Model of Interest Rates and Its Application to Treasury Bond Options." *Financial Analysts Journal* 46, no. 1 (January/Febuary): 33–39.

Bodie, Zvi, Dale F. Gray, and Robert Merton. 2007. "New Framework for Measuring and Managing Macrofinancial Risk and Financial Stability." NBER Working Paper.

Johnson, R.A., V. Srinivasan, and P.J. Bolster. 1990. "Sovereign Debt Ratings: A Judgmental Model Based on the Analytic Hierarchy Process." *Journal of International Business Studies* 21/1, 95–117

Chaumeton, Lucie, Gregory Connor, and Ross Curds. "A Global Stock and Bond Model." *Financial Analysts Journal* 52, no. 6 (November/December 1996): 65–74.

Cheng, Ping, Zhenguo Lin, and Yingchun Liu. 2011. "Heterogeneous Information and Appraisal Smoothing." *Journal of Real Estate Research* 33 (4): 443–469.

Cheung, Lily, Chris Howley, and Vivek Kapoor. 2007. "Rating Private Equity CFOs: Stochastic Market Cash Flows." Standard & Poor's.

de Servigny, A., and O. Renault. 2002. "Default Correlation: Empirical Evidence." Standard & Poor's Working Paper.

diBartolomeo, Dan. 1998. "Optimization with Composite Assets Using Implied Covariance Matrices." Northfield Working Paper. www.northinfo.com/documents/58.pdf.

diBartolomeo, Dan. 2010. "Equity Risk, Credit Risk, Default Correlation and Corporate Sustainability." *Journal of Investing*, December.

Driessen, Joost, Tse-Chun Lin, and Ludovic Phalippou. 2007. "A New Method to Risk and Return of Non-Traded Assets through Cash Flows." NBER Working Paper 14144.

Fama, Eugene, and Kenneth French. 1992. "The Cross-Section of Expected Stock Returns." *Journal of Finance* 33 (1): 3–56.

Getmansky, M., Andrew Lo, and Igor Makarov. 2004. "An Econometric Model of Serial Correlation and Illiquidity in Hedge Fund Returns." *Journal of Financial Economics* 74, no. 3 (December): 529–609.

Giesecke, Kay. 2003. "A Simple Exponential Model for Dependent Defaults." *Journal of Fixed Income* 13.

Giesecke, Kay. 2006. "Default and Information." *Journal of Economic Dynamics and Control* 30.

Hull, John, Izzy Nelkin, and John White. 2004. "Merton's Model, Credit Risk and Volatility Skews." *Journal of Credit Risk* 1.

Hull, John, and John White. 2001. "The General Hull-White Model and SuperCalibration." *Financial Analysts Journal* 57.

Kaplan, Steve, and Annette Schoar. 2005. "Private Equity Performance: Returns, Persistence and Capital Flows." *Journal of Finance* 60 (4): 1791–1823.

Leland, Hayne, and Klaus Bjerre Toft. 1996. "Optimal Capital Structure, Endogenous Bankruptcy, and the Term Structure of Credit Spreads." *Journal of Finance* 51.

Margrabe, William. 1978. "The Value of an Option to Exchange One Asset for Another." *Journal of Finance* 33 (1): 177–186.

Merton, R. C. 1974. "On the Pricing of Corporate Debt: The Risk Structure of Interest Rates." *Journal of Finance* 29:449–470.

Overbeck, Ludger, and Wolfgang Schmidt. 2005. "Modeling Default Dependence with Threshold Models." *Journal of Derivatives* 12.

Phalippou, Ludovic, and Oliver Gottschalg. 2007. "The Performance of Private Equity Funds." Wharton Financial Working Paper 05-42.

Qi, H., Y. A. Xie, S. Liu, and C. Wu. 2009. "Inferring Default Correlation from Equity Return Correlation." Proceedings of the 2009 European Financial Management Symposium on Risk Management in Financial Institutions.

Tasman, W. Graham. 2011. "Multi-Asset Class Simplification." *Risk Professional*, April.

Yaksick, Rudy. 1998. "Expected Optimal Exercise Time of a Perpetual American Option: A Closed Form Solution." *Journal of Financial Engineering* 4 (1).

Zeng, B., and J. Zhang. 2001. "An Empirical Assessment of Asset Correlation Models." Moody's KMV working paper.

Zhou, Chungsheng. 2001. "An Analysis of Default Correlations and Multiple Defaults." *Review of Financial Studies* 14.

CHAPTER 19

# R-Squared

*Jason MacQueen*

There are a number of domestic and international multifactor equity risk models now available to investors. This chapter reviews the three main methods currently used to build multifactor equity risk models. The main part of the chapter is theoretical and generic, and is intended to highlight the strengths and weaknesses of the different methods, but it also concludes with a review of R-Squared Risk Management's Short-Term Global Equity Risk model, available on FactSet.

## WHY BUILD STOCK RISK MODELS?

The first important point to make is that no one builds stock risk models because they care about individual stock risk. If they did, they almost certainly wouldn't use the same model for, say, 40,000 different stocks, but would perhaps go to the extent of building 40,000 different models, one for each stock.

Security analysts, for example, sometimes build simple spreadsheet models for each of the stocks they follow, in order to capture the idiosyncrasies of particular stocks. More typically, they build a series of models for companies in different industries, on the grounds that stocks within a particular industry will be subject to much the same common factor effects as one another, so that one generic model for each industry will be sufficient. They would use something like the dividend discount model and/or cash flow return on investment (CFROI, a metric used by Credit Suisse First Boston) to evaluate a stock or company individually. They most likely wouldn't or shouldn't try modeling stocks on some collective basis.

Equity risk models are a different case, however. We build a single risk model for all the stocks in our universe because we care about *portfolio risk*, and regard each stock in the universe simply as a possible holding in a portfolio. In portfolio risk analysis, we want each holding of the portfolio to be treated equally. This simple point turns out to have profound consequences, as we shall see later. There are some collective attributes that can be tallied to offer country, sector, or industry risk numbers, but generally the viewpoint of risk models is for portfolios.

## GENERIC RISK MODELING

Risk is usually defined as the variance of returns, so all stock risk models (and, indeed, all portfolio risk analyses) are based on an underlying model of return. In practice, almost all risk models are based on linear multifactor models of stock return. Such models have the virtues of simplicity, clarity, and tractability.

While it is conceptually possible to imagine other, more complex models of stock return (based on chaos theory, for example), there has not yet been any evidence that their greater complexity is outweighed by any significant improvement in the model forecasts. For the purposes of this chapter, we confine our attention to linear multifactor models of return and risk.

Throughout this exercise, it is important to remember that the ultimate goal is to build a stock risk model that will enable us to produce good forecasts of portfolio risk, and to analyze the risk structure of the portfolio. We begin with a completely generic linear multifactor model of stock return.

### Generic Multifactor Stock Return Model

$$R_{it} = \alpha_i + \sum_{f=1}^{K} \beta_{if} R_{ft} + \varepsilon_{it} \tag{19.1}$$

In this expression, $R_{it}$ is the return to stock $i$ over time period $t$, $R_{ft}$ is the return to factor $f$ over time period $t$, and $\beta_{if}$ is the exposure of stock $i$ to factor $f$, commonly known as the stock's beta on the factor.

The terms $\alpha_i$ and $\varepsilon_{it}$ represent the parts of the return to the stock that cannot be explained by its exposures to the factors. The first is a constant term (typically close to zero), and the second is the residual return, which, by construction, has a mean of zero.

Stock risk is defined as the variance of stock returns, so we can immediately derive an expression for stock variance by simply taking the variance of the preceding expression, which gives:

$$V_i = \sum_{f=1}^{K} \sum_{g=1}^{K} \beta_{if} \beta_{ig} C_{fg} + RSD_i^2 \quad (19.2)$$

This expression shows that, given a linear multifactor model of stock return, stock variance is determined by the betas of the stock on each of the factors, the factor covariance matrix, and the variance of the residual returns on the stock. Put simply, in this kind of model the overall risk of a stock consists of a part that is factor-related and a residual or stock-specific part.

It is worth noting that in most commercial equity risk models, the average explanatory power of the factor-related part varies from 20 percent to 40 percent. This is another reminder that the model is not being built because we care very much about individual stock risk; for a (reasonably well-diversified) portfolio, the explanatory power of these kinds of models is usually nearly 90 percent.

We have now said all that there is to say about the return and risk of *individual stocks*. Because our main focus is on portfolio risk analysis, however, we also need to consider how pairs of stocks will covary, so that these covariance effects can be properly taken into account when we compute portfolio risk.

As before, we can simply take the formula for stock return and derive the covariance between two stocks by simple algebra, from which we first obtain:

$$C_{ij} = \sum_{f=1}^{K} \sum_{g=1}^{K} \beta_{if} \, \beta_{jg} \, C_{fg} + Cov\left(\varepsilon_{it}, \varepsilon_{jt}\right) \quad (19.3)$$

Note, however, that it is standard practice to *assume* that the residual returns of each stock are uncorrelated with each other, and therefore don't contribute to the overall covariance between the two stocks (or, indeed, to portfolio risk).

This is actually quite a strong assumption: it is equivalent to asserting that the particular set of factors used in the risk model has captured *all* the systematic covariance between all the securities in the universe. We will return to this point later. For the time being, however, let us *assume* that:

$$Cov(\varepsilon_{it}, \varepsilon_{jt}) = 0 \quad (19.4)$$

for all stocks $i$ and $j$.

Then the covariance between two stocks $i$ and $j$ is simply given by:

$$C_{ij} = \sum_{f=1}^{K} \sum_{g=1}^{K} \beta_{if} \beta_{jg} C_{lg} \tag{19.5}$$

This expression says that any two stocks covary only insofar as they are both sensitive to the same common factors, which covary with each other.

### Generic Portfolio Holdings

A portfolio consists of holdings of $N$ stocks. Let $p_i$ be the proportional holding of stock $i$ in portfolio $P$ so that in absolute space (i.e., not relative to a benchmark), we have:

$$\sum_{i=1}^{N} p_i = 1 \tag{19.6}$$

This condition is usually known as the budget constraint, and it ensures that we have kept track of all the money we have to invest. Note that the portfolio holdings $p_i$ can be long (positive) or short (negative); all that matters is that they sum to 1.

### Generic Portfolio Return and Risk

The return on a portfolio over some time period is calculated as the weighted average of the returns on the stocks held in it, weighted by their holding sizes at the start of the period.

Into this initial expression we can then substitute our multifactor model for stock return, and some simple algebra will then give us the corresponding expression for portfolio return in terms of our multifactor model. Doing this gives us:

$$\begin{aligned} R_P &= \sum_{i=1}^{N} P_i R_{it} \\ &= \sum_{i=1}^{N} P_i \left( \alpha_i + \sum_{f=1}^{K} \beta_{if} R_{ft} + \varepsilon_{it} \right) \\ &= \alpha_p + \sum_{f=1}^{K} \beta_{pf} R_{ft} + \varepsilon_{pt} \end{aligned} \tag{19.7}$$

where the corresponding portfolio characteristics are calculated as follows:

$$\alpha_p = \sum_{i=1}^{N} p_i \alpha_i$$

$$\beta_{pf} = \sum_{i=1}^{N} p_i \beta_{if}$$

and

$$\varepsilon_{pt} = \sum_{i=1}^{N} p_i \varepsilon_{it} \tag{19.8}$$

This expression for portfolio return is now in exactly the same form as the original expression for stock return, so we can immediately derive portfolio risk in exactly the same way, giving the following expression for portfolio variance:

$$V_P = \sum_{f=1}^{K} \sum_{g=1}^{K} \beta_{Pf} \beta_{Pg} C_{fg} + \sum_{i=1}^{N} RSD_i^2 \tag{19.9}$$

This is our ultimate goal: to be able to first calculate, and then analyze, the risk of a portfolio using a multifactor model, and we now have an expression that enables us to do that (still assuming that the residual covariances are all zero). Rather than getting into the details of portfolio risk analysis, we will focus on the practicalities of producing the data values needed for this computation.

## PRACTICAL RISK MODELING

A brief inspection of the preceding expression tells us that building a multifactor risk model in practice therefore means producing the following three sets of numbers:

- The factor covariance matrix $C_{fg}$ $\forall f,g$ $(K \times K)$
- The factor exposures file $\beta_{if}$ $\forall i,f$ $(N \times K)$
- The residual risk vector $RSD_i$ $\forall i$ $(N \times 1)$

where $N$ is the number of stocks in the universe, and $K$ is the number of factors in the risk model.

The main intellectual effort lies in determining the first two of these. The residual risk of each stock usually falls out from the process of determining the factor loadings and factor covariances, although some firms also attempt to make further adjustments to the residual risks in the light of current market conditions.

Before we begin to build any risk model, however, there are some very important choices to make that will determine what kind of model we build and how good it will be at forecasting portfolio risk. Remember that all risk models are based on the multifactor model of stock return given earlier, and that, in practice, it will be derived from some observed historical data.

We always have the stock returns data, $R_{it}$. In one sense, these choices have to do with what other data (if any) we are going to use in the modeling process. Put another way, these choices are about whether we wish to prespecify the factors, and if we do, whether we are going to give ourselves the stock betas $\beta_{if}$ or the factor returns $R_{ft}$ as additional data.

## STATISTICAL FACTOR MODELS

Both the stock betas and the factor covariance matrix (and, hence, the residual risks) can be estimated from stock returns data by factor analysis or principal components analysis (PCA).

In this method, the historic stock returns for the whole universe of stocks are first converted into a historical covariance matrix over some look-back period. This covariance matrix (or, in some cases, the corresponding correlation matrix) is then transformed into a series of orthogonal factors, in descending order of importance, which between them will capture all the covariance in the stock universe. Note that, if we are modeling a universe of 20,000 stocks, we will transform the covariance matrix into 20,000 orthogonal factors.

However, by using the eigenvalues, which tell us how much of the overall variance is captured by each factor, we can then decide that the first $K$ factors capture most of the significant common factor effects present in the data. The rest of the statistical factors are simply discarded.

The second step in this modeling process is to do time-series regressions of each stock's returns against the set of $K$ statistical factor returns to determine the individual stock betas. Finally, the part of each stock's return history that is not captured by the $K$ risk model factors is used to determine each stock's specific, or residual, risk.

This type of model will, *by construction*, have the best possible fit with the in-sample data, although this is, of course, no guarantee that it will necessarily have the best fit in subsequent out-of-sample data. It does also provide comfort that no significant common factor effects have been left out of the model, since we can choose how many factors to include, and we will have a very good idea of how (un)important the discarded factors are.

However, it is often hard to give any kind of intuitive economic meaning to these statistical factors. For single-country risk models, the first factor often looks similar to the local market. Beyond the first factor, however, it is rarely obvious what economic realities the factors correspond to. Moreover, the results often vary considerably over different data sets and different time periods, leading to a worrying instability in the model.

The biggest problem with these kinds of models comes when portfolio managers are trying to explain to clients that their portfolios currently have a big bet on "factor 3" and bets against "factors 6 and 8." This is, at best, unhelpful to the clients, but also possibly quite alarming, particularly if the managers admit that they don't really know what these factors represent. They could never speak with a client about how they simultaneously know and don't know what explains the variance of return.

Vendors of statistical factor models usually try to overcome this problem by various methods of risk attribution. This involves some form of mapping from the statistical factors onto defined macroeconomic or fundamental factors. This can be done either at the factor level or at the beta level. In both cases, the point is to turn the exposures of the portfolio to the statistical factors into a set of factors that have some meaning and relevance for the portfolio manager (and client).

These kinds of risk models originated from trading desk applications. Traders sometimes need to construct a hedge against some set of stocks that they are about to take onto their books, or they need to construct short-term tracking baskets of stocks for some purpose. In these cases, there is no end client to whom the meaning of the factors has to be explained, and all the trader cares about is that the basket of stocks has the required tracking characteristics.

In fact, further consideration of this application helps to reveal what statistical factor models are particularly good for. In almost all these kinds of applications, the trader will be using the risk model to ensure that the position is *neutralized* against common factor movements that the trader has no control over, and that have the potential to affect the value of the trader's book. So an analysis of the risk characteristics of any portfolio that may be designed using the model would reveal that the trader had effectively achieved zero exposures to most or all of the statistical risk factors.

This suggests a potential application for institutional portfolio managers. Hybrid risk models combine a chosen set of defined factors, which have direct relevance to the factor bets the manager is taking, with statistical factors, whose dual purpose is to ensure that all remaining common factor effects are taken into account, and that the portfolio is neutral with respect to them.

Clearly, the problem described earlier, of having to explain to your client what "factor 3" represents, disappears if the manager can simply say that the portfolio has no exposure to it. We will return to the advantages of hybrid models later in this chapter.

## DEFINED FACTOR MODELS

The standard alternative to a purely statistical factor approach is to prespecify, or define, the factors that are to be used in the risk model. For example, if we are building a risk model for a particular equity market, such as Japan, we may wish to have a Japanese market factor and some Japanese industry factors in the model. Other possibilities would correspond to our ideas of what other common factor effects exist in the Japanese market, such as style effects, size, and so on.

There are a number of criteria that should govern the choice of factors in a risk model. The most important consideration, of course, is that the set of factors should span the full range of common factor effects present in the universe of securities we are trying to model. Other important criteria include observability (i.e., not choosing factors that are inherently unobservable), intuitive appeal (choosing factors that correspond to the portfolio manager's intuition as to what are the important sources of common factor effects), and data reliability.

From a technical point of view, we would ideally like the factors to be orthogonal to each other. This has the benefit of making the factor risk decomposition very clear, and is also much more likely to result in stable factor betas for individual stocks. Unfortunately, most of the usual suspects for risk model factors are fairly highly correlated in their natural state. In practice, therefore, the best solution is usually to transform the original factors into a block orthogonal matrix.

For example, there was a risk modeling company in the United Kingdom several years back named Quantec. In Quantec's Cross-Country (XC) Global risk model, there were three main types of factors, namely, currencies, global market and sector factors, and local country factors. In their natural state, each country factor (represented initially by its local market index) was highly correlated with the overall global market factor and with its local currency factor, as well as with whichever global sectors happened to dominate that particular market. This high degree of cross-correlation would normally lead to significant instability in the resulting stock betas.

However, before the factors were used in the risk model, they were orthogonalized on each other. Thus, the global market and sector factors were regressed on the currency factors to strip out currency-related effects, and the local country factors were regressed both on the currency factors and on the global market and sector factors. This meant that the resulting local country factor represented variance in the local market *net of* currency-related and global market- and sector-related effects. In essence, it represented the purely domestic volatility of the local market.

The factor covariance matrix is the central foundation of any risk model, and the right choice of factors is of fundamental importance both for accurate forecasting of tracking error and for analyzing the risk structure of portfolios in a useful way.

The factors chosen for any particular risk model should be relevant to the purposes for which it is being designed, should have intuitive appeal to the users of the risk model, and should satisfy common sense. Obviously, they will also need to be factors that capture the important dimensions of risk in the types of portfolios being analyzed. However, this requirement is rarely very restrictive in practice.

## ESTIMATE FACTORS OR ESTIMATE BETAS?

Once we have decided to prespecify the factors to be used in the model, we then have to choose whether to provide time-series data on the factor returns or cross-sectional data on the stock betas (the factor exposures).

In either case, once we have the stock returns and the chosen second set of data, we use the underlying model of stock return given by equation (19.10) to estimate the remaining data required to complete the risk model.

$$R_{it} = \alpha_i + \sum_{f=1}^{K} \beta_{if} R_{ft} + \varepsilon_{it} \tag{19.10}$$

Specifically, if we have given ourselves the factor return time series, the final step will be to run time-series regressions of the returns on each stock against the set of factor returns (after any orthogonalization), in order to estimate the stock betas, which will then be the regression coefficients.

If, on the other hand, we choose to obtain the stock betas directly from empirical data, the final step will be to run cross-sectional regressions, one for each month, of the returns to all stocks over the month against the set of factor betas at the beginning of the month. In this case, the regression coefficients will be estimates of the factor returns for that month. In this method, we then go on to chain-link the estimated factor returns to generate time series, and would then use these to derive the factor covariance matrix.

The essential point is that, in either case, there will be a loss of information and the introduction of estimation error at the regression stage of the process. In the first method, the estimation error will be in the estimated stock betas. In the second method, the estimation error will be in the estimated factor returns, and hence in the factor covariance matrix.

Note that both methods *presume* that the variables (either factor returns or stock betas) that are to be derived from empirical data are actually observable. In the first case, we can usually find reasonably good proxies for the returns to the chosen factors. Thus, the returns to a U.S. market factor, for example, can be readily proxied by the S&P 500, the Russell 3000, or the Wilshire 5000. However, in the second case, it is necessary to observe the exposures of *all* the stocks to *all* the factors, and this may easily require a huge amount of data collection and processing.

For example, for a global risk model with 50 factors, covering 20,000 stocks, either we would need to measure the returns to the 50 factors over 84 months (for a seven-year history) or we would need to observe 1,000,000 betas at the beginning of each month for 84 months. At the very least, it is clear that this second method leaves a lot more scope for observation errors to creep in.

Many risk model vendors seek to avoid this difficulty by simply using dummy variables for stock betas. Suppose a global risk model includes currency, country, and industry factors. Then a stock such as Deutsche Bank, which is priced in euros, is (obviously) a bank, and is domiciled in Germany, would be given a beta of 1 on the euro, a beta of 1 on Germany, and a beta of 1 on banking. Its betas to all other currency, country, and industry betas would be set equal to 0. This is very easy to do, and it only has to be done once, as these classifications will not change from month to month. Unfortunately, *it's just plain wrong*.

A moment's reflection will make it obvious that not all German stocks will have a beta of 1 on the German market, nor will all bank stocks have a beta of 1 on banking. Some stocks will have betas greater than 1 and some will have betas lower than 1. Even the capital asset pricing model (CAPM), possibly the simplest risk model ever invented, recognizes this simple fact!

Another (related) fallacy is that currency risk for any stock is simply determined by its currency of denomination, which is what is implied by setting a beta of 1 on the euro for Deutsche Bank, and all its other currency betas equal to 0. To do so ignores the fact that Deutsche Bank has revenues, costs, and income denominated in several different currencies, and also ignores the possibility that its own treasury department may engage in currency hedging.

A very clear example of this is to consider the currency betas of Japanese multinational stocks, such as Toyota, Sony, Panasonic, and Hitachi. These stocks will usually have betas to the Japanese yen of significantly less than 1, and may also be sensitive to the movements of other currencies, such as the euro or the U.S. dollar, as well. Meanwhile, more domestically oriented stocks such as Fuji Bank, Nippon Sheet Glass, or All-Nippon Airways have betas to the Japanese yen greater than 1.

Although this shortcut makes the task of providing 1,000,000 stock betas every time the risk model has to be updated very easy, it has the very significant disadvantage that it is wrong. To coin a phrase, *dummy variables are for dummies!*

However, even leaving this issue aside, there are profound differences in the results from risk models using either the approach of giving the factor returns and estimating the stock betas or the approach of giving the stock betas and estimating the factor returns. We will consider these differences first at the stock level, but then, more importantly, at the portfolio level.

## PRACTICAL CONSEQUENCES AT THE STOCK LEVEL

In the first method, the factor covariances (and their volatilities and correlations) should correspond directly with investors' experiences of the behavior of the factors, while the stock betas will have estimation errors. As a result, some of the stock betas will undoubtedly look a little strange.

On the other hand, while the second method will probably give better betas (unless they are dummy variables), the factor covariances will have estimation error in them, and will sometimes be somewhat counterintuitive.

In practice, bearing in mind that both the stock betas and the factor covariances are used in the calculation of stock risk, we should inevitably expect our estimates of stock risk, calculated as shown in equation (19.11), to have some estimation error in them.

$$V_i = \sum_{f=1}^{K} \sum_{g=1}^{K} \beta_{if} \beta_{ig} C_{fg} + RSD_i^2 \qquad (19.11)$$

## PRACTICAL CONSEQUENCES AT THE PORTFOLIO LEVEL

Something rather different happens at the portfolio level, and we should remember here that we are ultimately building our stock risk model in order to provide us with estimates of portfolio risk. We are not directly concerned with the possibility of estimation errors in individual stock risk.

Remember that portfolio risk is calculated as follows:

$$V_P = \sum_{f=1}^{K}\sum_{g=1}^{K} \beta_{pf}\,\beta_{pg}\,C_{fg} + \sum_{i=1}^{K} p_i^2\,RSD_i^2 \qquad (19.12)$$

and that the portfolio betas used in this expression are calculated as:

$$\beta_{pf} = \sum_{i=1}^{N} p_i\,\beta_{if} \qquad (19.13)$$

In the first method, the estimation error in the stock betas will, to some extent, be *diversified away* at the portfolio level, whereas in the second method, the estimation error in the factor covariance matrix is *not diversified away*, but remains the same at the portfolio level as it was at the stock level. All that is required for this to happen is that the estimation errors in the stock betas should be uncorrelated across different stocks, and this is usually the case. Note that the estimation errors in the stock residual risks will also tend to diversify away at the portfolio level.

For building stock risk models, the first method would therefore seem to be the better approach. In practice, the standard risk models commercially available not only use one of these two different methods, but also use different stock universes and different sets of factors, and make various other assumptions in their construction. This makes it very difficult to compare them directly, although it would be a relatively simple matter to build two risk models using the same set of stocks and factors, but each of the two different methods, in order to test whether the first method did, indeed, generate better estimates of portfolio risk than the second.

Alan Scowcroft and James Sefton of UBS did actually test this by taking a fixed universe of stocks, a given set of factors, and a fixed look-back period, and then building a time-series model, a cross-sectional model, and a statistical model, and then comparing how good each of the three models were at predicting out-of-sample portfolio risk. They found that the time-series method always dominates the other two methods.[1]

## A SHORT DIGRESSION

For the purposes of building multifactor risk models, then, the first method just described, which concentrates on getting the factors right at the expense of some errors in the stock betas, would seem to be the preferred approach. However, the alternative approach, of concentrating on getting the stock betas right and accepting errors in the factors, may be more appropriate for other purposes.

For example, if we are building a linear multifactor model of return for *stock selection*, we will care more about the individual stock betas than the factor returns.

Indeed, in many so-called multifactor stock selection models the only aspect of the factor returns that matters is their sign. A slight variation of equation (19.1) is the generic form of all linear multifactor stock selection models:

$$E[R_{it+1}] = E[\alpha_i] + \sum_{f=1}^{K} \beta_{ift} E[R_{ft+1}] \qquad (19.14)$$

In this equation, we have expected returns over the *next* period for the stock and the factors, rather than actual returns, and the stock betas at the end of the previous period. The expected value of the residual term is, of course, zero.

Most so-called multifactor stock selection models are actually just multiple screening filters. The *sign* of each factor is presumed to be known, and the modeling process reduces to simply screening some universe for the required high-beta or low-beta stocks.

Note that this simple-minded approach creates the artificial problem of how to weight the factors. Note also that these factors are rarely measured as returns, and the betas are rarely true factor exposures.

## HYBRID RISK MODELS

As is often the case in life, however, it turns out there is a catch. In this case, the catch is that we can use time-series regressions to estimate stock betas only *if we can reasonably assume that the betas are stable over time*—in other words, time stationarity, which is a constant theme throughout this book. For currency, country, and industry factors (in other words, for the factors that usually contribute the majority of each stock's variance), we can safely make this assumption.

On the other hand, for the kind of factors that active managers often use for their stock selection models, such as value, growth, momentum, and liquidity, we cannot make this assumption. Fundamental variables such as book-to-price ratios are interesting to portfolio managers *precisely because they are not stable over time*. We search for high book-to-price ratio stocks because we expect that other investors will eventually realize that they are cheap, and so drive their price up by buying them. In the process the portfolio will have outperformed the market, and the book-to-price ratio will have changed to some lower value. For these kinds of style or active factors, we have no choice but to use the cross-sectional method.

Hybrid risk models actually use a combination of cross-sectional factors, time series factors, and statistical factors to get the best features of each of the three different methods of building risk models.

The cross-sectional regression method is used for the active factors. The residual returns from this stage are then used in time-series regressions to determine the stock betas to currency, country, and industry factors. We then include a small number of statistical factors to catch any residual common factor effects that have not been captured by the defined factors. By doing this last step, we can be assured that the set of factors does, indeed, capture all of the systematic risk present in the universe of securities covered by the risk model, and therefore that the (residual) stock-specific risk really is idiosyncratic, and really is uncorrelated with anything else.

Users of hybrid risk models have the comfort of knowing that all the common factor risk had been accounted for (at least to the desired level of accuracy, depending on the number of statistical factors selected), together with the satisfaction arising from the ability to use the prespecified factors in the model to explicitly identify and quantify the factor bets being made at any moment in any given portfolio.

## THE R-SQUARED SHORT-TERM HYBRID RISK MODEL FOR GLOBAL EQUITIES

Hybrid risk models combine the explanatory power of pure statistical models with the intuitive factor definitions of a prespecified model. The R-Squared Short-Term Global Risk Model combines the most common active factors used in stock selection models with industry and country (or regional) factors, and with statistical factors, to gain the usability and relevance of defined factors with the explanatory power of statistical factors.

The risk model has four blocks of factors. First are the currency factors, used to capture each stock's significant currency sensitivities. Then there is a series of country- or region-specific active factors, where the betas represent a stock's exposure to the attributes most commonly used in stock selection models. Third is a double factor block where each stock's exposures to industry and country (or regional) factors are estimated. The final block consists of a small number of statistical factors.

After the currency block, the residual (and now currency invariant) stock returns are used to derive the active factor returns. Together with each stock's exposures to these factors, they will explain some portion of each stock's returns in each period. The stock returns that are left over are called the stock's active factor residual returns.

The country (or regional) and industry factors are built from these active factor residual returns by combining stock returns into capitalization-weighted portfolios of all well-behaved stocks in a particular region or industry. The country (or regional) and industry betas for individual stocks are derived by regressing each stock's returns on these factors (see details that follow).

Significantly, this means that, unlike many of the older types of specified factor models, we do not simply assume that a stock will have a beta of 1 on its own industry (or country) and a beta of 0 on all other industries (or countries). Dummy variables are for dummies! Instead, it recognizes that not all stocks in an industry (or country) will necessarily have the same exposure to the industry (or country) factor, and that stocks may have significant exposure to other industries (or countries) as well.

Priors are imposed by first regressing each stock's returns on its relevant currency, country (or regional), or industry factor returns (as appropriate). All other betas to factors in these groups are statistically checked for significance, to ensure that each stock has only nonzero betas on factors that actually affect its returns.

The statistical factors are principal components of the residual covariance matrix derived from the stock residual returns to the country (or regional) and industry factors. The statistical betas for each stock are then estimated by regressing the stock's residual returns on the statistical factors, and again testing for statistical significance.

## Data

All calculations are done on daily, exponentially time-weighted, log returns with a historical look-back period of 250 working days (about one year). No attempt is made to fill in for missing data. The time-weighting coefficient is such that the oldest return (one year ago) has about a quarter the weight of the most recent return (yesterday). The half-life of the time-weighting is around six months. This has the effect of making the model very responsive to recent changes in market volatility.

There are many ways to measure the most commonly used attributes, like value or growth. However, including each of them as separate factors would create problems of collinearity and instability in the model. The model therefore uses composite variables in these cases. See Table 19.1 for details.

**TABLE 19.1** Active factor definitions.

| Factor Name | Attribute(s) | Lower Limit | Upper Limit |
|---|---|---|---|
| Growth | Net Income per share | −1.5 | 1.5 |
| | Trailing earnings growth | −8.0 | 12.0 |
| | Forecasted earnings growth | −0.5 | 5.0 |
| Value | Dividend yield | 0.0 | 0.1 |
| | Earnings yield | −0.8 | 1.2 |
| | Book-to-price ratio | 0.0 | 10.0 |
| | Cash flow-to-price ratio | −0.8 | 1.2 |
| Short momentum | (OLS slope of past five days' price)/(Last night's price) | −0.08 | 0.08 |
| Long momentum | (OLS slope of past 20 days' price)/(Last night's price) | −0.06 | 0.06 |
| Liquidity | $(3V_{-1} + 2V_{-2} + V_{-3})/[0.3 * \text{sum}(V_{-1}$ to $V_{-20})] - 1$ where $V_{-x}$ is the trading volume $x$ days ago | −1.0 | 9.0 |

## Currency Factors

All stocks are first regressed on their home currency's returns in the base currency, rather than simply assuming that a stock will have a sensitivity of 1 to its home currency. The stock residual from this regression is then regressed on the remaining major currencies, and if there is a statistically significant sensitivity it is kept as an additional currency beta.

## Active Factors

Within each region, a multiple cross-sectional regression (day by day) is done with the stock returns from one day as the dependent variables and the composite or other normalized attributes from the previous day as the independent variables. The regression coefficients from these 250 regressions are concatenated to give the time series of returns to each of the active factors. The factor returns and the normalized attribute values (or stock betas) are then combined to give a time series of explained return for each stock, and this is then subtracted from the stock's actual returns to give its residual return series.

### Industry and Country/Regional Factors

All the stocks in each industry or region are combined to form a capitalization-weighted factor returns series. Stock sensitivities are calculated via a multiple stepwise regression with priors, on a stock-by-stock basis. Note that the model *does not* use dummy variables for country or region sensitivities. As the poets say, "Dummy variables are for dummies."

Priors are imposed by first regressing the stock's residual returns on the prior factor's returns. Then the stock's residual returns from this regression are regressed on the remaining factors in the block. A stock gets a prior on a factor if its returns were used to build that factor.

Most stocks have enough degrees of freedom in their returns history for a full set of factor betas to be estimated by regression. The results for these stocks are then used to help assign betas for stocks with incomplete return histories or missing data. Any prior is applied first. The residuals from this prior regression are then used in a multiple-stepwise regression on the remaining factors in the factor block. All betas generated by the multiple-stepwise regressions are statistically checked for significance (adjusted for the available degrees of freedom). For stocks with short histories, a peer group average of the betas of stocks in the same industry and same country is used.

### Statistical Factors

A full correlation matrix is derived from these stocks' residual return time series, and the first three principal components are extracted. As the economic meaning of the statistical factors is unknown, no priors are applied to the statistical factors. All stocks with sufficient degrees of freedom are eligible for regression on the statistical factors. As with the previous two blocks, multiple-stepwise regressions are done, again with degrees-of-freedom-adjusted statistical significance checking.

### Stock-Specific Risk

For most stocks, the stock-specific risk is simply the standard deviation of the final residual returns time series. This is not the case for those stocks that at any point in the block regressions had too few degrees of freedom to be regressed, and as a result were assigned averaged peer group betas. For these very short history stocks a similar averaging method is used to determine their stock-specific risk (see Tables 19.1 to 19.3).

**TABLE 19.2** Industry factor detail.

| Factor Number | Factor Name | Factor Mnemonic | Factor Code |
|---|---|---|---|
| 1 | Electronic Technology | ElecTech | 1300 |
| 2 | Consumer Durables | ConsDur | 1400 |
| 3 | Energy Minerals | EngyMiner | 2100 |
| 4 | Process Industries | ProcInd | 2200 |
| 5 | Health Technology | HlthTech | 2300 |
| 6 | Consumer Nondurables | ConsNDur | 2400 |
| 7 | Industrial Services | IndSrv | 3100 |
| 8 | Commercial Services | ComSrv | 3200 |
| 9 | Distribution Services | DistSrv | 3250 |
| 10 | Technology Services | TechSrv | 3300 |
| 11 | Health Services | HlthSrv | 3350 |
| 12 | Consumer Services | ConsSrv | 3400 |
| 13 | Retail Trade | RetlTrd | 3500 |
| 14 | Transportation | Trnspt | 4600 |
| 15 | Utilities | Util | 4700 |
| 16 | Finance | Fin | 4800 |
| 17 | Communications | Comms | 4900 |
| 18 | Nonenergy Minerals | NEngyMiner | 1100 |
| 19 | Producer Manufacturing | PrducerMnf | 1200 |

**TABLE 19.3** Regional and country factor detail.

| Factor Number | Factor Name | Factor Mnemonic | Factor Constituents |
|---|---|---|---|
| 20 | North America | NrthAm | US, CA |
| 21 | Latin America | LtnAm | PY, AR, BR, CL, CO, CR, CU, MX, NI, PA, PE, UY, VE |
| 22 | Britain and Ireland | GB_IE | GB, IE |
| 23 | Iberian Region | Iberia | ES, PT |
| 24 | Austria and Germany | DE_AT | DE, AT |

**TABLE 19.3** *(Continued)*

| Factor Number | Factor Name | Factor Mnemonic | Factor Constituents |
|---|---|---|---|
| 25 | France | FR | FR |
| 26 | Benelux | Benelux | LU, NL, BE |
| 27 | Italy | IT | IT |
| 28 | Nordic Region | Nordic | FI, NO, SE, DK, IS |
| 29 | Switzerland | CH | CH |
| 30 | Emerging Europe | EmEur | BG, TR, YU, EE, GR, HU, LV, LT, PL, RO, RU |
| 31 | Emerging Africa | | |
| 32 | Middle East | | |
| 33 | Japan | JP | JP |
| 34 | Australasia | | AL, NZ |
| 35 | Asia-Pacific ex Japan | | |
| 36 | Emerging Asia | | |

## SUMMARY

The whole point of building a stock risk model at all is to enable us to do portfolio risk analysis. This involves estimating, or forecasting, the overall risk of the portfolio, and then breaking it down either by contributions from different holdings or by contributions from different factor exposures.

The important tests of how good any risk model is, therefore, should be: first, how good are its forecasts of overall portfolio risk (either in absolute terms or relative to some benchmark), and second, how useful/relevant/intuitive is its decomposition of the risk structure of a portfolio?

In this chapter we have outlined the various alternative approaches currently being used to build linear multifactor risk models, together with a description of their respective strengths and weaknesses.

## NOTE

1. A. Scowcroft and J. Sefton, "Understanding Factor Models," *UBS Investment Research,* January 2006.

CHAPTER 20

# The Future of Risk Management and Analytics

**Steven P. Greiner, PhD; David Mieczkowski, PhD; William F. McCoy, CFA, PRM; Andrew Geer, CFA, FRM; Daniel S. Mathon, PhD, CFA; Viviana Vieli; Christopher Carpentier, CFA, FRM; Mido Shammaa, CFA, FRM; and Sameer R. Patel**

The role of technology in shaping risk management cannot be understated. Its evolution has taken risk management along with it. Imagine trying to estimate a factor model or perform a mean-variance optimization with a slide rule. Imagine again trying to sift through tick data for trading opportunities. Imagine trying to back-test any sort of strategy. Risk management was implicit because it had to be before computers. No one focused on correlation, because you couldn't compute correlations with a slide rule. Looking at any five- to 10-year span, it's hard to argue against the advances in risk management available to practitioners being due to the advancement of technology. In the 1980s, computer memory was measured in kilobytes; in the 1990s, megabytes; in the first decade of the 2000s, gigabytes; and now memory is measured in terabytes. It doesn't take a PhD to make an extrapolation that by the 2020s exabytes ($10^{18}$ bytes, of which $10^{15}$ would store the entire contents of all the libraries in the United States, leaving 1,000 times that much empty) will be the working descriptor for computer memory.

This is a dominant theme in investing in general, as there has always been vastly more pertinent information available than the resources capable of accounting for it. This is why the statements that markets are inefficient and that it is hard to consistently beat the market are not contradictory. If the information available is so much larger than the capacity of humans (even with the aid of machines) to process it, then markets will be inefficient by definition. Loan-level prepayment modeling was not an option in 1981, nor was mean-CVaR optimization, nor multivariate Garch. So technology will continue to advance, and risk management will advance along with it.

Moreover, the digitization of textual content will enable algorithms to exploit this data going forward. Most financial information is in the form of text to begin with. The implication is that the historical employment of statistics and mathematics in the world of computing will continue to advance toward combining word structure, natural language heuristics, and social networking and engineering to give greater flexibility and more explanatory variables to models. Classification schemes, cluster analysis, dendograms, trees, and associated statistics will become more routine in their usage. This can be seen in its early stages with the advent of news sentiment indicators by several companies these days, and the frequency of this topic at finance conferences. For example, the interpretation of leverage with Garch modeling is that negative news pushes returns downward to a greater extent than positive news pushes returns upward (on average). This is also one fundamental explanation for momentum investing: that bad news travels more slowly; hence stocks trending upward continue unabated for periods. Current technology allows only numerical exploitation of leverage in a Garch model, however. The day is coming when news itself may become the descriptor in the model. A second example surrounds language disparities between newspapers, which are very dissimilar from language in 10-Ks and 10-Qs. Moreover, there is naturally an increased sensitivity that occurs when one starts dealing with textual data, which may allow real differential sensitivities to be calculated on news events classification schema. This can then assist the analysis of firmwide exposure to entities, ensuring prompt response to market news across portfolios and asset classes. The processing of these differences can lead to risk models based solely on textual content and interpretation, but faster computing speed and more memory are necessary conditions before their deployment.

For a software company, we at FactSet have front-row seats when it comes to seeing how computational challenges impact modeling choices. Some of these choices have been discussed explicitly in this book. The use of linearization in the fixed income risk chapters was prompted, in part, because of a Monte Carlo within a Monte Carlo problem. This is difficult for even basic security valuation and much more challenging for risk management. Consider the difficulty in valuing an American swaption. Option exercise can occur at any time, but to determine the rational exercise strategy, one must know whether the option is worth more alive than dead. A brute force Monte Carlo approach doesn't work, because the problem quickly devolves into a near infinite Monte Carlo within Monte Carlo problem, while a tree-based approach has limitations in how many factors can reasonably be used to drive the forward curve (two is pushing it, and inclusion of a stochastic volatility will more than break a computer), because the number of nodes (and thus calculations) grows exponentially with the number of factors. Hence there is an intrinsic association between technology and risk management and with risk management and model selection, for one of the first things a quant learns in finance is the difference between a tractable model and unemployment.

In this chapter we offer a picture of where we believe risk management and risk analytics will evolve to in the near future. From our perch, we have an overview of what many vendors in the risk space are working on as well as our own research teams' efforts. In addition, we fold into this perspective some of the inducements to the practice from increased regulatory oversight and comment on what we see clients requesting from risk analytic providers where appropriate.

## THE INCREASING REGULATORY ENVIRONMENT

When the great financial crisis began in 2007, it was believed that regulatory oversight was widespread, pervasive, and preventive—locked and loaded, so to speak. We are forced to question why the regulators weren't aware of the systemic risks in the banking systems that had arisen by 2008. The Basel Accord in 1988 had already begun to address capital requirements, which became enforced in 1992 by the G-10. These became obsolete rather quickly, and Basel II was published in 2004, just about the time systemic risks were rising. Its premise was to provide banking regulators with a standard for bank capital to insure against the operational risks that banks were assuming in a growing globalization and interconnectedness of economies. Unfortunately, due to the usual politics of governance, it wasn't fully adopted until 2008 when the crisis hit. Since then Basel III has become the working document and was endorsed by the G-20 in November 2011 in Seoul. Even so, its comprehensiveness means adoption of Basel III's full provisions isn't scheduled until 2019.

In the United States, the Dodd-Frank Wall Street Reform and Consumer Protection Act was strung together in the usual congressional overreaction to a crisis and was signed into law in July 2010. This bill offers the greatest significant changes to financial regulation since the Great Depression—moreover, some would add, with very little thought to the extensiveness of it, or its ramifications. As of this writing, regulators are still compiling components of it, and its comprehensive nature makes uncertainty ubiquitous. For instance, the American Bankers Association's chairman, Steve Wilson, wrote a letter to Sheila Bair, the head of the Federal Deposit Insurance

Corporation (FDIC), indicating that provisions of the law are harmful for community banks and interfere with their providing products and services that their customers want and communities need—in particular, provisions on debit card interchange (a large source of income for community banks), new capital standards, reporting requirements, and risk retention. He actually stated that Dodd-Frank will put a thousand small banks out of business in the coming years. Dodd-Frank restricts the sources of capital even while regulators and bank examiners are demanding more capital. Where will these banks get it from? The success of the financial sector is not an end in itself, but a means to an end, which is to support the vitality of the real economy and the livelihood of the American people, Sheila Bair said. We hope legislatures' knee-jerk reactions aren't misinterpreted to be in sync with this statement, for much of Dodd-Frank is dubious policy.

Another governing body in Europe, Undertakings for Collective Investment in Transferable Securities (UCITS), created its first protocol in 1985. Its original raison d'être was to give asset management companies an EU-wide passport by establishing collective standards acceptable to each member state. By 2009, UCITS IV Directive was released and immediately approved by the European Parliament in January of that year. Outwardly, UCITS still establishes the passport criteria, but inwardly it has evolved to usurp jurisdiction over standards setting for risk management.

What these governing bodies have in common is increased enforcement of risk management protocols they themselves have established, without the concomitant fiduciary liability. That is, the regulators have thrown together various litmus tests for liquidity and crisis management, but have accepted none of the associated responsibility for failure. They leave that to the banks and asset managers. Thus there is a pretense from these regulating bodies of offering greater scrutiny and oversight, while in reality they've merely transferred their responsibility to their constituencies and have increased the hurdles for firms' doing business.

Additionally, the Securities and Exchange Commission (SEC) and Commodity Futures Trading Commission (CFTC) continue to attempt to address episodes of systemic and market risks via new rules for hedge funds and commodities traders. The ramifications of all this new regulation aren't certain yet, but the commonality is that there's significant pressure for firms to expand the methods and approaches for managing their business and portfolios through enterprise-wide risk management systems. The current environment and desire for greater regulation will mandate greater use of risk measures and statistics. Of course for risk vendors, risk managers, and quants, this is good news in general, but for asset managers, owners, pensions, and hedge funds, it increases their costs and liabilities of doing business. Unfortunately, to get to the heart of the matter, in regard to the overused Black Swan terminology referring to extreme events, we aren't going to better predict their occurrences regardless of how much regulation exists, which is the express purpose of regulation in the first place: to attempt to preempt systemic risk.

Risk measurement in a regulatory framework also foretells its irrelevancy. By its nature, a regulation must be one size fits all and unambiguous. However, risk management is a nuanced endeavor, and must be customized to the particular needs of the institution. Thus, risk in a regulatory environment is likely to be adopted by the unsophisticated, without the depth of understanding for full control. For the sophisticated (and wealthier institutions with access to the needed computing power), there should be better risk-adjusted returns. Also, financial innovation is often done to evade the intent of regulation while complying with the written law. Over time, the required risk measures would be weakened by the next generation of financial products to skirt the regulation.

## THE IMPACT OF REGULATIONS WITH TECHNOLOGY

Historically, it has been important to distinguish between sources of risk. There are the standard, day-to-day variations of returns in regular markets that Ben Graham has stated are normal and not associated with risk, and then the systemic stresses that regulators are concerned about. The sources of these risks are different, and the variation of security pricing (the actual changes due to the leverage effect, for instance) is different in the presence of systemic stresses. For example, during crisis, leverage means returns become more skewed due the asymmetric effect of bad news on volatility. The association between assets tightens, and correlations across assets (and classes) increase. Additionally, often liquidity dries up. More research into systemic market behaviors might be needed to lead to model development in this regard. The SEC-sponsored research into this topic should prove interesting. Likewise, as credit risk models evolve in their understanding of distress, we may expect to see more credit-related aspects bleed into market risk models. Credit risk analysis will still answer separate questions on loss, but the interaction of credit and market risk might be merged into market risk singularly. The contagion and bleeding of these risks into other asset classes is currently a hot topic. Multi-asset-class (MAC) risk is in its early beginnings and not at a level to offer great explanation of contagion during stress in general. More CPU speed, more memory, and parallelization will enable huge advances in this field.

As an aside, identifying areas from which alpha can still be obtained in times when correlations rise is also where fruitful efforts will be employed.

Pairwise correlations might have risen, making it harder to diversify and identify/exploit alpha in stressful market environments, but sources might differ (e.g., factor correlations going up or down) that can be exploited.

Until recently, getting single top-level numbers for a MAC portfolio came about by looking at asset classes separately and independently then aggregating risks. This will be certain to overestimate risk simply because it discounts the effects of diversification. True multi-asset-class modeling means getting all assets into the same analysis and identifying risk drivers, combining asset classes into a holistic analysis with explanatory factors, and allowing their covariance to be calculated and risk deciphered to account for real diversification. This has historically been very hard due to computational limitations and resource constraints. That is, the theory is there to develop sound models, but the algorithmic solutions take too long in practice to solve. The future will naturally lead to greater interaction among fixed income, equity, currency, and commodities financial engineers due to regulatory forces and the enabling of technology to allow for big models to be run in manageable wall-clock time.

## THE FUTURE VIEW

If we further extrapolate current trends, the obvious future leads to increasing complexity and usage of risk models and statistics. Models will become more nuanced and specific, using more complex mathematics to model nonnormal returns and their time variation, in turn requiring greater computational power. As of the time of this writing, many see returns from the overall market stymied for the foreseeable future, so investors will get more creative and need to search for places to find their returns outside of the standard equity and bond markets, similar to the invention of credit default swaps (CDSs) in the early 2000s. Investors may turn to more leveraged instruments and strategies, which lessens the effectiveness of the widely used normal distribution assumption. Risk analysis will need to pick up the nonnormality of returns and the obvious nonlinearity. For instance, the Committee of European Securities Regulators (CESR) recognizes that a variety of models exists for estimating value at risk (VaR) and each model has its own set of assumptions, advantages, and drawbacks. It is the responsibility of a UCITS applicant to select the appropriate VaR model. CESR is of the view that for a UCITS referring largely to financial derivatives presenting nonlinear risk features, the parametric VaR model is not appropriate and should rather refer to a historical simulation model or a Monte Carlo model to compute the risks. Hopefully, having learned from our more recent past, the need to understand these risks will be more important than ever.

Complete repricing and Monte Carlo methodologies will become more the norm, along with more of a focus on tail risk, if not by choice, perhaps by regulation.

While the accuracy is hoped to improve with these more sophisticated models, there are concerns. First, increased complexity leads to increasing model and software risk, while a second concern might be greater opacity. It may become harder to understand the underlying mechanisms driving the risk output. This is due to more complex models being more sensitive to initial conditions because they encompass nonlinear outputs with feedback, much borrowed from the theory of chaos and weather forecasting. In this way contagion effects can be modeled. In short, this may lead for the tendency of risk to become a black box number unless the integration of an educational curriculum on risk, and associated culture of risk management, is spread throughout more firms. With increasing complexity in risk modeling comes more domain expertise required to perform the operation, too. Consider model updating. The domain expert signs off on that portion of the model, but who verifies the macro integration and interactions? In light of this, independent model validation will become increasingly important and difficult. Indeed, many of the larger financial institutions are already beginning to staff dedicated internal model validation teams. The use of model validation services through third-party consultancies is also on the rise. There is also an increased operational risk with this approach similar to the difficulties software companies have with legacy code. That is, they become hostages to the model creators. Thus extra costs to mitigate this risk involve installing some element of redundancy and cross-training to hedge departure risk.

## NEW TYPES OF RISK MODELS

In terms of model development, the hope is for construction of several new types of models. First would be increasing use of mathematical networks. Currently, correlation is used to summarize relationships between companies and industries. While correlation is very useful, it is based on historical relationships that might not hold due to stationarity violations, and it does not specify mechanisms, either. However, direct relationships between companies, such as supplier/buyer, could be captured by mathematical networks. As we've stated, when fundamental analysts review a company, they simultaneously examine up and down the supply chain as well as the customer network, thereby ascertaining a qualitative assessment of covariance, usually unknowingly. This can be done more efficiently through the use of mathematical networks if the problem is specified correctly.

As we spoke about in Chapter 6, asset pricing models have historically relied almost entirely on linear association between returns and explanatory variables. In this sense, correlation and covariance are satisfactory measures of concordance even though they offer no comment on nonlinear association between assets. Though Arch/Garch processes later introduced the advantage of including autoregressive behavior of returns, this is still only minimally a nonlinear contribution, if that. Going forward, we might expect pricing models to begin to include nonlinear relationships, especially when dynamics are considered in shorter time frame analysis that high-frequency trading is encouraging. Once this need is satiated, we would expect to observe more practical use of copulas in the implementation of risk modeling, as only the copula can extract true overall association between assets beyond linear.

Additionally, multivariate Garch (M-Garch) techniques will come of age and will be employed more and more. The holdback of this technology now is mostly computing time. Though lack of convergence can happen in the traditional maximum likelihood solutions these days, the work-around to overcome these disadvantages involves even longer computing times. Today that issue is solved through faster but less convergent algorithms and approximate methods that come with higher estimation errors. Imagine what could be computed with CPU speeds and parallelization offering orders of magnitude calculations under the same wall-clock time.

Whether or not Moore's law holds and raw CPU processing power increases exponentially, parallelization of computing resources has only just begun to be harnessed. Many tasks in finance are amenable to parallelization, so while the CPU time needed to run ever more complex algorithms may rise substantially, the wall-clock time needed can actually go down. As the cost of purchasing additional CPU power continues to fall over the next five to 10 years, the rise of the massively parallel computing environment is inevitable. Grid computing is already being implemented in most large institutions, but we are still just on the cusp of the type of cheap computational power needed to contemplate Monte Carlo within a Monte Carlo, or optimization within an optimization. Having this type of computing power is going to make *feedback* and *contagion* the buzzwords of tomorrow, as *fat-tailed* and *Black Swans* are the buzzwords of today.

In addition to parallelization, big data is going to be a dominant theme in risk management and in investment management in general, and data fetching, which is one predominant rate-determining step (of several) in risk modeling today, may not go away tomorrow. However, all this cheap data storage capacity means that the running record of the past will become ever more detailed. Every little nuance of model output can be saved and reread with another model to offer insight and interpretation. This will again mean that risk professionals will be able to create ever more detailed models, and that new financial signals will abound. For one example of how all this new technology might be harnessed, one has to look no further than the reigning *Jeopardy* champion, IBM's Watson. Artificial intelligence and machine learning are now possible at a level that makes economic simulation with realistic, rational optimizing individual agents a real possibility, and then, after combining this with textual categorization and language interpretation, risk management may become a living being.

Ultimately, all of these financial models that risk managers employ are a marriage of hardware with software. The trend in hardware development has been toward ever greater speed and storage capacity. The trend in software has been toward ever greater ability for programmers to specialize and to collaborate. Additionally, the complexity of the problems solved on a computer seems to grow with the CPU speed. That is, an optimization on a computer in 2002 that took two hours takes two minutes in 2012, so there are so much more complex calculations that can be performed in the one hour and 58 minutes of wall-clock time remaining in 2012. Thus the progressive increase in CPU velocity is enabling financial engineers to attack larger and larger problems, solved under the identical wall-clock time. For risk management clients, this means the turnaround for portfolio analysis in real time is that much deeper, more extensive, and more descriptive than ever before, and this is accelerating. One would add this also results in addressing more sophisticated outcomes that the risk management industry is facing these days and questioning, as a result of both theoretical advances as well as technological advancements. Of course the theory-technology interaction has feedback mechanisms, too, in that as CPU speed and software parallelization allow the solution of more difficult problems, finance theory will advance to propose new, perhaps more difficult questions.

As we've seen computers commoditized over the years, so too have we seen the models themselves become more commoditized. Open source code has found its way into many businesses, and finance will ultimately be forced to incorporate some of the elements of the open source philosophy. We will see the beginning of this in the next five to 10 years, as risk vendors make their models more and more open and as the components become more specialized. Rather than treat models as black boxes and highly proprietary, risk vendors may be forced to open their models and framework up to their clients, which will ultimately encourage improvement and contributions from their own individual perspectives. We are seeing that at FactSet now with the ability for clients to create their own risk models through our Alpha-Testing platform. For example, professional investors used to spend all their time on alpha and return estimation, but now we're beginning to see equal interest and attention spent on risk analysis and a clamoring for more tools to assist with this exercise. The attention historically given to alpha by asset managers is increasingly being eaten by attention given to losing money and to risk. We're nearing an equal apportioning of attention.

Alas, even by 2020, 20/20 hindsight won't be available to help investors avoid the financial hazards that seem to be affecting markets with greater frequency and intensity and for longer periods of time. Consider that over the prior 10 to 15 years the investable universe for many has expanded greatly. Due to technology and innovative financial engineering, the increased number of asset classes and strategies available will create a need to include them into the risk modeling process. Ever since the credit crisis we've been seeing managers pay attention to assets outside their regular charter more and more. Risk management therefore will become even more important in the investment process and will invariably become an integral part of it, all the way from outlining the investment policy to portfolio construction and to performance attribution, where the risk of asset classes will play a key part in the allocation of funds and managers. Increased computational power and the continuing influx of physical science professionals into the field will lead to new risk measurement tools and optimization methods, but enthusiasm for these new techniques needs to be tempered with good judgment and experience. One might worry about products and strategies designed to arbitrage the risk management process rather than truly mitigate risks. This potential for confusion of the risk management objectives can arise when the compensation schemes for asset managers hinge solely on outperformance. We do not know of any risk manager compensated by the size of the losses avoided as yet.

The combination of cheaper technology, the commoditization of risk models, and greater installation of risk management systems far and wide will lead to more investors employing multiple risk models. Today, cost is a major deterrent and the advantages of having simultaneously both shorter-term and longer-term risk models are simply prohibited. However, shorter-term risk assessment, as an additional viewpoint to long-term risk, yields great advantages. The question arises as to whether the investing mandate can utilize short-term risk models, since large institutional investors, asset owners, and pension funds cannot quickly make trades to adjust to higher-frequency risk forecasts. However, risk modeling is offering opinions these days on how to hedge risks and adjust the portfolio during the construction and rebalancing process so as to insure against the shorter-term volatilities. Moreover, even for a large investor who rebalances monthly, being aware of the trend in risk is as important as knowing the level. For example, the level of a long-horizon risk model may be used in portfolio optimization (i.e., optimizing to a given tracking error [TE] level). A shorter-horizon daily updating risk model will have higher sensitivity to immediate risks and offer insight to where risks are trending that the longer-horizon model may miss. Thus if a manager sees risks increasing with a shorter-horizon model, optimizing to a lower than normal tracking error during the portfolio rebalancing process at the end of the month might be prudent. The manager would still use the longer-horizon risk model during portfolio optimization, but would optimize to the TE level at the bottom of its allowable range, for instance. In any event, we predict increased usage of multiple opinions ascertained through the use of several risk models.

## STRESS-TESTING YOUR WAY TO EVENT RISK PREPAREDNESS

Today, the only way to get a handle on systemic risks is through performing what-ifs through stress-testing. The one thing regulators insist on that has the strongest backing by just about everyone involves stress-testing. It's not just a means to determine downside risk, but also a way to examine overall portfolio positioning (relative or absolute) in order to ensure that positions are reflecting the manager's outlook, especially when it comes to economic forecasts. It yields information about the relative scale of losses and about their volatility, and also offers insight into potential mechanisms for losses. It can offer clues as to whether some event is a 65 basis points event, or a 5.5 or 20 percent event. Stress-testing is also one of the few areas where regulators are mandating its usage, without stipulating the recipe for its application. Their guidelines are more like open questions than dictatorial rhetoric. This leaves much room for innovative development that risk vendors are rapidly exploiting. Since much of stress-testing can involve large-scale computing, we see vigorous use of this technology going forward as computing power increases vastly. By the 2020s, the average asset manager will probably spend as much time running stress tests as doing risk forecasts.

Similar to the evolution of technology in the automotive industry, where state-of-the-art components are tried on racing cars first, in finance the institutional investors lead the charge in sophistication of product. Hence, on the retail front, the combination of increased awareness of investment risk and proliferation of cloud computing will lead to a democratization of the risk management tools. We see increasing demand from retail investors and their advisers for many of the techniques currently used by institutions. At conferences we present at, increasingly consultants and retail clients ask for "light risk model" versions now. Will Mr. and Mrs. Kim want to know with 95 percent confidence the minimum age that they can retire at and still achieve all of their retirement goals? Wouldn't you? In fact, William Sharpe's company, Financial Engines, does just that. It offers (almost) institutional analytics to mom-and-pop portfolios. Morningstar also offers today to the retail investor what was institutional-like portfolio analysis in times past. These examples support the precedent of what tools the professional investor has today that will become the retail investor's friend in the future.

The risk management tools and analytics being developed today in conjunction with the evolution of technology and forceful regulation are pushing the implementation of better risk models toward helping identify the cause, measure the effect, and hedge risks that were unknown just a short time ago. We see increased demand for risk modeling and no slowing of its technological advancement.

# Index

Active weight
  active exposure versus, 21, 33, 70–71, 498–499
  FX exposure, 141
  implied alpha, 411, 413
  in RM design example, 56–57
  solutions via mean variance, 22
Alpha
  Buffet RM strategies, 15
  enhanced MVO, 440, 443, 444–445
  estimation error, 184–185
  exposure versus experienced risk, 46, 48
  fundamental investing, 411, 413
  Garch, 222
  portfolio optimization, 20–21
  risk forecast expectations, 24
  separating from beta, 202, 220
Alpha models, 55–56, 194, 220
APT RM system. *See* SunGard APT RM system
Asset association, 183–197. *See also* Covariance matrices
  copulas, 184, 193–196, 229, 404, 574
  estimation error, 184–185, 187–192, 217
  linear and nonlinear, 183–184
  shrinkage, 22, 62, 82, 127, 185–193, 206
Asset classes, 87–118
  equities (*see* Equities)
  fixed income (*see* Fixed income)
  multi-asset-class portfolios (*see* Multi-asset-class (MAC) portfolios)
Asset cross-correlation. *See* Correlations
AXA Rosenberg, 47–48
Axioma risk models, 483–506
  accuracy of, 489–491
  Alpha Alignment Factor (AAF), 444
  background, 483–484
  CAPM beta, 202
  daily updates, 76, 487
  estimation error, 185
  exposure specification, 205
  flexibility of risk model, 486, 488–489, 491–492
  fundamental investing, 408–410
  innovations, 492–495
  portfolio rebalance scenario, 495–506
  portfolio versus security level, 76–82
  reporting, 484–485

Baron-Adesi Whaley (BAW) options pricing, 151, 153, 161–162
Barra. *See* MSCI-Barra
Berkshire Hathaway, 14–16, 155–156
Beta
  capital asset pricing model (CAPM), 202
  currency hedging, 40
  customized hybrid risk models, 213–217
  estimation error and, 555–559
  exposure and stationarity, 33
  factors versus, 555–557
  illiquid markets, 533, 535
  multifactor models, 202–205
  as risk measurement, 14–15, 49
  separating from alpha, 202, 220
Binomial tree models, 104, 163–165, 269, 532
Black-Scholes formula
  callable bond options, 103–104
  original paper, 147–148
  stochastic differential equations, 267–268, 271
Black Swans. *See also* Crisis of 2008
  asset association and, 183, 185
  extinction-level events (ELEs), 50
  RM predicting, 51–52, 195
  September 2011 stress-tests, 395–398
  stationarity and, 3, 19
Brinson attribution method, 70–71, 418
Buffett, Warren, 14–16, 49, 486

Capital asset pricing model (CAPM), 194, 202, 508, 533, 556
Caplets, 271–272, 327–329, 345
China, 27, 28–29, 363
Coherent risk measures, 370, 372, 450
Collateralized mortgage obligations (CMOs)
  idiosyncratic bond risk, 348–352
  option-adjusted spreads, 288–289
  overview, 111–112
  spread risk factor model, 296, 312–322
Commodities, 121–138
  estimation universe, 128, 129, 137
  futures, 121–123, 144
  model methodology, 123–126, 143–144
  model results, 129–138
  risk calculation, 126–129
Conditional duration, 281–282
Conditional value at risk (CVaR), 451, 452
Confidence intervals
  on confidence intervals, 375
  Garch, 227–228
  model accuracy, 489
  risk report accuracy, 53–55, 60–61, 80–81
  VaR surface as function of, 223
Constant elasticity of variance (CEV) models, 329–332
Contagion, 17, 571, 573, 574
Contango, 122
Contingent claims models, 528–529
Convexity
  calculations, 236, 237
  credit default swaps (CDSs), 176–177
  currency risk, 355–356
  government bond futures, 168–172
  interest rate risk exposures, 273, 281
  overview, 101, 105–106
Copulas, 184, 193–196, 229, 404, 574
Correlations
  APT statistical factor models, 473–474, 479–480
  asset and equity return, 530
  Axioma innovations, 494
  Buffet RM strategies, 15
  copula versus, 194–195, 404
  corporate securities, 106, 549
  default correlations, 529–531
  of factors, 466–468
  in fundamental investing, 404–405
  interest rates, 276
  interest rate volatility risk, 337–340
  tail correlations, 19–20
Counterparty risks, 527
Covariance matrices
  all-encompassing, 83–84
  Black Swans and, 185
  Buffet RM strategies, 15
  customized hybrid risk models, 214
  enhanced MVO, 432–433
  estimation error, 184–185, 187–192, 217
  extrema accentuated, 21–22, 62, 206
  extrema minimized, 22, 62, 82, 127, 185–193, 206
  FactSet model, 196–197
  historical, 552
  for linear associations, 184
  multifactor models, 204, 206, 555
  parametric approach, 20
  stationarity assumptions, 19
Covariance structural regime, 184
Credit default swaps (CDSs), 108–110, 176–177, 404
Credit risk, 97, 527–529, 571
Crisis of 2008
  asset association and, 183
  correlations of CDSs, 404
  Gaussian copula, 194–196
  multi-asset-class portfolios, 82–83
  protection from, 452–453
  RM to forefront, 13, 47–49
  stress-tests, 389, 393–398
Currency risk
  Axioma currency model, 494–495
  currency exposure, 34–35
  currency unions, 359–367
  exchange rates by country, 38–39
  hedges, 37–47
  hedges for exposure, 353–359
  overview, 138–143, 352–353
  size of markets, 27
Customized hybrid risk models (CHRMs), 212–218

Debasing currency, 10–11, 139
Debt
  countries compared, 27–29
  debasing currency, 10
  MF Global and euro sovereign, 24
Decomposing risk
  APT factor models, 472
  Axioma risk models, 497–500

CAPM beta, 202
Northfield MAC example, 540–543
returns only, 229
as risk management, 523
systematic versus idiosyncratic, 87–88, 371–372
Default correlations, 529–531
Derivatives
APT RM system, 477–479
counterparty risks, 527
credit default swaps, 176–177
currency risk, 116
Eurodollar futures, 177–179
fixed income derivatives overview, 165–167
forward curve for pricing, 115
government bond futures, 167–172
interest rate caps, 271–272, 327–328, 344
interest rate swaps, 172–176
Northfield Information Systems, 531–532
risk forecasting, 344–345
size of market, 27
stress-test of portfolio, 389–398
term structure dynamics for pricing, 257–258
underlying versus derivative price, 372
Dimensionality, 128, 204, 206, 209
Dimensionality reduction techniques, 430–431
Dodd, David, 200
Dodd-Frank Wall Street Reform and Consumer Protection Act (2010), 48–49, 569–570
Dollar hedge, 40–45, 354, 357–359, 366
Duration
cheapest to deliver, 166
complex securities, 112–114
credit default swaps (CDSs), 109–110
currency risk, 355–356
effective duration (*see* Effective duration)
interest rate risk, 273–277, 281–282
interest rate sensitivity, 106
key rate duration (*see* Key rate duration)
overview, 96–103, 236, 237
principal component durations (PCDs), 277
Duration-constrained expected tail loss (ETLD), 282
Duration-constrained value at risk (VarD), 282
Earnings per share (EPS), 403
Effective duration
definition, 236, 273
government bond futures, 168
option-adjusted spread and, 313
sensitivity to interest rates, 102, 112–113
spread duration versus, 296
Efficient frontier, 430, 441
Enhanced mean-variance optimization (EMVO)
constraints, 432–440, 443, 445–447
extreme tail loss optimization, 450–452
factor alignment problems (FAPs), 443–445, 458
further improvements, 441–443
multiperiod model, 449–450
multiportfolio optimization, 448–449
nonlinear instruments into, 452–453
optimizer selection, 456–458
overview, 432–434
Equities, 87–96
equity risk as portfolio risk, 547–548
factor models, 466–469
financial statement variables, 90–92
fixed income versus, 97–98
macroeconomic risk, 88–89
risk calculations, 92–96
systematic versus idiosyncratic risk, 87–88
Estimation error
betas and, 555–559
covariance matrices, 184–185, 187–192, 217
definition, 61–62
enhanced MVO, 441
portfolio versus security-level, 75–76
Eurozone debt-to-GDP levels, 28
*Ex ante* forecasts
definition, 70
use of, 371, 377, 511
Excess return (XS) time series, 409
Expectations of RM, 24–25, 54–58
Expected tail duration, 281–282
*Ex post* measures, definition, 68–70
Exposure
active weight versus, 21, 33, 70–71, 498–499
definition, 33
experienced risk versus, 37–47
exposure analysis (*see* Exposure analysis)
foreign exchange, 34–35

Exposure (*continued*)
  fundamental investing, 405, 410
  interest rate risk, 273–277
  interest rate volatility risk, 342–344
  models for specifying, 205
  multifactor models, 200–205
  regressions in risk model, 36–37
  spread exposure, 295–296
Exposure analysis
  in example RM design, 56–57
  insights from, 50
  for judging managers, 46
  risk model exposure, 34–35
  stress-testing and, 144
  volatility and diversification, 499
Extinction-level events (ELEs), 50. *See also* Black Swans
Extreme tail loss (ETL), 431, 450–452

Factor models
  derivatives, 477–479
  equities, 466–469
  interest rate risk, 258–267
  interest rate volatility risk, 259
  multi-asset-class portfolios, 466, 467–468, 471, 474–477
  multifactor models, 200–206, 212, 551–555
  multifactor prespecified, 199–205, 466–467, 554–555
  principal component analysis (PCA), 204, 205–212, 258–267
  spread risk, 312–322
  statistical factor models, 465–468, 471, 474–477 (*see also* SunGard APT RM system)
Fat tails
  interest rate movements, 341
  returns having, 19, 410
  stationarity assumptions, 19–20
  underlying properties, 22–23
Fixed income (FI), 96–117, 233–249
  APT modeling, 475
  bond idiosyncratic risk, 346–352
  characteristics of, 235–236
  convexity (*see* Convexity)
  corporate securities, 103–107
  credit analysis, 107–110
  definition of *fixed*, 98
  duration (*see* Duration)
  equity versus, 96–98
  immunization, 102
  linearization, 236–240 (*see also* Taylor linearization)
  securitized bonds, 110–114
  spot yield curve, 103
  statistical analysis for, 114–117, 349
Fixed income derivatives
  credit default swaps (CDSs), 108–109, 176–177
  Eurodollar futures, 177–181
  government bond futures, 167–172
  interest rate swaps, 172–176
  overview, 165–167
Foreign exchange. *See* FX (foreign exchange)
Forward curve
  derivatives pricing, 115
  historically bootstrapped, 263–266, 276
  implied forward curve, 275
  interest rate volatility risk, 337–342
  no arbitrage conditions, 269–270
  spot curves and, 256
  spot rate decomposition, 261
Forward LIBOR, 256, 270–271, 275, 327–328
Forward price, 254–255
Forward rates
  correlation, 276
  currency hedging, 39
  Eurodollar futures, 166, 177
  future interest rate expectations, 265–266
  historical forward curves, 263
  holding period return, 254–257
  no arbitrage conditions, 269–271
Forward volatility, 272, 328–336, 338–346
Fundamental investing, 401–428
  characteristics of, 401–403
  optimization, 421–428
  risk controls, 403–405
  risk management strategies, 405–421
  role of risk models, 486
Funds of funds (FoFs), historical risk models, 219–221
FX (foreign exchange)
  currency risks, 139–143, 352–359
  exposure, 34–35, 141–142
  hedging, 37–47, 139, 140–142
  trading volume, 27

Garch, 221–229, 267, 574
Gaussian approximations, overview, 18–19, 23

Gaussian copula, 194–196
GIIPS (Greece, Italy, Ireland, Portugal, Spain)
debt-to-GDP, 28
euro-sovereign model, 309–310
in example RM design, 56
hypothetical departure, 359–367
Global Industry Classification Standards (GICS), asset exposure, 21, 36
Graham, Benjamin, 14–15, 49–50, 95, 200, 486, 571
Great Financial Crisis (GFC), 48. *See also* Crisis of 2008
Gross domestic product (GDP), 26, 28–29

Hazard rates, 109
Hedging
bonds, 116
dollar hedge, 40–45, 354, 357–359, 366
with fixed income derivatives, 166–167
foreign exchange, 37–47, 139, 140–142
government bond futures, 168–171
interest rate risk, 276
against true exposures, 75
worst-case value at risk for, 453
Historical risk models, 219–221
Holding periods, 88, 140
Holdings decomposition, 446–447

Identification of risk, 4, 5
Idiosyncratic risk
bonds, 346–352
commodities, 128
customized hybrid risk models, 218
equities, 87–88, 92, 96
fixed income, 117
illiquid markets, 533
multifactor models, 203, 212
spread risk, 304
use of, 371–372, 377
Illiquid investments
private equity, 532–535
real estate, 536–540
Implied alpha, 185, 411, 413, 440, 444
Independent and identically distributed (i.i.d.)
alpha estimates as, 21
companies as, 15
forward rates, 262
portion of total risk, 371
Inflation
currency risk, 139
debasing currency, 11
Interest rate caps, 271–272, 327–328, 344
Interest rate derivatives (IRDs), 345
Interest rate parity, 359–367
Interest rate risk, 251–282
characteristics of, 251–252
exposures, 273–277
factor models, 258–267
hedging, 166, 168–171
Northfield Information Systems, 526–527
principle component analysis, 115
risk forecasting, 278–280
short rate models, 268–269
stochastic differential equations, 267–273
term structure, 252–258
volatility affect on, 105–106
Interest rate volatility risk, 325–346
callable bond price, 105–106
exposure, 342–344
factor models, 259
forecasting, 336–342, 344–346
Gaussian shock volatility, 267
Ho-Lee and Black-Derman-Toy models, 104
overview, 325–326, 345–346
stochastic differential equations, 271–273
term structure of volatility, 327–336
volatility processes, 270
Internet bubble, 13, 50
Investing
criteria establishment, 6
fundamental investing (*see* Fundamental investing)
momentum investing, 402, 568
quantamental investing, 403
quantitative investing (*see* Quantitative investing)
technical investing, overview, 401, 402
value investing, 14

Japan
accuracy in reporting, 62
debt-to-GDP ratio, 29
Deming in, 5
as U.S. debt owner, 27

Key rate duration
fixed income, 102, 113, 114, 248–249
government bond futures, 168

Key rate duration (*continued*)
  hedging, 167
  interest rate exposures, 273–277, 283, 342
  interest rate volatility exposure, 344
  risk forecasting, 278
  spread duration and, 236

LIBOR market model (LMM), 270–271, 327–328, 329
Liquid assets cushion per UCITS, 3
Lloyd's of London, 3–4

Marginals, 375–377, 413
Market risk, definition, 97
Markets, sizes of, 26–29
Markowitz, Harry, 21, 184, 369, 371, 429
Matched pair analysis, 534–535
Mean-conditional value at risk (mean-CVaR), 19, 22–23
Mean-fat-tail, 19
Mean-variance optimization (MVO)
  algorithms for, 453–456
  for asset returns, 19
  enhanced MVO (*see* Enhanced mean-variance optimization (EMVO))
  mean-CVaR outperforming, 22–23
  overview, 429–430
  risk modeling, 20–21
  security-level forecasts, 76
Measurement of risk. *See* Risk measures
Media perceptions of RM, 7–8, 13
Merton inputs, 309
Merton model
  bond idiosyncratic risk, 350–351
  contingent claims, 528
  credit analysis, 107
  euro-sovereign spreads, 312
  highly nonlinear, 234
  structural approach, 292–294, 296–298, 305–306
MF Global, 24
Model risk
  of bond price calculator, 250
  of model complexity, 573
  option-adjusted spreads, 288, 295
  overview, 23–24, 61–63
  sensitivities and, 238
  uncertainty as, 524
Models. *See* Risk models
Momentum investing, 402, 568
Monte Carlo VaR
  bond idiosyncratic effects, 348
  currency risk, 354
  efficient repricing method versus, 249
  FactSet tools, 374–375, 389
  nonnormality of returns, 372
  prepayment risk, 322
Mortgage-backed securities (MBSs)
  agency MBSs, 312–316, 319–322, 348–350
  composite pool returns, 117
  forward curve for pricing, 115
  hedging, 172
  option-adjusted spreads, 288–292, 295–296, 312–316, 319–322, 324
  overview, 110–114
  price discovery, 324
  test portfolio analysis, 241–248
  value at risk, 114, 238–240
MSCI-Barra
  CAPM beta, 202
  estimation error, 185
  exposure specification, 205
  history of, 20–21, 199–200, 507–508
  against other models, 511, 516
  reporting, 510–520
  risk model details, 36, 508–510
Multi-asset-class (MAC) portfolios. *See also* Northfield Information Systems (NIS)
  APT statistical factor models, 471, 474–477
  example risk profile, 540–543
  fixed income and equity models, 98, 107
  future modeling, 572
  R-Squared equity risk model, 196
  shrinkage and, 187
  statistical factor modeling, 466, 467–468
  total risk view, 82–84
Multifactor models. *See* Factor models
Munger, Charlie, RM strategy, 15
Mutual funds, size of market, 27

Nationally Recognized Statistical Rating Organization (NRSRO), 107
Nonquantifiable risks, 16–18
Normal approximations, overview, 18–19, 23
Normal backwardation, 122
Northfield Information Systems (NIS), 523–544

complex instruments and derivatives, 531–532
default correlation, 529–531
exposure specification, 205
fixed income risks, 526–529
history of, 200
MAC example risk profile, 540–543
MAC unified framework, 524–526, 538
monthly updates, 76, 81, 380
other models versus, 511, 516
portfolio versus security level, 76–82
private equity, 532–535
real estate, 536–540
stress-testing, 380–386, 392
Numeraire, change of, 271
Nyquist sampling theorem, 73–74

Offsetting risk, 5
Optimization. *See* Portfolio optimization
Option-adjusted spread (OAS)
mortgage-backed securities, 288–292, 295–296, 312–316, 319–322, 324
NIS credit risk, 527–528
spread risk, 312–315, 317–320
Options
fixed income derivatives (*see* Fixed income derivatives)
on government bond futures, 171–172
implied volatility model, 151–161
pricing, 145–148, 151, 153, 161–165
volatility smile, 147, 148, 149–151

Parameter estimation error, 524. *See also* Estimation error
Parametric covariance estimation, 20, 95–96
Par curve
interest rates, 257, 283
spot curve versus, 114–115
volatility and, 327
Physicists versus financial economists, 8
Portfolio insurance, 145–147
Portfolio managers (PM)
asset selection by, 6
compensation of, 46–47
risk managers versus, 24, 47, 49
risk model reporting, 510–520
Portfolio optimization, 429–458
asset allocation, 21, 71, 403
fundamental investing, 421–428
mean-variance optimization (*see* Enhanced mean-variance optimization (EMVO); Mean-variance optimization (MVO))
multiperiod model, 449–450
multiportfolio optimization, 448–449
optimizer selection, 456–458
robust optimization, 441–442
statistical resampling, 21–22, 441
Portfolio risk measures. *See* Risk measures
Prepayment risk, 313–316, 322, 527
Price-earnings ratio (P/E), 62, 90, 201, 402
Price-to-book ratio (P/B), 33, 62, 90, 201, 202, 456
Principal component analysis (PCA)
commodities, 128
equities, 95–96
fixed income, 115
interest rate risk, 278
interest rate volatility risk, 337–342
multifactor models, 204, 205–212
statistical factor models, 258–267
Principal component durations (PCDs), 277
Private equity, 532–535
Probabilities
real-world versus risk-neutral, 258
risk management as, 2, 4, 17
Professional organizations for RM, 7

Quantamental investing, 403
Quantifiable risks, 16–18
Quantitative investing
correlations of assets, 404
overview, 401, 402–403
role of risk models, 485–486

Rachev, Svetlozar, 18
Random return matrix, 211
Ratings and default risk, 107
Real estate, 536–540
Regulatory risk management
Committee of European Securities Regulators (CESR), 572
credit crisis of 2008, 48–49
Dodd-Frank Wall Street Reform and Consumer Protection Act (2010), 48–49, 569–570
dwarfing asset loss, 6
effects to come, 569–571
risk disclosures, 34
stress-testing, 577

Regulatory risk management (*continued*)
  systematic risk and, 2–3, 49, 569–570
  UCITS and liquid assets, 2–3
  value at risk model selection, 572
Return on equity (ROE), 402
Reverse optimization, 411
Risk. *See also specific risks*
  beyond volatility, 49–51
  common, 200–202
  common versus asset-specific, 125
  common versus security-specific, 23–24, 75–82, 87–88
  definition, 5, 524
  experienced risk as realized, 46
  Graham definition, 14
  modeling (*see* Risk models)
  quantifiable, 16–18
Risk-based performance attribution, 418, 421
Risk horizon
  for bonds, 117
  forecast reliability and, 54, 72–75
Risk management (RM)
  culture of, 4–5, 24
  data necessary for, 4
  defining, 5, 16–18
  example of RM design, 55–58
  expectations of, 24–25, 54–55, 55–58
  failure stories, 11–13
  future of, 567–578
  history of, 3–8, 47–49
  investments versus banks, 523
  managing risks of, 23–25
  media perceptions, 7–8, 13
  as opportunity set, 25–29
  portfolio versus security level, 23–24, 75–82, 87–88, 547–551
  primary roles of, 51–53
  as probability management, 2, 4, 17
  professional organizations, 7
  regulatory RM (*see* Regulatory risk management)
  success stories, 8–11
  trends versus levels, 23, 24–25, 52
Risk managers
  compensation of, 576
  portfolio managers versus, 24, 46–47, 49
  veto rights in portfolios, 24, 47, 49, 520
Risk measures, 369–398
  beta as, 14–15
  coherent risk measures, 370, 372, 450
  commonly used measures, 68–69, 370–375
  forecasting chosen measures, 71–75
  group- or security-level, 69–70
  list of measures, 68–69, 377
  marginal contribution, 375–377, 413
  necessity of, 4, 5, 59
  quantifiable, 16–18, 64–66
Risk models, 199–229. *See also specific models and risks*
  AXA Rosenberg bug, 47–48
  commodities, 123–126
  customized hybrid, 212–218
  equities, 92, 466–469
  factor models (*see* Factor models)
  future of, 571–577
  Garch, 221–229, 267, 574
  generic return models, 548–551
  historical, 219–221
  hybrid risk models, 559–563
  model risk (*see* Model risk)
  multifactor in practice, 551–554 (*see also* Factor models)
  reduced form, 290–292
  regression order, 36
  risk horizon and, 72–75
  role of, 485–486
  selection of, 200
  stability and accuracy, 84–86
  stationarity centrality, 85–86, 559
  structural, 290, 292–294
  update frequency, 76, 81, 380, 487
  validation of, 573
Risk parity, 499
RM. *See* Risk management (RM)
Robust optimization, 441–442
Roll yield, 83, 121–123, 144
R-Squared, 547–563
  customized hybrid risk models, 213
  daily update, 76
  factor models, 552–555
  factors versus betas, 555–557
  generic modeling, 547–552
  government bond futures, 169–175
  MAC risk model, 196
  model details, 205, 560–563
  options and derivatives, 178, 180
  other models versus, 511, 516
  portfolio versus security level, 76, 80–83, 547–551
  stress-testing, 380–386, 394–397

SABR-LMM model, 332–336, 337–340, 343
Second-order cone programming (SOCP), 454–455, 456–458
Securities and Exchange Commission
  AXA Rosenberg investigation, 47–48
  new regulation, 570
*Security Analysis* (Graham & Dodd), 200
Security association. *See* Asset association
Seignorage, 10
Sharpe ratio, 133, 187, 294, 388, 439
Shrinkage, 22, 62, 82, 127, 185–193, 206
Shrinkage target, 442
Six Sigma, 5
Sizes of markets, 26–29
S&P 500–VIX correlation, 11
Specification error, 61, 62, 95, 186, 200
Spot curves
  cash flow exposure, 114
  coupon stripping, 257
  definition, 103, 282–283
  effective duration, 236–237, 273
  error, 347
  factor models, 259–265
  forward curves and, 115
  interest rate risk and, 168, 325–326, 342
  interest rate risk forecasting, 276, 278
  option-adjusted spreads, 288, 324
  overview, 253–254
  short rate models, 268
  spread duration, 296
  spread of bonds, 294, 312
Spot LIBOR, 256, 327
Spot rates
  bond value, 286
  correlation, 276
  decomposition of, 261
  forward price and, 255–256
  forward rates and, 266
  Ho-Lee/Black-Derman-Toy models, 104
  from key rates, 274–275
  spot FX rates, 353, 363
  swap rates, 257
  volatility and, 327
  yield to maturity, 253
Spot volatility, 271–272, 327–331
Spot yield curves. *See* Spot curves
Spread residuals, 346–352
Spread risk, 285–322
  derived spread approach, 297–307
  diversity against covariance, 107
  euro-sovereign spreads, 308–312
  factor model approach, 312–322
  overview, 285–290
  reduced form models, 290–292
  spread duration, 109–110, 296
  spread exposure, 295–296
  structural models, 292–294, 305
Static spread, 286
Stationarity
  of asset association, 183, 195
  in flood insurance, 9
  as optimization assumption, 19
  risk model centrality, 85–86, 559
  time stationarity and VIX, 12
Statistical factor models, 465–468, 471, 474–477. *See also* SunGard APT RM system
Statistics
  independent and identically distributed (i.i.d.) (*see* Independent and identically distributed (i.i.d.))
  for mortgage-backed securities, 114–117
  RM as probability management, 2, 4, 17
  statistical resampling of portfolios, 21–22, 441
Stochastic differential equations (SDEs), 271–273
Stock markets, sizes of, 25–29
Stress-testing
  in example RM design, 57–58
  future of, 577–578
  measurement of risk, 65–68
  regulatory criteria, 377–378, 577
  as RM role, 50, 51–52, 54
  use of, 378–398
SunGard APT RM system, 465–480
  core universe selection, 469–470
  derivatives and nonunderlying securities, 477–479
  equities factor models, 468–469
  factor model overview, 465–468
  MAC factor model estimation, 474–477
  number of factors, 470–471
  other models versus, 511, 516
  risk profile estimation, 471–474
  stress-testing, 392
  user-defined assets, 479–480
Survivorship bias, 85
Swap (par) rate, 256–257, 276
Swaptions, 167, 336, 344

Synthetic security, 477–478
Systematic risk
  customized hybrid risk models, 218
  equities, 87–88
  principal component analysis, 211–212
  regulation and, 2–3, 49, 569–570
  spread risk, 304
  statistical factor models, 466
  use of, 371–372, 377

Tail correlations, 19–20. *See also* Fat tails
Taleb, Nassim, 3, 17, 50, 194–195
Taylor linearization
  interest rate risk, 276–277, 278, 281–282
  test of, 240–249
Taylor rule for monetary policy, 266
Technical investing, overview, 401, 402
Technology, and RM, 238, 567–569, 571–572, 574–578
Tented pattern, 113
Term structure of spot rates, 253
Time series
  APT perpetual futures, 480
  betas via regression, 33, 36–37, 203–205, 211–212, 552, 555, 559
  customized hybrid risk models, 213, 216, 217
  fundamental investing, 409, 410–411
  principal component analysis and, 260
  risk trend through time, 25, 61
  yield curve time series, 475
Total Quality Management (TQM), 5
Tracking error (TE)
  description of, 63–65
  fixed return excluded, 98
  fundamental investing, 408–410
  real estate portfolios, 537
  use of, 371, 377
Trade scheduling, 449–450
2008 financial crisis. *See* Crisis of 2008

Uncertainty
  cash flow uncertainties, 285–286, 289, 290–291
  definition, 524
  risk and, 59–63
Unconstrained conditional expected tail duration (ETD), 282
Unconstrained duration at VaR (DVaR), 282
Undertakings for Collective Investment in Transferable Securities (UCITS)
  liquidity risk specifications, 2–3
  standards for RM, 570
  stress-testing criteria, 377–378
  value at risk model selection, 572
U.S. debt market, 27

Value at risk (VaR)
  Black Swans and, 195–196
  default correlation, 300–305
  as downside risk measure, 450–452, 453
  for fixed income, 96
  fixed return included, 98
  mean-conditional VaR (mean-CVaR), 19, 22–23
  model selection, 572
  Monte Carlo VaR (*see* Monte Carlo VaR)
  on mortgage-backed securities, 114, 238–240
  Taylor approximation versus, 248–249
  use of, 372–375, 377
  worst-case value at risk (WCVaR), 451–452, 453
Variance risks, 87
Venture capital, 532–535
VIX RM failures, 11–13
Volatility
  Axioma dynamic volatility adjustment, 493
  beta as measure, 14–15
  corporate securities, 106
  currencies, 143
  exposure versus dollar hedging, 45
  interest rate derivative pricing, 327
  interest rate volatility risk (*see* Interest rate volatility risk)
  leverage effect, 229
  as normal, 14, 49
  options volatility smile, 147, 148, 149–151
  spot volatility, 271–272, 327–331
Volatility regime, 184

Winsorizing, 202, 214
Worst-case value at risk (WCVaR), 451–452, 453

Yield curves, 114–115, 467, 475, 476–477, 526–527